Read this first!

Here's how to find the incredible wedding and special event information in *Here Comes The Guide:*

• Event Venues

Sites are organized by region and city, with illustrated descriptions and details about capacities, fees and services. To find a specific site, see the index starting on page 541.

• Useful Questions to Ask Venues & Event Professionals

Not sure what to ask a potential event location, photographer, caterer, etc.? Our lists of questions on pages 21–42 will make it easier for you to interview them and help you decide who to hire.

Don't forget to check out HereComesTheGuide.com!

HereComesTheGuide.com has the most up-to-date information on event venues, services, and bridal trunk shows and fairs—as well as lots of photos and virtual tours. And if you have a certain type of location or event professional in mind, you'll really appreciate our amazingly useful search engine. We make it easy to find exactly what you're looking for.

Our Cover Photographer

Our cover photo was shot by Joey Kennedy. To find out more about him and his work, *Here Comes The Guide's* editor had a conversation with him:

Q *How did you get into wedding photography?*

A I've always been an artist at heart. I started out as a painter, but I switched to photography as a way to express myself creatively. After teaching photography for seven years, I began shooting weddings full time in 2009 and I'm still passionate about it!

Q *So, what keeps you passionate?*

A It's the people! I literally get a new family every week and, to me, family is everything. I shoot a lot of photos of family members as well as the bride & groom and wedding party. I love making art, but at the end of the day capturing the entire family and all the details is what's incredibly important to me.

Q *What's your photographic style?*

A I would say it's "Fine Art". My work is more cinematic than journalistic, and I use both digital and film to create a timeless look. I provide my clients with just enough direction to help elicit the best photos without actually posing anyone. For example, I choose places to shoot based on the quality of the light, and then I simply allow people to be themselves. I find shooting with "natural light" more inspiring, and it's far less intimidating than bringing in big lights and other equipment.

Q *Why do couples enjoy working with you so much?*

A I've been told that clients like my style of communication, and can see that I really care about them. I also have an intense work ethic; I put a lot of effort into getting every shot I possibly can, and no matter how difficult it is I never stop trying. I always think about what I would want done, so I'm very invested. There's no autopilot for me! I'm going to work incredibly hard for you, and hopefully make great art, too!

Q *Destination weddings are a big part of what you do, right?*

A Definitely! I shoot nationwide, especially in California where the light, atmosphere and people are really special. The landscape, the weather…it's all perfect! I think my style and sensibilities are a great fit for the West.

Q *How has your own life experience influenced your photography?*

A Last year, I almost lost my mother. Thankfully she survived, but that changed how I shoot weddings. Now, I make a point of setting up a special time for family photos. I want the pictures I take to become even more valued as the years go by because they show people who may not be around in the future. As clients grow older, they'll want to look at those photos again and again. They'll remember what it was like to see their parents and grandparents on that day, photographed in beautiful light with authentic emotion. When you have great images, they will fill your heart!

Joey Kennedy's work has been featured in *Once Wed, Style Me Pretty, The Knot Magazine* (regional and national), *Weddings Unveiled Magazine, Munaluchie Bridal Magazine, Green Wedding Shoes,* and *Wedding Chicks.*

What Makes Us Different?

We do most of your homework for you.

1. We actually visit the venues in *Here Comes The Guide*.

We check out 95% of our event sites in person before we include them in *The Guide*.

2. We write every venue description with you in mind.

Each site description is based on our personal experience, so it's informative, accurate and often entertaining.

3. We provide real pricing for venues, along with nitty-gritty details about each site's capacity, services and amenities.

This makes it easy to create a list of your top contenders, and by the time you contact or visit a location you're totally informed!

4. We save you a ton of time.

By putting so much comprehensive information all in one place, we save you hours … days … maybe months of searching for event locations. And, you can actually do most of your planning without leaving home!

HereComesTheGuide.com has it ALL:

- **Virtual Tours**

  Most of the event sites we feature on **HereComesTheGuide.com** have virtual tours! It's *the* way to explore wedding locations on your own time (and in your pajamas).

- **Photos of Hundreds of Wedding Venues and Services**

  Each location and event professional has their own photo gallery.

- **Fee Info for Every Venue**

  HereComesTheGuide.com provides pricing for facility rental, catering and other costs.

- **CERTIFIED BY THE GUIDE Event Services**

  We don't just feature any old caterer or DJ. We've carefully checked out each event professional.

- **Local Bridal Shows**

  Find out what events are happening near you, like fab food tastings and fashion shows. Did you have something better to do this weekend?

- **Wedding Dress Trunk Shows and Samples Sales Calendar**

  Want to browse an entire collection of the latest designer wedding dresses? How about a discount on an in-stock bridal gown? This is the place to find special designer and sales events.

- **MyGuide**

  Log in to organize your **HereComesTheGuide.com** search results. You can save and share your favorite locations and event services (and we won't give out your email address—period).

- **Guest Accommodations, Honeymoon Locations & Rehearsal Dinner Venues**

  Need to book a block of rooms for your out-of-town guests? Looking for the perfect honeymoon or rehearsal dinner spot? Find them all on HereComesTheGuide.com.

Our website also includes many venues that are so new they aren't even in this book!

What People Say

"I went out and spent the money on your book without hesitation. I'm so glad I did! I've gotten some great ideas and was able to create an outline for my budget. Not only did I find great reception locations in your book, but I think I found my rehearsal dinner place as well. It was a gold mine!"

—*Liz Davis, Bride*

"I went to about ten locations that are in your book and found that the site descriptions were pretty accurate. I'm amazed at how well you were able to capture the feeling of a place and put it into words."

—*Stephanie Stevensen, Bride*

"I'm in the process of helping my daughter research sites for her wedding reception and your website has been hugely helpful! The location information is thorough and consistent, making comparing the different locations so easy. We have found places to check out that we never would have thought of on our own. Thanks so much for all the work you must have done to put all this information together!"

—*Gail C., Mother of the Bride*

"Having recently gotten married, I have a special appreciation for *Here Comes The Guide.* It was extremely helpful during my time of planning. The quick descriptions painted a beautiful picture of each and every venue, and were very helpful in narrowing down the search by budget, criteria and location. I feel this is a very important tool for every busy bride and still recommend it to all my engaged friends."

—*A Southern California Bride*

"I got married in August and cannot stress how much help *Here Comes The Guide* was to me. I was often able to receive more information from your site than from my contacts with the actual locations and vendors! Especially since I was planning a Northern California wedding from Southern California, you saved me A TON of legwork."

—*Jamie Juster, Bride*

"I have finally found a website that has it all! I'm planning my wedding from out of state and your event locations search is the best! I've been looking for a website that has all the information in one place. Thank you!!!"

—*Sarah, Bride*

About Here Comes The Guide

"I just had to let you know how WONDERFUL your website is. **I was amazed to finally find a website with REAL information**. Other wedding websites just gave me names and phone numbers, and I still had to do all the research on my own. Yours gave me all the nitty-gritty stuff I needed to know to find locations and vendors. With only two sessions at your website, my wedding was planned. Amazing!"

—*Christina R., Bride*

"I have to tell you, I was blown away by your website. It's so beautiful and professionally done. The detail you provide is just enough so that the browser doesn't get bogged down in minutiae. **Your site is such a great resource that I've started telling everybody about it.** I've seen tons of wedding sites, so I know that you've come up with something that's really different."

—*Kimberly P., Bride*

"I completely love your website and look forward to the book. **This is the only resource that is so detailed on California sites, and it makes it so much easier to plan from a long distance.** *Here Comes The Guide* is the best source of information."

—*Jocelyn, Bride*

"**I absolutely love your website. It's warm, feminine and has what one might call 'simple elegance.'** Great job! I refer friends to your website all the time—for weddings, showers and of course, birthdays. Keep up the fabulous work."

—*Maria, Bride*

"I love your site! Most other sites that I visited seemed to have a hidden agenda to steer me towards only what benefited them. **This site is non-biased and easy to use. Thank you!**"

—*Elisa Parra, Bride*

"Thanks for providing this invaluable resource! **I'll be using the site for corporate event planning**—I don't know what I did without it!"

—*Mary, Corporate Planner*

"**This is a wonderful website, with all the details that a bride looks for when she's searching for a reception location.** It's well organized and incredibly useful. I wish there were more sites like this one. THANK YOU!!!"

—*Amy, Bride*

We Need Your Help

- **Tell venues that you're using *Here Comes The Guide*.**

  When you contact the places we feature, let them know that you heard about them through *The Guide*.

- **Help us keep our information current.**

  We'd appreciate it if you'd contact us with your comments, corrections, suggestions and complaints. Your feedback helps us maintain the accuracy of our information.

- **Let us know if you discover a great venue that's not featured in *Here Comes The Guide*.**

  Please call or email us if you find an event site you think we should include in our book and on our website.

Hopscotch Press, Inc.

510/548-0400   fax 510/548-0144

info@HereComesTheGuide.com
HereComesTheGuide.com

Information Is Always Changing

Everything changes:
pricing, services, décor,
landscaping and even ownership.

We've tried to make the information in this book completely accurate, but it's not possible. Locations give us incorrect facts and figures, change ownership or management, revamp their pricing and policies, and sometimes go out of business. Truth is, things in the event industry can turn upside down overnight.

So how can you make sure that you're getting correct information? It's simple:

- When you tour venues, bring your book with you or use your smartphone or tablet to quickly refer to each location's page on **HereComesTheGuide.com** for the most up-to-date info.

- When you contact a location, show or read the information in *Here Comes The Guide* to the facility's representative to verify that it's still current.

- Get everything that's been agreed on in writing, and review it carefully before you sign any contract!

Here Comes The Guide

Fifteenth Edition

Copyright © 2017–2018
Published by Hopscotch Press, Inc.
Printed in the U.S.A.

Here Comes The Guide, Northern California®

Fifteenth Edition

Jan Brenner, *Co-Author/Editor-in-Chief*
Jolene Rae Harrington, *Co-Author/Editor*

Meredith Monday Schwartz, *Chief Executive Officer*
Sharon Carl, *Production Director*
Maggie Munki, *Production Specialist*
Jennifer Ahearn, *Online Media Director*
Angela Mullan, *Regional Sales Lead*
Stephanie Bush, *Regional Sales Manager*
Jessica Robins, *Regional Sales Manager*
Amy Sanderson, *Regional Sales Manager*

Inside Illustrations: *Jon Dalton and Michael Tse*

Library of Congress Control Number: 2016953398
ISBN 978-1-885355-24-9

Here Comes The Guide®

Fifteenth Edition

Acknowledgments

Our deepest appreciation goes to our writers, Jolene Rae Harrington (also an invaluable editor), Laurie Turner, and Annie Cooper. Without them none of our books would ever get written.

The illustrations in *Here Comes The Guide* are created by our artist, Jon Dalton. Using both computer graphics and fine art skills, he transforms photographs of the facilities into the distinctive line drawings that give *The Guide* its unique style.

And as always, we are eternally grateful to our clients and our readers. Your support year in and year out keeps *Here Comes The Guide* a popular resource.

Table of Contents

Really, Really Important Information

Questions To Ask

Part One: Event Venues

Regional Areas and Cities

Maps

Index

Certified By The Guide

Preface

When I graduated from college in 1973 (pre-internet!), I thought I'd never have to do another endless research project again. Boy, was I wrong. Compared to looking for a place to get married, term papers were a piece of cake. I began my quest optimistically enough, but after a couple of days of frantic and fruitless networking (my wedding date was a mere three months down the road!), the enormity of my task started to sink in. It had taken me 33 years to find the right guy, and it was beginning to look like it might take an equally long time to find the right place.

Going into high gear, I reached out and touched just about everyone I knew, along with quite a few total strangers. Friends and friends of friends didn't have any recommendations that suited our particular needs, and although wedding consultants had information, they were reluctant to part with their lists of sites unless I hired them to plan my wedding. I even called some caterers, florists and cake makers, but they were usually too busy to give me in-depth descriptions of places over the phone. Some chambers of commerce had organized wedding location lists ready to mail out; others had nothing and knew nothing.

After days of phoning, all I had was a patchwork quilt of information. I still hadn't found *the* place, and finally had to face the painful truth: there was no central resource or comprehensive, detailed list. I became anxious. With a full-time job I was hardly free to conduct an exhaustive search, and I realized that I would never be able to find out about the vast majority of interesting or unusual wedding sites, let alone thoroughly evaluate them! My frustration was exacerbated by the fact that it was August and the wedding date in October was drawing closer with each passing day.

As luck would have it, my sister mentioned that her hairdresser had gotten married on a yacht in San Francisco Bay. Hallelujah! That's it! I cried. What a great idea! I'd never even thought about a floating wedding and had no idea you could do such a thing.

We got married on a hot, sunny day behind Angel Island in San Francisco Bay. The captain performed the ceremony on the bow, and afterwards the yacht tooted its horn, the crew let loose multicolored balloons, and a "Just Married" sign was thrown over the stern. As we swept past Alcatraz Island, Sausalito and the Golden Gate and Bay Bridges, our guests relaxed in the sun, enjoying drinks and hors d'oeuvres. What a wonderful day! Even my parents' friends had a great time, and wrote us after the wedding to let us know how much they'd loved their outing on the water.

Serendipity was largely responsible for making my wedding memorable, but you don't have to rely on luck. I created *Here Comes The Guide* so that others wouldn't have to experience what I went through, and I hope it makes your search for the perfect location easy and painless.

Lynn Broadwell
Founder

Really, Really Important Information

Introduction

Little did we know when we wrote *Here Comes The Guide, Northern California* in 1989 that we would receive such an overwhelming response from our readers. The first edition sold out in less than a year, and as public demand grew we hustled to get the second edition in print. Thanks to our enthusiastic readership of engaged couples, savvy party hostesses and event planners, *The Guide* continues to be a bestseller!

So what makes this book so popular?

We've done most of your homework for you.

We present comprehensive, solid information: a full description and illustration of each location, plus details about fees, capacities and services. Our wide selection of facilities includes delightful places that you might not have found on your own.

This book cuts your search time by 90%.

Instead of having to call or email dozens of facilities and ask the same questions over and over again, you can look up many of the answers in *The Guide*. Once you've narrowed down your list of potential sites, you can contact them to schedule an in-person visit. Not only does *The Guide* save you time, it often saves you money by letting you comparison shop!

We screen our venues.

We personally evaluate almost every property in *Here Comes The Guide,* sending a professional writer to 95% of our sites to make sure they meet our criteria. (Yes, we actually turn down locations that don't satisfy our requirements.)

We're experienced.

We've been writing and publishing *Here Comes The Guide* since 1989. We're proud that our publication has become the essential resource for weddings—and just about any kind of event in California.

If you can't find the perfect venue in *Here Comes The Guide,* check out our website at HereComesTheGuide.com.

You'll have access to all the information in the *Here Comes The Guide* book online and a lot more:

- **More Northern California venues,** along with photo gallery slideshows and virtual tours. You'll be able to tour hundreds of sites in your pajamas!

- **Even more venues in other regions of the U.S.,** like Southern California, New England, Chicago and Hawaii, just to name a few.

- **Plenty of event services,** with lots of photos of floral designs, cakes, makeup and hair—you name it!

- **Trunk Shows & Sample Sales Calendar** for the latest wedding attire styles and savings.

- **Bridal Fair Calendar** with details about upcoming extravaganzas and wedding showcases.

- **Venues for Rehearsal Dinners, Etc.** Need a place to hold your rehearsal dinner, bridal shower, day-after brunch or other intimate gathering? We've got lots of suggestions (with photos and details, of course!)

- **Guest accommodations/room block options** plus photos and details.

- **Honeymoon destinations,** including romantic photos and practical info.

Navigation is a snap, and our searchable database lets you find event sites by city, type, capacity, view, etc., and event professionals by company name, region or service category. A special *MyGuide* feature lets you save your favorites and share them with friends and family.

And check back often—we regularly update our website with event locations and services that aren't featured in the book!

Understanding Our Information

Explanation of Main Headings

Each venue description in *Here Comes The Guide* follows the same format. To help you understand the information presented, we've provided an explanation of the main headings in the same order as they appear.

Description

Once you've selected a geographical area and you're clear about your needs, then thoroughly review all the sites listed in your area of preference. The descriptions are written to give you a sense of what places are like, from ambiance to physical layout. However, before reading the descriptions, you may want to check the *Capacity* and *Fees & Deposits* sections to determine which places seem to be a good fit from a size and budget perspective. If a facility is still a viable option after you've read the entire two-page editorial, flag it for easy reference when planning to contact and visit sites later on. You can also go to our website, HereComesTheGuide.com and log in to MyGuide to save and share your favorites.

Ceremony Capacity

Standing and seated capacities are sometimes included for ceremonies since these numbers may be totally different than the corresponding numbers for receptions.

Reception Capacity

By now you should have a rough idea of how many people will be attending. If not, it's time to zero in on the number, since many facilities want a deposit based on an estimated head count. Look at the capacity figures for each event location. Seated or sit-down capacity refers to guests seated at tables. Standing capacity refers to a function where the majority of guests are not formally seated, such as a champagne/hors d'oeuvres reception (though there may be cocktail tables and/or lounge furniture). Keep track of those facilities that are compatible with your guest count, or add them to your MyGuide favorites. If you're planning well in advance and don't have your guest list whittled down yet, then you'll just have to estimate and refine the count as the date draws near. There is a world of difference in cost and planning effort between an intimate party of 60 and a large wedding with over 200 guests, so pin down your numbers as soon as you can.

Meeting Capacity

In general, the seated capacity for meetings is listed as a range or a maximum. Sometimes, specific spaces are named along with their individual capacities. Occasionally, seating configurations are also provided: *theater-style* (auditorium row seating with chairs arranged closely together), *classroom-style* (an organized table-and-chair arrangement, usually in rows) and *conference-style* (seating around tables).

Fees and Deposits

We've tried to make the information regarding costs as accurate as possible. However, keep in mind that we can't list the fees for all of the services a venue offers. Also, while packages tend to be more inclusive, they may not cover the full cost of your event—especially when you add in extras like appetizers or rentals. It's important to find out as soon as possible exactly what is—and isn't—included with any service or package you're considering in order to accurately assess how your venue choice will impact your budget.

It's a good idea to confirm pricing with the facility you're calling. If you're planning far in advance, anticipate price increases by the time you contract with a venue. Once you're definite about your location, you should lock in your fees in a contract, protecting yourself from possible rate increases later. Make sure you ask about every service provided and are clear about all of the extras that can really add up. Facilities may charge you for tables, chairs, linens, plateware and silverware, glassware and additional hours. Don't be surprised to see tax and service charges in fixed amounts applied to the total bill if the facility provides restaurant or catering services. Although it may seem redundant to include the phrase "tax, alcohol and service charge are additional" in each entry, we find that most people forget (or just don't want to accept the painful reality) that 23–33% will be applied to the food & beverage total.

> **Look at the information regarding fees and deposits and remember that these figures change regularly and usually in one direction—up!**

Sometimes a deposit is nonrefundable—a fact you'll definitely want to know if the deposit is a large percentage of the total bill. And even if it's refundable, you still need to read the cancellation policy thoroughly. Make sure you understand the policies that will ensure you get your cleaning and security deposit returned in full and, again, get everything in writing.

Food costs vary considerably. Carefully plan your menu with the caterer, event consultant or chef. Depending on the style of service and the type of food being served, the total food bill can vary dramatically—even if you're getting quotes from the same caterer. If, for example, you're having a multi-course seated meal, expect it to be the most expensive part of your event.

Alcohol is expensive, too, and you may be restricted in what you can serve and who can serve it. Some venues don't allow you to bring your own alcoholic beverages, and even if they do permit it you may be limited to beer, wine or champagne. Many places discourage you from bringing your own (BYO) by charging an exorbitant corkage fee to remove the cork and pour. Other places have limited permits that don't allow them to serve alcohol or restrict them from serving certain kinds; some will let you or the caterer serve alcohol, others require someone with a license. Make sure you know what's allowed. Decide what your budget is for alcohol and determine what types you're able to provide. And keep in mind that the catering fees you are quoted rarely include the cost of alcohol. If you provide the alcohol, make sure you keep your purchase receipts so you can return any unopened bottles.

So how much will your event cost? Hopefully not more than you can afford! There are a lot of variables involved in coming up with an estimated total for your event. Just make sure you've included them all in your calculations and read all the fine print before you sign any contract.

Availability
Some facilities are available 7am to 2am; others offer very limited "windows." If you'd like to save some money, consider a weekday or weeknight reception, or think about having your event in the off-season (often November, or January through March, but varies depending on the region). Even the most sought-after places have openings midweek and during non-peak months—and at reduced costs. Facilities want your business and are more likely to negotiate terms and prices if they have nothing else scheduled. Again, read all the fine print carefully and mark those facilities that have time slots that meet your needs. If the date you

have in mind is already booked, it doesn't hurt to ask if someone actually confirmed that date by paying a deposit or signing a contract. If they haven't, you may be in luck.

Services/Amenities and Restrictions

Most facilities provide something in the way of services and many have limitations that may affect your function. For instance, they may not allow you to have amplified music outdoors or bring your own caterer.

We've attempted to give you a brief description of what each venue has to offer and what is restricted. Because of space limitations, we've shortened words and developed a key to help you follow our abbreviated notations. Once you're familiar with our shorthand, you'll be able to read through all the data outlined at the bottom of each entry and flag each facility that meets your requirements.

Services/Amenities Key

CATERING
- **in-house:** the facility provides catering (for a fee)
- **in-house, no BYO:** the facility provides catering; you cannot bring in your own
- **preferred list:** you must select your caterer from the facility's approved list
- **in-house or BYO:** the facility will provide catering or you can select an outside caterer of your own
- **BYO, licensed:** arrange for your own licensed caterer

KITCHEN FACILITIES
- **ample** or **fully equipped:** large and well-equipped with major appliances
- **moderate:** medium-sized and utilitarian
- **minimal:** small with limited equipment; may not have all the basic appliances
- **setup** or **prep only:** room for setup and food prep, but not enough space or utilities to cook food
- **n/a:** not applicable because facility provides catering or doesn't allow food

TABLES & CHAIRS
- **some provided** or **provided:** facility provides some or all of the tables and chairs
- **BYO:** make arrangements to bring your own

LINENS, SILVER, ETC.
- same as above

RESTROOMS
- **wheelchair accessible** or
- **not wheelchair accessible**

DANCE FLOOR
- **yes:** an area for dancing (hardwood floor, cement terrace, patio) is available
- **CBA, extra charge:** a dance floor can be brought in for a fee

BRIDE'S & GROOM'S DRESSING AREA
- **yes:** there is an area for changing
- **no:** there's no area for changing
- **limited:** smaller space, not fully equipped as changing room
- **CBA:** can be arranged

PARKING
- **CBA:** can be arranged
  other descriptions are self explanatory

ACCOMMODATIONS
  If overnight accommodations are available on site, the number of guest rooms is listed.
- **CBA:** the facility will arrange accommodations for you

OUTDOOR NIGHT LIGHTING
- **yes:** there is adequate light to conduct your event outdoors after dark
- **access only** or **limited:** lighting is sufficient for access only

OUTDOOR COOKING FACILITIES
- **BBQ:** the facility has a barbecue on the premises
- **BBQ, CBA:** a barbecue can be arranged through the facility
- **BYO BBQ:** make arrangements for your own barbecue
- **n/a:** not applicable

CLEANUP

- **provided:** facility takes care of cleanup
- **caterer:** your caterer is responsible
- **caterer or renter:** both you and/or your caterer are responsible for cleanup

AUDIOVISUAL/MEETING EQUIPMENT

- **full range:** facility has a full range of audiovisual equipment
- **no:** no equipment is available
- **BYO:** bring your own equipment
- **CBA:** equipment can be arranged

- **CBA, extra fee:** equipment can be arranged for an extra fee

VIEW

We've described what type of view is available for each facility.

- **no:** the facility has no views to speak of

OTHER

Description of any service or amenity that is not included in above list.

Restrictions Key

ALCOHOL

- **in-house, no BYO:** the facility provides alcoholic beverages (for a fee) and does not permit you to bring your own
- **BYO:** you can bring your own alcohol
- **corkage, $/bottle:** if you bring your own alcohol, the facility charges a fee per bottle to remove the cork and pour
- **WCB only:** *(or any combination of these three letters)* only wine, champagne and beer are permitted
- **licensed server:** the server of alcohol must be licensed

SMOKING

- **allowed:** smoking is permitted throughout the facility
- **outside only:** smoking is not permitted inside the facility
- **not allowed:** smoking is not permitted anywhere on the premises
- **designated areas:** specific areas for smoking have been designated

MUSIC

Almost every facility allows acoustic music unless stated otherwise. Essentially, restrictions refer to amplified music.

- **amplified OK:** amplified music is acceptable without restriction
- **outside only:** no amplified music allowed inside

- **inside only:** no amplified music permitted outside
- **amplified OK with limits or restrictions:** amplified music is allowed, but there are limits on volume, hours of play, type of instruments, etc.

WHEELCHAIR ACCESS

Accessibility is based on whether the event areas (not necessarily the restrooms) of a facility are wheelchair accessible or not.

- **yes:** the facility is accessible
- **limited:** the facility is accessible but with difficulty (there may be a step at the entrance, for example, but all of the rooms are accessible)
- **no:** the facility is not accessible

INSURANCE

Many facilities require that you purchase and show proof of some insurance coverage. The type and amount of insurance varies with the facility, and some facilities offer insurance for a minimal charge.

- **liability required, certificate required** or **proof of insurance required:** additional insurance is required
- **not required:** no additional insurance is required
- **may be required:** sometimes additional insurance is required

Valuable Tips

Selecting an Event Venue

Before you jump into the venue descriptions in *Here Comes The Guide,* identify what kind of celebration you want and establish selection criteria early. Here are some basics:

Your Venue's Geographical Location

For many couples, it's important that the location they select is easy for the majority of their guests to get to. However, whether you're hosting your event close to home or planning a destination wedding in another city, state or country, you need to think about the logistics of getting everyone to your event site.

Special Considerations in Northern California

Guests may be traveling a considerable distance by car to get to your party destination. Sure, they can use Google Maps or their vehicle's GPS to get directions to your venue, but those resources aren't always 100% reliable. Given the Northern California freeway system and traffic congestion, you'll save your guests lots of time and trouble if you provide, along with the invitation, specific directions on a separate map drawn to scale. Include symbols indicating north, south, etc. and the names of the appropriate off-ramps. If you're not sure about exits, landmarks or street names, take a dry run of the route to make sure everything on your map is accurate and easy to follow. If your function occurs after dark, do the test drive at night so you can note well-lit landmarks that will prevent your guests from getting lost—both coming to your event and going home.

If you're having a Friday evening event, take commuters into account, especially if your event site is in an area that gets bumper-to-bumper traffic. One solution is to schedule your get-together after 7pm when freeways are less congested.

Even if you have few constraints when picking a location, it's still worth considering the total driving time to and from your destination. When it's more than two hours, an over-night stay may be necessary, and you may be limited to a Saturday night event, since your nearest and dearest won't be able to spend hours on the road during the week. If you're going to need lodging for some of your guests during your celebration, be sure to check out the "Guest Accommodations/Room Blocks" section on HereComesTheGuide.com for suggestions and info. If you have guests arriving by plane, it's certainly helpful if there's an airport nearby, and if your co-workers, friends or family enjoy drinking try to house them close to the event site or have contact numbers handy for transportation via taxis or Uber.

There's no reason why you can't contemplate a special event in the Santa Cruz Mountains or in a wine cave in Calistoga. Just remember that if you're planning a wedding that's not local, a venue's on-site coordinator or a wedding planner can really help: Many are experienced in handling destination events and can be a great asset.

Budget

Many couples aren't very experienced with event budgeting and don't know how to esti-mate what locations, products and services will ultimately cost. If you're not sure what you can realistically afford, we recommend talking to a professional event planner or wedding coordinator early in the planning stages. You don't have to make a big financial or time commitment to use a professional; many will assist you on an hourly basis for a nuts-and-bolts session to determine priorities and to assign costs to items on your wish list.

Part of being realistic involves some simple arithmetic. Catering costs, for example, are usually calculated on a per-person basis. The couple who has $10,000 and wants to invite 250 guests should know that $40 per guest actually won't go very far. Tax and gratuity combined usually consume 23–33% of the food & beverage budget. If you subtract that 30% from $40, you have $28 left. If you also serve alcohol at $12/person, you're down to $16/person for food. That's usually not enough for appetizers and a seated meal, let alone location rental fees, entertainment, flowers, printed invitations, photography, etc.

Before you make any major decisions or commit any of your funds for specific items, take a serious look at your total budget, make sure it can cover all your anticipated expenses, and leave a little cushion for last-minute items. If your budget doesn't cover everything, it's time for some hard decisions. If you have a very large guest list and a small pocketbook, you may need to shorten the list or cut back on some of the amenities you want to include. No matter who foots the bill, be advised that doing the homework here really counts. Pin down your costs at the beginning of the planning stage and get all estimates in writing.

> **The important point is that if you know what kind of event you want and are clear about your budget, your search will be faster and easier.**

Style

Do you know what kind of event you want? Will it be formal or informal? A traditional wedding or an innovative party? Will it be held at night or during the day? Indoors or outdoors? Is having a garden ceremony or gourmet food a deal breaker? By identifying the geographical area and the most important elements of your dream wedding before you start looking for a venue, you can really narrow down your search.

Guest Count

How many people are anticipated? Many facilities request a rough estimate 60–90 days in advance of your function—and they'll want a deposit based on the figure you give them. A confirmed guest count or guarantee is usually required 72 hours prior to the event. It's important to come up with a solid estimate of your guest list early on in order to plan your budget and select the right ceremony or reception spot.

It's also important to ensure that the guest count you give the facility *before* your event doesn't change *during* your event. Believe it or not, it's possible to have more people at your reception than you expected. How? Some folks who did not bother to RSVP may decide to show up anyway. In one case we know of, the parents of the bride got an additional bill for $1,200 on the event day because there were 30 "surprise" guests beyond the guest count guarantee who were wined and dined. To prevent this from happening to you—especially if you're having a large reception where it's hard to keep track of all the guests—it's a good idea to contact everyone who did *not* RSVP. Let them know as politely as possible that you will need to have their response by a given date to finalize food & beverage totals.

Seasonal Differences

Northern California, for all its (pardon the expression) faults, has got some great advantages weather-wise. Outdoor special events, ceremonies and receptions can take place throughout most of the year, and from September to November you can anticipate sunny skies and warm temperatures. However, when the mercury rises in inland areas, watch out. A canopy or tables with umbrellas are essential for screening the sun. In fact, you should ask each facility manager about the sun's direction and intensity with respect to the time of day and month your event will take place. Guests will be uncomfortable facing into the sun during a ceremony, and white walls and enclosed areas bounce light around and can hold in heat. If your event is scheduled for midday in July, for example, include a note on your location map to bring sunglasses, hat and sunscreen. If you also mention words like "poolside," "yacht deck" or "lawn seating" on the map, it will help guests know how to dress. In summer, you might want to consider an evening rather than a midday celebration. Not only is the air cooler, but you may also get an extra bonus—a glorious sunset.

If you're arranging an outdoor party November through April, or in the foothills or mountain areas, expect cooler weather and prepare a contingency plan. Despite our region's favorable Mediterranean climate, it has rained in May, June and July, so consider access to an inside space or a tent (and factor in any additional cost that might require).

Special Requirements

Sometimes places have strict rules and regulations. If most of your guests smoke, then pick a location that doesn't restrict smoking. If alcohol is going to be consumed, make sure it's allowed and find out if bar service needs to be licensed. If dancing and a big band are critical, then limit yourself to those locations that can accommodate them and the accompanying decibels. Do you have children, seniors or disabled guests, vegetarians or folks who want kosher food on your list? If so, you need to plan for them, too. It's essential that you identify the special factors that are important for your event before you sign a contract.

Locking in Your Event Date

Let's say it's the first day of your hunt for the perfect spot, and the second place you see is an enchanting garden that happens to be available on the date you want. You really like it but, since you've only seen two locations, you're not 100% sure that this is *the* place. No problem. You decide to keep your options open by making a tentative reservation. The site coordinator dutifully pencils your name into her schedule book and says congratulations. You say thanks, we have a few more places (like 25) to check out, but this one looks terrific. Then off you go, secure in the knowledge that if none of the other sites you visit pans out, you still have this lovely garden waiting for you.

The nightmare begins a couple of weeks, or perhaps months, down the road when you've finished comparison-shopping and call back the first place you liked to finalize the details. So sorry, the coordinator says. We gave away your date because a) oops, one of the other gals who works here erased your name by mistake (after all, it was only *penciled* in), b) we didn't hear back from you soon enough, or c) you never confirmed your reservation with a deposit.

For the tiniest instant you picture yourself inflicting bodily harm on the coordinator or at least slapping the facility with a lawsuit, but alas, there's really not much you can do. Whether a genuine mistake was made or the facility purposely gave your date to another, perhaps more lucrative party (this happens sometimes with hotels who'd rather book a big convention on your date than a little wedding), you're out of luck. To avoid the pain (and ensuing panic) of getting bumped, here's what we suggest: Instead of just being penciled in, ask if you can write a refundable $100–250 check to hold the date for a limited time. If the person in charge is willing to do this but wants the full deposit up front (usually nonrefundable), then you'll need to decide whether you can afford to lose the entire amount if you find a more appealing location later on. Once the coordinator or sales person takes your money, you're automatically harder to bump. Make sure you get a receipt that has the event date, year, time and space(s) reserved written on it, as well as the date your tentative reservation runs out. Then, just to be on the safe side, check in with the facility weekly while you're considering other sites to prevent any possible "mistakes" from being made. When you finally do commit to a place, get a signed contract or at least a confirmation letter. If you don't receive written confirmation

> **If you try to pick a venue before you've made basic decisions, selection will be a struggle and it will take longer to find a spot that will make you happy.**

within a week, hound the coordinator until you get it, even if you have to drive to the sales office and stand there until they hand it over to you. And even after you've plunked down your money and have a letter and/or contract securing your date, call the coordinator every other month to reconfirm your reservation. It pays to stay on top of this, no matter how locked in you think you are. If you don't hear back from your contact in a reasonable time frame despite repeated attempts, you should contact the facility or catering sales department directly to confirm that your coordinator still works there. If she/he doesn't, find out who is responsible for managing your event, and verify that your contract (and the must-have details) are still in place.

Parking

Parking is seldom a critical factor if you get married outside an urban area, but make sure you know how it's going to be handled if you're planning a party in a parking-challenged place like downtown San Francisco, San Jose or Berkeley.

A map is a handy supplement to any invitation, and there's usually enough room on it to indicate how and where vehicles should be parked. Depending on the location, you may want to add a note suggesting carpooling or mention that a shuttle service or valet parking is provided. If there's a fee for parking, identify the anticipated cost per car and where the entry points are to the nearest parking lots. The last thing you want are surprised and disgruntled guests who can't find a place to stash their car, or who are shocked at the $20–40 parking tab.

Professional Help

If you're a busy person with limited time to plan and execute a party, pick a facility that offers complete coordination services, from catering and flowers to decorations and music. Or better yet, hire a professional event or wedding coordinator. Either way, you'll make your life much easier by having someone else handle the details. And often the relationships these professionals have with vendors can end up saving you money, too.

Food and Alcohol Quality

Food and alcohol account for the greatest portion of an event's budget; consequently, food & beverage selections are a big deal. Given the amount of money you will spend on this category alone, you should be concerned about the type, quantity and quality of what you eat and drink. If in-house catering is provided, we suggest you sample different menu options prior to paying a facility deposit. If you'd like to see how a facility handles food setup and presentation, ask the caterer to arrange a visit to someone else's party about a half hour before it starts. It's wise to taste wines and beers in advance, and be very specific about hard alcohol selections.

Hidden Costs

This may come as a surprise, but not all services and event equipment are covered in the rental fee, and some facilities hide the true cost of renting their space by having a low rental fee. It's possible to get nickeled and dimed for all the extras: tables, chairs, linens, dance floor, cake cutting, valet service and so forth. You can also end up paying more than you expected for security and cleanup. All these additional charges can really add up, so save yourself a big headache by understanding exactly what's included in the rental fee and what's not before you sign any contract.

Bonus Info

If you're not sure what to ask potential venues and event professionals, check out our "QUESTIONS TO ASK" section starting on page 21. We've put together lists of questions that come in very handy when you're interviewing potential event locations, photographers, caterers, etc.

Tips for Previewing a Venue

Make Appointments.

If you liked what you read about a venue in *The Guide,* then we recommend you make an appointment to see that location rather than just driving by. Sometimes an unremarkable-looking building will surprise you with a secluded garden or hidden courtyard. And sometimes the opposite is true—you'll love the stunning façade, but the interior isn't your style.

Incidentally, we've withheld the addresses of privately owned properties. Should you happen to know where any of these facilities is located, we urge you to respect the owner's or manager's privacy and make an appointment instead of stopping by.

When you do call for an appointment, don't forget to ask for specific directions, including cross streets. You can also look up the location on *HereComesTheGuide.com* and print out a detailed street map. Try to cluster your visits so that you can easily drive from one place to another without backtracking. Schedule at least an hour per facility and leave ample driving time. You want to be efficient, but don't over-schedule yourself. It's best to view places when you're fresh and your judgment isn't clouded by fatigue.

Bring along *The Guide* or use your phone or tablet to access our website.

We've listed the street address for each site, and our illustrations in the book often make it easier to identify the venues you're planning to see. And if you bring the book or use your smartphone or tablet to look up venues on HereComesTheGuide.com, you can double-check our information with the site representative.

Bring a notebook—paper or digital!

You can make notes in your copy of *Here Comes The Guide,* but have a small notebook or digital device handy, too. Keep track of the date, time and name of the person providing the information, and then read back the info to the site representative to confirm that what you heard is correct. Remember to have your notes with you when you review your contract, and go over in detail what you were told versus what's in the contract before you sign anything.

Take pictures.

Video is particularly useful for narrating your likes, dislikes and any other observations while you're shooting a venue. However, if you're just taking still photos, make sure you have a system for matching shots to their respective locations. You'd be surprised how easy it is to confuse photos. Make sure your phone or other gear is charged and bring whatever else you need to make it all work properly.

File everything.

Many facilities will hand you pamphlets, menus, rate charts and other materials. Develop a system for sorting and storing the information that keeps your notes, photos and handouts together, clearly labeled and easily accessible.

Bring a checkbook or credit card.

Some of the more attractive venues book a year to 18 months in advance. If you actually fall in love with a location and your date is available, plunk down a deposit to hold the date.

Working With a Venue

Confirm All the Details

When you make the initial phone call or email, confirm that the information presented in *Here Comes The Guide* is still valid. Show or read the information in our book to the site's representative, and have him or her inform you of any changes. If there have been significant increases in fees or new restrictions that you can't live with, cross the place off your list and move on. If the facility is still a contender, request a tour.

Once you've determined that the physical elements of the place suit you, it's time to discuss details. Ask about services and amenities or fees that may not be listed in the book and make a note of them. Outline your plans to the representative and make sure that the facility can accommodate your particular needs. If you don't want to handle all the details yourself, find out what the facility is willing and able to do, and if there will be an additional cost for their assistance. Venues often provide planning services for little or no extra charge. If other in-house services are offered, such as flowers or wedding cakes, inquire about the quality of each service provider and whether or not substitutions can be made. If you want to use your own vendors, find out if the facility will charge you an extra fee. For more help with working with a location, see our "Questions to Ask a Wedding Venue" on page 26.

The Importance of Rapport

Another factor to consider is your rapport with the person(s) you're working with. Are you comfortable with them? Do they listen well and respond to your questions directly? Do they inspire trust and confidence? Are they warm and enthusiastic or cold and aloof? If you have doubts, you need to resolve them before embarking on a working relationship with these folks—no matter how wonderful the facility itself is. Discuss your feelings with them, and if you're still not completely satisfied, get references and call them. If at the end of this process you still have lingering concerns, you may want to eliminate the facility from your list even though it seems perfect in every other way.

On the other hand, don't let your rapport with a banquet coordinator or site rep sway you to book a venue you aren't in love with—there's a lot of turnover in the hospitality industry, and you may call Brittany one day only to—surprise!—be referred to Brian. So if Brittany was your main reason for choosing this place, you could be in for a big disappointment if you and Brian don't hit it off and suddenly the venue's shortcomings really stand out.

Signing a Contract

It's easy to get emotionally attached to a location, but remember that it's not a done deal until you sign a contract. Now's the time to be businesslike and put your emotions aside. If you can't do that, get a non-emotional partner, friend or relative to help you review the small print and negotiate changes before you sign. Remember all those notes you took when you first visited the site? Compare them with what's actually written in the contract. No matter what someone told you about the availability of a dance floor, the price of pastel linens, or the ceremony arch, you can't hold the facility to it until the contract is signed. Places revise their prices and policies all the time, so assume that things may have changed since you originally saw the site or talked to a site representative.

If you're not happy with the contract, prepare to negotiate. Before your appointment with whoever has the power to alter the contract, make an itemized list, in order of importance, of the changes you want. Decide what you're willing to give up, and what you can't live without. If in the end the most important things on your list cannot be addressed to your satisfaction, this is probably not the right place for you. It's better to find another location than to stay with a facility that isn't willing to work with you.

Insurance Considerations

Nowadays, if someone gets injured at an event or something is damaged at or near the event site, it's likely that someone will be sued.

In order to protect themselves and spread the risk among all parties involved, facilities often require additional insurance and/or proof of insurance from service professionals and their clients.

Event sites and service professionals (such as caterers) are very aware of their potential liability and all have coverage of one kind or another. Many of the properties we represent will also require you, the renter, to get extra insurance.

What's funny (or not so funny) is that as more and more event sites require extra liability and/or a certificate of insurance, fewer insurance companies are willing to issue either one—even if you're covered under a homeowner's policy. At this point, insurance carriers don't want to attach extra clauses to your policy to increase coverage for a single event, and most, if not all, companies are unwilling to add the event site's name to your existing policy as an additional insured.

Don't despair. Even though it's hard to come by, you can get extra insurance for a specified period of time, and it's relatively inexpensive.

Obtaining Extra Insurance

- **The first thing to do is read your rental contract carefully.** Make sure you understand exactly *what's* required and *when* it's required. Most facilities want $1,000,000–2,000,000 in extra liability coverage. If you don't pay attention to the insurance clauses early in the game, you'll have to play catch-up at the last moment, frantically trying to locate a carrier who will issue you additional insurance. And, if you don't supply the certificate to the facility *on time,* you may run the risk of forfeiting your event site altogether.

- **The second thing is to ask your event site's representative if the site has an insurance policy through which you can purchase the required extra coverage.** If the answer is yes, then consider purchasing it—that's the easiest route (but not necessarily the best!). The facility's extra insurance coverage may not be the least expensive and it may not provide you with the best coverage. What you need to ask is: "If one of my guests or one of the professionals working at my event causes some damage to the premises or its contents, will this extra insurance cover it?" If the answer if yes, get it in writing.

- **The third thing, if the answer is no, is to find your own coverage.** We suggest you avoid random searches online and call one of these two insurance providers:

   1) WedSafe at 877/723-3933. This company insures weddings and private events. You can reach them at their toll free number or online at wedsafe.com. They offer coverage for wedding cancellation and/or liability.

2) WedSure®, a division of R.V. Nuccio & Associates, Inc. at 1-800-ENGAGED or www.WedSure.com. They specialize in insuring special events. Their website FAQs outline what's offered, and you can also contact them to clarify details and get a personalized quote.

Coverage starts at $95 for a wedding; the total cost will depend on what you want. Rob Nuccio's coverage is underwritten by Fireman's Fund.

Here are some of the items a typical policy might cover:

- Cancellation or postponement due to: weather, damage to the facility, sickness, failure to show of the caterer or officiant, financial reasons—even limited change-of-heart circumstances!

- Photography or videography: failure of the professional to appear, loss of original negatives, etc.

- Lost, stolen or damaged gifts

- Lost, stolen or damaged equipment rentals

- Lost, stolen or damaged bridal gown or other special attire

- Lost, stolen or damaged jewelry

- Personal liability and additional coverage

- Medical payments for injuries incurred during the event

If you use this service, call or email to let us know whether you're happy with them. We'd love to get your feedback.

It Can't Happen To Me

Don't be lulled into the notion that an event disaster can't happen to you. It could rain when you least expect it. Or your well-intentioned aunt might melt your wedding dress while ironing out a few wrinkles. Wouldn't it be nice to know that your dress, wedding photos, equipment rentals and gifts are covered? Naturally, a New Year's Eve party or a high school prom night is riskier than a wedding, but we could tell you stories of upscale parties where something did happen and a lawsuit resulted.

So even if extra insurance is not required, you may still want to consider additional coverage, especially if alcohol is being served. *You are the best predictor of your guests' behavior.* If you plan on having a wild, wonderful event, a little additional insurance could be a good thing.

Recycling

Do Your Part!

If you're wondering why we're including a brief item about recycling in a book like *Here Comes The Guide,* it's because parties and special events often generate recyclable materials as well as leftover food and flowers.

You and your caterer can feel good by donating the excess, and recycling plastic bottles, glass, paper, etc. An added benefit is that food donations are tax deductible for either you or the caterer. And if you recycle, the cost for extra garbage bins can be eliminated or reduced. Call your local recycling center to arrange a pickup.

Food donations can be distributed to teenage drop-in centers, youth shelters, alcoholic treatment centers, rescue missions, and AIDS hospices, as well as senior, homeless and refugee centers. Flowers will brighten the day of patients or residents at your favorite local hospital, hospice or senior center.

IMPORTANT: There are regulations that apply to the kinds of foods that can be donated and how they need to be packaged. If you plan to donate your leftovers, it's best to talk to your caterer about it or call the places where you'd like to donate *prior* to your event to find out what their requirements for preparation and drop-off are. Look online to find Northern California food banks and homeless shelters that take food donations.

For more valuable tips about going green, read our article "It's A Nice Day for a Green Wedding." You'll find it in the Wedding Ideas section on HereComesTheGuide.com!

Working With Event Professionals

Hiring a Caterer: Get References and Look for Professionalism

If you're selecting your own caterer, get references from friends and acquaintances or, better yet, contact any of the caterers featured on HereComesTheGuide.com. We've thoroughly screened these companies and can assure you that they're in the top 5% of the industry in terms of quality and service. We keep all of their references on file, so you can contact us and ask questions about them.

Every caterer is different. Some offer only pre-set menus while others will help you create your own. Menus and prices vary enormously, so try to have a good idea of what you want and what you can spend before interviewing prospective caterers. After you've talked to several caterers and have decided which ones to seriously consider, request references from each one and call them. Ask not only about the quality of the food, but about the ease of working with a given caterer. You'll want to know if the caterer is professional—fully prepared and equipped, punctual and organized. You may also want to know if the caterer is licensed, prepares food in a kitchen approved by the Department of Health, or carries workmen's compensation and liability insurance. And don't forget to inquire about the cleanup—did the staff remove all the equipment and garbage in a matter that was acceptable? Although this level of inquiry may seem unnecessary, responses to these questions will give you a more complete picture of how a caterer runs his or her business, and will help you determine which one is best suited for your event.

Facility Requirements for Caterers

Facilities often have specific requirements regarding caterers—they may have to be licensed and bonded, out by 11pm or fastidiously clean. Before you hire a caterer, make sure that he or she is compatible with your site. In fact, even if the facility does not require it, it's a good idea to have your caterer visit the place in advance to become familiar with any special circumstances or problems that might come up. You'll notice throughout *Here Comes The Guide* the words "in-house" or "select from list" after the word *Catering*. Sites that have an exclusive caterer or only permit you to select from a preferred list do so because each wants to eliminate most of the risks involved in having a caterer on the premises who is not accustomed to working in that environment. Exclusive or preferred caterers have achieved their exalted status because they either provide consistently good services or they won the catering contract when it went out to bid. Whether you're working with one of your facility's choices or your own, make sure that your contract includes everything you have agreed on before you sign it.

Working with an Event Planner or Wedding Coordinator

Opting to hire a professional planner may be a wise choice. A good consultant will ask you all the right questions, determine exactly what you need, and take care of as much or as little of your affair as you want. If you'd like to feel like a guest at your own event, have the consultant manage everything, including orchestrating the day of the event. If you only want some advice and structure, hire a planner on a meeting-by-meeting basis.

Most of the principles used in selecting a caterer apply to hiring an event coordinator. Try to get suggestions from friends or facilities, follow up on references the coordinators give you, compare service fees and make sure you and the coordinator are compatible. The range of professionalism and experience varies greatly, so it really is to your advantage to investigate each coordinator's track record. You can save a lot of time by starting with the coordinators featured on HereComesTheGuide.com

Again, once you've found someone who can accommodate you, get everything in writing so that there won't be any misunderstandings down the road. Although engaging a professional to "manage" your event can be a godsend, it can also be problematic if you turn the entire decision-making process over to them. Don't forget that it's your party, and no one else should decide what's right for you.

For lists of questions to ask potential wedding venues and vendors, go to page 21 in this book. You can also find them on HereComesTheGuide.com.

Questions To Ask
Venues and Event Professionals

(including Here Comes The Guide's Wedding Checklist)

Here Comes The Guide's Wedding Checklist

10–12 Months To Go...

☐ Visit HereComesTheGuide.com and start planning your wedding!

☐ Work out your budget and establish your top priorities—where to save/where to splurge.

☐ Find ideas. Start browsing bridal blogs and magazines (or visit Pinterest.com/HCTG) to identify your wedding style and color palette.

☐ Compile your preliminary guest list (you'll need that guest count!).

☐ Choose your wedding party—who do you want by your side at the altar?

☐ Find a venue for your ceremony and reception, and reserve your date.

☐ Now that you have a date, tell everyone to save it! For destination weddings or weddings around a holiday, consider sending out Save-the-Date cards or emails. Or create your own wedding website, and let your invitees know about it.

☐ Find a dress and begin assembling the perfect accessories. Need inspiration? Attend a bridal fair or trunk show.

☐ Already feeling overwhelmed? Consider hiring a Wedding Coordinator.

☐ Assemble an all-star vendor team. We'd start with:
  • Caterer
  • Photographer/Videographer
  • Officiant
  When you hire a vendor, get all the details in writing!

☐ Another way to minimize stress: Start dreaming up your honeymoon…and check out our "Plan A Honeymoon" section on HereComesTheGuide.com.

6–9 Months To Go...

☐ Continue researching, interviewing and booking vendors. And don't forget, when you hire one make sure to put everything in writing!

  • Decide on arrangements with your Floral Designer.
  • Do a tasting and choose your wedding cake with your Cake Designer.
  • Hire the DJ/Entertainment for your ceremony, cocktail hour and reception.
  • Discuss the style and wording of your wedding invitations with a Stationer.

☐ Create your gift registry (and don't forget to update your wedding website!).

☐ Arrange hotel room blocks for out-of-town guests and book your own suite for the wedding night. See HereComesTheGuide.com for room block options.

☐ Shop for bridesmaid/flower girl dresses and give your attendants clear instructions on how to place their orders.

☐ Arrange and book any necessary transportation.

☐ Go over bridal shower/bachelorette details and the guest list with the person(s) hosting your party.

3–5 Months To Go...

☐ Book the rehearsal and rehearsal dinner locations (see HereComesTheGuide.com for rehearsal dinner options). If you're including entertainment or specialty details like a groom's cake, now's the time to lock in these elements.

☐ Put together your rehearsal dinner guest list.

☐ Make childcare arrangements for your guests' kids.

☐ Reserve all necessary party rentals and linens.

☐ Order wedding favors for your guests.

☐ Shop for and reserve men's formalwear.

☐ Concentrate on finalizing the:
  • Guest list. Get everyone's mailing address.
  • Invitation wording. Confirm your invitation text with the Stationer, and consider additional stationery (programs, menu cards, place cards, thank-you cards, etc.).

Schedule a pickup date for your invites.

- Ceremony readings and vows.
- Menu, beverage and catering details.
- Timeline of the reception formalities.

☐ Do a Makeup & Hair trial and book your stylists. While you're at it, come up with your own beauty and fitness regimen to be camera-ready for the big day.

☐ Shop for and purchase your wedding rings.

☐ Finalize honeymoon plans and obtain all necessary documents (are you sure your passports are up to date?).

6–8 Weeks To Go...

☐ You're getting close…mail out those invitations! Have a game plan for recording the RSVPs and meal choices.

☐ Touch base with your vendors to confirm date, deposits and details.

☐ Start researching marriage license requirements and name-change paperwork.

☐ Begin your dress fittings. Be sure to buy the appropriate undergarments beforehand.

☐ So you think you *can't* dance? Consider taking a dance lesson with your fiancé—a good way to break in your bridal shoes!

☐ Give the wedding party a nudge—make sure they've ordered all necessary attire.

☐ Write thank-you cards for shower gifts and any early wedding gifts received.

3–5 Weeks To Go...

☐ Send out rehearsal dinner invitations. If your get-together will be informal, feel free to send an Evite.

☐ Finalize and confirm:

- Wedding vows and readings with your Officiant.
- Shot list with your Photographer/ Videographer.
- Song list for ceremony, cocktail hour and reception with your DJ and/or Band/ Musicians.

- Timeline for the reception and who's giving the toasts.
- Wedding night and honeymoon accommodations.

☐ Obtain marriage license and complete name-change documents, if applicable.

☐ Pick up your wedding rings and proofread any engraving!

☐ If you're the traditional type, do you have something old, new, borrowed and blue?

☐ Purchase your guest book, toasting flutes, cake servers, unity candle, and all that good stuff.

☐ Buy gifts (optional) for the wedding party and parents of the bride and groom.

☐ Have your final dress fitting. Bring your shoes and accessories for the full impact.

☐ Sigh. Hunt down whoever hasn't RSVP'd yet.

1–2 Weeks To Go...

☐ Give your caterer/venue the final guest count.

☐ Arrange seating and create the seating chart and/or place cards.

☐ Pick up your gown. Swoon.

☐ Confirm arrival times and finalize the wedding timeline with vendors and the wedding party—make sure your MOH has a copy, too.

☐ Put together your own Bridal Emergency Kit.

☐ Speaking of emergencies: Check the weather report, and if things look iffy contact your venue to make sure a contingency plan is in place.

☐ Start packing for your honeymoon. (See "weather report" above.)

☐ In desperate need of a facial or massage? Now's the time to squeeze one in.

The Day Before...

☐ Make sure all wedding-day items are packed/ laid out and ready to go! (Don't forget the rings and marriage license!)

☐ Figure out tips and final payments for vendors. Put them in clearly marked envelopes and give them to the Best Man or another person you trust to hand out at the reception.

☐ Assign someone to pack up your gifts/ belongings after the reception (don't forget the top tier of your cake!).

☐ Thank your BFF for agreeing to return your groom's tux and other rental items the day after the wedding.

☐ Enjoy a mani-pedi.

☐ Attend the rehearsal and dinner. Now's the time to give out wedding party gifts.

☐ Try to go to bed early...you need your beauty sleep tonight.

Wedding-day advice...

☐ Allow plenty of time to get ready.

☐ Do the rounds at your wedding—greet everyone and thank them for coming.

☐ Take a deep breath. Stop to appreciate your new spouse and the day that you spent so much time planning!

After the Honeymoon/Back to Reality...

☐ Write and send thank-you cards. (Don't procrastinate!)

☐ Complete your registry and exchange any unwanted or duplicate gifts.

☐ Have your wedding dress cleaned and preserved by a reputable company.

☐ Keep in touch with your Photographer/ Videographer to work on albums, DVDs, etc.

☐ Enjoy wedded bliss...

Questions to Ask a Wedding Venue

Here Comes The Guide is a fantastic resource to help you find the location to host your wedding, rehearsal dinner or company party. Even with all the info we provide, though, you'll need to address your specific needs with each venue you visit to come up with a winner.

The following list of questions and tips will help you navigate through your location search (for a printable version, go to HereComesTheGuide.com). Use them as a guide while you're talking with a site contact or reviewing a site information packet. Feel free to add questions that relate to your particular event (e.g. "Can my dog be the ring bearer in my ceremony?") Make sure to get everything in writing in your final contract! **Don't forget to have a notebook, digital device or your planning binder handy so that you can record answers to all these questions.**

1. What dates are available in the month I'm considering?

2. How many people can this location accommodate?

3. What is the rental fee and what is included in that price? Is there a discount for booking an off-season date or Sunday through Friday?

4. How much is the deposit, when is it due, and is it refundable? What's the payment plan for the entire bill?

5. Can I hold my ceremony here, too? Is there an additional charge? Is the ceremony site close to the reception site? Are there changing areas for the bride and groom? How much time is allocated for the rehearsal?

6. Is the site handicap accessible? (To be asked if you have guests with mobility issues.)

7. What's the cancellation policy? *NOTE: Some places will refund most of your deposit if you cancel far enough in advance, since there's still a chance they can rent the space. After a certain date, though, you may not be able to get a refund—at least not a full one.*

8. What's your weather contingency plan for outdoor spaces?

9. How long will I have use of the event space(s) I reserve? Is there an overtime fee if I stay longer? Is there a minimum or maximum rental time?

10. Can I move things around and decorate to suit my purposes, or do I have to leave everything as is? Are there decoration guidelines/restrictions? Can I use real candles? *TIP: Keep the existing décor in mind when planning your own decorations so that they won't clash. If your event is in December, ask what the venue's holiday décor will be.*

11. What time can my vendors start setting up on the day of the wedding? Is it possible to start the setup the day before? How early can deliveries be made? How much time will I have for décor setup? Does the venue provide assistance getting

gifts or décor back to a designated car, hotel room, etc. after the event has concluded?

12. Do you provide a coat check service (especially important for winter weddings)? If not, is there an area that can be used and staffed for that purpose?

13. Is there an outdoor space where my guests can mingle, and can it be heated and/or protected from the elements if necessary? Is there a separate indoor "socializing" space?

14. Do you have an in-house caterer or a list of "preferred" caterers, or do I need to provide my own? Even if there is an in-house caterer, do I have the option of using an outside caterer instead?

15. If I hire my own caterer, are kitchen facilities available for them? *NOTE: Caterers charge extra if they have to haul in refrigerators and stoves.*

16. Are tables, linens, chairs, plates, silverware and glassware provided, or will I have to rent them myself or get them through my caterer?

17. What is the food & beverage cost on a per-person basis? What is the tax and service charge?

18. Can we do a food tasting prior to finalizing our menu selection? If so, is there an additional charge?

19. Can I bring in a cake from an outside cake maker or must I use a cake made on the premises? Is there a cake-cutting fee? If I use a cake made on site is the fee waived? Do you provide special cake-cutting utensils?

20. Can I bring my own wine, beer or champagne, and is there a corkage fee if I do? Can I bring in other alcohol?

21. Are you licensed to provide alcohol service? If so, is alcohol priced per person? By consumption? Are there additional charges for bar staff? Is there a bar minimum that must be met before the conclusion of the event? What is the average bar tab for the number of people attending my event? *NOTE: Some facilities (private estates and wineries in particular) aren't licensed to serve hard*

alcohol. You may need to get permission from the location to bring in an outside beverage catering company.

22. Are there restrictions on what kind of music I can play, or a time by which the music must end? Can the venue accommodate a DJ or live band? *TIP: Check where the outlets are located in your event space, because that will help you figure out where the band can set up and where other vendors can hook up their equipment. You don't want the head table to block the only outlet in the room.*

23. Is there parking on site? If so, is it complimentary? Do you offer valet parking, and what is the charge? If there is no parking on site, where will my guests park? Are cabs easily accessible from the venue? If a shuttle service is needed, can you assist with setting it up? *TIP: You should have the venue keep track of the number of cars parked for your event and add the total valet gratuity to your final bill so that your guests won't have to tip.*

24. How many restrooms are there? *TIP: You should have at least 4 restrooms per 100 people.*

25. Do you offer on-site coordination? If so, what services are included and is there an additional charge for them? Will the coordinator supervise day-of? How much assistance can I get with the setup/décor?

26. What security services do you offer? Do I need to hire my own security guards, or does the site hire them or have them on staff? *TIP: In general, you should have 2 security guards for the first 100 guests and 1 more for every additional 100 guests.*

27. Does the venue have liability insurance? *NOTE: If someone gets injured during the party, you don't want to be held responsible—if the site doesn't have insurance, you'll need to get your own. For info on insurance go to page 14.*

28. Can I hire my own vendors (caterer, coordinator, DJ, etc.), or must I select from a preferred vendor list? If I can bring my own, do you have a list of recommended vendors? *TIP: Check out the prescreened vendors featured on HereComes-TheGuide.com. They're all top event professionals who have passed our extensive reference check and been Certified By The Guide.*

29. What overnight accommodations do you provide? Do you offer a discount for booking multiple rooms? Do you provide a complimentary room or upgrade for the newlyweds? What are the near-est hotels to the venue? *TIP: Some venues have partnerships with local hotels that offer a discount if you book a block of rooms.*

30. Do you have signage or other aids to direct guests to my event?

31. Do you have a recycling policy?

More Tips:

- If you really love the site, ask the venue representative to put together a proposal with all the pricing and policies—including the tax and service charge—so you have an idea of the basic cost.

- Use your cell phone (or a digital camera) to take photos or videos of the locations you visit, so that you have a record of what you liked or didn't like about them. And if you're planning to visit more than a few venues, it's a good idea to snap a photo of each one's sign when you arrive—that way you won't get confused about which place is which when you review your photos later.

- Pay attention to the venue as a whole: Check out everything, including the restrooms, the foyer, the dressing rooms, the outdoor lighting and even the kitchen. You want to be sure your vision can be realized at this location. If possible, make arrangements with the site representative to visit the venue when it's set up for a wedding.

- GET EVERYTHING IN WRITING. Your date is not officially reserved until you sign a contract and, in many cases, give a deposit—even if a site contact says you don't need to worry about it. Once you've found THE PLACE, make sure you ask what is required to get your booking locked in and then follow through on satisfying those requirements. And don't assume that just because the site coordinator said you can have 4 votive candles per table you'll get them. Before you sign a contract, read the fine print and make sure it includes everything you and the site contact agreed on. As new things are added or changed in your contract, have the updated version printed out and signed by you and the site representative. Also, document all your conversations in emails and keep your correspondence.

Questions to Ask a Wedding Photographer

You've put so much time and effort into planning your wedding you'll want every special moment captured for your photo album. But how do you know which photographer is right for you? Whether you're considering any of our *Certified By The Guide* wedding photographers or another professional, you need to do your homework.

Here are the questions you should ask those photographers who've made your short list, to ensure that the one you ultimately choose is a good fit for you and your wedding.

The Basics

1. Do you have my date available? *NOTE: Obviously, if the answer is NO and you're not willing or able to change your date, don't bother asking the rest of these questions.*

2. How far in advance do I need to book with you?

3. How long have you been in business?

4. How many weddings have you shot? Have you done many that were similar to mine in size and style?

5. How would you describe your photography style (e.g. traditional, photojournalistic, creative)? *NOTE: It's helpful to know the differences between wedding photography styles so that you can discuss your preferences with your photographer. For descriptions of the various styles, see the next page.*

6. How would you describe your working style? *NOTE: The answer should help you determine whether this is a photographer who blends into the background and shoots what unfolds naturally, or creates a more visible presence by taking charge and choreographing shots.*

7. What do you think distinguishes your work from that of other photographers?

8. Do you have a portfolio I can review? Are all of the images yours, and is the work recent?

9. What type of equipment do you use?

10. Are you shooting in digital or film format or both? *NOTE: The general consensus seems to be that either format yields excellent photos in the hands of an experienced professional, and that most people can't tell the difference between film and digital images anyway. However, film takes longer to process than digital.*

11. Do you shoot in color and black & white? Infrared? *NOTE: Photographers who shoot in a digital format can make black & white or sepia versions of color photos.*

12. Can I give you a list of specific shots we would like?

13. Can you put together a slideshow of the engagement session (along with other photos the couple provides) and show it during the cocktail hour? What about an "instant" slideshow of the ceremony?

14. What information do you need from me before the wedding day?

15. Have you ever worked with my florist? DJ? Coordinator, etc.? *NOTE: Great working relationships between vendors can make things go more smoothly. It's especially helpful if your videographer and photographer work well together.*

16. May I have a list of references? *NOTE: The photographer should not hesitate to provide this.*

The Shoot

17. Are you the photographer who will shoot my wedding? If so, will you have any assistants with you on that day? If not, who will be taking the pictures and can I meet them before my wedding? *NOTE: You should ask the questions on this list of whoever is going to be the primary photographer at your event, and that photographer's name should be on your contract.*

18. Do you have backup equipment? What about a backup plan if you (or my scheduled photographer) are unable to shoot my wedding for some reason?

19. If my wedding site is out of your area, do you charge a travel fee and what does that cover?

20. Are you photographing other events on the same day as mine?

21. How will you (and your assistants) be dressed? *NOTE: The photographer and his/her staff should look professional and fit in with the style of your event.*

22. Is it okay if other people take photos while you're taking photos?

23. Have you ever worked at my wedding site before? If not, do you plan to check it out in advance? *NOTE: Photographers who familiarize themselves with a location ahead of time will be prepared for any lighting issues or restrictions, and will know how best to incorporate the site's architectural elements into the photos.*

24. What time will you arrive at the site and for how long will you shoot?

25. If my event lasts longer than expected, will you stay? Is there an additional charge?

Packages, Proofs and Prints

26. What packages do you offer?

27. Can I customize a package based on my needs?

28. Do you include engagement photos in your packages?

29. What type of album designs do you offer? Do you provide any assistance in creating an album?

30. Do you provide retouching, color adjustment or other corrective services?

31. How long after the wedding will I get the proofs? Will they be viewable online?

32. What is the ordering process?

33. How long after I order my photos/album will I get them?

34. Will you give me the negatives or the digital images, and is there a fee for that?

Contracts and Policies

35. When will I receive a written contract? *TIP: Don't book a photographer—or any vendor—who won't provide a written contract.*

36. How much of a deposit do you require and when is it due? Do you offer a payment plan?

37. What is your refund/cancellation policy?

38. Do you have liability insurance?

Questions to Ask Yourself:

1. Do I feel a connection with this photographer as well as his/her photos? Are our personalities a good match?

2. Am I comfortable with this person's work and communication style?

3. Has this photographer listened well and addressed all my concerns?

Check references. *Ask the photographer for at least 5 references, preferably of couples whose weddings were similar to yours in size and/or style. Getting feedback from several people who have actually hired the photographer in question can really help you decide if that person is right for you. Be sure to check out the photographers on HereComesTheGuide.com. They're some of the best in the business and have all been Certified By The Guide.*

Photography Style Glossary

Though there are no standard "dictionary definitions" of photographic styles, it's still a good idea to have an understanding of the following approaches before you interview photographers:

Traditional, Classic: The main idea behind this timeless style is to produce posed photographs for display in a portrait album. The photographer works from a "shot list," ensuring he or she covers all the elements the bride and groom have requested. To make sure every detail of the shots is perfect, the photographer and his/her assistants not only adjust their equipment, but also the background, the subject's body alignment, and even the attire.

Photojournalism: Originally favored by the news media, this informal, reality-based approach is the current rage in wedding photography. Rather than posing your pictures, the photographer follows you and your guests throughout the wedding day, capturing events as they unfold to tell the story of your wedding. He or she has to be able to fade into the background and become "invisible" in order to snap these candid or unposed photos, and must also possess a keen eye and a willingness to do what it takes to get the shot.

Illustrative Photography: This style, which is often used for engagement photos, is a pleasing blend of traditional and photojournalistic, with an emphasis on composition, lighting and background. The photographer places subjects together in an interesting environment and encourages them to relax and interact. Illustrative captures some of the spontaneity of candids, while offering the technical control of posed shots.

Portraiture: Traditional photographers generally excel at the precision required in portraiture—formal, posed pictures that emphasize one or more people. Couples interested in a more edgy result may prefer Fine Art Portraiture, with its dramatic lighting, unique angles and European flavor.

High Fashion: Commercial photographers excel at creating striking, simple photographs that dramatize the subject—and, of course, her clothes! Though not a style generally included in wedding photography, you may want to choose a photographer with high fashion experience if looking artsy and glamorous while showing off your dress is important to you.

Natural Light: Rather than using a camera flash, photographers use the natural light found in a setting, usually daylight. The look is warm and, well, natural—yet the photographer must be skilled to deal with shadows and other lighting challenges.

Questions to Ask a Wedding Planner

In the first flush of joy after your engagement, you probably began browsing wedding websites, social media sites like Pinterest, and magazines. If you soon felt buried by a blizzard of checklists and a daunting array of decisions, you and your fiancé might want to think about hiring a professional wedding planner.

Depending on your budget and needs, you can contract:

- a full-service planner to arrange every detail

- someone to assist you only in choosing your wedding location and vendors

- a day-of coordinator (which really means 30 days before your wedding)

NOTE: Many locations have in-house coordinators, but make sure you're clear on exactly what level of service they provide. Venue coordinators usually just handle day-of issues and offer a list of their preferred vendors, so having your own planner may still be a great help.

Even though hiring a planner is an added cost, they often end up saving you money in the long run. And no doubt about it—the right wedding planner can definitely save you time and stress (priceless!).

Before interviewing potential wedding planners, you and your fiancé should have an idea of:

- How much money you have in your budget
- How many people you would like to invite
- Your preferred wedding date
- Your vision for your wedding *(NOTE: If you aren't sure yet don't worry—getting help with this is one of the reasons why you're hiring a wedding planner!)*

After each interview is complete, ask yourselves:

- Did we feel heard?
- Does the planner understand our vision?
- Did we get a strong sense he/she will work with our budget?
- Was there a good connection and did our personalities mesh well?

Listen to your gut. If an interview doesn't feel right, then maybe that person just isn't a good fit for you. Your wedding planner is the vendor you'll be spending the most time with, so it's important to pick someone who's compatible with you and your fiancé.

Now, here are THE QUESTIONS!

Getting to Know a Planner

1. Do you have our wedding date open? If so, do you anticipate any issues with the date such as weather, travel for our guests, difficulty booking a venue, etc.?

2. What made you want to be a wedding planner?

3. Describe the most challenging wedding you planned and how you handled the problems that came up.

4. How would you rate your problem-solving skills?

5. How would you rate your communication skills?

6. Are you a certified wedding planner? If so, where did you get certified? What is your educational background?

7. Are you a member of any wedding association(s)? If so, does your association require you to satisfy yearly education requirements?

8. How long have you been in business? Do you have a business license?

9. How many full-scale weddings have you planned? When was your last one?

10. How many wedding clients do you take on in a year? How many do you expect to have during the month of our wedding?

11. Is wedding planning your full-time job? If it's part-time, what is your other job?

Working With the Venue

12. Have you ever worked at the venue we've chosen?

13. If our event is outdoors, what contingency plan would you have for bad weather? (Describe an event where you had weather issues and how you resolved them.)

Hiring Other Vendors

14. Are we required to book only the vendors you recommend or do we have the freedom to hire someone even if you haven't worked with them before?

15. Do you take a commission or discount from any of the vendors you would refer us to?

16. Will you be present at all of the vendor meetings and will you assist us in reviewing all of the vendor contracts and making sure everything is in order?

17. Will you invoice us for all the vendor fees or will we need to pay each one of them ourselves?

18. For the vendors who will be on site the day of our wedding, can I provide you with checks for final payment that you will distribute to them?

19. If issues arise with the vendors before, during or after our wedding, will you handle them or are we responsible for this?

Scope of Work

20. What kind planning do you offer? Logistical only (i.e. organizational—handling things like the timeline and floor plan) or Design and Logistical (i.e. bringing a client's vision to life as well as taking care of all the organizational aspects of the wedding)?

21. If you just do logistical planning, can you refer us to a vendor who can assist us with event design? *(NOTE: Floral designers often do full event design, as do vendors who specialize in design.)*

22. Will you handle every aspect of the planning or can we do some things on our own? In other words, what parts of the planning will we be responsible for?

23. Will you be the person on site the day of our wedding or will it be another planner? How many assistants will you have?

24. In case of an emergency that prevents you from being at our wedding, who will be the backup planner? What are their qualifications?

25. What time will you arrive and depart on the day of our wedding?

26. Will you stay on site after our wedding to make sure everything has been broken down and all vendors have left the location?

27. Will you provide us with a timeline of the wedding and a floor plan of the wedding venue?

28. Do you offer different package options or is everything customized based on what we're looking for?

29. How many meetings and phone calls are included in our package?

30. Is the wedding day rehearsal included in your services?

31. Do any of your packages include planning the rehearsal dinner and/or post-wedding brunch? If not, would you provide that service and what would be the extra cost to include it in our contract?

32. Do any of your packages include honeymoon planning? If not, would you provide that service and what would be the extra cost to include it in our contract?

33. Do any of your packages include assistance with finding my wedding dress and wedding party attire? If not, would you provide that service and what would be the extra cost to include it in our contract?

Getting Down to Business

34. Once we book with you, how quickly can we expect to receive the contract?

35. After we give you our budget, will you provide us with a breakdown of how the money is going to be allocated?

36. As changes are made to our plans, will you update us with a revised estimate and updated contract?

37. How do you charge for your services? Hourly, percentage of the wedding cost, or flat rate?

38. Can you provide a detailed list of all the items included in your fee?

39. What is your payment policy? Do you accept credit cards?

40. How much of a deposit is required to book your services? When is the final payment due?

41. Are there any fees that won't be included in your proposal that we should be aware of?

42. What is your refund or cancellation policy?

43. Can you provide a list of references? *NOTE: Any experienced coordinator should be able to give you plenty of references. For a list of Coordinators/ Wedding Planners you can trust, see the ones we've featured on HereComesTheGuide.com. They've all passed our difficult certification process with flying colors! Brides and grooms told us how much they loved working with them, so we wanted to recommend them to you.*

44. Can you provide us with a portfolio and/or video of weddings you have done?

Questions to Ask a Caterer

Besides your location, the food and drink for your wedding bash will probably consume the largest portion of your wedding budget. Catering costs are usually presented as "per-person" charges, sometimes abbreviated in wedding brochures as "pp" after the amount. But be aware—the per-person charge often doesn't include everything: Tax and the gratuity (sometimes called the "service charge") might be extra, and there may also be separate per-person charges for the meal, drinks, hors d'oeuvres, and even setup. So your actual per-person charge might end up being considerably more than you expect. Bring your calculator along when meeting with potential caterers to help you arrive at the real bottom line.

There's more to consider. Nowadays, many caterers offer a range of services in addition to catering. Some are actual "event producers," providing props, special effects, décor—in other words, complete event design. They might also be able to assist in finding a location, coordinating your affair, or lining up vendors. One thing a caterer can't do, however, is cook up a 5-course Beef Wellington dinner for $20 per person. When planning your menu, be realistic about what you can serve given your budget and the size of your guest list.

A lot of factors come into play when selecting a caterer, so don't be afraid to ask as many questions as you need to. You can refer to the following list, whether your potential caterer works at your event facility or you're hiring them independently.

The Basics

1. Do you have my date open?

2. How many weddings do you do per year, and how long have you been in business?

3. Have you done events at my location? *TIP: If you haven't chosen your location yet, ask the caterer if they can help you select one.*

4. Are you licensed by the state of California? Are you licensed to serve alcohol?

5. Will I need any permits for my event? If so, will you handle obtaining them?

6. Will you provide a banquet manager to coordinate the meal service or an on-site coordinator who will run the entire event?

7. Can you assist with other aspects of the wedding like selecting other vendors, event design (e.g. specialty lighting, elaborate décor, theme events, etc.)?

Food & Presentation

8. Given my budget, guest count and event style, what food choices would you recommend? Do you specialize in certain cuisines?

9. Do we have to work off a preset menu or can you create a custom menu for our event? If I have a special dish I'd like served, would you accommodate that?

10. Do you offer event packages or is everything à la carte? What exactly do your packages include?

11. Do you use all fresh produce, meat, fish, etc.? Can you source organic or sustainably farmed ingredients?

12. Can you accommodate dietary restrictions, such as kosher, vegan, etc.?

13. What décor do you provide for appetizer stations or buffet tables?

14. Do you offer package upgrades such as chocolate fountains, ice sculptures, espresso machines or specialty displays?

15. Can you do theme menus (e.g. barbecue, luau, etc.)? Would you also provide the décor?

16. What's the difference in cost between passed appetizers and appetizer stations? What's the price difference between a buffet and a sit-down meal? If we have a buffet, are there any stations that cost extra, like a carving station? *NOTE: Don't automatically assume that a buffet is going to be the less expensive option. Ask your caterer which type of service is more affordable for you, given the menu you're planning.*

17. How much do you charge for children's meals?

18. How much do you charge for vendor meals?

19. Do you do wedding cakes? If so, is this included in the per-person meal price or is it extra?

20. Can you show me photos of cakes you've done in the past?

21. If I decide not to serve cake, can you provide a dessert display instead?

22. If we use an outside cake designer, do you charge a cake-cutting fee?

23. Do you do food tastings and is there an extra charge for this?

24. Do you handle rental equipment such as tables, chairs, etc.?

25. What types of linens, glassware, plates and flatware do you provide? *NOTE: Some low-budget caterers have basic packages that use disposable dinnerware instead of the real thing, so make sure you know exactly what you'll be getting.*

26. Can you provide presentation upgrades such as chair covers, lounge furniture, Chiavari chairs, etc.? What would be the additional fees?

27. What is your policy on cleanup? *TIP: Be very clear about what "cleanup" means and who's responsible for handling it—and be sure to get it in writing. We've heard many tales about caterers that left dirty dishes, trash and uneaten food behind. In most cases, when you rent a location it will be YOUR responsibility to leave the place in acceptable condition. You want to spend your wedding night with your honey, not picking up empty bottles from the lawn!*

28. If there is leftover food from my event, can we have it wrapped up for guests to take home or have it delivered to a local shelter?

Drink

29. Do you provide alcoholic beverages and bartenders? Can you accommodate specialty cocktails?

30. What brands of alcohol will be served?

31. Can we provide the alcohol and you provide the bar labor?

32. Do you charge a corkage fee if we provide our own wine or champagne?

33. How do you charge for alcoholic and non-alcoholic beverages? Per consumption or per person? Which is more cost-effective?

34. Is the champagne toast after the ceremony included in your meal packages or is it extra?

35. Will your staff serve the wine with dinner?

36. How long will alcohol be served?

37. Is coffee and tea service included with the per-person meal charge? What brands of each do you offer and do they include decaf and herbal tea options?

Business Matters

38. What is the ratio of servers to guests?

39. How will the servers be dressed?

40. How is your pricing broken down (e.g. food, bar, cake-cutting, tax, gratuity)? *NOTE: Usually tax and a service charge are tacked on to your final cost. The service charge, which can range 18–23%, is used to tip the staff. And in many states, the service charge itself is taxable.*

41. How much time do you require for setting up and breaking down my event, and are there extra fees for this?

42. If my event runs longer than contracted, what are your overtime fees?

43. What is the last date by which I can give you a final guaranteed guest count?

44. What is your payment policy? Do you accept credit cards?

45. How much of a deposit is required to hold my date? When is the final payment due?

46. Are there any fees that won't be included in the proposal that we should be aware of?

47. Once we book with you, how quickly can we expect a contract? And if we make changes to menu choices or other items, will you update us with a revised estimate and contract?

48. What is your refund or cancellation policy?

49. Can you provide a list of recent references? *TIP: See the caterers we feature on HereComesTheGuide.com. These pre-screened companies provide great food and service, and they all passed our rigorous certification process with flying colors.*

Questions to Ask a Floral Designer

Floral designers do much more than just supply the bouquet! They help create the look and mood for your wedding ceremony, as well as centerpieces and other table decorations for the reception. They add the floral flourishes for the wedding party (don't forget that corsage for Grandma!), and some may even work with your cake designer to provide embellishments.

Before sitting down with a floral designer, you should already have reserved your ceremony and reception venue. That way you'll be able to discuss how much additional floral décor will be needed to either achieve a specific look at your site or complement an existing garden and/or room aesthetic.

Another must: Don't design the wedding bouquet until you've ordered your wedding dress. Since that task will hopefully be completed at least 6 months before your wedding date (hint, hint!), you should have plenty of time to work out the details of both your accessories and floral décor.

So where to start? Do a little research prior to interviewing floral artists by visiting the websites or shops of vendors you're considering. You want to know that whomever you hire can create bouquets and arrangements that suit your style. (And do explore our "Brides Want to Know: Bouquet Brainstorm" article on HereComesTheGuide.com for more GUIDElines and inspiration.)

Once you've compiled your short list of contenders, use these questions to zero in on your final choice:

The Basics

1. Do you have my date open?

2. Have you done events at my ceremony and reception location(s) before? If not, are you familiar with the sites?

3. How long have you been in business?

4. How many weddings have you done?

5. Where did you receive your training?

6. How many other weddings or events will you schedule on the same day?

7. Will you be doing my arrangements yourself or would it be another floral designer?

8. What design styles (e.g. ikebana, traditional, modern, trendy, European, Oriental) do you work in?

9. Can you work with my budget?

10. What recommendations can you give me to maximize my budget?

11. Do you offer specific packages or is everything customized?

12. Can you provide me with 3–4 recent wedding clients that I can contact for references?

The Flowers

13. What flowers are in season for the month I am getting married?

14. Based on my color scheme and budget, what flowers do you recommend?

15. Is there a difference in price if I use one type of flower vs. a mixed arrangement or bouquet?

16. If I request it, can you provide any organic, pesiticide-free or sustainably grown varieties? *TIP: Organic roses cost more, but last so much longer!*

17. What are the different kinds of wraps (called "collars" in florist-speak) you can do for my bouquet?

18. What about coordinating boutonnières, bridesmaid flowers, and centerpieces? Can you suggest anything special to coordinate with the theme/venue/season of my event?

19. What other décor can you provide (aisle runner, candelabras, trees, arches, votives, mirrors, etc.)? How will these items affect the overall cost?

20. If I give you a picture of a bouquet and/or arrangement that I like, can you recreate it?

21. Do you have photos or live examples of florals designed in the style I want?

22. Can you do sketches or mockups of the arrangements you've described before I sign the contract? If so, is there an additional fee for this?

23. Will you work with my cake designer if I decide to add flowers to my wedding cake? If so, is there an additional setup fee for this?

24. How far in advance of the wedding will you create the bouquets and arrangements, and how are they stored?

25. Can you assist me in the preservation of my bouquet after the wedding? If not, can you recommend someone?

The Costs

26. Do you charge a delivery fee?

27. Do you have an extra charge for the setup and breakdown of the floral décor?

28. Is there an extra fee if I need you to stay throughout the ceremony to move arrangements to the reception site?

29. Are there any additional fees that have not already been taken into account?

The Contract

30. How far in advance do I need to secure your services? What is the deposit required to secure my date?

31. Will you provide me with an itemized list of all the elements we've discussed, along with prices?

32. When can I expect to receive my contract from you?

33. What is your refund policy if for some reason I need to cancel my order?

Useful Tips:

- Prior to meeting with potential floral designers: have your color scheme finalized; create a list of the kinds of flowers you like; and have some examples (pictures from magazines, the web, etc.) of the kind of bouquets and arrangements that appeal to you.

- After you've met with each floral designer ask yourself, "Did the florist answer all my questions to my satisfaction?" "Do I feel like the florist really listened and understood my vision?" "Am I comfortable with this person?"

- Once you've booked your floral designer you'll want to provide them with a picture of your dress and swatches or photos of the bridesmaids dresses and the linens you'll be using.

Don't forget to browse our Floral Designers on HereComesTheGuide.com! They all got rave reviews during our rigorous certification process, and received the Certified By The Guide seal of approval.

Questions to Ask a Cake Designer

Next to your dress, the cake is probably a wedding's most important icon. And whether you want a traditional multi-tiered confection, a miniature Statue of Liberty (hey, that's where he proposed!) or a cupcake tower, your wedding cake should reflect your personality. Use the following questions as a guide when evaluating a potential cake designer. If you're not familiar with cake terms, please see the cake glossary on page 37.

Business Matters

1. Do you have my wedding date open?

2. How many wedding cakes do you schedule on the same day? *NOTE: You want to feel comfortable that your designer is sufficiently staffed to handle the number of cakes they've scheduled to deliver and set up on your date.*

3. How do you price your cakes? By the slice? Does the cost vary depending on the design and flavors I choose?

4. What is your minimum per-person cake cost?

5. What recommendations can you give me to maximize my budget?

6. Do you have a "menu" of cakes and prices that I can take with me?

7. What are the fees for delivery and setup of the cake? Do you decorate the cake table, too?

8. What do you do if the cake gets damaged in transit to or at my reception site?

9. Do you provide or rent cake toppers, a cake-cutting knife, cake stands, etc.? What are the fees?

10. How far in advance should I order my cake?

11. How much is the deposit and when is it due?

12. When is the final payment due?

13. Are there any additional fees that I should be aware of?

14. What is your refund policy if for some reason I need to cancel my order? What if I'm not happy with the cake?

15. When can I expect to receive my contract from you?

Background Check

16. How long have you been in business? Are you licensed and insured?

17. How many weddings have you done?

18. Where did you receive your training?

19. Can you provide me with 3–4 recent brides that I can contact for references? *TIP: Check out the cake vendors featured on HereComesTheGuide.com.*

They're some of the best cake designers in Northern California and they've all been Certified By The Guide.

The Cake

20. Do you have a portfolio of your work I can view, and did you make all the cakes in it?

21. What are your specialties?

22. Can you design a custom cake to match my theme, dress or color scheme, or do I select from set designs?

23. If I provide you with a picture of what I'd like, can you recreate it? Does it cost extra for a custom design?

24. I have an old family cake recipe. Can you adapt it for my wedding cake design?

25. If I don't have a clear vision of what I would like, can you offer some design ideas based on my theme and budget?

26. What flavors and fillings do you offer?

27. What are the different ingredients you typically use? Do you offer all organic or vegan options? *TIP: Quality ingredients cost more, but the investment is worth it—the cake will taste better.*

28. Do you have cake tastings? Is there a charge?

29. Do you do both fondant and buttercream icing?

30. Are there any other icing options I should consider? Which do you recommend for my cake design?

31. Can you create sugar paste, gum paste or chocolate flowers? If I decide to have fresh flowers on my cake will you work with my florist or will you obtain and arrange the flowers yourself?

32. Will you preserve the top tier of my cake for my first wedding anniversary or do you provide a special cake for the occasion?

33. Can you make a groom's cake? Is this priced the same as my wedding cake?

34. How much in advance of the wedding is the cake actually made? Do you freeze your cakes? *NOTE: Wedding cakes usually take at least a couple of days to make.*

Useful Tips:

- Arrange a consultation with your potential cake designer in person, and do a tasting before you sign a contract. *NOTE: Not all cake tastings are complimentary.*

- Make sure your cake designer specializes in wedding cakes. A wedding cake is generally much more elaborate than a birthday cake from your local bakery. Your cake professional should have special training in constructing this type of cake.

- In general, you should order your cake 6–8 months prior to your wedding.

- You might be able to save money by choosing one overall flavor for your cake, or by having a small cake for display and the cake cutting accompanied by a sheet cake to serve to your guests. Some cake designers may even offer a "dummy" or fake cake layer (usually made from styrofoam) to add an extra tier (or more) to your cake without too much extra expense. Talk to your cake designer to see how you can get the most bang for your wedding cake buck.

Wedding Cake Glossary

Icings

Buttercream: It's rich and creamy, is easily colored or flavored, and is used for fancy decorations like shells, swags, basketweaves, icing flowers, etc. Since it's made almost entirely of butter (hence the name), buttercream has a tendency to melt in extreme heat, so it's not recommended for outdoor weddings.

Fondant: Martha Stewart's favorite. This icing looks smooth and stiff and is made with gelatin and corn syrup to give it its helmet-like appearance (it's really very cool looking). It looks best when decorated with marzipan fruits, gum paste flowers, or a simple ribbon, like Martha likes to do. Although not as tasty as buttercream or ganache, fondant does not need refrigeration so it's the perfect icing to serve at your beach wedding.

Royal Icing: A mix of confectioner's sugar and milk or egg whites, royal icing is what the faces of gingerbread men are decorated with. It's white, shiny and hard, and does not need to be refrigerated. It's used for decorations like dots and latticework.

Ganache: This chocolate and heavy cream combination is very dark, and has the consistency of store-bought chocolate icing. It can be poured over cakes for a glass-like chocolate finish or used as filling (it stands up wonderfully between cake layers). Due to the ingredients, however, it's unstable—don't use it in hot or humid weather or the icing will slide right off the cake.

Whipped Cream: Delicious, but by far the most volatile, fresh whipped cream is usually not recommended for wedding cakes because they have to be out of the fridge for so long. If you really want to use it (it looks extremely white and fresh, which goes beautifully with real flowers) just keep it in the fridge until the very last second.

Decorations

Marzipan: An Italian paste made of almonds, sugar and egg whites that is molded into flowers and fruits to decorate the cake. They're usually brightly colored and very sugary. Marzipan can also be used as icing.

Gum Paste: This paste, made from gelatin, cornstarch, and sugar, produces the world's most realistic, edible fruit and flower decorations. Famous cake designers like Sylvia Weinstock are huge fans of gum paste. One nice benefit: these decorations last for centuries in storage.

Piping: Piping is ideal for icing decorations like dotted Swiss, basketweave, latticework, and shells. It comes out of a pastry bag fitted with different tips to create these different looks, which can range from simple polka dots to a layered weave that you'd swear is a wicker basket.

Pulled Sugar: If you boil sugar, water, and corn syrup it becomes malleable and the most beautiful designs can be created. Roses and bows that have been made from pulled sugar look like silk or satin—they're so smooth and shiny.

Dragees: These hard little sugar balls are painted with edible gold or silver paint, and they look truly stunning on a big ol' wedding cake.

Questions to Ask a DJ or Live Entertainment

Too often choosing the entertainment is left to the end of your overwhelming "Wedding To-Do List"—but it shouldn't be. Not only does music set the appropriate mood, but a skilled Master or Mistress of Ceremonies will gracefully guide your guests from one spotlight moment to another. And practically speaking, the best performers are often booked well in advance—so shake your groove thing, or you may be stuck doing the chicken dance with Uncle Edgar.

To get you started, we've put together this list of questions that will help you evaluate a DJ, band, or other entertainer. Note that rather than interviewing a specific performer or DJ yourself, you might be dealing with an entertainment agency rep.

The Basics

1. Do you have my date open?

2. Have you done events at my ceremony and/or reception location before? If not, are you familiar with them?

3. How long have you been in business? *NOTE: If you are interviewing a live band, you'll want to ask how long the musicians have played together. However, if you work with a reputable agency, instead of booking a specific band you'll most likely be getting seasoned professionals brought together for your event. Even though all the band members may not have played together before, they're professional musicians who are able to work together and sound fantastic anyway. The key is to make sure you book the specific singer and/or bandleader that you liked in the demo. The players will take their cues from them.*

4. How many weddings have you done? How many do you do in an average weekend?

5. What sets you apart from your competition?

6. Are there any other services that you provide, such as lighting design?

7. How far in advance do I need to secure your services?

8. Can you provide me with 3–4 recent wedding clients that I can contact for references?

Pricing and Other Business Details

9. What is your pricing? Does this include setup and breakdown between ceremony and reception locations?

10. How much is the deposit and when is it due? When is the final payment due?

11. If the event lasts longer than scheduled, what are the overtime charges?

12. What is the continuous music charge? *NOTE: For bands, bookings traditionally run for 4 hours divided into 4 sets, each lasting 45 minutes with a 15-minute break. If you want "continuous music," i.e. with band members trading breaks, there is usually an additional charge.*

13. When can I expect to receive my contract from you?

14. Are there any additional fees that could accrue that I am not taking into account, like travel expenses or charges for special musical requests? (One performer was asked to prepare an entire set of songs from *Phantom of the Opera!* Yes, he charged extra.)

15. What is your refund policy if for some reason I need to cancel or alter my date?

16. Do you carry liability insurance? *NOTE: This usually only applies to production companies that also supply lighting, effects, etc.*

17. If I hire musicians for the ceremony and want them to play at the wedding rehearsal, what is the extra charge?

The Music

18. Do you have a DVD of your music or a video link to a prior wedding where you performed?

19. Can you assist me in choosing the music for my processional, recessional, father-daughter dance, etc.?

20. How extensive is your music library or song list? What genres can you cover? Can I give you a specific list of songs I want or don't want played?

21. Are we guaranteed to have the performer(s) of our choice at our event? *SEE NUMBER 3 ABOVE. As mentioned, many bands hired by an agency are made up of members who may not play together regularly. Even set bands often have substitute players. If there are specific performers (singer, harpist, guitarist, etc.) that you want, make sure that your contract includes them. Of course, illness or other circumstances may still preclude their being able to perform at your event.*

22. If the DJ or one of the band members scheduled for my event is unable to perform for some reason, do you have a backup replacement ready to go?

23. Can you provide wireless mics for the ceremony?

24. Does any of your equipment require special electrical outlets that I need to inform my wedding site about?

25. Do you bring backup equipment?

26. What kind of space or stage do you require for the DJ or band? If my site doesn't provide what you need, will you make arrangements for the stage or am I responsible for renting it? *NOTE: a band will require a specific amount of square feet per band member.*

27. How much time will you need for setup, sound check and breakdown on the day of the event?

28. What music will be provided during the breaks? *NOTE: If you have a preference, make it known. If you want them to play your own digital music, be sure to inquire about system compatibility with your CD, iPod, etc.*

29. How many people will you staff for my event?

Useful Tips:

- Discuss with your site manager any restrictions that might affect your event, like noise limits, a music curfew and availability/load of electrical circuits. Also check with your facility and caterer about where and what to feed the performers.

- All professional entertainers have access to formalwear (if they don't, that's your first clue they're not professionals!) However, it is YOUR responsibility to be specific about how you expect your performers to be dressed. Any extraordinary requests (period costumes, all-white tuxes, etc.) are normally paid for by the client.

- Make notes of your general music preferences before you meet with your DJ, bandleader, etc. For example: "Classical for the ceremony, Rat Pack-era for the cocktail hour and a set of Motown during the reception." Not only will this help you determine which entertainment professionals are a good match for you, it will guide them in preparing your set list. *TIP: The DJs and Entertainers on HereComesTheGuide.com are first-rate. They all got great reviews during our certification process, and we're happy to recommend them.*

For PDF versions of these QUESTIONS TO ASK, visit www.HereComesTheGuide.com

Questions to Ask When Ordering Your Wedding Invitations

Letterpress, thermography, engraved, matte, jacquard, glassine… ordering invites will mean learning a few new vocabulary words (see page 42). You'll also need to learn about all the components that you might want to include in your invitation, as well as what other printed materials could be part of your wedding scenario. With so many details to consider, you'll depend on a creative wedding invitation professional to clue you in on the jargon, and guide you in choosing invites that reflect your wedding style. After all, nothing sets the tone for an event like an impeccably designed wedding invitation.

This list of questions has been compiled to help ensure that no detail is left unaddressed (no pun intended), whether you're working with a stationery boutique, an online vendor, or a graphic designer.

Getting To Know Your Invitation Professional

1. How long have you been in business?

2. What is your design background? *NOTE: This may or may not involve formal training. Remember, "good taste" isn't necessarily something that can be taught!*

3. What types of printing processes do you offer and which do you specialize in? Which do you recommend for my budget and style?

4. Is your printing done in-house or do you outsource it? *NOTE: Printing is usually less expensive if it's outsourced. However, a possible benefit of in-house printing is a quicker turnaround time, which could come in especially handy if any reprinting (say, due to an error) is required.*

5. Do you offer custom invitations as well as templated styles? Is there a fee if I want to order a sample of either an existing invitation style or a custom design? If so, how much?

6. If I choose a custom wedding invitation, what are my options for color, paper type, ink and fonts? What is the word limit for the text?

7. Can I also order my table numbers, place cards, escort cards, ceremony programs, menus, etc. from you?

8. Do you offer a package or a discounted price if I order all of the invitation components at the same time? (For a complete list of what might be included, see the next page.)

9. If I want to include a picture or graphic on my save-the-date card or invitation, can you accommodate that? If so, does the image need to be saved in a specific format? Do you have photo retouching available, and if so, what is the price range? Can your photo specialist also convert color images to black & white or sepia? Is there an additional cost?

10. Are there any new styles, trends and color combinations I might consider? Which are the most popular? What kinds of handmade or artisanal paper do you offer? *NOTE: The answers to these questions will give you a sense of how creative and up-to-the-minute your invitation professional is.*

11. Can my invitations be printed on recycled paper and/or with soy-based ink?

12. Based on the paper I select and the number of pieces involved, what would it cost to mail my wedding invitation? *NOTE: If you use a non-standard sized envelope, postage may be more expensive.*

Getting Down To Business

13. Once I place my order, how long will it take to have the completed invitations delivered? Do you have rush-order available and what are the extra fees? If you are ordering from an online company, ask: What are the shipping methods available to me, and their respective costs?

14. If the invitation involves multiple pieces, can you assemble them? If so, is there an additional fee? How will the assembly affect my delivery date?

15. Do you offer an invitation addressing service? If so, what is the charge for this? What lettering style options are available? Will the lettering push back my delivery date?

16. When is payment due?

17. I will have an opportunity to sign off on my invitation proof before you send my order to print, right?

18. Once I've signed off on the proof, I expect the printed invitations to match the approved sample. If they don't (i.e. an error was made after I signed off on the proof), will my invitations be corrected and reprinted at no additional cost? How much additional time will it take to redo my order if there is a problem with it?

19. What is your refund policy if for some reason I need to cancel my order?

20. When can I expect to receive my contract from you?

21. Can you provide me with the contact information of 3–4 recent wedding clients who I can call or email for references?

Possible Printed Invitation Components

(Don't panic ... most of the extra elements are OPTIONAL!!)

- Save-the-Date Cards

- Wedding Announcement

- Wedding Invitation Components:
  - Outer Envelope
  - Optional Inner Envelope
  - Optional Belly Band
  - Invitation
  - Reception Card, if held at a different location than the ceremony
  - Directions/Map
  - Response Card & SASE (self-addressed stamped envelope)

- Thank-You Cards

- Shower Thank-You Cards

- Other Invites:
  - Engagement Party
  - Shower
  - Bachelor/Bachelorette Party
  - Rehearsal Dinner
  - After Party

- Wedding Program

- Pew Cards

- Place Cards

- Table Cards

- Menus

- Napkins, Matchbooks or Labels for favors

Useful Tips:

- Ordering your invitations over the phone increases the possibility of mistakes, so order in person if possible. If you order your invitations from an online company, make sure your contract states that they will correct mistakes they make for free.

- Insist on getting a proof. Have at least two other people review all your proofs before you sign off on them—it's amazing what a fresh pair of eyes will see!

- If ordering online, remember that color resolution can vary drastically between computers. The best way to guarantee the exact color you want is to ask that a sample be snail-mailed to you.

- Order 20–30 extra save-the-dates and/or invitations with envelopes in case you have to add to the guest list or you make a mistake when assembling or addressing the envelopes.

- Save-the-date cards should be sent out 6–9 months prior to your wedding.

- Invitations should be sent out 6–8 weeks prior to your wedding.

- Consider working with one stationer or graphic designer for all of your printed materials. He or she will guide you in making sure all of the components convey a consistent design concept. Not that they have to be identical, but as Joyce Scardina Becker observes in *Countdown to Your Perfect Wedding,* "It's like making a fashion statement: All of the accessories in your wardrobe should coordinate and fit together nicely."

- To Evite or not to Evite? For the main event, even we progressives at *Here Comes The Guide* come down on the side of tradition and say go with real paper and snail mail—even if your budget determines that you have to DIY. However, if your overall wedding style is relaxed and casual, then we think Evites are fine for the supporting events, such as your Bachelorette Party. We like Evite's built-in RSVP system and creative style options.

Invitations Glossary

A glossary of common printing terms.

Printing Terms

Letterpress: Letterpress printing dates back to the 14th century, and involves inking the raised surface of metal type or custom-engraved plates and then applying the inked surface against paper with a press. When used with the right paper (thick, softer paper results in a deeper impression), typefaces and colors, letterpress creates an elegant product with a stamped, tactile quality. This process offers lots of options, but can cost more than other methods. Also, photographs and metallic inks generally don't work well with letterpress.

Embossing: Using a metal die, letters and images are pressed into the paper from behind, creating a raised "relief" surface, imparting added dimension to the invitation design. Usually used for large initials or borders. Ink or foil may be applied to the front of the paper so that the raised letters and images are colored.

Blind embossing: No ink or foil is applied, so the embossed (raised) image is the same color as the paper.

Thermography: This popular printing method uses heat to fuse ink and resinous powder, producing raised lettering. Though it looks almost exactly like engraved printing, thermography is much less expensive. This process will not reproduce detail as sharply as engraving will. The powder is added after the ink is applied, generally with an offset press, so the use of paper or metal offset plates affects quality here, too.

Engraving: Engraving is generally the most formal and expensive printing option. The image is etched into a metal plate, and the ink held in the etched grooves is applied to the paper with a press. The resulting raised image is comprised entirely of ink sitting on the surface of the paper. The ink applied is opaque, making it possible to print a lighter colored ink on a darker colored paper. Engraving is not the best printing choice if you have a photo or illustration that requires a screen.

Offset printing: Most printing these days is offset, which means the original image is transferred from a plate to a drum before it is applied to the paper. This process produces print that sits flat on the surface. There are many levels of quality with this method: If your printer uses paper printing plates, the job will cost less but the result may be fuzzy, inconsistent lettering. Metal plates yield much sharper, crisper type.

Digital printing: In this method the computer is linked to the printing press and the image is applied to paper or another material directly from a digital file rather than using film and/or plates. Digital is best for short-run, quick jobs. This can also be a good option if you want to use full color.

Foil stamping: Foil is applied to the front side of the paper, stamped on with a metal die. Foils can be metallic or colored, shiny or dull. They are usually very opaque, and this is a great way to print white on a dark colored paper.

Calligraphy: This is the perfected art of writing by hand. Often associated with fancy, curlicue script, calligraphy can be done in several genres and styles.

Paper Terms

Matte: A paper coating that's flat and non-reflective (no gloss).

Jacquard: Screen-printed paper that creates an illusion of layering; for example, paper that looks like it's overlaid with a swatch of lace.

Parchment paper: This paper is somewhat translucent and often a bit mottled to mimic the appearance of ancient, historical documents made out of animal skin. It's excellent for calligraphy.

Linen finish: Paper with a surface that actually mimics linen fabric. If you look closely, you see lines of texture going both horizontally and vertically on the surface.

Rice paper: Not actually made of rice, this paper is extremely thin and elegant.

Glassine: A very thin, waxy paper. Thinner than vellum (see below), its surface is slick and shiny, whereas vellum is more translucent. Glassine is best suited for envelope use, while vellum is sturdy enough to be printed on directly for invitation use.

Vellum: A heavier, finely textured, translucent paper made from wood fiber. Similar to parchment, it was originally made from the skin of a calf, lamb or baby goat and used for writing and painting during the pre-printing age.

HereComesTheGuide.com

search   BOOKSTORE | ABOUT | ADVERTISE WITH US | HELP   MYGUIDE REGISTRATION | LOGIN

Here Comes THE GUIDE

START HERE   VENUES   VENDORS   IDEAS   CHECKLISTS   BRIDAL SHOWS + EXPOS

FIND A *Venue*

Woodland Hills Country Club
San Fernando Valley

FIND A *Vendor*

Colleen Riley Photography
Northern California

SERIOUSLY USEFUL *wedding info*
— SINCE 1989 —

Deals + DISCOUNTS

Hayley Anne Photography
Receive 50% off a Santa Cruz
engagement session when you mention
Here Comes The Guide!...
And get more wedding vendor deals here.

Anaheim Hills Golf Course Clubhouse
Anaheim Hills Golf Course Clubhouse is
offering discounted rates on
Friday/Sunday evenings and Saturday...
And get more wedding venue deals here.

Orange County Wedding Discount

Ask the Anaheim Hills Golf
Course Clubhouse about their
discounted rates on

LET'S GET IT
Started ...

You've gotta visit our website!
Here's what you'll find:

- A fast and easy way to search for the perfect venues and vendors.

- Information about new venues that aren't in the book!

- Lots of locations for rehearsal dinners, honeymoons and accommodations (room blocks!) for your event.

- More great wedding and special event services!

- Direct links to the event venues and vendors we feature.

- Tons of photos and videos. Real Wedding galleries, too!

- Virtual tours of most venues.

- Information about bridal fairs.

- Wedding dress trunk shows and sample sales calendar.

Event Venues

Northern California

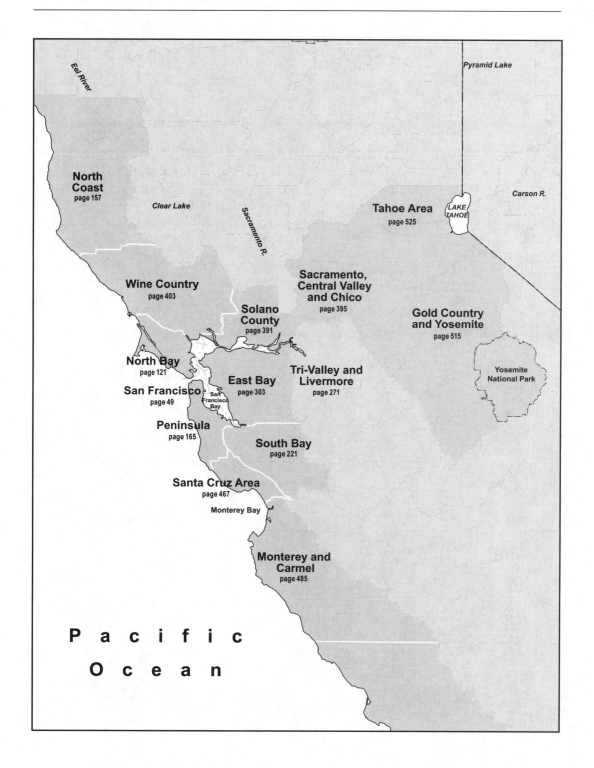

Eel River

Pyramid Lake

North Coast
page 157

Clear Lake

Sacramento R.

Tahoe Area
page 525

Carson R.

LAKE TAHOE

Wine Country
page 403

Solano County
page 391

Sacramento, Central Valley and Chico
page 395

Gold Country and Yosemite
page 515

Yosemite National Park

North Bay
page 121

East Bay
page 303

Tri-Valley and Livermore
page 271

San Francisco
page 49

San Francisco Bay

Peninsula
page 165

South Bay
page 221

Santa Cruz Area
page 467

Monterey Bay

Monterey and Carmel
page 485

P a c i f i c

O c e a n

San Francisco

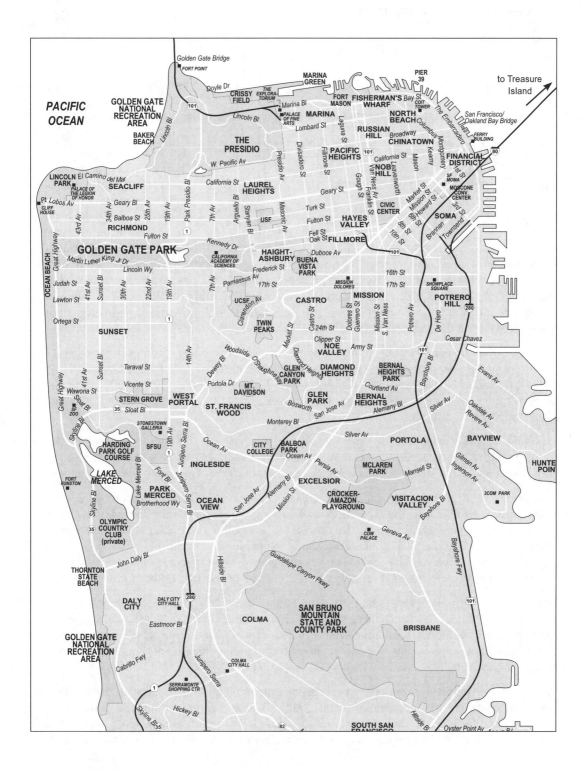

Argonaut Hotel

Waterfront Hotel

495 Jefferson Street, San Francisco
415/345-5552 Catering Department
www.argonauthotel.com
emearls@noblehousehotels.com

● Rehearsal Dinners	● Corp. Events/Mtgs.
● Ceremonies	● Private Parties
● Wedding Receptions	● Accommodations

As befits its prime waterfront location on Fisherman's Wharf, the Argonaut Hotel easily seduces visitors with an abundance of seaside and historic charm. A recent makeover has transformed the Argonaut—one of the main occupants of a landmark 1907 building that had once housed the wharf's largest fruit and vegetable cannery—into a chic boutique hotel. The building's exposed brick and wooden beams have been incorporated into the interior's playful design concept, which takes its inspiration from the luxury cabins of Gold Rush-era steam ships bound for San Francisco. And like the excited passengers arriving here for the first time, your family and friends will be looking forward with anticipation to your celebration at the Argonaut.

First off, out-of-towners will be captivated by the iconic surroundings, and even locals will find themselves rediscovering its allure. The hotel overlooks the green stretch of the SF Maritime National Historical Park, as well as numerous antique vessels docked along the water's edge. Everyone will want to capture classic photos in front of a cable car, or the bay with Alcatraz and the Golden Gate Bridge in the distance.

Once inside, guests relax in the light and airy lobby, which is a playful interpretation of the ocean-journey motif. Navy blue deck chairs flank antique-style steamer trunks, and a working astronomer's clock above the stately fireplace mantle contributes to the Argonaut's nostalgic character.

The lobby's nautical theme is echoed in the prefunction foyer, where guests enjoy the cocktail hour. Receptions follow in the Golden Gate Ballroom, which recalls the formality of first-class ocean travel when one always dressed for dinner. Yet be assured, the ambiance is neither stuffy nor ho-hum: Chandeliers are shaped like giant ships' compasses and beautifully textured wall coverings reminiscent of woven jute add exotic, seafaring flavor. The spacious ballroom has a flexible layout, and can be sectioned off for a wedding ceremony or used altogether for one grand gala.

You can also tie the knot outdoors in the Del Monte Courtyard. The bride makes her entrance down a brick staircase, and exchanges vows with her groom in front of the legendary skyline. The adjoining Maritime Room, with large windows and lofty ceilings, hosts social hours or intimate receptions. Brick walls, rough wooden columns and maritime-inspired accents lend an informal though no less authentic atmosphere.

All the hotel's events feature superb coastal cuisine from the Blue Mermaid Restaurant and Bar next door. The chef welcomes customized menus, but who could resist including one of the signature chowders and fresh, sustainably caught seafood dishes? This trendy dining spot is also available for private events, and has a patio that can be tented for rehearsal dinners or casual get-togethers.

Want more novelty? The hotel's first floor houses the San Francisco Maritime National Historical Park Museum Visitors Center, a unique social hour venue. Interactive displays of nautical memorabilia let guests drink in the neighborhood's storied past along with their champagne. The Argonaut's event pros can even arrange an intimate soiree aboard the tall ship Balclutha moored nearby.

After the festivities, guests retire to luxuriously outfitted accommodations, most with postcard views. Together with its 4-diamond service and amenities, the Argonaut offers an epic destination wedding experience.

CEREMONY CAPACITY: The Argonaut holds up to 270 seated guests both indoors and outdoors.

EVENT/RECEPTION CAPACITY: The hotel accommodates 320 seated or 450 standing guests indoors (270 with a dance floor).

MEETING CAPACITY: With over 8,500 square feet of private space, the Argonaut can accommodate groups ranging 10–300 guests.

FEES & DEPOSITS: 25% of the estimated event total is required to secure your date and time. A second deposit is due 30 days prior to the event, and the estimated final balance is due 3 days prior. The ceremony fee starts at $1,000 and the reception room fee starts at $1,200. Wedding packages start at $130/person and include a champagne toast, passed hors d'oeuvres, 1-hour open house bar, 2-course meal, wine service throughout dinner, and a complimentary suite for the newlyweds on their wedding night. Special guest room rates may be negotiated. A 23% service charge and tax are additional.

AVAILABILITY: Daily until midnight; early morning hours by arrangement. Closed on Thanksgiving, Christmas, and New Year's Day.

SERVICES/AMENITIES:

Catering: in-house
Kitchen Facilities: n/a
Tables & Chairs: provided, Chiavari chairs
Linens, Silver, etc.: provided
Restrooms: wheelchair accessible
Dance Floor: provided
Bride's & Groom's Dressing Areas: yes
AV/Meeting Equipment: full range available through PSAV

Parking: valet or public garage
Accommodations: 252 guest rooms
Outdoor Night Lighting: yes
Outdoor Cooking Facilities: no
Cleanup: provided
View: SF cityscape, SF Bay and park
Other: event coordination

RESTRICTIONS:

Alcohol: in-house
Smoking: outside only
Music: amplified OK indoors with volume restrictions

Wheelchair Access: yes
Insurance: Not required but recommended. Outside vendors need to provide insurance.
Other: no glitter, rice or birdseed

This is important! Tell locations you're reading HERE COMES THE GUIDE and ask if our information is still current.

51

Asian Art Museum

Museum

200 Larkin Street, San Francisco

415/581-3777

www.asianart.org/about/rent-space
facilityrentals@asianart.org

● Rehearsal Dinners	● Corp. Events/Mtgs.
● Ceremonies	● Private Parties
● Wedding Receptions	○ Accommodations

The historic and regal building that houses San Francisco's Asian Art Museum is as captivating as the art inside. A massive stone Beaux-Arts structure—which was built in 1917 and functioned as the city's main library for decades—stands four stories high with columns, stairs, and inscriptions completing its stately façade. Gleaming marble surfaces, beautifully carved stone arches, and antique light fixtures greet visitors in the lobby and grace the sophisticated special event spaces beyond.

The stunning transformation from book repository to museum was masterminded by Italian architect Gae Aulenti, who is perhaps best known for taking a defunct train station in Paris and turning it into the award-winning Musée D'Orsay.

Through the central archway leading off the lobby, guests encounter the opulent Grand Staircase and Loggia, which still retain an early 1900s elegance. Two flights of gently ascending travertine marble steps lead up to the Loggia, an airy arcade that overlooks the staircase and has a decorative barrel-vaulted ceiling. The glass cases that line its walls display an array of distinctive Asian ceramics, and remind us that this is indeed a museum. Some couples have married on the stairs, which look amazing when decorated with candles and flowers; with this setup, wedding attendees observe the ceremony from the Loggia above, as if gazing upon royalty. Once the service concludes, cocktails, passed champagne and hors d'oeuvres are served in the Loggia, where tall tables, candles and special linens personalize the space. During this time, your guests can explore the art galleries situated on either side of the Hall, where a world-class collection of works from China, Japan and Korea awaits.

For an elegant sit-down dinner and dancing, the adjacent Samsung Hall is equally classy. Vast and square-shaped, it continues the visual theme of columns and plenty of marble, but also boasts enormous windows crisscrossed with intricate metalwork. A huge bronze chandelier illuminates the festivities from high above. When you add linen-clad tables, mood lighting and the dulcet sounds of a string quartet, the hall feels positively palatial.

If you prefer a contemporary setting, the museum has a pair of almost identical courts on the lower level that are connected by two open hallways. Known as the North and South Courts, they were completely remodeled during the museum construction, and present a striking contrast to the historic sections of the facility. Their thoroughly modern and minimalist design features clean lines, a marble floor, and an angular ceiling of skylights nearly three stories above. Because of their considerable size, the courts lend themselves to a wide range of event options: wedding ceremonies, sit-down dinners, buffets with food stations, and cocktail parties. You can even create a lounge atmosphere by bringing in a bar, conversational groupings of couches, and tables and chairs.

Before the festivities begin, brides who want a secluded spot in which to get ready or relax can utilize the lovely Peterson Room on the first floor. A lavish private room, it has Oriental rugs and Asian-inspired décor that's very Zen.

There are many advantages to planning an event at the Asian Art Museum, but the main one is this: No matter where you hold your celebration, you're surrounded by beauty. The building has so much style and history (not to mention its world-renowned art collection) that you don't have to add much to make your celebration dazzling.

CEREMONY, EVENT/RECEPTION & MEETING CAPACITY: The Museum accommodates a maximum of 400 seated or 1,500 standing guests, though not all in one room. Samsung Hall and the Loggia hold up to 250 seated guests (225 when including space for a dance area), and up to 350 standing. Each Court holds up to 200 seated or 250 standing guests. The Galleries may be rented in conjunction with the event spaces. Food and beverages are not permitted in the galleries.

Please inquire about outdoor tent options to increase maximum capacity.

FEES & DEPOSITS: A nonrefundable $5,000 deposit is required to secure your date. The balance is due 30 days prior to the event. The rental fee ranges $3,500–20,000 depending on the space(s) reserved.

AVAILABILITY: Weddings (including setup, event, and load-out) are contracted from 5:15pm–1:30am year-round, except Thursday nights. Corporate events (including setup and loadout) are contracted from 5:15pm–midnight year-round, except Thursday nights.

SERVICES/AMENITIES:
Catering: select from list
Kitchen Facilities: prep only
Tables & Chairs: through caterer
Linens, Silver, etc.: through caterer
Restrooms: wheelchair accessible
Dance Floor: built-in or BYO through caterer
Bride's Dressing Area: yes
AV/Meeting Equipment: CBA, extra charge

Parking: valet or public garage
Accommodations: no guest rooms
Outdoor Night Lighting: yes
Outdoor Cooking Facilities: yes
Cleanup: through caterer
View: artwork

RESTRICTIONS:
Alcohol: BYO, licensed server
Smoking: outside only
Music: amplified OK

Wheelchair Access: yes
Insurance: liability required
Other: no glitter, rice or birdseed

Bently Reserve and Conference Center

Historic Bank

301 Battery Street, San Francisco
415/294-2226

www.bentlyreserve.com
jim.bruels@bentlyreserve.com

- Rehearsal Dinners
- Ceremonies
- Wedding Receptions
- Corp. Events/Mtgs.
- Private Parties
- Accommodations

We always get asked about mansions in San Francisco and, to tell you the truth, there aren't many that can accommodate a large wedding reception indoors. Although the Bently Reserve is not exactly a mansion, it does possess the elegant, understated grandeur you'd expect from a palatial estate. And it can handle quite a crowd.

Originally part of the lobby of the 1924 Federal Reserve Bank of San Francisco, the Banking Hall where events are held is truly awe-inspiring. This remarkable space, lined with two rows of 25-foot-tall Ionic columns, recalls both the affluence of the Roaring 20s and the Gatsby Era's penchant for reveling amid luxury: The hall is lavished in real and faux European marble; the entry doors are solid bronze; and two spectacular bronze chandeliers draw your eyes up to the soaring 34-foot coffered ceiling. For a supremely theatrical entrance, descend the imperial bronze-and-marble double stairway, which flows from the mezzanine down to the gleaming marble main floor.

Ceremonies here are nothing short of majestic. The built-in architectural elements, like the columns and mezzanine, provide a natural framework for staging your vows. Add your own embellishments—sheer draping, floral displays, and luminarias along the wedding aisle, for example—to heighten the glamorous, chapel-like ambiance. Whether you're entertaining an intimate group for a rehearsal dinner or a gala for up to 800, you'll be celebrating in high style.

The landmark venue's most recent addition is the versatile Couples Lounge, where wedding parties can get ready and couples can relax in private before the big event. The room is both chic and comfortable, and a 46≤ flat screen TV linked to a camera inside the Banking Hall allows couples to view the arrival of their guests and other preparations taking place in the hall.

A stunning mix of both modern and traditional, the Bentley Reserve is included in the National Register of Historic Places. So if you have an extended guest list and are searching for a unique and impressive location in The City, you couldn't ask for a better spot.

CEREMONY CAPACITY: The main hall seats 350 guests, and the Conference Center seats up to 70.

EVENT/RECEPTION & MEETING CAPACITY: The Banking Hall accommodates 250 seated theater-style, 350 seated banquet-style or up to 650 standing guests; the Conference Center holds up to 70 guests and has 8 separate meeting spaces.

FEES & DEPOSITS: The Banking Hall rental fee ranges $6,300–12,000 depending on the day of the event. A refundable $1,000 security deposit is payable with the signed license agreement. The Conference Center's rental fee for special events is based on the time and day of the event and the size of the group, and is subject to availability.

AVAILABILITY: Sunday–Thursday, 8am–midnight; Friday and Saturday until 1am. Tours of the facility are by appointment only.

SERVICES/AMENITIES:
Catering: select from preferred list
Kitchen Facilities: fully equipped
Tables & Chairs: caterer
Linens, Silver, etc.: caterer
Restrooms: wheelchair accessible
Dance Floor: yes
Bride's Dressing Area: yes
AV/Meeting Equipment: full range CBA

Parking: adjacent garage, discounted on evenings and weekends
Accommodations: nearby hotels
Outdoor Night Lighting: yes
Outdoor Cooking Facilities: no
Cleanup: renter
View: no
Other: coat check room

RESTRICTIONS:
Alcohol: exclusive bar service through *Best Beverage Catering*
Smoking: outside only
Music: amplified OK indoors

Wheelchair Access: yes
Insurance: liability required
Other: no glitter or confetti

The Chapel

777 Valencia Street, San Francisco
415/551-5142
www.thechapelsf.com
events@thechapelsf.com

Special Event Venue

● Rehearsal Dinners	● Corp. Events/Mtgs.	
● Ceremonies	● Private Parties	
● Wedding Receptions	Accommodations	

Put your name in lights and be ready to take the stage at this extraordinary wedding and event venue in the very heart of San Francisco's colorful Mission District. Definitely historic, now totally hip, this 1914 building was voted one of the "10 Most Beautiful Music Venues in California" by *California Home + Design Magazine*. It actually boasts a playhouse-quality marquee and professional stage as well as unique and exciting spaces for hosting celebrations that consistently produce rave reviews.

Fans will tell you this place rocks, and they're right. It's evident as soon as you walk through the big double doors and step into the spacious entrance vestibule, ideal for a coat check, registration, and lots of mingling. Straight ahead you'll find the imposing hall that gives The Chapel its name. It makes quite an impact with its 40-foot ceiling, handsome hardwood floors, built–in black granite bar, and performance-caliber stage, lights and sound. Perfect for fabulous out-of-the-box, one-of-a-kind affairs—from weddings to fashion shows or day conferences to rock operas—this ultra-cool environment also features a 24-foot screen with theater-quality projector, a green room and dressing rooms for behind-the-scenes prep, and a VIP box. A generous mezzanine and balcony with its very own bar, additional reception area, and excellent stage and chapel views further adds to your options.

To the left of the entrance vestibule, the main bar is an equally flexible and inspiring multifunctional setting. Great for a wedding shower, an engagement party, a product demo, meet-up and more, it's clearly "happy hour" all the time here. Floor-to-ceiling windows, a hardwood floor and a black granite bar, which wraps around one side of the room all the way to a cozy lounge, give it a dynamic, party vibe day and night. Whether it's used on its own or as a pre- or après-function location for main chapel festivities, it's sure to enliven the scene.

It's also a terrific spot to showcase some of the bites and beverages for which this venue is famous. In fact, a short walk through the large sliding doors will land you in the Vestry, The Chapel's restaurant, where the talented and experienced staff serve up tasty family-style dinners, mouth-watering multi-course banquets, passed or stationary hors d'oeuvres, multicultural brunches, and all kinds of holiday fare. Vegetarian, vegan or gluten-free? This trend- and health-savvy kitchen will creatively accommodate your special needs. The restaurant's outdoor patio can be set up with its own bar and rented out for smaller groups, and there's a beautiful private dining room for more intimate functions.

We've actually seen The Chapel in full wedding swing and can report that gatherings here are an unquestionable blast. As one happy party host put it, "I'm impressed with the diversity of ways to utilize the space. The menu at the Vestry is, in a word, Yum!"

And then there's the very satisfied groom who declared, "Making the decision to have our wedding at The Chapel is one of the best, most regret-free choices we've ever made."

CEREMONY CAPACITY: The chapel can seat 150 indoors.

EVENT/RECEPTION CAPACITY: The facility holds 150 seated or 400 standing indoors, and 80 seated or 120 standing outdoors.

MEETING CAPACITY: The site can accommodate 200 seated guests.

FEES & DEPOSITS: 50% of the estimated event total is required to reserve your date, and the balance is due 3 days prior to the event. The venue rental fee starts at $6,000 and varies depending on the spaces reserved, and the day and time of the event. The food & beverage minimum starts at $6,000. Meals start at $10/person and wedding packages start at $40/person. Tax, alcohol, a 20% service charge, and a San Francisco Employer Mandate surcharge are additional.

AVAILABILITY: Year-round, daily, 9am–2am.

SERVICES/AMENITIES:

Catering: in-house
Kitchen Facilities: n/a
Tables & Chairs: provided
Linens, Silver, etc.: provided
Restrooms: wheelchair accessible
Dance Floor: provided
Bride's Dressing Area: yes
AV/Meeting Equipment: provided

Parking: on street, garage nearby
Accommodations: no guest rooms
Outdoor Night Lighting: CBA
Outdoor Cooking Facilities: no
Cleanup: provided
View: no
Other: event coordination

RESTRICTIONS:

Alcohol: provided
Smoking: not allowed
Music: amplified OK indoors

Wheelchair Access: limited
Insurance: liability required

City Club of San Francisco

Historic Club

155 Sansome Street, San Francisco
415/362-2480
www.cityclubsf.com
catering@cityclubsf.com

● Rehearsal Dinners	● Corp. Events/Mtgs.
● Ceremonies	● Private Parties
● Wedding Receptions	Accommodations

Just walking into the lobby of this former Stock Exchange Tower, situated in the heart of the Financial District, gives you an inkling of what's to follow. One glance at the highly polished black-and-green marble floors, black-and-white marble walls and gold ceiling and you feel instantly surrounded by glamour.

Elevators whisk you up to the 10th floor, and the entrance to The City Club itself. Here, even the elevator doors—framed in bronze and decorated in silver, bronze and brass appliqué—offer an elegant example of this facility's attention to detail. The club (which occupies the 9th through 12th floors) features one of the most striking and exquisite Art Deco interiors we've seen, including a remarkable stairwell painted with an original 30-foot-high Diego Rivera fresco. Furnishings are original Art Deco pieces and appointments are generously clad in black marble, silver and brass. The ceiling is stunning, covered with burnished gold leaf squares. Sophisticated with just the right amount of glitz, this is an exceptional place for a wedding ceremony and/or reception, special event or corporate affair.

CEREMONY CAPACITY: The 10th floor (Cafe) can accommodate 220 seated or 300 standing guests; the 11th floor (Main Dining Room) 240 seated or 300 standing. The 9th Floor suites accommodate 120 seated or 150 standing, while the 12th Floor suites hold 100 seated or 120 standing.

EVENT/RECEPTION & MEETING CAPACITY: For receptions, the entire club (10th and 11th floors) may be reserved. The club holds 20–460 seated or up to 500 for a standing reception on two floors.

FEES & DEPOSITS: For special events, the facility fee for a 5-hour block of time ranges $1,500–5,000. Smaller spaces are available on the 9th and 12th floors for weeknight events, prices vary accordingly. The food & beverage minimum ranges $10,000–25,000. Curfew is 2am and the overtime charge is $500/hour. On weeknights, Monday–Friday, the food & beverage minimum ranges $6,000–12,000. The minimum varies depending on the month and day of the event. Tax and a 23% service charge are additional. Member sponsorship and benefits are available.

AVAILABILITY: Year-round, Monday–Friday, 7:30am–2am. On Saturday and Sunday, 8am–2am.

SERVICES/AMENITIES:

Catering: in-house, no BYO
Kitchen Facilities: n/a
Tables & Chairs: provided; styles and quantities vary
Linens, Silver, etc.: provided
Restrooms: wheelchair accessible
Dance Floor: yes
Bride's Dressing Area: yes
AV/Meeting Equipment: full AV services are available

Parking: CBA
Accommodations: no guest rooms; affiliate club hotels
Outdoor Night Lighting: access only
Outdoor Cooking Facilities: no
Cleanup: provided
View: San Francisco skyline

RESTRICTIONS:

Alcohol: in-house
Smoking: in smoking room only
Music: amplified OK

Wheelchair Access: yes
Insurance: not required

Overwhelmed? Use the search criteria on www.HereComesTheGuide.com to narrow down your choices.

Cliff House

1090 Point Lobos, San Francisco
415/666-4027
www.cliffhouse.com
virginia@cliffhouse.com

Historic Waterfront Restaurant

● Rehearsal Dinners	● Corp. Events/Mtgs.
● Ceremonies	● Private Parties
● Wedding Receptions	Accommodations

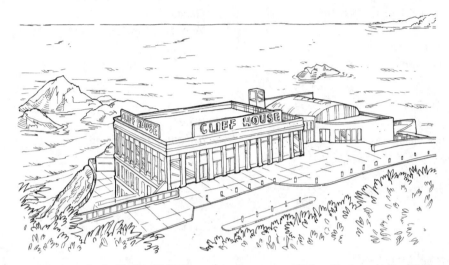

For over a century and a half, the Cliff House has been one of The City's most familiar and beloved landmarks. Generations of San Franciscans have brought visiting friends and relatives to this spot to show off the glorious westernmost part of the city. Drawn here by the spectacular ocean views and the waves crashing along the rocky shore, they often stopped in at the restaurant for a hot meal after a blustery walk on Ocean Beach, or to watch a particularly lovely sunset over a glass of wine.

What most people don't realize is that the Cliff House is also a remarkable place for a wedding or special event. Originally built in 1863, it's gone through a number of incarnations in its long and illustrious life and is now more captivating than ever.

The 1909 building at the core of the current venue has been uncovered and restored, and the new Sutro Wing on the north side (named for the famous public bathhouse that flourished nearby in the early 1900s) has been designed as an upscale restaurant. This clever addition's two-story windows frame the truly breathtaking views, while an opalescent floor-to-ceiling sea-glass mosaic reflects the shimmery light of the ocean and evokes the pearly inside of an abalone shell. An exhibition kitchen, which expands the open feeling, is visible from nearly everywhere in the room. Two large Italian ceramic panels, which depict ladies bathing and once hung in the Sutro Baths, have been restored and now grace the restaurant.

The completely separate Terrace Room in the 1909 section, however, is the place for weddings. All of the glories of a Pacific sunset to the west and misty Ocean Beach stretching southward can be viewed through floor-to-ceiling windows on two sides. If you hold your ceremony on the private Terrace, you'll have the beach and the Pacific as your backdrop while you face Seal Rock. Afterwards, invite your guests inside the Terrace Room for cocktails followed by dinner and dancing. A palette of muted sand dune tones is carried through the chairs, carpet and window treatments; seven large framed mirrors run along the wall opposite the windows, brightening the room and reflecting the view. (Consider having your cake table in front of one of the mirrors.) There's often an extended dusk here—the kind you get when you're out at sea. With any luck, that lingering glow will illuminate the room all during your reception. An adjacent dedicated kitchen turns out updated classic cuisine for your private party, so there's no conflict with restaurant dining.

Come rediscover this uniquely San Franciscan treasure. Its mesmerizing clifftop location and exceptional sea views make it well worth the trip.

CEREMONY CAPACITY: The Terrace Deck and Terrace Room each accommodate 120 seated guests.

EVENT/RECEPTION & MEETING CAPACITY: The Terrace Room can hold 120 seated or 150 standing guests.

FEES & DEPOSITS: For events, a nonrefundable $3,500 deposit (which is applied towards the final bill) is required when reservations are confirmed. The estimated event total is due 8 weeks prior to the event; the balance is payable at the end of the function. A guest count confirmation is due 2 weeks in advance. Food service is provided. Per-person costs run $65–75 for buffets, $50–75 for seated dinners. Beverages, ceremony package, setup fee, tax and a 20% service charge are additional.

For business meetings, a room rental fee may apply. The fee varies depending on the day of the week, event duration and food & beverage total.

AVAILABILITY: Year-round, daily, 8am–1:30am. The Terrace Room is not available Sunday before 6pm or on major holidays.

SERVICES/AMENITIES:

Catering: in-house, no BYO
Kitchen Facilities: n/a
Tables & Chairs: provided
Linens, Silver, etc.: provided
Restrooms: wheelchair accessible
Dance Floor: yes, extra charge
Bride's Dressing Area: no
AV/Meeting Equipment: no

Parking: nearby lots, valet parking after 5pm $10/vehicle
Accommodations: no guest rooms
Outdoor Night Lighting: no
Outdoor Cooking Facilities: no
Cleanup: provided
View: ocean
Other: wedding and event coordination

RESTRICTIONS:

Alcohol: in-house
Smoking: outdoors only
Music: amplified OK indoors

Wheelchair Access: yes
Insurance: not required

Commodore Cruises & Events

Yachts

Boarding at Alameda, Pier 40 SF, and 19 other ports in the Bay Area
510/337-9000

www.commodoreevents.com
events@commodoreevents.com

- Rehearsal Dinners
- Ceremonies
- Wedding Receptions
- Corp. Events/Mtgs.
- Private Parties
- Accommodations

If you're a lover of ocean liners, cruise ships, yachts, and all the grandeur and pampering they imply, why not charter one of Commodore Cruises' six luxury yachts for your milestone event? Boarding from their home port in Alameda, Pier 40 and 19 other ports in the San Francisco Bay area, their fleet has maintained the fine tradition of white glove entertaining at sea for over 30 years.

The *Cabernet Sauvignon* is the Grande Dame of San Francisco Bay. It possesses four enormous decks: a spacious lounge deck, a dining deck for sit-down dinners or buffets, a large dance-floor deck equipped with an excellent sound system and magnificent bar, and an open-air sky deck that's perfect for viewing the city skyline. A private stateroom provides a changing space for brides and bridesmaids.

Commodore's trio of Mega Yachts is extremely versatile. The *Pinot Noir,* with its long white bar and mirrored ceilings resembles a chic set straight out of a James Bond movie. Its equally stunning sister yacht, the *Chardonnay,* boasts a large dance floor on the second deck. Couples who desire an intimate outdoor ceremony might want to consider the *Merlot.* Popular because it serves groups large and small, it has a dance floor on the second deck that spills out onto the open-air deck, creating a wonderful indoor/outdoor flow.

The *Fumé Blanc,* a three-deck replica of a New York State steamship, features a 30-foot dance floor, roomy viewing platforms on the bow, and a 340-guest capacity. And lastly, the Zinfandel treats guests to fabulous 360-degree views from a dining deck with floor-to-ceiling windows.

All vessels offer well-appointed settings for dining, gorgeous wraparound views of the bay, and multiple menu options for a wide variety of social and corporate functions. Plus Commodore Cruises & Events works with a selection of highly rated vendors to help you create the wedding or special event of your dreams. Before booking any other venue, make reservations for one of Commodore's open houses where you can "Meet the Fleet." *Bon Voyage!*

CEREMONY, EVENT/RECEPTION & MEETING CAPACITY: Maximum capacity is 340 guests aboard the *Fumé Blanc* and 350 aboard the *Cabernet Sauvignon.* Many events are hosted with 20–130 guests aboard smaller yachts.

FEES & DEPOSITS: A nonrefundable deposit of 25% of the estimated event total is required to reserve your date. Another 25% is due 120 days prior to the event, and the balance is due 14 days prior. Fees, including meals, a full bar and 3–4 hours aboard, range $65–200/person. The yachts are also available à la carte.

AVAILABILITY: Year-round, anytime.

SERVICES/AMENITIES:

Catering: in-house or BYO

Kitchen Facilities: fully equipped

Tables & Chairs: provided

Linens, Silver, etc.: provided, upgrades available

Restrooms: some wheelchair accessible

Dance Floor: yes

Bride's Dressing Area: yes

AV/Meeting Equipment: provided

Parking: large free lot

Accommodations: hotels near all ports

Outdoor Night Lighting: yes

Outdoor Cooking Facilities: n/a

Cleanup: provided

View: entire San Francisco Bay

Other: wedding cakes, florals, referrals

RESTRICTIONS:

Alcohol: in-house, or BYO with corkage fee

Smoking: on open-air decks only

Music: sound system and in-house DJs available

Wheelchair Access: yes

Insurance: not required

Conservatory of Flowers

Historic Conservatory

100 John F. Kennedy Drive, San Francisco
415/845-2394
www.conservatoryofflowers.org/events/weddings
sordway@sfcof.org

● Rehearsal Dinners	● Corp. Events/Mtgs.
● Ceremonies	● Private Parties
● Wedding Receptions	○ Accommodations

If you're looking for a symbolic place to begin your marriage, you can't beat the Conservatory of Flowers in Golden Gate Park. This seemingly fragile, multi-faceted gem of a building with a thriving, ever-growing, organic heart, has suffered fire, earthquakes and windstorms—and yet, it's still standing after 130 years.

In December 1995, a Pacific storm with 100-mile-an-hour winds shattered 40 percent of the frosty white glass panels, and damaged the framework so badly that the entire structure had to be dismantled and reassembled using a mixture of old and replacement wood beams. Luckily, a rebuilt and thoroughly revitalized Conservatory was able to reopen in the fall of 2003.

The Vestibule is the entry to the Conservatory and a lovely entrée to your event. While you're serving cocktails in this peaked roof section, take a look at the surrounding glass: It's not all white or clear, but punctuated by jewel-like insets of green, tiger lily orange, ruby and delphinium blue.

From the Vestibule, go through the Lowland Tropics, the large central gallery with the gorgeous pointed cupola housing the enormous century-old philodendron and a dense mix of other tropical plants. The cool Highland Tropics gallery contains a collection of delicate high-altitude orchids. The Aquatic Plants gallery has a water lily pond with little waterfalls and fantastic *Victoria amazonica* lily pads—the kind that grow so large they're depicted in fairy-tale books with children sitting on them.

Inside Potted Plants, the wooden arbor is tailor-made for exchanging vows. It's flanked by potted palms, and the vines overhead drip with star-shaped lavender flowers. Throughout this gallery are hibiscus plants with showy blooms in yellows, pinks, oranges and reds, and orchids in all the crazy variety of sizes, shapes and colors that orchids exhibit. Huge pots of Dr. Suessian, spiky-stemmed Madagascar Palms sit here, and two banks of plants with a mesmerizing diversity of leaf textures, shapes and patterns run the length of the room.

Just past Potted Plants is Special Exhibits, a large open gallery dominated by the ethereal, spun-sugar look of the Conservatory's structure. Depending on the availability of this space, ceremonies take place here among changing plant exhibitions; past exhibits have featured butterflies, carnivorous and poisonous plants, and local history.

The Orchid Pavilion is ideal for larger, sit-down dinner functions, events or meetings. Outdoor ceremonies and tented events for up to 300 people can be held on the Conservatory's lawn or platform.

Flower lovers will find no better place for a celebration than this Conservatory. It's a uniquely beautiful San Francisco landmark.

CEREMONY CAPACITY: The Conservatory can accommodate up to 50 standing indoors and 300 seated outdoors.

EVENT/RECEPTION & MEETING CAPACITY: The Conservatory holds up to 200 standing. The Orchid Pavilion holds 160 for a seated dinner or 200 for a standing reception. Smaller celebrations as well as larger tented events can be accommodated; call for details.

FEES & DEPOSITS: 25% of the rental fee is required to reserve your date. The balance is due 30 days prior to event date. The rental fee ranges $2,500–20,000 depending on the space, guest count, and length of time rented.

AVAILABILITY: Year-round, daily, 6pm–midnight. Daytime hours are available with some restrictions.

SERVICES/AMENITIES:

Catering: select from list
Kitchen Facilities: prep only
Tables & Chairs: white wooden folding chairs and rectangular tables provided
Linens, Silver, etc.: BYO or through caterer
Restrooms: wheelchair accessible
Dance Floor: wood flooring throughout
Bride's Dressing Area: no
AV/Meeting Equipment: BYO or through vendor

Parking: reserved parking included, street parking available
Accommodations: no guest rooms
Outdoor Night Lighting: access only
Outdoor Cooking Facilities: caterer build-out
Cleanup: caterer
View: landscaped grounds, Golden Gate Park

RESTRICTIONS:

Alcohol: BYO, licensed server
Smoking: not allowed
Music: amplified OK indoors with restrictions

Wheelchair Access: yes
Insurance: liability required

de Young Museum

Landmark Museum

50 Hagiwara Tea Garden Drive, Golden Gate Park, San Francisco
415/750-3683
www.famsf.org
deyoungevents@famsf.org

- Rehearsal Dinners
- Ceremonies
- Wedding Receptions
- Corp. Events/Mtgs.
- Private Parties
- Accommodations

For an event as captivating as a work of art, the de Young Museum is unquestionably the right venue. Founded in 1895 and situated in the heart of San Francisco's Golden Gate Park, the completely redesigned museum has been transformed into an ultra-cool contemporary frame for fine art and outstanding functions.

Entrance is through the courtyard installation by famed sculptor Andy Goldsworthy. An invitingly lit lobby, featuring Italian stone floors and Ruth Asawa sculptures, is a fitting place to greet guests with champagne before whisking them up nine stories to the Hamon Observation Tower. Here, surrounded by walls of glass, delighted celebrants can savor cocktails, hors d'oeuvres and music. While mingling, they'll admire unimpeded 360-degree panoramic views of San Francisco's downtown skyline, the Golden Gate Bridge, the sparkling Pacific, and Golden Gate Park.

Your guests will also be impressed by the spectacular architecture of the concourse-level event spaces and galleries. The walls soar two stories high in dramatic Wilsey Court, a perfect fit for an über-elegant wedding reception, dinner dance or upscale corporate affair. Designed by renowned Swiss architects Herzog & de Meuron, its inspired use of angles, openness and art gives the space a fluid vitality. A grand staircase to the upper galleries is ideal for regal entrances and photo ops. And don't forget that you can include the de Young's magnificent exhibitions, if you choose. The adjacent Piazzoni Murals Room, with burnished Italian landscapes adorning its walls, can serve as a special lounge, a separate bar and entertainment area, or an exclusive private chamber for more intimate gatherings.

But why stop there? For an artsy vibe with a whimsical twist, take your party to the de Young Café, de Young Terrace, and Barbro Osher Sculpture Garden, which can be used separately or in combination. Have your ceremony on the broad sculpture garden lawn amid playful artworks and fanciful landscaping, host cocktails on the adjacent terrace, then dine and dance in the café. One of the museum's most popular event spaces, it transforms to suit your mood: casual, formal, festive or even sultry. Striking touches like the colorful hand-blown glass lamps suspended overhead remind you that no matter where you go in the de Young art is everywhere, contributing a dynamic dimension to your celebration.

CEREMONY & MEETING CAPACITY: Indoors, spaces hold up to 400 seated guests. Outdoors, the Garden seats up to 200 for a ceremony.

EVENT/RECEPTION CAPACITY: Indoors, spaces hold up to 400 seated or 2,500 standing guests.

FEES & DEPOSITS: 50% of the rental fee is due at the time of booking. The rental fee starts at $5,000 and varies depending on the space reserved.

AVAILABILITY: Year-round, daily. Special events take place in a 4-hour block between 6:30pm and 1am. Daytime rental is available in limited blocks during museum hours. Overtime fees are additional.

SERVICES/AMENITIES:

Catering: select from preferred list
Kitchen Facilities: fully equipped
Tables & Chairs: some provided
Linens, Silver, etc.: through caterer
Restrooms: wheelchair accessible
Dance Floor: provided
Bride's & Groom's Dressing Areas: no
AV/Meeting Equipment: some provided

Parking: valet or public garage
Accommodations: no guest rooms
Outdoor Night Lighting: access only
Outdoor Cooking Facilities: no
Cleanup: provided
View: park, garden, pond, cityscape
Other: event coordination

RESTRICTIONS:

Alcohol: BYO
Smoking: not allowed
Music: amplified OK

Wheelchair Access: yes
Insurance: liability required

Want to know WHAT TO ASK a potential location or vendor? Check out our Questions to Ask starting on page 21.

E&O Kitchen & Bar

Restaurant

314 Sutter Street, San Francisco
415/693-0303

www.eosanfrancisco.com
events@eosanfrancisco.com

- ● Rehearsal Dinners
- ● Ceremonies
- ● Wedding Receptions
- ● Corp. Events/Mtgs.
- ● Private Parties
- ○ Accommodations

One of San Francisco's favorite dining and event spaces just got even better. Located amid galleries, boutiques and topnotch hotels just a block from Union Square, the tremendously popular restaurant formerly known as E&O Trading Company has been re-envisioned and re-introduced to fans and new customers as E&O Kitchen & Bar.

Tonya Bellusci, designer of San Francisco's District and Oakland's Pican restaurants, was commissioned to update the environment with a more relaxed Southeast Asian feel. Inspired by the beaches of Bali, Thailand and Sri Lanka, the new vibe incorporates shades of earth, gray and gold along with subtle tropical accents.

The spacious foyer, which leads seamlessly to the long open bar, is airy and inviting and creates a lounge area ideal for music, cocktails and plenty of guest interaction. This is no doubt the perfect place to sample the wondrous concoctions of the venue's expert mixologist—how about a Gazebo…or perhaps a Blushing Geisha? Guests can mingle effortlessly here, nibbling on an inventive array of appetizers or simply sipping a glass of wine or champagne.

The hip new floor plan encourages flow, and everyone will be able to move freely through the restaurant as they dine on treats like succulent wood-grilled satays, ahi poke, plump little dumplings, and other delicious Pacific Rim specialties. You'll find all the design elements E&O is known for—sleek bar, exhibition kitchen, soaring ceilings—here in the main dining area.

Planning an intimate affair? A new private dining room has been added on the ground floor. It features Asian-influenced décor, a flat screen TV and a fabulous antiqued carved wooden door to ensure that your party will not be disturbed.

Downstairs in the Cinnabar Room, so named for the distinctive red color of the walls, the atmosphere is decidedly den-like and clubby. The wood-beamed ceiling, black marble bar, and velvet and leather chairs add to the aura of comfort and privacy.

For extra-large company dinners or smaller family gatherings, the mezzanine level is ideal. Past the shimmering, waterfall-like wall mosaic, up the stairs or elevator, the handsome U-shaped mezzanine affords a dazzling command of the main floor dining room, attractive Sutter Street views, and private and semiprivate dining in the E&O Room and North Mezzanine.

The flexible layout allows you to use individual spaces or combine them to suit your celebration. However, if you're hosting a large event or you just want the whole restaurant to yourself, you have the option of entertaining and dining on all three levels.

E&O is easy to reach via public transportation, and the adjacent Stockton-Sutter Garage makes parking convenient. Guests staying in nearby hotels will love the fact that everything is within walking distance—they can do a little shopping or visit a few galleries on their way to your event.

CEREMONY CAPACITY: The facility seats 70 for a ceremony.

EVENT/RECEPTION CAPACITY: Private dining spaces hold up to 275 seated or 400 standing guests.

MEETING CAPACITY: The restaurant accommodates up to 200 seated guests.

FEES & DEPOSITS: 50% of the estimated event total is required to reserve your date, and the balance is due at the end of the event. Meals range $60–90/person. Tax, alcohol, a 21% service charge, and a 4% San Francisco Employer Mandate surcharge are additional.

AVAILABILITY: Year-round, daily, 11:30am–11pm.

SERVICES/AMENITIES:

Catering: in-house, no BYO
Kitchen Facilities: n/a
Tables & Chairs: provided
Linens, Silver, etc.: provided
Restrooms: wheelchair accessible
Dance Floor: CBA
Bride's Dressing Area: no
AV/Meeting Equipment: some provided

Parking: public garage
Accommodations: no guest rooms
Outdoor Night Lighting: no
Outdoor Cooking Facilities: no
Cleanup: provided
View: SF cityscape
Other: event coordination, on-site florals

RESTRICTIONS:

Alcohol: in-house, no BYO
Smoking: outside only
Music: amplified OK indoors

Wheelchair Access: yes
Insurance: not required

Exploratorium

Pier 15, San Francisco
415/528-4500

www.exploratorium.edu/rentals
events@exploratorium.edu

Landmark Museum

● Rehearsal Dinners	● Corp. Events/Mtgs.
● Ceremonies	● Private Parties
● Wedding Receptions	Accommodations

For a jaw-dropping event that will wow young and old, you simply must consider the Exploratorium in its all-new venue at Pier 15 on San Francisco's Embarcadero. Packed with exciting exhibits—and 100,000 square feet of indoor/outdoor event space—the new Exploratorium is making a huge splash on our ever-popular Bayscape.

Situated right on the water between Fisherman's Wharf and the Ferry Building, the museum's nine-acre campus occupies Pier 15. The super-popular interactive museum of science, art and human perception includes the Kanbar Forum (a cabaret-style performance space), numerous indoor galleries, the Outdoor Gallery, the Fisher Bay Observatory Gallery & Terrace, a restaurant, café, and museum shop—all of which can be used individually or in combination for your spectacular celebration.

What we love about this venue is that, true to its mission, it was designed with the latest developments in sustainable architecture and has been awarded an LEED Platinum Certification! With a goal of being the largest net-zero energy museum in the U.S., it offsets its energy use with "green" features like solar panels and a bay water heating and cooling system. We also like the way it allows for so much movement and flow. You can thread your event through the exhibits in a manner that entertains and engages. Whether you're planning a wedding, gala, corporate extravaganza, product launch, film screening, dinner-dance, meeting or any other kind of gathering, you'll find just the right spot in this tremendously flexible and dynamic setting.

Weddings, for example, might begin with a ceremony in the Fisher Bay Observatory Gallery, a gorgeous glass-walled jewel box of a room on the second floor of the only entirely new structure on the pier. This exquisite chamber affords nearly 360-degree views that include Treasure Island, the Bay Bridge, the Transamerica Pyramid and Coit Tower, and it contains an oculus—a giant glass eye in the ceiling from which to view the heavens. Sliding glass doors open onto the Outdoor Terrace, where more soothing bay views frame cocktails, passed hors d'oeuvres, dinner or dancing under a tent or a canopy of sky.

Three more galleries offer unique entertainment experiences. Your guests can chat, stroll, dine and dance their way through one or all of them, depending on your vision. The Life Sciences come alive in the East Gallery, a beautiful space for an intimate seated dinner or reception with enormous windows overlooking the bay. The expansive Bechtel Central Gallery is perfect for larger affairs where the exploration of sight, sound and perception is sure to stimulate interaction.

The Osher West Gallery, which integrates exhibits on psychology and art, houses the museum's iconic Tactile Dome. It can be used in tandem with the adjacent Kanbar Forum—which has a stage, a state-of-the-art sound and projection system, theater- or cabaret-style seating and a permanent bar—or with other galleries to engender the sense of wonder, amazement, joy and play that makes an event here unforgettable.

And do remember: The Exploratorium's expertise in interaction and perception extends to its energetic and imaginative event staff. Whether it's picking out party favors from the Museum Shop, inventing new ways to utilize the galleries and exhibits, or carefully orchestrating a festive flow, they'll know how to transform your great ideas into a truly inspiring celebration.

CEREMONY CAPACITY: Indoor ceremony spaces can accommodate 1–300 seated guests. The outdoor Observatory Terrace holds up to 125 guests.

EVENT/RECEPTION CAPACITY: Individual galleries hold up to 150–300 seated or 200–1,200 standing. The entire facility can accommodate up to 1,000 seated or 3,500 standing.

MEETING CAPACITY: Meeting spaces hold up to 200 seated theater-style.

FEES & DEPOSITS: 50% of the rental fee is required to reserve your date. The balance is due 3 months prior to the event. The evening gallery rental fee starts at $8,000 and varies depending on the galleries rented, number of guests and total contracted hours.

AVAILABILITY: Year-round, daily except Thursday, starting at 5:30pm.

SERVICES/AMENITIES:

Catering: select from approved list
Kitchen Facilities: prep only
Tables & Chairs: through caterer
Linens, Silver, etc.: through caterer
Restrooms: wheelchair accessible
Dance Area: provided or through caterer
Bride's Dressing Area: CBA
AV/Meeting Equipment: CBA, extra charge
Other: access to hundreds of hands-on exhibits

Parking: valet, public lots or on-street
Accommodations: no guest rooms
Outdoor Night Lighting: access only, BYO
Outdoor Cooking Facilities: through caterer
Cleanup: caterer
View: cityscape of Transamerica Pyramid and Coit Tower; bay views including Bay Bridge and Treasure Island

RESTRICTIONS:

Alcohol: through caterer, licensed server required
Smoking: outdoors only on the street
Music: amplified OK with restrictions

Wheelchair Access: yes
Insurance: liability required
Other: decorations require prior approval; no glitter, balloons, confetti, birdseed or rice

Fairmont San Francisco

Hotel

Atop Nob Hill, San Francisco
415/772-5186
www.fairmont.com/sanfrancisco
emilie.lynch@fairmont.com

- Rehearsal Dinners
- Ceremonies
- Wedding Receptions
- Corp. Events/Mtgs.
- Private Parties
- Accommodations

As the first hotel to open after the 1906 earthquake, Fairmont San Francisco became the main gathering place and grand centerpiece of the City by the Bay. Since then, this extraordinary hotel continues to be a mecca for guests from all over the world and one of San Francisco's most treasured landmarks.

Over the last century, Fairmont San Francisco has undergone many changes, but an $85 million centennial restoration and $25 million guest room renovation not only brought back architect Julia Morgan's stunning turn-of-the-century interior, it added all the modern amenities you'd expect in a world-class hotel.

The lobby is now both larger and lighter in tone, and is splendidly understated with rich plum and gold hues. The original white-and-gray marble floor (lifted out slab by slab, cleaned and meticulously replaced) has been given a high sheen. The gold leaf on the 26-foot-high ceilings has been enhanced, and the ornate moldings have been cleaned and restored. Multiple pilasters and columns, painted in a *trompe l'oeil* marble finish, are highlighted with gold leaf accents. Informal clusters of period-style furniture, rich in detail with lots of tassels and trim, dot the lobby. The adjacent Laurel Court has become a warm and elegant restaurant and bar where your guests will enjoy mingling over drinks and hors d'oeuvres.

Two of the most grand and glamorous spaces in the hotel are the Venetian and Gold ballrooms. Both are light and airy, with elaborately ornamented vaulted ceilings, gold leaf detailing, and crystal chandeliers. The Pavilion Room has picture windows that overlook Fairmont's rooftop garden, a sublime spot for exchanging vows. The Crown Room, named for its spectacular location on the top floor of the tower, boasts one of the best views in the city: Tall wraparound windows reveal a sweeping 270-degree panorama of the Golden Gate and Bay Bridges, Coit Tower, Alcatraz, Downtown and the Twin Peaks. The setting here is impressive enough, but if you really want to have the ultimate reception, opt for the Presidential Service—each table has its own white-gloved waiter.

For a truly elite event, consider the 6,000-square-foot Penthouse Suite, a palatial residence spanning the entire eighth floor of the main building. Following a $2 million enhancement, this incredible venue features a living room with a grand piano, a formal dining room that seats 60, a two-story circular library, a billiard room, a breathtaking terrace with sweeping views of the San Francisco skyline and bay, and three oversized bedrooms. When you reserve the Penthouse, you and your guests have exclusive use of it and are free to flow from one space to another throughout the celebration.

If your event is on an intimate scale, Fairmont has a variety of beautiful smaller banquet rooms. More casual rehearsal dinners and post-wedding gatherings are often held in the Tonga Room & Hurricane Bar, which consistently receives awards for hosting San Francisco's best happy hour and offers exceptional island-inspired cuisine in a tropical setting.

CEREMONY CAPACITY: Seven indoor ceremony sites accommodate 5–500 seated guests. The Roof Garden holds 170 seated.

EVENT/RECEPTION CAPACITY: The hotel's event spaces can accommodate 5–900 seated or 150–2,500 standing guests indoors.

MEETING CAPACITY: There are 22 rooms that hold 35–1,500 guests seated theater-style or 12–1,000 seated classroom-style.

FEES & DEPOSITS: A nonrefundable deposit is required when reservations are confirmed. 30% of the estimated event total is due 90 days prior to the event. An additional deposit of 45% of the estimated total is due 30 days prior, with the remaining balance due 14 days before the event. Dinner wedding packages start at $170/person. Lunch packages range $115–200/person. Tax, alcohol and service charge are additional. For ceremonies, a $3,500–18,000 fee may be charged depending on the room(s) selected and extent of setup. The bride and groom receive a complimentary suite for the night of the event. Group rates for overnight guests can be arranged.

AVAILABILITY: Year-round, daily, 8am–2am.

SERVICES/AMENITIES:

Catering: in-house, no BYO
Kitchen Facilities: n/a
Tables & Chairs: provided
Linens, Silver, etc.: provided
Restrooms: wheelchair accessible
Dance Floor: provided
Bride's & Groom's Dressing Areas: yes
AV/Meeting Equipment: full range CBA

Parking: adjacent garages, valet CBA
Accommodations: 592 guest rooms
Outdoor Night Lighting: yes
Outdoor Cooking Facilities: no
Cleanup: provided
View: SF Bay, city skyline, Bay and Golden Gate Bridges
Other: event planning, on-site florist

RESTRICTIONS:

Alcohol: in-house, no BYO
Smoking: outdoors only
Music: amplified OK indoors

Wheelchair Access: yes, elevator
Insurance: not required

First Unitarian Universalist Church of San Francisco   *Historic Church*

1187 Franklin Street, corner of Franklin and Geary, San Francisco
415/776-4580 x202

www.uusf.org
reservations@uusf.org

● Rehearsal Dinners	● Corp. Events/Mtgs.
● Ceremonies	● Private Parties
● Wedding Receptions	Accommodations

As you drive past the bustling corner of Geary and Franklin Streets, you'll notice a beautiful old building that contrasts sharply with its modern neighbors. Built of sandstone in the Gothic Revival-Romanesque style, the First Unitarian Universalist Church of San Francisco looks as if it has existed for over a hundred years—and it has.

Although this is the church's third location in the city, it has occupied this corner since 1889. The First Unitarian Universalist Church marries all loving couples, and does not discriminate based upon gender or spiritual belief.

In the sanctuary, Gothic and modern design elements create an atmosphere that is open and airy, yet visually stimulating. White plaster walls, set with exquisite stained-glass rose windows, soar up to meet the tracery of the carved beam ceiling hung with wrought-iron and gilt chandeliers. On the chancel, the imposing carved Gothic chairs, pulpit and lectern are lightened by a delicate abstract metal candelabra hung on the wall behind them. A custom-built 3,100-pipe organ—said to be one of the best on the West Coast—sits regally in the choir loft. For an extra touch of magic, six-foot-tall candelabras can be fitted into brackets at the ends of the pews, giving an ethereal glow to your ceremony.

The 70-seat Chapel is ideal for smaller weddings. Octagonal in shape, its tall concrete walls are inset with narrow, stained-glass windows in shades of blue and gold, and hung with Oriental rugs and wall hangings. What makes the Chapel truly unique, however, is its fabulous acoustics. Not only do they enhance every type of music from harp to string quartet, they give the Chapel a feeling of real intimacy, and ensure that your guests will hear even your softest-spoken words.

The 35-seat Fireside Room, with fireplace, beamed ceilings and wood paneling is a cozy spot for intimate weddings, receptions or business functions. A favorite place for wedding photos and outdoor celebrations is the Allyne Courtyard, a sunny space whose focal point is a free-form bronze fountain, surrounded by flowering trees and plants.

For indoor events, the Church has two large function areas. The Thomas Starr King Room is named after the Church's beloved minister from 1860 to 1864. This spacious room has a parquet floor, impressive pyramidal beamed skylight hung with wood-and-opaque-glass light fixtures, and a recessed stage area that is perfect for a bride's table or DJ setup. The artwork on the walls is changed monthly. The adjacent Martin Luther King Room, named after the civil rights leader, is a smaller version of the Starr King Room, and sliding doors allow you to combine the two if desired.

Perhaps the most impressive thing about the First Unitarian Universalist Church is its acceptance of diverse faiths, cultures and lifestyles. You are invited to work with their clergy to create a ceremony that celebrates your values and the unique commitment you are making. So, whether you want a traditional wedding with organ music accompanying your procession, or a less conventional ceremony, you're sure to find a warm welcome at the First Unitarian Universalist Church.

CEREMONY CAPACITY: The Sanctuary can accommodate up to 375 seated guests.

EVENT/RECEPTION & MEETING CAPACITY: The church's two reception rooms combined hold up to 270 seated or 300 standing guests indoors.

FEES & DEPOSITS: 50% of the rental fee is required to reserve your date; the balance is due 30 days prior to the event. An $800–2,000 ceremony fee includes 1 hour for rehearsal, 2 hours for setup, 1 hour for photos after the ceremony, the organist, and a wedding ceremony coordinator. The rental fee for receptions and business functions ranges $700–1,500 depending on the guest count and space rented. Events running past 10pm incur additional fees.

AVAILABILITY: Year-round, daily, 8am–10pm.

SERVICES/AMENITIES:
Catering: BYO
Kitchen Facilities: prep only
Tables & Chairs: provided
Linens, Silver, etc.: BYO
Restrooms: wheelchair accessible
Dance Floor: yes
Bride's & Groom's Dressing Areas: provided
AV/Meeting Equipment: TV, microphones, sound system, CD/DVD capability

Parking: nearby garages
Accommodations: no guest rooms
Outdoor Night Lighting: n/a
Outdoor Cooking Facilities: n/a
Cleanup: through caterer
View: inner courtyard
Other: event coordination

RESTRICTIONS:
Alcohol: BYO
Smoking: outdoors only
Music: amplified OK indoors only

Wheelchair Access: yes
Insurance: not required

The wedding vendors on our website are the best in the business. How do we know? Read page 553.

Foreign Cinema

Restaurant

2534 Mission Street, San Francisco
415/648-7600 X24

www.foreigncinema.com
janine@foreigncinema.com

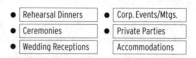

- Rehearsal Dinners
- Ceremonies
- Wedding Receptions
- Corp. Events/Mtgs.
- Private Parties
- Accommodations

Dinner and a movie … it's the quintessential first date that's probably launched more relationships than any other activity. So what could be more perfect than celebrating the most important day of your relationship by playing out your own romantic wedding scene at Foreign Cinema in San Francisco?

This dynamic and thoroughly original venue in the Mission District has become a magnet for foodies, cinephiles, and loyal locals by artfully editing together critically acclaimed cuisine with several unique dining environments—including a glorious courtyard where films are projected on an exterior wall. If you buy out the restaurant, all of these spaces become yours for the Big Night.

A small marquee-style awning marks the entrance to the restaurant, where two stainless steel doors usher you down a seductively lit hallway, flickering with votive candles. If you're having your ceremony here, your guests will be invited outside to the canopied center Courtyard, which provides a nice long aisle for a dramatic bridal entrance. After the service, friends and family can enjoy a sumptuous cocktail reception in the Modernism West Gallery, a loft-like space with a two-story ceiling. Lining the crisp white walls is an impressive display of visually exciting artwork, which gives the setting a cultural edge and provides a great backdrop for photos. There's a chic bar at one end, and along the other are floor-to-ceiling windows inset with glass doors that lead to a cozy Zen-like Upper Patio. Some couples opt to host their entire event in the Gallery.

For larger groups, the festivities continue across the Courtyard with dinner in the rustically elegant Dining Room, whose wood-framed windows open to the outdoors, creating a nice connection between the two spaces. A newly remodeled bar area features a Brazilian barrocca soapstone counter atop a colorfully tiled base that harmonizes with avocado-hued banquettes. The wood floor, fireplace and very cool chandeliers—whose lighting elements are actually truck headlights—give the room a warm, yet trendy feel.

Overlooking it all is the Mezzanine, which can serve as a VIP lounge, an intimate rehearsal dinner spot, or a retreat for the bride and groom … all with great views of the action below. And part of that action is the open kitchen, because Foreign Cinema, being chef-owned, is very focused on maintaining the high level of its popular California-Mediterranean dishes, prepared in inventive ways with only fresh, organic ingredients.

Finally, top off a wonderful evening with dancing in the Gallery and nightcaps in the Courtyard while your favorite movie or a slideshow of your own love story is projected on the wall.

CEREMONY CAPACITY: The facility holds 100 seated guests indoors or outdoors.

EVENT/RECEPTION CAPACITY: The venue can accommodate up to 170 seated or 350 standing guests.

MEETING CAPACITY: Meeting rooms hold 70 seated guests.

FEES & DEPOSITS: A deposit (amount varies) is required to secure your date, and the balance is due at the conclusion of the event. The food & beverage minimum ranges $2,000–35,000 depending on the space reserved and the day of the week. Menus range $64–115/person. Tax, alcohol and a 20% service charge are additional. A facility fee may apply.

AVAILABILITY: Year-round, daily. Call or email for specifics on available times.

SERVICES/AMENITIES:

Catering: in-house
Kitchen Facilities: n/a
Tables & Chairs: provided
Linens, Silver, etc.: provided
Restrooms: wheelchair accessible
Dance Floor: provided
Bride's Dressing Area: no
AV/Meeting Equipment: CBA

Parking: on-street, valet, garage nearby
Accommodations: no guest rooms
Outdoor Night Lighting: yes
Outdoor Cooking Facilities: none
Cleanup: provided
View: garden courtyard
Other: on-site florals, event coordination, film projection available

RESTRICTIONS:

Alcohol: in-house
Smoking: not allowed
Music: amplified OK with restrictions

Wheelchair Access: yes
Insurance: not required

Fort Mason Center

Historic Event Center

2 Marina Boulevard, Landmark Building A
Fort Mason Center, San Francisco

415/345-7500

www.fortmason.org
www.fortmason.org/venuerental/rfp
sales@fortmason.org

Rehearsal Dinners	● Corp. Events/Mtgs.
● Ceremonies	● Private Parties
● Wedding Receptions	Accommodations

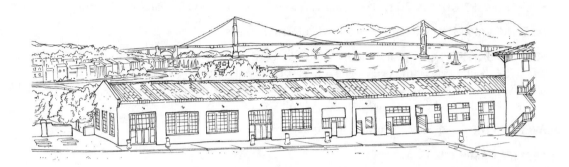

Fort Mason Center embodies what most people love about San Francisco—a nearness to nature (especially the bay), novel architecture and a sense of the past. Located on some of the most prime real estate in the city, the center's historic buildings sit adjacent to the Marina Green, right on the water, with postcard-worthy vistas of the Golden Gate Bridge, Alcatraz, and the Marin Headlands. Its well-preserved structures and piers recall its military past, but in the 1970s the site was re-purposed as an urban national park and Fort Mason Center was established. It's since become a hub for nonprofit arts organizations, and also houses galleries, bookstores and restaurants. In addition, the center has many unique venues that host events of all types and sizes.

Among the most popular sites for intimate weddings is the Firehouse, a lovely freestanding hall tucked away in the far northeast corner of the complex. Considered a hidden gem thanks to its near complete privacy and divine views, it edges right up to the bay on one side and a pine-covered hill on the other. Inside, high-ceilinged rooms dress up nicely for seated dinners, buffets and dancing.

For larger festivities, the recently renovated Gallery 308 represents the height of industrial chic. Its open floor plan, with polished concrete floors and vaulted ceilings, becomes a blank canvas for your own creative event styling. Windows not only bring in natural light during the day, but capture spectacular seascape panoramas, including the iconic Golden Gate Bridge. At night, the view becomes a galaxy of twinkling lights from the city, yachts and bridge.

The General's Residence—which has entertained luminaries such as General MacArthur and two presidents—has been restored to its former splendor. A sprawling lawn behind the building hosts ceremonies with sweeping bay views, while floor-to-ceiling windows throughout the interior bring those legendary vistas indoors. The residence is an intriguing blend of past and present: The Foyer evokes nostalgic grandeur with its fireplace and magnificent crystal chandelier, yet the Dining Room and Ballroom both have a breezy, contemporary simplicity.

The grandest of galas are easily accommodated in the fully customizable Festival Pavilion. Outfitted with hi-tech amenities and convenient annexes for storage, catering prep or VIP retreats, the spacious Pavilion is a flexible option for both corporate conferences and mega celebrations. The historic waterfront structure also commands classic views of Alcatraz and the San Francisco Bay.

Though Fort Mason Center effortlessly accommodates those tying the knot, it also has a strong mission to serve the local community. Booking an event here helps ensure that this landmark—and its affiliated arts organizations—remains for future generations to enjoy. This added benefit is not lost on socially conscious couples who realize that it's possible to get married in high style and support a nonprofit in the process.

CEREMONY CAPACITY: Gallery 308 can accommodate up to 400 seated guests, the Firehouse 100 seated, and the General's Residence 200 seated.

EVENT/RECEPTION CAPACITY: Gallery 308 holds 250 seated or 400 standing guests, the Firehouse 80 seated or 100 standing, the General's Residence 130 seated in the dining room or 450 standing in the entire venue, and the Festival Pavilion up to 2500 seated or standing guests.

MEETING CAPACITY: Gallery 308 seats 400 guests theater-style.

FEES & DEPOSITS: 50% of the rental fee is required to secure your date, and the balance is due 45 days prior to the event. The rental fee ranges $1,000–8,000 depending on the time of the event and the space reserved.

AVAILABILITY: Year-round, daily, 8am–midnight.

SERVICES/AMENITIES:

Catering: BYO
Kitchen Facilities: limited
Tables & Chairs: provided
Linens, Silver, etc.: some provided
Restrooms: wheelchair accessible
Dance Floor: portable provided
Bride's Dressing Area: CBA
AV/Meeting Equipment: some provided

Parking: large lot, on-street; valet CBA
Accommodations: no guest rooms
Outdoor Night Lighting: access only
Outdoor Cooking Facilities: CBA
Cleanup: renter
View: panorama of San Francisco Bay, Alcatraz Island, cityscape and coastline
Other: picnic area, event coordination

RESTRICTIONS:

Alcohol: BYO
Smoking: not permitted
Music: amplified OK indoors

Wheelchair Access: yes
Insurance: liability required

Great American Music Hall

Historic Music Hall

859 O'Farrell Street, San Francisco
415/255-7395
www.gamh.com
shana@slims-sf.com

- Rehearsal Dinners
- Ceremonies
- Wedding Receptions
- Corp. Events/Mtgs.
- Private Parties
- Accommodations

Standing beneath marble columns, ornately gilded balconies and an elaborate frescoed ceiling, it's easy to imagine this building's allure when it first came on the scene as a flashy French restaurant and San Francisco's grandest nightclub. Opening in 1907 on the heels of the great earthquake, the 5,000-square-foot concert hall symbolized the city's renewed optimism. The popular club flourished for a quarter century in this incarnation, then became the Music Box, where Sally Rand performed her famous fan dances, and later served as a Moose Lodge and yet another French restaurant.

In 1972 it was reborn as the Great American Music Hall, and in 1994 a complete facelift restored the club to its original rococo grandeur. For more than 25 years the hall has showcased the talents of music and comedy greats such as Ray Charles, the Grateful Dead, Bonnie Raitt, Jay Leno, Whoopi Goldberg and Robin Williams. Its intimate setting and wonderful acoustics continue to make it a favorite of music lovers throughout the Bay Area.

In addition to countless concerts, the Hall has hosted corporate bashes, fundraisers, holiday parties, product launches and weddings. Its flexible layout—one large room with balconies, a stage, huge oak dance floor and two full bars—makes it party-friendly, and there's not a bad seat in the house. The Music Hall also comes equipped with a state-of-the-art lighting and sound system and all the necessary staff.

Couples getting married here use the stage for the ceremony, with their "audience" seated in chairs on the dance floor. Once the knot has been tied, the rows of chairs are removed and the Hall is ready for the next phase of the celebration. Tables have been set up for dining all around, and even on the balconies if you like. With a band or a DJ making music on the stage and your guests dancing in the center of the room, the festivities can carry on into the night.

The Great American Music Hall offers a couple of very cool options that take the fun factor up a notch: They'll put the name of your company, your group, your families, or a special message on their marquee (who wouldn't get a kick out of seeing your name in lights?). Considering a theme event? The Hall is the perfect setting for a glitzy casino night, a Barbary Coast bash, or a Phantom of the Opera Night. Swing or '60s dance parties work well here, too.

Close to Union Square and only 10 blocks from Moscone Center, the Music Hall is conveniently situated for post-convention events. The space adapts comfortably to the size of your group, whether you have 50 or 600 guests.

While you can enhance the mood here with lounge furniture and uplights on the columns, the Great American Music Hall is really quite scintillating all by itself. The only building of its kind in The City, it provides a unique window into San Francisco's colorful, exuberant past.

CEREMONY & EVENT/RECEPTION CAPACITY: The Hall can accommodate 50–350 seated and up to 600 standing guests for a reception. Ceremonies can take place on the stage.

MEETING CAPACITY: Up to 250 seated guests with an unobstructed view of the stage.

FEES & DEPOSITS: Half the required event minimum plus a refundable $500 security deposit are due when reservations are confirmed; the balance is payable 2 business days prior to the event. Facility rental rates are as follows: Sunday–Wednesday $7,200 with an additional food & beverage minimum of $3,000; Thursday–Saturday $8,900 with an additional food & beverage minimum of $5,000. Food & beverage minimums are subject to a service charge and current sales tax. Holiday rates may be subject to an additional surcharge.

There are additional fees for miscellaneous services and various rental items. Evening rental rates include a house manager, bartenders, cocktail waitresses, sound and lighting technicians, security staff, an on-site event coordinator and more. If you use the in-house catering, all servers and culinary staff are included and meal pricing is as follows: hors d'oeuvres start at $20/person, dinners at $45/person; alcohol, tax and service charge are additional.

AVAILABILITY: Year-round, daily, flexible start and end times.

SERVICES/AMENITIES:

Catering: in-house or BYO
Kitchen Facilities: fully equipped
Tables & Chairs: cocktail tables and chairs are provided or rented
Linens, Silver, etc.: call for details
Restrooms: wheelchair accessible
Dance Floor: yes
Bride's Dressing Area: 3 dressing rooms
AV/Meeting Equipment: microphones, screen, built-in stage, state-of-the-art sound and lighting systems

Parking: valet, garage, nearby lots, on-street
Accommodations: no guest rooms
Outdoor Night Lighting: access only
Outdoor Cooking Facilities: no
Cleanup: provided
View: no
Other: event coordination, entertainment

RESTRICTIONS:

Alcohol: in-house
Smoking: no
Music: amplified OK

Wheelchair Access: yes
Insurance: required
Other: no birdseed, rice or confetti; no stick-on name tags

Hamlin Mansion

2120 Broadway, San Francisco
415/389-8069

www.parties-sf.com
moira@parties-sf.com

Historic Pacific Heights Mansion

- ● Rehearsal Dinners
- ● Ceremonies
- ● Wedding Receptions
- ● Corp. Events/Mtgs.
- ● Private Parties
- ☐ Accommodations

Now and then you may come across a school that occupies a mansion, but only the Hamlin School has a Pacific Heights address with a spectacular panoramic view of the Golden Gate and San Francisco Bay.

The mansion in this case is Stanwood Hall, one of three buildings that make up the school. Designed by Julius Kraft, the 24-room house was constructed in 1901 for James Leary Flood, son of the Nevada silver king, and was part of the last wave of mansion building in The City. Its Italian Baroque exterior is distinguished by Ionic columns, pilasters and pedimented windows arranged in formal symmetry, characteristic of the early 1900s Revival style that succeeded the late Victorians.

Granite steps, flanked by two gray marble lions (nicknamed Leo and Leona by Hamlin students), lead to a mosaic and marble vestibule and a pair of oak-and-plate-glass doors. Beyond the vestibule is the two-story Great Hall, a space with columns and wall-to-wall oak paneling that's practically custom-made for ceremonies. The bride makes her entrance by walking down a magnificent staircase, illuminated by a large art glass window with four chipped-glass "jewels" embedded in it. Guests are seated throughout the hall, and there's room on the balcony above for an additional group of onlookers. Or, you can exchange vows outside on the Great Lawn, where views of San Francisco Bay and Marin create a stunning backdrop.

Cocktails are usually served after the ceremony, giving guests an opportunity to explore the entire house, upstairs and down. Directly beyond the Great Hall is the Library, a warm room with a dark mahogany-paneled interior, striking black marble and gold fireplace and great bay vistas. Note the carved wood garland over the doorway as you enter. In contrast to the Library is the adjacent Solarium. This mosaic-and-glass space, filled with light and capped by three small Tiffany glass cupolas, also looks out to the bay and Marin County. Upstairs, there's a mezzanine that overlooks the Great Hall.

Receptions are held on the level below the main floor in the Dining Area, whose East and West Dining Rooms can be reserved individually or combined for large parties. The décor is simple, yet elegant, with ivory walls and maple floors. Large windows provide bay views and natural light during the day, while wall sconces cast soft light at night. If you'd like a more romantic ambiance, candles are permitted.

For over a century, the Hamlin Mansion has impressed all who enter its doors with its classic lines and rich appointments. You'll find that these qualities also make it a wonderful place for an upscale wedding, party or corporate event.

CEREMONY CAPACITY: The Great Hall holds 100 seated, with space around the balcony for an additional 80 standing. Outdoors, the Great Lawn holds 200 seated guests.

EVENT/RECEPTION & MEETING CAPACITY: The Mansion accommodates a maximum of 200 seated guests in two adjoining dining rooms. The largest one, the West Dining Room, holds up to 150 seated.

FEES & DEPOSITS: A refundable $1,000 security/cleaning deposit is required when the contract is signed. For weddings, a $7,500 rental fee covers use of the facility for 5 hours and is payable 2 months prior to the event. Food services are provided, please choose from our list. Valet is required from 2 approved vendors, and ranges $550–2,800 depending on the guest count. 2 house managers and a party manager are required at an extra fee.

AVAILABILITY: Year-round, weekdays after 6:30pm, weekends and school holidays all day.

SERVICES/AMENITIES:

Catering: select from preferred list, no BYO
Kitchen Facilities: n/a
Tables & Chairs: some provided
Linens, Silver, etc.: provided, extra charge
Restrooms: wheelchair accessible
Dance Floor: yes
Bride's Dressing Area: yes
AV/Meeting Equipment: no

Parking: valet required, extra charge
Accommodations: no guest rooms
Outdoor Night Lighting: access only
Outdoor Cooking Facilities: no
Cleanup: caterer
View: panorama of SF Bay
Other: baby grand piano, coordination, lawn area

RESTRICTIONS:

Alcohol: in-house or BYO
Smoking: outdoors only
Music: amplified OK; music curfew 10pm–Thursday, 11:30pm Friday–Saturday; bands have a 5-piece instrument maximum

Wheelchair Access: elevator
Insurance: recommended
Other: no rice, rose petals or bubbles

Want to find more venues and services? Check out our informative website, www.HereComesTheGuide.com.

83

Hornblower Cruises & Events

Yachts

San Francisco and Berkeley

415/438-8300

www.hornblowerweddings.com
sfsales@hornblower.com

● Rehearsal Dinners	● Corp. Events/Mtgs.
● Ceremonies	● Private Parties
● Wedding Receptions	Accommodations

Offering some of the most stunning views in the world, the San Francisco Bay is a wedding destination in itself. When you're out on its vibrant blue waters, there are picture-perfect panoramas wherever you look: landmarks like the Bay Bridge, Golden Gate Bridge, and sun-washed Alcatraz Island; the forested Marin headlands; and San Francisco's famous skyline. One of the best ways to merge these scenic glories with a topnotch celebration is with Hornblower Cruises & Events. From glamorous yachts to a replica of a turn-of-the-century coastal steamer, Hornblower's wide range of vessels combine the facilities of a fine restaurant with the excitement of a bay cruise. Whether you're planning a fabulous affair for 1,500 people or an intimate get-together with your closest friends, one of Hornblower's San Francisco Bay-based fleet will provide a spectacular setting.

The *Commodore Hornblower,* a 75-foot custom-built wood yacht, comes with two decks and two bars. The *Empress Hornblower,* is a 84-foot vessel reminiscent of river ferryboats. Outfitted with the rich woods and shining brass typical of the Hornblower fleet, she features indoor decks, an awning-covered outdoor deck, two dance floors and two bars. The *Sunset Hornblower* is a 98-foot ship that was recently refurbished. She has two decks appointed with mahogany and brass, as well as two bars.

The most contemporary member of the Hornblower fleet is the 150-foot, sleek and modern *San Francisco Spirit*. Live large on this 400-person craft, with elegant appointments that create a luxurious atmosphere.

The 183-foot *California Hornblower* is patterned after early 19th-century steamships and is the flagship of the Hornblower fleet. Boasting three decks, dining salons, spacious promenade decks and multiple dance floors, she can handle even the largest gathering with style.

One of the most impressive vessels is the 292-foot *San Francisco Belle*. Originally a casino riverboat, she's been remodeled to accommodate sizable groups for special events. She's designed with three large interior decks and an expansive sundeck.

All Hornblower events include linens, china and flatware. Their staff can handle as many of your wedding details as you desire, from personalized menus to photography and custom floral displays. If you get married on board, you have the additional option of using one of Hornblower's captains who are licensed ministers. With more than 50,000 special events and private parties to their credit, Hornblower Cruises & Events knows how to make the most of an unforgettable setting, and provide all the finery to make your celebration truly memorable.

CEREMONY, EVENT/RECEPTION & MEETING CAPACITY: Depending on the vessel selected, Hornblower's fleet can accommodate 20–1,050 seated or 50–1,500 standing guests. The largest seated dining capacity on one deck is 350 people.

FEES & DEPOSITS: 50% of the estimated total is required to book a vessel. A confirmed guest count is due 14 working days prior to the event; the final balance is due 10 working days prior. Custom weddings and wedding packages are available. Reception packages start at $98/person and include a 2-hour cruise, meal service, champagne toast, tax, service charge, and landing fee. Prices are subject to change.

AVAILABILITY: Year-round, daily, anytime.

SERVICES/AMENITIES FOR ALL VESSELS:

Catering: in-house
Kitchen Facilities: n/a
Tables & Chairs: provided
Linens, Silver, etc.: provided
Restrooms: wheelchair accessibility varies per vessel
Dance Floor: available
Bride's Dressing Area: no
AV/Meeting Equipment: CBA, extra fee

Parking: various paid/public locations
Accommodations: no guest rooms
Outdoor Night Lighting: varies
Outdoor Cooking Facilities: no
Cleanup: provided
View: the entire San Francisco Bay and skyline, Alcatraz and all bridges

RESTRICTIONS:

Alcohol: in-house with packages, or corkage $20/bottle
Smoking: allowed on outside decks
Music: provided or BYO; amplified OK

Wheelchair Access: varies per vessel
Insurance: not required
Other: no rice or fire on boats

Hotel Kabuki

Hotel

1625 Post Street, San Francisco
415/614-5416 Catering Department

www.hotelkabuki.com
www.jdvhotels.com
rbacon@jdvhotels.com

- Rehearsal Dinners
- Ceremonies
- Wedding Receptions
- Corp. Events/Mtgs.
- Private Parties
- Accommodations

Elegantly balancing both Western and Eastern influences, the Hotel Kabuki is a serene retreat in the heart of historic Japantown. This Joie de Vivre property has a modern, sophisticated interior, filled with elements that also reflect the refined beauty of the past.

A distinctively Japanese tone is set by the Summer Garden, a calm enclave featuring a koi pond and waterfall surrounded by a perfectly manicured landscape. This is a lovely spot for wedding photos.

On every floor you'll discover displays of priceless art, some of it dating back to the 1700s. Downstairs on the Garden Level, the impressive Imperial Ballroom features hand-painted Japanese murals, custom-made chandeliers and sconces, and a parquet dance floor. Through a large picture window you have a view of the Spring Garden, an artful arrangement of rocks and lush ferns. Prefunction cocktails are often served in the Imperial Ballroom Foyer, whose walls are lined with exquisite, one-of-a-kind Japanese artworks.

Back up on the Lobby level is the hotel's junior ballroom, the Sakura Room. This space is notable for its shoji-coffered ceiling and view of the Summer Garden through a floor-to-ceiling window. Natural light flows into the room during the day, and at night adjustable lighting allows you to create whatever ambiance you like. The Garden, softly lit in the evening, is a tranquil addition to the mood you've created. Additional rooms, some with garden vistas, are available for smaller functions.

The Hotel Kabuki is pet-friendly, and it's located in one of San Francisco's most vibrant areas. Shopping, dining, the Sundance film theater complex, and a variety of music venues are all within walking distance. Union Square, the Golden Gate Bridge, Golden Gate Park, Chinatown and the famed cable cars, as well as the Fillmore district, are also nearby. Just a block and a half away is the famous Kabuki Springs and Spa—try one or two exotic body treatments (think green tea wrap and Javanese Frangipani oil massage) or an acupuncture session, and you and your friends will look and feel cool, calm and collected for your trip down the aisle.

Whether you're planning an intimate rehearsal dinner, a gala reception or a post-wedding brunch, Hotel Kabuki's variety of options, multilingual staff and emphasis on personalized service will make it a success.

CEREMONY CAPACITY: Several ceremony spaces accommodate 100–350 seated guests indoors.

EVENT/RECEPTION CAPACITY: The hotel holds 15–350 seated or 30–1,000 standing guest indoors.

MEETING CAPACITY: Meeting spaces can accommodate 12–350 seated guests.

FEES & DEPOSITS: A deposit is required to reserve your date and is applied to the balance. Per-person food costs, not including wine, start at $45 for lunch and $55 for dinner. Alcohol, tax and a 22% service charge are additional.

AVAILABILITY: Year-round, daily, anytime.

SERVICES/AMENITIES:

Catering: in-house; Indian, kosher, other cuisine also available
Kitchen Facilities: n/a
Tables & Chairs: provided
Linens, Silver, etc.: provided
Restrooms: wheelchair accessible
Dance Floor: yes
Bride's & Groom's Dressing Areas: yes
AV/Meeting Equipment: full-service AV and business center

Parking: Japan Center garage (low rates)
Accommodations: 218 guest rooms
Outdoor Night Lighting: access only
Outdoor Cooking Facilities: n/a
Cleanup: provided
View: Japanese tea gardens
Other: full-service event coordination, piano, stage

RESTRICTIONS:

Alcohol: in-house, corkage negotiable
Smoking: outside only
Music: amplified OK

Wheelchair Access: yes
Insurance: not required

Hotel Nikko San Francisco

Hotel

222 Mason Street, San Francisco
415/394-1183
www.hotelnikkosf.com
www.restaurantanzu.com
catering@hotelnikkosf.com, anzu@hotelnikkosf.com

- Rehearsal Dinners
- Ceremonies
- Wedding Receptions
- Corp. Events/Mtgs.
- Private Parties
- Accommodations

Guests and visitors from all over the world stroll across Hotel Nikko's vast, art-filled lobby and lounge in its velvet chairs. Through enormous windows they can watch the city bustle by, as the soothing sound of a cascading fountain provides a calming contrast to the whirl of activity outside.

High-rise hospitality and a reputation for service and style have long been the hallmarks of this popular hotel, a sophisticated downtown hostelry that can quite literally look down on its neighbors. A favorite spot for grand gatherings, its 25 floors of public and private spaces offer opportunities for entertaining that most smaller establishments can't match. In addition to the 510 tastefully appointed guest rooms and 22 suites, there are good-sized, subdividable meeting rooms, which are great for social and corporate functions.

But the Nikko Grand Ballroom on the third floor is the *pièce de résistance*—at over 6,600 square feet, it's perfect for affairs of up to 300 guests. Its Asian contemporary décor, featuring richly textured and burnished wall coverings, dark mahogany floor-to-ceiling doors, and ethereal tulle-inspired chandeliers, will create a warm ambiance for your celebration. The ballroom can be sectioned into three smaller salons: Each one is suitable for a large function in its own right, and can be creatively transformed for a grand reveal or customized theme. The Ballroom Foyer, with its floor-to-ceiling windows, provides an airy, prefunction reception area that can also be enhanced with festive elements.

For high-profile parties with a clubbier feel, ascend to Hotel Nikko's 25th floor where an elegant aerie of glass showcases panoramic bay views in an atmosphere of style and restraint. From the floor-to-ceiling windows of the Golden Gate Room one can see Marin County and the Golden Gate Bridge. Bay View Room vistas include the hotel's Financial District and Union Square neighbors, the wooded East Bay hills, and the silvery Bay Bridge. The Peninsula Room looks south, past AT&T Park, all the way to San Bruno Mountain. Down on the 5th floor, the Outdoor Patio is a stunning choice for an intimate ceremony or cocktail reception. Here, guests can enjoy a glass of bubbly al fresco while savoring the surrounding cityscape.

ANZU Restaurant and Bar lends itself beautifully to an intimate wedding, rehearsal dinner, post-wedding brunch or bridal shower. The entire restaurant can be reserved exclusively for your affair, and the dramatic bar and upscale modern furnishings create a captivating setting so no other decoration is needed.

But the strongest suit of this excellent downtown hotel is service. Legendary Asian hospitality has always been a big part of its legacy, and decades of experience show in the way the expert staff custom caters and creates events with the kind of flair and focus that has earned lofty accolades. From innovative menu design and the careful arrangement of flowers to the care and feeding of its distinguished clientele, the attention to detail is exacting. It's no wonder Hotel Nikko partygoers and guests often book return engagements.

CEREMONY CAPACITY: The Nikko Ballroom holds 600 seated guests and the Golden Gate Room holds 120 seated. Various other spaces are available with capacities ranging 10–200 seated guests.

EVENT/RECEPTION CAPACITY: The hotel can accommodate 70–600 seated or 100–1,000 standing guests indoors. ANZU Restaurant and Bar holds up to 100 seated or 150 for a standing reception. The 5th Floor Outdoor Patio can host up to 50 for a cocktail reception.

MEETING CAPACITY: 16 different spaces (20,000+ sq. ft.) hold up to 600 seated guests.

FEES & DEPOSITS: 10% of the estimated event total is required to reserve your date. 50% of the estimated total is due 3 months prior to the event, and the balance is due the week of the event. Several wedding packages are offered and include hors d'oeuvres, meal, wedding cake, champagne toast, and complimentary suite for the bride and groom. Also included are floor-length linens, silver service, mirror and votive candles on tables. Packages start at $90/person. Tax, alcohol and service charge are additional.

AVAILABILITY: Year-round, daily, 6am–2am.

SERVICES/AMENITIES:

Catering: in-house, no BYO
Kitchen Facilities: n/a
Tables & Chairs: provided
Linens, Silver, etc.: provided
Restrooms: wheelchair accessible
Dance Floor: yes
Bride's & Groom's Dressing Areas: yes
AV/Meeting Equipment: full range

Parking: valet CBA or several garages nearby
Accommodations: 532 guest rooms
Outdoor Night Lighting: no
Outdoor Cooking Facilities: no
Cleanup: provided
View: panoramic cityscape and SF Bay
Other: event coordination

RESTRICTIONS:

Alcohol: in-house or BYO, corkage fees apply
Smoking: not allowed
Music: amplified OK

Wheelchair Access: yes
Insurance: not required

James Leary Flood Mansion

Historic Mansion

2222 Broadway, San Francisco
415/292-3142
www.floodmansion.org
info@floodmansion.org

● Rehearsal Dinners ● Corp. Events/Mtgs.
● Ceremonies ● Private Parties
● Wedding Receptions ☐ Accommodations

The Flood Mansion is a symphony of classical styles— Italian Renaissance, Rococo, Tudor and Georgian. This elegant building, constructed in 1915, has remained well preserved since Mrs. Flood donated her home to the Religious of the Sacred Heart in 1939. Although the building is now used as a private school, it's available for special events after school hours and on weekends.

The Mansion is impressive: Its Grand Hall is 140 feet long with marble floors and unrivaled views of the bay; the architecturally complex Reception Room boasts a magnificent coffered ceiling, painted murals in golds, blues and greens, a marble fireplace, and a parquet floor. And, weather permitting, a pretty enclosed courtyard off of the Grand Hall is available for outdoor gatherings. The Flood Mansion is definitely the place for a stately and elegant party.

CEREMONY CAPACITY: The courtyard holds 170 seated and the Grand Hall 200 seated.

EVENT/RECEPTION CAPACITY: The entire main floor accommodates 165 seated comfortably or 300 standing guests for a cocktail reception. The courtyard holds 200 standing guests.

MEETING CAPACITY: The main floor can accommodate 200 seated.

FEES & DEPOSITS: 50% of the rental fee plus a refundable damage deposit are required to secure your date, and the rental balance and a certificate of insurance are due 1 month prior to the event date. The rental fee starts at $10,000.

AVAILABILITY: March, April, May and mid-August through December. Available days vary from month to month so please contact the venue for details. Guests and catering staff must vacate the premises by 11pm Sunday–Thursday, or midnight Friday and Saturday.

SERVICES/AMENITIES:
Catering: select from preferred list
Kitchen Facilities: ample
Tables & Chairs: BYO
Linens, Silver, etc.: BYO
Restrooms: wheelchair accessible
Dance Floor: yes
Bride's Dressing Area: CBA
AV/Meeting Equipment: BYO

Parking: valet parking or shuttle service required
Accommodations: no guest rooms
Outdoor Night Lighting: access only
Outdoor Cooking Facilities: no
Cleanup: caterer
View: SF Bay, Golden Gate Bridge and Alcatraz
Other: grand piano, 70″ flat screen TV

RESTRICTIONS:
Alcohol: BYO, must use licensed server
Smoking: not allowed
Music: amplified OK indoors, Sunday–Thursday until 9:30pm or Friday–Saturday until 10:30pm

Wheelchair Access: yes
Insurance: extra liability required

This is important! Tell locations you're reading HERE COMES THE GUIDE and ask if our information is still current.

91

Jewish Community Center of San Francisco

Community Center

3200 California Street, San Francisco
415/292-1269
jccsf.org/events
privateevents@jccsf.org

● Rehearsal Dinners	● Corp. Events/Mtgs.
● Ceremonies	● Private Parties
● Wedding Receptions	Accommodations

Known for its warmth and inclusivity, the JCCSF is open to everyone and welcomes secular and same-sex weddings. When you walk through their doors, you'll be greeted like a friend or family member, and couples planning a wedding will be pleased to discover that the building is as impressive as the staff. Made of sand-colored brick and tawny Jerusalem limestone, it spans almost an entire city block, fits gracefully into the neighborhood, and offers some unique spaces for a celebration.

The heart of the venue is the light-filled three-story Atrium. An airy mobile, appropriately named Ruach (Bridge of Breath), sails overhead. Its slender steel arches are fitted with panels of dichroic glass that shine different colors depending on how the light strikes them. There are various interpretations of the sculpture, but many like to think it symbolizes the bridge joining the couple and connecting their two families. The floor is paved with more Jerusalem limestone in tones ranging from light almond to amber. If you'd like to be married on site, you can descend the glass-walled staircase from the second floor and have your ceremony in front of the Sheva Middot, an inspirational 30-foot sculpted wall that highlights the seven core values of the JCCSF, as well as life-affirming quotations from other religions and cultures. Or, if you're tying the knot elsewhere, use this space as a prefunction area for cocktails. There is a platform for musicians, and you can set up a bar here as well.

Both of the JCCSF's reception rooms open to the Atrium. Kanbar Hall, the larger of the two, has a dramatically high ceiling, walls of rich paprika-red fabric, tall soundproof windows and a full-sized stage. It's also outfitted with state-of-the-art lighting and sound systems (a technician can be arranged, too). The theater seating normally used for performances or lectures is fully retractable and disappears during events. If you have a live band, they can play on the stage with a dance floor set right below.

Smaller receptions are held in the Fisher Family Hall, brightened by white and papyrus-colored walls and light filtering in from the Atrium through one wall of frosted glass. Like Kanbar Hall, it has a complete audiovisual system, and its blond parquet sprung-wood floor is perfect for dancing.

Note that other conference rooms are available on the second floor if you're planning a Ketubah signing, Bedecken or Tisch. Also, there are three separate kitchens, one of which will suit your event: a kosher meat kitchen, a dairy/vegetarian kitchen and a non-kosher kitchen.

The JCCSF has some perks you will love: First and foremost is its own parking garage, a real bonus in this parking-challenged town. Second, the performers' Green Room makes a terrific dressing room—with multiple mirrors and a sitting room (even a mini-fridge), you and your bridesmaids have ample space for prep and touch-ups.

Organized in 1877, the JCCSF is the oldest Jewish center on the West Coast and, while its main mission is to foster a Jewish community, it extends its hospitality to all. So, whatever your background, they invite you to come and build a little community of your own.

CEREMONY CAPACITY: The Atrium holds up to 150 seated guests.

EVENT/RECEPTION CAPACITY: The Center holds up to 300 seated or 360 standing guests.

MEETING CAPACITY: The Center can seat 460 guests, theater-style.

FEES & DEPOSITS: 50% of the rental fee along with a refundable security deposit is required to secure your date, and the balance is due 30 days prior to the event. The rental fee ranges $185–4,400 depending on the space, day and time reserved.

AVAILABILITY: Year-round, daily, 8am–midnight.

SERVICES/AMENITIES:

Catering: select from list or BYO
Kitchen Facilities: 3 (kosher meat, dairy/vegetarian, non-kosher)
Tables & Chairs: provided
Linens, Silver, etc.: BYO or through caterer
Restrooms: wheelchair accessible
Dance Floor: CBA
Bride's Dressing Area: yes
AV/Meeting Equipment: CBA

Parking: parking garage
Accommodations: no guest rooms
Outdoor Night Lighting: access only
Outdoor Cooking Facilities: no
Cleanup: caterer or renter
View: no
Other: full sound and lighting

RESTRICTIONS:

Alcohol: BYO, must use licensed server
Smoking: outside only
Music: amplified OK

Wheelchair Access: yes
Insurance: general and liquor liability required
Other: no pork or shellfish allowed

Julia Morgan Ballroom
at the Merchants Exchange

Historic Landmark

465 California Street, San Francisco
415/591-1826

www.juliamorganballroom.com
lillian@juliamorganballroom.com

- Rehearsal Dinners
- Ceremonies
- Wedding Receptions
- Corp. Events/Mtgs.
- Private Parties
- Accommodations

The Julia Morgan Ballroom at the Merchants Exchange is not just one of San Francisco's most iconic event venues; it's also a link to the city's unique and compelling history. Located in the heart of the bustling Financial District, the building radiates elegance from the street to the lobby and beyond. With a design pedigree from three of America's most renowned architects, a legacy of hosting many of the city's most important events, and state-of-the-art technological amenities, the Julia Morgan Ballroom succeeds at being both quintessentially San Francisco and an ideal choice for your celebration.

Your experience begins on California Street, with cable cars whirring up Nob Hill. As you step through the Merchant Exchange building's street-level doors and into the barrel-vaulted lobby, you're transported to an era of lavish detail and impeccable taste: The space shines with marble, gold leaf and bronze, while abundant natural light streams in through the curved glass ceiling.

Gleaming new elevators whisk you quickly up to the 15th floor and the landmark Julia Morgan Ballroom, the masterwork of American architectural titans Willis Polk, Daniel Burnham and Julia Morgan. Here, your privacy and exclusivity are ensured—there are no busy hotel corridors to contend with, no intrusions from the outside world.

Guests first enter through a classic foyer and proceed naturally to the opulent bar and lounge, featuring gilded ceilings and fireplaces of carved stone at each end. The 27-foot curved marble bar sweeps you toward the ballroom and a breathtaking reveal…

Light flows into the stunning 4,370-square-foot ballroom through a wall of soaring floor-to-ceiling arched windows that afford a view of the glittering cityscape, while mirrors on the opposite wall reflect the light. The view overhead is equally impressive—the ceiling is an intricate honeycomb of painstakingly crafted mahogany octagonals. Rich, paneled walls continue the refined aesthetic with classic columns worked directly into the wood. At the far end, a 20-foot stone fireplace provides a striking backdrop and a final touch of grandeur.

Weddings at the Julia Morgan Ballroom are not simply planned; they're designed. The experienced staff, who have choreographed events for U.S. presidents, foreign dignitaries, business legends and stars of film, music and sports, are experts at creating custom events. Dedicated to excellence and discretion, they'll ensure that your wedding or special occasion includes your personal touches and reflects your vision.

With its prime location amid fine hotels, notable restaurants, and cultural attractions, the ballroom gives event-goers easy access to the best of everything San Francisco has to offer, as well as numerous public transportation options and plenty of evening parking.

CEREMONY & EVENT/RECEPTION CAPACITY: Ceremonies and receptions can be held in the Lobby, Ballroom or Lounge. The Julia Morgan Ballroom holds up to 350 seated or 800 standing. The Lounge area holds 60 seated or 350 standing.

MEETING CAPACITY: For large meetings, the Ballroom holds approximately 450 theater-style or 350 conference-style. There are 2 smaller seminar rooms that can accommodate 12–20 seated conference-style.

FEES & DEPOSITS: 25% of the rental fee plus the food & beverage minimum is required to secure your date. The rental fee for use of the entire 15th floor starts at $10,500. The rental fee for only the Lounge area is $4,500; for smaller meeting rooms, the fee starts at $600. There is special pricing for Friday and Sunday celebrations; call for details. Meals start at $75/person. Tax, alcohol and service charge are additional.

AVAILABILITY: Year-round, daily. Hours are by arrangement.

SERVICES/AMENITIES:

Catering: by in-house chef
Kitchen Facilities: fully equipped
Tables & Chairs: provided; mahogany Chiavari chairs and barstools available
Linens, Silver, etc.: provided
Restrooms: wheelchair accessible
Dance Floor: provided (mahogany)
Bride's & Groom's Dressing Areas: yes
AV/Meeting Equipment: available

Parking: street parking, nearby garages or valet
Accommodations: no guest rooms
Outdoor Night Lighting: access only
Outdoor Cooking Facilities: no
Cleanup: provided
View: downtown San Francisco cityscape
Other: full-service event production, WiFi, event lighting, stage, setup and breakdown

RESTRICTIONS:

Alcohol: in-house
Smoking: outdoors only
Music: amplified OK

Wheelchair Access: yes
Insurance: certificate required
Other: no rice, birdseed, glitter or sparklers

Legion of Honor Museum

Landmark Museum

100 34th Avenue, Lincoln Park, San Francisco
415/750-3698
www.famsf.org
legionevents@famsf.org

● Rehearsal Dinners	● Corp. Events/Mtgs.
● Ceremonies	● Private Parties
● Wedding Receptions	○ Accommodations

Whether you're seeing the Legion of Honor for the first time or the tenth, you can't help but be a little awe-struck. The majestic neoclassical building, standing on the highest point of Lincoln Park, represents San Francisco at its absolute best: great architecture, fine art, romance, and stunning coastal views.

Weddings often begin with a ceremony on the Balustrade Lawn, a promontory where couples exchange vows against a breathtaking panorama of the Golden Gate Bridge, the Marin Headlands, and the Pacific Ocean. Or, if palatial is your preference, get married in the regal Court of Honor. Sunrise to sunset, the light is forever changing in this expansive piazza with its soaring wraparound colonnade. August Rodin's famous sculpture, *The Thinker,* sits alone at the entrance, animating the space with its dynamic form.

The Legion of Honor is home to more than 70 Rodin sculptures, and it's the only place on earth where you and your guests may dine and dance sumptuously among the sculptor's masterpieces. They reside in three adjacent galleries with vaulted ceilings—a series of event spaces of princely proportions. Celebrating in any one of these chambers will give your gathering a luxurious feel. But combine all three for unprecedented grandeur: Have cocktails in one gallery, dining in another and dancing in the third. However, you'll probably want to have that first dance, center stage, under the museum's magnificent rotunda, whose gorgeous marble floor is available for just that purpose. You might also opt to include a favorite musical selection played by the museum's designated organist on the Legion's very own walnut, ivory and ebony Skinner pipe organ—one of the finest in the world and a working work of art. Its 4,500 pipes have been seamlessly integrated into the very structure of the museum.

Downstairs on the Terrace Level other interesting choices await. How about a cocktail reception amid the treasures in the dramatic Hall of Antiquities? Guests can meet and mingle surrounded by pottery, sculpture, glass vessels and metalwork created by early artists from Greece, Rome, Egypt and the Ancient Near East. There's room for a large bar, and waiters can serve up champagne and passed hors d'oeuvres here before celebrants step into the adjoining Legion Café to dine.

The Legion Café, with its abundant windows and glass doors, and art-accented walls is an inviting environment for any affair. You can use the whole room or just a section of it for a more intimate atmosphere. Doors open onto the herb-scented Café Terrace. Attractive brickwork grounds the airy space, an elegant stone balustrade frames it, and silvery olive trees create a natural canopy.

It feels so removed from the stresses and pressures of everyday life, you might well imagine that you've been spirited away to Paris's Luxembourg Gardens or some other leafy paradise.

The Legion of Honor houses some of the most beautiful art in the world, which elevates every event that's held here. No matter what your occasion—wedding, corporate gala or private party—it will unfold brilliantly in this exquisite Beaux-Arts setting.

CEREMONY CAPACITY: The Balustrade Lawn to the right of the museum entrance, and the Court of Honor, hold up to 350 seated guests each. The indoor Rodin Gallery can accommodate 160 seated, and the Florence Gould Theater seats 316.

EVENT/RECEPTION CAPACITY: The Café holds 220 seated or 300 standing guests. An additional 140 may be added to that capacity by tenting the sculpture garden at an extra charge. There are three Rodin Galleries that combined hold 180 seated or 350 standing; 130 guests may be seated in the central Rodin Gallery. The Entire Museum can be rented for a standing reception of 650 guests.

MEETING CAPACITY: The museum's Florence Gould Theater holds 316 seated theater-style, plus 3 wheelchair spaces and 2 companion seats.

FEES & DEPOSITS: 50% of the facility fee and a signed agreement are due at the time of booking. The rental fee starts at $6,000 and varies depending on the rental package selected. The balance and final guest count are due at least 60 days prior to the event.

AVAILABILITY: Year-round, daily, starting at 6:30pm. Additional hours are available for an extra fee.

SERVICES/AMENITIES:

Catering: select from preferred list
Kitchen Facilities: setup or prep only
Tables & Chairs: some provided
Linens, Silver, etc.: BYO
Restrooms: wheelchair accessible
Dance Floor: provided
Bride's Dressing Area: CBA, extra fee
AV/Meeting Equipment: CBA, extra fee

Parking: large lot
Accommodations: no guest rooms
Outdoor Night Lighting: yes
Outdoor Cooking Facilities: n/a
Cleanup: provided
View: Lincoln Park, Pacific Ocean, Golden Gate Bridge and Marin Headlands

RESTRICTIONS:

Alcohol: BYO, licensed and insured server
Smoking: not allowed
Music: amplified OK with volume restrictions

Wheelchair Access: yes
Insurance: certificate required

Loews Regency San Francisco

Hotel

222 Sansome Street, San Francisco

415/276-9637

www.loewshotels.com/regency-san-francisco/meetings/weddings
sage.mcrae@loewshotels.com

- Rehearsal Dinners
- Ceremonies
- Wedding Receptions
- Corp. Events/Mtgs.
- Private Parties
- Accommodations

Loews Regency San Francisco, a Forbes Four Star Hotel, creates a soothing and sophisticated environment in the center of one of the world's most unique cities. Impeccable service and unparalleled views make for outstanding events, and an exceptional experience for guests.

A feeling of calm envelopes guests as they enter the dramatic Italian travertine marble lobby. From here, a striking grand staircase, outfitted with curved glass and mapa burlwood veneer, leads them up to the second level where most celebrations are held. With more than 5,000 square feet of beautifully designed, versatile, and technologically enhanced event spaces, the hotel easily accommodates private parties and lavish weddings—which are a specialty—as well as pre- and post-wedding celebrations.

For a stunning ceremony, host it on the 40th-floor Sky Deck. At this height you're presented with a postcard panorama normally only enjoyed by birds: views of the Golden Gate Bridge, Coit Tower and Alcatraz Island. A spectacular "Cocktails in the Clouds" enhancement allows you and your guests to remain on the 40th floor for a post-ceremony cocktail reception, giving you more time to savor the magnificent vista. There are a variety of unique options for tying the knot indoors, as well.

Receptions take place in your choice of three distinctive, contemporary rooms, all with floor-to-ceiling windows that let in abundant natural light. Re-imagined in 2017, they feature an elegant "light on water" theme, realized in a neutral color palette of shades of gray with metallic accents. The Library manages to be sleek, yet warm, with its mix of modern artwork and suede details. The Embassy & California Rooms are paneled in antique mirrors, and appointed with touches of silver and gold, rich textures, and whimsical lighting elements. Of course, wherever you celebrate in the hotel, their professional planners will ensure that your affair is executed with the uncompromising attention to detail for which Loews Regency San Francisco is renowned.

Cuisine at this hotel is also a top priority. The culinary team always uses the freshest local ingredients and is happy to customize your menu, including wine pairings. In addition, you can choose from an extensive array of carefully crafted cocktails and an award-winning wine list.

The guest rooms and suites occupy the top 11 floors of this 48-story building (the third tallest in San Francisco), and afford expansive vistas of the bay, both bridges, Alcatraz Island, Marin, the East Bay, and the city itself. Two of their signature suites have large terraces where newlyweds can linger over breakfast the next morning. The Spa, an 8,000-square-foot haven, includes a fitness center, a couple's suite, and three treatment rooms. An array of flexible packages lets you personalize your spa time and enjoy a rejuvenating experience before and after your event.

Although it's the epitome of modern design and state-of-the-art technology, Loews Regency San Francisco still offers the warm, attentive service of a boutique hotel. And it's within walking distance of Union Square, the Ferry Building, and Fisherman's Wharf. We think it's a wonderful choice, not only for a special occasion, but for a romantic getaway any time of the year.

CEREMONY & EVENT/RECEPTION CAPACITY: The California Room accommodates 90 seated or 110 standing guests; the Embassy Room holds 120 seated or 130 standing; and the Library holds 60 seated or 70 standing. The Boardroom holds 40 seated or 50 standing. The 40th floor Sky Deck seats 110 for a ceremony, or holds 75 standing for a cocktail reception.

MEETING CAPACITY: Several spaces accommodate 15–250 seated guests.

FEES & DEPOSITS: 25% of the estimated event total is required to secure your date, and the balance is due 30 days prior to the event. The rental fee starts at $750 and varies depending on the space, day and time rented. Ceremony event space starts at $3,000. Wedding packages start at $195/person, and include a 1-hour cocktail reception with premium bar, and house wines during dinner. Upgrades to the bar package and wines, and after-dinner beverages are available for an extra fee. Tax and a 22% service charge are additional.

AVAILABILITY: Year-round, daily, anytime.

SERVICES/AMENITIES:

Catering: in-house, no BYO
Kitchen Facilities: n/a
Tables & Chairs: provided
Linens, Silver, etc.: provided
Restrooms: wheelchair accessible
Dance Floor: portable provided
Bride's Dressing Area: CBA
AV/Meeting Equipment: CBA

Parking: on street, valet, or nearby garages
Accommodations: 155 view guest rooms
Outdoor Night Lighting: CBA
Outdoor Cooking Facilities: no
Cleanup: provided
View: panorama of Golden Gate Bridge, Alcatraz, Coit Tower, the Transamerica Building, and the Bay Bridge from the 40th floor Sky Deck
Other: event coordination, spa services

RESTRICTIONS:

Alcohol: in-house, BYO wine and champagne with corkage fee
Smoking: outdoors only
Music: amplified OK with restrictions

Wheelchair Access: yes, elevator
Insurance: not required

Overwhelmed? Use the search criteria on www.HereComesTheGuide.com to narrow down your choices.

Marines' Memorial Club

Historic Club and Hotel

609 Sutter Street, San Francisco

415/830-9135

www.marineclub.com
lisajimenez@marineclub.com

- Rehearsal Dinners
- Ceremonies
- Wedding Receptions
- Corp. Events/Mtgs.
- Private Parties
- Accommodations

The Marines' Memorial Club is a hidden jewel in San Francisco's exciting Union Square area. This California Spanish Revival beauty was built in 1926, and in 1946 became a memorial to the Marines who lost their lives during World War II. Today, the landmark is a nonprofit club for veterans and their families—and also a fine hotel and special event facility.

The club's rich architectural heritage, first-class food and service, and nostalgically elegant décor bring extra dimensions to any celebration. The entire 10th and 11th floors are dedicated to sophisticated and unique banquet and meeting spaces. Weddings on the 11th floor might begin with a ceremony in the exquisite, take-your-breath-away Crystal Ballroom. A vaulted hand-painted ceiling holds three massive crystal chandeliers. Their ornate prisms shimmer over the gleaming candelabra, and the ballroom's oval shape lends a soft intimacy to the magnificent space. For ceremonies, the staff sets up a raised dais flanked by a pair of ficus trees festooned with twinkle lights. After the service, guests retire to the Crystal Lounge, connected to the ballroom by a foyer. Everyone toasts the happy couple, while taking in the sweeping city view from the Lounge's wall of vaulted windows. (Tear your eyes away from the luminous cityscape for a moment, and admire the Lounge's gold-leafed and frescoed ceiling.) When it's time to dine, guests return to the Crystal Ballroom, which has been transformed with themed linens, silver candelabra centerpieces, and a dance floor.

An equally impressive option awaits on the 10th floor. There's a stately majesty about the Commandant's Ballroom, thanks to a 22-foot-high intricately painted and coffered ceiling, wood detailing, and striking iron chandeliers with matching sconces. Enhancing this ballroom's splendor are vaulted east-facing windows that capture a sparkling city vista. Just as with the Crystal Ballroom, the Commandant's serves as the setting for both ceremonies and lavish receptions. During the cocktail hour, the nearby Heritage and Regimental Rooms, which are connected by an adjoining foyer, are set for cocktail service. Guests can get their drinks from bars set up in either room, then relax at cocktail tables holding flickering votive candles. The Regimental Room looks out toward Nob Hill, and is clad in mahogany paneling. A built-in bar comes in handy during a cocktail hour or rehearsal dinner, and a working fireplace adds to the clubby atmosphere. The Heritage Room enjoys views of Nob Hill and downtown, and Art Deco chandeliers convey a bit of whimsy. Returning to the Commandant's Ballroom for the reception and dancing completes the evening's revelry.

Events at the Club are catered in-house, and feature gourmet contemporary American cuisine. Renovated guest rooms and suites provide a comfortable overnight stay. Newlyweds love Suite #403's oversized tub-for-two; its spacious living room and wall of mirrors are great for pre-wedding primping. The Leatherneck Steakhouse on the 12th floor showcases a stunning panorama with glimpses of the bay over towering skyscrapers—what a dynamic spot for a rehearsal dinner! Though shopping and nightlife is right outside the Club's door, the Marines' Memorial is marvelously self-contained: it also has a health club, an indoor pool, a library, a museum, and its own theater! Whether you are a veteran or civilian, you're sure to find a warm welcome at this timeless club.

CEREMONY & EVENT/RECEPTION CAPACITY: The club holds 25–270 seated guests indoors.

MEETING CAPACITY: Several spaces can accommodate 30–300 seated guests.

FEES & DEPOSITS: For weddings, a nonrefundable deposit is required to reserve the banquet room. There's no rental fee if you meet a food & beverage minimum; however, house catering is required. A guest count along with the estimated event balance is due 7 business days prior to the event. Ceremonies are $1,750 for Friday or Sunday, $2,250 for Saturday. Wedding reception packages, which include open bar, hors d'oeuvres, champagne and wine service, salad and entrée service and cake cutting, range $115–173/person depending on the menu selection. Brunch, Luncheon or hors d'oeuvre receptions start at $80/person. Tax and a service charge are additional.

For meetings and business functions, the rental fee for meeting rooms varies depending on the room(s) and/or services selected. Call for additional information regarding food & beverage charges.

AVAILABILITY: Year-round, daily, 7am–11pm. There are overtime charges for events running more than 5 hours.

SERVICES/AMENITIES:
Catering: in-house, no BYO
Kitchen Facilities: n/a
Tables & Chairs: provided
Linens, Silver, etc.: provided
Restrooms: wheelchair accessible
Dance Floor: yes
Bride's Dressing Area: CBA
AV/Meeting Equipment: CBA

Parking: nearby garage
Accommodations: 138 guest rooms
Outdoor Night Lighting: access only
Outdoor Cooking Facilities: no
Cleanup: provided
View: Nob Hill, SF cityscape and Union Square
Other: full event coordination; ethnic cuisine available upon request

RESTRICTIONS:
Alcohol: in-house
Smoking: not allowed
Music: amplified OK

Wheelchair Access: yes, elevator
Insurance: required for DJs and entertainers

Presidio Event Venues

103 Montgomery Street, The Presidio, San Francisco

415/561-5444

www.presidio.gov
events@presidiotrust.gov

National Park Event Venues

● Rehearsal Dinners	● Corp. Events/Mtgs.
● Ceremonies	● Private Parties
● Wedding Receptions	● Accommodations

The Presidio is a genuine local treasure. A national park with a proud legacy as a premier military base, it also boasts an iconic San Francisco Bay view that includes the Golden Gate Bridge and Alcatraz. Architecturally significant buildings have been lovingly restored and are arrayed among 1,491 acres, where gardens, forests, and wildlife flourish. Naturally, such a spectacular setting is perfect for memorable weddings, and this National Historic Landmark District has plenty of scenic venues to choose from.

For a romantic ceremony, many couples are drawn to the park's two historic chapels. The stately Spanish Mission-style Presidio Chapel rests on a forested hillside overlooking the bay. Photo ops abound out on the tiled garden patio, and the resplendent vaulted redwood sanctuary is lined with 12 arched, stained-glass windows. In contrast, the quaint Chapel of Our Lady is a simple, white wood-frame structure with a stunning surprise: Two of its walls are constructed entirely of multicolored glass block panels. Behind the altar, a massive floor-to-ceiling window frames lush greenery and towering eucalyptus, an inspirational backdrop for saying your vows. At both chapels, you're welcome to use your own officiant, musicians, and cultural style.

A scenic stroll from either venue takes you to the Golden Gate Club, nestled among groves of cypress and pine. This 1940s-era paragon of Mission design has plenty of period details to give your gala real character. Receptions are dazzling in the Ventana Room, whose curving two-story window wall hugs a green meadow edged with trees, while the bay shimmers in the distance. The lofty cathedral ceiling and large fireplace, combined with the natural environment just outside, impart a sense of serenity.

But there's a rival for your reception dreams—the prestigious Presidio Officers' Club. Formerly reserved for army brass, this gracious Mission Revival-style building now hosts civilian celebrations. The handsome Moraga Hall, with its upscale furnishings and vintage fireplace, makes a sleek prefunction gathering spot. The main attraction, however, is on the upper floor: the comfortably appointed View Terrace, which captures the Presidio's sweeping bay vista. Inside the adjoining Ortega Ballroom, floor-to-ceiling windows and an L-shaped balcony merge your fête with that phenomenal view.

For a wedding with country flair, the unique Log Cabin can't be beat. Built in 1937, this former non-commissioned officers' club resembles a grand hunting lodge with a fieldstone foundation and log-lined walls. The expansive front lawn is ideal for open-air ceremonies with a lovely view of the San Francisco skyline and peeks of the blue Pacific through the surrounding woods. Inside, you can't help but admire the cabin's handcrafted appeal: A soaring ceiling is supported by beams and columns made of polished tree trunks, and giant wagon wheel chandeliers illuminate a spacious dance floor. Put candles everywhere and crank up the huge gas fireplace, and your reception will glow with rustic elegance.

The park has so many options that you'll be grateful for the guidance of Presidio Event Venues' caring professionals, as well as their exceptional in-house catering. Couples can also enjoy an abundance of activities and amenities before and after their big day, including a charming historic inn, golf course, spa, award-winning restaurants, and a trampoline gym and rock-climbing facility to name a few.

If you're planning to leave your heart in San Francisco, there really is no better place than the Presidio for a destination wedding in The City.

CEREMONY CAPACITY: The Golden Gate Club seats up to 250, and the Log Cabin up to 150 indoors or on the lawn. The Chapel of Our Lady seats up to 200, the Presidio Chapel 144.

EVENT/RECEPTION CAPACITY: With a buyout, the Golden Gate Club holds up to 400 seated or 800 standing. The Log Cabin accommodates 150 seated or 200 standing and the Officers' Club Ballroom holds 160 seated or 250 standing. The Chapel of Our Lady's courtyard can host a cocktail reception for up to 200 standing guests.

MEETING CAPACITY: The Golden Gate club seats up to 280, the Log Cabin up to 150, the Officers' Club Ortega Ballroom up to 300, and the Chapel of Our Lady up to 200.

FEES & DEPOSITS: A nonrefundable $350 booking fee is required to secure your date and will be applied to the total rental fee. 50% of the event rental fee is due with a signed permit. The event rental fee balance, insurance fee and security deposit are due 180 days prior to the event date. The rental fee ranges $1,200–9,000 depending on the space, day and time reserved, as well as the type of event. Please visit www.presidio.gov for current rate information.

AVAILABILITY: Year-round, daily. Not available on national holidays, Christmas Eve or Day, New Year's Eve or Day, Thanksgiving or the day after, and the 4th of July.

SERVICES/AMENITIES:

Catering: in-house or select from preferred list
Kitchen Facilities: limited, prep only at most venues
Tables & Chairs: BYO, CBA or through caterer
Linens, Silver, etc.: BYO or through caterer
Restrooms: wheelchair accessible at most venues
Dance Floor: available at some venues
Bride's Dressing Area: CBA at some venues
AV/Meeting Equipment: BYO or limited CBA

Parking: lot nearby, restrictions may apply
Accommodations: Inn at the Presidio
Outdoor Night Lighting: access only
Outdoor Cooking Facilities: no
Cleanup: renter, caterer and vendors
View: SF Bay, Golden Gate Bridge, San Francisco skyline and Presidio Forest at some locations

RESTRICTIONS:

Alcohol: in-house, or choose from preferred list
Smoking: outdoors only
Music: amplified OK with volume restrictions

Wheelchair Access: yes at most venues
Insurance: extra liability required
Other: votive candles, decorations and any tent installations or equipment on lawn require prior approval

Presidio Golf Course and Clubhouse

Golf Course & Clubhouse

300 Finley Road at Arguello Gate, The Presidio, San Francisco
415/561-4661 X207

www.presidiocafe.com
tlyons@presidiogolf.com

- Rehearsal Dinners
- Ceremonies
- Wedding Receptions
- Corp. Events/Mtgs.
- Private Parties
- Accommodations

Since 1776, the Presidio has guarded the Golden Gate, first for Spain, then Mexico, and finally for the United States. Then, as now, the Presidio was one big beautiful piece of California coastland. Today, its 1,500 acres of eucalyptus, cypress, pine forest, coastal wild flowers, and ocean and bay views are a national park site, and the 7,000-square-foot Clubhouse is a fine place to host a wide spectrum of events.

The Clubhouse has a casually refined look that makes you want to step inside. The interior, a blend of Mission-style architecture and Maybeck-inspired, landscape-friendly details, features cathedral ceilings, exposed fir beams, cherrywood trim and paneling, and a large limestone fireplace. Five French doors extend its largest dining area onto the Tented Terrace, which is perfect for any style of function from barbecue to black-tie. From here you also have an excellent view of the final green of the Presidio's historic 18-hole golf course. President Theodore Roosevelt reviewed the command on the Presidio Golf Links in 1903, and many a golfer of note—including TR himself, Dwight Eisenhower, Bing Crosby and Arnold Palmer—has played through on its fairways.

Of course, the close proximity of Bentgrass greens and well-maintained parklands is a powerful lure. Party plans could easily include a bit of golf practice or a short nature hike. But more likely, guests will simply want to sit back and enjoy the fresh air and the vista—lush green lawns, pine and eucalyptus groves, and the lovely neighborhood homes, all looking very low-rise from this vantage point on a gentle crest.

The Palmer Room (named for Arnold Palmer, of course!), provides cozier quarters just right for smaller meetings, breakfasts, luncheons or dinners, and the Palmer Terrace and lawn—with its garden setting and pine-curtained bay views—allows celebrants to take the dining and good times outdoors.

CEREMONY CAPACITY: The Outdoor Terrace holds up to 150, the South Lawn accommodates 220, and the Palmer Lawn holds 130 seated guests.

EVENT/RECEPTION CAPACITY: The Cafe accommodates 80 seated or 125 standing guests, the Palmer Room 40 seated or 50 standing, and the entire Clubhouse 130 seated or 150 standing. The Clubhouse and Tented Terrace combined seat 200.

MEETING CAPACITY: The Palmer Room seats up to 50 guests theater-style or 30 guests conference-style. The entire facility holds 120 seated.

FEES & DEPOSITS: For events, 50% of the estimated event total is required to reserve your date; the balance is due 10 days prior to the event. Room rental fees change per season, but range $500–1,000 for a daytime event to $5,000 for use of the Clubhouse and Tented Terrace. Meals range $25–50/person for lunch and $55–125/person for dinner. Tax, alcohol and a 21% service charge are additional, as is a $3/person cake-cutting fee.

AVAILABILITY: Year-round, daily, dawn until midnight.

SERVICES/AMENITIES:

Catering: in-house, no BYO
Kitchen Facilities: n/a
Tables & Chairs: provided
Linens, Silver, etc.: provided
Restroom: wheelchair accessible
Dance Floor: provided
Bride's Dressing Area: no
AV/Meeting Equipment: CBA, extra charge

Parking: large complimentary lot
Accommodations: no guest rooms
Outdoor Night Lighting: no
Outdoor Cooking Facilities: no
Cleanup: provided
View: fairways, park
Other: event coordination

RESTRICTIONS:

Alcohol: in-house or corkage $15/bottle
Smoking: outside only
Music: amplified OK indoors

Wheelchair Access: yes
Insurance: not required

San Francisco Design Center Galleria

Event Facility

101 Henry Adams Street, San Francisco
415/490-5861

www.sfvenues.com
jwagner@sfdesigncenter.com

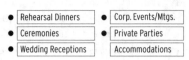

● Rehearsal Dinners	● Corp. Events/Mtgs.
● Ceremonies	● Private Parties
● Wedding Receptions	Accommodations

The exterior of the Galleria building at the San Francisco Design Center gives you no clue as to what's inside—all you see are sky and trees reflected in a gleaming, four-story façade of more than 700 individual glass panes. Walk through the front doors, however, and you get a sense of what the world would be like if top designers were in charge.

The main event area is directly ahead of you, and it becomes immediately clear that the building's architects made excellent use of the four stories they had to play with. They've created a soaring atrium with a retractable skylight that literally brings the outdoors inside: On nice days, fresh air and sunshine flood in. The whole space radiates warmth and contemporary sophistication thanks to the open feeling, Italian tile floor and exposed brick walls.

Weddings shine here, whether they're intimate or grand. Smaller receptions have plenty of room to spread out on the main floor, which seems to expand upward to the dramatic 60-foot ceiling. The polished light maple hardwood floor in the center can be used for dining or dancing, while the raised stage is ideal for a band or DJ. There's a built-in beverage bar as well. If you plan to wine and dine hundreds, you can also set tables on the three levels of balconies rising on all sides. Guests thoroughly appreciate the elevated seating, as it provides the perfect vantage for watching the festivities below.

Want to exchange vows here, too? Why not! The atrium makes a lovely setting for a ceremony. Place elegant flower arrangements or rose petals along the aisle, set potted trees laced with lights around the perimeter, or leave the interior just as it is.

The Galleria looks great without decorations, but you can transform it any way you like: Hang a fabric canopy overhead…add colored uplights and a monogram…dazzle your guests with a performer suspended from the ceiling. Asian and Indian weddings often bring in a dance troupe. The accommodating staff welcomes out-of-the-box thinking and encourages you to indulge your imagination.

In addition to weddings, this site can host almost any kind of event. On weekdays the Galleria showcases designer furniture, but on weeknights and weekends it comes into its own as a party venue. Cirque parties with tents and performers fit right in, as do speakeasy events. With its state-of-the-art light system, stage and versatile seating configurations, it's especially suitable for corporate galas, cocktail receptions, and holiday parties. Not surprisingly, the Galleria has been discovered by high-tech, multimedia companies and the media, who love the possibilities it offers. They frequently bring in fantastic props and produce large-scale audiovisual presentations to launch a new website or product.

There are so many pluses to this unique location you can do practically anything with it, and entertain groups of 100 to 1,600! So go ahead and fantasize—truth is, for any event where you want a quality production with endless options, the Galleria has the resources, the space and, above all, the style.

CEREMONY CAPACITY: The Galleria holds 400 seated guests.

EVENT/RECEPTION & MEETING CAPACITY: The Galleria can accommodate up to 850 seated or 1,600 standing guests; the first floor holds 400 seated or 1,000 standing, and 3 additional floors hold up to 200 seated or standing guests each (depending on sightlines).

FEES & DEPOSITS: 50% of the rental fee is required as a deposit to secure your date; the balance is payable 90 days prior to the event. The rental fee starts at $7,000 Sunday–Friday, and $8,000 on Saturday, and varies depending on the guest count and floors rented. Light technicians (at $50/hour per technician) are available. A facility manager and security guards are required; call for specific rates.

AVAILABILITY: Year-round, weekday evenings 6pm–2am, and weekends 8am–2am.

SERVICES/AMENITIES:

Catering: select from list or BYO with approval
Kitchen Facilities: no
Tables & Chairs: provided for up to 300 guests
Linens, Silver, etc.: through caterer
Restrooms: wheelchair accessible
Dance Floor: yes
Bride's & Groom's Dressing Areas: yes
AV/Meeting Equipment: lighting system

Parking: on-street, pay lots
Accommodations: no guest rooms
Outdoor Night Lighting: access only
Outdoor Cooking Facilities: CBA
Cleanup: basic janitorial cleanup included in rental fee
View: no

RESTRICTIONS:

Alcohol: in-house
Smoking: outside only
Music: amplified OK

Wheelchair Access: yes
Insurance: liability insurance required

Want to know WHAT TO ASK a potential location or vendor? Check out our Questions to Ask starting on page 21.

San Francisco Film Centre

Event & Film Center

39 Mesa Street, Suite 107, The Presidio, San Francisco
415/561-3456
www.sffilmcentre.com
info@sffilmcentre.com

● Rehearsal Dinners	● Corp. Events/Mtgs.
● Ceremonies	● Private Parties
● Wedding Receptions	☐ Accommodations

The San Francisco Film Centre is an in-demand urban event venue that also happens to be in one of the city's most beautiful settings. It occupies an elegant Mission-style building originally designed to house enlisted men and officers stationed at the Presidio. Although it never fulfilled its function as a military residence, it's found another calling: In 1999 the Film Centre undertook an extensive renovation, and today it's a multi-use facility providing a variety of resources to the public as well as the film and media community.

Events are held in the amazingly versatile Palm Room. Fresh white walls and columns along with Australian Eucalyptus hardwood floors lend a sophistication to the space. During the day sunlight streams in through attractively shaded multipaned windows, illuminating the room and making the floors gleam (subtle track lighting makes them shimmer at night). East and west windows afford views of the Golden Gate Bridge, the Main Post and the Presidio's meticulously landscaped grounds. Floor-to-ceiling French doors open onto a covered Spanish-tile veranda, creating a wonderful indoor-outdoor flow. This terrace is distinguished by 13 graceful arches and wrought-iron railings, and when the weather is warm or heaters are added it's ideal for a cocktail reception. Some parties turn it into a lounge with comfy couches and chairs.

We think the Palm Room is quite inviting as is, but you're encouraged to give it your personal stamp and indulge your imagination. For example, use colored uplights and the adjustable track lighting to set the mood or match your décor, or place couches and carpets in one section for a clubby atmosphere. Another plus: the room's excellent acoustics are great for a DJ or band.

The most popular place for exchanging vows is at the top of the stairs in front of the centre's historic arched doors, which make a perfect frame for the couple as well as a unique backdrop for photos. Guests are seated on the lawn below, and the iconic Golden Gate Bridge is visible in the distance. Other ceremony options include the veranda and a smaller lawn on the opposite side of the building. Whichever site you choose, it's just a short walk to your reception in the Palm Room.

In addition to weddings, the Film Centre is also a great choice for film screenings, fundraisers, art installations, corporate functions and parties of all kinds. The Palm Room can be sectioned into breakout areas, while the veranda is frequently used for a buffet setup or wine tasting. Retreats often conduct sessions out on the lawns, and the Conference Room is available for the bridal party or for smaller meetings and groups. There's even an intimate Screening Room that seats 24 for a lecture or presentation. Downstairs, a professionally equipped catering kitchen adds to the long list of amenities that give the centre its marvelous flexibility.

Gorgeous surroundings, a wonderful venue, and plenty of parking are all part of your experience at the San Francisco Film Centre—and you get to celebrate in the city but feel like you're miles from one.

CEREMONY CAPACITY: Outdoor lawn areas hold up to 150 seated guests. Small ceremonies may be held on the Veranda.

EVENT/RECEPTION CAPACITY: The Palm Room accommodates up to 180 seated, 150 with dancing or 250 standing guests; the Veranda holds up to 150 standing.

MEETING CAPACITY: The Palm Room seats up to 250 guests theater-style or 100 classroom-style.

FEES & DEPOSITS: 50% of the rental fee is required to reserve your date, and the balance is due 30 days prior to the event. The Palm Room rental fee ranges $3,000–5,000 for an 8-hour time frame; extra time is $250/hour. A discounted rate is available for weekday events.

AVAILABILITY: Year-round, daily, 7am–midnight.

SERVICES/AMENITIES:

Catering: select from preferred list or BYO
Kitchen Facilities: fully equipped
Tables & Chairs: BYO or through caterer
Linens, Silver, etc.: BYO or through caterer
Restrooms: wheelchair accessible
Dance Floor: hardwood floor
Bride's Dressing Area: yes
AV/Meeting Equipment: CBA, extra charge

Parking: large lot
Accommodations: no guest rooms
Outdoor Night Lighting: yes, on veranda
Outdoor Cooking Facilities: CBA
Cleanup: caterer
View: Main Post and Golden Gate Bridge, Presidio Officers' homes

RESTRICTIONS:

Alcohol: in-house
Smoking: outside only
Music: amplified OK indoors only

Wheelchair Access: yes
Insurance: liability required

Sir Francis Drake Hotel

Hotel

450 Powell Street, San Francisco

415/395-8526

www.sirfrancisdrake.com
catering@sirfrancisdrake.com

- Rehearsal Dinners
- Ceremonies
- Wedding Receptions
- Corp. Events/Mtgs.
- Private Parties
- Accommodations

The Sir Francis Drake Hotel's 21-story, Gothic-style tower just off Union Square and its Beefeater-attired doormen have been beloved San Francisco attractions since 1928.

Stepping into the Drake's opulent Italian Renaissance lobby is just like stepping back into the 1920s: Marble staircases, walls and pillars convey a stately air; crystal chandeliers shine and the lofty, ornately detailed ceiling sparkles with gold leaf. The main event spaces, the Empire Ballroom and the Franciscan Room, have a high-society, Age of Innocence ambiance, and all were beautifully renovated in 2013. In the gold-and-ivory Empire Room, exquisite hand-painted murals turn the walls into works of art. Overhead, three crystal chandeliers suspended from a vaulted ceiling painted with ribbons of gold leaf give the room a delicate amber glow. The adjoining wood-paneled Walnut Room, with its club-like, Edwardian atmosphere and built-in bar, makes a great prefunction space.

Located just off the mezzanine, the spacious and grand Franciscan Room is an excellent choice for a formal wedding. It's a regal setting, featuring a 21-foot ceiling with intricate gold embossing, chandeliers, windows draped with blue silk curtains, and columns with carved gold capitals. Guests can enjoy cocktails and hors d'oeuvres on the adjacent mezzanine, which offers a cozy fireplace and a bird's-eye view of the vibrant hotel lobby below.

And for those who have a yen for a panoramic 180-degree view of San Francisco, try the recently renovated Starlight Room on the 21st floor. It not only has a built-in dance floor and shiny baby grand piano, it features floor-to-ceiling windows that wrap around the room, making it seem like you're floating in the clouds.

Steeped in 80 years of history, the Drake is a true classic. Brides may fall in love with its enchanting vintage architectural details, but they'll also appreciate the modern amenities and personal service this landmark hotel has to offer.

CEREMONY & EVENT/RECEPTION CAPACITY: The hotel accommodates 50–220 seated or 200–350 standing guests indoors.

MEETING CAPACITY: The Hotel has 17,000 square feet of meeting and conference space with 14 different rooms accommodating groups from 10 to 350 people.

FEES & DEPOSITS: For weddings, a nonrefundable deposit is required to confirm your date. Half the food & beverage total is payable 3 months prior to the event; the balance and guest count guarantee are due 3 days prior. Wedding packages range $125–210/person and include open bar, passed hors d'oeuvres, champagne, wine, wedding cake and a 3-course dinner. Tax, and a 24% service charge are additional. Per-person prices for seated meals are as follows: luncheons start at $69, dinners at $82, luncheon buffets at $69, and dinner buffets at $95. Alcohol, tax and a 24% service charge are additional. The bride and groom receive a complimentary suite, and group discounts for overnight guests can be arranged.

Fees for meetings and business functions vary depending on rooms and services selected; call for specifics.

AVAILABILITY: For special events and business functions, year-round, daily, 6am–midnight. Weddings usually take place on Saturdays 11am–5pm or 6pm–midnight; other days have more flexible time frames. The Starlight Room is available for buyouts. Contact the wedding consultant for specifics.

SERVICES/AMENITIES:

Catering: in-house, no BYO

Kitchen Facilities: n/a

Tables & Chairs: provided

Linens, Silver, etc.: provided

Restrooms: wheelchair accessible

Dance Floor: provided

Bride's & Groom's Dressing Areas: no

AV/Meeting Equipment: provided

Parking: nearby garages or valet, extra fee

Accommodations: 416 guest rooms

Outdoor Night Lighting: n/a

Outdoor Cooking Facilities: n/a

Cleanup: provided

View: Starlight Room has 180-degree view of San Francisco skyline

Other: event coordination, baby grand piano

RESTRICTIONS:

Alcohol: in-house, no BYO

Smoking: designated areas

Music: amplified OK

Wheelchair Access: yes, elevator

Insurance: liability required

Other: no rice, open flames or fog machines

Swedenborgian Church

Landmark Chapel

2107 Lyon Street at Washington, San Francisco

415/346-6468

www.sfweddings.org
events@sfswedenborgian.org

- Rehearsal Dinners
- Ceremonies
- Wedding Receptions
- Corp. Events/Mtgs.
- Private Parties
- Accommodations

Built in 1895 in Pacific Heights by a coterie of artists, architects and spiritual seekers, the historic Swedenborgian Church is rustic and charming in the Arts and Crafts tradition. There's a huge brick fireplace inside and, lit with candles, the interior is exceptionally beautiful and serene. Floors, walls and ceilings are wood, and the arching overhead beams are good-sized madrone tree trunks. In lieu of conventional pews, handmade Mission-style maple chairs are provided.

Many of San Francisco's most important (if not famous!) personages were once affiliated with this church, such as Robert Frost, who went to Sunday School here. The founders of the Sierra Club were all active associates, including John Muir. The Sierra Club's legendary landscape painter, William Keith, painted four large murals that line the north wall of the sanctuary, and Phoebe Hearst (William Randolph Hearst's mother) is represented by her donation of a rare cast-iron copy of Peter Vischer's 15th-century "Praying Madonna."

Adjacent to the chapel is a turn-of-the-century Craftsman house whose Garden Room, Fireside Room and Dining Room are used for receptions. Both the Fireside and Dining Rooms have working fireplaces. In front of the house, a quiet garden with a small pool, trees, benches and flowers provides a pretty spot for gatherings and wedding photos.

The Swedenborgian Church offers traditional, contemporary and interfaith ceremonies, with weddings usually scheduled three hours apart.

CEREMONY CAPACITY: The chapel holds 120 seated or 150 standing.

EVENT/RECEPTION CAPACITY: The house holds up to 90 seated or 120 standing guests.

MEETING CAPACITY: The house can accommodate up to 100 people for a meeting.

FEES & DEPOSITS: A nonrefundable deposit of 50% of the rental fee (plus a $400 security deposit if you're booking a reception) is required to reserve your date, and the balance is due 30 days prior to the event. The fee for a ceremony only ranges $1,000–2,000 depending on the day of the week, spaces used, and number of guests. The reception only fee is $3,000. A ceremony & reception runs $4,000–5,000 depending on the day. For complete rental details, please visit the "Make a Reservation" page on Swedenborgian Church's website.

AVAILABILITY: Receptions can be scheduled by arrangement. Guests must vacate the premises by 9pm.

SERVICES/AMENITIES:

Catering: BYO or select from preferred list
Kitchen Facilities: fully equipped
Tables & Chairs: provided
Linens, Silver, etc.: BYO
Restrooms: wheelchair accessible
Dance Floor: yes, small receptions only
Bride's Dressing Area: yes
AV/Meeting Equipment: n/a

Parking: on street, garage nearby
Accommodations: no guest rooms
Outdoor Night Lighting: access only
Outdoor Cooking Facilities: no
Cleanup: caterer
View: garden

RESTRICTIONS:

Alcohol: BYO wine, champagne or beer; no hard alcohol permitted
Smoking: not allowed on premises
Music: amplified ok indoors with restrictions

Wheelchair Access: limited
Insurance: not required
Other: no rice, seeds, flower petals or bubbles

Terra Gallery and Event Venue

511 Harrison Street, San Francisco

415/896-1234

www.terrasf.com
info@terrasf.com

Art Gallery & Event Venue

- Rehearsal Dinners
- Ceremonies
- Wedding Receptions
- Corp. Events/Mtgs.
- Private Parties
- Accommodations

The collective creativity of entrepreneurs, artists and tech whizzes has made SOMA the hippest neighborhood in The City, vibrating with a diversity of businesses, restaurants, clubs and galleries.

One of the most intriguing of these is Terra Gallery & Event Venue, a collection of galleries and event spaces that epitomizes the synergy of art and technology. At this urban-chic venue, just blocks from the Bay Bridge, you're encouraged to turn your celebration into a work of art—literally. The whole place is like a big blank canvas on which you can paint whatever vision you have in mind. Terra's two diverse levels have separate entrances, so you can reserve a floor individually or take over all the galleries and offer your guests multiple environments.

Terra Gallery's upper floor has a spacious, open feeling thanks to 5,000 square feet of Brazilian cherry hardwood floors, white brick walls and support columns rising 20 feet to the ceiling, and floor-to-ceiling windows at the end of the room. Light pours in during the day, and at night city lights turn the wall of glass into a vast glittering tableau—a dreamy backdrop for a wedding ceremony. A carpeted area with leather furniture and a baby grand piano lets guests relax and enjoy the view.

Equally impressive is Mer, a lounge-style space on the lower floor that gives off the ultra-hip vibe of a private club. Serpentine bars inlaid with glass tiles let the staff serve up signature cocktails with style and ease. A built-in oak stage at one end holds your entertainment, while guests dance on the gleaming hardwood floor. Mer adjoins a 3,000-square-foot landscaped patio, which can be left open to the stars or elegantly tented. Bamboo, lush foliage and water features evoke a garden atmosphere for a cocktail reception.

Terra's staff will work with you and your planners to ensure that your wedding is seamlessly choreographed. You're welcome to incorporate the current exhibit's paintings into your event, or turn Terra into your own personal gallery by exhibiting blown-up photos of the bride and groom on the walls, or projecting a slide show set to music. Terra's state-of-the art Bose sound system, gallery lighting and multimedia capabilities allow for the ultimate in customization. And if you're having a destination wedding here, they're able to provide a live feed to guests who can't attend.

You're free to bring your own licensed caterer, and there's plenty of nearby parking with valet service available upon request. To make it easy for out-of-town guests who want to take advantage of nearby museums, entertainment and sightseeing, Terra has partnered with local hotels for special group rates.

Terra's versatility makes it an inspired choice for just about any type of event. Whether you desire a quiet and refined affair or a totally theatrical experience, Terra has all the elements.

CEREMONY CAPACITY: Terra Gallery holds up to 300 seated guests; Mer accommodates 200 seated.

EVENT/RECEPTION CAPACITY: Terra Gallery holds 350 seated guests or 725 standing; Mer accommodates 200 seated or 725 standing.

MEETING CAPACITY: Terra Gallery holds 400 seated guests; Mer accommodates 200 seated. When both floors are used, 400 can be seated theater-style with a breakout area for 200.

FEES & DEPOSITS: A $2,000 deposit is required to reserve your date. The balance is due 30 days prior to the event. The rental fee ranges $6,500–15,000 depending on date of the event, guest count, facility usage and type of organization.

AVAILABILITY: Year-round, daily; timing is customized to your needs.

SERVICES/AMENITIES:

Catering: BYO or CBA
Kitchen Facilities: 2 prep kitchens
Tables & Chairs: BYO or CBA
Linens, Silver, etc.: BYO or CBA
Restrooms: wheelchair accessible
Dance Floor: provided at no charge
Bride's & Groom's Dressing Areas: yes
AV/Meeting Equipment: CBA, extra fee

Parking: garages nearby or valet CBA
Accommodations: nearby hotels
Outdoor Night Lighting: CBA
Outdoor Cooking Facilities: yes
Cleanup: CBA
View: cityscape, landscaped grounds
Other: contemporary art on display; increased bandwidth in/out available at competitive rates

RESTRICTIONS:

Alcohol: in-house
Smoking: outside only
Music: amplified and live music OK indoors

Wheelchair Access: yes
Insurance: required, CBA

The wedding vendors on our website are the best in the business. How do we know? Read page 553.

W San Francisco

Hotel

181 Third Street, San Francisco
415/817-7884

www.wsanfrancisco.com/weddings
wsanfrancisco.weddings@whotels.com

- Rehearsal Dinners
- Ceremonies
- Wedding Receptions
- Corp. Events/Mtgs.
- Private Parties
- Accommodations

Hip, fresh and vibrant, this multifaceted boutique hotel in San Francisco's artistic epicenter offers floor after floor of entertaining options for your extraordinary upcoming event.

It all begins at the lobby level, where the eclectic and electric mix of iconic design and contemporary luxury that characterizes W Hotels worldwide is immediately apparent. Arranged more like a home than a lobby, W's capacious Living Room brings suggestions of the cityscape and the artsy SF MOMA ambiance indoors in the sophisticated use of black and gray, the silvery and neon accents, and lighting that transitions naturally from day to night. This chic, lounge-like setting with its metal-and-glass fireplace and racy black bar is a guaranteed ice-breaker, so start the party with a DJ and cocktails here … or use the restaurant, TRACE, with its focus on sustainability and innovation, for cocktails and dining.

But don't stop here. A swift ascent by stair or elevator will take you to the next dazzling level—the mezzanine-style floor that overlooks the Living Room. A delicate fiber-optic chandelier waterfalls from the third-floor ceiling down through both spaces tying them together. In the Upstairs Bar, your guests can sip cocktails while watching the scene below. The long, all white LED-lit bar is a showstopper. Silver bead-curtained cabanas with Living Room views and private seating are a very subtle nod to San Francisco in the '60s and lend this sleek space a sultry charm. Need more room to mingle? How about dinner, dancing or cocktails in the Industry Room and its intimate prefunction area, another great spot from which to view the first-floor action.

There's more. The third floor features two glamorous Great Rooms with a pearl white and silver color scheme, avant-garde lighting, floor-to-ceiling windows, full AV capability and a generous prefunction foyer. Both rooms can be combined for banquets and galas. Or consider the three Workrooms, which can also be used together if the occasion warrants, along with their own prefunction space. For certain celebrations you might want to book the whole floor, which also includes a Strategy Room and a Studio. Even the halls here are suitable for entertaining. You could wander around them for hours, relaxing in wingback chairs or tuning in to music in the Chill Pods—try one, they make a cool backdrop for photos!

The newly renovated fourth-floor Social Terrace is one of San Francisco's most dynamic event settings. Sheltered by a sleek pavilion designed in W's signature contemporary style, the Social Terrace is a dramatic location for ceremonies, dining or even dancing. The vibe is modern luxury with an urban edge, and a birds-eye panorama of the city lights is a scintillating bonus.

Really, this is a venue so mind-blowing in possibilities you will just have to see it to believe it. So, check it out. The experienced event staff are poised and eager to help you invent an unforgettable affair. And when the party is over, your next adventure can begin here, too: You and your guests will love unwinding in one of the stylish guest rooms or suites and sampling W Hotels' famous Whatever/Whenever service.

CEREMONY CAPACITY: The W San Francisco holds 300 seated guests indoors.

EVENT/RECEPTION CAPACITY: The hotel accommodates 200 seated or 400 standing indoors.

MEETING CAPACITY: Meeting spaces hold 240 seated.

FEES & DEPOSITS: 20% of the estimated event total is required to secure your date. The balance is due 2 weeks before the event. The rental fee ranges $500–2,000 depending on the space reserved and guest count. Wedding packages start at $185/person and may be customized. Meeting room rental and all food & beverage orders are subject to tax and a 24% service charge.

AVAILABILITY: Year-round, daily, call for details.

SERVICES/AMENITIES:

Catering: in-house
Kitchen Facilities: n/a
Tables & Chairs: provided
Linens, Silver, etc.: silver provided; linens CBA, extra fee
Restrooms: wheelchair accessible
Dance Floor: provided
Bride's Dressing Area: CBA
AV/Meeting Equipment: state-of-the-art provided; full on-site PSAV team available

Parking: valet only
Accommodations: 404 guest rooms, pets are welcome
Outdoor Night Lighting: CBA
Outdoor Cooking Facilities: no
Cleanup: provided
View: cityscape
Other: event coordination, spa services, stylized bars

RESTRICTIONS:

Alcohol: in-house
Smoking: designated areas only
Music: amplified OK

Wheelchair Access: yes
Insurance: liability required

The Westin St. Francis San Francisco
on Union Square

Historic Hotel

335 Powell Street, San Francisco
415/774-0450
www.westinstfrancis.com
mmsfo.metroleads@startwoodhotels.com

- Rehearsal Dinners
- Ceremonies
- Wedding Receptions
- Corp. Events/Mtgs.
- Private Parties
- Accommodations

Commonly referred to as the Grand Dame of Union Square, The Westin St. Francis has been a symbol of elegance in San Francisco for more than a century. Its many rooms, some featuring exquisite historic detailing and others reflecting more modern luxury, have hosted beautiful wedding ceremonies, grand receptions, and business events of all types.

In the hotel's turn-of-the-century Landmark Building, you'll find stunning ballrooms with gilt pillars, intricately carved ceilings, and a hundred years' worth of history. They include: the Borgia Room, a jewel-box chamber with oak-paneled walls, a six-foot-tall marble fireplace, and a vaulted, delicately painted ceiling (originally the hotel's chapel, it's perfect for a wedding ceremony); the St. Francis Suite (just right for a smaller ceremony and reception); and the Colonial Room, appointed with Italian murals, elaborate candelabras, and gold-leafed columns separating regal opera balconies. Large events are held in the Grand Ballroom, which is easily transformed by your choice of décor and can accommodate up to 800 guests. Receptions often start with cocktails in the Colonial Room, then flow into the adjacent Grand Ballroom for the main affair.

If you prefer a more contemporary ambiance, hold your celebration in the Tower Building. Its two premier spaces, Victor's and Alexandra's, are a pair of sophisticated settings on the 32nd-story Imperial Floor. Five glass elevators overlook spectacular downtown panoramas as they whisk guests up to this sky-high getaway. Boasting breathtaking floor-to-ceiling views that extend from the Bay Bridge to the Golden Gate, these private rooms also dazzle at night: Glowing chandeliers and hundreds of sparkling pin-spots provide adjustable lighting to match your mood. Gold Chiavari chairs, custom Wedgwood china and your own Imperial Floor concierge make having an event up here a sublime experience.

The possibilities at The Westin St. Francis are almost endless. Are you looking for Old San Francisco glamour or something more modern? If you can't decide, why not combine the past and the present with a ceremony in the Borgia Room followed by dinner and dancing in Alexandra's. Whatever spaces you select, your event will most certainly be magical.

CEREMONY CAPACITY: The hotel can accommodate 20–800 seated guests.

EVENT/RECEPTION CAPACITY: The St. Francis has 32 banquet rooms with 56,000 square feet of event space; some of the larger rooms hold 80–800 seated or up to 1,200 standing guests.

MEETING CAPACITY: The facility's 32 rooms seat 20–1,000 theater-style, 15–800 classroom-style or 10–50 conference-style.

FEES & DEPOSITS: For social events, a nonrefundable deposit based on the estimated event total is required when the contract is signed; the remaining balance and a final guest count are due 72 business hours prior to the event. Wedding packages start at $185/person ($209/person for the Imperial Floor), and include hors d'oeuvres, 4-hour bar, 2-course meal, wedding cake, champagne toast, wine with meal, and a specialty suite for the bride and groom. Tax and a 24% service charge are additional. A ceremony setup fee may be required. Customized wedding and bar mitzvah packages can be arranged; kosher catering under strict rabbinical supervision is available. Persian and Indian catering are also available.

AVAILABILITY: Year-round, daily, anytime, including holidays.

SERVICES/AMENITIES:

Catering: in-house

Kitchen Facilities: n/a

Tables & Chairs: provided

Linens, Silver, etc.: provided

Restrooms: wheelchair accessible

Dance Floor: provided

Bride's & Groom's Dressing Areas: suite provided

AV/Meeting Equipment: full range; AV extra charge

Parking: limited on-site; many nearby garages

Accommodations: 1,195 guest rooms

Outdoor Night Lighting: n/a

Outdoor Cooking Facilities: n/a

Cleanup: provided

View: sweeping cityscape from upper floors

Other: kosher, Indian and Persian catering; wedding cakes

RESTRICTIONS:

Alcohol: in-house

Smoking: outside of hotel only

Music: amplified OK

Wheelchair Access: yes

Insurance: not required

North Bay

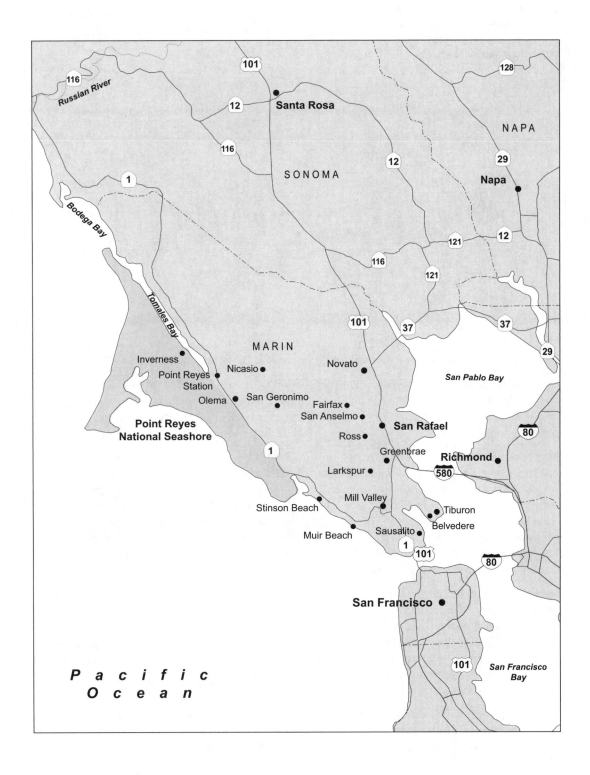

Kimball Hall
at St. Stephen's Episcopal Church

3 Bay View Avenue, Belvedere/Tiburon

415/435-4501

www.ststephenschurch.org
satoko@ststephenschurch.org

Reception Hall and Church

- Rehearsal Dinners
- Ceremonies
- Wedding Receptions
- Corp. Events/Mtgs.
- Private Parties
- Accommodations

You can't help but have an "Ah, yes!" reaction when you step onto the campus of Kimball Hall and St. Stephen's Episcopal Church, nestled into a shady hillside on lush Belvedere Island.

As you enter, you walk through a beautiful fountain courtyard bounded on one side by the hall and on the other by the church. Planted with Japanese maples, camellias, ferns and rhododendrons, it's an inviting and serene spot for mingling over cocktails or hosting an intimate al fresco ceremony or reception.

Most receptions and large events are held in Kimball Hall, a brilliantly designed space that makes you feel like you're inside an exquisite, light-splashed wooden box. The floors are simple blond wood, the walls are softwood in varying shades, and the gently curved ceiling is trimmed with eye-pleasing lattice. Natural light passes through the courtyard-facing glass wall as well as the windows that overlook Belvedere Lagoon, Tiburon and Angel Island, giving the airy room an inner glow. With such an artfully conceived interior, the venue can accommodate any color palette. The hall opens onto the courtyard, which can provide additional seating for large receptions or a quiet place for guests to relax during your celebration.

For a formal church ceremony, the sanctuary at St. Stephen's is ideal. The soaring concrete columns and walls of its gothic architecture suggest a sacred space and eloquently convey a powerful—even tangible—sense of the Divine. A heavenly blue ceiling crowns the long, high nave, and slender vertical bands of stained glass filter sunlight down onto the church's wooden altar. Hand-carved torchières holding votive candles line the aisle, softly lighting the way as the bride walks toward her groom. At the same time, music played on the massive pipe organ fills the building, long noted for its superb acoustics.

The hall, courtyard and church are a lovely combination of spaces that complement each other perfectly. From the pageantry and solemnity of the wedding ceremony to the festive dining and dancing that follow, everyone who celebrates with you here will remember the experience with pleasure.

CEREMONY CAPACITY: The church holds up to 250 seated guests indoors. Please ask about requirements for use of the St. Stephen's Church sanctuary.

EVENT/RECEPTION CAPACITY: Kimball Hall accommodates up to 150 seated guests or 120 with room for dancing. The courtyard provides additional seating for up to 60.

MEETING CAPACITY: Meeting spaces seat 125 guests.

FEES & DEPOSITS: A $1,000 deposit is required to book your date, and the balance is due 10 days prior to the event. The rental fee ranges $1,500–$5,000 depending on the number of hours reserved and whether both the church and hall are rented.

AVAILABILITY: Year-round, daily, except the week before Easter and the week before Christmas. The church is available 11am–10pm except Thursdays (11–6pm) and Sundays (3pm–9pm).

SERVICES/AMENITIES:

Catering: select from preferred list
Kitchen Facilities: fully equipped
Tables & Chairs: some provided or through caterer
Linens, Silver, etc.: through caterer
Restrooms: wheelchair accessible
Dance Floor: provided
Bride's & Groom's Dressing Areas: yes
AV/Meeting Equipment: some provided

Parking: large lot, on-street
Accommodations: no guest rooms
Outdoor Night Lighting: limited
Outdoor Cooking Facilities: BBQ CBA
Cleanup: renter removes garbage from premises
View: garden patio, hills, lagoon, fountain
Other: grand piano, clergy on staff, pipe organ, event coordination

RESTRICTIONS:

Alcohol: BYO wine, beer or champagne
Smoking: not allowed
Music: amplified OK with restrictions

Wheelchair Access: yes
Insurance: liability required

Deer Park Villa

367 Bolinas Road, Fairfax
415/456-8084

www.deerparkvilla.com
weddings@deerparkvilla.com

Historic Wooded Restaurant

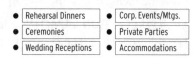

- Rehearsal Dinners
- Ceremonies
- Wedding Receptions
- Corp. Events/Mtgs.
- Private Parties
- Accommodations

In 1927, Joe and Antoinette Ghiringhelli held their wedding-night dinner at a restaurant tucked into the hills of Fairfax. Charmed by the special property—originally opened in 1916 as a lodge—the young newlyweds made a promise to each other that one day they would own it. In 1937 their dream became a reality. To celebrate, Joe planted a grove of redwood trees, which have since grown into an "Enchanted Forest" of towering giants that have sheltered hundreds of couples as they exchange wedding vows.

The bride's day begins in the adorable Bridal Suite, which once served as the Villa's carriage house. There's a full bathroom, cedar closet, and lots of windows—all accented by vintage furnishings, art, and décor. If you opt to take photos around the grounds before the festivities begin, your photographer will surely thank you—the light here is lovely at any time of day, and you're likely to capture some shots of the Villa's namesake deer, who are frequent (and welcome!) visitors.

As guests begin to arrive, they'll be guided by attendants down a shady gravel path to a parking area surrounded by trees and picturesque outbuildings. From there, they'll make their way toward the heart of the property where the Enchanted Forest stands.

The trees form a large circle, becoming a natural cathedral that feels both sacred and celebratory. You can say "I do" beneath an arbor or chuppah, or let the beauty of the redwoods serve as your altar. After the ceremony, the grove will be set for dinner so you and your guests can continue to enjoy the setting. It's especially pretty as night falls, when market lights, high in the boughs, form a softly glowing canopy.

During the cocktail hour, guests mingle at the outside bar, which overlooks a sweet, handmade stone water feature depicting a fairytale bridge and turret. The bar is backed by a series of shelves just begging to be personalized—couples have decorated them with family photos, candles, and lighted marquee signs. Guests can also play bocce ball, roast s'mores around fire pits, or retreat to the Zen Grove, a peaceful spot with a circular flowerbed at its center that can be set with chairs, tables, or lounge furniture.

After dinner, the party moves to the Dance Hall. This large room occupies a section of Deer Park's historic restaurant, named "Bootlegger's Lodge" in a colorful nod to the Prohibition Era. (They host rehearsal dinners here, too!) 1920s-inspired art and tchotchkes line the walls, and wrought-iron lamps and sconces cast just the right amount of light on the hardwood dance floor. The Dance

Hall also houses The Lodge Bar, which stays open late so you and your guests can wind down the evening without feeling rushed.

The venue celebrated its centennial anniversary in 2016, and is lovingly run by a third generation of the Ghiringhelli family. When couples wed at Deer Park Villa, they become part of its enduring romantic story.

CEREMONY CAPACITY: The site can seat 200 indoors or 350 outdoors.

EVENT/RECEPTION CAPACITY: The facility holds 200 seated or 300 standing indoors, and 350 seated or 350 standing outdoors.

MEETING CAPACITY: The facility can accommodate 300 seated guests.

FEES & DEPOSITS: Wedding packages range $6,000–10,000 depending on the day and time of the event, guest count, and spaces reserved. They include the bridal room, redwood grove, outdoor fire pit, lounge, heaters and bar, tables & chairs, indoor & outdoor dancing locations, and complimentary parking. Full bar and beverage packages, as well as an in-house DJ, are also available. Flexible deposit and payment plans are arranged on an individual basis. Please check with the venue for additional pricing info.

Rates for business functions, meetings or other types of events vary; contact the venue for more details.

AVAILABILITY: Year-round.

SERVICES/AMENITIES:

Catering: select from approved list
Kitchen Facilities: fully equipped
Tables & Chairs: provided
Linens, Silver, etc.: through caterer
Restrooms: wheelchair accessible
Dance Floor: portable provided
Bride's Dressing Area: yes
AV/Meeting Equipment: some provided

Parking: large, complimentary, supervised lot; available daytime and overnight
Accommodations: 6 guest rooms
Outdoor Night Lighting: yes
Outdoor Cooking Facilities: BBQ CBA
Cleanup: caterer
View: forest, fountain, garden, landscaped grounds
Other: outdoor fire pit lounge, heaters, lounge bar & deck area

RESTRICTIONS:

Alcohol: in-house
Smoking: designated areas only
Music: amplified OK

Wheelchair Access: yes
Insurance: liability required

Want to find more venues and services? Check out our informative website, www.HereComesTheGuide.com.

125

Mill Valley Community Center

180 Camino Alto, Mill Valley
415/383-1370
www.millvalleycenter.org
jmurphy@cityofmillvalley.org

Community Center

● Rehearsal Dinners	● Corp. Events/Mtgs.
● Ceremonies	● Private Parties
● Wedding Receptions	Accommodations

How blessed is Mill Valley? Let us count the ways: dramatic location at the foot of Mt. Tamalpais; redwood groves; proximity to the bay and San Francisco; sophisticated citizenry and small-town feel.

And, since April 2001, add the Mill Valley Community Center to that list—it's become the town's pride and joy. Every day, from early morning to late evening, people flock here to swim, dance, work out or attend meetings.

The two-building complex, connected by arcades and enclosed walkways, is clad in olive-green wood siding that calls to mind the leaves of the oak trees on nearby hills. While it has the inviting silhouette of an Adirondack-style resort from 100 years ago, this structure deftly combines wood, concrete, painted steel, copper and glass to create a facility with all the light-admitting spaciousness and crispness of good modern architecture.

The center's main event space is the Cascade Room, and to reach it visitors first pass through a dramatic entrance atrium. Their eyes are immediately drawn up to a vaulted ceiling supported by four slender concrete pillars. The atrium's distinctive reddish-gray slate floor is made of stone quarried in China. (The floor generates steady inquiries from landscapers whose clients have fallen in love with the slate and want to know where they can get some for themselves.)

The generous use of glass in the Cascade Room is particularly effective at night, when light pours out through the windows. Motorists on the nearby main road often slow down to look in longingly on its festive scenes, and imagine themselves dancing the night away in this warm, bright place. By day, the two-story space is lit by sunlight falling through the tall windows that run the length of its side walls. The cathedral-style ceiling is supported by laminated wood trusses, an airy architectural element that makes the room soar. Perhaps the nicest touch is the wood floor, left uncarpeted to allow the richness of its eucalyptus floorboards to dazzle the eye. They range along a spectrum of earthy reds, from reddish-browns and near maroons to lighter-colored planks. An adjoining professional kitchen can accommodate any catering operation.

The large patio on the east side of the Cascade Room has no walls or fences, so people don't feel hemmed in. It runs right up to a three-acre lawn (part of a community playing field), so that in one step you can move from stone to grass. This is a well-thought-out design that provides a sense of space, and invites parties to spill happily beyond the patio. The level lawn is a fine place to pitch a tent or two if you want to host an outdoor event.

Smaller rooms are available for wedding-related activities, including the Terrace Room, which can handle a cocktail party or small dinner. Wedding parties can also rent the whole facility if they'd like, including the 25-yard swimming pool, Jacuzzi, giant water slide and adjoining patio.

Mill Valley has always had a nice hum, and this well-maintained facility only adds to it. People instinctively sense it's a great place to hold a celebration.

CEREMONY CAPACITY: The Cascade Room seats 300 guests, and the lawn area seats 200.

EVENT/RECEPTION CAPACITY: The center can accommodate up to 285 seated or 400 standing guests indoors.

MEETING CAPACITY: The facility has 9 rooms that can seat 2–400 theater-style, or up to 200 classroom-style.

FEES & DEPOSITS: For special events, a refundable $100–500 deposit is required when the contract is signed. The rental fee for the Cascade Room ranges $140–225/hour on weekdays and $2,400–3,400 on weekends (for an 8-hour block). Other rooms range $30–150/hour. An attendant fee runs $15–20/hour for weeknights after 6pm, and weekends 8am–midnight.

AVAILABILITY: Year-round, daily, 8am–midnight.

SERVICES/AMENITIES:

Catering: BYO
Kitchen Facilities: commercial kitchen
Tables & Chairs: provided for 285 guests
Linens, Silver, etc.: BYO or caterer
Restrooms: wheelchair accessible
Dance Floor: hardwood floor in Cascade Room
Bride's Dressing Area: CBA
AV/Meeting Equipment: lectern, TV, screen, dry erase boards, microphone and sound system, portable stage

Parking: large complimentary lot
Accommodations: no guest rooms
Outdoor Night Lighting: CBA
Outdoor Cooking Facilities: CBA
Cleanup: some provided
View: Mt. Tamalpais
Other: baby grand piano

RESTRICTIONS:

Alcohol: BYO
Smoking: outside only
Music: amplified OK indoors; OK outdoors with curfew and volume restrictions

Wheelchair Access: yes
Insurance: certificate required
Other: decorations require approval

Mountain Home Inn

Retreat

810 Panoramic Highway, Mill Valley
415/381-9000
www.mtnhomeinn.com
mountainweddingevents@gmail.com

●	Rehearsal Dinners	●	Corp. Events/Mtgs.
●	Ceremonies	●	Private Parties
●	Wedding Receptions	●	Accommodations

Perched on a forested ridge between the lofty peaks of Mt. Tamalpais and Mill Valley 1,000 feet below, the Mountain Home Inn has been enticing guests with stunning views and rustic charm for over a century.

This bed and breakfast was built in 1912 as a mountain getaway for San Franciscans seeking an escape to nature, and has since served the entire Bay Area as a welcome stop for hiking enthusiasts, writers, lovers and even celebrities (Jack London and the Grateful Dead have stayed here). An abundance of wood, both inside and out, lends warmth to all the rooms, as do numerous fireplaces and homey details like the vintage photos of the inn framed on guest room doors.

Everyone who comes here is mesmerized by the breathtaking panorama from the Upper Deck: A vast redwood forest flows down and away to the distant foothills of Mt. Tam, and on a clear day you can see past Tiburon and Angel Island to the East Bay. Although the inn is only 25 minutes from The City, it feels like it's at the edge of the wilderness. No wonder so many couples decide to get married here.

When you book your wedding at Mountain Home Inn, you can have exclusive use of the venue, which includes indoor and outdoor event spaces on three levels plus ten guest rooms. You're free to choreograph your day any way you like, but it has to be said that the Upper Deck, with its spectacular vista and endless sky overhead, is the premier spot for any warm-weather ceremony or reception. If the temperature drops, couples get married in front of the fireplace in the cozy Mountain View Room, where large picture windows frame all three peaks of Mt. Tamalpais. Other ceremony options include the nearby woods and beach (permits are required for these sites). The terraced gardens just below the deck are filled with purple Mexican sage, rosemary and salvia, making them a lovely setting for photos.

Cocktails and hors d'oeuvres are generally served either outside right in front of the inn or downstairs in the Bayview Room, which has French doors that open to a view-filled terrace. While your guests are mingling, tables for the reception are set up on the deck or in the Mountain View

Room. Simple decorations such as candles, leaves and tree branches are easy to come by and complement the natural surroundings.

All of the guest rooms face east, so your family and friends will wake up to the sunrise. Some of the rooms also have Jacuzzi tubs, fireplaces and terraces. Mountain Home Inn's sister property, the English Country-style Pelican Inn, is only ten minutes away and offers a convenient place for a rehearsal dinner or post-wedding brunch. A shuttle can be arranged to transport your guests between the inn and any other local lodging.

Mountain Home Inn offers a number of wedding packages, and their on-site wedding coordinator is happy to customize a package for you. She can also assist in organizing activities for your guests, such as hiking on Mt. Tam, cycling, picnicking or going to the beach. Designated a Bay Area Green Business, the inn keeps its grounds pesticide-free, uses eco-friendly cleaning products and supports local farmers and artisans.

CEREMONY CAPACITY: The inn holds 100 seated guests indoors (upstairs and downstairs) and 100 seated outdoors.

EVENT/RECEPTION CAPACITY: The facility accommodates 100 seated or standing outdoors, and 50 seated or standing indoors.

MEETING CAPACITY: Meetings spaces seat up to 30 guests.

FEES & DEPOSITS: 33% of the total event cost is required to reserve your date, and the balance is due on the day of the event. The rental fee ranges $500–3,000 depending on the season. Meals start at $45/person for 3 courses; and $55/person for 4 courses. Tax, alcohol, staff wages and a 20% service charge are additional.

AVAILABILITY: Year-round, daily.

SERVICES/AMENITIES:

Catering: in-house
Kitchen Facilities: n/a
Tables & Chairs: provided
Linens, Silver, etc.: provided
Restrooms: wheelchair accessible
Dance Floor: CBA or BYO
Bride's Dressing Area: yes
AV/Meeting Equipment: CBA or BYO

Parking: large lot, on-street
Accommodations: 10 guest rooms
Outdoor Night Lighting: yes
Outdoor Cooking Facilities: no
Cleanup: provided
View: panorama of ocean, mountains, hills, forest, valley and cityscape
Other: event coordination

RESTRICTIONS:

Alcohol: beer and wine provided
Smoking: not allowed
Music: amplified OK

Wheelchair Access: yes
Insurance: not required

Rancho Nicasio

1 Old Rancheria Road, Nicasio
415/264-6859
www.ranchonicasio.com
maxbrown@ranchonicasio.com

Historic Restaurant & Grounds

- Rehearsal Dinners
- Ceremonies
- Wedding Receptions
- Corp. Events/Mtgs.
- Private Parties
- Accommodations

In the Broadway play *Brigadoon,* an enchanted village appears on the Scottish moors for a single day each century, then disappears for another 100 years. In the geographic center of Marin County, the little town of Nicasio must look like a Brigadoon to the frazzled city dwellers who often happen upon it during rambling weekend drives. Fortunately, Nicasio, set in a secluded valley and surrounded by grassy hills, woods and placidly grazing ranch animals, never fades from view (except, perhaps, on the rare foggy day). Although travelers who discover it leave reluctantly, they're consoled by the thought that this little country retreat is only half an hour away from the clamor of Highway 101.

Often they come back to get married, heading straight for Rancho Nicasio, the town's heart and soul. You can't miss it: Set at the north side of Nicasio's New England-style town square, Rancho Nicasio is the busiest and most important building in town. That's because it's the area's all-in-one post office, general store, bar, restaurant and social center. Even without the hubbub surrounding it, Rancho Nicasio's Spanish-style white stucco façade, red trim, sloping tile roof and long porch (where locals invariably gather to schmooze) set it apart from its Victorian neighbors.

Two settings create Rancho Nicasio's appeal for weddings. Indoors, the Rancho Room, with its beautiful wooden ceiling trusses, brass-trimmed fixtures and permanent oak dance floor, has a built-in stage equipped with professional lighting and sound (Rancho Nicasio is West Marin's main live music venue). Curtains on the north wall open to a view of a deep green lawn, a vine-festooned gazebo, a shady grove of pines, and distant pastures, farm buildings and soft-shouldered knolls. There's a touch of whimsy, too: The moose head above the fireplace wears different hats throughout the year.

Just outside the Rancho Room, an open-air deck looks out over Rancho Nicasio's grand lawn, which has been the memorable venue for many a wedding. Remember, Marin has one of the best climates in the world, and Nicasio sits at its sunny center. Couples love exchanging vows outdoors—usually in front of the gazebo—while musicians play across the way on a small stage. Afterwards, guests socialize by the full-service al fresco bar on the lawn's east side, or enjoy the aroma of food cooking on the two big grills next to it. A professional chef provides on-site catering.

Besides the lawn and the Rancho Room, Rancho Nicasio also boasts Marin's quintessential western barroom. There are lots of animal heads on the walls, wagon wheel chandeliers, a long oak bar with glass mirrors, a brick fireplace, dark wood trusses and knotty pine paneling. The bar adjoins a meeting room that has its own private, oak-sheltered deck—a splendid rehearsal dinner location. (There's even a cottage tucked away at the far end of the green that's ideal for the bridal party. It has a tub and shower, full-length mirror, living room and bedroom.)

Locals brag that Rancho Nicasio "is 25 minutes from everywhere." The couples who come here from "everywhere" leave with lifelong memories. They look back on having pledged their love under a canopy of warm country light, enveloped by happy friends and great music. It's just the kind of experience you'd expect to have at Marin's own Brigadoon.

CEREMONY CAPACITY: The lawn holds up to 250 seated guests. Indoors, the Rancho Room holds up to 160 seated.

EVENT/RECEPTION CAPACITY: Outdoors, Rancho Nicasio accommodates up to 250 guests; indoors, up to 160 seated.

MEETING CAPACITY: Event spaces seat up to 160.

FEES & DEPOSITS: A nonrefundable deposit is required to reserve your date, and the balance is due on the day of the event. The rental fee starts at $500. The rental fee and package pricing vary depending on the guest count, space rented, day of the week, time of the event, and time of year. All-inclusive wedding packages range $18,000–25,000 for up to 150 guests. Tax and gratuity are additional.

AVAILABILITY: Year-round, except Christmas and New Year's Day.

SERVICES/AMENITIES:
Catering: in-house, no BYO
Kitchen Facilities: n/a
Tables & Chairs: provided
Linens, Silver, etc.: provided
Restrooms: wheelchair accessible
Dance Floor: yes
Bride's Dressing Area: yes
AV/Meeting Equipment: CBA, extra charge
Other: on-site event planner, professional sound and lighting technician on staff, on-site music coordinator for assistance with musical entertainment and bands

Parking: on site
Accommodations: no guest rooms
Outdoor Night Lighting: CBA
Outdoor Cooking Facilities: chefs can prepare a buffet on the outdoor brick barbecue
Cleanup: provided
View: 5-acre site; landscaped grounds; panorama of hills and valley

RESTRICTIONS:
Alcohol: in-house, full bar
Smoking: designated outdoor areas only
Music: amplified OK indoors, outdoors CBA; stages available both inside and outside

Wheelchair Access: yes
Insurance: typically not required

StoneTree Golf Club
A Bay Club Property

Golf Club

9 Stonetree Lane, Novato
415/209-6296
www.bayclubs.com/stonetree
events.bcst@bayclubs.com

● Rehearsal Dinners	● Corp. Events/Mtgs.
● Ceremonies	● Private Parties
● Wedding Receptions	Accommodations

For years, Marin County's tree-studded Black Oak Point was where the Bay Area's Renaissance Faire revelers gathered each September to recreate Elizabethan England. These days the area's beautiful oak woods sweep down to the striking Clubhouse at StoneTree Golf Club, the Bay Club's premier North Bay golf and events property. With its stone columns, picture windows, rafter beams, and handsome dark furniture, the Clubhouse evokes the grand lines of a luxury mountain lodge.

This is a place carefully designed to host weddings and other events, indoors and out. The attractive entrance hall has an elegant, understated ambiance and is highlighted by an expansive window at the far end that drinks in the light, flanked by a romantic floor-to-ceiling stone fireplace. Throughout the building, warm-hued walls are accented by rich, dark-stained wood. From the entrance hall, guests can head off to the 77 Bar & Lounge or to the Ballroom, the Clubhouse's main reception space.

Every view from the Ballroom is absolutely lovely, ranging from a spring-fed waterfall, three ponds, and Black Point's towering oaks to the intricate stonework alongside the Club's main road. The Ballroom can be split into smaller spaces, and features an adjacent arcaded balcony that's visible through tall windows and accessible through French doors. The balcony's sheltering colonnade, formed by tapering wood pillars set on stone bases, reinforces the feeling of being in a grand lodge.

Ceremonies may be held on the golf course fairway or tee box, each affording panoramic vistas that extend from Mt. Tamalpais and the San Rafael hills to the south, all the way north to Marin's wooded ridges and Black Point's oak woods. The golf course undulates over terrain that's an artful mix of sharply manicured greens and natural vegetation. Wedding parties often begin with the ceremony and/or cocktail hour on the golf course, then move on to the Ballroom for dinner.

With architecture that inspires, but never overwhelms, StoneTree Golf Club makes people feel that they're a part of a grand occasion. That sensibility, combined with beautiful views and masterful catering, makes this renowned property a prime North Bay wedding venue.

CEREMONY CAPACITY: The golf course fairway and tee box each accommodate up to 230 guests.

EVENT/RECEPTION CAPACITY: The Ballroom can be divided to hold 80 seated guests on one side and 150 seated on the other for a total of 230 guests.

MEETING CAPACITY: The Ballroom seats up to 230 guests.

FEES & DEPOSITS: 25% of the estimated event total is required to secure your date, and the balance is due 7 days prior to the event. The venue rental fee ranges $3,000–10,000 depending on venue space required. Customized wedding packages range $59–199/person. Tax, alcohol and a 21% service charge are additional.

Rates for business functions, meetings or other types of events vary. Please contact the venue for more details.

AVAILABILITY: Year-round, daily, 6am–2am, except Christmas Day.

SERVICES/AMENITIES:

Catering: in-house
Kitchen Facilities: n/a
Tables & Chairs: provided
Linens, Silver, etc.: provided
Restrooms: wheelchair accessible
Dance Floor: portable provided
Bride's & Groom's Dressing Areas: yes
AV/Meeting Equipment: CBA, extra fee

Parking: 2 large complimentary lots
Accommodations: no guest rooms
Outdoor Night Lighting: CBA
Outdoor Cooking Facilities: CBA
Cleanup: provided
View: coastal range, Mt. Tamalpais, Mt. Burdell, Big Rock Ridge, golf course

RESTRICTIONS:

Alcohol: in-house, or BYO wine and champagne with corkage fee
Smoking: designated areas outdoors
Music: amplified OK indoors, OK outdoors until 2am

Wheelchair Access: yes
Insurance: not required
Other: no rice, confetti, birdseed or sparklers; limited real flower petals are permitted

---

This is important! Tell locations you're reading HERE COMES THE GUIDE and ask if our information is still current.

133

Unity In Marin

600 Palm Drive, Hamilton Center, Novato
415/475-5000
www.unityinmarinweddings.org
events@unityinmarin.org

Chapel and Banquet/Events Facility

●	Rehearsal Dinners	●	Corp. Events/Mtgs.
●	Ceremonies	●	Private Parties
●	Wedding Receptions		Accommodations

Step back in time to the sun-kissed days when California belonged to Spain and town centers displayed flowing fountains, colonnades, bell towers, gardens and charming baroque façades. Unity In Marin invites you to do just that. Nestled in the rolling hills of southern Novato, this Marin County wedding venue includes a multi-use Chapel area, the versatile Unity Hall for receptions, a commercial kitchen, and a lawn and garden courtyard.

The chapel, which blends pleasingly with the Spanish Colonial-style buildings in the adjacent town center, is surrounded by roses, wisteria, palms and a broad lawn. Its soaring interior welcomes ceremonies and/or receptions, with light-colored walls and cushioned chairs for flexible seating. Windows line the top of each side wall, bringing in views of the ever-changing sky. Pendant chandeliers, suspended from a spectacular exposed-wood-beam ceiling, cast up and down lighting. The room's ambiance is further enhanced by an ethereal half-dome ceiling over the maple-floored chancel/stage area.

The balcony is backlit by a colorful stained-glass window with an arch of clear glass beneath it. Old pews from the original Hamilton Chapel have been restored for additional seating. To the side, a state-of-the-art media booth controls a world-class sound system, theater lights and a rear-lit projection screen. The 8 x 10 screen, designed to be a discreet architectural element over the chancel area, appears as an opaque window when not in use. With this sophisticated AV system, you can project favorite photos, engagement pictures, videos or background images prior to or during the ceremony or reception.

In the vestibule area, there's a soundproof family or "cry" room. This carpeted area has a picture window that allows families with babies or crying children a comfortable place from which to view the ceremony. Adjoining the chapel is a bride's room with its own bathroom and full-length mirror, perfect for treasured moments of privacy and as a place to change before and after the wedding.

Unity Hall is ideal for receptions and banquets, and can also be partitioned into four smaller meeting rooms. Floor-to-ceiling windows and multiple doors offer views of the courtyard, while other windows look out to the back hillside. The countertops and granite serving counter work well for buffets, and the adjacent full-size commercial kitchen can accommodate any caterer.

Garden-style weddings are easily arranged in the courtyard, which has a fountain as its centerpiece. This outdoor space is enclosed by colonnaded walkways that provide shade and can also be used for a buffet or cocktail table setup. With unobtrusive built-in lighting and sound, the courtyard can be used any time of day.

The campus' newest addition is the Meditation Garden, a beautiful backdrop for photos. A wisteria-covered trellis beckons you down a winding path through naturally landscaped gardens. Wooden benches along the way encourage you to relax and enjoy the surrounding native trees, flowers and greenery.

Unity In Marin is both romantic and spiritually uplifting. When you come by for a visit, take a moment to sit on a bench near the fountain and appreciate how deftly this venue has melded past and present together. We think its combination of carefully rendered classical Mission architecture and cutting-edge facilities is hard to beat.

CEREMONY CAPACITY: Several spaces accommodate 50–300 seated guests. The chapel seats up to 300 and Unity Hall seats up to 145.

EVENT/RECEPTION CAPACITY: Unity In Marin can accommodate 80–200 seated or 150–275 standing guests indoors, and 80–300 seated or 400 standing outdoors. The chapel holds 200 for a sit-down banquet.

MEETING CAPACITY: The chapel seats up to 80 classroom-style. Unity Hall holds up to 145 seated theater-style or 50 seated conference-style.

FEES & DEPOSITS: 50% of the rental fee is required to reserve your event date. The rental balance and a refundable $150–900 security deposit are due 30 days prior to the event. The venue rental fee starts at $1,500 and varies depending on the spaces selected, date of the event and guest count.

AVAILABILITY: Year-round, daily, 7am–midnight; extended hours can be negotiated.

SERVICES/AMENITIES:

Catering: select from preferred list, or BYO licensed and full-service
Kitchen Facilities: commercial, fully equipped
Tables & Chairs: CBA
Linens, Silver, etc.: BYO or caterer
Restrooms: wheelchair accessible
Dance Floor: CBA
Bride's Dressing Area: yes
AV/Meeting Equipment: WiFi internet access, state-of-the-art AV; lighting and sound available, extra fee

Parking: ample, complimentary
Accommodations: no guest rooms, nearby hotels
Outdoor Night Lighting: yes
Outdoor Cooking Facilities: no
Cleanup: renter or caterer
View: courtyard and Novato hills
Other: ministers available

RESTRICTIONS:

Alcohol: BYO or through caterer
Smoking: designated areas only
Music: amplified OK indoors, outdoors with limits

Wheelchair Access: yes
Insurance: liability required

Marin Art & Garden Center

Art Center & Garden

30 Sir Francis Drake Boulevard, Ross
415/454-1301
www.magc.org
rental@magc.org

- ● Rehearsal Dinners
- ● Ceremonies
- ● Wedding Receptions
- ● Corp. Events/Mtgs.
- ● Private Parties
- Accommodations

The Marin Art & Center, an 11-acre historic estate in the exclusive town of Ross, is a dream come true for anyone seeking exquisitely landscaped gardens and a serene, private atmosphere. Within these lush grounds are various indoor and outdoor sites for weddings, parties, meetings, workshops and other special occasions.

The Livermore Pavilion is a wonderful venue for large celebrations. Spacious and airy, it affords an uninterrupted view of the gardens through a wall of windows. Rustic stone gas-jet fireplaces add warmth both inside the room and on the adjoining deck, which is shaded by an attractive awning. The Pavilion is air-conditioned and can be divided into two smaller spaces, making it ideal for corporate meetings. An adjacent lawn area and gravel patio feature overhead café lighting, so they're a great choice for outdoor dining and events.

The inviting Garden Room opens to an expansive garden area. When the weather is warm, you won't be able to resist having your event outside. The garden is enclosed by ivy-covered walls, live oaks, redwoods and Japanese maples. Below these trees, huge mossy boulders, heavenly bamboo and flourishing shrubs heighten the woodsy feeling. Buffet service or a string quartet can be set up on a slightly raised area, shaded by redwoods. In the evening, soft lighting and the twinkling stars above create a magical ambiance.

For couples getting married at the center, the grounds provide a host of appealing options for ceremonies. The popular Gazebo Lawn offers the charm of a traditional white wooden gazebo, set on a swath of velvety grass and surrounded by a rare dawn redwood as well as elm and horse chestnut trees. The Fountain area is perfect for an al fresco ceremony, reception or party. Here, a large fountain pool sends its glittering spray into the air. A floral rainbow of daylilies, blue catnip, verbena, Santa Barbara daisies and iris blooms around the fountain, all enclosed by an aggregate-concrete path. On one side, a forest of mature elms, Lombardy poplars, deodar cedars and honey locusts forms a backdrop behind a curving wooden bench beneath a pergola.

Though its fabulous gardens and tranquil setting make the Marin Art & Garden Center seem a world away, it's centrally located near Highway 101 and only 20 minutes from San Francisco. When you have your event here, you not only have a chance to "get away from it all," you also experience a little piece of Paradise close to home.

To contact Marin Art & Garden Center by mail, the address is PO Box 437, Ross, CA 94957.

CEREMONY CAPACITY: Indoor and outdoor spaces hold 300+ seated guests.

EVENT/RECEPTION CAPACITY: The center can seat 200 indoors or 300 outdoors.

MEETING CAPACITY: The Livermore Pavilion seats 225 theater-style and the Garden Room seats 50 theater-style.

FEES & DEPOSITS: Half of the total rental fee is required to secure your date; the rental balance and a refundable $500 cleaning/security deposit are due 1 month prior to the function. The rental fee ranges $4,700–6,600 depending on the space selected. A buyout wedding package is $9,000, which guarantees full exclusivity on the day of your wedding.

AVAILABILITY: Year-round, weekends, 8am–10pm at the Livermore Pavilion and the Garden Room.

SERVICES/AMENITIES:

Catering: select from preferred list only

Kitchen Facilities: ample, fully equipped

Tables & Chairs: provided, no extra fee

Linens, Silver, etc.: BYO or through caterer

Restrooms: wheelchair accessible

Dance Floor: yes

Bride's Dressing Area: yes

AV/Meeting Equipment: sound systems, AV screens, mics, wireless internet

Parking: large lot and on-street; shuttle or valet required for larger events

Accommodations: nearby hotels

Outdoor Night Lighting: yes, overhead café lights

Outdoor Cooking Facilities: yes, on asphalt only

Cleanup: through caterer or renter

View: gardens, pond, hills, Mt. Tamalpias

Other: parasols, Chiavari chairs ($4/chair)

RESTRICTIONS:

Alcohol: BYO, must use licensed server

Smoking: outdoors only

Music: amplified OK with restrictions

Wheelchair Access: yes

Insurance: liability required

Other: no rice or birdseed

San Francisco Theological Seminary

Seminary

105 Seminary Road, San Anselmo
415/451-2843

www.seminaryevents.com
dcarey@sfts.edu
events@sfts.edu

● Rehearsal Dinners	● Corp. Events/Mtgs.
● Ceremonies	● Private Parties
● Wedding Receptions	● Accommodations

When they first see a photograph of this place, many people remark that it looks like a castle on a wooded Scottish brae or a medieval village in central Europe. It's easy to understand why this seminary on a hill evokes such romantic associations. First there's Montgomery Memorial Chapel, a graceful stone church near the seminary's main entrance that is one of its two most popular wedding sites. Then, up the hill, there's Stewart Memorial Chapel at Geneva Hall, a splendid white church with an arcade, a soaring campanile, a terrace that overlooks a breathtaking view, and stained-glass windows whose intense colors rival those of Europe's cathedrals.

In between the two ceremony venues is a tree-shaded campus with grand lawns, weathered moss-covered stone walls, classrooms, Victorian homes for faculty members and rock-faced administration buildings that evoke the allure of historic citadels. The most popular reception site is the Geneva Hall terrace, a curving sweep of stone that provides one of the most stunning panoramas in Marin: the north flank of Mt. Tamalpais; Ross Township's redwood-covered ridges; Red Hill; the seminary's signature stone academic buildings; and views down the Ross Valley.

There's a more prosaic form of beauty here, too: Because the seminary is a religious nonprofit entity, it can offer its beautiful grounds and facilities at prices that are considered quite competitive by Marin County standards.

The seminary has another deal sweetener—a Victorian home available for small prenuptial parties or a pre-wedding stay. You can rest overnight at the seminary, then awaken fresh the next morning, knowing you don't have to travel anywhere for the big day. The seminary also has a 28-room dorm-style retreat center, which allows close friends and family to lodge together. Keeping so many of your loved ones nearby makes it easy to turn your wedding into a destination weekend.

Besides a choice of romantic chapels and the campus' overall enticing feel, couples also like the unlimited parking and almost universal accessibility for their disabled guests. This site is like a good day that just keeps getting better. First, the drive here takes you through some of Marin's loveliest, leafiest neighborhoods, and then the campus itself charms you with its meandering lanes, compelling architecture and one-of-a-kind vistas in a county famous for its views. Once it wins you over, any other venue just won't feel as right.

CEREMONY, EVENT/RECEPTION & MEETING CAPACITY: The venue accommodates up to 170 seated or standing guests both indoors and outdoors.

FEES & DEPOSITS: A nonrefundable deposit of 50% of the estimated event total is required to secure your date, and the balance is due 2 months prior to the event. The rental fee ranges $1,200–3,800 depending on the space rented.

AVAILABILITY: Year-round. Call for details.

SERVICES/AMENITIES:

Catering: select from preferred list
Kitchen Facilities: none
Tables & Chairs: provided
Linens, Silver, etc.: through caterer
Restrooms: wheelchair accessible
Dance Floor: through caterer
Bride's & Groom's Dressing Areas: yes
AV/Meeting Equipment: some provided

Parking: large lot or on-street
Accommodations: 33 guest rooms
Outdoor Night Lighting: access only
Outdoor Cooking Facilities: no
Cleanup: caterer or renter
View: mountains, meadow, garden, forest
Other: pianos, picnic area

RESTRICTIONS:

Alcohol: through caterer
Smoking: not allowed
Music: amplified OK indoors and outdoors with restrictions

Wheelchair Access: yes
Insurance: liability required

The Clubhouse at Peacock Gap

Golf & Country Club

333 Biscayne Drive, San Rafael
415/453-4910 X1

www.peacockgapgolfclub.com
eventsdir@peacockgapclubhouse.com

- Rehearsal Dinners
- Ceremonies
- Wedding Receptions
- Corp. Events/Mtgs.
- Private Parties
- Accommodations

The Clubhouse at Peacock Gap enjoys an enviable location. Situated in the heart of Marin County in the charming town of San Rafael, it's easy to get to. But perhaps more importantly, its prime hilltop setting takes full advantage of the gorgeous surroundings, including China Camp State Park to the north and west.

Guests are welcomed into the Craftsman-inspired Clubhouse through its impressive lobby, with plush wood and leather furnishings, an oversized stone fireplace, and spectacular views of the hills through floor-to-ceiling windows. After some pre-ceremony mingling, guests make their way to the ceremony site—an expansive lawn overlooking the hills and golf course. A permanent four-posted wooden pergola, which sits at the lawn's edge, can be draped with fabric, hung with lights or flowers, or used as a *chuppah*.

Following an al fresco cocktail hour on the Back Patio—a trellis-covered deck flanked by stone pillars and cozy fire pits—it's time to celebrate, and you've got great options. The three Salons inside the Clubhouse can be used individually or combined to make a grand ballroom with a high, recessed ceiling and a state-of-the-art AV setup that features a pair of enormous dropdown screens with mounted projectors. Each of the Salons has sliding glass doors that may be opened to the patio during nice weather, letting in fresh breezes from the San Francisco and San Pablo bays. The one at the far end of the Clubhouse also has an entire wall of floor-to-ceiling windows that look out to the terrace.

You'll find lots of helpful bonus amenities here, too. A well-appointed Bridal Room boasts a full-length mirror, large vanity mirrors with three different light settings (your makeup artist will be in heaven!), a generous closet for storing dresses and valuables, and plenty of space to spread out with your bridesmaids. The Groom's Room has everything the guys need to relax while they do their own prep, including a big-screen TV. The Clubroom, located adjacent to the main Clubhouse, is great for intimate gatherings or can be set up to entertain your littlest guests.

Add to these perks the expert coordination of Peacock Gap's caring and attentive staff, and you've got all the elements needed for an effortless wedding day in one of Northern California's most desirable spots.

CEREMONY CAPACITY: The venue can seat 600 indoors or 450 outdoors.

EVENT/RECEPTION CAPACITY: The Event Reception Area holds 600 seated or 1,200 standing indoors, and 450 seated or 1,000 standing outdoors.

MEETING CAPACITY: 4 meeting rooms accommodate 20–500 seated guests.

FEES & DEPOSITS: 25% of the estimated event total is required to secure your date. An additional 50% is due 90 days prior to the event, and the balance is due 14 days prior. Room rental fees range $500–6,000 depending on the space and time reserved. Meals range $29–56/person; bar packages are available at $18–52/person. Tax and a 22% service charge are additional. An outdoor ceremony site is available.

AVAILABILITY: Year-round, daily, anytime.

SERVICES/AMENITIES:

Catering: in-house
Kitchen Facilities: n/a
Tables & Chairs: provided
Linens, Silver, etc.: provided
Restrooms: wheelchair accessible
Dance Floor: portable provided
Bride's & Groom's Dressing Areas: yes
AV/Meeting Equipment: provided

Parking: large lot
Accommodations: no guest rooms
Outdoor Night Lighting: CBA
Outdoor Cooking Facilities: no
Cleanup: provided
View: Mt. Tamalpais, valley, trees; panorama of mountains, hills and fairways
Other: firepits, terrace area

RESTRICTIONS:

Alcohol: provided, or BYO wine with corkage fee
Smoking: designated areas only
Music: amplified OK

Wheelchair Access: yes
Insurance: not required

Overwhelmed? Use the search criteria on www.HereComesTheGuide.com to narrow down your choices.

Falkirk Mansion

Historic Mansion

1408 Mission Avenue, San Rafael
415/485-3328
www.falkirkculturalcenter.org
falkirk.rentals@cityofsanrafael.org

● Rehearsal Dinners	● Corp. Events/Mtgs.
● Ceremonies	● Private Parties
● Wedding Receptions	Accommodations

Magnificent oaks and magnolias frame the historic Falkirk Mansion, a lovely Queen Anne Victorian in the heart of Marin. Built in 1888, the house is the creation of Clinton Day, the architect who designed the Stanford University campus chapel. In keeping with the style of the day, it has a complex and intriguing roof line of gables and chimneys, variously shaped bays and plenty of decorative details.

The property was purchased in 1906 by Captain Robert Dollar, a Scotsman who'd made his fortune in timber and shipping. He added many features to the estate, including the brick steps and pond, rolling lawns, the greenhouse and a carriage house. A civic-minded man, he donated generously to both San Rafael and his hometown of Falkirk, Scotland—hence the name of the Mansion.

Today, Falkirk Cultural Center serves as a historic site, contemporary art gallery, cultural and educational center, as well as a popular spot for weddings. You can have your ceremony in the outdoor Wedding Garden, on the sprawling lawns or in the parlor. The Mansion's interior is beautifully rendered in rich redwood paneling, and features ornate mantelpieces, hardwood floors and elegant wall coverings. When you reserve the Mansion, you have use of the entire first floor. The foyer has a huge decorative fireplace and floor-to-ceiling stained-glass windows. Have your reception indoors or, during warmer months, dine and dance on the veranda. This secluded wooden porch is enclosed by camellia bushes and an ancient oak. It doesn't matter how you orchestrate your wedding; Falkirk will imbue it with intimacy and a century's worth of Victorian charm.

CEREMONY CAPACITY: The Parlor holds 50 seated or 75 standing guests; outdoors the site can accommodate 125 seated.

EVENT/RECEPTION CAPACITY: October–April, the standing capacity is 100 and the seated capacity is 50–60 guests. April–October, the house and veranda hold up to 125 guests.

MEETING CAPACITY: Indoors, the venue holds 60 seated theater-style or 20 seated conference-style; outdoors it holds 80 seated theater-style.

FEES & DEPOSITS: A refundable $500 deposit is required to reserve your date. Rental fees are due 45 days prior to the event. Saturday rates for a 6-hour minimum block are $200/hour from April 15–October 14, and $150/hour from October 15–April 14. Friday night and Sunday rates year-round are $100/hour, with a 4-hour minimum. Weekday rates vary; call for more information. Special rates can be arranged for nonprofits.

AVAILABILITY: Year-round. Saturday 1pm–midnight; Sunday-Friday 8am–midnight.

SERVICES/AMENITIES:

Catering: select from approved list or BYO
Kitchen Facilities: minimal
Tables & Chairs: provided
Linens, Silver, etc.: BYO
Restrooms: wheelchair accessible
Dance Floor: no
Bride's Dressing Area: yes
AV/Meeting Equipment: limited

Parking: large public lot
Accommodations: no guest rooms
Outdoor Night Lighting: yes
Outdoor Cooking Facilities: no
Cleanup: caterer
View: wooded park and grounds

RESTRICTIONS:

Alcohol: BYO
Smoking: restricted area only
Music: amplified OK to 90 decibels

Wheelchair Access: yes
Insurance: extra liability required
Other: no candles, decorations restricted

Maple Lawn Estate

1312 Mission Avenue, San Rafael
415/295-LAWN (5296)

maplelawnevents.com
maplelawnevents@gmail.com

Historic Mansion and Lawn

● Rehearsal Dinners	● Corp. Events/Mtgs.
● Ceremonies	● Private Parties
● Wedding Receptions	Accommodations

A pair of hand-stacked stone pillars mark the entry to Maple Lawn, a rambling Victorian house and grounds that was once the home of one of the area's leading families. Built with 19th-century mining riches, the residence was often the scene for "must attend" social and civic soirées. Happily today, under the current ownership of the San Rafael Elks, this grand estate continues to set a gold standard for gracious events.

Maple Lawn's *pièce de résistance* is the expansive Magnolia Terrace, an absolute jewel of a garden area off to the side of the blue-and-white mansion. As you enter through an ornate, iron gate, the first thing that greets you is a profusion of colorful blooming hedges. Just ahead is a raised, canopied terrace, and stretching out beyond that is an incredibly lush lawn surrounded on three sides by mature magnolia and camellia trees. Running straight through the center of the grass is a wide brick promenade adorned with two multi-tiered fountains topped dramatically with Greek goddesses.

What a spectacular setting this makes for your ceremony, as friends and family seated on the lawn watch you walk down that center aisle to meet your groom beneath a neoclassical arch. After vows are exchanged, everyone is invited to toast your new life with a glass of bubbly on the terrace. Slightly elevated and separated from the grass by box hedges and flower-filled urns, this shady spot is perfect for enjoying cocktails and hors d'oeuvres. Then dinner is served at tables on the lawn, followed by dancing back on the terrace under the twinkle-lit canopy.

Beautiful as the grounds are, there are pleasures to be found inside the house as well. To start with, you'll surely be smitten with a bride's room that's the epitome of femininity. Large enough for all your attendants to gather and relax, its décor includes an antique Victorian vanity table, a carved white marble fireplace, and high ceilings with lots of crown molding. The groomsmen get to play men of leisure in the "old school" Card Room Lounge with its adjacent wood-paneled Billiards Room.

At the front of the house, there's an airy Solarium and cozy porch overlooking pine trees that would make a delightful spot for a bridal shower or bridesmaid's breakfast. And the clubby Drake's Bar, complete with burgundy leather wingback chairs, early American paintings and a vintage mural of Sir Francis Drake arriving in the Bay Area, could be just right for a rehearsal dinner.

If you'd prefer an indoor reception, check out the regal-sized Boyd Banquet Room, which boasts a coved ceiling with the original brass-and-crystal chandeliers that illuminated many historic parties. But even if you don't entertain inside, do take advantage of the polished wooden doors (replete with brass doorknockers), central staircase and porte-cochère as romantic photo backdrops unique to Maple Lawn.

CEREMONY CAPACITY: The site holds 180 seated guests indoors and 300 seated outdoors.

EVENT/RECEPTION CAPACITY: The facility can accommodate 200 seated or 250 standing indoors and 300 seated or 500 standing outdoors.

MEETING CAPACITY: Meeting rooms hold up to 100 seated guests.

FEES & DEPOSITS: A nonrefundable $1,000 deposit is required to reserve your date, and the balance is due 2 weeks prior to the event or upon contract execution, whichever comes first. Rental packages start at $4,300 and vary depending on the day and time of the event, the space reserved and number of guests. Alcohol, tax and a 20% service charge are additional.

AVAILABILITY: Year-round, daily.

SERVICES/AMENITIES:

Catering: select from preferred list or BYO, extra fee
Kitchen Facilities: fully equipped
Tables & Chairs: provided
Linens, Silver, etc.: through caterer
Restrooms: wheelchair accessible
Dance Floor: provided
Bride & Groom's Dressing Areas: yes
AV/Meeting Equipment: BYO

Parking: large lot, garage nearby
Accommodations: no guest rooms
Outdoor Night Lighting: yes
Outdoor Cooking Facilities: BBQ on site
Cleanup: provided and/or caterer
View: forest, fountain, garden, landscaped grounds
Other: event coordination

RESTRICTIONS:

Alcohol: in-house
Smoking: designated areas only
Music: amplified OK with restrictions

Wheelchair Access: limited
Insurance: liability required

Unitarian Universalist Congregation of Marin

Church

240 Channing Way, San Rafael

415/479-4131

www.uumarin.org
events@uumarin.org

● Rehearsal Dinners	● Corp. Events/Mtgs.
● Ceremonies	● Private Parties
● Wedding Receptions	Accommodations

Exploring Marin County can be a lifetime passion, especially as you discover the region's wonderful hidden vistas, many of which are seldom publicized in guidebooks and tourist literature. One of those little-known views can be enjoyed at the Unitarian Universalist Congregation of Marin, a place that welcomes couples of any faith or sexual orientation (great for interfaith marriages and same-sex unions).

From its hilltop setting high above Terra Linda, the center offers a grand panorama of the north flank of Mt. Tamalpais that most people will never see. Superb as the view is, however, the heart of this venue is a simple, tranquil courtyard graced by a grove of mulberry trees whose broad leaves spread bountiful shade over a lush lawn. A curving three-level terrace rises toward an arbor-topped knoll along two sides of the space, and an ornamental pool and fountain in the center teems with goldfish and water lilies. Water gurgles over a sandstone ledge and spills into the pool creating a calming, almost musical sound.

Beginning at the courtyard, a gravel path winds up past flowers, herbs and succulents to a flagstone-paved area on top of the knoll. With a tall oak and an arbor as backdrops, this is a compelling spot for photos. From this height you can see a quintessential Marin panorama: Terra Linda and Mt. Tam to the west and southwest; the wooded hills that run south of Santa Venetia from Civic Center to China Camp; and a commanding view of San Pablo Bay.

The center's Fellowship Hall is the most popular site for dining and dancing (or for winter indoor ceremonies). It has a high ceiling of pine beams and rafters, an oak floor and picture windows on three sides, including one that looks out over Terra Linda and that impressive Mt. Tam view. The more modest Fireside Room is warm and intimate, ideal for a small wedding or reception. Its focal point is a tall sandstone-faced fireplace, flanked by picture windows that look out to a dense oak wood. The room has direct access to the courtyard, and in winter a roaring fire makes it especially inviting. Whichever space you use, your guests can party till 11pm.

Caterers will find counter space galore and a professional range in the large kitchen, and UUCM is happy to refer brides to a preferred list of seasoned vendors.

Their first look at the courtyard is usually all it takes to convince many couples to get married here. But if more reasons are needed, the center's outstanding views, affordability, and beautiful setting quickly clinch their decision.

CEREMONY CAPACITY: The Courtyard and Fellowship Hall hold up to 200 seated guests.

EVENT/RECEPTION CAPACITY: The Courtyard and Fellowship Hall each accommodate up to 200 seated or 250 standing guests.

MEETING CAPACITY: The Fellowship Hall seats 12–200 guests.

FEES & DEPOSITS: For a wedding, a $950 deposit is required to reserve your date. The package fee is due 4 weeks prior to the event. Packages range $2,150–2,700 depending on the space rented and the day and time of the event. There is a 25% discount for December–February weddings. Packages include use of entire facility, attendant, tables and chairs (for up to 150 guests), custodial service (setup, breakdown and cleanup). The Saturday wedding package includes use of the facility for a half day the Friday before to decorate, rehearse, etc. Up to 125 outdoor chairs are provided at no additional cost. For rentals and other services, select from their preferred vendor list. Hourly rental of the facility is also available; call for pricing.

AVAILABILITY: Year-round. Monday–Saturday, 7am–11pm and Sunday, 2pm–11pm.

SERVICES/AMENITIES:

Catering: select from preferred list
Kitchen Facilities: fully equipped
Tables & Chairs: provided indoors
Linens, Silver, etc.: BYO or through caterer
Restrooms: wheelchair accessible
Dance Floor: provided
Bride's Dressing Area: yes
AV/Meeting Equipment: some provided

Parking: large lot and on-street
Accommodations: no guest rooms
Outdoor Night Lighting: limited, BYO, CBA
Outdoor Cooking Facilities: BBQ CBA
Cleanup: provided
View: panorama of bay, woods and mountains
Other: grand piano, clergy on staff, picnic area

RESTRICTIONS:

Alcohol: BYO
Smoking: outside only
Music: amplified OK

Wheelchair Access: yes
Insurance: liability required

Cavallo Point
The Lodge at the Golden Gate

Historic Landmark

601 Murray Circle, Fort Baker, Sausalito

415/339-4776

www.cavallopoint.com
weddings@cavallopoint.com

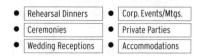

- Rehearsal Dinners
- Ceremonies
- Wedding Receptions
- Corp. Events/Mtgs.
- Private Parties
- Accommodations

It's been awarded honor status by the National Trust for Historic Preservation, and has LEED Gold Certification from the U.S. Green Building Council. The property is also ranked #2 Best Hotel In California by *Travel+Leisure* and is the "Sense of Place" winner of the *National Geographic* World Legacy Award. History, ecology and luxury all seem to blend seamlessly together at Cavallo Point Lodge, the meticulously restored Colonial Revival complex tucked away like a gorgeous surprise at the northern foot of the Golden Gate Bridge.

The views are breathtaking from anywhere on this property set on 75,000 acres of sunny national parkland, but especially from the Mission Blue Chapel. Named after an endangered California butterfly, this pristine, cream-colored structure stands high on a hillside covered with tufted grasses and California native plants. Its adjoining terrace is ideal for light-hearted gatherings, and affords a vista of San Francisco, the sparkling bay, and the towers of the Golden Gate Bridge rising above the pines and eucalyptus through tiaras of clouds.

There are no pews in the chapel, which has large picture windows, gleaming honey-colored floors, and a low stage that make it an excellent setting for anything from a meeting of the minds to a wedding ceremony or reception. But perhaps you'll want to take your celebration outdoors to the Mission Blue Lawn, where your guests can enjoy an elegant hilltop affair or an exchange of vows framed by the incomparable natural panorama.

At the foot of the hill, the Callippe Terrace—named for the endangered Callippe butterfly—is another prime party venue. This one comes with a welcoming fire pit, comfortable seating and a lovely view of historic Fort Baker. Team it up with the Callippe Ballroom and the Callippe Foyer for an ultra-grand indoor-outdoor fête. The foyer alone is roomy enough for cocktails and dancing. Large, lounge-like alcoves flanking the doors add to the sense of grandeur. If you need a place for additional activities, the handsome Silverspot Room on the opposite side of the ballroom can be used as a minitheater, a children's playroom and more.

Not enough possibilities? The lodge offers an amazing 14,000 square feet of adaptable function rooms and formal meeting space. Traipse upstairs to where the balconied Verbena Room and

Foyer, La Mariposa Borracha Room and the Cavallo Point Cooking School kitchen multiply ways to maximize your event experience. Imagine serving cocktails or dinner in a graceful salon with fireplace and thrilling wraparound views, or a group lesson in the art of fine cuisine in the warmth of a spotless, professionally equipped, wine country-style kitchen.

Added to all this are day-of accommodations for the bride, a luxurious Healing Arts Center & Spa, the award-winning Murray Circle restaurant, the Farley Bar and a dreamy veranda designed for sitting back and soaking up the wild beauty of the surrounding terrain. You won't want to leave the grounds and you don't have to. The magnificently renovated two-bedroom family-friendly suites and guest rooms and glamorous contemporary lodgings are a great place for you and your guests to settle in and relax for a weekend…or embark on an extended stay full of fun-filled exploration. Rest assured, any journey that begins here is bound to be a glorious one.

CEREMONY CAPACITY: The facility holds 208 seated guests, indoors or outdoors.

EVENT/RECEPTION CAPACITY: The site can accommodate 180 seated or 250 standing indoors, and 250 seated or standing outdoors. Outdoor events require a tent from a third-party rental company.

MEETING CAPACITY: Meeting rooms hold 200 seated theater-style, or 180 banquet-style.

FEES & DEPOSITS: 50% of the total event cost is required to reserve your date, and the balance is due 30 days prior to the event. The rental fee ranges $6,500–9,500 depending on the season and the number of guests. Meals, including wine, beer and wedding cake, range $225–275/person. Tax, alcohol and a 23% service charge are additional.

AVAILABILITY: Year-round.

SERVICES/AMENITIES:

Catering: in-house
Kitchen Facilities: n/a
Tables & Chairs: provided, CBA
Linens, Silver, etc.: provided, CBA
Restrooms: wheelchair accessible
Dance Floor: portable provided
Bride's Dressing Area: yes
AV/Meeting Equipment: provided, CBA
Other: on-site wedding cake, spa services, picnic area

Parking: large lot
Accommodations: 142 guest rooms
Outdoor Night Lighting: CBA
Outdoor Cooking Facilities: BBQ CBA
Cleanup: provided
View: garden patio, landscaped grounds; panorama of fields, hills, cityscape, coastline, forest, mountains, ocean and park

RESTRICTIONS:

Alcohol: BYO with corkage fee
Smoking: designated areas only
Music: OK with restrictions

Wheelchair Access: yes
Insurance: not required

Want to know WHAT TO ASK a potential location or vendor? Check out our Questions to Ask starting on page 21.

149

The Spinnaker Restaurant
and Banquet Facility

Waterfront Restaurant

100 Spinnaker Drive, Sausalito
415/332-1500 Main or 415/332-8792 Special Events
www.thespinnaker.com
specialevents@thespinnaker.com

- Rehearsal Dinners
- Ceremonies
- Wedding Receptions
- Corp. Events/Mtgs.
- Private Parties
- Accommodations

A well-known landmark along downtown Sausalito's waterfront, The Spinnaker Restaurant has been a favorite dining destination for over 55 years. This popular venue, which sits on piers right over the water, also boasts a delightful banquet facility that offers the same excellent cuisine, topnotch service and spectacular bay views.

Although the banquet facility adjoins the restaurant, it's completely separate from the main dining room and has its own entrance as well as a dedicated kitchen that caters solely to your special event. And like the restaurant, it has plenty of floor-to-ceiling windows and glass doors that let diners savor sweeping vistas of Belvedere, Angel Island, Alcatraz, the Bay Bridge and San Francisco's skyline from anywhere in the room.

The warm interior, in shades of cream and rose, is complemented by a high, distinctive, wood-slat ceiling. Sliding glass doors open onto an outdoor deck that provides an additional 1,000 square feet of bayside event space. Sailboats glide past almost close enough to touch, their colorful spinnakers and white sails billowing in the breeze.

The practical attributes of The Spinnaker Banquet Facility are as compelling as the views. This versatile venue is spacious enough to accommodate a large wedding reception or holiday party (with a band and dance floor) or can easily be set up with lecture-style seating, a stage and a podium for business functions. It can also be configured for smaller, more intimate gatherings, such as bridal shower luncheons, anniversary parties or birthday celebrations.

The Spinnaker is known for orchestrating memorable occasions tailored to their clients' individual needs. Their expert event planning services include arranging everything from florals and photography to music or other entertainment. They offer a variety of reception packages, and their signature menus—which feature fresh seafood, gourmet meats, local specialties and savory vegetarian options—cater to every culinary preference.

Quiet and tasteful, The Spinnaker Banquet Facility is an inviting waterfront venue that makes the most of its picturesque surroundings.

CEREMONY & EVENT/RECEPTION CAPACITY: The deck holds 75 seated or 90 standing guests, the banquet room 160 seated or 220 standing.

MEETING CAPACITY: The Banquet Room seats 200 theater-style or 160 conference-style.

FEES & DEPOSITS: To reserve your date, a nonrefundable $1,500 deposit is required (which is applied towards the event balance). The food & beverage balance is payable at the event's completion. The food & beverage minimum is $2,000 Monday–Thursday daytime; $3,000 Monday–Thursday evening; $4,500 Friday, Saturday and Sunday daytime; $5,000 Friday & Sunday evening; and $9,000 Saturday evening. In-house catering is provided. Buffets or seated meals run $55–65/person; alcohol, tax and a 19% service charge are additional. A $1,400 room charge, $200 bartending fee and $250 dance floor fee may apply. For ceremonies, there's a $450 setup charge.

For business luncheons and dinners, or for smaller groups, special rates can be arranged.

AVAILABILITY: Year-round, daily, 7am–midnight, in 4-hour blocks.

SERVICES/AMENITIES:

Catering: in-house, no BYO
Kitchen Facilities: n/a
Tables & Chairs: provided
Linens, Silver, etc.: provided
Restrooms: wheelchair accessible
Dance Floor: CBA, extra fee
Bride's Dressing Area: no
AV/Meeting Equipment: PA, microphones

Parking: valet parking
Accommodations: no guest rooms
Outdoor Night Lighting: on deck
Outdoor Cooking Facilities: no
Cleanup: provided
View: San Francisco Bay and bridges
Other: event coordination, cakes, music CBA

RESTRICTIONS:

Alcohol: in-house or corkage $15–17/bottle
Smoking: designated areas
Music: amplified OK

Wheelchair Access: yes
Insurance: not required

Stinson Beach Community Center

Community Center & Chapel

32 Belvedere Avenue, Stinson Beach
415/868-1444
www.stinsonbeachcommunitycenter.org
info@stinsonbeachcommunitycenter.org

- Rehearsal Dinners
- Ceremonies
- Wedding Receptions
- Corp. Events/Mtgs.
- Private Parties
- Accommodations

Stinson Beach is one of the Bay Area's natural treasures. This curving stretch of white sand extends three miles along Marin County's Pacific coastline and has a visual advantage many other beaches lack: To reach it, you drive down a scenic mountain road whose views are often as dramatic as those along the French Riviera. But even better than Stinson Beach's gratifying appearance is the little town that has grown up beside it: a quiet seaside community whose very existence is a restorative balm to almost any visitor's hectic life.

This is a beautiful place for a wedding, and the best place to celebrate is at the Stinson Beach Community Center, a building that's been at the heart of Stinson Beach's civic life for decades. Located just off Shoreline Highway, up from the fire station and next door to Stinson Beach Community Church, the center looks like a small lodge. The exterior is finished with brown wood siding with white trim. Wood predominates inside, too: Three impressive trusses under a ceiling of pine rafters span the center's large sunny interior, the walls have four-foot-high wainscoting, and the floors are Canadian maple hardwood. Delightful murals of sunlit clouds are painted on the east and west walls, adding a whimsical touch. Across the room from the entrance, the center's focal point is a tall light-brick fireplace capped with a huge log mantel. On either side of it are large wood-trimmed windows and French doors.

The French doors open out to a patio enveloped by nature. A flower- and bush-lined fence runs along one side, separating it from a gurgling creek edged with fragrant cedars, mulberry trees and pines. While flowerbeds and potted plants adorn the patio, its most compelling visual attribute is a magnificent maple tree whose trunk has grown out horizontally. The trunk—easily 2.5 feet in diameter—runs parallel to the ground for about 20 feet, finally coming to rest on the pavement, where it extends three long branches 30 feet up into the air. It's an impressive conversation piece, to say the least.

Some couples marry on nearby Stinson Beach, while others opt for a ceremony in the church next to the center. The church's bright interior of light fir walls and pews soars to pointed arches, and the altar is backed by floor-to-ceiling glass. A mezzanine accommodates an organ and a choir. The church has an intimate feel inside and a small-town look outside, with its wooden siding and steeply angled roof culminating in a little belfry.

Stinson Beach has a best-of-both-worlds air about it. Although it's only a 45-minute drive from San Francisco, it's just far enough removed to possess an enticing away-from-it-all quality. And, it may be just the place to have a memorable, uncomplicated wedding day.

To contact Stinson Beach Community Center by mail, the address is PO Box 158, Stinson Beach, CA 94970.

CEREMONY CAPACITY: The Community Center holds 150–200 seated guests with room for 299 standing. The Chapel holds 115 seated guests and up to 130 including standing guests.

EVENT/RECEPTION & MEETING CAPACITY: The Community Center holds 200 seated or 299 standing. Tenting can be arranged to increase capacity.

FEES & DEPOSITS: For special events, a $500 security deposit is required to secure your date. The rental fee ranges $2,600–3,000 and includes a block of time from 8am to midnight plus full use of the industrial kitchen, basic cleaning, and an event monitor. The Chapel rents for $500/day and includes a rehearsal the day prior to the ceremony.

Please call for affordable meeting rates.

AVAILABILITY: Year-round, daily, 8am–midnight.

SERVICES/AMENITIES:
Catering: BYO or CBA
Tables & Chairs: provided, call for details
Kitchen Facilities: new, fully equipped
Linens, Silver, etc.: BYO
Restrooms: wheelchair accessible
Dance Floor: hardwood floor indoors
Bride's Dressing Area: yes
AV/Meeting Equipment: sound system (plug in with headphone jack)

Parking: Center's parking area and on-street
Accommodations: nearby hotels and beach house rentals
Outdoor Night Lighting: on porch and patio
Outdoor Cooking Facilities: CBA
Cleanup: caterer, basic cleanup provided
View: Stinson Beach hills, part of Mt. Tamalpais
Other: grand piano, organ

RESTRICTIONS:
Alcohol: BYO
Smoking: outside only
Music: amplified OK until 11pm, call for details

Wheelchair Access: yes
Insurance: certificate required

Corinthian Yacht Club

Historic Yacht Club

43 Main Street, Tiburon
415/435-4812 x12
www.corinthiancatering.com
alicia@cyc.org

● Rehearsal Dinners	● Corp. Events/Mtgs.
● Ceremonies	● Private Parties
● Wedding Receptions	Accommodations

The setting of the Corinthian Yacht Club is truly spectacular. Even its members, who've been coming here for years, never fail to be awed by its sweeping view. It's easily one of the great panoramas in all of California, taking in Tiburon's rustic downtown, the deep waters of Raccoon Strait, Angel Island's wooded profile, the silvery Bay Bridge, the high hills and towers of San Francisco, Alcatraz' ship-like silhouette, and Belvedere Island's leafy slopes and grand mansions. Only steps away, in the club's harbor, spars and spinnakers bob everywhere and there's a steady flow of craft setting out to ply the bay or return home from it.

This beloved Marin landmark—a Colonial Revival building with a shimmering white façade and soaring 40-foot columns—could be tempted to let its prime waterfront address do all the work. But the club has never rested on its scenic laurels. "Location, location and location" is matched with a high level of service, thanks to a cadre of employees who have worked here for years. Their experience shows in their uncanny ability to anticipate guests' needs, providing little touches that may not be much in the larger scheme of things, but are remembered over the years by grateful clients: glasses that get refilled without prompting or perhaps a server conjuring up a special platter of hors d' oeuvres for the bride and groom when they've arrived late to their cocktail hour.

The club welcomes private events hosted by members and non-members alike. Bridal parties can take over the entire second story, an ensemble of four distinctive spaces that flow together beautifully. People love to circulate here, knowing that each area they stroll to presents its own visual reward. Start with the Grand Ballroom, a redwood-paneled room with a 22-foot-high ceiling, large stage for musicians, imposing stone fireplace, and an oak floor that's ready for dancing no matter how you configure the dining tables. The adjoining Sun Porch, which runs along one side of the ballroom, affords unobstructed views of the main dining area as well as a dramatic bay vista through giant picture windows. With such an impressive backdrop, the Sun Porch is also a favorite site for the cake cutting. It accesses an outdoor deck that not only presents a fine harbor and breakwater view, but can function as a bar or reception space, too. Both the deck and Grand Ballroom have doorways to a separate cocktail area with a granite-topped bar and a collection of nautical-motif plaques, pendants and photos that create an enjoyable yacht-club feel.

The Corinthian Yacht Club is a unique Bay Area venue where you don't have to choose between the site and the service—your guests will take away wonderful memories of both.

CEREMONY CAPACITY: The enclosed Sun Porch accommodates 90 seated with additional room for 10 standing guests. A Ballroom ceremony is available with a room flip for an additional charge with a maximum of 150 seated.

EVENT/RECEPTION CAPACITY: The Grand Ballroom seats 200 guests with a small dance floor or 250 without a dance floor, with room for an additional 50 seated on the adjoining enclosed Sun Porch.

MEETING CAPACITY: The Grand Ballroom can seat 250 guests theater-style, and 150 classroom-style.

FEES & DEPOSITS: A $3,500 deposit is required at the time of booking and is applied towards the total event cost. The facility rental fee ranges $2,000–6,000, depending on the guest count and the date of the event. There is a guest minimum for all events, which ranges 100–150 depending on the event date. The fee covers a 5-hour block for the event plus additional time for setup and breakdown; extra event hours are $600/hour. Setup and cleanup fees are $250 and there's a security fee of $250. A payment of 80% of the estimated total is due 6 weeks prior to the event date with the remaining balance due the week following the event, after the final beverage bill has been tallied.

Catering is provided exclusively in-house; menu prices start at $65/person plus a 20% service charge and tax. On average, bar prices start at $30/person based on consumption, including service and tax.

AVAILABILITY: The Ballroom is available daily 9am–11pm.

SERVICES/AMENITIES:
Catering: in-house, no BYO
Kitchen Facilities: n/a
Tables & Chairs: provided
Linens, Silver, etc.: china, silverware, glassware provided; linens available for an extra charge
Restrooms: wheelchair accessible
Dance Floor: yes
AV/Meeting Equipment: projector and screen, podium, sound system, wireless microphone

Parking: public lot nearby, no non-member parking on site
Accommodations: no guest rooms
Outdoor Night Lighting: yes
Outdoor Cooking Facilities: yes
Cleanup: provided
View: San Francisco Bay and skyline, Angel Island, Alcatraz, and Bay Bridge

RESTRICTIONS:
Alcohol: in-house, or BYO wine and champagne with an $18/bottle corkage fee
Smoking: outside on decks only
Music: amplified OK with volume restrictions

Wheelchair Access: yes, all levels
Insurance: not required
Other: security required

North Coast

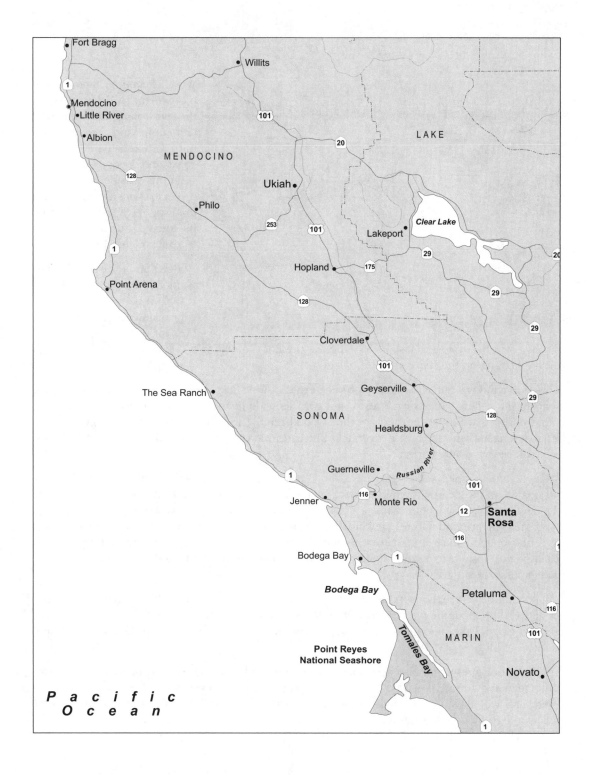

Fort Bragg

Willits

1

Mendocino
Little River

Albion

MENDOCINO

101

20

LAKE

128

Ukiah

Philo

253

101

Lakeport

Clear Lake

29

Hopland

175

29

128

29

Cloverdale

101

Geyserville

29

SONOMA

Healdsburg

128

Guerneville

Russian River

101

Jenner

116

Monte Rio

12

Santa
Rosa

1

116

Bodega Bay

1

Bodega Bay

Petaluma

116

MARIN

101

Point Reyes
National Seashore

Tomales Bay

Novato

P a c i f i c
O c e a n

1

Bodega Harbour Yacht Club

Yacht Club

565 Smith Brothers Road, Bodega Bay
707/875-3519 X400

www.bodegayachtclub.com
avineyard@kempersports.com

- Rehearsal Dinners
- Ceremonies
- Wedding Receptions
- Corp. Events/Mtgs.
- Private Parties
- Accommodations

West of Petaluma, there's a scenic two-lane road that takes you through rolling hills and past dairy farms and sheep ranches until you reach the Sonoma coast and Bodega Bay. This beautiful seaside outpost has a relaxed, small-town charm that's perfectly epitomized by its local landmark, Bodega Harbour Yacht Club.

Housed in a historic cedar-plank building, the Yacht Club is tucked between a copse of cypress trees and the bay. The building rests on sturdy pilings directly over the water, so visitors looking out the floor-to-ceiling windows often feel as though they're floating on the sea.

These tall windows frame the yacht club's centerpiece stone fireplace, whose bold fieldstone façade soars to the ceiling. Guests can't resist sitting on its wide hearth to chat and enjoy refreshments, either during a welcome reception or the cocktail hour. The entire space, including the supporting columns and crossbeams, is strikingly finished in knotty cedar, and the overall effect is one of rustic elegance and warmth.

Though some couples exchange vows at St. Teresa's church (immortalized by photographer Ansel Adams) in the nearby town of Bodega, many choose to wed next to the fireplace in front of the bayfront windows, often while a glorious sunset paints the horizon. For those who want to combine romance and nature, the club also offers ceremonies right on the beach. In fact, this is the only venue in all of Sonoma County with its own beach ceremony site! For the reception, the party moves upstairs to a wood-lined mezzanine-style room overlooking the first floor's dramatic glass-and-stone surfaces.

An exciting new reception option is the adjacent Waterfront Pavilion, which hosts large parties of up to 300 right at the water's edge. With the sound of the waves lapping just a few feet away, and the glow of the moonlight on the bay visible through the clear side panels, the atmosphere is quite alluring.

You and your guests will also appreciate the professional catering services, including a customized menu and cuisine prepared by the chef of the club's own Bluewater Bistro. The experienced event staff will assist you throughout the planning process, and know how to make the most of this wonderfully unique location.

Few places like Bodega Harbour Yacht Club exist on the waterfront between San Francisco and Mendocino. Its architectural beauty, bayside location and scenic harbor views make it a natural for couples seeking a tranquil, yet inspirational, setting.

CEREMONY CAPACITY: The facility can accommodate 80 seated indoors and 300 seated outdoors.

EVENT/RECEPTION CAPACITY: The club holds 140 seated or 175 standing guests. Outdoors, the Waterfront Pavilion seats 300 guests.

MEETING CAPACITY: Meeting spaces accommodate up to 100 seated guests.

FEES & DEPOSITS: A deposit in the amount of $1,000 is required at the time of reservation. 50% of the estimated total is due within 90 days of the event, 90% is due within 7 days, and the remaining balance is due on the day of the event. These payments are nonrefundable. For a reception only, the club rental fee is $2,500 for a 5-hour period. For a reception and ceremony, the fee is $3,500 (5 hours plus ceremony time). Buffets range $44–60/person; alcohol, tax and a 20% service charge are additional.

AVAILABILITY: Year-round, daily including holidays, 8am–midnight.

SERVICES/AMENITIES:

Catering: in-house, no BYO

Kitchen Facilities: n/a

Tables & Chairs: provided

Linens, Silver, etc.: provided

Restrooms: wheelchair accessible

Dance Floor: hardwood floor lower level

Bride's Dressing Area: no

AV/Meeting Equipment: PA, podium, screen

Parking: on-street and complimentary lot

Accommodations: no guest rooms, hotels nearby

Outdoor Night Lighting: yes

Outdoor Cooking Facilities: no

Cleanup: provided

View: Bodega Bay and marina

Other: some coordination

RESTRICTIONS:

Alcohol: in-house, or BYO wine and champagne corkage $20/bottle

Smoking: outside only

Music: amplified OK indoors until 11pm

Wheelchair Access: yes

Insurance: certificate required

Secret Gardens

Private Garden

Corner East Shore & Bay Flat Roads, Bodega Bay

406/581-4814

www.bodegabaysecretgardens.com
bodegabaysecretgardens@gmail.com

- Rehearsal Dinners
- Ceremonies
- Wedding Receptions
- Corp. Events/Mtgs.
- Private Parties
- Accommodations

When we passed through the Secret Gardens' humble iron gate, we felt as if we had encountered Narnia—the magical, otherworldly kingdom that C.S. Lewis wrote of in his famed children's books. Entering the gardens, you're immersed in a world of unbridled beauty. In every direction the eye is delighted: here the abundant blooms of rhododendrons, irises and camellias; over there delicate Japanese maples, cherry trees and towering redwoods. A year-round running brook unspools the length of the gardens, pausing now and again to calm itself in one of several lovely ponds. It took 10 years to wrangle this magnificent garden from a tenacious coastal jungle, but the effort was worth it: today it's truly an idyllic place to hold a celebration.

A variety of scenic spots are available to tie the knot, but most couples prefer to marry on a gorgeous redwood deck with an attached redwood Ceremonial Arch. After the ceremony, folks can lose themselves along the gardens' meandering paths before joining the feasting and festivities at the handsome pavilion at the far side of the gardens.

Although the Secret Gardens is ideal for outdoor weddings, it's also excellent for any number of events—seminars, retreats, bar mitzvahs and anniversaries. Overnight accommodations are easily arranged with both luxury hotels and more modest accommodations available nearby.

The Secret Gardens, a place whose extraordinary beauty has made it anything but secret, has been featured in HGTV, A&E, Town and Country Magazine, radio and other media! So if your heart is set on a garden party, call sooner rather than later—this is a venue that books up quickly!

CEREMONY & EVENT/RECEPTION CAPACITY: The Ceremony Area holds 150 seated guests and the Pavilion up to 150 seated.

MEETING CAPACITY: Meetings spaces accommodate up to 150 guests.

FEES & DEPOSITS: 50% of the rental fee is required to reserve your date, and the balance plus a $950 security deposit are due 1 month prior to the event. Engagement photos and a 1-hour rehearsal are included. The weekend rental fee starts at $5,900; call for midweek rates. Extra hours are available.

AVAILABILITY: Daily, mid-April through mid-November.

SERVICES/AMENITIES:

Catering: select from preferred list, or BYO
Kitchen Facilities: yes, limited outdoor
Tables & Chairs: provided, extra fee
Linens, Silver, etc.: through caterer
Restrooms: wheelchair accessible
Dance Floor: 2 large dance areas
Bride's & Groom's Dressing Areas: yes
AV/Meeting Equipment: BYO
Other: complimentary sound system for the ceremony area

Parking: ample on-street and in private lot, local shuttle service recommended
Accommodations: nearby hotels and rental homes
Outdoor Night Lighting: yes
Outdoor Cooking Facilities: yes, area available
Cleanup: caterer or renter
View: gardens, pond, creek and redwoods

RESTRICTIONS:

Alcohol: BYO, insurance required, no corkage fees
Smoking: designated area only
Music: amplified OK until 10pm

Wheelchair Access: yes
Insurance: certificate required

Sea Ranch Lodge

Restaurant & Lodge

60 Sea Walk Drive, The Sea Ranch
800/732-7262 or 707/785-2371
www.searanchlodge.com
weddings@searanchlodge.com

● Rehearsal Dinners	● Corp. Events/Mtgs.
● Ceremonies	● Private Parties
● Wedding Receptions	● Accommodations

In the early morning, a light mist veils the coast. Weathered redwood buildings float into view, hugged by deep green stands of cypress trees. Far below, the sea crashes against the rocks, and the rugged, serpentine coastline fades away into the fog. You blink, half expecting that when you open your eyes it will all disappear. But it doesn't. And you begin to understand why so many people consider The Sea Ranch a magical place.

Perched high on a bluff, the Sea Ranch Lodge is part of a small community of individualists who cherish the soothing solitude of this North Coast haven. And for those who don't have the luxury of living here permanently, the lodge provides a temporary getaway. It's also a coveted location for a wedding.

Getting married outdoors here is an exhilarating experience. The short path down from the lodge that brings you to the two ceremony sites cuts through a meadow of golden grass bordered by wildflowers in purple, yellow and white. As you walk, you hear the surf pounding and smell the ocean's scent in the air. Bihler Point is a breathtaking, secluded spot on the bluffs with a panoramic view of the ocean. However, there's only standing room for 25 people; no chairs or other furniture are permitted. Most ceremonies take place on nearby Black Point Lawn, where you can tie the knot followed by cocktails next to a charmingly rustic 1890s barn that overlooks the shoreline extending for miles in both directions. For a spiritual touch at either site, have a bagpiper or flutist play a special melody.

If you'd rather have your celebration inside the lodge, the facility has two interconnecting spaces, each with redwood walls and ocean views. The two-level Fireside Room is perfect for a cozy reception, elopement, renewal of vows or rehearsal dinner. A large river rock fireplace dominates one wall, while art from the Spindrift Gallery is showcased on another. A huge picture window and a skylight let in natural light. The adjacent Solarium is an intimate atrium used for cocktails, hors d'oeuvres and mingling. Completely enclosed by glass, it affords a floor-to-ceiling view of the meadows, ocean and sky.

Larger receptions are held in a festive party tent, which is set up near the guest rooms. Bordered by a high, weathered fence and fronted by greenery, it feels quite private. The spacious pole tent, included in one of Sea Ranch Lodge's wedding packages, comes with a dance floor, oak bar, flooring, heat, sound, and more. Twinkling perimeter lights add sparkle at night, and you can customize the décor, too, with paper lanterns, crystal chandeliers, long farm tables, or whatever suits the style of your event.

The beauty of The Sea Ranch, aside from its abundant natural attributes, is that you and your guests can stay here long enough to really relax and enjoy it. Recently renovated with stylish contemporary appointments, guest rooms are uncluttered and comfortable; all have ocean views and most have fireplaces (but, to preserve the tranquility, none have televisions). Diversions include exploring the many beaches, hiking along miles of trails, and playing golf on The Sea Ranch's links-style course. Black Point Grill serves all meals, which feature internationally inspired California cuisine with an emphasis on the freshest local ingredients.

Not getting married? Don't let that stop you from coming to the Sea Ranch Lodge. The setting is just as uplifting for a romantic weekend, corporate retreat, or family reunion. Let's face it, when the earth was created, some places ended up much more enchanting than others. This is one of them.

CEREMONY CAPACITY: The outdoor oceanfront ceremony site accommodates 2–130 guests. Indoors, the Fireside Room seats up to 50, which makes it perfect for a small wedding, commitment ceremony, elopement or renewal of vows.

EVENT/RECEPTION CAPACITY: The Fireside Room holds 60 seated, and tented space can hold 61–130 seated guests.

MEETING CAPACITY: The Fireside Room seats 50 theater-style, or 33 conference- or classroom-style.

FEES & DEPOSITS: A nonrefundable deposit of the site fee is required to secure your date. The site fees start at $750 and varies depending on the type of event and guest count. Wedding dinner packages start at $130/person. There is also an all-inclusive elopement package for 2–15 people that ranges $3,550–5,550 depending on the number of guests. Selected dog-friendly rooms are available; there is a one-time charge of $50/pet with a limit of 2 pets per room.

AVAILABILITY: Year-round, daily, anytime.

SERVICES/AMENITIES:

Catering: in-house
Kitchen Facilities: n/a
Tables & Chairs: provided
Linens, Silver, etc.: provided
Restrooms: wheelchair accessible
Dance Floor: included in tent package
Bride's & Groom's Dressing Areas: CBA
AV/Meeting Equipment: wireless internet access, projectors

Parking: ample
Accommodations: 19 guest rooms
Outdoor Night Lighting: access only
Outdoor Cooking Facilities: n/a
Cleanup: provided
View: Pacific Ocean, coastline, meadows, cypress trees
Other: event coordination, spa treatments in private treatment rooms, recreational activity planning and more; call for details

RESTRICTIONS:

Alcohol: in-house, or BYO with corkage fee
Smoking: not permitted
Music: amplified OK with restrictions

Wheelchair Access: yes
Insurance: CBA

Peninsula

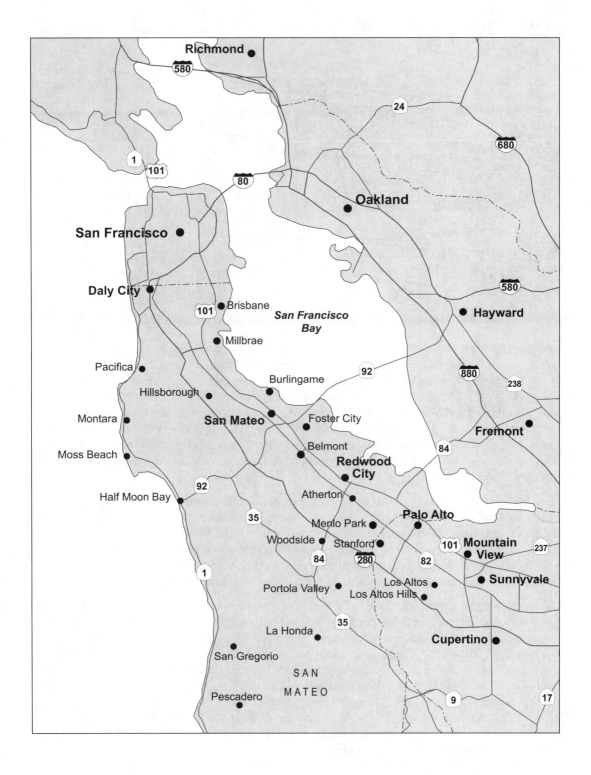

Mission Blue Center

Community Center

475 Mission Blue Drive, Brisbane
415/508-2140

www.brisbaneca.org/living/community-center
tvaccaro@ci.brisbane.ca.us

● Rehearsal Dinners	● Corp. Events/Mtgs.
● Ceremonies	● Private Parties
● Wedding Receptions	○ Accommodations

Brisbane is like the librarian in romantic comedies whose beauty—until the doofus leading man finally figures out to take off her glasses and undo her hair—remains unseen. It's hidden away in a nook of Mt. San Bruno and isolated by wetlands from the tens of thousands of commuters who pass by it daily on Highway 101.

But those who leave the freeway and do some exploring will find an unspoiled little town that climbs up its hill like an Italian fishing village. Brisbane has its share of wealth, but it has yet to be yuppified or see its main street turned into a stretch of chain stores. You sense right away that this is a tight-knit place that knows it has a good thing going. Part of that good thing is Mission Blue, the community center the town built in 2000. It has everything a building of its type should have, including appealing architecture, a great hillside location with a fine view, and the ability to seamlessly accommodate a wedding and reception. There's a poetic touch, too: Mission Blue is named after a rare butterfly whose preservation inspired the saving of open space on Mt. San Bruno, the imposing palomino-colored ridge that dominates the view from the center's terrace.

Mission Blue's main entrance takes you to a soaring glass-walled foyer that's often used for a post-ceremony champagne reception. It opens into the spacious room at the center's heart, cleverly designed with visual cues that separate it into two distinct areas. The first half of the room, with its hardwood floor and light-colored walls, is perfect for an indoor ceremony or dancing. The second half, carpeted and tiled, and painted a slightly darker color, is ideal for dining. The two areas can be partitioned or used in combination, and are easily accessed from the nearby full-service kitchen.

Glass doors lead from the interior to a beautifully fashioned, stone-finished terrace that runs the length of Mission Blue's west and north sides. It sweeps out from the building toward a well-kept lawn that many couples have used to recite their vows. Standing on the terrace, you can look across a valley to Mt. San Bruno, and south to a view of Brisbane's little houses clambering up the hill. There are fine design touches everywhere, including a wooden pergola at one end of the lawn and a colonnade along the terrace whose eye-catching beams and supports call to mind the sophisticated carpentry of a Chinese temple. Planters and flowerbeds abound, and the simple black railing that stands between the lawn and the hillside is sculptural in form. Even Mission Blue's exterior colors have a sensual appeal—the olive green, creamy white and light chocolate tones give it an almost luscious appearance.

This site's architects certainly understood how to create a welcoming place: Mission Blue is a harmonious interplay between space and light, colors and materials, indoors and outdoors. But when you have your celebration here, you won't be thinking about how all the elements work so well together—you'll just be having a great time.

CEREMONY CAPACITY: Mission Blue Center seats up to 200.

EVENT/RECEPTION & MEETING CAPACITY: The Center holds 200 seated at tables or 300 seated theater-style. The large room can be broken into smaller spaces.

FEES & DEPOSITS: A refundable $500 cleaning deposit is required to reserve your date; the balance is due 21 days prior to the event. The rental fee is $410/hour; discounts are available for Brisbane residents and for partial-hall rentals.

AVAILABILITY: Year-round, daily, 8am–midnight.

SERVICES/AMENITIES:

Catering: BYO
Kitchen Facilities: full kitchen
Tables & Chairs: provided
Linens, Silver, etc.: BYO
Restrooms: wheelchair accessible
Dance Floor: yes
Bride's Dressing Area: CBA
AV/Meeting Equipment: wall-mounted projection screen, LCD projector, PA system, CD/DVD player, stage

Parking: 40-space lot and on-street
Accommodations: no guest rooms
Outdoor Night Lighting: access only
Outdoor Cooking Facilities: no
Cleanup: renter
View: Mt. San Bruno and bay

RESTRICTIONS:

Alcohol: BYO
Smoking: outdoors only
Music: amplified OK

Wheelchair Access: yes
Insurance: liability required
Other: no wall decorations

Fairview Crystal Springs

Golf Club

6650 Golf Course Drive, Burlingame
650/546-6170
www.fairviewevents.com/crystal-springs
crystalsprings@fairviewevents.com

- Rehearsal Dinners
- Ceremonies
- Wedding Receptions
- Corp. Events/Mtgs.
- Private Parties
- Accommodations

One of the most picturesque wedding sites in the Bay Area has something very few people ever have the privilege of seeing: a bird's-eye view of the protected land around Crystal Springs Reservoir. Access to this jewel of a lake and the heavily wooded semi-wilderness that encircles it is limited to forest rangers and city officials.

But if you wed outdoors at Fairview Crystal Springs, you are among the rare outsiders who get to enjoy this breathtaking vista—and with it comes much more than simple bragging rights. The ceremony site, a sprawling meadow at the southern end of the Crystal Springs Golf Course, has a gazebo that stands on a grassy knoll overlooking the reservoir. The view from here is sensational, with glistening waters below and tree-covered ridges behind it. In the distance, high hills slope toward the bay. There are no houses in sight, and deer often graze nearby. The backdrop is so spectacular that the gazebo needs little adornment. There's plenty of room for a limo to drop off the bride, and if she wants to add a little more pizzazz to the moment, she can even arrive in a horse-drawn carriage. A smooth earthen aisle cuts through a beautifully tended lawn to the gazebo, where the couple exchanges vows.

The reception takes place up a tree- and greens-lined road at the banquet center, set at the edge of gentle terraces that drop off toward the reservoir. Guests arrive via a red-carpeted terrace that captures a sweeping panorama down to the fairways. Best of all is spotting the deer that placidly graze the course.

The primary dining spot is the Vista Room. Its entire west wall is windows, and glass doors open to the adjoining Vista Deck, a large glassed-in area shaded by a canopy that makes a sublime setting for an outdoor cocktail hour. Whether you're celebrating inside or out, the expansive view takes in the woods to the west and the neighboring hills and the golf course's gorgeous landscape to the north.

Fairview Crystal Springs offers a range of all-inclusive packages that put the venue with a million-dollar view within reach of the average couple. Plus the flexible packages make planning your event here a breeze, since you can customize the options to suit both your budget and your vision.

The elements for a fabulous day are here in splendid array: the gazebo in its unforgettable surroundings; a personable, attentive staff; good food; fresh, sea-kissed air (the ocean is only a few ridges away); and nature's intense blues and greens. Lastly, nearby Highway 280 makes Crystal Springs easily accessible from San Francisco, the Peninsula and the South Bay. Now, that's a list that should satisfy anyone.

CEREMONY CAPACITY: The venue accommodates up to 300 guests indoors or outdoors.

EVENT/RECEPTION CAPACITY: Indoors, the Vista Room holds 300 seated or standing guests.

MEETING CAPACITY: Event spaces accommodate 50–300 seated guests.

FEES & DEPOSITS: 25% of the estimated total event cost is required to reserve your date. An additional 25% is due 120 days prior to the event and the balance (based on your final guest count) is due 10 days prior. All payments are credited towards your final balance and are nonrefundable and nontransferable. The ceremony fee starts at $599, and completely customizable wedding packages start at $43/person,. These include invitations, DJ, dinner and more. For most packages, a champagne toast and wine with dinner are included and a hosted bar is extra. Tax and a 22% service charge are additional.

AVAILABILITY: Year-round, anytime.

SERVICES/AMENITIES:

Catering: in-house
Kitchen Facilities: n/a
Tables & Chairs: provided
Linens, Silver, etc.: provided
Restrooms: wheelchair accessible
Dance Floor: yes
Brides Dressing Area: yes
AV/Meeting Equipment: some provided

Parking: large lot
Accommodations: no guest rooms
Outdoor Night Lighting: yes
Outdoor Cooking Facilities: no
Cleanup: provided
View: fairways, lake, meadows, mountains
Other: event coordination, in-house wedding cake and florals, clergy on staff

RESTRICTIONS:

Alcohol: in-house
Smoking: outside only
Music: amplified OK with some restrictions

Wheelchair Access: yes
Insurance: not required
Other: no rice, confetti or glitter; no open flames

Want to find more venues and services? Check out our informative website, www.HereComesTheGuide.com.

169

Hyatt Regency San Francisco Airport

Hotel

1333 Bayshore Highway, Burlingame
650/696-3025

sanfranciscoairport.hyatt.com
thomas.toomey@hyatt.com

● Rehearsal Dinners ● Corp. Events/Mtgs.
● Ceremonies ● Private Parties
● Wedding Receptions ● Accommodations

Less than half an hour from San Francisco and minutes from the airport, this first-class hotel has recently undergone a spectacular, multimillion-dollar transformation. It's now more popular than ever for high-profile conventions and corporate functions, and brides in search of convenience and lots of options will find the red carpet is rolled out for weddings, too.

First impressions really count, and the Hyatt Regency in Burlingame wows you at the entrance with its soaring Atrium. Rising skyward more than nine stories, this architecturally intriguing space has all of its event and casual seating areas harmoniously arranged on a raised level in the center. Here, guests can relax and mingle in the cabanas or Sky Lounge, and check out the new 3SIXTY Bar, Bistro and Market while enjoying a 360-degree view of the entire Atrium, which is filled with natural light from the vast, skylight "ceiling" 110 feet above. A refreshing change from the typical hotel lobby, the Atrium is not only a great place to people-watch, it's also a unique spot for a cocktail reception.

If you're the kind of person who has as many friends in real life as you do on Facebook and you'd like to invite all of them to share your special day, then the Grand Peninsula Ballroom is for you. Start with cocktails and hors d'oeuvres in the open, airy Grand Foyer. At the appointed hour, four sets of double doors will be opened to reveal the recently updated ballroom. Cool and contemporary, with fabric-covered walls, a coffered ceiling, and a warm gray color scheme, it provides a sophisticated backdrop that will complement any occasion. Amazing "chandeliers" made of undulating glass, that look like works of art and change color at the touch of a button, are just part of the state-of-the-art sound and lighting system. You can add uplighting for an even more dramatic effect. If you'd like to get married at the hotel, part of the ballroom's 18,000 square feet may be sectioned off for a lovely ceremony site, complete with its own entrance.

Tucked away in another section of the lobby level is the Regency Ballroom and its adjoining foyer. Sleekly modern in design, it also features neutral décor and its own striking, color-controlled chandeliers.

For a celebration setting that's a bit less conventional, there's the tented Poolside Pavilion. Completely climate controlled, this "bride's favorite" is fronted by a graceful, wisteria-covered arbor and looks out to the shimmering pool.

The new Cypress and Sequoia rooms off the Atrium level provide additional options for events. Both spaces benefit from large windows that let in plenty of light, and if you're hosting cocktails in the Atrium, it's a smooth transition into the adjoining Sequoia Room for dinner and dancing.

The Hyatt offers a range of packages, and their catering team is happy to custom-tailor a menu for your event, as well as accommodate cultural or ethnic needs. Plus, if you take advantage of their flexible Personal Preference Dining option, your friends and family will be able to select their favorite entrée from among four choices. In addition to having a great time at your wedding, your out-of-town guests will appreciate all the hotel's amenities, including a fully renovated and expanded fitness center and pool, as well as 3SIXTY Bistro, Bar and Market, and free trolleys to area attractions.

CEREMONY CAPACITY: The hotel holds up to 2,500 seated guests indoors.

EVENT/RECEPTION & MEETING CAPACITY: The facility can accommodate 1,500 seated or 1,800 standing guests indoors and 250 standing outdoors.

FEES & DEPOSITS: 25% of the total event cost is required to secure your date and the balance is due 15 days prior to the event. The rental fee ranges $500–2,500 depending on the space reserved. Meals range $56–86/person. Tax, alcohol and a 24% service charge are additional.

AVAILABILITY: Year-round, daily, 6am–2am.

SERVICES/AMENITIES:

Catering: in-house
Kitchen Facilities: n/a
Tables & Chairs: provided
Linens, Silver, etc.: provided
Restrooms: wheelchair accessible
Dance Floor: provided
Bride's Dressing Area: CBA
AV/Meeting Equipment: provided

Parking: large lots
Accommodations: 789 guest rooms
Outdoor Night Lighting: CBA
Outdoor Cooking Facilities: no
Cleanup: provided
View: garden, landscaped grounds, pool area
Other: event coordination

RESTRICTIONS:

Alcohol: in-house, no BYO
Smoking: outside only
Music: amplified OK

Wheelchair Access: yes
Insurance: not required

Kohl Mansion, "The Oaks"

2750 Adeline Drive, Burlingame
650/762-1134 or 650/762-1137

www.kohl-mansion.com
ddevin@mercyhsb.com
tbaldocchi@mercyhsb.com

Historic Mansion & Grounds

● Rehearsal Dinners		● Corp. Events/Mtgs.	
● Ceremonies		● Private Parties	
● Wedding Receptions		Accommodations	

Commissioned by Frederick Kohl and his wife in 1912, the Kohl Mansion was built on 40 acres of oak woodlands in Burlingame. Kohl, heir to a shipping fortune, loved to entertain and created this grand estate to include a manor house, pool, rose garden, tennis courts, greenhouses, and a large carriage house. Now, decades later, the elegant rosebrick Tudor mansion is again available for parties, and has many inviting rooms for weddings, special events, business functions and picnics.

The wood-paneled Library features a large marble fireplace, bookcases and graceful French doors that open to a center courtyard. The room's Gothic bay window catches the light filtered through the oaks on the lawn just beyond. The sizable Great Hall, a copy of the Arlington Tudor Hall in Essex, England, was built for music and entertaining. Its very high ceiling, oak paneling and walnut floor create a fine acoustical setting for music. A lighter twin of the Library, the spacious and airy pale green Dining Room has delicate, pristine-white plaster relief on the walls and ceiling. This marvelous dining environment shares the Library's view of the oak-studded lawn through its own bay windows.

The Morning Room, with white lattice walls and a black-and-white marble floor, adds a touch of formality to the East Wing. It overlooks the English Rose Garden and surrounding manicured grounds, where guests can stroll over the lawn or sample hors d'oeuvres on the large terrace. The Kohl Mansion is, indeed, a fabulous facility for anyone planning a stylish event.

CEREMONY & EVENT/RECEPTION CAPACITY: Various rooms in the mansion hold 50–200 seated and 75–300 standing guests. The patio and lawn areas each accommodate 300 seated or standing.

MEETING CAPACITY: Event spaces accommodate 50–200 seated guests.

FEES & DEPOSITS: To reserve your date, half the rental fee is due at the time of booking; the remainder is due 90 days prior to the event. The rental fee ranges $7,000–14,250 depending on the guest count and date of event. It covers an 8-hour minimum and includes a $500 refundable security deposit and a $500 setup fee.

AVAILABILITY: From mid-August through June, parties and special events are held after 3pm on weekdays, and anytime on Saturday and Sunday. July through mid-August, every day, anytime. Meetings can be held year-round, time frames subject to availability.

SERVICES/AMENITIES:

Catering: select from preferred list
Kitchen Facilities: full
Tables & Chairs: provided
Linens, Silver, etc.: BYO
Restrooms: wheelchair accessible
Dance Floor: provided
Bride's Dressing Area: yes
AV/Meeting Equipment: podium, stage

Parking: large lots, valet required for over 200 guests
Accommodations: no guest rooms
Outdoor Night Lighting: no
Outdoor Cooking Facilities: BYO
Cleanup: caterer
View: San Francisco Bay and coastal hills
Other: baby grand piano, swimming pool, tennis courts, children's room, coatcheck room

RESTRICTIONS:

Alcohol: BYO, licensed bartender required
Smoking: outside only
Music: amplified OK indoors, acoustic only outdoors; time restrictions vary depending on the day of the week; sound check required hourly

Wheelchair Access: yes
Insurance: certificate required or CBA for a small fee

Crowne Plaza Foster City-San Mateo

Hotel

1221 Chess Drive, Foster City
650/295-6129

www.eventscp.com
sales@cpfcc.com

● Rehearsal Dinners	● Corp. Events/Mtgs.
● Ceremonies	● Private Parties
● Wedding Receptions	● Accommodations

"Location, location, location!" may be the byword of people who deal in real estate, but hoteliers are pretty hip to the idea, too. That's certainly the case at the Crowne Plaza Foster City-San Mateo, a bustling newly renovated 351-room hotel conveniently situated at a major Bay Area crossroads. Right off the western end of the San Mateo Bridge, and just minutes south of San Francisco International Airport, it's easily accessible from The City, South Bay, East Bay and the Peninsula. Free parking and a complimentary airport shuttle to SFO are provided, and nearby restaurants, shopping and parks add even more to the hotel's appeal.

But a great location is only part of what makes the Crowne Plaza a thriving site for weddings. The five-story garden atrium certainly has brides talking. Its most impressive feature has to be the room-length waterfall along the east side: Four streams of water cascade among flower-strewn rocks, creating a soothing and arresting backdrop. For obvious reasons, many couples love having their ceremony in here. Brides often descend dramatically from above in one of the hotel's glass elevators, then walk to a wooden bridge at the center of the atrium to exchange vows. Palms, ficus and other plants give this glassed-in area a tropical feel.

Receptions usually start in the Magellan Foyer where cocktails are set up, and then move into the adjoining ballroom, which can be divided into four sections depending on the size of your event. Rehearsal dinners and post-wedding brunches are often held on site, too. The Marco Polo Room, directly off the atrium, is especially well suited for smaller gatherings where family and close friends want to mingle and catch up with each other. An abundance of rich wood creates a lot of warmth, and the glass wall facing the atrium can be curtained for privacy or left open for people watching.

Bridal suites, which are a standard part of the hotel's wedding package, are located in the Executive Tower, a twin building reached via a covered driveway. The Crowne Club there has a cocktail and hors d'oeuvre serving area that you can reserve for an intimate reception. The adjacent Bay View Ballroom, which hosts dinners and dancing and is sometimes used for ceremonies, is a favorite with smaller wedding parties. For musical entertainment, bring your own band or DJ or, if your event is on a Friday or Saturday night, you have another option: Accompany your guests over to the Clubhouse Bistro just off the atrium, where the house DJ rocks the crowd two nights a week.

The final component of this hotel's appeal is its experienced wedding staff. They're not only flexible about letting you decorate early so you'll have plenty of time to spare, they also go out of their way to accommodate the needs of almost any ethnic group. For example, when there's a traditional Chinese wedding, which involves a pre-ceremony tea ritual, the staff here always sets aside a proper space for it.

The wedding manager says the first thing she asks any prospective client is, "What is it that you want to do?" When she gets the answer to that question, she and her team quickly go about the business of making each reception reflect the couple's wishes.

CEREMONY CAPACITY: The Atrium holds 50 seated guests.

EVENT/RECEPTION CAPACITY: Various rooms hold up to 650 seated or 800 standing guests. Smaller events for 25 people can be accommodated; call for detailed configuration options.

MEETING CAPACITY: Event spaces accommodate 25–550 seated guests.

FEES & DEPOSITS: A deposit is required to reserve your date and a second deposit, which is equal to 50% of your estimated event total, is due 4 months after the original booking date; the final balance is due 10 days prior to the event. There are no separate room rental fees. Packages range $45–130/person. A 20% service charge and tax are additional. A ceremony setup fee and a cake-cutting fee may also apply. Group room rates are available, as is a complimentary bridal suite for the wedding couple.

AVAILABILITY: Year-round, daily, 6am–1am.

SERVICES/AMENITIES:

Catering: in-house; outside ethnic caterers may be allowed
Kitchen Facilities: n/a
Tables & Chairs: provided
Linens, Silver, etc.: provided
Restrooms: wheelchair accessible
Dance Floor: yes
Bride's & Groom's Dressing Areas: yes
AV/Meeting Equipment: full range

Parking: complimentary self-parking
Accommodations: 351 guest rooms
Outdoor Night Lighting: CBA
Outdoor Cooking Facilities: no
Cleanup: provided
View: bay views from some spaces
Other: event coordination, ethnic weddings

RESTRICTIONS:

Alcohol: in-house
Smoking: outside only
Music: amplified OK indoors

Wheelchair Access: yes
Insurance: not required

Oceano Hotel and Spa

280 Capistrano Road, Half Moon Bay
650/726-5400

www.oceanohalfmoonbay.com
nancyn@oceanohalfmoonbay.com

Waterfront Hotel and Spa

- Rehearsal Dinners
- Ceremonies
- Wedding Receptions
- Corp. Events/Mtgs.
- Private Parties
- Accommodations

A quaint, artsy Main Street... miles of shoreline trails and natural habitats... world-class golf, surfing and fishing.... As if there wasn't enough to love about Half Moon Bay, we've discovered another reason to come to this seaside getaway: The Oceano Hotel & Spa. Located just 30 minutes from San Francisco, this spectacular boutique-style hotel is nestled between the picturesque Pillar Point Harbor and the Santa Cruz Mountains.

Guests are greeted in the newly redesigned lobby, where nautical accents and modern furnishings reflect the beauty of the California coast. This airy space is bathed in natural light from its vaulted atrium ceiling and surrounded by three stories of guest rooms. These spacious accommodations, which feature high ceilings, fireplaces, and plantation-style furniture, invite guests to relax in luxury. Thoughtful amenities like Aveda bath products, a plush spa-quality bathrobe, and organic bamboo sheets add to the experience. Each Deluxe Suite has an oceanview balcony where you can enjoy the peaceful sound of the waves rolling in.

With all it has to offer, The Oceano Hotel isn't just a great place to stay—it's also ideal for hosting a grand wedding. From the rehearsal dinner to the ceremony and reception, wedding events can all be custom-tailored to make each one unique.

The lovely Wedding Garden, with its graceful Italian cypress trees and sweeping views of the harbor, sets the stage for an outdoor ceremony. A stone pathway leads to a white gazebo that's perfect for exchanging vows.

Afterwards, family and friends mingle over gourmet appetizers and cocktails on the landscaped lawn before entering The Oceano's newest reception space, The Gate House. It captures the rustic charm of a coastal barn with wooden beams, wrought-iron chandeliers, and hardwood floors. French doors open to a scenic patio that showcases a stone fireplace.

The Oceano Grand Ballroom and Atrium provides another impressive backdrop for a one-of-a-kind wedding reception. This elegant banquet space is embellished with ornate crown molding, Art Deco wall sconces and a trio of crystal chandeliers. The soothing neutral palette—soft gold, vanilla and a touch of sea green—lends an upscale ambiance. When it is time for dancing, guests step through custom floor-length curtains into the Atrium, a stylish annex aglow in moonlight from a skylit ceiling.

While its sophisticated guest rooms and event spaces make The Oceano an exceptional destination wedding venue, perhaps the most endearing aspect of this sea-inspired sanctuary is its warm and enthusiastic service. Their dedicated on-site wedding planners will work with you every step of the way to ensure you have a wonderful celebration, and the entire staff is genuinely eager to make your visit to Half Moon Bay a memorable one.

CEREMONY CAPACITY: The hotel holds 250 seated indoors and 350 seated outdoors.

EVENT/RECEPTION CAPACITY: The hotel accommodates 250 seated or 450 standing guests indoors and 400 seated or 800 standing outdoors.

MEETING CAPACITY: The hotel seats 250 guests.

FEES & DEPOSITS: 30% of the total event cost is required to reserve your date, and the balance is due 2 weeks prior to the event. The rental fee ranges $1,000–6,000 depending on the space selected. Meals range $95–150/person. Tax, alcohol and a 20% service charge are additional.

If you've booked your event at Oceano, you will also receive 2 free wedding rooms: one for the night before the event, and the honeymoon suite for your wedding night. Please contact the location for more details.

AVAILABILITY: Year-round, daily, 6am–11pm.

SERVICES/AMENITIES:

Catering: in-house

Kitchen Facilities: n/a

Tables & Chairs: provided

Linens, Silver, etc.: provided

Restrooms: wheelchair accessible

Dance Floor: provided

Bride's Dressing Area: yes

AV/Meeting Equipment: provided

Parking: large lot

Accommodations: 95 guest rooms

Outdoor Night Lighting: no

Outdoor Cooking Facilities: n/a

Cleanup: provided

View: landscaped grounds, garden, courtyard; panorama of mountains, ocean/bay and fields

Other: spa services, picnic area, shopping promenade, event coordination

RESTRICTIONS:

Alcohol: in-house, or BYO with corkage fees

Smoking: not allowed

Music: amplified OK with restrictions

Wheelchair Access: yes

Insurance: not required

Other: no birdseed, rice, glitter or confetti

This is important! Tell locations you're reading HERE COMES THE GUIDE and ask if our information is still current.

Hillsborough Racquet Club

Historic Club

252 El Cerrito Avenue, Hillsborough
650/343-2062
www.hillsboroughracquetclub.org
hrcrentals@yahoo.com

● Rehearsal Dinners	● Corp. Events/Mtgs.
● Ceremonies	● Private Parties
● Wedding Receptions	Accommodations

The Hillsborough Racquet Club has a wonderful ambiance—polished and dignified, but without any stiffness or stuffiness. HRC's members are proud of their private club and enjoy its unique spaces, from the ballroom, patio and bar, to the indoor badminton court. When you host your wedding here, you have exclusive use of the facility during your event, along with an experienced manager to provide discreet assistance.

Built in 1913 as a polo club, the Hillsborough Racquet Club is located in a lovely residential neighborhood surrounded by elms, cypresses and laurel hedges. The entrance faces away from the street, and it's not until you walk around to it that you see the club's beautiful architectural elements. The building's design is based on the classical Greek Doric order with clean, elegant lines. A handsome portico curves along the front, opening to a patio with flowerbeds and the main entrance. Visitors enter a domed, parquet-floored foyer with hallways that lead to a bridal changing room, a servers' entrance, dining and music rooms, and the ballroom.

The ballroom is the heart of the club and it's easy to see why. It's large and airy, but not overwhelming—ideal for dinner and dancing. Interior designers enjoy the room's good "bones"—the walls are finished in off-whites and ornamentation is simple and subdued. The room's main visual focuses are a large working fireplace capped with a Tudor arch on one side, and a wall of windows and French doors on the opposite side that open to the patio. This sunny space, sheltered by a shade tree and lined with flowers and small hedges, is a wonderful spot for cocktails and outdoor dining.

Adjoining the ballroom is a bar and a "domino room." The bar is backed by a mirror that reflects light pouring in from the windows. Next door, the domino room has a very clubby feel and makes a fine place to sit and relax, or to take a break from the festivities.

The dining room has a fireplace, brass chandelier and "hounds and hunters" prints on the walls. In the adjacent music room, a grand piano stands against a light-loving wall of windows that can serve as a backdrop for small ceremonies. (Couples may wed in the ballroom, too, and HRC is close to several neighborhood churches.) French doors in this room also lead to the patio, creating a nice indoor/outdoor flow.

Other pluses are the large staging kitchen off of the dining room, and the changing room/ladies' lounge next to the foyer.

The members are happy to share their club with you for your special occasion, whether it be a wedding, anniversary party, or other celebration. What's more, you'll get the attention you deserve, since HRC never hosts more than one function per weekend.

CEREMONY & EVENT/RECEPTION CAPACITY: The ballroom holds 165 guests seated at tables with room for a dance area. When all five rooms of the club are used together, there is space for 225 seated. The patio holds up to 50 seated or 70 standing guests.

MEETING CAPACITY: The ballroom seats 225 guests theater-style.

FEES & DEPOSITS: A $1,000 deposit is required to reserve your date. 50% of the rental fee is due 6 months prior to the event, and the balance is due 3 months prior. The rental fee ranges $4,500–5,000 (depending on the guest count) for a 5-hour block of time. An extra hour is allowed for a wedding ceremony ($500 ceremony fee). December events incur an additional $500 charge for holiday decorations.

AVAILABILITY: Year-round, daily (except Thursdays) until 11pm.

SERVICES/AMENITIES:

Catering: BYO

Kitchen Facilities: warming kitchen

Tables & Chairs: provided

Linens, Silver, etc.: through caterer

Restrooms: wheelchair accessible

Dance Floor: yes

Bride's Dressing Area: yes

AV/Meeting Equipment: BYO

Parking: ample on site

Accommodations: no guest rooms

Outdoor Night Lighting: CBA

Outdoor Cooking Facilities: through caterer

Cleanup: caterer and resident manager

View: landscaped terrace

Other: exclusive use of facility during event

RESTRICTIONS:

Alcohol: BYO

Smoking: outdoors only

Music: amplified OK indoors with restrictions

Wheelchair Access: yes

Insurance: liability required

Los Altos History Museum

51 South San Antonio Road, Los Altos
650/948-9427 x12

www.losaltoshistory.org
mperry@losaltoshistory.org

History Museum & Special Event Facility

● Rehearsal Dinners	● Corp. Events/Mtgs.	
● Ceremonies	● Private Parties	
● Wedding Receptions	Accommodations	

Not so very long ago, apricot orchards, vineyards, and walnut groves cloaked the fertile plains of the Peninsula, and dairy farms and greenhouses dotted the hillsides. The transition from pristine agricultural paradise to Silicon Valley hub is skillfully realized at the Los Altos History Museum, where the past comes alive right before your very eyes. We thought this place was so interesting and so lovely that we would come here even if we weren't planning a special event. But make no mistake—there's plenty here to entice party-givers of all types.

In a model of team spirit, a group of Los Altos go-getters banded together to create this local museum, a captivating window in time set among acres of delightful parks and gardens. Open since spring 2001, the History Museum resides in a folksy, wood-plank building. The vaulted entryway and the indoor balcony, which encircles the three-story space, generate an open, welcoming look and feel. Most of the main floor is taken up by the Changing Exhibits Gallery, which features visiting collections, some on loan from notable institutions like the Smithsonian. Up a winding staircase to the permanent exhibit you'll find engaging interactive displays of Los Altos area history. There's more history just across the landscaped courtyard in the landmark J. Gilbert Smith History House. This adorable Craftsman-style shingled farmhouse from 1905 sets a nostalgic tone for your outdoor wedding or special event.

Surrounding both buildings, the pretty museum gardens offer several spots to enjoy the inspiring beauty of flowers in bloom, treetops swaying in the breeze, and squirrels scampering about their natural habitat. Why not exchange marriage vows under the dappled shade of oak trees? The front yard of the History House is a darling scene for memorable photos, the newlyweds framed by an archway wrapped in wild roses, or the wedding party posed on the broad porch steps in an old-fashioned tableau. In fair weather, you may want to hold your reception outdoors too, skillfully arranged by the museum's expert event coordinator.

A more formal outdoor ceremony and reception site is the spacious red-brick courtyard between the main Museum and the quaint façade of the History House. Your walk down the aisle is accented by antique-style verdigris lamps, potted blooms and delicate saplings, and a redwood pergola lets you say your vows while facing the lush garden. Afterwards, you can dine outdoors and even have your first dance under the stars.

Then the party moves through sliding glass doors into the Changing Exhibits Gallery, where polished blond wood floors and historic or art exhibits lend an air of distinction to your celebration. Here, the cake is served and guests can dance the night away. Those who prefer quieter pursuits might meander upstairs to enjoy the interactive displays, artifacts and vintage clothing, or step outside for a stroll along the moonlit garden lanes. This is the way museums should be—hands-on, fun, and fascinating. To further enhance your event, arrange a guided tour of the History House. The quaintly furnished rooms replicate in amazing detail the lifestyle of a 1930s farm family. You'll feel like you stepped through a time tunnel into the simple, wholesome world of a bygone era.

The Los Altos History Museum is more than just a peek into the past; it's also a vision of the future, a future that embraces family, community, and traditional values, while honoring a connection to the land. When you hold your special celebration here, you'll become part of this ideal tomorrow, because the proceeds from your event go towards supporting the museum and its grounds for generations to come.

CEREMONY CAPACITY: The Garden seats 200 guests, and the Changing Exhibits Gallery seats 60.

EVENT/RECEPTION CAPACITY: The Garden accommodates 200 seated or standing, and the Changing Exhibits Gallery 60 seated or 150 standing.

MEETING CAPACITY: The Gallery seats 60 theater-style or classroom-style.

FEES & DEPOSITS: The entire rental fee, along with a $1,350 security and rentals deposit and an $825 application fee, is required to reserve your date. The rental fee starts at $5,400. Liability insurance and an alcohol permit fee are also required.

AVAILABILITY: Friday–Sunday, 4pm–11pm, first weekend in May through first weekend in October. Outdoor setup access at 3pm.

SERVICES/AMENITIES:

Catering: select from preferred list
Kitchen Facilities: moderate
Tables & Chairs: provided; extra fee
Linens, Silver, etc.: through caterer
Restrooms: wheelchair accessible
Dance Floor: hardwood floor or brick patio
Bride's & Groom's Dressing Areas: yes
AV/Meeting Equipment: provided, extra fee

Alcohol: BYO, licensed and insured server
Smoking: not allowed
Music: amplified OK indoors and outdoors until 8pm with volume restrictions

Parking: large complimentary lot
Accommodations: no guest rooms
Outdoor Night Lighting: yes
Outdoor Cooking Facilities: through caterer
Cleanup: through caterer
View: garden courtyard, Peninsula coastal hills and landscaped grounds
Other: coordination, docent-led tours

RESTRICTIONS:

Wheelchair Access: yes
Insurance: extra liability required
Other: no rice, birdseed, confetti or glitter

Allied Arts Guild

Historic Landmark & Garden

75 Arbor Road at Cambridge, Menlo Park
650/322-2405

www.alliedartsguild.org
events@alliedartsguild.org

- Rehearsal Dinners
- Ceremonies
- Wedding Receptions
- Corp. Events/Mtgs.
- Private Parties
- Accommodations

The Allied Arts Guild is an extraordinary place. It hits you instantly as you walk through the entry and gaze at the fountains, the wrought-iron details, colorful frescos and intricate tilework. The beautiful and tranquil gardens draw you further into the central courtyard, where you say to yourself, "I can't believe I'm in Menlo Park."

No wonder. This serene oasis is a historic landmark located amidst three and a half acres that were once part of an original Spanish land grant. Allied Arts is so hidden, you'd never know that it's located here, tucked away in a quiet, residential neighborhood not far from the Stanford University campus. The founders' original dream of a European-style crafts guild was realized in 1929 by California artist Pedro deLemos and architect Gardner Dailey. Both were responsible for creating the gardens, buildings and shops of the complex, and adhering to a romantic palette with a strong Spanish emphasis.

After more than 70 years, the site holds a major place in California history. Luckily for all of us, this jewel-of-a-venue has been recently and completely restored back to its original splendor. The complex is designed in the Spanish Colonial style, with meandering courtyards and terraces, burbling fountains, and handsome buildings with white plaster walls topped by terracotta tiles. The lush gardens were inspired by gardens in Granada, Spain, with an emphasis on color, fragrance and seasonal flowers. During the summer months, a floral profusion of intense color makes a great background for wedding photos. Just imagine getting married outdoors in a spot called "Garden of Delight," encircled by Blue Nile lilies, aster, salvia and hydrangeas or "The Court of Abundance," with splashing fountain surrounded by gold and yellow marigolds, wallflowers and nasturtiums!

If the weather is uncooperative, you can have your ceremony or reception indoors in the Dining Room or Sunset Room. Both have rustic, high-beamed ceilings and wrought-iron chandeliers. The cement floors are worthy of note: They were painstakingly handcarved by Pedro deLemos to look like stone. The homey Spanish fireplaces are made of adobe, and when a fire is burning, they give the rooms a warm glow.

You can rent one part of the complex, or go for broke and celebrate by renting the entire facility. You'd be hard pressed to find a more relaxed and striking setting on the Peninsula with both indoor and outdoor event spaces. And there's an added benefit: Because Allied Arts is a nonprofit organization, all proceeds are donated to the Lucile Packard Children's Hospital at Stanford—which means a significant portion of your rental fees are tax deductible!

CEREMONY & EVENT/RECEPTION CAPACITY: The site accommodates 150 seated or standing, indoors or outdoors.

MEETING CAPACITY: The site holds 120 seated guests (up to 44 seated conference-style).

FEES & DEPOSITS: Ceremonies start at $3,000; for receptions the use fee ranges $5,000–8,000. Weekday events range $1,000–3,000.

AVAILABILITY: Year-round, Monday–Saturday, 8am–10pm.

SERVICES/AMENITIES:

Catering: select from preferred list
Kitchen Facilities: moderate
Tables & Chairs: some provided
Linens, Silver, etc.: through caterer
Restrooms: wheelchair accessible
Dance Floor: CBA
Bride's Dressing Area: yes
AV/Meeting Equipment: provided

Parking: on-site lot for 120 cars, and on-street
Accommodations: no guest rooms
Outside Night Lighting: yes
Outdoor Cooking Facilities: CBA
Cleanup: provided
View: garden, landscaped grounds, historic architecture

RESTRICTIONS:

Alcohol: in-house or BYO
Smoking: designated area only
Music: amplified OK indoors, acoustic only outdoors

Wheelchair Access: yes
Insurance: certificate required
Other: no birdseed or rice; no swimming

Rosewood Sand Hill

Hotel

2825 Sand Hill Road, Menlo Park
650/561-1549
www.rosewoodsandhill.com
sandhill@rosewoodhotels.com

- Rehearsal Dinners
- Ceremonies
- Wedding Receptions
- Corp. Events/Mtgs.
- Private Parties
- Accommodations

Elegantly Californian in design and impressively international in reputation, Rosewood Sand Hill is nestled on 16 lush acres in the heart of Silicon Valley. It's a place where high-tech and venture capital jet setters love to relax … and we think it's just the spot for a fabulous Bay Area wedding.

Two nearby airports provide easy access, and there's a stunning array of premier indoor and outdoor event spaces, spas, restaurants, and guest accommodations to choose from. Plus the resort-like setting, amidst generous courtyards and gardens with views of the Santa Cruz Mountains, makes it a divine destination—and one you don't want to miss.

Celebrations in this breezy oasis of style unfold with an effortless refinement and expertise. How could it be otherwise? Most of the sophisticated event areas are ever so private, sequestered in the sumptuous sprawl of the main building's lower level. And Rosewood's hilltop location means inspiring vistas from expansive terraces and lawns.

Of course, our choice for a smashing reception or gala would be the 2,769-square-foot Rosewood Ballroom. Featuring hand-stenciled silk paneling, chandeliers, and a 16-foot ceiling, it opens to its own foyer and terrace where guests can mingle over cocktails while savoring the garden and mountain views. The adjacent Vista Lawn, which is bordered by gardens and mature trees and backed by a majestic mountain panorama, is custom-made for an al fresco ceremony.

Planning something a little more intimate? Consider the beautifully appointed Eucalyptus Room and its spacious foyer. Like the handsome Dogwood and Valley Oaks Boardrooms nearby, it can be used with the graceful Portico, a versatile outdoor "living room" with a rose garden surround and gorgeous mountain and garden views. In fact, the natural flow from interior to exterior environments is one of the hallmarks of this remarkable property. Even the more compact Courtyard Rooms near the hotel's entry fountain offer open breezeways and a tranquil, trellised terrace.

Short strolls around the grounds reveal other idyllic enclaves: The Cypress and Birch Gardens with their fountains and greenery, the treelined passages—even the pool—are all conducive to splendid parties, which the catering staff is well versed in delivering. Needless to say, the cuisine and service are flawless … and photo ops are everywhere.

The best part of the Rosewood experience: Their topnotch facilities and overnight accommodations (including suites and villas) allow you and your guests to enjoy not just the big day, but all of your pre- and post-wedding festivities, too. So don't stress. Arrive a day or two early and stay for several more. Take the time to luxuriate in all that this sanctuary has to offer.

CEREMONY CAPACITY: The site holds 300 seated indoors and 300 seated outdoors.

EVENT/RECEPTION CAPACITY: The site accommodates 220 seated or 350 standing guests indoors and 400 seated or 600 standing outdoors.

MEETING CAPACITY: Meeting spaces seat up to 300.

FEES & DEPOSITS: 25% of the estimated event total is required to reserve your date, and the balance is due 30 days prior to the event. Rental and ceremony fees start at $1,000 and vary depending on day and time of the event, space selected, your guest count, and other factors. Meals range $125-350/person. Tax, alcohol and a service charge are additional.

AVAILABILITY: Year-round, daily, anytime. Call for details.

SERVICES/AMENITIES:
Catering: in-house
Kitchen Facilities: n/a
Tables & Chairs: provided
Linens, Silver, etc.: provided
Restrooms: wheelchair accessible
Dance Floor: provided
Bride's Dressing Area: CBA
AV/Meeting Equipment: CBA

Parking: complimentary self-parking and day valet; overnight valet parking $25/night
Accommodations: 121 guest rooms
Outdoor Night Lighting: CBA
Outdoor Cooking Facilities: BBQ CBA
Cleanup: provided
View: fountain, garden patio, landscaped grounds, pool area; panorama of the Santa Cruz Mountains
Other: on-site wedding cake

RESTRICTIONS:
Alcohol: in-house
Smoking: not allowed
Music: amplified OK with restrictions

Wheelchair Access: yes
Insurance: liability required

Overwhelmed? Use the search criteria on www.HereComesTheGuide.com to narrow down your choices.

185

Westin San Francisco Airport

Hotel

One Old Bayshore Highway, Millbrae
650/872-8118

www.westin.com/san-francisco-airport
vidzal@westinsfoairport.com

- Rehearsal Dinners
- Ceremonies
- Wedding Receptions
- Corp. Events/Mtgs.
- Private Parties
- Accommodations

The name Westin San Francisco Airport Hotel is a bit of a misnomer, because even though it's close to the airport this venue is really more like an elegant resort. With its refined décor, warm ambiance and long list of amenities, it's one of the Peninsula's most popular places for weddings, receptions and parties.

Set on the cusp of a palm-lined drive near the edge of the bay, and just two minutes from the airport, the Westin is surprisingly quiet and peaceful. Even the lobby has a calming influence, designed in warm natural shades and outfitted with modern, comfortable furnishings and lush floral arrangements.

From here it's a short walk to the banquet rooms, and by the time you reach them, you're expecting something sophisticated and tasteful. You won't be disappointed. The Westin Ballroom, where most weddings, large meetings and special events take place, is very lovely. Brides are usually overjoyed with the décor and have been known to exclaim, "Oh, this will match my dress perfectly!" That's because the walls are papered in a neutral champagne-and-taupe print that gives off a subtle gold sheen, and the coffered ceiling is white. One of the most striking features of this ballroom is the lighting. Instead of traditional chandeliers, there are fixtures fashioned from white globes seemingly "scattered" behind a veil of pearl strands. When the lights are dimmed, you feel like you're gazing at clusters of stars, shining through golden clouds. Additional romantic lighting comes from alabaster-and-brass wall sconces. Although the ballroom can be divided into four sections, only one event at a time is scheduled so you can tailor the size of the space to fit your needs.

The expansive foyer area in front of the ballroom is not only refreshing to the eye, it's large enough to be set up with fountains, plants and an hors d'oeuvre buffet and still have plenty of room left over for a crowd to mingle comfortably. And if you have kids at your event, you'll be ever grateful to the Westin—they make a room for childcare available just off the foyer.

Smaller weddings and meetings are held in the Bayshore Ballroom, an intimate space with crystal chandeliers, alabaster wall sconces, and floor-to-ceiling windows overlooking the pool atrium. The atrium itself is ideal for cocktail parties and more informal receptions. Huge potted ferns and rubber trees, as well as colorful flowers set around the pool, soak up the sunlight from the vaulted skylit "ceiling" and create a tropical ambiance.

Two dozen other rooms are available for functions, and award-winning chefs will create custom, culturally diverse menus. Guests staying overnight sleep well, thanks to the Westin's super-comfy Heavenly Bed and triple-paned windows that create a virtually soundproof environment. There's one more amenity just for weddings: a customized web page for each couple to facilitate reserving guest rooms and providing information to attendees.

The combination of beautiful facilities, excellent food and personal service generates lots of repeat business for the hotel. Their "Letters To The Hotel" binder includes pages of laudatory comments such as, "The Westin is the only place to hold an event in San Mateo County! Period!" and "My daughter's dream of a perfect wedding day came true!" Read them all and you come away with a sense that guests feel quite welcomed here and very well taken care of. It's absolutely clear why they return to the Westin time after time—for many of them it's like coming home.

CEREMONY CAPACITY: The Bayshore Ballroom holds 200 and the Westin Ballroom holds 300.

EVENT/RECEPTION CAPACITY: The hotel can accommodate 48–410 seated or 125–600 standing guests indoors.

MEETING CAPACITY: The Westin has over 22,000 square feet of function space, including 31 flexible rooms, from ballrooms and salons to suites and boardrooms. Spaces can accommodate 4–700 guests for business events.

FEES & DEPOSITS: For weddings, a nonrefundable $5,000 deposit is required to secure your date; the balance is due 3 days prior to the event. There are 3 wedding packages ranging $75–125/person that include centerpieces, champagne reception and toast, 3-course meal, hors d'oeuvres, wine with meal, overnight accommodations and breakfast for the bride and groom. All menus can be customized; wedding menus range $75–125/person. Tax and a 24% service charge are additional. A ceremony setup charge starts at $500.

For other social events or business functions, prices vary depending on the menu and services selected; call for specific rates. Meeting packages are also available.

AVAILABILITY: Year-round, daily including holidays, until 1am. For Saturday weddings, time frames are 11am–5pm or 6pm–1am.

SERVICES/AMENITIES:
Catering: in-house, no BYO
Kitchen Facilities: n/a
Tables & Chairs: provided
Linens, Silver, etc.: provided
Restrooms: wheelchair accessible
Dance Floor: provided
Bride's & Groom's Dressing Areas: guest room CBA
AV/Meeting Equipment: full range and business center, in-room data port lines

Parking: ample, gated and secure lots
Accommodations: 400 guest rooms
Outdoor Night Lighting: access only
Outdoor Cooking Facilities: no
Cleanup: provided
View: no
Other: event coordination, baby grand piano, ice sculpture, wedding cakes, limo service, customized web page

RESTRICTIONS:
Alcohol: in-house, or BYO wine and champagne corkage negotiable
Smoking: outside only
Music: amplified OK

Wheelchair Access: yes
Insurance: not required
Other: no rice, birdseed, glitter or confetti

La Costanera—Contemporary Peruvian Cuisine   *Waterfront Restaurant*

8150 Cabrillo Highway, Montara
650/728-1600

www.lacostanerarestaurant.com
eric@lacostanerarestaurant.com

- Rehearsal Dinners
- Ceremonies
- Wedding Receptions
- Corp. Events/Mtgs.
- Private Parties
- Accommodations

La Costanera, a Michelin-starred culinary destination just north of Half Moon Bay, is an upscale all-in-one event venue with gourmet panache. Perched on a bluff above Montara Beach, this gorgeous restaurant is nothing short of a masterpiece. The three-level, 10,000-square-foot building is shaped like half of a modern Mesoamerican pyramid, with slanting windows and skylights that embrace a breathtaking ocean view. Its overall design reflects a contemporary global aesthetic, artfully blending rustic, natural elements—rich woods, sea shells, distressed metal—into the décor of the geometrically shaped rooms. Cleverly styled furnishings and accents, such as old-fashioned maps inlaid into some of the tabletops and nautically inspired mobiles, convey an antique seafaring flair. The effect is beautifully original.

La Costanera's layout offers supreme event versatility, and you can buy out the entire restaurant for your event or reserve individual sections. The main floor houses the restaurant and a semiprivate dining area called the Greenhouse, with its own fireplace and atrium. Glass doors open to an oceanview patio, complete with fire pit, for outdoor dining or an intimate ceremony. Back inside, a staircase leads to a skylit balcony that overlooks the action on the main floor. This private enclave can host rehearsal dinners, showers or small gatherings.

The lower level holds the bar and lounge, a very cool space for receptions, social hours and after-parties—La Costanera can stay open until 2am. A long bar serves up the drinks (we recommend the house-made sangria or their pisco sour, a Peruvian cocktail that's one of our all-time favorites). Gleaming tile floors and Oriental carpets enhance the space's exotic luxe; a sunken lounge area, normally outfitted with velour couches and club chairs, can be cleared ahead of time for dancing. Glass doors open onto a beachfront patio, whose glorious panorama of sea and sky makes it quite the romantic spot for ceremonies. A footpath leads directly to the sand, so while your guests are sipping sangria, you and your bridal party can pose for photos alongside the waves.

The food and drink is as impressive as the setting. Chef-owner Carlos Altamirano already has two critically acclaimed restaurants to his credit, Mochica and Piqueos, and this latest venture is sure to add to his culinary fandom. Altamirano's fusion dishes reflect his country's Asian and Mediterranean influences, and introduce some fascinating indigenous components like yucca fries, sweet plantains and blue potatoes. Seafood is the star here, but entrées like lamb chops in mint chimichurri sauce will keep carnivores contented, too. La Costanera brilliantly showcases Peru's national dish, *cebiche,* in a dozen or so provocative interpretations, and they even have a cute cart to serve it up to your guests. Round out the appetizers with an assortment of tapas and anitcuchos (South American-style skewers), and you have a cocktail hour that's pure foodie fun. Just don't forget the pisco! La Costanera has an entire menu of pisco variations, ensuring your signature cocktail will be unique (mojitos are so 2008…).

The expert staff will help you navigate the novel food and drink options, and can assist with event extras—entertainment, late-night service, valet parking, flowers, favors and more. With its hip vibe, cutting-edge cuisine and stunning atmosphere, La Costanera is definitely a venue to put on your short-list.

CEREMONY CAPACITY: The restaurant holds 150 seated guests indoors and 100 seated outdoors.

EVENT/RECEPTION CAPACITY: The facility can accommodate 270 seated or 400 standing indoors and 50 seated or standing outdoors.

MEETING CAPACITY: Meeting rooms hold 200 seated guests.

FEES & DEPOSITS: 25% of the total event cost is required to secure your date. The rental fee ranges $400–3,500 depending on the space reserved. Meals range $50–125/person. Tax, alcohol and a 20% service charge are additional.

AVAILABILITY: Year-round, Tuesday–Sunday, 5pm–midnight.

SERVICES/AMENITIES:

Catering: in-house
Kitchen Facilities: n/a
Tables & Chairs: provided
Linens, Silver, etc.: provided
Restrooms: wheelchair accessible
Dance Floor: provided
Bride's Dressing Area: CBA
AV/Meeting Equipment: BYO

Parking: large lot
Accommodations: no guest rooms
Outdoor Night Lighting: yes
Outdoor Cooking Facilities: none
Cleanup: provided
View: coastline, mountains, ocean/bay
Other: event coordination

RESTRICTIONS:

Alcohol: in-house, or BYO with corkage fee
Smoking: outdoors only
Music: amplified OK with restrictions

Wheelchair Access: yes
Insurance: liability required

Crowne Plaza Cabaña Palo Alto

Hotel

4290 El Camino Real, Palo Alto
650/628-0138
www.cabanapaloalto.com
sales.catering@cabanapaloalto.com

- Rehearsal Dinners
- Ceremonies
- Wedding Receptions
- Corp. Events/Mtgs.
- Private Parties
- Accommodations

The Crowne Plaza Cabaña is a rarity: It's the only hotel on the Peninsula with a breezy resort style and vintage Hollywood feel. And while it's been completely updated with new décor and modern amenities, this carefree oasis retains much of the relaxed elegance and innovative design elements that made it a 1960s California classic.

Each of the event spaces has something special to offer. The flexible Mediterranean Ballroom, which can host a gala of 800 or be sectioned into salons for more intimate celebrations, is visually striking. Step inside and the first thing you notice is the incredible "chandeliers", set into the deeply coffered ceiling. Although they're constructed of white, frosted glass, these extraordinary works of art look like fluidly draped fabric that changes shape as you dim or amplify the lighting. The room is done in a soft taupe, a neutral backdrop that complements any color scheme and beautifully showcases dramatic uplighting. A series of doors open to a spacious and sun-drenched natural stone courtyard that's perfect for a smaller ceremony, cocktail hour, or al fresco reception. It can be used alone or in conjunction with the ballroom.

On the second floor you'll find the chic Cyprus Room, the hotel's most sought-after venue. With its unique oval shape, wraparound floor-to-ceiling windows, and distinctive touches, this room's charms are hard to resist. During the day, natural light streams in through the windows, which provide a bird's-eye view of the lush trees all around, as well as the courtyard and turquoise swimming pool below. At night, lights may be dimmed for a soft, romantic ambiance.

The Cyprus Room opens to the Sun Deck, which accommodates overflow reception seating and also works well for a wedding ceremony or social hour. Four Cabaña Suites next to the deck provide even more options: For example, you might reserve one for the bride's changing room and another for a hospitality room. One of the suites connects to the Sun Deck, creating a wonderful indoor-outdoor flow.

Speaking of "outdoor", the pool deck is a classy spot for an event. Tiled in a fabulously retro teal-and-off-white checkerboard design, and bordered by swanky cabañas, palms trees, and large planters filled with vibrant flowers, it harkens back to a time when movie stars lounged around the sparkling pool with drink in hand, ready to see and be seen.

A variety of smaller rooms are available, too, so you should be able to find a space that perfectly suits your occasion. In addition, the attentive staff will work with you to deliver the event you envision.

The Crowne Plaza Cabaña has been impressing its guests for over 50 years, and it continues to do so with inspired service, upscale guest rooms and suites, and all the amenities you could want. In fact, locals love this place so much they often come here on weekends for a family staycation!

CEREMONY CAPACITY: The hotel accommodates up to 800 seated guests indoors and 400 seated outdoors.

EVENT/RECEPTION CAPACITY: The facility holds 640 seated and 800 standing indoors; 350 seated and 750 standing outdoors.

MEETING CAPACITY: Event spaces accommodate 800 seated guests.

FEES & DEPOSITS: 25% of the estimated event total is due with the signed contract, and the balance is payable 30 days prior to the event. The ceremony fee starts at $500 and varies depending on the site reserved and the level of customization. Wedding packages start at $68/person. Tax, alcohol and a 22% service charge are additional. Room rental fees may apply if certain minimums are not met.

AVAILABILITY: Year-round, daily, 6am–midnight.

SERVICES/AMENITIES:

Catering: in-house or approved outside ethnic caterer
Kitchen Facilities: fully equipped
Tables & Chairs: provided
Linens, Silver, etc.: provided
Restrooms: wheelchair accessible
Dance Floor: yes
Bride's & Groom's Dressing Areas: yes
AV/Meeting Equipment: provided

Parking: large lot
Accommodations: 184 guest rooms and 11 suites
Outdoor Night Lighting: yes
Outdoor Cooking Facilities: no
Cleanup: provided
View: pool, courtyard, grounds
Other: event coordination

RESTRICTIONS:

Alcohol: in-house
Smoking: outside only
Music: amplified OK indoors

Wheelchair Access: yes
Insurance: not required

Elizabeth F. Gamble Garden

Historic Home & Garden

1431 Waverley Street, Palo Alto
650/329-1356 x202

www.gamblegarden.org
admin@gamblegarden.org

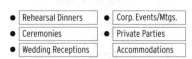

- Rehearsal Dinners
- Ceremonies
- Wedding Receptions
- Corp. Events/Mtgs.
- Private Parties
- Accommodations

The Elizabeth F. Gamble Garden is one of the most perfect garden ceremony/reception sites we've seen. Miss Gamble, granddaughter of the co-founder of the Procter & Gamble Company, willed the home and its grounds to the City of Palo Alto. The estate is now run by the Elizabeth F. Gamble Horticultural Foundation.

The main house is a 1902 Edwardian-style structure built in a lovely, older residential area of Palo Alto. Inside, a dining room, drawing room and library are available for receptions. Each room has been carefully restored using colorful, turn-of-the-century reproduction wallpapers. Dark natural wood wainscoting has been returned to its original splendor and there are graceful, molded ceilings and nicely finished oak floors throughout. Each room has its own fireplace. A set of French doors in the Library opens onto a brick porch that leads down to the first of many beautifully landscaped spaces.

Our favorite spots are the formal and informal gardens—the collective work of a full-time horticulturist and 300 volunteers. Each separately landscaped area feels like a private secret garden: The rose garden (with its 100 species of roses), the wisteria garden, and the Victorian grotto—separately or combined—provide elegant settings for small wedding ceremonies and receptions.

After the ceremony, guests are invited to gather at the Tea House, where hors d'oeuvres and beverages are served. The bride and groom often slip away from the festivities at this time for a quiet moment together in the Gazebo, an Edwardian-inspired garden house.

The reception is usually held at the Carriage House. While the buffet is set up inside, guests are seated on the adjoining brick terrace. Five sets of French doors make it easy for people to move indoors and out, giving them the feeling of being in a garden pavilion.

Miss Gamble succeeded in creating a place of serenity and beauty. We recommend it highly.

CEREMONY CAPACITY: The Wisteria Garden, Rose Garden, Tea House Patio and Carriage House each hold 50 seated or standing guests; the Drawing Room holds 30 seated or standing.

EVENT/RECEPTION & MEETING CAPACITY: The facility accommodates up to 50 guests (75 are allowed twice a month depending on the weather and the type of event).

FEES & DEPOSITS: For events, the rental fee and a signed contract are required to reserve your date. The rental fee for an 8-hour block on Saturday or Sunday is $1,200 May–October, and $100/hour November–April with a 6-hour minimum. The rental fee Monday–Friday is $100/hour during the day, and there's a $600 minimum on weekday evenings.

For meetings and business functions, fees vary based on rooms rented and rental time frames; call for more details.

AVAILABILITY: Year-round, daily. For weddings, Saturday and Sunday, noon–10pm and Monday–Friday 4pm–10pm. For other weekday functions, Monday–Thursday, 9am–5pm and Friday, 9am–4pm.

SERVICES/AMENITIES:

Catering: BYO
Kitchen Facilities: fully equipped
Tables & Chairs: BYO
Linens, Silver, etc.: BYO
Restrooms: wheelchair accessible
Dance Floor: yes
Bride's Dressing Area: yes
AV/Meeting Equipment: screen, wireless

Parking: lot
Accommodations: no guest rooms
Outdoor Night Lighting: yes
Outdoor Cooking Facilities: no
Cleanup: renter or caterer
View: Edwardian gardens

RESTRICTIONS:

Alcohol: BYO wine, beer or champagne; no beer kegs in main house
Smoking: not allowed
Music: acoustic only; no amplified or recorded music

Wheelchair Access: yes
Insurance: required
Other: rose petals only (no rice, birdseed, etc.)

Want to know WHAT TO ASK a potential location or vendor? Check out our Questions to Ask starting on page 21.

Garden Court Hotel

Hotel

520 Cowper Street, Downtown Palo Alto
800/824-9028 or 650/323-1912

www.gardencourt.com
eventservices@gardencourt.com

- Rehearsal Dinners
- Ceremonies
- Wedding Receptions
- Corp. Events/Mtgs.
- Private Parties
- Accommodations

Garden Court Hotel is the only luxury boutique hotel in Downtown Palo Alto, and it's an excellent choice for a local or destination wedding. Nestled on a treelined street and designed around an open-air courtyard and fountain, the venue has a contemporary-chic, elegant ambiance and provides an amazing backdrop for your special event. Their professional staff is also renowned for personable service with extraordinary attention to detail.

All of the hotel's event spaces offer a relaxed, indoor/outdoor flow and may include fire, a fountain or lighting as individual features or in combination—the ideal mix of amenities for California-style entertaining. You can gather around the fire for s'mores, float flowers in the fountain, hang lanterns overhead along with the existing string lights or showcase your personal style by adding your own special touches. Celebrations hosted in the Courtyard Ballroom on the ground floor often begin around the adjacent patio and fountain, where your signature cocktail and passed hors d'oeuvres are served. Then guests are invited into the spacious ballroom for the main reception, leaving the courtyard open for guests to enjoy a respite after dinner and during dancing.

The newly renovated Grove Ballroom on the second floor boasts floor-to-ceiling arched windows on three sides. An outdoor balcony runs the length of the room and overlooks downtown Palo Alto and a lush landscape design. Guests are free to step outside to mix and mingle before, during and after the main event in the ballroom. Several unique spaces on this floor can be used to set up a specialty dessert station or bar.

At Garden Court Hotel, the guest experience is well thought out: With the venue's prime location in the immediate city center, your family and friends will have access to plenty of entertainment options between organized activities, and they'll find a variety of cafes and shops nearby. Plus, there's an energetic, high-tech vibe to the whole town.

A complimentary wedding-night stay at Garden Court Hotel and a complimentary honeymoon in Spain (offered through their Spanish partnerships; certain requirements and restrictions apply) are available for qualifying couples.

CEREMONY CAPACITY: The Grove Ballroom accommodates 210 seated or 290 standing. The Courtyard Ballroom holds 120 seated or 200 standing.

EVENT/RECEPTION & MEETING CAPACITY: For a reception, various rooms accommodate 8–230 seated or 8–300 standing. For a meeting, the hotel seats 8–60 conference-style or 8–200 theater-style. Removable dividing walls can vary the room size.

FEES & DEPOSITS: A nonrefundable deposit based on your event is due at the time of booking, when a payment schedule for the estimated event balance is also determined. The final payment is due 10 days prior to your event. Facility fees vary depending on the day of the week and event space reserved. Menu and beverage packages range $65–95/person. A 20% service charge and tax are additional.

Facility fees for meetings and corporate events vary based on group size, room(s) selected and catering requirements. Please call for more details; a customized estimate and an event packet will be sent directly.

AVAILABILITY: Year-round, daily, 7am–midnight.

SERVICES/AMENITIES:
Catering: in-house
Kitchen Facilities: n/a
Tables & Chairs: provided
Linens, Silver, etc.: provided
Restrooms: wheelchair accessible
Dance Floor: provided
Bride's Dressing Area: CBA, extra fee
AV/Meeting Equipment: full range CBA, extra fee

Parking: complimentary valet, large lot, free street parking on weekends
Accommodations: 62 guest rooms and suites
Outdoor Night Lighting: yes
Outdoor Cooking Facilities: no
Cleanup: provide
View: open-air courtyard and fountain or Downtown Palo Alto

RESTRICTIONS:
Alcohol: in-house or BYO wine and champagne; corkage per bottle applied
Smoking: outside only
Music: amplified OK indoors only, outdoors acoustic music only

Wheelchair Access: yes
Insurance: not required
Other: no birdseed or rice

Lucie Stern Community Center

Community Center

1305 Middlefield Road, Palo Alto
650/463-4900
www.cityofpaloalto.org/luciestern
lscc@cityofpaloalto.org

- Rehearsal Dinners
- Ceremonies
- Wedding Receptions
- Corp. Events/Mtgs.
- Private Parties
- Accommodations

With its white-stucco archways, red-tile roof and vibrant courtyard, the Lucie Stern Center is a quintessential example of Spanish-Mediterranean architecture. Originally built in 1934 as a community theater, this welcoming venue now offers a variety of options for weddings and special events.

One of the most popular areas for gathering during a celebration is the Courtyard, a brick-paved retreat surrounded by lush greenery. Enhancing this picturesque setting is the majestic theater, standing tall in the background—it's evocative of a centuries-old Spanish church.

From the courtyard, guests walk through double glass doors into the spacious Lucie Stern Center Ballroom, complete with a beautiful hardwood floor, dark wood wainscoting and two floral-tiled fireplaces. Designed in a rustic, hacienda style, the room features a cathedral ceiling with exposed wooden beams and six cylindrical chandeliers crafted of black wrought iron. Seven large, dramatic windows frame views of the facility's verdant front lawn and allow natural light to filter into the room.

If your wedding is small and informal, consider hosting it in the attractive Community Room, whose windows overlook a Mission-style promenade. Two sets of French doors open to a patio that's enclosed by stucco and vine-covered walls and a wooden colonnade. This private outdoor space has a two-tiered lawn bordered by an array of colorful flowers—the upper level is the ideal spot for your ceremony or live entertainment. For a more intimate setting, reserve the Fireside Room. Accessed by another set of French doors off of the patio, its focal point is an impressive brick-and-stucco fireplace.

From the blooming white roses at the courtyard entry to the open-air promenade and Mission-style rooms, the Lucie Stern Community Center is a charming location for any occasion. We encourage you tour the building and grounds, and discover the many possibilities available for your event.

CEREMONY CAPACITY: The center holds 300 seated guests indoors or up to 250 seated outdoors.

EVENT/RECEPTION CAPACITY: The center accommodates 200 seated or 300 standing guests indoors or up to 150 seated or 200 standing outdoors.

MEETING CAPACITY: The center seats up to 300 guests theater-style.

FEES & DEPOSITS: One third of the rental fee is required to secure your date, and the balance is due 30 days prior to the event. The rental fee starts at $2,500 and varies depending on the space and day rented, and the duration of the event. Visit www.cityofpaloalto.org/luciestern for more details.

AVAILABILITY: Year-round, daily, 6am–midnight.

SERVICES/AMENITIES:

Catering: BYO
Kitchen Facilities: fully equipped
Tables & Chairs: most provided
Linens, Silver, etc.: BYO or through caterer
Restrooms: wheelchair accessible
Dance Floor: ballroom
Bride's Dressing Area: no
AV/Meeting Equipment: BYO or CBA

Parking: ample on site
Accommodations: no guest rooms
Outdoor Night Lighting: yes
Outdoor Cooking Facilities: through caterer
Cleanup: caterer or renter
View: garden patio

RESTRICTIONS:

Alcohol: BYO wine, beer or champagne
Smoking: outside only
Music: amplified OK with restrictions

Wheelchair Access: yes
Insurance: general liability required, may be purchased through the venue

MacArthur Park

Restaurant & Historic Landmark

27 University Avenue, Palo Alto
650/321-9996
www.macarthurparkpaloalto.com
barbara@macpark.com

- Rehearsal Dinners
- Ceremonies
- Wedding Receptions
- Corp. Events/Mtgs.
- Private Parties
- Accommodations

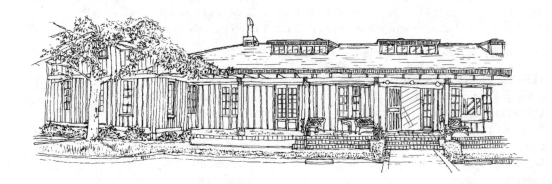

MacArthur Park has long been recognized for its classic American cuisine, but what many people don't know is that this award-winning Palo Alto restaurant is also a fabulous venue for special events—everything from engagement parties and rehearsal dinners to wedding receptions.

The historic building that houses MacArthur Park was designed in 1918 by renowned architect Julia Morgan (who later became famous for her architectural masterpiece, Hearst Castle). It originally served as a recreation facility where WWI troops would meet with their sweethearts and spouses, so it seems quite fitting that today it's popular for wedding celebrations.

MacArthur Park's simple yet elegant design is a fine example of Morgan's craftsman style, and showcases many beautiful period details. The main dining room has a vaulted ceiling with exposed wood trusses and beams, and an enormous brick fireplace anchors each end of the space. Interior balconies provide additional dining areas and give guests a bird's-eye view of the festivities below. The décor is neutral and timeless: The room is painted in a rich, soothing shade of café au lait…dark brown wood chairs contrast with white linens…original framed artwork graces board and batten walls.

The very attractive private dining rooms are well-suited for more intimate events like rehearsal dinners and business meetings, and feature the same warm tones and wall treatments as the main dining room. Several sets of French windows are framed by long drapes that, when closed, filter the natural light flowing in, creating an almost ethereal effect.

For outdoor functions, take a peek at the enclosed courtyard, an aggregate patio set with white chairs and matching linen-covered tables. Striped fabric awnings shade guests from the sun, and heat lamps take the chill off during cooler months or evening affairs.

MacArthur Park's crowd-pleasing American menu options incorporate local, seasonal ingredients and can be customized for your wedding. And, of course, the venue's experienced and knowledgeable event team will do their best to ensure that you and your guests have a truly memorable experience.

CEREMONY CAPACITY: The Patio accommodates 100 seated or 150 standing; the Main Dining Room area, including lofts, holds up to 250 seated.

EVENT/RECEPTION & MEETING CAPACITY: The Main Dining Room seats up to 250 guests, with balconies. The patio courtyard holds 100 seated or 150 for a standing reception. Lofts hold 28 guests each. The Julia Morgan Room seats 40 and the Camp Fremont Room seats 24. The new Veteran Room holds 100 seated or 120 standing guests.

FEES & DEPOSITS: A deposit is required to secure your date. There is no fee to reserve the restaurant for a day event. Food service is provided. Seated functions, including food, beverages, tax and service charges, run $65–100/person. A food & beverage minimum will apply.

For business functions and meetings, call for more information and rates.

AVAILABILITY: Year-round, 7 days a week.

SERVICES/AMENITIES:

Catering: in-house, no BYO
Kitchen Facilities: n/a
Tables & Chairs: provided
Linens, Silver, etc.: provided
Restrooms: wheelchair accessible
Dance Floor: CBA, extra fee
Bride's Dressing Area: no
AV/Meeting Equipment: CBA, extra fee

Parking: valet extra charge, large lot nearby
Accommodations: no guest rooms
Outdoor Night Lighting: yes
Outdoor Cooking Facilities: no
Cleanup: provided
View: no
Other: event coordinator on site

RESTRICTIONS:

Alcohol: in-house
Smoking: not permitted
Music: amplified OK

Wheelchair Access: yes
Insurance: not required

Palo Alto Hills Golf & Country Club

Country Club

3000 Alexis Drive, Palo Alto

650/917-5117

www.pahgcc.com
catering@pahgcc.net

- Rehearsal Dinners
- Ceremonies
- Wedding Receptions
- Corp. Events/Mtgs.
- Private Parties
- Accommodations

Set high in the rolling hills above Silicon Valley and nestled next to the Arastradero Open Space Preserve, the Palo Alto Hills Golf & Country Club boasts spectacular Bay Area vistas. And although this is one of the most prestigious private clubs in the United States, you don't have to be a member to host a special event here.

The country club is known for its welcoming atmosphere, and its Grand Ballroom could not be more inviting. Considered one of the loveliest spaces on the Peninsula, it's an ideal setting for any celebration. Windows on three sides showcase the golf course, signature 18th-hole green and cascading waterfall (a fabulous backdrop for a wedding ceremony and photos). The venue is also spacious enough to accommodate a seated reception for 275 with a dance floor.

The ballroom opens onto a landscaped terrace that's popular for wedding ceremonies, rehearsal dinners or post-ceremony cocktail receptions. Your guests will appreciate both the fresh air and the irresistible View: verdant fairways bordered by majestic redwoods, pine and oak trees. The park-like setting not only brings nature into your event, it offers endless photo opportunities.

For smaller gatherings, reserve the sophisticated Members Dining Room, whose warm cherrywood walls are crisscrossed with a distinctive pattern of brass inlay. In the evening, add a romantic glow with candles on the tables, or simply enjoy the captivating panorama of city lights sparkling against the night sky.

Two meeting rooms, which can be used individually or combined, are available for rehearsal dinners.

The chef takes pride in using the freshest ingredients and supporting many local and organic farms and vendors. He and his staff have created three distinct wedding packages, but if you have something else in mind they're happy to customize a menu for your occasion.

Impeccable service is the top priority at the Palo Alto Hills Golf & Country Club. Whether you're planning an elegant black-tie affair, a casual poolside party or something in between, you'll be impressed with their entire staff, from the valet parking attendants to the professional event coordinator who will help you personalize your festivities.

CEREMONY, EVENT/RECEPTION & MEETING CAPACITY: The clubhouse holds up to 275 seated or 400 standing guests, both indoors and outdoors.

FEES & DEPOSITS: The rental fee ranges $500–3,000 depending on the day of the week. Meals range $85–130/person. All wedding packages include a 1-hour hors d'oeuvre reception, salad course, entrée, champagne toast and cake-cutting. Tax, alcohol and a 20% service charge are additional.

AVAILABILITY: Year-round.

SERVICES/AMENITIES:

Catering: in-house
Kitchen Facilities: n/a
Tables & Chairs: provided
Linens, Silver, etc.: provided
Restrooms: wheelchair accessible
Dance Floor: provided
Bride's Dressing Area: yes
AV/Meeting Equipment: provided, extra fee

Parking: self-parking or valet, extra fee
Accommodations: no guest rooms
Outdoor Night Lighting: yes
Outdoor Cooking Facilities: n/a
Cleanup: provided
View: bay, fairways, grounds, hills, pool, waterfall
Other: event coordination

RESTRICTIONS:

Alcohol: in-house, or BYO wine with corkage fee
Smoking: outdoors only
Music: amplified OK

Wheelchair Access: yes
Insurance: not required

The wedding vendors on our website are the best in the business. How do we know? Read page 553.

The Palo Alto Wedding & Event Center

Ballroom

4249 El Camino Real, Palo Alto

650/493-4249 x124

www.weddingandeventcenteratpaloalto.org
eventmanager@paloaltoelks.org

● Rehearsal Dinners	● Corp. Events/Mtgs.
● Ceremonies	● Private Parties
● Wedding Receptions	Accommodations

Fresh and exciting, the Palo Alto Wedding & Event Center is located in the heart of Silicon Valley, just one mile south of Stanford University and minutes from the area's foremost technology and venture capital companies. Opened in 2011 as part of the Palo Alto Elks Lodge, it's become a popular venue for weddings as well as other social, corporate and community functions.

The atmosphere is a welcoming one. As you enter through the spacious atrium, you immediately notice the high ceiling, splendid front wall of windows, and striking contemporary staircase that leads to the second-level facilities. But don't go upstairs just yet.

First explore the ground floor where the Grand Ballroom radiates a clean, crisp elegance. The 23-foot ceiling lends it an unquestionable grandeur, but there's nothing stuffy about this space: It's fully equipped with state-of-the-art internet, AV and lighting capabilities in keeping with the property's high-tech environment. Clerestory windows, a beautiful built-in dance floor, and creamy, fabric-covered walls further elevate the room's tone. There's also a full catering kitchen and a two-sided bar that can simultaneously serve both the ballroom and the bistro/ballroom foyer. Want to host part of your festivities outdoors? The poolside terrace and lawn is an ideal place for a ceremony or cocktails and hors d'oeuvres in a relaxed, California palm and garden surround.

Upstairs the mood is equally airy and uplifting. The Palo Alto Room, with its two walls of floor-to-ceiling windows and gorgeous white oak floors, is versatile enough to accommodate any kind of event, and its neutral cream-and-champagne interior complements any décor. Sun-splashed by day, moonlit by night, it's a stunning blank canvas for whatever light and sound enhancements you might want to introduce. If you like, it can be divided into two smaller chambers for more intimate gatherings. Also on this level, the Card Room is often used for a small ceremony or as a private space for the bride and her bridesmaids or the groom and his men.

All in all, you'll find over 9,000 square feet of handsomely appointed and surprisingly affordable event space here, along with an experienced event staff dedicated to making your celebration the best it can be. Top it off with the benevolent energy of the Elks and their focus on fraternity, charity and good works, and you can be certain you and your guests will be in excellent hands.

CEREMONY, EVENT/RECEPTION & MEETING CAPACITY: The center holds up to 260 seated or standing guests in the Grand Ballroom, 150 seated or standing in the Palo Alto Room, and 200 seated or standing outdoors.

FEES & DEPOSITS: The venue rental fee, which ranges $1,000–3,000 depending on the space reserved, is required to secure your date. The balance is due on or before the day of the event. Dinners start at $38/person, breakfast and lunch are also available. Wedding packages, which include the rental fee and meals, start at $100/person. Tax, alcohol and a 20% service charge are additional.

Rates for business functions, meetings or other types of events vary. Please contact the venue for more details.

AVAILABILITY: Year-round, daily, 6am–midnight.

SERVICES/AMENITIES:
Catering: in-house
Kitchen Facilities: n/a
Tables & Chairs: provided
Linens, Silver, etc.: provided
Restrooms: wheelchair accessible
Dance Floor: provided
Bride's Dressing Area: yes
AV/Meeting Equipment: some provided

Parking: large lot
Accommodations: no guest rooms
Outdoor Night Lighting: yes
Outdoor Cooking Facilities: BBQ on site
Cleanup: provided
View: garden patio, pool area
Other: grand piano, in-house florals, event coordination

RESTRICTIONS:
Alcohol: in-house, or BYO wine with a $15 corkage fee
Smoking: not allowed
Music: amplified OK with restrictions

Wheelchair Access: yes
Insurance: not required

The Sea by Alexander's Steakhouse
at Dinah's Garden Hotel

4269 El Camino Real, Palo Alto
650/213-1117
www.theseausa.com
contact@theseausa.com

Restaurant & Hotel

- Rehearsal Dinners
- Ceremonies
- Wedding Receptions
- Corp. Events/Mtgs.
- Private Parties
- Accommodations

For decades, Dinah's Garden Hotel has been known for its imaginative accommodations, tucked amidst five luxuriantly landscaped acres brimming with sparkling waterfalls. Recently, Dinah's teamed up with The Sea by Alexander's Steakhouse, a new venture from the acclaimed restaurant group. The partnership has added delectable dining, as well as an array of event spaces that exude modern elegance with Asian flair.

A wedding here might begin with an intimate ceremony on a spacious L-shaped terrace. Say your vows in the redwood section, bordered by planter boxes filled with greenery. Guests look on from chic white leather chairs, shaded by canvas umbrellas. Then toast the momentous occasion in the adjoining tiled section beneath a vaulted awning, where high-top cocktail tables and stylish lounge furniture create a congenial atmosphere.

Receptions unfold in The Sea's ballroom, a refined space whose Brazilian cherrywood floor is polished to a warm gleam. Recessed lighting, a soaring cathedral ceiling and multipaned clerestory windows lend a luminous grandeur. There's plenty of room for dancing, and the latest tech capabilities—including "surround sound"—expand your entertainment options.

Like the ballroom, the main dining room's clean, contemporary aesthetic achieves a look of uncomplicated sophistication. The bar and lounge is a fun place to mingle before or after the main event. Next to the lounge is the Gulf Room, where frosted glass panes and embroidered black curtains create privacy. A slanted ceiling and geometric nooks showcasing floral arrangements add architectural interest. With a capacity of up to 50 seated guests, the Gulf Room hosts rehearsal dinners or intimate receptions with grace and ease. Another option is the Boardroom, whose floor-to-ceiling glass looks out to the Patio—a nice spot to host cocktails before moving inside for dinner.

The centerpiece of The Sea is, of course, the food. Under the leadership of Executive Chef Yu Min Lin, who previously helmed a Michelin-rated restaurant, The Sea is dedicated to taking the freshest seasonal ingredients and transforming them into an extraordinary culinary adventure. Yu Min meticulously sources all his seafood, selecting only the best wild and sustainably harvested products.

Kick off your cocktail hour with epicurean treats like hamachi shots or Wagyu beef rolls. For the main course, the seafood entrées are the most popular, but creative vegetarian dishes and high-quality steaks are also available. An extensive wine list and specialty cakes by The Sea's Executive

Pastry Chef round out the offerings. Throughout, the well-trained staff delivers synchronized service for a seamless dining experience.

The hotel displays the same originality and attention to detail as the restaurant. A stroll through Dinah's Garden Hotel takes you past romantic gardens filled with koi ponds, waterfall grottos and quaint footbridges. To further enhance your stay, each of Dinah's 129 guest rooms is individually decorated with world-class art and priceless collectibles. Lagoon rooms embrace lush foliage and the sound of flowing water. The opulently arrayed Signature Suites boast luxurious amenities such as a steam room, private decks, and a working model train. The morning after, enjoy brunch at Dinah's Poolside Restaurant, a local favorite.

With everything you need to hold a memorable wedding weekend all in one place, this peninsula oasis is a winning combination.

CEREMONY CAPACITY: The facility accommodates up to 120 seated guests outdoors on the terrace.

EVENT/RECEPTION CAPACITY: Indoors, the facility holds 150 seated, 250 standing; outdoors, 60 seated or 120 standing.

MEETING CAPACITY: Event spaces seat 150 guests.

FEES & DEPOSITS: 20% of the total event cost is required to reserve your date, and the event balance is due on the day of the event. The food & beverage minimum ranges $3,500–20,000 depending on the day and time of the event. Meals range $95–110/person. Tax, alcohol and a 20% service charge are additional. If you cancel within 15 days of your event date, the 20% deposit will be kept by the venue.

AVAILABILITY: Year-round, daily.

SERVICES/AMENITIES:

Catering: in-house
Kitchen Facilities: n/a
Tables & Chairs: provided
Linens, Silver, etc.: provided
Restrooms: wheelchair accessible
Dance Floor: yes
Bride's & Groom's Dressing Areas: yes
AV/Meeting Equipment: provided

Parking: large lots
Accommodations: 129 guest rooms
Outdoor Night Lighting: yes
Outdoor Cooking Facilities: no
Cleanup: provided
View: garden, pool area, waterfall, pond
Other: event coordination

RESTRICTIONS:

Alcohol: in-house
Smoking: designated area only
Music: amplified OK with restrictions

Wheelchair Access: yes
Insurance: not required

Sheraton Palo Alto

Hotel

625 El Camino Real, Palo Alto
650/328-2800 x7005
www.sheraton.com/paloalto
ktobin@pahotel.com

● Rehearsal Dinners	● Corp. Events/Mtgs.
● Ceremonies	● Private Parties
● Wedding Receptions	● Accommodations

Picture a clear, rocky stream running beneath footbridges, past lush ferns and flower gardens. Sounds more like a combination of the mountains and a tropical island than Palo Alto, but that's exactly where it is. At the Sheraton Palo Alto, each of the event spaces has its own unique look, from the Spanish-tiled, glass-enclosed courtyard to the glamorous, modern ballroom. The hotel is located on a commercial boulevard within walking distance of downtown Palo Alto, but because it's set back off the road and imaginatively landscaped, the Sheraton maintains an air of exclusivity.

A stroll through the mostly glass lobby, suffused with light from windows and skylights, takes you to the large swimming pool area. It's the perfect spot for a splashy cocktail hour: A brick-paved patio is bordered by trees and gardenias, and at night the pool is illuminated by underwater lights and the trees glow with twinkle lights.

The Reception Room is in its own wing, and features two large crystal chandeliers, a dance floor and vaulted ceiling. Foldout glass doors open onto an adjoining lawn, which is equally suited for ceremonies or stargazing. A semicircular wall encloses the lawn, so only your group can access it.

Justine's Ballroom is actually two spacious banquet rooms separated by a beautiful glass-enclosed interior courtyard designed with Spanish tile, white stucco archways, arched mirrors and a glass ceiling. The setting makes a picturesque backdrop for your ceremony, photographs and even the cake cutting. Use the banquet room that opens onto a streamside patio for cocktails, then spread out into both dining rooms for dinner. Another appealing venue is the Cypress Ballroom, an imperial room highlighted by custom carpeting, contemporary chandeliers and softly lit shadowboxes.

With its variety of event spaces, the Sheraton Palo Alto gives you plenty of options, and their creative and experienced staff guarantee to work wonders on your special day.

CEREMONY CAPACITY: The hotel can accommodate 150–300 seated or 200–350 standing guests indoors, and up to 120 seated or 200 standing outdoors.

EVENT/RECEPTION CAPACITY: The site holds 150–350 seated or up to 500 standing guests indoors and 110 seated or 200 standing outdoors.

MEETING CAPACITY: Small meeting rooms and parlors are available in addition to 3 larger spaces that seat 30–300 guests.

FEES & DEPOSITS: For weddings and special events, 25% of the estimated event total is required to secure your date. The balance is due 10 days prior to the event. Lunches start at $45/person and wedding packages start at $82/person. Alcohol, a 22% service charge and tax are extra. The wedding couple receive a complimentary room with champagne. Group rates can be arranged for overnight wedding guests. For meetings, room rental fees start at $400.

AVAILABILITY: Year-round, daily, anytime.

SERVICES/AMENITIES:

Catering: in-house; some ethnic caterers permitted
Kitchen Facilities: n/a
Tables & Chairs: provided
Linens, Silver, etc.: provided
Restrooms: wheelchair accessible
Dance Floor: portable indoors or Piazza Courtyard
Dressing Areas: CBA
AV/Meeting Equipment: full range CBA

Parking: large lot, valet available
Accommodations: 350 guest rooms and suites
Outdoor Night Lighting: yes
Outdoor Cooking Facilities: n/a
Cleanup: provided
View: flower gardens, fountain, koi ponds
Other: event coordination

RESTRICTIONS:

Alcohol: in-house, or corkage $15/bottle, $25/magnum
Smoking: outdoors only
Music: amplified OK

Wheelchair Access: yes
Insurance: not required
Other: no birdseed or rice; no fog machines

Westin Palo Alto Hotel

Hotel

675 El Camino Real, Palo Alto
650/321-4422 X7005
www.westin.com/paloalto
ktobin@pahotel.com

● Rehearsal Dinners	● Corp. Events/Mtgs.
● Ceremonies	● Private Parties
● Wedding Receptions	● Accommodations

It may look like simply another nice hotel from the outside, but as soon as you step into the marble-clad lobby of the Westin Palo Alto you experience its extraordinary appeal. This boutique-style venue combines clean, harmonious Feng Shui with a cosmopolitan sophistication that is warmed by understated Mediterranean architecture. Facing the entrance, a sleek marble staircase is flanked by a tableau of up-lit Oriental ferns in creamy ceramic vases. Above you, a ceiling inset with a serene shade of sky-blue introduces the hotel's design motif: *celestial*.

The expansive feeling of connection to heavenly elements is most artfully realized in the hotel's peaceful garden courtyards. Each is defined by two five-storied façades, whose guest room windows are embellished with wrought-iron balconies and pastel-hued shutters that recall Old World town squares. The Court of the Moon & Stars is favored by many brides for ceremonies because of its striking water feature: Along one ivy-decked wall, a row of fountain urns the color of cobalt blue overflow with water into a rectangular pool. At night, white globes glow like full moons in the background. Opposite this wall are French doors opening to a luxurious fireplace suite, often reserved by the bridal couple for the perfect grand entrance. Your attendants and overnight guests might stay in the other rooms overlooking the courtyard, turning it into your own private party haven.

But feel free to spread your event out into other delightful enclaves. The Court of the Sun features a bronze sundial at its center, cheerful yellow umbrellas, and a trellis climbing with golden honeysuckle. A large celadon fountain urn gurgles at the center of the Court of the Wind, while reeds and grasses arch along one wall as if bending to a gentle breeze. Either of these are pleasant spots for a social hour or an al fresco reception; or serve cocktails in the Court of Water around the swimming pool!

Indoor receptions are equally charming in the sumptuous Siena-Carrara Ballroom, commodious enough to accommodate your exclusive fête while still keeping things cozy. Leave the doors open, and guests can meander into the tastefully appointed Foyer, furnished with club chairs and sofas for relaxed conversation.

The Westin Palo Alto caters to intimate celebrations, that convivial kind of gathering where you're actually well-acquainted with each guest. Since yours is the one and only event on site, the Westin staff is dedicated to making it quite special indeed.

You would expect a venue with such style and personal service to be very costly; however, Westin offers reasonably priced wedding packages that include champagne and butler-passed hors d'oeuvres for the social hour; plated gourmet dinner with wine; elegant centerpieces; and a complimentary suite for the newlyweds. Speaking of wedding nights: Most of the hotel suites include romantic touches like a fireplace and whirlpool tub, and all rooms have Westin's signature Heavenly Bed, which boasts "10 layers of comfort"…so if you and your new spouse decide to leave the "do not disturb" sign on your door indefinitely, everyone will understand.

CEREMONY CAPACITY: The Courtyard holds 50 seated guests; the Siena-Carrara Ballroom 100.

EVENT/RECEPTION CAPACITY: The Siena-Carrara Ballroom holds up to 60 seated or 100 standing; the Courtyard up to 50 seated or 60 standing.

MEETING CAPACITY: Event spaces accommodate 12–80 seated guests.

FEES & DEPOSITS: 25% of the estimated event total is required to reserve your date, and the balance is due 10 days prior to the event. The rental fee ranges $300–800 depending on the food & beverage minimum. Lunches start at $46/person, wedding packages start at $86/person. Tax, alcohol and a 22% service charge are additional. All packages include a 1-hour cocktail reception, a champagne toast for all guests, wine service during dinner, elegant centerpieces, and a complimentary guest room for the wedding couple with a bottle of champagne.

AVAILABILITY: Year-round, daily, anytime.

SERVICES/AMENITIES:

Catering: in-house
Kitchen Facilities: n/a
Tables & Chairs: provided
Linens, Silver, etc.: provided
Restrooms: wheelchair accessible
Dance Floor: provided
Dressing Areas: CBA
AV/Meeting Equipment: CBA

Parking: large lot, valet available
Accommodations: 184 guest rooms
Outdoor Night Lighting: yes
Outdoor Cooking Facilities: no
Cleanup: provided
View: pool, courtyard, fountain, grounds
Other: event coordination

RESTRICTIONS:

Alcohol: in-house, or BYO with $15/bottle corkage
Smoking: outside only
Music: amplified OK with restrictions

Wheelchair Access: yes
Insurance: not required

Want to find more venues and services? Check out our informative website, www.HereComesTheGuide.com.

209

Woman's Club of Palo Alto

Historic Woman's Club

475 Homer Avenue, Palo Alto
650/321-5821

womansclubofpaloalto.org
rentals@womansclubofpaloalto.org

- Rehearsal Dinners
- Ceremonies
- Wedding Receptions
- Corp. Events/Mtgs.
- Private Parties
- Accommodations

On June 20, 1894, 24 women gathered to organize the Woman's Club of Palo Alto. Their goals were friendship, self-improvement, and community involvement. Within the first four years of the club's existence, they founded the city's first reading room and library, as well as its first elementary school and high school.

Their dream of having their own clubhouse, however, was not realized until 1916. After 12 years of fundraising, they built their Tudor-Craftsman-style "home" for $10,590. At the time, they worried that it was too far removed from the center of town, but its location in a quiet residential neighborhood has proved a felicitous one.

Weddings are held in the Ballroom, a simply designed space with grand proportions. On two sides, tall windows flood the room with light, which reflects off polished maple floors. Eight brass-and-glass fixtures suspended from the high ceiling, and dark wood wainscoting and trim throughout add period character. Have your ceremony on the stage, which is framed by a red velvet curtain and illuminated by footlights. A Steinway grand piano is available for musical accompaniment. Buffets are usually set up in the adjacent Fireside Room, aptly named for its tiled fireplace, and joined to the Ballroom by folding French doors. A small side patio lets guests step outside for a little fresh air.

The founders of the Woman's Club of Palo Alto may not have envisioned their clubhouse as a setting for private events, but today the landmark building has become just that. Its elegant ballroom and chef's kitchen make it a popular and affordable spot for weddings, corporate functions, and other celebrations.

CEREMONY, EVENT/RECEPTION & MEETING CAPACITY: The Ballroom and Fireside Room hold 150 seated guests for a banquet, or 200 seated theater-style.

FEES & DEPOSITS: For weekend special events or weddings, the $3,000 full-day rental fee and a $1,000 security deposit are due with your signed contract.

For weekday meetings and multi-day bookings, the rate is $300/hour with a minimum of 6 hours.

AVAILABILITY: Year-round.

SERVICES/AMENITIES:

Catering: BYO
Kitchen Facilities: fully equipped
Tables & Chairs: provided
Linens, Silver, etc.: BYO
Restrooms: wheelchair accessible
Dance Floor: on stage, in Ballroom
Bride's Dressing Area: yes
AV/Meeting Equipment: WiFi, AV

Parking: on-street and nearby lots
Accommodations: no guest rooms
Outdoor Night Lighting: access only
Outdoor Cooking Facilities: BYO BBQ
Cleanup: caterer
View: residential neighborhood
Other: air conditioning

RESTRICTIONS:

Alcohol: BYO
Smoking: outdoors only
Music: amplified OK indoors only until 10pm

Wheelchair Access: yes
Insurance: liability required

Valley Presbyterian Church

Church

945 Portola Road, Portola Valley
650/851-2848

www.valleypreschurch.org
wedding@valleypreschurch.org

Rehearsal Dinners	Corp. Events/Mtgs.
● Ceremonies	Private Parties
Wedding Receptions	Accommodations

From its breathtaking sanctuary to its wooded grounds, Valley Presbyterian Church draws on the purity of the natural world to enhance your spiritual experience. "There's a sense of peace here," explains one congregant. "You feel like a part of nature, and thus closer to God." Being welcoming and inclusive, this church invites all couples to celebrate their wedding here.

The heart of Valley Presbyterian Church is the awe-inspiring sanctuary—its simplicity and unpretentious beauty evoke serenity and wonder. Guests enter through four heavy wooden doors, richly carved with images of New Testament figures. Oak pews are upholstered with green fabric, and the A-frame pine ceiling is accented by dark beams. Polished riverbed stones in the washed aggregate floor echo the sanctuary's earthy aesthetic, while stone planters filled with greenery line the interior.

However, it's the soaring sanctuary windows behind the communion table that take your breath away. They frame a grove of majestic redwood trees reaching heavenward. Guests face this magnificent forest scene, while from the steps below the communion table the bridal party enjoys its own striking tableau: the six-foot-tall stained-glass window above the front doors depicting a simple golden Celtic cross in a blue-toned mosaic. When light shines through it, the amber cross is reflected across the church onto the view of the redwoods, and seems to float mysteriously in the air—a sparkling vision that heightens the mood of peaceful reverence.

The church comes with the services of a minister, coordinator, organist, wedding hostess and hostess assistant. Every couple that marries at Valley Presbyterian attends a one-day Marriage Preparation Workshop, as well as a separate private meeting with their assigned officiant. All are welcome here, and though a Valley Presbyterian minister will be the main officiant of the wedding, you may invite a guest minister to assist with the ceremony. Also included, but optional, are candelabras with candles, a unity candle, white silk florals for the communion table, pew decorations and an aisle runner.

Valley Presbyterian Church believes in giving back to the community, and is known for its outreach and children's programs. This is a church that actively promotes family, community, and spiritual values—a promising environment for starting a new life together.

CEREMONY CAPACITY: The Sanctuary holds 225+ guests. Call for details.

FEES & DEPOSITS: A nonrefundable $1,200 deposit is required to reserve your date. The fee is $2,050 for a 2½-hour time frame. Fees are subject to change without notice. Couples need not be members of Valley Presbyterian Church; however, it is necessary that the ceremony be a Christian service.

AVAILABILITY: Year-round. Ceremonies on Saturday begin at 10am, noon, 2:30pm and 5pm, and on Sunday at 2:30pm and 5pm. Rehearsals take place on the Friday before the wedding. To arrange a weekday or evening wedding, please contact the Wedding Coordinator.

SERVICES/AMENITIES:

Catering: n/a

Kitchen Facilities: n/a

Tables & Chairs: n/a

Linens, Silver, etc.: n/a

Restrooms: wheelchair accessible

Dance Floor: n/a

Bride's & Groom's Dressing Areas: yes

AV/Meeting Equipment: n/a

Parking: lot for 175 guests

Accommodations: no guest rooms

Outdoor Night Lighting: yes

Outdoor Cooking Facilities: n/a

Cleanup: provided

View: redwood forest

RESTRICTIONS:

Alcohol: not permitted

Smoking: not allowed

Music: acoustic only

Wheelchair Access: yes

Insurance: not required

Other: no birdseed or rice

San Mateo County History Museum

Museum

2200 Broadway, Redwood City
650/299-0104 X225

www.historysmc.org
sue@historysmc.org

● Rehearsal Dinners	● Corp. Events/Mtgs.
● Ceremonies	● Private Parties
● Wedding Receptions	Accommodations

Domes are wondrous things, and there's no end to our fascination with them. Fortunately, you don't have to go to Rome (St. Peter's), Washington, DC (the Capitol) or Istanbul (the Hagia Sophia) to get a great dome fix—or even to get married beneath one. Just take the much shorter trip to Redwood City, where the San Mateo County History Museum has preserved one of the Bay Area's most remarkable domes.

The museum inhabits the venerable 1910 county courthouse, a sandstone structure that retains all of the dignity of that era, with its tile floors, Corinthian columns and tall, stately doors opening to Exhibit Galleries and the beautifully restored Courtroom A. The overwhelming centerpiece, however, is its magnificent dome. A towering concoction of skylit glass panes colored brilliant red, green, amber and opaque white, it rises above sculpted eagles and ornamental arches to a constellation of gold stars on a deep blue background. The dome is a full-tilt, rock-your-head-back-on-your-shoulders-and-stare-at-it-in-wonder kind of thing. Get married under it and you'll be talking about it for years to come.

Many couples also use the rotunda for their ceremony and reception. If your party is a large one, take advantage of the balcony-like second floor, which doubles as another dining space. Here guests not only have a better vantage of the gorgeous glass overhead, they can stroll over to the railing and enjoy a bird's-eye view of the festivities below.

Courtroom A also makes a fabulous setting for a ceremony or sit-down dinner. You reach it via a grand staircase distinguished by marble-topped risers, brass railings and mahogany banisters. Couples love its elegance and often pose for wedding photos on it. The courtroom has rich oak moldings and furnishings, including the traditional long railing that separates the jury and bar members from the public. Overhead, the ceiling features an oblong skylight of green, red and gray-blue glass arranged in abstract floral patterns. Stylized plaster wreaths of fruits and grains border the skylight, and four heavy Federal-style chandeliers with scalloped sconces hang low from the ceiling. Large oak-framed windows along two walls come down almost to the floor, and a Roman-style pediment spans the main entrance. The thick English carpet, red with gold highlights, feels absolutely wonderful underfoot. The original clerk, bailiff and judge's benches are still there, as are the jury chairs. This immensely refined room bestows an extra element of grace on any wedding.

The rotunda is so phenomenal that it needs little decoration, and the same goes for Courtroom A. For an added diversion (and fee), arrange to have the museum's exhibits open to your guests. If you love history or simply want something delightfully unconventional, it would be hard to beat this domed museum.

CEREMONY CAPACITY: Courtroom A holds 100 seated guests and the Rotunda holds 150 seated.

EVENT/RECEPTION CAPACITY: The entire courthouse holds 400 standing guests. Courtroom A accommodates up to 170 for a seated reception.

MEETING CAPACITY: The museum seats up to 120 guests for meetings.

FEES & DEPOSITS: A $750 deposit is required to reserve your date, and the balance is due 30 days prior to the event. The rental fee ranges $3,200–5,000 depending on the spaces reserved, services selected and staffing needed for the event.

AVAILABILITY: Year-round, daily. Monday all day; Tuesday–Sunday, 5pm–midnight.

SERVICES/AMENITIES:

Catering: select from preferred list
Kitchen Facilities: full catering kitchen
Tables & Chairs: tables provided, extra fee
Linens, Silver, etc.: CBA
Restrooms: wheelchair accessible
Dance Floor: yes
Bride's Dressing Area: yes
AV/Meeting Equipment: full range CBA, including teleconferencing and internet access

Parking: on-street or large lot, free after 6pm
Accommodations: no guest rooms
Outdoor Night Lighting: yes
Outdoor Cooking Facilities: no
Cleanup: caterer and janitorial staff
View: park, hills, fountain, grounds
Other: access to exhibits, extra fee

RESTRICTIONS:

Alcohol: BYO
Smoking: not allowed
Music: amplified OK indoors

Wheelchair Access: yes
Insurance: required

The Mountain Terrace

17285 Skyline Boulevard, Woodside
650/851-1606

www.themountainterrace.com
info@themountainterrace.com

Special Event Facility

● Rehearsal Dinners		● Corp. Events/Mtgs.
● Ceremonies		● Private Parties
● Wedding Receptions		Accommodations

Whether you're driving down from San Francisco or up from San Jose, the final six miles to The Mountain Terrace are sensational. They ascend a mountainside on state route 84, one of California's most magnificent sections of highway. The winding road is flanked by sturdy old oaks, dense fragrant redwood groves and huge chateau-like mansions. There are spectacular bay and ridge views at several spots along the way and, in a couple of places, imposing trees thrust their branches out across the road to form living archways.

If the last leg of the trip is a revelation, a second surprise awaits at the top. Where Highway 84 meets up with redwood-edged Skyline Blvd., there's a small crossroads settlement. The Mountain Terrace is an unassuming wooden building at the far end of this little village. However, as they say, appearances can be deceiving: The Mountain Terrace's prosaic exterior conceals glories inside. Once you cross the parking lot and pass through a redwood arbor, what you see takes your breath away: a brilliant green acre of lawn, shimmering in the sunlight, rimmed by oaks and dozens of soaring redwoods. At its far boundary, where the mountain begins to slope to the lowlands, it draws your eyes to a sweeping view of the southern part of San Francisco Bay all the way down to the Fremont hills.

By itself, the lawn makes a perfect spot for an outdoor wedding and reception. But there's more—once you've taken in the lawn, you turn to see a large two-level redwood deck. Right away you know it would make a superb setting for a stand-up reception, sit-down dinner or any kind of function in between. On its upper level, a trellis shelters half the deck. The lower deck, only a couple of steps down from the upper, has a deftly crafted octagonal-shaped extension that's perfect for cocktails or a dinner buffet. Just beyond the deck there are more oaks (one with a tree swing) shading chairs beneath them. The little grove makes a perfect nook partygoers can use to take a break from the main festivities while not losing touch.

There's still more: Glass doors connect the deck to a substantial indoor space, divided into a dining room and a bar/dance area by a large stone fireplace. The antique bar, made of solid oak, has hefty Doric columns carved into it and is backed by a massive three-part mirror. The room's hardwood floor invites carefree dancing (there's an area where a band or DJ can set up). The dining area looks out through picture windows onto the deck and lawn. In winter, with a roaring fire inside and mist-shrouded redwoods outside, it makes a cozy wedding and reception site by itself.

As a facility, The Mountain Terrace is a "three-fer": stunning lawn and view, inviting interior and grand redwood deck. Then there's the drive up, which will put your guests in such a good mood, by the time they arrive they'll be ready to fully enjoy the charms of this very special place.

CEREMONY CAPACITY: The meadow accommodates up to 400 seated guests.

EVENT/RECEPTION CAPACITY: Indoors, the site holds 130 seated. Outdoors, the patio holds up to 200 seated; the decks and lawn seat up to 300. When combined, the indoor and outdoor spaces accommodate a maximum of 350 seated guests.

MEETING CAPACITY: Meeting spaces seat up to 160 guests.

FEES & DEPOSITS: A refundable $500 security deposit plus the rental fee is required to secure your date, and the balance is payable prior to the event. The rental fee ranges $2,000–8,000 depending on the date and time reserved. Meals start at $65/person. Tax, alcohol and service charge are additional.

Meeting packages for up to 100 include: an 8-hour facility rental, tables, chairs, LCD projector with screen, flip charts, accessories, WiFi, continental breakfast, lunch and refresh breaks.

Corporate event packages may include: a cocktail reception; picnic, lunch or dinner; wine tasting party; cooking challenge or team building events.

AVAILABILITY: Year-round, daily.

SERVICES/AMENITIES:

Catering: in-house
Kitchen Facilities: fully equipped
Tables & Chairs: provided for up to 150 guests
Linens, Silver, etc.: china, glassware and flatware provided for up to 200; linens arranged by venue, extra fee
Restrooms: wheelchair accessible
Dance Floor: indoor area
Bride's Dressing Area: yes
AV/Meeting Equipment: provided

Parking: on-site lot or shuttle
Accommodations: no guest rooms
Outdoor Night Lighting: yes
Outdoor Cooking Facilities: CBA, extra fee
Cleanup: provided
View: redwoods, partial bay view

RESTRICTIONS:

Alcohol: in-house
Smoking: designated areas
Music: amplified OK indoors only, outdoors acoustic only

Wheelchair Access: yes
Insurance: not required

This is important! Tell locations you're reading HERE COMES THE GUIDE and ask if our information is still current.

217

Thomas Fogarty Winery and Vineyards

Hilltop Winery

19501 Skyline Boulevard, Woodside
650/851-6772

www.fogartywinery.com
events@fogartywinery.com

● Rehearsal Dinners	● Corp. Events/Mtgs.
● Ceremonies	● Private Parties
● Wedding Receptions	Accommodations

If we were to rate venues on a scale from 1 to 10, Fogarty Winery would be a 10! Located off Skyline Boulevard, it has to be one of the best places we've seen, not only for weddings but for private parties and corporate functions, too.

Commanding an extraordinary panorama of the bay and Peninsula, the winery sits high on a ridge in a quiet vineyard setting. As you arrive, vineyards and a picturesque pond come into view. At the top of the ridge is a large lawn, beautifully landscaped around the perimeter—a perfect spot for an outdoor ceremony.

Receptions and special events are held in the Hill House and/or the outdoor Pavilion. True to its name, the former steps down the hill and is designed with incredible attention to detail, featuring a stone fireplace, fine woodwork, skylights, a wine bar and a professional kitchen. From comfortable seating indoors, as well as from the semi-glass-enclosed terrace, you can see for miles—past the vineyards all the way to the distant bay.

Adjacent to the Hill House is the Pavilion, a covered redwood deck suspended over the hillside. Calling it a "covered deck" may be something of an understatement: This 4,000-square-foot architectural treat is constructed of teal-painted columns and beams which support a peaked cedar roof inset with skylights. You have a 270-degree view of the surrounding oak-dotted hills, the Chardonnay vineyards below, and the bay. The Pavilion is ideal for cocktails and hors d'oeuvres or an open-air seated reception—no matter how hot the day is, there's always a breeze blowing here.

For small private dinners, the Redwood Room is light and airy. It's outfitted with custom-built "barrel" tables, handcrafted leather chairs, a wood-burning stove and full kitchen—and it affords a panoramic view of the bay. If you'd like to have a meeting in these glorious surroundings, hold it in the Board Room or the Hill House. Lovely landscaping completes the picture, enhancing every event that's hosted at the winery. We can't recommend this facility highly enough.

CEREMONY CAPACITY: The Garden or the covered Pavilion each hold up to 216 seated guests.

EVENT/RECEPTION CAPACITY: The Hill House accommodates 216 seated without space for dancing, or 180 with dancing. The Pavilion holds up to 216 seated guests.

MEETING CAPACITY: Event spaces seat 20–216 guests.

FEES & DEPOSITS: For weddings, 50% of the rental fee is required as a nonrefundable deposit, due when the reservation is confirmed; the balance is payable 6 months prior to the event. The rental fee includes use of the lawn area, bridal suite, groom's room, Hill House, and the Pavilion for 8 or 9 hours. Only one wedding is booked per day. April–October, the wedding rental fee for the entire facility is $8,000 Monday–Friday and $8,500–11,500 Saturday–Sunday. November–March the fee is $7,000.

For other special events and business functions, fees vary depending on spaces selected, event duration, day of the week and season. Call for rates.

AVAILABILITY: Year-round, daily. For weddings and receptions, weekends 8am–11pm. For corporate events, any day 7am–11pm. Closed Thanksgiving, Christmas and New Year's Days and Eves.

SERVICES/AMENITIES:

Catering: select from preferred list
Kitchen Facilities: fully equipped
Tables & Chairs: some provided
Linens, Silver, etc.: BYO
Restrooms: wheelchair accessible
Dance Floor: inside Hill House
Bride's & Groom's Dressing Areas: yes
AV/Meeting Equipment: full range

Parking: valet available, extra fee
Accommodations: no guest rooms
Outdoor Night Lighting: yes
Outdoor Cooking Facilities: CBA
Cleanup: caterer
View: panorama of SF Bay and all major mountain peaks
Other: site manager, wine tasting

RESTRICTIONS:

Alcohol: wine, sparkling wine, and beer provided, no BYO
Smoking: outside only
Music: must select band or DJ from preferred list; acoustic only on lawn area

Wheelchair Access: yes
Insurance: certificate required for weddings & private events

South Bay

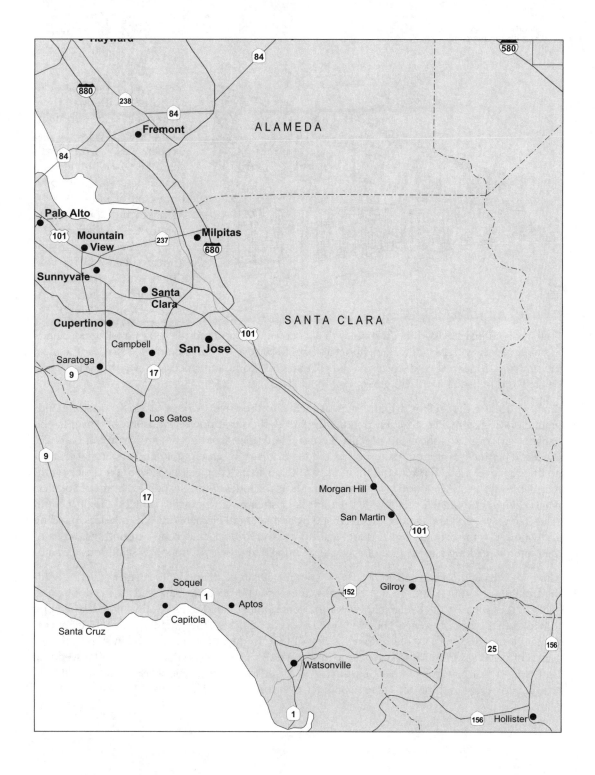

Villa Ragusa

35 South Second Street, Campbell
408/364-1900

www.villaragusa.com
events@villaragusa.com

Special Events Facility

Rehearsal Dinners	● Corp. Events/Mtgs.
● Ceremonies	● Private Parties
● Wedding Receptions	Accommodations

Some couples opt for a small wedding, with just their nearest and dearest in attendance. Then there are those exuberant souls who want to share their once-in-a-lifetime experience with everyone, from next of kin and good friends to third cousins twice removed. If you fall into the latter category, we've got a great suggestion for you: Check out Villa Ragusa, located in the historic downtown section of Campbell.

Built in traditional Mediterranean style, with a stucco façade and red-tile roof, Villa Ragusa blends in so seamlessly with its vintage neighbors it's hard to believe it's only been here since 2001. Inside, the simple European-style décor gives the villa an Old World ambiance, yet everything is freshly painted and polished to a high gloss.

When you enter the facility, a grand staircase leads to the Foyer, whose flawless limestone-and-granite floor glistens like a frozen pond. Four wooden double doors lead from the Foyer to the immense room that is the heart of Villa Ragusa. Here, the visual details are spare but carefully chosen. The thick carpeting, patterned in shades of maroon, green, gold and cream, looks as if no one has ever walked on it, and the dark wood bar that occupies one side of the space is immaculate and gleaming. Round frosted-glass-and-brass chandeliers are suspended from the coffered white ceiling, and arched windows let natural light stream in. The walls, painted in soft neutral shades of gray-green and cream, are enlivened by architectural elements such as pilasters, molding and wooden wainscoting. French doors lead to a covered deck that wraps around two sides of the building, making a great place for guests to mingle and enjoy Campbell's salubrious climate.

Although Villa Ragusa can accommodate 600 people, it can be divided into smaller galleries holding from 100 to 400 seated guests. Naturally, they provide portable bars and dance floors, and some of the galleries are available for wedding ceremonies. Villa Ragusa is also more than happy to book other types of events. They've hosted everything from Little League dinners to giant corporate parties, and the City of Campbell is one of their frequent clients. Last, but not least, there's plenty of parking in the 350-space garage just down the street. So go ahead and send a wedding invitation to that cousin from back east that you haven't seen since you were five years old, and anyone else you can think of. There's room for everyone up at Villa Ragusa.

CEREMONY CAPACITY: The Campbell Gallery holds 300 seated, and the West Gallery holds 250 seated.

EVENT/RECEPTION & MEETING CAPACITY: Event spaces accommodate 100–600 seated guests.

FEES & DEPOSITS: For events, a nonrefundable $2,000 deposit is required to reserve your date and the final balance is due 10 days prior to the event. Beverage packages range $6–28/person, and include beverages and bar service. The ceremony fee is $1,500, including chairs, setup and use of the facility. Wedding packages start at $66/person.

AVAILABILITY: Year-round. Sunday–Thursday, 7am–11pm; Friday–Saturday, 7am–midnight.

SERVICES/AMENITIES:

Catering: in-house
Kitchen Facilities: n/a
Tables & Chairs: provided
Linens, Silver, etc.: provided
Restrooms: wheelchair accessible
Dance Floor: hardwood and 2 portable floors available
Bride's Dressing Area: yes
AV/Meeting Equipment: mic/podium, stage and riser at no additional charge; other AV equipment CBA for extra fee

Parking: public, free parking nearby
Accommodations: no guest rooms
Outdoor Night Lighting: access only
Outdoor Cooking Facilities: no
Cleanup: caterer
View: downtown Campbell
Other: some event coordination

RESTRICTIONS:

Alcohol: in-house; or BYO, $10/bottle corkage
Smoking: outside only
Music: amplified OK until midnight

Wheelchair Access: yes
Insurance: not required
Other: no confetti or glitter; decorations require approval

Fortino Winery and Event Center

Winery

4525 Hecker Pass Highway, Gilroy
408/842-3305

www.fortinowinery.com
debbi@fortinowinery.com

- Rehearsal Dinners
- Ceremonies
- Wedding Receptions
- Corp. Events/Mtgs.
- Private Parties
- Accommodations

Acres of vineyards, rolling hills, ancient California live oaks ... you'll feel the smile on your face and the lift in your spirits even on the approach to Fortino Winery. Located along the Santa Clara Wine Trail, this family-owned and community-oriented establishment has been producing fine wine and equally fine celebrations for decades.

Gatherings generally unfold on the lovely Redwood Terrace directly behind the winery. A popular summer music venue, it also happens to be just the spot for wedding ceremonies, receptions, and other social and corporate events. A low stage backed by towering redwoods provides the perfect focal point for the huge patios and vast sweep of lawn. In summer, a full vineyard sunshade keeps things cool. Sheer enough to shield without blocking your view of the sky, it's accented by market lights that add twinkle to the wink of the moon and the stars.

The variety of spacious settings affords plenty of room for dining, games, entertainment, and dancing. What's remarkable, though, is that this large expanse of patio and lawn has such an intimate backyard feel. Maybe it's the redwood fence or the flowerbeds ... or, perhaps it's special touches like the little memorial apple tree where cherished family members are quietly remembered that lend it such warmth. Whatever the reason, you'll definitely feel at home—whether you're a bride in the glamorous bride's room, a groom enjoying a toast with a few special friends under the front patio arbor, or early arrivals sampling a flight of Fortino's award-winning wines in the rusticly charming tasting room. Adults and kids can even play bocce ball and kick back at the picnic tables beneath the giant eucalyptus trees next to the vineyard.

And, if for some reason dining and dancing outdoors is not in your cards, you can move the party indoors and celebrate in the handsome Barrel Room. Entrance is through the broad, 40-foot-high Barrel Door, made by owner Gino Fortino. Comprised of wood from 60-year-old barrels, it has magnificent hand-hewn, wrought-iron hinges. Gino is also responsible for the simple and—according to past guests—simply delicious menu offerings made and served up on the premises. In keeping with the winery's Old World roots, food here is Italian style. Your choices include hors d'oeuvres, the Classic Italian buffet, Fortino's own Dinner Buffet or their Family Style or Wine Country Dinner.

One thing you're sure to notice: Wherever you are on this property, the welcoming vibe is uncanny. It's as if Gino is personally inviting you to relax, while the winery's kind and attentive staff help him carry on the family tradition of hospitality. It's no wonder wedding couples and other guests come back often over the years for birthdays, anniversaries, holiday parties—eventually even their own children's weddings…and a whole new generation of fun.

CEREMONY CAPACITY: The facility holds 100 seated guests indoors and 250 seated outdoors.

EVENT/RECEPTION CAPACITY: The facility accommodates 110 seated or 200 standing indoors and 300 seated or 450 standing outdoors.

MEETING CAPACITY: Meeting spaces hold 150 seated guests.

FEES & DEPOSITS: An $800 deposit is required to reserve your date. The full facility fee is due 90 days later. The balance is due 10 days prior to the event. Rental fees range $1,800–3,400 depending on the guest count and the space rented. Meals range $34–65/person. Tax (on food and alcohol) and an 18% service charge are additional.

AVAILABILITY: Year-round: indoors, October–April; outdoors, May–October.

SERVICES/AMENITIES:

Catering: in-house
Kitchen Facilities: n/a
Tables & Chairs: provided
Linens, Silver, etc.: provided
Restrooms: wheelchair accessible
Dance Floor: provided
Bride's Dressing Area: yes
AV/Meeting Equipment: CBA

Parking: large lot
Accommodations: no guest rooms
Outdoor Night Lighting: yes
Outdoor Cooking Facilities: no
Cleanup: provided
View: garden courtyard, landscaped grounds, valley; surrounded by large redwoods, hills and vineyards
Other: event coordination

RESTRICTIONS:

Alcohol: in-house
Smoking: designated areas only
Music: amplified OK with restrictions

Wheelchair Access: yes
Insurance: liability required

Wedgewood Eagle Ridge

Event Center at Golf Club

2951 Club Drive, Gilroy
866/966-3009

www.wedgewoodbanquet.com
events@wedgewoodbanquet.com

Rehearsal Dinners	● Corp. Events/Mtgs.
● Ceremonies	● Private Parties
● Wedding Receptions	Accommodations

About 35 minutes south of San Jose lies Wedgewood Eagle Ridge, a sophisticated special event facility that offers a dynamic combination of scenic vistas, high-quality amenities and surprising affordability.

From inside an exclusive gated community high in the hills above Gilroy, Eagle Ridge enjoys a sweeping panorama of the tranquil countryside and lush fairways of the neighboring golf course. The impressive driveway is lined with stately palm trees, and as you approach the Clubhouse you're greeted by warm, rose-scented breezes.

Crisp, manicured hedgerows and a wisteria-entwined veranda accent this graceful, two-story structure, which is done in Monterey Colonial style with white clapboard siding and green shutters. As refreshing as a cool glass of summertime lemonade and quite cheerful any time of year, the Clubhouse effortlessly blends in with its surroundings along with the 100-year-old oaks that shade the landscape.

Behind the Clubhouse, a great swath of lawn ringed by slender cypress trees serves as a beautiful ceremony site. Large stone urns mark a pavered wedding aisle just begging for rose petals. A stacked flagstone stage topped with a romantic white pergola frames the couple as they say their vows, and friends and family look on with the tree-cloaked hills as a picturesque backdrop.

Inside, the venue is every bit as charming. In the Lounge, you'll find a freestanding double fireplace of brick and wood; a large marble-and-wood bar; and circular wrought-iron chandeliers hanging from a vaulted, open-beamed ceiling. Guests can relax and sip cocktails in overstuffed leather chairs before moving into the dining room for dinner. And yes, these spaces also have plenty of windows to showcase the fabulous view!

Though Eagle Ridge is visually stunning, one of its most valuable assets is Wedgewood's trademark on-site coordination. Their expert staff choreographs all the elements, including customizing their five flexible wedding packages to suit your vision. Along with varied and generous menus, the packages offer any combination of invitations, flowers, cake, entertainment and officiant—all of which have been carefully selected for maximum value and satisfaction.

Relaxed elegance, a gorgeous rural setting, budget-friendly and service-oriented … it's no wonder South Bay wedding couples are escaping to Wedgewood Eagle Ridge for their dream celebration!

CEREMONY CAPACITY: The lawn area holds up to 225 seated guests, and the club seats 225 indoors.

EVENT/RECEPTION & MEETING CAPACITY: The banquet room accommodates 225 seated or standing.

FEES & DEPOSITS: 25% of the estimated total event cost is required to reserve your date. An additional 25% is due 120 days prior to the event and the balance (based on your final guest count) is due 10 days prior. All payments are credited towards your final balance and are nonrefundable and nontransferable. All-inclusive, completely customizable wedding packages start at $46/person. Tax, alcohol and a 21–22% service charge are additional.

AVAILABILITY: Year-round, daily, 6am–11pm.

SERVICES/AMENITIES:

Catering: in-house
Kitchen Facilities: n/a
Tables & Chairs: provided
Linens, Silver, etc.: provided
Restrooms: wheelchair accessible
Dance Floor: yes
Bride's Dressing Area: yes
AV/Meeting Equipment: some provided

Parking: large lot
Accommodations: no guest rooms
Outdoor Night Lighting: yes
Outdoor Cooking Facilities: no
Cleanup: provided
View: fairways, foothills
Other: event coordination, in-house wedding cake and florals, clergy on staff

RESTRICTIONS:

Alcohol: in-house
Smoking: outdoors only
Music: amplified OK

Wheelchair Access: yes
Insurance: not required
Other: no rice, confetti or glitter; no open flames

Overwhelmed? Use the search criteria on www.HereComesTheGuide.com to narrow down your choices.

227

Nestldown

Private Estate

Los Gatos Mountains, address withheld to ensure privacy.
408/353-5311

www.nestldown.com
request@nestldown.com

● Rehearsal Dinners	● Corp. Events/Mtgs.
● Ceremonies	● Private Parties
● Wedding Receptions	Accommodations

A bride at Nestldown descends a broad stairway through redwoods to a lakeside amphitheater where she will say her vows. About halfway down, she experiences a sublime moment when, for a few seconds, she can look up to the tops of the soaring trees and feel as though she's suspended among them, a bird waiting to glide to earth.

This is not the only ethereal moment she or her groom and guests will enjoy here. Nestldown, an enchanted hideaway in a mountain forest, evokes magic over and over.

Years ago it was a fruit farm in the Santa Cruz Mountains that grew apples, peaches and kiwis. Its current owners have spent the past 20 years creating a wonderland of gardens, whimsical sculptures, topiary figures, and fanciful structures on 35 acres at the property's heart. The result is a place where so many things delight and amaze: redwoods standing gray under morning clouds that suddenly blaze cinnamon in sunlight; flowers splashed along every path; barely-there trails and unexpected stairways that lead the curious to bentwood benches and chairs set smack in the middle of the forest. But all of these sensory treats are just preludes to the beauty of Nestldown's outdoor chapel and the breathtaking architecture of its signature building, The Barn.

You reach the chapel on an earth-and-wood staircase that meanders down a forested hillside. Its destination is a flagstone-paved amphitheater, sheltered by trees and ferns, that faces a wisteria-covered pergola. The pergola, set at the edge of a small, forest-fringed lake, is built from redwood saplings with their bark left on. It's so natural in appearance that it looks as though it sprang by itself from the ground. Just beyond it is another grace note, a wooden bridge, Japanese in its simplicity, that arches over a rivulet at the foot of a small waterfall.

Post-ceremony celebrations take place in The Barn and on its adjoining lawn. The Barn is one of the most beautiful wooden structures built in Northern California in recent years. Almost everybody who enters it for the first time gasps at the interior of this soaring glass-and-fir structure. The interior rises to a steep-pitched ceiling, supported by slender wooden columns. The timbers, stained a glowing reddish-amber, still have the wonderful smell of fresh-cut wood lingering about them. Gardens and trees hug two sides of The Barn. Flowers bloom year-round—geraniums, red hot salvias, alyssum, candytufts, begonias, violas, irises and calla lilies—and there are fanciful critters everywhere: A brass bear peers out from one garden and in another a topiary serpent undulates through a sea of long, slender-bladed fescue. A large koi pond in front of The Barn is lined with willows and birch, and embellished by a brass stork. Just off The Barn's terrace, a grand meadow sweeps out to a copse of redwoods where a hand-carved wooden bench reveals the image of three cavorting bears.

Nestldown is sheer exhilaration. You feel a giddy sense of expectation and joy, as you discover nature's best so skillfully combined with the fruit of human imagination.

CEREMONY CAPACITY: The outdoor chapel, Foxglove Meadow, and the Main Lawn each seat 200 guests. The Barn seats 200.

EVENT/RECEPTION & MEETING CAPACITY: Indoors, the facility holds 200 seated or standing guests. There are several outdoor spaces that hold up to 200 seated. Smaller events can also be accommodated.

FEES & DEPOSITS: 50% of the rental fee is required to secure your date; the balance is due 60 days prior to the event. The rental fee ranges $7,500–20,000 depending on the guest count, space reserved and time of year.

AVAILABILITY: January–mid-December, daily, 9am–11pm; dancing must end by 9:45pm. On Thursdays and Sundays, January–April and November–December, events must end by 10pm. The facility is closed for events from mid-December to December 30th.

SERVICES/AMENITIES:

Catering: select from list
Kitchen Facilities: prep only
Tables & Chairs: provided for up to 200 guests
Linens, Silver, etc.: through caterer
Restrooms: wheelchair accessible
Dance Floor: yes
Bride's Dressing Area: yes
AV/Meeting Equipment: full AV CBA

Parking: on-site for up to 100 cars; shuttle CBA
Accommodations: no guest rooms
Outdoor Night Lighting: some areas
Outdoor Cooking Facilities: CBA
Cleanup: provided
View: pond, meadow, redwoods, garden

RESTRICTIONS:

Alcohol: BYO, licensed server
Smoking: designated area only
Music: amplified OK indoors

Wheelchair Access: yes
Insurance: certificate required
Other: no rice, birdseed, or latex balloons

Toll House Hotel

140 South Santa Cruz Avenue, Los Gatos
408/884-1044
www.tollhousehotel.com
jennifer.barbosa@metwestterra.com

Boutique Hotel

- Rehearsal Dinners
- Ceremonies
- Wedding Receptions
- Corp. Events/Mtgs.
- Private Parties
- Accommodations

Nestled at the base of the Santa Cruz Mountains, the Toll House Hotel in Los Gatos offers a friendly, unpretentious atmosphere and quaint charm. Its shingled walls, cheerful balconies and mansard-roofed clock tower give it an old-fashioned feel. Those planning a special event appreciate its convenient location—it's within easy walking distance of downtown shops and restaurants, 30 minutes from Santa Cruz, and 60 minutes from Monterey Bay via Highway 17.

The hotel has both indoor and outdoor event areas. Inside, the aptly named Capitola Room is tailor-made for corporate functions. The Summit Ballroom is used for weddings and receptions and has plenty of space for dancing. Prefunction events are held in the adjacent Lobby, whose overstuffed green damask chairs and loveseats tempt you to relax and contemplate the classical paintings hung on the walls. There's also Verge Restaurant and Lounge, the Toll House's California fusion restaurant.

In the center of the Toll House Hotel, the sunny courtyard is a favorite place for weddings and receptions. A splashing fountain adds refreshing coolness. On the second floor, a small deck overlooks the courtyard. This is also a nice spot for weddings and related events, and rehearsal dinners are frequently held here. The five adjoining rooms that open onto this deck are often rented by the wedding party or close friends. No need for a designated driver when the party is right outside your room!

The Toll House's relaxed atmosphere makes it popular for bar and bat mitzvahs as well. It's the kind of place that's posh enough to make adults feel really pampered, but casual enough to make children feel at home, too.

CEREMONY CAPACITY: The Courtyard holds 200 seated; the Ballroom 160 seated.

EVENT/RECEPTION CAPACITY: The Courtyard accommodates 200 seated and the Ballroom 120 seated with dance floor, or up to 150 without.

MEETING CAPACITY: Event spaces accommodate 14–180 seated guests.

FEES & DEPOSITS: A nonrefundable deposit equal to 25% of the event total is required to reserve your date; the balance is payable 1 month prior to the event. Room rental fees range $225–1,900 depending on the guest count, catering costs, and room(s) selected.

They offer 3 all-inclusive wedding packages that range $100–200/person. Full bar service is available.

AVAILABILITY: Year-round, daily, 7am–11pm.

SERVICES/AMENITIES:

Catering: provided, no BYO
Kitchen Facilities: n/a
Tables & Chairs: provided
Linens, Silver, etc.: provided
Restrooms: wheelchair accessible
Dance Floor: in Courtyard and Ballroom
Bride's Dressing Area: no
AV/Meeting Equipment: CBA

Parking: complimentary garage
Accommodations: 115 guest rooms
Outdoor Night Lighting: yes
Outdoor Cooking Facilities: no
Cleanup: provided
View: Santa Cruz Mtns., Old Town Los Gatos
Other: event and wedding coordination

RESTRICTIONS:

Alcohol: provided, no BYO
Smoking: designated areas
Music: indoors only

Wheelchair Access: yes
Insurance: not required
Other: no confetti, birdseed, rice or glitter

Guglielmo Winery

Winery

1480 East Main Avenue, Morgan Hill
408/779-2145
www.guglielmowinery.com
eventcenter@guglielmowinery.com

● Rehearsal Dinners	● Corp. Events/Mtgs.	
● Ceremonies	● Private Parties	
● Wedding Receptions	Accommodations	

There is practically no event that this versatile venue can't handle. Weddings, private and corporate parties, and rehearsal dinners in the popular Villa Emile Event Center keep this historic family winery hopping all year long. They even host a Harvest Festival every August complete with a grape stomping competition, and a Holiday Gift Faire in December.

Emilio Guglielmo, whose family passed down their winemaking craft for generations in Italy, came to the Santa Clara Valley in 1908 and by 1925 had established his winery in Morgan Hill. Today, Emilio's three grandsons run the award-winning winery, and their custom-designed event space, Villa Emile, is a pleasing complement to it. Creativity is encouraged here, and the staff will help you custom-design your event including personalized labels for small bottles of wine you can use as favors or gifts.

Villa Emile is immediately adjacent to the winery itself. Pass through the iron gates, topped by a stained-glass window with the family name "Guglielmo" encircled by grapevines, and you'll find yourself in the courtyard. This area consists of a cobblestone patio bordered by beds of assorted flowers, an ideal place for small parties or pre-dinner drinks and hors d'oeuvres. Nearby is a granite bar where wine, champagne and beer are served under an arbor covered by a luxuriant 85-year-old grapevine.

A redwood pergola and cobblestone path link the courtyard to a larger cobblestone event space, where tables and chairs can be set up under their expansive white tent. At one end of the area is an enormous covered stage supported by rugged sandstone pillars (perfect for live music or a DJ). In front of the stage, a spacious dance floor invites you to get out there and boogie. At the other end of the area is a charming red-tile-roofed arbor, where couples often exchange their wedding vows. To the right, a separate building houses a beautifully appointed dressing room for the bride and her attendants. A small balcony off this room overlooks the vineyard and rolling hills, and is a favorite spot for wedding photos.

The structures here—all built out of terracotta stucco—seem to have sprung from the earth as naturally as the grapevines themselves, and their red-tile roofs are reminiscent of Tuscany. Geraniums, lilies-of-the-Nile, and petunias add colorful accents in front of the stage and along the paths. In this lovely setting, with its relaxed, Old World ambiance, you and your guests will feel that time spent at Guglielmo Winery is time well spent indeed.

CEREMONY CAPACITY: Indoors, the Heritage Room holds up to 125 seated or 150 standing. Outdoors, the white tent accommodates 300 seated or standing.

EVENT/RECEPTION CAPACITY: The Heritage Room seats 60 and the white tent holds up to 300.

MEETING CAPACITY: The Heritage Room seats 50 theater-style or 30 conference-style.

FEES & DEPOSITS: For weddings, the rental fee starts at $1,000 for indoor events and $3,000 for outdoor events, and varies depending on the space rented, day and time of the event, and guest count. For meetings, business functions and other types of events, please contact the venue for pricing.

AVAILABILITY: Year-round.

SERVICES/AMENITIES:

Catering: select from list
Kitchen Facilities: refrigeration
Tables & Chairs: provided
Linens: provided, white only; other colors extra fee
Restrooms: wheelchair accessible
Dance Floor: cement floor near stage
Bride's & Groom's Dressing Areas: yes
AV/Meeting Equipment: BYO

Parking: ample, lot nearby
Accommodations: no guest rooms
Outdoor Night Lighting: yes
Outdoor Cooking Facilities: no
Cleanup: caterer or renter
View: vineyards and surrounding hills
Other: event coordination

RESTRICTIONS:

Alcohol: in-house (beer, wine and champagne only); no BYO
Smoking: designated areas
Music: amplified OK until 9:30pm

Wheelchair Access: yes
Insurance: certificate required

The Corinthian Event Center

Historic Private Club

196 North Third Street, San Jose
408/938-2323
www.corinthiangrandballroom.com
jdavis@corinthiangrandballroom.com

● Rehearsal Dinners	● Corp. Events/Mtgs.	
● Ceremonies	● Private Parties	
● Wedding Receptions	Accommodations	

Located in the heart of historic downtown San Jose, this 1924 landmark is no ordinary venue. As you walk up the broad granite steps, past the enormous urns and soaring columns, you can't help but be impressed by the stately elegance of its neoclassic design.

That impression carries through to the interior spaces as well. The Corinthian Room is the event center's main ballroom, and it has all the elements of a true ballroom. You enter through a foyer, regally outfitted with a crystal chandelier and a hand-painted wood-beam ceiling. Once inside the Corinthian Room, you're struck by its grand proportions and majestic features. The 60-foot ceiling has massive wood beams, and is inset with alternating panes of blue glass and intricately detailed panels of gold leaf grillwork. Six extraordinary wrought-iron-and-glass lanterns hang from the ceiling like giant luminous earrings, while five 30-foot palm trees embedded with twinkle lights add sparkle. At one end of the room is a stage with a carved stone proscenium arch framing red velvet curtains; at the other end is a carved granite balcony, where just-married couples often dance their first dance. Banquettes along the sides of the room make cozy seating areas, and there's a raised section that's ideal for the head table. The hardwood dance floor is permanently ensconced in front of the stage.

Smaller functions take place in the Gold and Silver Rooms or the Phoenix Lounge. All have crystal chandeliers, cream walls, and ceilings baffled for sound. You can reserve these spaces individually, or combine them to make one long room that's perfect for a corporate meeting or small social event. The Olympia Room, a large private room with white walls and pastel detailing, is available for small meetings and as a bride's dressing area.

Whether you're getting married or planning a company meeting or party, the center's staff will help you orchestrate it. And if you're inviting out-of-town guests, they'll appreciate being close to many of San Jose's best hotels and cultural activities.

CEREMONY CAPACITY: The Gold and Silver Rooms combined hold up to 100 seated guests; the Olympia and Decathlon Rooms each hold 60 seated, and the Corinthian Room seats 300.

EVENT/RECEPTION CAPACITY: The facility holds 5–300 seated or up to 500 standing guests indoors. The ballroom can accommodate 300 seated or 500 standing.

MEETING CAPACITY: Event spaces accommodate 5–350 seated guests.

FEES & DEPOSITS: For special events and weddings, a nonrefundable $2,000 deposit secures your date and is required when reservations are made. Full payment is due 5 days prior to your event. For 5 hours' use, the rental fee ranges $500–3,500 depending on the space selected. There is a ceremony setup charge. In-house catering is provided: Meals start at $46/person; alcohol, tax and a 20% service charge are additional. Note: There is a food & beverage minimum which varies depending on the day of the week, a $12,000 minimum is required for functions held on Saturday evenings. All wedding events have private use of the event center when the food & beverage minimum is met. Off-site catering is also available.

For business functions, weekday morning and afternoon rental rates run $150–1,000 depending on the room(s) selected. Food pricing will vary depending on the type of function, guest count and event duration.

AVAILABILITY: Year-round, daily, 7am–midnight. Weddings are in 5-hour blocks; extra hours may be available for an additional $500/hour.

SERVICES/AMENITIES:

Catering: in-house
Kitchen Facilities: n/a
Tables & Chairs: provided
Linens, Silver, etc.: provided
Restrooms: wheelchair accessible
Dance Floor: yes
Bride's Dressing Area: CBA
AV/Meeting Equipment: AV provided; other CBA, extra fee

Parking: on-street or nearby garage, free on weekends and weekdays after 6pm
Accommodations: no guest rooms
Outdoor Night Lighting: yes
Outdoor Cooking Facilities: no
Cleanup: provided
View: no
Other: event coordination

RESTRICTIONS:

Alcohol: in-house
Smoking: outside only
Music: amplified OK indoors

Wheelchair Access: yes
Insurance: not required
Other: no helium balloons in Corinthian Room; no confetti, birdseed or rice indoors

Want to know WHAT TO ASK a potential location or vendor? Check out our Questions to Ask starting on page 21.

Fairmont San Jose

Hotel

170 South Market Street, San Jose
408/998-1900
www.fairmont.com/san-jose
glenn.comp@fairmont.com

● Rehearsal Dinners ● Corp. Events/Mtgs.
● Ceremonies ● Private Parties
● Wedding Receptions ● Accommodations

For over 100 years Fairmont Hotels have represented luxury and extraordinary service, and Fairmont San Jose lives up to this reputation admirably. Winner of the AAA Four Diamond Award, Fairmont San Jose offers not only the elegant décor, luxurious accommodations and exemplary service that has made the chain famous around the world, but an entire floor of ballrooms and meeting spaces tailor-made for sophisticated celebrations and business functions.

Planning a sit-down dinner for 1,000 guests, or a banquet for 800? Then you'll want to check out the 13,000-square-foot Imperial Ballroom and the 8,000-square-foot Regency Ballroom. Both of these majestic spaces feature 20-foot molded ceilings with crystal chandeliers, and the Imperial Ballroom is accompanied by a Foyer that's lovely enough for a wedding ceremony or prefunction cocktail party. It's full of natural light, thanks to an enormous arched window overlooking César Chavez Plaza. For ceremonies, a stage is set up beneath the fanciful wrought-iron-and-crystal chandelier that hangs from the Foyer's vaulted ceiling, and guests are seated in a "theater in the round" configuration. A host of smaller rooms are available for more intimate gatherings, whether festive or business oriented. All are similar in décor to the Imperial and Regency Ballrooms, but with more modest 12-foot ceilings. Many of them have large windows with views of the Plaza or the trees lining First Street, giving the rooms an open, airy feel.

One of the most delightful spaces at the Fairmont is the Club Regent. Formerly a dinner theater, its octagonal shape and curtained stage give this room plenty of personality, while split-level seating makes it surprisingly intimate and versatile. It's ideal for sit-down receptions of up to 240, since the room's unique layout allows guests to be seated around a central head table, making everyone feel close to the "action." But it's also a favorite spot for bar and bat mitzvahs, since the kids can cut loose on the main floor, while adults observe the festivities from the upper level (the Club Regent would also be great for a graduation party, or any event where different generations might each like their own space).

As you would expect from an award-winning hotel, the Fairmont provides much more than just beautifully appointed ballrooms and meeting spaces. They're one of the only hotels in the South Bay to offer kosher catering, and they specialize in Asian, Indian and Persian weddings. Perks for brides and grooms include a complimentary bridal suite and a tulle-draped stage to showcase the wedding cake. One more bonus: The fabulous lobby, with its marble columns, statuary, chandeliers and floral displays, makes an opulent backdrop for your wedding photos.

With all the amenities we've listed above, plus a great central location in the heart of Silicon Valley, it's easy to see why Fairmont San Jose has been awarded such high accolades. Don't be afraid to expect perfection at this first-rate establishment—you won't be disappointed. After all, this is the Fairmont!!

CEREMONY CAPACITY: There are 22 rooms that accommodate 10–1,000 seated guests.

EVENT/RECEPTION CAPACITY: The hotel's 22 banquet rooms hold 30–1,000 seated or 50–3,200 standing guests. In addition, the Club Regent holds 240 seated or 300 standing.

MEETING CAPACITY: The hotel offers over 65,000 square feet of meeting space, with 22 rooms that accommodate 28–1,400 seated guests.

FEES & DEPOSITS: For weddings, a nonrefundable $3,000 minimum deposit is required to secure your date. 75% of the anticipated total is due 45 days prior to the event, and the balance is payable 5 business days prior. Rental charges vary depending on the room size and the event time frame. There are 4 wedding packages ranging $110–150/person, which usually include hors d'oeuvres, a 2-course dinner, wedding cake, champagne toast, and bridal suite. Tax and service charges are extra.

For business functions, all services are customized. Call for more information and rates. The hotel has an on-site full-service business center.

AVAILABILITY: Year-round, daily including holidays, until 1am.

SERVICES/AMENITIES:
Catering: in-house; outside caterers allowed only for Indian cuisine and must be approved
Kitchen Facilities: n/a
Tables & Chairs: provided
Linens, Silver, etc.: provided
Restrooms: wheelchair accessible
Dance Floor: provided
Bride's & Groom's Dressing Areas: CBA
AV/Meeting Equipment: full range AV

Parking: valet or nearby parking lots
Accommodations: 805 guest rooms
Outdoor Night Lighting: CBA
Outdoor Cooking Facilities: CBA
Cleanup: provided
View: César Chavez Park, Circle of Palms
Other: wedding cakes

RESTRICTIONS:
Alcohol: in-house, no BYO
Smoking: allowed outdoors
Music: amplified OK until 1am

Wheelchair Access: yes
Insurance: not required
Other: no fog machines

Hayes Mansion

200 Edenvale Avenue, San Jose
408/362-2342
www.hayesmansion.com
msabedra@hayesmansion.com

Historic Mansion & Grounds

● Rehearsal Dinners   ● Corp. Events/Mtgs.
● Ceremonies   ● Private Parties
● Wedding Receptions   ● Accommodations

There must be 1,001 places for romantic photographs in the award-winning Hayes Mansion. The front of the impressive mansion is an obvious choice, but there are picturesque inglenooks, gorgeous doorways with beveled glass insets and shining wood trim, graceful archways, mysterious stairways lit with art deco fixtures, and lawns and flowers a-plenty. And that's just in the daytime—by night it's a completely different and dramatic experience.

Built in 1905 for Mary Hayes Chynoweth and designed by architect George Page, it's a marriage of Queen Anne, Mission and Mediterranean styles. Oddly enough, these diverse architectures meld together well, resulting in a beautifully preserved jewel of a building.

Hold your ceremony on the front lawn and let the entire mansion, with its grand entryway and four-story central tower, create the backdrop. Or get married at one of the entrances to the East or West Lawns, each with a carved archway and sweeping steps. If an intimate indoor wedding is your preference, exchange vows in the Willow Glen Room, standing in front of a marble fireplace beneath a gleaming wooden arch. These are just a tiny sampling of your many ceremony options.

Reception possibilities range from several smaller rooms like the Parlors, all the way up to the Grand Hayes Ballroom, which enjoys its own separate building. Serve cocktails and hors d'oeuvres in the vast foyer of the ballroom, whose French doors open to a vista of the lawn and Mansion. Then dine elegantly in the ballroom, with its 20-foot ceilings, chandeliers, stage, drop-down screens, projectors, sound system, dance floor—the works.

Hayes Mansion offers several banquet packages with an amazing array of delicacies. Some of the featured dishes are: mini beef wellingtons with mushroom duxelles and a truffle reduction; dungeness crab crusted Pacific salmon; and pepper crusted filet mignon with lobster tail. The selection of vegetarian dishes is equally enticing.

Wedding packages include a luxury guest room in the mansion for the bride and groom (minimum guest count applies). Relaxing in your plush surroundings, you could easily imagine you're the privileged guest of Mary Hayes Chynoweth, enjoying the good life at the turn of the 20th century. There are also 214 spacious rooms for your guests, many with views of the Santa Cruz Mountains. For a delightful twist on bridesmaid gifts, surprise your entourage with a day at the spa. All the stresses of planning a wedding will slip away as you unwind with a soothing massage, manicure and pedicure, or indulge in a multitude of other beautifying treatments.

One of the charms of the Hayes Mansion is its lack of restrictions. The facility once hosted a wedding with a live elephant, so it's unlikely you can come up with anything that they can't accommodate (though the management says you're welcome to try). The range of event spaces runs the gamut from grand and impressive to intimate and homelike, and from enormous swaths of lawn and scenery to small, sun-dappled patios. The only problem you'll have is trying to choose between so many seductive possibilities.

CEREMONY CAPACITY: The San Jose Room, Westwood Patio and Guadalupe Room each seat up to 140 guests; the Edenvale Room seats 200, and the East Lawn up to 600 seated or 900 standing.

EVENT/RECEPTION CAPACITY: Various rooms hold 10–450 seated or 50–900 standing; the entire mansion can accommodate 1,200 for a standing reception. Patio areas seat 10–100, and the East Lawn holds 800 seated or 1,200 standing.

MEETING CAPACITY: There are 24 rooms, some of which seat up to 720 guests theater-style.

FEES & DEPOSITS: For weddings, the entire facility fee is required to book your date. 50% of the estimated total is due 60 days prior to the event and the balance due 14 days prior (however, a customized payment schedule can be arranged). The facility fee starts at $750 and pricing varies depending on the room selected. Customized wedding packages for 100 guests range $125–225/person and include. hors d'oeuvres, salad, 2 entrées, wedding cake and overnight accommodations for the bride and groom. Ceremony packages start at $250 for 30 minutes and include padded chairs, rehearsal and setup.

For other special events and business functions, 50% of the estimated total is required to confirm reservations; another 30% is due 60 days prior to the event; and the remaining event balance is payable 14 days prior. The rental fee ranges $1,500–9,000 depending on the guest count and space(s) selected. Meals start at $75/person. Alcohol, tax and a 23% service charge are additional.

AVAILABILITY: Year-round, daily, anytime. Weddings take place on Fridays, Saturdays and Sundays; other days and time frames may be negotiated.

SERVICES/AMENITIES:

Catering: in-house, outside specialty cuisine caterers ok with approval

Kitchen Facilities: fully equipped, extra fee

Tables & Chairs: provided

Linens, Silver, etc.: provided

Restrooms: wheelchair accessible

Dance Floor: provided

Bride's & Groom's Dressing Area: provided, extra fee

AV/Meeting Equipment: computer networking capabilities and wireless, high-speed internet service provided; extra fee for video conferencing equipment, lighting packages, LCD packages, and microphones

Parking: complimentary valet; large lots

Accommodations: 214 guest rooms and suites

Outdoor Night Lighting: limited

Outdoor Cooking Facilities: no

Cleanup: provided

View: Santa Cruz Mountains

Other: outdoor pool, tennis, volleyball; full-service day spa, fitness center

RESTRICTIONS:

Alcohol: in-house packages available

Smoking: designated areas

Music: amplified OK, outdoors until 10pm

Wheelchair Access: yes

Insurance: liability required

Other: no birdseed, rice, glitter or confetti

Hotel De Anza and La Pastaia

Hotel & Restaurant

233 West Santa Clara Street, San Jose
408/494-4714

www.hoteldeanza.com
brobinson@destinationhotels.com.

- Rehearsal Dinners
- Ceremonies
- Wedding Receptions
- Corp. Events/Mtgs.
- Private Parties
- Accommodations

The Hotel De Anza is not only a historic hotel, it's one of San Jose's most beautiful event facilities. Art Deco splendor—gold accents, etched glass and distinctive fixtures—is everywhere. Serve pre-party cocktails in the Hedley Club, the De Anza's classic lounge. This extraordinary space has a highly detailed ceiling painted in golds, raspberries and blues. An enormous stone fireplace glows in winter, illuminating the room's large paintings, eclectic furnishings and glass-backed bar.

French doors lead to the adjacent Palm Court Terrace, a sheltered courtyard enclosed by terracotta-colored walls covered with ivy. Two fountains set into the walls add the sweet sounds of water flowing; palms, ferns and flowers around the perimeter lend the freshness and color of a garden. A canopied ceiling and heat lamps protect guests from the elements, making the Terrace attractive for events year-round.

For an indoor event, have a dazzling reception in the De Anza Room, a magnificent space with warm gold walls, hand-stenciled with gold-leaf leaves. The ceiling's concrete beams are intricately painted in shades of gold, burgundy, blue and green, and a beautiful mural on a freestanding screen adds more color.

The hotel's restaurant, La Pastaia (which means "pasta maker" in Italian), is a feast for the senses. Vibrant red walls showcase a collection of antique travel posters, while a stone floor and an abundance of slate tile throughout provide an earthy contrast. The exhibition kitchen area is tantalizing: a long marble counter is laden with delectable desserts and fresh-baked bread, and a wood-burning oven glows continuously at one end.

Small alcoves with a combination of banquettes and tables are cozy, intimate nooks. Create your own menu—no matter what you select, your guests will appreciate the genuine Italian cuisine, professionally served in a Tuscan-chic atmosphere.

And when the festivities are over, you can honeymoon in the hotel's luxurious Penthouse, whose sumptuous bathroom beckons with a black marble floor, marble counters and a whirlpool bathtub large enough for four. We can't say enough about the Hotel De Anza and La Pastaia; take your time when visiting so that you can fully savor this one-of-a kind place.

CEREMONY CAPACITY: The Palm Court Terrace holds 200 seated or 250 standing, and the De Anza Room holds 100 seated or standing guests.

EVENT/RECEPTION CAPACITY: The Palm Court Terrace holds 200 seated or 250 standing, the De Anza Room holds 100 seated or standing, and La Pasta Restaurant holds 100 seated or 150 standing.

MEETING CAPACITY: There are 5 meeting rooms that accommodate 10–200 seated guests.

FEES & DEPOSITS: For weddings, a deposit is due when the facility is booked, and the balance is payable 1 week prior to the event. A payment plan can be arranged. Catering is provided exclusively by *La Pastaia*. There is a $5,000–15,000 food & beverage minimum for the Palm Court Terrace, depending on the season, day and time of the event. Menus can be customized. Alcohol, tax and a 20% service charge are additional.

AVAILABILITY: Year-round, daily, 7am–midnight.

SERVICES/AMENITIES:

Catering: in-house, no BYO
Kitchen Facilities: n/a
Tables & Chairs: provided
Linens, Silver, etc.: provided
Restrooms: wheelchair accessible
Dance Floor: CBA, extra fee
Bride's Dressing Area: CBA
AV/Meeting Equipment: AV equipment provided, other CBA

Parking: nearby lots and valet
Accommodations: 100 guest rooms including penthouse
Outdoor Night Lighting: yes
Outdoor Cooking Facilities: no
Cleanup: provided
View: San Jose skyline from upper floors
Other: event coordination, custom wedding cakes

RESTRICTIONS:

Alcohol: provided
Smoking: outside only
Music: amplified OK until 11pm outdoors or 12:30am indoors

Wheelchair Access: yes
Insurance: not required

Mexican Heritage Plaza

School of Arts & Culture

1700 Alum Rock Avenue, San Jose
408/794-6240
www.mhplaza.com
kelly@mhplaza.com

● Rehearsal Dinners	● Corp. Events/Mtgs.
● Ceremonies	● Private Parties
● Wedding Receptions	Accommodations

The Mexican Heritage Plaza, a six-acre jewel located in a bustling section of San Jose, is a beacon of neighborhood pride and veritable feast for your senses. Viewed from the street, its distinctive adobe-hued tower and modern building complex barely hint at the treasures you'll find within this dynamic culture and education center. The artfully designed property revels in its mix of vibrant murals, architectural flourishes, tranquil gardens and soothing water features. But it's the whole-hearted homage to family and community, expressed artistically throughout the property, that stirs your soul and makes this exciting venue such a compelling choice for a wedding.

From the moment you arrive, you see the fun and unexpected ways in which Mexico's heritage is celebrated, from the colorful mosaic walkway at each entrance, to the Aztec symbols adorning a fountain at the side entry. A gate here leads to the beautifully landscaped garden and water areas.

The Main Garden is utterly charming, with a wide lawn planted with rows of stately palms and an adobe brick wall draped in ivy and red trumpetvine flowers. Set into the wall are large niches decorated with handcrafted tiles imprinted with photo transfers of local ancestors and historic events. Woven together, they create a tapestry of life from generation to generation. With your own nearest and dearest gathered to witness your rite of passage, this makes a particularly meaningful ceremony site. As an alternative, you can exchange vows in front of the adjacent Rose Garden. Your guests will be seated beneath a lovely arbor that's covered with an array of blooms and ringed by flowering trees. Separating these two captivating settings is a serene reflecting pool, complete with feathery marsh grass, a small waterfall and surrounding patio.

Either of these areas is also perfect for a cocktail reception, especially at night when twinkle lights or hidden spots add a bit of magic. Or take advantage of the site's modern, state-of-the-art theater building by utilizing the glass-enclosed Theater Lobby. With its massive, brightly painted wooden bar, Day of the Dead figurines and tribal theater masks adorning the walls, it makes for a festive scene.

You're in for a treat when it comes to options for your main reception as well. The dazzling Pavilion has a dramatic, stepped pyramid-style ceiling that reflects more than a nod to Aztec influences. The room's four walls are made up of glass doors that can fold away leaving only the corner pillars, creating an indoor-outdoor feel (with the advantages of a great sound system and climate control). If you're craving a totally al fresco party under the stars, set up your dining and dancing in the Plaza itself. No matter what spaces you choose you can't go wrong here: From expansive backdrops for large groups to unique nooks for more intimate gatherings, every spot at the Mexican Heritage Plaza has its own allure.

CEREMONY CAPACITY: The site holds 300 seated indoors and 200 seated outdoors.

EVENT/RECEPTION CAPACITY: The facility can accommodate 200 seated or 500 standing indoors and 900 seated or 2,000 standing guests outdoors.

MEETING CAPACITY: Meeting spaces hold 250 seated.

FEES & DEPOSITS: One third of the total event cost is required to secure your date, and the balance is due 90 days prior to the event. The rental fee ranges $3,900–6,500 depending on the time of year, guest count and space reserved. Clients who mention Here Comes The Guide when booking will receive a 10% discount off the rental fee.

AVAILABILITY: Year-round, daily. Events must end by midnight.

SERVICES/AMENITIES:

Catering: select from preferred list
Kitchen Facilities: prep only
Tables & Chairs: provided
Linens, Silver, etc.: through caterer or BYO
Restrooms: wheelchair accessible
Dance Floor: available in most areas
Bride's & Groom's Dressing Areas: upon request
AV/Meeting Equipment: some provided; AV equipment CBA

Parking: large lots, on street
Accommodations: no guest rooms
Outdoor Night Lighting: yes
Outdoor Cooking Facilities: no
Cleanup: in-house contractor required
View: fountain, garden courtyard, landscaped grounds

RESTRICTIONS:

Alcohol: BYO, security required (restrictions apply)
Smoking: 20 feet away from facility
Music: amplified OK

Wheelchair Access: yes
Insurance: liability required

The wedding vendors on our website are the best in the business. How do we know? Read page 553.

The Pavilion Event Center at Boulder Ridge

Event Center

1000 Old Quarry Road, San Jose
408/323-9900 x125
www.boulderridgegolfclub.com
events@boulderridgegolfclub.com

● Rehearsal Dinners	● Corp. Events/Mtgs.
● Ceremonies	● Private Parties
● Wedding Receptions	Accommodations

At the top of a picturesque road that starts at Almaden Lake and heads up into the Santa Theresa Hills, there's a wedding venue that's sure to entice you with its spectacular, unobstructed views in virtually all directions.

Perched high on a plateau overlooking Boulder Ridge golf course, The Pavilion Event Center was named for the dramatic sandstone rock formations that dot the hillside fairways. These striking boulders, which were part of land that was once home to the Ohlone Indians, now contribute to this location's unique landscape.

The Pavilion's rough-hewn stone and earth-colored exterior blends organically with the natural tones of the Santa Cruz Mountains in the distance. Spreading out in front of the building is a verdant lawn, adorned with several Craftsman-style arbors, each framing a different vista. The Welcome Arbor, with its nearby fountain, faces north, presenting arriving guests with a bird's-eye view of downtown San Jose's skyline. The Bridal Arbor, which you can enhance with your choice of flowers, garlands, crystals, or other decorations, becomes the focal point when everyone takes their seats and turns to watch the bride begin her walk down the aisle. Vows are exchanged at the Gazebo, facing west towards the Almaden Valley, allowing the setting sun to form the perfect, glowing backdrop for the ceremony.

After the "I do's", invite everyone to enjoy cocktails and hors d'oeuvres on the adjoining Terrace, where a large granite-topped bar is a great place to get the party started. Since there's something interesting to catch your eye no matter where you look, it may be hard to tear your friends and family away from the scenery, but even after they sit down to dinner in the Pavilion they're never far from the natural beauty and twinkling lights outside.

Wraparound windows framed in hand-stained sustainable wood cover two sides of the dining room and a floor-to-ceiling fireplace with stone hearth dominates the fourth. Chandeliers with mottled glass shades and California *plein air* paintings reinforce the indoor/outdoor motif of the open, airy space.

An on-site coordinator will help you choreograph your event from start to finish, but she's also happy to work with your own wedding planner. And when it comes to food, the chef can customize your menu, including ethnic specialties.

Before your shuttle or limo whisks you away to your new life, take a quiet stroll under the stars with your beloved—a truly romantic end to a memorable celebration.

CEREMONY CAPACITY: The facility holds 200 seated outdoors or 200 seated indoors with no reception space.

EVENT/RECEPTION CAPACITY: The site can accommodate 200 seated guests indoors with a dance floor.

MEETING CAPACITY: Meeting spaces hold 200 seated guests.

FEES & DEPOSITS: A $2,000 deposit is required to reserve your date and the balance is due 14 business days prior to the event. Full wedding packages start at $160/person and include the site rental fee, parking shuttle, ceremony and banquet chairs, hors d'oeuvres, entrée, champagne toast, house wine, beer, soft drinks, wedding cake, service charge and sales tax.

AVAILABILITY: Year-round, daily, 7am–11pm. Site visits are by appointment only. Please call 408/323-9900 x125 or email events@boulderridgegolfclub.com.

SERVICES/AMENITIES:

Catering: in-house
Kitchen Facilities: n/a
Tables & Chairs: provided
Linens, Silver, etc.: provided
Restrooms: wheelchair accessible
Dance Floor: (15' x 15') provided
Bride's Dressing Area: yes
AV/Meeting Equipment: CBA

Parking: large lot
Accommodations: no guest rooms
Outdoor Night Lighting: yes
Outdoor Cooking Facilities: none
Cleanup: provided
View: fairways, landscaped grounds; panorama of mountains, hills and valley
Other: spa services, parking shuttle, event coordination

RESTRICTIONS:

Alcohol: in-house or BYO wine, $25 corkage fee; no outside liquor or beer
Smoking: outdoors only
Music: amplified OK with restrictions

Wheelchair Access: yes
Insurance: recommended

San Jose Woman's Club

Historic Woman's Club

75 South Eleventh Street, San Jose
877/852-7774 X1

sjwomansclub.org
rentals@sjwomansclub.org

● Rehearsal Dinners	● Corp. Events/Mtgs.	
● Ceremonies	● Private Parties	
● Wedding Receptions	Accommodations	

With its façade of tall arched windows and imposing entryway, the San Jose Woman's Club building makes a graceful impression. Completed in 1929, the Spanish-style structure has hosted a wide variety of events over the years, including wedding ceremonies, receptions, concerts, corporate retreats, and fundraising dinners.

The foyer, with its fireplace niche and tiled stairway, is often used for small ceremonies; the stairs serve as both an entrance for the bride and an attractive backdrop for memorable photos. It's also a relaxed space for sipping champagne and mingling.

The Ballroom, however, is the building's *pièce de résistance*. A high, slightly vaulted ceiling spans the enormous room, and light from a wall of tall arched windows brings out the shine on the maple floor. The floor itself is unusual in that it has a special "spring" construction to enhance dancing. Up above, the beams crisscrossing the ceiling are all hand-stenciled, and the ornate parchment-and-wrought-iron chandeliers glow amber when lit. You can exchange vows on the curtained stage, while your favorite tune is played on the Steinway baby grand piano.

The Ballroom has plenty of space for a large reception, but if you need additional seating, the adjacent Tea Room comes in very handy. Separated from the Ballroom by two sliding glass pocket doors, it has easy access to the kitchen via a pass-through counter at one end. Like the Ballroom, its pastel unadorned walls make a neutral backdrop for potted plants and flowers. The club offers a great deal of flexibility, not only for weddings, but for private parties, seminars, concerts or lectures—and its fees are very affordable.

CEREMONY CAPACITY: The club holds 400 seated theater-style.

EVENT/RECEPTION CAPACITY: The Ballroom holds 350 seated guests, and the Tea Room holds 100 seated banquet-style.

MEETING CAPACITY: The Ballroom seats 400 theater-style and the Tea Room seats 125 theater-style. The Fireside Room holds 25 seated conference-style.

FEES & DEPOSITS: A deposit of half the facility fee is required to hold your date. The facility fee ranges $700–3,200 depending on the room and day reserved. The balance of the facility fee and a security deposit are due 90 days prior to the event. Security personnel are required at $55 per officer (1 officer for up to 150 guests, 2 for more than 150 guests). For more detailed information, please call 877/852-7771 x1.

For weekday business functions or meetings, the rental rate varies depending on the guest count and event duration. Call for specifics.

AVAILABILITY: Year-round.

SERVICES/AMENITIES:

Catering: select from preferred list or BYO, extra fee

Kitchen Facilities: plating only

Tables & Chairs: provided

Linens, Silver, etc.: BYO

Restrooms: wheelchair accessible

Dance Floor: in Ballroom

Bride's Dressing Area: yes

AV/Meeting Equipment: podium, stage with lights

Parking: adjacent lot, on-street

Accommodations: no guest rooms

Outdoor Night Lighting: yes

Outdoor Cooking Facilities: BYO

Cleanup: renter

View: no

RESTRICTIONS:

Alcohol: BYO, licensed server

Smoking: outside only

Music: amplified OK with restrictions; amplification not required in many cases as acoustics are superb

Wheelchair Access: yes

Insurance: certificate required; special event insurance available

Other: no rice, birdseed or confetti; no tacks or tape on walls

Silver Creek Valley Country Club

Country Club

5460 Country Club Parkway, San Jose
408/239-5888
www.scvcc.com
catering@scvcc.com

- Rehearsal Dinners
- Ceremonies
- Wedding Receptions
- Corp. Events/Mtgs.
- Private Parties
- Accommodations

Whoever invented the phrase "storybook wedding" must have attended one at Silver Creek Valley Country Club (SCVCC). Every last detail at this upscale facility has been carefully thought out to ensure the most memorable experience possible for all guests.

Driving into the club, you pass through a master-planned gated community. Here, swaying palms keep watch over sprawling houses that echo the earth tones of nearby Mount Hamilton and the adjoining foothills. At the end of a long, curving driveway stands the main clubhouse, a golden-hued edifice reminiscent of an Italian villa. Inside, every visitor experiences stunning grandeur and personalized service.

As you make your way through the expansive foyer, what really commands your attention is the imposing and ornate rotunda. Encircled by gold-tipped wrought iron and capped by a vast domed skylight, it soars over dual curving staircases that descend to the floor below. (Note that photographers love to pose the wedding party on the landing halfway down the stairs. Flooded with light, it's a prime spot for photos.)

French doors off the foyer lead to the Yerba Buena Ballroom, Silver Creek's main event space. Like the rest of the building's valley-facing side, this unusual crescent-shaped room features a back wall made entirely of glass. Every guest enjoys spectacular views of the championship golf course and the evergreen valley beyond, and at night thousands of twinkling lights from the surrounding homes yield a panorama that's even more dramatic.

The Ballroom's neutral décor creates a complementary backdrop for any event: Walls are painted white and beige, and ivory drapes frame windows. Overhead, five modern chandeliers cast a warm glow, while a cream-colored tile floor in the center invites everyone to dance.

If you have a smaller-sized gathering, or you'd like to serve cocktails and hors d'oeuvres while pictures are being taken, consider the adjoining Chaboya Lounge. This L-shaped space boasts a wood-paneled, granite-topped bar, cozy fireplace, and a terracotta patio that shares the club's sweeping vistas.

Have you always dreamed of saying your vows in an exotic South Sea setting? Silver Creek Valley Country Club can save you the plane fare. It's just a short pleasant walk from the clubhouse to a majestic waterfall, where couples exchange vows on a raised flagstone Ceremony Landing at the base of this triple-level water feature. Or get married in front of the Cypress Dome with your guests seated on a rolling expanse of lawn. The site itself is certainly photogenic, but photographers also like to snap pictures of the bride and bridesmaids arriving via golf cart, as well as the just-marrieds departing for the reception in the same fashion.

From the tasteful furnishings to the friendly, accommodating staff, Silver Creek Valley Country Club offers still more amenities that will make planning your wedding easy and enjoyable. Put yourself in the hands of the club's on-site event coordinators, and prepare for a "storybook wedding" that has the happiest of endings.

CEREMONY CAPACITY: The outdoor ceremony area holds up to 300 seated guests.

EVENT/RECEPTION CAPACITY: The club accommodates 300 seated or 500 standing guests indoors.

MEETING CAPACITY: Meeting rooms seat up to 250 guests.

FEES & DEPOSITS: The rental fee for weddings and events ranges $4,000–15,000 depending on the event date. The rental fee for meetings starts at $250. Meals range $34–128/person. Tax, alcohol and a 20% service charge are additional. Valet parking service is available upon request.

AVAILABILITY: Year-round, daily, 8am–midnight.

SERVICES/AMENITIES:

Catering: in-house; outside ethnic cuisine caterers ok with approval
Kitchen Facilities: n/a
Tables & Chairs: provided
Linens, Silver, etc.: provided
Restrooms: wheelchair accessible
Dance Floor: provided
Bride's Dressing Area: only available before the ceremony
AV/Meeting Equipment: CBA, extra charge

Parking: self-parking or valet, extra charge
Accommodations: no guest rooms
Outdoor Night Lighting: yes
Outdoor Cooking Facilities: n/a
Cleanup: provided
View: panorama of valley and hills
Other: event coordination

RESTRICTIONS:

Alcohol: in-house, no BYO
Smoking: outdoors only
Music: amplified OK indoors and outdoors

Wheelchair Access: yes
Insurance: required for outside ethnic cuisine caterer
Other: no rice, birdseed, glitter or confetti

The Tech Museum of Innovation

Museum

201 South Market Street, San Jose
408/795-6221
www.thetech.org
maureenl@thetech.org
esanchez@thetech.org

● Rehearsal Dinners	● Corp. Events/Mtgs.
● Ceremonies	● Private Parties
● Wedding Receptions	Accommodations

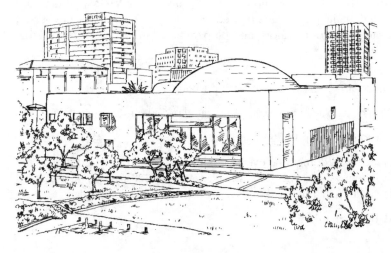

All you people who yawn at the prospect of going to a museum listen up: The Tech is not just a museum, it's an adventure. In fact, The Tech may be the most exciting thing to happen to the South Bay in years.

Located in downtown San Jose, facing Plaza de Cesar Chavez and just across from the Fairmont Hotel, this bright mango building houses 300 high-tech interactive exhibits that will energize the most jaded visitor. And wonder of wonders—if you host an event here, the exhibits are available for your guests' enjoyment!

Events are held in the museum lobby, the exhibit galleries, and the Hackworth IMAX Dome Theater. You can reserve any combination of spaces or rent the entire museum. The lobby is a fantastic place for a large party: It's a three-level atrium with a 45-foot cylindrical tower rising up through it and, when used in conjunction with the adjacent New Venture Hall, it can accommodate 500 for a sit-down dinner.

The galleries lend themselves to standing receptions. They're thoroughly modern, displaying a mix of steel, glass and plastic, with walls and ceilings painted in jewel shades of purple, yellow and blue. Each gallery has a different theme: In *Social Robots,* you get to build (and accessorize) your own robot. At the award-winning *Body Metrics* exhibit, visitors can check out wearable sensor kits and track and manipulate their own biometric data. The world's first interactive exhibit on bioengineering, *BioDesign Studio,* lets guests use biology as technology to make colorful mixes of DNA and bricks out of mushrooms. Favorites like the *Jet Pack Chair* and the *Earthquake Shake Platform* are always crowd-pleasers.

In addition to these extraordinary galleries, The Tech has one more cutting-edge gem that will dazzle you and your guests: the Hackworth IMAX Dome Theater. The only one of its kind in Northern California, it features a giant hemispherical screen whose image dwarfs that of a conventional theater and puts the audience in the center of the action. Outfitted with state-of-the-art audiovisual equipment, the theater can be reserved exclusively for a performance or presentation, but we recommend you also use it for viewing an IMAX film: Take the ultimate off-trail adventure into America's great outdoors in *National Parks Adventure.* Get a breathtaking portrait of Earth from space in *Beautiful Planet,* or learn about the profound ways aviation has transformed our lives in *Living in the Age of Airplanes.*

The Tech aims to inspire the innovator in everyone, yet even if you don't come away wanting to be a scientist when you grow up, you'll have to admit that this place makes traditional meeting rooms and party themes feel obsolete. Part of the next generation of museums, The Tech triumphs at making science, math and technology not only accessible, but positively fun.

CEREMONY CAPACITY: The New Venture Hall holds up to 300 seated indoors, and the Rooftop Terrace holds 200 seated outdoors.

EVENT/RECEPTION CAPACITY: The Tech can accommodate 500 seated or 2,500 standing guests.

MEETING CAPACITY: The Large Group Meeting Room holds up to 65 seated guests, and the New Venture Hall, 400 seated. The Noyce Center for Learning seats a maximum of 125 and can be divided into three separate meeting rooms that can be configured to seat 24–60 people.

FEES & DEPOSITS: 50% of the rental fee and a $1,000–2,500 security/cleaning deposit are required to secure your date. The rental fee ranges $500–12,500 depending on the space(s) reserved. Exclusive use of the Hackworth IMAX Dome Theater can be arranged at an additional cost. Fees are based on a 4-hour time period; for longer events, there will be an extra hourly charge. Meals start at $20/person. Tax, alcohol and service charge are additional.

AVAILABILITY: Year-round, daily, 6pm–midnight. Closed Christmas Day.

SERVICES/AMENITIES:

Catering: in-house, or select from list
Kitchen Facilities: prep only
Tables & Chairs: BYO or through caterer
Linens, Silver, etc.: through caterer
Restrooms: wheelchair accessible
Dance Floor: CBA
AV/Meeting Equipment: CBA, extra charge

Parking: Convention Center garage, nearby lots
Accommodations: no guest rooms
Outdoor Night Lighting: no
Outdoor Cooking Facilities: no
Cleanup: through caterer
View: no
Other: on-site coordinator

RESTRICTIONS:

Alcohol: in-house
Smoking: outdoors only
Music: amplified OK

Wheelchair Access: yes
Insurance: certificate required

Want to find more venues and services? Check out our informative website, www.HereComesTheGuide.com.

251

The Terrace at Willow Glen

Event Facility

San Jose, address withheld to ensure privacy.

408/838-3485

www.ttawg.com
info@ttawg.com

Rehearsal Dinners	●	Corp. Events/Mtgs.
● Ceremonies	●	Private Parties
● Wedding Receptions		Accommodations

Situated on a quiet street and surrounded by sunny lawns and shade trees, the Terrace at Willow Glen is just three miles from downtown San Jose but it could easily be worlds away.

Established in 2007, this is the city's first commercial "Green Building", which means that the owners, architects, developers and contractors incorporated sustainable energy and environmental design goals early in the building process. The result is a location that's pleasing to be in year-round, and beautifully equipped for hosting a range of events including weddings, quinceañeras, and company parties.

The main entrance is through the airy International Brotherhood of Electrical Workers (IBEW) Meeting Hall lobby, where big double doors lead into the spacious banquet room. In addition to providing 6,000 interior square feet, it opens to a huge walled terrace for outdoor ceremonies and cocktails. It's lovely when strung with bistro lights or accented with lounge chairs, and there's even a stainless-steel natural gas grill for cooking up some barbecue.

Inside or out, your privacy is ensured. The banquet room's three walls of UV-treated windows and glass doors screen out heat and add seclusion by day. At night, heavy drapes can be drawn to cocoon you inside, while custom illumination may be created by having your DJ or decorator bring in spots, stage cans, and gobo projections. The room also comes with full AV, an in-ceiling projector, and a 10-foot dropdown screen behind the stage for your video presentation or photomontage.

Oh, and did we mention that you can actually play music till midnight here? Bongos or horns, banda or DJ, mariachi or rock, acoustic or amplified—it's all good!—so go ahead and party late on the large dance floor.

As for dining, this site's big prep kitchen is a caterer's dream. And, speaking of catering, while you can bring in your own, the property's staff is ready, not only to stage your event, but to provide some tempting banquet options as well, be they American or international. To make planning even easier, they offer all-inclusive packages, or you can have them customize one for you. At the Terrace at Willow Glen, they live by the concepts of enhancement and transformation!

"Everyone is so different," says the facility's Event Manager. "They come with their own vision, and we bring it to life."

CEREMONY & MEETING CAPACITY: The site holds 400 seated guests indoors and 225 seated outdoors.

EVENT/RECEPTION CAPACITY: The facility can accommodate 400 seated or standing indoors and 200 seated or standing outdoors.

FEES & DEPOSITS: A deposit is required to reserve your date. The venue rental fee starts at $6,500 for Saturday or Sunday and $5,500 for weekdays. All-inclusive wedding packages start at $60/person; tax, service charge, and a discretionary gratuity are additional. Some packages include alcohol.

AVAILABILITY: Year-round, Monday–Friday 5:30pm–midnight, Saturday and Sunday 8am–midnight.

SERVICES/AMENITIES:

Catering: in-house or BYO
Kitchen Facilities: prep only
Tables & Chairs: provided
Linens, Silver, etc.: provided or through caterer
Restrooms: wheelchair accessible
Dance Floor: provided
Bride's Dressing Area: yes
AV/Meeting Equipment: provided

Parking: large complimentary lot
Accommodations: no guest rooms
Outdoor Night Lighting: yes
Outdoor Cooking Facilities: BBQ on site
Cleanup: provided or caterer
View: garden courtyard
Other: event coordination available, extra fee

RESTRICTIONS:

Alcohol: in-house or BYO
Smoking: outdoors only
Music: amplified OK indoors only with restrictions

Wheelchair Access: yes
Insurance: liability required

The Villages Golf and Country Club

Golf & Country Club

5000 Cribari Lane, San Jose
408/223-4688
www.thevillagesgcc.com
theclubhouse@the-villages.com

- Rehearsal Dinners
- Ceremonies
- Wedding Receptions
- Corp. Events/Mtgs.
- Private Parties
- Accommodations

We've heard the sad tale before: You'd love to have a country club wedding, but there's one tiny little problem—you don't belong to a country club. Lucky for you, membership isn't required at The Villages Golf and Country Club. Perched in the hills above southeastern San Jose, this facility has everything you're looking for: a handsome Spanish Mission-style clubhouse; lovely banquet rooms; well-tended gardens, and a verdant, meticulously groomed golf course. You get all this, plus a variety of wedding packages, at a price that won't make you dip into your honeymoon fund.

In the clubhouse, you'll find three special event rooms that can be used separately or in combination. Though all three have a versatile cream-and-tan color scheme and elegant chandeliers, each one has its own distinct design elements: The Oak Room features a gleaming hardwood oak dance floor; the Sunset Room has a large window that takes advantage of the view of the Santa Clara Valley; and the Fairway Room boasts panoramic golf course views. Adjacent to this trio of rooms is a foyer area with a grand piano. The Oak and Fairway Rooms are particularly lovely when used together, but no matter what configuration of these areas you choose, they're all brimming with sophisticated country club ambiance.

So, now that we've introduced you to the Villages Golf and Country Club, you won't have to give up your dream of a country club wedding. And if there's no wedding in your future, but you'd still like to book your event here, go right ahead—the flexible, competent staff can help you with whatever type of gathering you've got in mind. The price is right, the setting is fabulous, and they'll be happy to see you even if you don't have a membership card.

CEREMONY CAPACITY: Indoor and outdoor ceremony space is available. Contact the facility for more details.

EVENT/RECEPTION & MEETING CAPACITY: The clubhouse holds up to 250 seated with a dance floor. This space can be divided into smaller reception areas.

FEES & DEPOSITS: A nonrefundable $2,400 room rental deposit is required to reserve your date. The estimated event total is due 7 working days prior to the event. Meals range $48–75/person; tax, alcohol and a 20% service charge are additional. Security services are required at the rate of $250/officer.

AVAILABILITY: Year-round, daily, 6am–11pm.

SERVICES/AMENITIES:

Catering: in-house, no BYO

Kitchen Facilities: n/a

Tables & Chairs: provided

Linens, Silver, etc.: provided

Restrooms: wheelchair accessible

Dance Floor: hardwood floor

AV/Meeting Equipment: projection screen

Parking: large lot

Accommodations: no guest rooms

Outdoor Night Lighting: yes

Outdoor Cooking Facilities: no

Cleanup: provided

View: golf course, Santa Clara Valley, city lights

Other: on-site coordinator, PA system

RESTRICTIONS:

Alcohol: in-house; or BYO wine, $15/bottle corkage

Smoking: outdoors only

Music: amplified OK indoors only

Wheelchair Access: yes

Insurance: not required

Other: no rice or open flames

David's Restaurant & Banquet Facility

Restaurant and Event Facility

5151 Stars & Stripes Drive, Santa Clara
408/986-1666 x21

www.davids-restaurant.com
jean@davids-restaurant.com
jeandavidsrestaurant@gmail.com

- Rehearsal Dinners
- Ceremonies
- Wedding Receptions
- Corp. Events/Mtgs.
- Private Parties
- Accommodations

For many couples, nothing says romance like a golf course, and for them there's David's Restaurant and Banquet Facility, two neighboring venues on the Santa Clara Golf Course that share the same beautiful panorama of velvety green fairways.

With its sharply steepled roof, wood-beamed ceiling and huge windows overlooking the greens, the restaurant feels like a cathedral—especially at night by candlelight. During cold weather, the natural stone fireplace makes a beautiful backdrop for an indoor ceremony, but on a sunny day you might prefer to get married outside on the adjacent patio.

Just steps away is David's Banquet Facility, which has five rooms facing the fairways. Clean and modern, with baffled wood ceilings, stylish chandeliers, wood trim, and large picture windows, the rooms can be opened up into one grand space with a fireplace at either end, or partitioned into smaller spaces for a more intimate event. Stage your ceremony on the grassy landscaped area next to the fairway, or in front of one of the granite-faced fireplaces. A long foyer with a high ceiling provides plenty of room for pre-banquet cocktails.

David's can arrange any type of affair, from an informal barbecue to an elegant sit-down dinner, with equal ease. They specialize in Continental cuisine, offering a choice of 44 hors d'oeuvres, from petit beef Wellington suxelles to sushi. Feast on entrées as elaborate as chicken Voldostano with prosciutto and gruyère cheese, or as simple and delicious as broiled salmon filet. For vegetarians, there is an array of choices, like stuffed red bell pepper and charbroiled polenta with fresh seasonal squash.

Other options include international custom menus and a variety of buffets, from Mexican or Italian-style to the Grand Buffet with a wide selection of hors d'oeuvres, salads, pastas and entrées. Buffet desserts, such as chocolate-dipped strawberries, double lemon cake and mini éclairs, are an irresistible finale to a great meal.

Its golf course location lends David's an open, breezy, out-in-the-country feeling; yet it's right in the heart of Silicon Valley, within walking distance to major hotels. David's has over 35 years of restaurant and banquet experience and can handle every detail of your event. If you want to make planning your celebration easier, put yourself in their capable hands.

CEREMONY, EVENT/RECEPTION & MEETING CAPACITY: The location holds up to 500 seated or 600 standing guests, indoors or outdoors.

FEES & DEPOSITS: A $1,000 deposit is required to reserve your date, and the balance is due 7 days prior to the event. The rental fee ranges $0–1,000 depending on the space, day, and time rented. Meals range $30–45/person. Tax, alcohol and a 20% service charge are additional.

AVAILABILITY: Year-round, daily, 7am–midnight or later.

SERVICES/AMENITIES:

Catering: in-house
Kitchen Facilities: n/a
Tables & Chairs: provided
Linens, Silver, etc.: provided
Restrooms: wheelchair accessible
Dance Floor: provided
Bride's & Groom's Dressing Areas: yes
AV/Meeting Equipment: provided

Parking: large lot
Accommodations: no guest rooms
Outdoor Night Lighting: yes
Outdoor Cooking Facilities: BBQ
Cleanup: provided
View: park, garden, landscaped grounds
Other: event coordination, on-site florals, chair covers

RESTRICTIONS:

Alcohol: in-house
Smoking: outside only
Music: amplified OK

Wheelchair Access: yes
Insurance: not required

Freedom Hall and Gardens

Gardens and Event Facility

Santa Clara, address withheld to ensure privacy.

408/379-FREE (3733)

www.freedomhall.com
info@freedomhall.com

Rehearsal Dinners	Corp. Events/Mtgs.
● Ceremonies	Private Parties
● Wedding Receptions	Accommodations

You would never in a million years guess that it was there. It's woodsy and flowery, with splashing fountains—perfect for taking the most idyllic of wedding photos. Yet the recently remodeled Freedom Hall and Gardens is right in the middle of Silicon Valley's high-tech empire in Santa Clara. What could be more convenient?

On weekends, this little oasis is as private and quiet as a desert island. Tucked away amid the silent office buildings, it's practically invisible to anyone passing by. But oh what this place has to offer: a fountain-pond surrounded by carpets of colorful flowers; natural stone formations; towering redwoods and weeping willows; and butterflies flitting across the pond by the rocky waterfall.

Ceremonies here are lovely. Picture your guests seated on the lawn at one end of the pond. You glide across the bridge spanning the water in front of them, and down the grassy aisle to stand in front of the fountain with your husband-to-be. Your music plays (via the professional outdoor sound system) as clouds drift through the blue sky overhead.

After exchanging vows, you and the wedding party walk the few yards to Freedom Hall, whose floor-to-ceiling windows command a panorama of the gardens. While the guests assemble, you wait in the Bride's Room, decorated with glass cases displaying a collection of wedding favors commemorating every wedding at Freedom Hall since the first one in 1995. You make your grand entrance through the bridal arch into the hall.

Dinner is served in the completely transformed Hall, which now features a gleaming hardwood floor, a granite bar, and Tuscan-inspired wrought-iron chandeliers. But the facility's most beautiful "decoration" is its view of the gardens. Guests are free to stroll outside, champagne glasses in hand, and meander along the winding brick paths through the redwoods.

Although the setting is quite appealing, what you don't see is the well-coordinated operation behind the event. Freedom Hall and Gardens hosts 170 weddings a year, and they know their stuff. The venue is Diamond-certified, which means that brides and grooms who were married here have been interviewed by an independent organization to determine the rate of customer satisfaction. Freedom Hall has consistently achieved a near-perfect score. It's not surprising that Freedom Hall and Gardens was voted "Best Wedding Reception Facility" by magazine from 2007 through 2016, and it was also inducted into their "Hall of Fame" in 2014.

The cuisine features classic American dishes such as a chef's carving station with New York roast steak, chicken Madeira, rice pilaf, pasta marinara, steamed vegetables and fresh-baked breads. There's a selection of passed hors d'oeuvres such as jumbo prawns, stuffed mushrooms and blue cheese pastries. As for dessert, any menu you choose includes complimentary chocolate-dipped strawberries as a sweet surprise before the wedding cake.

If you yearn for a ceremony in the redwoods, but your practical side requires a central location, Freedom Hall and Gardens offers both. You and your guests get the charm of a forest sanctuary, while being within walking distance of the Santa Clara Marriott and Great America. This place has everything you need.

CEREMONY & EVENT/RECEPTION CAPACITY: The site holds up to 250 guests maximum, indoors or outdoors.

MEETING CAPACITY: Meetings do not take place at this location.

FEES & DEPOSITS: A $3,000 deposit is required, and the balance is due 2 weeks prior to the event. There are no separate rental fees. The price per person, including the meal and alcohol, starts at $79. There is a 100-person minimum. Tax and a 20% service charge are additional.

AVAILABILITY: Year-round. Friday 6:30pm–midnight; Saturday and Sunday 10am–midnight; weekdays by special arrangement.

SERVICES/AMENITIES:

Catering: in-house
Kitchen Facilities: n/a
Tables & Chairs: provided
Linens, Silver, etc.: provided
Restrooms: wheelchair accessible
Dance Floor: provided
Bride's Dressing Area: yes
AV/Meeting Equipment: n/a

Parking: large lot
Accommodations: no guest rooms
Outdoor Night Lighting: yes
Outdoor Cooking Facilities: no
Cleanup: provided
View: garden, pond, fountain, grounds
Other: event coordination, on-site wedding cake, professional DJ

RESTRICTIONS:

Alcohol: in-house with package
Smoking: designated areas only
Music: amplified OK

Wheelchair Access: yes
Insurance: not required

This is important! Tell locations you're reading HERE COMES THE GUIDE and ask if our information is still current.

259

Hilton Santa Clara

Hotel

4949 Great America Parkway, Santa Clara
408/562-6703

www.hiltonsantaclara.com
joseph.jenci@hiltonsantaclara.com

- Rehearsal Dinners
- Ceremonies
- Wedding Receptions
- Corp. Events/Mtgs.
- Private Parties
- Accommodations

The Silicon Valley isn't the first place most people think of when planning a wedding or social gathering, and that's a shame. It means they're missing out on one of the nicest hotels in the area—the Hilton Santa Clara. Given its location, it's been a popular place for high-tech industry meetings, but it also has a number of features that make it an excellent choice for a special occasion.

The Hilton Santa Clara's exterior has the sleek, modern good looks you'd expect a large upscale hotel to have, but when you enter the lobby, you'd swear you were in an exclusive boutique hotel. Utilizing Classical, Art Nouveau and modern design elements, the lobby has an enticing air of relaxed, understated luxury. The neutral color scheme is anything but bland, while marble floors, wall panels and blond wood molding add natural luster to the room. Wall sconces, standard lamps and light fixtures, all made of sinuously curving wrought iron and frosted glass, make a stunning visual statement. Wherever you look, there is something to captivate your eye: two life-sized sculptures that could have been done by Rodin or Degas, richly colored and textured upholstery, framed prints and paintings.

All of the function areas in the Hilton Santa Clara reflect the imaginative style and attention to detail displayed in the lobby. There are two large ballrooms available for weddings and events: the 2,800-square-foot Sierra and the 1,500-square-foot Coastal. Each ballroom can be divided into three smaller rooms if desired. Another option for smaller, more casual get-togethers is La Fontana Lounge, just off the lobby. Softly lit by fixtures hanging from the coffered ceiling and enlivened by modern paintings, it's made-to-order for cocktail parties, receptions and "welcome" parties. By special arrangement, and depending on availability, you can rent the Concierge Room, a sort of super-deluxe "den" where guests watch TV, play games or just sit and chat over drinks. It's the perfect place for family and friends to relax after the reception.

In our opinion, the Hilton Santa Clara needs no more to recommend it than what we've already described, but we can't help mentioning just a few more benefits. They have a superb staff that can assist you in everything from menu selections to room rentals for your guests. The bridal package includes a complimentary suite for the bride and groom. And the Hilton Santa Clara's location can't be beat—California Great America theme park and the San Francisco 49ers' new Levi's Stadium are literally steps away, and the VTA lightrail stops right outside the hotel, giving you access to all the attractions of downtown San Jose. Should you wish to venture further afield, major freeways leading to the Monterey Peninsula or San Francisco are within easy reach. With all it has to offer, this Hilton qualifies as one of the South Bay's undiscovered treasures.

CEREMONY CAPACITY: The Coastal Ballroom holds 115 and the Sierra Ballroom 250.

EVENT/RECEPTION & MEETING CAPACITY: The Coastal Ballroom accommodates 60–100 seated or 200 standing, and the Sierra Ballroom 150–200 seated or 250–300 standing.

FEES & DEPOSITS: For weddings, a $2,000 nonrefundable deposit is required when the contract is signed. The event balance is due 2 weeks prior to the event, and a final guest count is due 1 week prior.

There is a variety of packages from which to choose. Prices range $66–99/person. Tax and a 24% service charge are additional. All packages include hors d'oeuvres, butler-passed champagne or sparking cider during the cocktail hour, champagne toast, 2 bottles of house wine per table, elegant floor-length linens and your choice of colored napkins and overlays, 2-course dinner and complimentary cake-cutting service. Complimentary wedding-night accommodations are provided for the bride and groom.

AVAILABILITY: Year-round, daily including holidays, 6am–midnight.

SERVICES/AMENITIES:

Catering: in-house
Kitchen Facilities: n/a
Tables & Chairs: provided
Linens, Silver, etc.: provided
Restrooms: wheelchair accessible
Dance Floor: yes
Bride's & Groom's Dressing Areas: guest room
AV/Meeting Equipment: CBA

Parking: complimentary
Accommodations: 280 guest rooms
Outdoor Night Lighting: access only
Outdoor Cooking Facilities: no
Cleanup: provided
View: Great America amusement park
Other: on-site wedding coordinator

RESTRICTIONS:

Alcohol: in-house; or BYO wine, $15/bottle corkage
Smoking: outside only
Music: amplified OK, volume limits after 11pm

Wheelchair Access: yes
Insurance: not required
Other: no open flames or fog machines; decorations need approval

Montalvo Arts Center

Historic Mansion & Grounds

15400 Montalvo Road, Saratoga
408/961-5856

www.montalvoarts.org/rentals
kkirkpatrick@montalvoarts.org

● Rehearsal Dinners		● Corp. Events/Mtgs.
● Ceremonies		● Private Parties
● Wedding Receptions		Accommodations

Nestled against a wooded slope in the secluded Saratoga Hills is Montalvo Arts Center, a lovely complex that holds a veritable treasure trove of venues for corporate events, private parties and, of course, weddings!

An inviting one-way road leads up to the center, and as you round the last turn you get your first glimpse of the expansive manicured lawns, colorful gardens, and Montalvo's beautiful Villa. Built in 1912 as the private residence of Senator James Duval Phelan, the Mediterranean-style estate is now a National Register Historic Landmark.

One of the property's most popular ceremony sites is the Love Temple, set inside the Italianate Garden at the bottom of the Great Lawn. A wide, rose-lined brick path flanked by antique marble statues leads to this open-air, white-columned pavilion, and couples wed in view of the surrounding garden with the Villa and woods in the background.

Directly behind the Villa, the Oval Garden offers a lush, intimate setting complete with classical statuary and wisteria-covered pergolas. A brick pathway serves as the center aisle, and a columned arcade makes a stately backdrop for exchanging vows. A third ceremony option is the new West Lawn Garden, which can accommodate 300+ guests.

While the newlyweds are photographed on the picturesque grounds, family and friends enjoy the cocktail hour either in the West Lawn Garden or the scenic Spanish Courtyard. Receptions follow on the Villa's broad veranda, where everyone is treated to splendid garden vistas and the occasional visiting deer.

The Villa's interior is equally impressive. All of the first floor's adjoining rooms open onto the veranda, creating a wonderful flow to your event. The huge Main Hall at the center of the house boasts a high, beamed ceiling and gilded chandeliers. An enormous fireplace topped with a tile and carved-wood mantel is usually set with flickering votives. The Hall is often used for dancing, its many French doors left open so that the music carries out to guests relaxing in the adjacent courtyard and on the veranda.

Other unique gathering spots include the handsome Library, paneled with rare New Zealand walnut. A working fireplace, soaring bookshelves and a grand piano are just a few of the Library's attractions. The bridal couple sometimes displays family photos on the Library's large desk, and arranges the wedding gifts on a built-in marble bar. Then there's the Dining Room, a cozy salon with a century-old fireplace and richly paneled walls.

Perhaps the Villa's most charming space is the Solarium, the perfect niche to showcase the wedding cake. Floor-to-ceiling windows along the north and east walls frame the scenery and let in abundant natural light, while the other walls are covered in 100-year-old lattice wood. The original terracotta tile floor, inlaid with floral patterns, enhances the vintage ambiance.

And that's not all: The entire upstairs is reserved for the bridal party and their immediate family. The three spacious suites include a lavish Bride's Room, with its own balcony overlooking the Great Lawn.

CEREMONY CAPACITY: The Oval Garden accommodates 250 seated, the West Lawn Garden seats 300-350, and the Side Veranda seats 130 in case of inclement weather. The Love Temple capacity is 150.

EVENT/RECEPTION CAPACITY: Indoors, the Villa holds 190 seated or 200 standing; outdoors, it's 300 seated or 1,000 standing. For other special events and business functions, the venue can accommodate up to 2,000. Events with over 300 guests may incur an additional cost and require special arrangements with the Events Manager.

MEETING CAPACITY: Meeting venues accommodate groups of 4–300 people; the Villa's main floor holds up to 100. The Carriage House Theatre can accommodate up to 300 people seated theater-style. The outdoor Garden Theatre accommodates 1,200 guests. The upper Villa has 3 large rooms that can be used for staff meetings or dressing rooms. The Cottage accommodates up to 14 guests.

FEES & DEPOSITS: For weddings, the rental fee ranges $14,000–20,000. Half the total fee is required when the site is booked; the balance is payable 6 months prior to the event along with a refundable security deposit and a certificate of insurance. For a Love Temple or Oval Garden ceremony only, the rental fee is $5,000. Please call for info about corporate rental fees and weekday rates. Special rates may apply for last-minute events.

AVAILABILITY: Ceremonies are held year-round and take place 10am–1pm. Ceremony/receptions are held year-round, in 9–12-hour blocks. All-day rentals are also available. For other special events and business functions, contact the Events Manager.

SERVICES/AMENITIES:
Catering: select from preferred list
Kitchen Facilities: ample
Tables & Chairs: provided
Linens, Silver, etc.: caterer
Restrooms: wheelchair accessible
Dance Floor: yes
Bride's & Groom's Dressing Areas: yes
AV/Meeting Equipment: WiFi; full range CBA, extra fee

Parking: valet may be required for over 200 guests, carpooling is encouraged
Accommodations: no guest rooms, hotel partners
Outdoor Night Lighting: yes
Outdoor Cooking Facilities: BYO
Cleanup: caterer
View: manicured lawns, formal gardens, historic sculptures and Santa Clara Valley vista

RESTRICTIONS:
Alcohol: through caterer
Smoking: outdoors only, designated area
Music: amplified OK with restrictions until 10pm

Wheelchair Access: yes
Insurance: certificate required

Saratoga Country Club

Country Club

21990 Prospect Road, Saratoga
408/253-0340 x215

www.saratogacc.com
sstephens@saratogacc.com

● Rehearsal Dinners	● Corp. Events/Mtgs.
● Ceremonies	● Private Parties
● Wedding Receptions	○ Accommodations

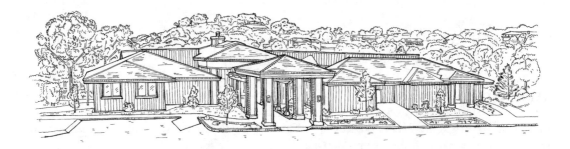

Perched high in the wooded hills above the Santa Clara Valley, the Saratoga Country Club offers everything you need for a superb wedding or festive gathering: beautiful surroundings, a romantic ceremony spot, a casually elegant clubhouse and fabulous food. And best of all, you don't have to be a member to host your event here.

The ceremony site, on top of a gentle hill, is one reason couples gravitate to the club. Surrounded by panoramic hillside views, it's as pretty as a wedding bouquet. The centerpiece is a majestic, one-of-a-kind, 15-foot-high white wrought-iron domed gazebo, set on cobblestones. Encircled by a large lawn and enclosed by a decorative fence, it's a private haven for family and friends to witness your exchange of vows. After the ceremony, it's just a short walk to the clubhouse reception by way of a spectacular lighted staircase with white railings, flanked by pines and oleanders!

The contemporary clubhouse is a well-appointed two-story structure painted in soft beige that harmonizes with the encompassing hillsides. An imposing portico and pergola-shaded walkway add drama to the building's entrance, where the exquisitely crafted cherrywood and cut-glass double doors are reminiscent of the work of Frank Lloyd Wright. In the Main Dining Room, the cream-colored walls are awash in sunlight, thanks to plenty of large windows interspersed with stately columns. French doors lead to spacious decks overlooking the verdant golf course below and the Santa Clara Valley in the distance. There's also a dance floor and stage area, and the soft, neutral beige-and-white color scheme of the dining room allows you to dress it up or down to your taste. Needless to say, this facility is not limited to wedding receptions; in fact, when we viewed it, it was set up for a graduation party with bright colored napkins, star-garlanded centerpieces and displays of yearbook photos and other school-related decorations. The dining room is also available during the week for any type of function.

Are all these great features beginning to intrigue you? Well, let us sweeten the pot just a little bit more. When you book your event at the Saratoga Country Club, you also get the services of events manager extraordinaire, Sherry Stephens. Her assistance is invaluable, especially for weddings. Every year, she updates a minutely detailed wedding guide outlining everything you need to know to plan your wedding, from a reception schedule to a list of preferred vendors. She's a calming influence for brides and a welcome resource for advice. Sherry even provides a detailed map to send out with your invitations, in case some of your guests are directionally impaired (the country club's secluded location is just minutes from highways I-280, SR-85 and I-880). So, schedule a trip to the Saratoga Country Club. Even if you're not a member, you'll be given VIP treatment!

CEREMONY CAPACITY: The Lawn Area holds up to 250 seated guests.

EVENT/RECEPTION & MEETING CAPACITY: The Dining Room accommodates 250 seated guests. Conference rooms are available for smaller groups.

FEES & DEPOSITS: A nonrefundable deposit, based on a percentage of the room rental fee and/or catering costs, is required when the contract is signed. The balance may be paid in installments, depending on the amount of time remaining between the signing of the contract and the date of the event, with the final payment due 10 days prior to the event. Any additional balance accrued is due at the end of the event. Room rental fees range $360–2,600 depending on the space(s) rented. (Be sure to ask about any special offers!) Banquets range $40–58/person and buffets start at $64/person. Tax, alcohol and a 20% service charge are extra.

AVAILABILITY: Year-round, daily, 7am–1am.

SERVICES/AMENITIES:

Catering: in-house, no BYO
Kitchen Facilities: n/a
Tables & Chairs: provided
Linens, Silver, etc.: provided
Restrooms: wheelchair accessible
Dance Floor: yes
Bride's Dressing Area: yes
AV/Meeting Equipment: CBA, extra fee

Parking: ample on site
Accommodations: no guest rooms
Outdoor Night Lighting: no
Outdoor Cooking Facilities: no
Cleanup: provided
View: golf course and Santa Clara Valley
Other: event coordination

RESTRICTIONS:

Alcohol: in-house, no BYO
Smoking: outdoors only
Music: amplified OK with restrictions

Wheelchair Access: yes
Insurance: not required
Other: no rice or birdseed

Saratoga Foothill Club

Historic Women's Club

20399 Park Place, Saratoga
408/867-3428

www.saratogafoothillclub.com
lbeesley@msn.com

● Rehearsal Dinners	● Corp. Events/Mtgs.
● Ceremonies	● Private Parties
● Wedding Receptions	○ Accommodations

On a quiet residential street near the crossroads of Big Basin and Sunnyvale/Saratoga Roads lies the Saratoga Foothill Club, a 1915 Arts and Crafts-style landmark. Designed by Julia Morgan as a women's club, it houses the oldest social organization in Saratoga. With a brown-shingled façade, sloping roof and decorative windows, it's one of the most distinguished small redwood structures in California: In 1978, the club received the distinction of being listed in the National Register of Historic Landmarks.

Equally noteworthy is the club's adjoining paved courtyard, dubbed the neighborhood's "Secret Garden." The cozy enclave is dotted with Japanese maples, whose summer-to-autumn crimson foliage provides a burnished backdrop for wedding ceremonies. On one side, a long wooden arbor is adorned with mature wisteria vines whose graceful lavender blooms debut in early spring. Beneath the arbor, a bench formed by twisted branches is an eye-catching place to gather the bridal party for photographs. Lush Japanese privets hedge the courtyard, lending privacy and a peaceful vision of greenery to the scene.

The club's interior further enhances the venue's appeal. A formal redwood foyer ushers guests into a hall that's ideal for a buffet reception or sit-down dining. The hardwood floor, half-timbered walls and 30-foot-high vaulted ceiling convey a quaint, chapel-like charm. (In fact, this room is sometimes used for ceremonies during the cooler months.) A bank of striking multipaned windows frames a view of the leafy courtyard, while just above, sunlight streams down from an elaborate circular window, setting the entire space aglow. The wedding cake looks picture-perfect in front of the windows, which highlight the newlyweds during the cake cutting. The room also has a raised platform stage that can hold musicians, a DJ, or even a decorated head table. Glass-transomed wooden doors open to an anteroom with a brick fireplace, a convenient spot to put a buffet table. Here and there authentic period fixtures—like rich wood paneling or eye-catching lamps—add vintage flair.

With its beautiful architectural details and overall feeling of comfort and warmth, the Saratoga Foothill Club offers a unique and intimate environment for celebrations.

CEREMONY CAPACITY: The patio seats 150 outdoors, and the club seats 200 indoors.

EVENT/RECEPTION CAPACITY: The site accommodates 150 seated banquet-style or 200 seated theater-style indoors, and 150 seated or 200 standing guests outdoors.

MEETING CAPACITY: The Main Room holds 200 seated theater-style.

FEES & DEPOSITS: A refundable $1,000 security deposit is required when reservations are made. The rental fee ranges $600–2,100. There is only one event per day. Wedding packages (based on 100 guests) start at $4,995 and include buffet, service, china, linens, cake, DJ, and beverage package.

AVAILABILITY: Year-round, daily, 9:30am–10pm.

SERVICES/AMENITIES:

Catering: in-house by *Panetta's Catering*
Kitchen Facilities: moderate
Tables & Chairs: provided
Linens, Silver, etc.: through caterer
Restrooms: wheelchair accessible
Dance Floor: yes
Bride's Dressing Area: yes
AV/Meeting Equipment: BYO

Parking: call for details
Accommodations: no guest rooms
Outdoor Night Lighting: yes
Outdoor Cooking Facilities: no
Cleanup: caterer or renter
View: of coastal hills and courtyard
Other: air conditioning; baby grand piano available

RESTRICTIONS:

Alcohol: BYO wine, champagne and beer in bottles or cans; no kegs
Smoking: on patio only
Music: amplified OK with volume limits

Wheelchair Access: yes
Insurance: certificate required

Overwhelmed? Use the search criteria on www.HereComesTheGuide.com to narrow down your choices.

267

Saratoga Springs

Resort

22801 Big Basin Way, Saratoga
408/867-3016 x51
saratoga-springs.com/wedding
jennifer@saratoga-springs.com

● Rehearsal Dinners		● Corp. Events/Mtgs.	
● Ceremonies		● Private Parties	
● Wedding Receptions		Accommodations	

Imagine celebrating the best day of your life in a veritable forest, with the ambient sounds of birds in the trees and leaves rustling in a cool afternoon breeze. Then, as night falls, a thousand stars twinkle overhead as you glide around a dance floor set into a rocky hillside. For many brides, a natural environment like this is far more stirring than any ballroom adorned with crystal chandeliers. And best of all, it can be found just minutes from San Jose.

The drive to Saratoga Springs takes you right through the upscale, horse-loving community of Saratoga, a tourist favorite. Just three blocks long, the village is known for one-of-a-kind boutiques, wide pedestrian sidewalks and two country inns, which come in handy for any friends and relatives who may want to make a weekend of it.

Leaving town, the road winds around and crosses a spring-fed stream as it heads towards the tree-studded foothills and Saratoga Springs itself, the oldest privately owned picnic grounds in the area. Once a booming logging center, these bucolic woodlands later became a stopping point for travelers making the arduous journey by wagon to the beach. Nowadays, the fifth generation of the Giannini family has updated the site's amenities, yet kept the woodsy ambiance for hosting affordable weddings and special events. Although there are several unique locales on the 125-acre preserve, two in particular offer the kind of awe-inspiring vistas that led Sierra Club founder John Muir to call the great outdoors "God's big show."

Cathedral Grove, named for the spectacular way the majestic redwoods and towering box elders lean towards each other—their branches form an arch like the ceiling of a Gothic church—is both private and very quiet. This lush hideaway provides lots of shade with a hint of dappled light filtering through the leafy canopy above. Soothing sounds of water are all around, coming from a brook in the gorge and two nearby creeks. In fact, you'll cross one of them as you make your entrance over a bridge to exchange vows with your groom in front of a dramatic rock cliff.

The grove, which can comfortably accommodate 150 guests, has ample room for dancing, a DJ setup, and ceremony or reception seating at long, family-style tables where your guests will enjoy the venue's signature barbecue buffet. Although many couples like the rustic setting just as it is, you can easily glam it up if you want. The on-site wedding planner can arrange to hang Japanese lanterns or flickering candles and have the trees and bridge spangled with pinpoint lights.

Speaking of bridges, one of the area's most recognizable landmarks, Longbridge, frames another choice wedding venue. This graceful stone span, built in 1904 on one of the highest elevations on the property, creates a stunning visual backdrop for either your ceremony or reception. From this site, the panoramic views are fantastic. Plus, the hillside dancing area to the right is surrounded by nature in all its glory.

Saratoga Springs is blessed with lots of wonderful photo spots, but the place where you can best capture the spirit of your day may be the romantic islet in Redwood Grove where two creeks, rather fittingly, join together as one.

CEREMONY CAPACITY: The facility holds 650 seated guests outdoors.

EVENT/RECEPTION & MEETING CAPACITY: The site accommodates 1,000 guests outdoors, seated or standing.

FEES & DEPOSITS: A $3,000–4,000 deposit is required to secure your date and the balance is due 10 days prior to the event. The rental fee ranges $0–3,950 depending on the day and time of the event, the space reserved, and whether minimum catering requirements are met. Meals range $40–85/person. Tax and service charges are additional.

AVAILABILITY: Year-round, daily, 8am–11pm.

SERVICES/AMENITIES:
Catering: in-house
Kitchen Facilities: n/a
Tables & Chairs: some provided
Linens, Silver, etc.: CBA
Restrooms: wheelchair accessible
Dance Floor: CBA
Bride's Dressing Area: CBA
AV/Meeting Equipment: BYO

Parking: large lot
Accommodations: no guest rooms
Outdoor Night Lighting: yes
Outdoor Cooking Facilities: BBQ on site
Cleanup: provided
View: creek, forest, hills, landscaped grounds, meadow, and park
Other: picnic area, event coordination

RESTRICTIONS:
Alcohol: in-house, or BYO with corkage fee
Smoking: outdoors only
Music: amplified OK with restrictions

Wheelchair Access: yes
Insurance: not required

Tri-Valley and Livermore Wine Country

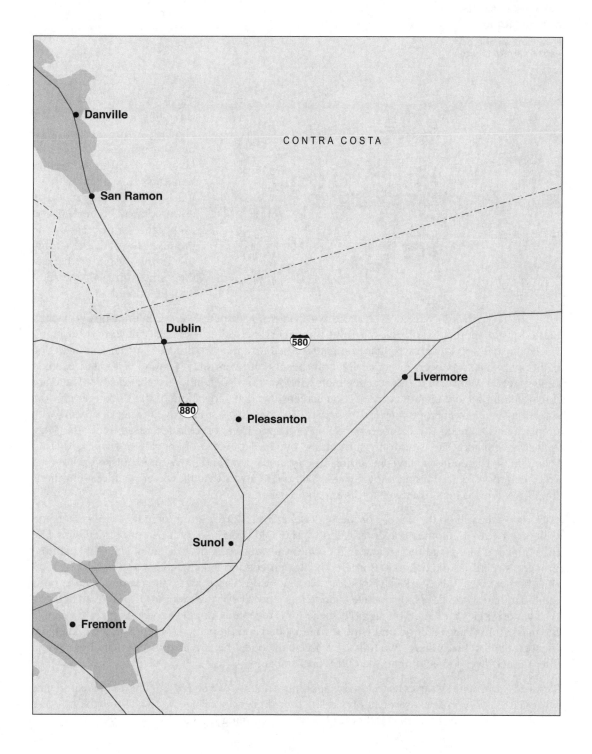

Bella Rosa at Garré Vineyard & Winery
and Martinelli Event Center

Vineyard & Winery

7986 Tesla Road, Livermore
925/371-8200

www.garrewinery.com
garre@garrewinery.com

- Rehearsal Dinners
- Ceremonies
- Wedding Receptions
- Corp. Events/Mtgs.
- Private Parties
- Accommodations

Garré Vineyard & Winery is a bit like a small village—a charming one surrounded by grapevines. One of the Livermore Valley's original wineries, this gem, with its Italian Wine Country style, has always drawn a crowd. Maybe it's because of the café on the premises, the park-like setting, the Tasting Room or the jazz they serve up with the food and the bocce ball.

That popularity has increased even more with Garré's Martinelli Event Center, a private facility located just a short drive up the hill from the winery. Set on an elevated vineyard, it's a grand Hacienda-style venue with wrought-iron gates, a bell tower, and palm trees at the entrance. The ballroom, which has been designed for both beauty and versatility, features a vaulted beamed ceiling, wood wainscoting and accents, high windows, and contemporary chandeliers. There are three built-in, remote-controlled projection screens (for that slide show of the bride and groom), as well as wireless microphones for the toasts. The building's stone-paved inner courtyard with fireplace and fountain is ideal for a bar setup and appetizers, or for a reception under the stars. A nearby ceremony site is not only surrounded by vines, but also offers views of vineyard-laced rolling hills. The entire facility—including an enormous patio and lawn, an exquisite bridal suite, and a comfortable groom's dressing area—is laid out in a way that allows for seamless transitions from ceremony to hors d'oeuvres to dining and dancing.

Back down the hill on the winery property is Bella Rosa, Garré's stunning new event center, and Oak Staging Area, another gorgeous wedding site. Old-fashioned 19th-century streetlamps line the paths and illuminate the area at night. One walkway leads up to a small stage beneath the property's centuries-old oak tree. Bordered by flowerbeds and Italian cypress and backed by rows of Cabernet vines, this is a lovely spot for a ceremony. Just steps away, the event center features a full bar, hardwood floors, distinctive chandeliers, and vineyard views through large arched picture windows. It's an incredibly flexible space for a reception, and a marvelous place to sample the masterful pairings of food and wine recommended and prepared by their Executive Chef and highly trained culinary staff. Two full-size bocce ball courts that are lit at night offer a before- and after-dinner diversion, adding to the Old World ambiance.

Tours of Garré Winery's event sites are by appointment only. We suggest that to really experience what Garré is like, make a reservation for lunch or dinner, too. That way you'll be able to stroll the grounds, take in the views, and taste their award-winning food and wine.

CEREMONY CAPACITY: The Martinelli Event Center seats up to 200 guests, and Bella Rosa seats up to 370.

EVENT/RECEPTION CAPACITY: The New Café holds up to 80 seated, the Café Courtyard up to 100, the Martinelli Center up to 200, and Bella Rosa up to 370.

MEETING CAPACITY: Spaces are available for 12–370 guests. Facilities include conference capabilities.

FEES & DEPOSITS: 15% of the estimated event total is the nonrefundable deposit required to reserve your date, and the balance is due 2 weeks prior to the event. The most popular all-inclusive packages range $90–150/person.

AVAILABILITY: Year-round, daily, anytime.

SERVICES/AMENITIES:

Catering: in-house

Kitchen Facilities: n/a

Tables & Chairs: provided, Chiavari chairs at both event centers

Linens, Silver, etc.: provided

Restrooms: wheelchair accessible

Dance Floor: yes

Bride's & Groom's Dressing Areas: yes

AV/Meeting Equipment: video projectors, DVD, amplifier, electronically operated projection screen, program speakers, wireless microphone, and wireless connections are available at both event centers

Parking: ample on site

Accommodations: no guest rooms

Outdoor Night Lighting: yes

Outdoor Cooking Facilities: no

Cleanup: provided

View: vineyards, valley, mountains, meadow, fountain, gardens

RESTRICTIONS:

Alcohol: in-house; full bar at both event centers

Smoking: outdoors only

Music: amplified OK outdoors until 10pm

Wheelchair Access: yes

Insurance: liability required

Crooked Vine and Stony Ridge Winery

Winery

4948 Tesla Road, Livermore
925/449-0458
www.crookedvine.com
janet@crookedvine.com

- Rehearsal Dinners
- Ceremonies
- Wedding Receptions
- Corp. Events/Mtgs.
- Private Parties
- Accommodations

The Livermore Valley, one of the country's oldest winemaking regions, is less than an hour from San Francisco and so picturesque that at some point you start fantasizing about owning a vineyard … or having a friend who does. Fortunately, within minutes of entering Crooked Vine and Stony Ridge Winery, you feel you are among friends because their passion, commitment and *joie de vivre* are contagious.

Owned by the Corbett family, this boutique winery has produced a dazzling array of varietals from century-old grapevines. At the same time, they've created a charming setting where you can celebrate your wedding in style—and have the entire property to yourselves.

As your guests arrive, they're ushered down a treelined pathway to a pair of tall redwood gates, emblazoned with an iron-forged version of the "crooked vine" logo. Inside those gates is a self-contained event site with three separate areas. To the left is the Barrel Room, with its stone-pillared façade and latticework arbor at the entry. To the right is the spacious Garden Courtyard, a shaded, stone-floored reception patio. And directly ahead is the manicured Ceremony Lawn, where friends and family await your walk down the aisle to a raised, Craftsman-style gazebo bordered by fragrant lavender and silvery shrubs.

Once vows have been sealed with a kiss, it's time to raise a toast with a flute of the venue's signature sparkling wine. Cocktails and appetizers can be served al fresco, but most brides opt for the climate-controlled Barrel Room. High ceilings, concrete floors and rows of stacked barrels bedecked with romantic tea lights set the scene. A black granite bar runs the length of one wall and framed paintings of colorful vineyards hang above it. At the center of the room, oak barrels are set up as cocktail tables. A dramatic focal point—and a popular backdrop for photos—are the two massive, antique, hand-carved barrels depicting joyful nymphs and cherubs at play among the vines.

If you can slip away, you and your groom will also want to take advantage of some other cool photo ops, by taking a walk through neat rows of sangiovese vines in front of the tasting room, or posing with the winery's mint condition 1930s car and early 1940s pickup truck.

Then rejoin everyone for dinner in the Garden Courtyard beneath the twinkling lights strung overhead. Your menu will be expertly paired with wine selections from their much-lauded reds and whites.

As night falls, take the party back inside where the great acoustics of the Barrel Room will get everybody dancing. And for those out-of-towners who want to explore the Livermore/Dublin area the next day (but not too early), the folks at Crooked Vine will be happy to help them choose from among the region's many points of interest.

CEREMONY & EVENT/RECEPTION CAPACITY: The facility can accommodate 100 seated or 200 standing indoors and 200 seated or standing outdoors.

MEETING CAPACITY: Meeting spaces hold 100 seated guests.

FEES & DEPOSITS: 50% of the rental fee and a refundable damage deposit are required to reserve your date, and the balance is due 90 days prior to the event. The rental fee for events starts at $3,500 for Friday or Sunday, and $5,000 for Saturday, and varies depending on the time of the event, guest count and space rented.

AVAILABILITY: Year-round, daily, 11am–10pm.

SERVICES/AMENITIES:

Catering: select from preferred list
Kitchen Facilities: none
Tables & Chairs: provided
Linens, Silver, etc.: through caterer
Restrooms: wheelchair accessible
Dance Floor: available
Bride's Dressing Area: yes
AV/Meeting Equipment: some provided

Parking: large lot
Accommodations: no guest rooms
Outdoor Night Lighting: yes
Outdoor Cooking Facilities: no
Cleanup: provided
View: garden courtyard, landscaped grounds, hills, vineyards
Other: picnic area

RESTRICTIONS:

Alcohol: in-house
Smoking: designated areas only
Music: amplified OK with restrictions

Wheelchair Access: yes
Insurance: liability required

Murrieta's Well

Wine Estate

3005 Mines Road, Livermore
925/456-2425

www.murrietaswell.com
catering@wentevineyards.com

● Rehearsal Dinners	● Corp. Events/Mtgs.
● Ceremonies	● Private Parties
● Wedding Receptions	Accommodations

"Romantic" is the word that is sure to come to mind when you first set eyes on this heavenly wine estate, tucked away in a pastoral fold of picturesque Livermore Valley. Named for the artesian well where Joaquin Murrieta (the notorious Robin Hood of El Dorado) and his band of desperados purportedly watered their horses, this history-rich property is just the place for a memorable event.

Your festivities can begin and/or end on the graceful Vineyard Terrace. A visual delight, it's artistically and fragrantly framed in native California plantings and bright bursts of blooms—red and white tree roses, hanging flowers, and colorful flowerbeds—and by the surrounding vineyard that's the source of the property's handcrafted wines. This sweeping outdoor venue, with broad patios and lawns, is ideal for a wedding ceremony, reception, or almost any event. Here, you can celebrate California style—under a canopy of brilliant blue or a sky full of stars—or tent the space if you desire.

For a show-stopping entrance and tasteful transition, use the mosaic staircase accented with antique Spanish tiles that descends, via an artfully planted hillside, from the upper deck lounge to the Vineyard Terrace. It overlooks Murrieta's fountain—and it's a red-carpet-caliber stop for photos.

The enchanting 100+-year-old winery building, with its huge double doors and second-story balcony, provides a striking backdrop, whether you're dining and dancing on the Terrace and lawns … or inside in the appropriately named Barrel Room. This rustic, yet refined, space features heavy wood beams and pillars, a high ceiling, natural stone walls, and ancient wine barrels, all of which create a dramatic ambiance. A series of glittering chandeliers and gilt-framed mirrors lend a bit of glamour, and you can add twinkling lights and vines wrapped around the wooden pillars for a theatrical touch, transporting your guests to another place and time. In fact, even the simplest additions—white-clad tables, glassware and cutlery, elegant arrangements of flowers— look remarkable in this room.

At the back of the Barrel Room, a staircase leads up to the broad tasting room foyer where a wide breezeway gives guests a private place to take a breather from all the excitement. This comfortable, nicely appointed outdoor lounge also makes a great spot for the bride and her entourage to relax before the wedding. Meanwhile, Murrieta's award-winning restaurant and events catering staff (set up out of sight on the second floor) whisk up and down the stairs with their perfect, mouthwatering pairings of fabulous food and estate-produced wines.

Murrieta's Well is carrying on a tradition of growing grapes and making wine that began back in the 1800s. When you host your event at this estate, you'll enjoy a taste of its storied past and an authentic wine country experience.

CEREMONY CAPACITY: Outdoor spaces seat up to 110 guests.

EVENT/RECEPTION & MEETING CAPACITY: Indoor and outdoor spaces hold up to 110 seated or 150 standing guests.

FEES & DEPOSITS: A nonrefundable 1,000–5,500 deposit is required to reserve your date. 50% of the estimated final balance is due 6 months prior to the event, and the balance is payable 2 weeks prior; all incurred expenses are due the day of the event. The rental fee ranges $1,000–5,500 depending on the day and season. *Wente Catering* provides sit-down dinners and buffets, including a custom-designed wedding cake. These range $85–95/person. Tax, beverages, rentals and a 20% service charge are additional.

AVAILABILITY: Year-round indoors, daily, 6pm–11pm.

SERVICES/AMENITIES:

Catering: in-house
Kitchen Facilities: n/a
Tables & Chairs: provided
Linens, Silver, etc.: provided
Restrooms: wheelchair accessible
Dance Floor: CBA
Bride's & Groom's Dressing Areas: no
AV/Meeting Equipment: CBA

Parking: large lot
Accommodations: no guest rooms
Outdoor Night Lighting: yes
Outdoor Cooking Facilities: no
Cleanup: provided
View: vineyards, garden, hills
Other: event coordination, custom-designed wedding cake

RESTRICTIONS:

Alcohol: in-house
Smoking: outside only
Music: amplified OK until 10pm

Wheelchair Access: yes
Insurance: liability required

Want to know WHAT TO ASK a potential location or vendor? Check out our Questions to Ask starting on page 21.

Poppy Ridge Golf Course

Golf Course and Clubhouse

4280 Greenville Road, Livermore
925/447-6779
www.poppyridgegolf.com/weddings
events@poppyridgegolf.com

● Rehearsal Dinners	● Corp. Events/Mtgs.
● Ceremonies	● Private Parties
● Wedding Receptions	Accommodations

Grapevines line a narrow private road that winds through gently sloping hills to a graceful hacienda-style clubhouse. Set on a hill, the tile-roofed building overlooks the pristine fairways and greens of the Poppy Ridge Golf Course. First opened for play in 1996, the 27-hole course and restaurant is the sister facility of top-ranked Poppy Hills Golf Course in Pebble Beach and, like the flower it's named for, it epitomizes the sunny charm of the Golden State.

Rustic-style double doors open to a peaceful lobby, a perfect ambiance for conjuring up heartfelt messages for the guest book. A few steps further, sunlight cascades through skylights, an appropriate introduction to the spacious restaurant that adjoins the far side of the lobby. The restaurant features a vaulted ceiling and is a picturesque place for weddings, company parties, tournament banquets and more. It comes with a full walk-up bar, and two walls of floor-to-ceiling windows that showcase breathtaking views. The north window boasts a commanding vista of the Chardonnay and Zinfandel courses, with Mt. Diablo in the background.

In addition to its enviable panorama, the restaurant has also earned high marks from repeat clientele for excellent food: Mouthwatering menus for hors d'oeuvres, sit-down dinners and buffets include tempting entrées that incorporate fresh, local ingredients and are accompanied by handcrafted sauces. The Executive Chef selects the menu for each event with the utmost care and consideration. Equal attention is paid to all other aspects of your celebration: The site fee—an incredible value—includes an event planner and on-site coordinator, bartenders, and all the props for the right presentation. And, of course, the staff is expert at helping you personalize your occasion and executing every detail.

If you'd prefer to entertain outdoors, reserve one of the building's wide, sun-splashed terraces with their unobscured backdrops of glistening lakes and lush greens. There's plenty of room for a ceremony on the inviting East Terrace, set with a beautiful white arbor and chairs for your guests.

Whatever the occasion, scenic Poppy Ridge Golf Course is a glorious setting for making merry.

CEREMONY CAPACITY: Poppy Ridge holds up to 170 seated guests, indoors or outdoors.

EVENT/RECEPTION CAPACITY: Indoors, Poppy Ridge seats up to 170, although that capacity can increase with the dance floor on the patio option (June–September). The indoor/outdoor seated capacity is 200 guests.

MEETING CAPACITY: Spaces are available that hold up to 150 guests.

FEES & DEPOSITS: The rental fee, which ranges $300–3,000 depending on the type of event, is required to reserve your date. The balance is due 14 days prior to the event. Some of the many services and amenities included in the rental fee are listed below in the Services/Amenities section. Meals range $44–53/person. Tax, alcohol and service charge are additional. There is a site fee for meetings; please contact the venue for more details.

AVAILABILITY: Year-round, daily, 6am–midnight. Site tours by appointment.

SERVICES/AMENITIES:

Catering: in-house, no outside catering
Kitchen Facilities: full kitchen
Tables & Chairs: included
Linens, Silver, etc.: included
Restrooms: wheelchair accessible
Dance Floor: included
Bride's Dressing Area: yes
AV/Meeting Equipment: no audio; projector, extra charge

Parking: for up to 300 cars
Accommodations: partner nearby hotels
Outdoor Night Lighting: yes
Outdoor Cooking Facilities: yes
Cleanup: provided
View: vineyards, fairways, hills, ponds, Livermore valley, landscaped grounds
Other: event coordination, patio heaters, colored napkins, chargers and garden arch included in rental fee

RESTRICTIONS:

Alcohol: beer, champagne and spirits provided or BYO wine and champagne with corkage fee
Smoking: outdoors only
Music: amplified OK

Wheelchair Access: yes
Insurance: liability required

Ravenswood Historic Site

Victorian Country Estate

2647 Arroyo Road, Livermore

925/373-5703

www.larpd.org
facilities@larpd.org

Rehearsal Dinners	● Corp. Events/Mtgs.
● Ceremonies	● Private Parties
● Wedding Receptions	Accommodations

If you're in search of a romantic estate surrounded by vineyards for your upcoming special occasion, this gem of a venue set in the Livermore Valley Wine Country is an obvious choice.

Built in 1891 by Christopher Augustine Buckley, Sr., who was known as the "Blind Boss" of San Francisco politics (yes, he was actually blind), it's part of the 100-acre landholding that once served as his family's summer home. Today, in addition to the handsomely restored Main House, the property features a lovely Carriage House and Cottage as well as gardens, apple orchards, vineyards, lawns, and scenic walks that serve as a glamorous Victorian-style frame for all types of events. Like the grand private residences of a far more opulent age, this site takes visitors back to an elegant era, one where time stops and memories that last are made.

Festivities can be staged indoors or out, weather permitting. With its graceful white gazebo (perfect for saying "I do"), shade trees and white Victorian-era streetlamps, the broad North Lawn behind the Main House is a dreamy setting for ceremonies. The smaller front lawn, where the couple can exchange vows at the top of the wide Main House stairs, and the home's huge double parlor provide similarly picturesque options.

Cocktails and appetizers may be served in a variety of locations, too: around the fountain on the front lawn, on the North Lawn, or in either or both of the two large parlors inside. The spacious U-shaped veranda that wraps around most of the central structure is also tailor-made for indulging in a glass of champagne and passed hors d'oeuvres while enjoying the garden, orchard and vineyard views along with the breezes and birdsong.

As for dining and dancing, indoor and al fresco possibilities abound. Set up tables on the North Lawn for an outdoor banquet or barbecue, or deck the halls of the Main House's handsome interior. Oak floors and wainscoting, fireplaces, pocket doors, chandeliers, and other period details lend the rooms of this historic home a special charm. There's even a spacious and secluded chamber downstairs that can be employed as a private haven for the bride and her wedding party.

No matter where you wander on the property, you'll discover all kinds of photogenic spots to pause or pose. But what we find most appealing about this site are the many ways you can personalize the venue and its sprawling visitor-friendly grounds. There's plenty of room for kids to play in the meadows and orchards without feeling confined, while still in full view of their families; for elders to sit a spell on the benches and admire the garden views; for couples to stroll arm-in-arm along the treelined paths; or for friends and family to gather and enjoy every unforgettable moment of your celebration.

CEREMONY, EVENT/RECEPTION & MEETING CAPACITY: The site holds 70 seated or standing guests indoors and 150 seated or standing outdoors.

FEES & DEPOSITS: A $500 deposit is required to reserve your date, and the balance is due 30 days prior to the event. The rental fee ranges $580–3,000 depending on the day of the event and your resident status (whether or not you are a Livermore resident).

AVAILABILITY: Year-round, daily, times vary.

SERVICES/AMENITIES:

Catering: BYO
Kitchen Facilities: fully equipped
Tables & Chairs: provided
Linens, Silver, etc.: BYO or through caterer
Restrooms: wheelchair accessible
Dance Floor: yes
Bride's Dressing Area: yes
AV/Meeting Equipment: BYO

Parking: large lot
Accommodations: no guest rooms
Outdoor Night Lighting: access only
Outdoor Cooking Facilities: BBQ CBA
Cleanup: caterer or renter
View: garden, landscaped grounds; panorama of hills and vineyards
Other: picnic area, gazebo

RESTRICTIONS:

Alcohol: BYO
Smoking: designated area only
Music: amplified OK

Wheelchair Access: yes
Insurance: liability required

Shrine Event Center

Banquet Facility

170 Lindbergh Avenue, Livermore
925/454-0094

www.shrineeventcenter.com
sales@shrineeventcenter.com

● Rehearsal Dinners	● Corp. Events/Mtgs.
● Ceremonies	● Private Parties
● Wedding Receptions	Accommodations

Towering palms, graceful willow trees, and lush grounds welcome you into the spacious Shrine Event Center. The grand ballroom is larger than most event facilities in the area, and it can take on any theme you have in mind.

Events often begin in the Lounge, where two built-in bars with mirrored backsplashes make serving cocktails both attractive and easy. Matching nearby counters can hold the appetizer or dessert display. The Lounge is also a fun retreat for after-dinner cordials.

The Lounge leads directly into the Lindbergh Ballroom, the centerpiece of the venue. Open, airy and contemporary, the ballroom features a dramatic vaulted ceiling with polished wooden beams. Rows of fabric swags overhead lend a soft, elegant look. At one end of the ballroom, an east-facing stage is perfect for your band or DJ.

One of the best things about the Shrine Event Center is its adaptability. The ballroom accommodates a wide range of events, from a corporate seminar to a beautiful wedding. For a sophisticated gala, deck the space out in white linen and crystal. If you're planning something more informal, like a luau-style banquet, the room easily transforms into a Caribbean paradise with vibrant colors and tropical décor. Add tulle, flowers, or twinkle lights as the spirit moves you. Track lighting on dimmers allows you to adjust the mood throughout your party. There's also a retractable screen for showing a photo or video montage, and even a disco ball in case you want to turn it up a notch when the dancing gets going. Their Sales Manager will work with you to design your event, and can recommend vendors to help you bring your ideas to life.

If you like, host both your ceremony and reception in the ballroom, where movable room dividers let you create separate areas if desired. Large conferences or banquets can combine adjacent breakout rooms with the ballroom, and seat up to 950 guests theater-style. The center's professional sound system with exceptional speakers is another plus, especially for corporate events.

The Shrine Event Center is easily accessible by freeway I-580 and close to the Livermore Municipal Airport, local hotels (one within walking distance), shopping, restaurants, parks and golf courses—something your out-of-town guests will appreciate. Plus, there are plenty of nearby wineries, hiking trails and other attractions to keep your family and friends happily occupied before and after your event.

Flexibility, convenience, affordability, complimentary on-site parking—and you can bring your own caterer and alcohol! With so much to offer, it's no wonder this venue is in demand!

CEREMONY CAPACITY: Ceremonies may be held upon request.

EVENT/RECEPTION CAPACITY: The main ballroom accommodates 450 seated for dining and dancing. Adjoining side rooms each seat 50 guests.

MEETING CAPACITY: The facility holds up to 950 guests seated theater-style.

FEES & DEPOSITS: A nonrefundable deposit is required to hold your date. The rental fee, which includes a 5-hour event plus 2 hours for setup and 1 hour post-event for cleanup, ranges $1,100–4,000 depending on the date and number of guests. A Shrine coordinator, security guards, and a refundable $1,000-minimum security deposit are required for every event; fees vary based on the type of event and guest count.

AVAILABILITY: Year-round, daily.

SERVICES/AMENITIES:
Catering: BYO licensed and pre-approved or select from list
Kitchen Facilities: fully equipped
Tables & Chairs: provided
Linens: available, or BYO
Silver, China etc.: through caterer or BYO
Restrooms: wheelchair accessible
Dance Floor: yes
Bride's Dressing Area: yes
AV/Meeting Equipment: AV equipment CBA, extra charge

Parking: large complimentary lot
Accommodations: nearby hotels
Outdoor Night Lighting: yes
Outdoor Cooking Facilities: yes
Cleanup: caterer, renter and some provided
View: East Bay foothills

RESTRICTIONS:
Alcohol: through caterer or BYO licensed server, no corkage fee or service charge
Smoking: outside only
Music: amplified OK

Wheelchair Access: yes
Insurance: certificate required

Wente Vineyards
Event Center, Golf Course & Vineyard Lawn

5050 Arroyo Road, Livermore
925/456-2425

www.wentevineyards.com
catering@wentevineyards.com

Restaurant & Golf Course

- Rehearsal Dinners
- Ceremonies
- Wedding Receptions
- Corp. Events/Mtgs.
- Private Parties
- Accommodations

Situated in a picturesque canyon at the southern end of the Livermore Valley, Wente Vineyards Restaurant, Event Center and Golf Course is surrounded by grapevines, sycamore groves and rolling hills. The site, with its beautifully landscaped grounds, is a versatile setting for corporate retreats, special events, and of course, Tri-Valley Wine Country weddings!

Founded 125 years ago, Wente Vineyards is the country's oldest continuously operated family-owned winery. It's no wonder, then, that the architecture reflects a sense of California history. White Spanish-style stucco buildings are accented with tile roofs and floors, and terracotta pots full of flowering plants set a cheery tone. The event center includes the Cresta Blanca Room, where indoor receptions are held, and the adjacent Terrace Lawn, a pretty spot for a garden wedding ceremony. There's space here, too, for an elegantly tented reception. Or use an open-sided tent for dancing, and set up tables and chairs outside to enjoy the view, which includes the changing seasonal colors of the sycamore trees.

Speaking of views: One of the best can be had on the new Vineyard Lawn near a pond at the golf course's 18th hole. Ceremonies and receptions on this green expanse can accommodate up to 1,000 of your nearest and dearest; in the background, lush vineyards and the golden Sandstone Hills cast a romantic spell.

Wente's award-winning restaurant casts a spell of its own. Three private dining rooms and terraces with vineyard views accommodate intimate receptions, rehearsal dinners, bridal showers or any other celebration. Wente, which has been Green Certified by Alameda County, has earned much critical acclaim for its cuisine, wine and sustainability. (They're among the first wineries in the state to be recognized by the recently established Certified California Sustainable Winegrowing Alliance.) Menus focus on simple foods with complex flavors, and incorporate the freshest locally grown and organic ingredients. Experienced staff will assist you with menu choices and wine selection, as well as recommendations for event services such as photography, floral design and overnight accommodations.

Wente also offers private wine tastings in their wine caves (a superb idea for your rehearsal dinner) and customized wine labeling for wedding favors. Sometimes event hosts organize a round of golf on Wente's Greg Norman-designed course, located just a chip shot away from the Conference Center. In keeping with their environmental sensitivity, the course was recently designated a "Certified Audubon Cooperative Sanctuary" by the Audubon International Program.

With its first-rate facilities, acres of vineyards and warm, Mediterranean ambiance, Wente is an extremely popular event site. They book up quickly, so don't wait too long to pay this East Bay oasis a visit.

CEREMONY CAPACITY: The Lawn and Garden can accommodate 350 seated; the Charles Wetmore and Cresta Blanca Rooms each hold 60–150 seated.

EVENT/RECEPTION CAPACITY: The site seats 15–150 indoors, and 20–1,000 outdoors.

MEETING CAPACITY: Various spaces seat 16–100 guests.

FEES & DEPOSITS: For weddings, a nonrefundable $1,000–5,500 deposit is required to reserve your date. 50% of the estimated event cost is due 6 months prior to the event, and the event balance is payable 2 weeks prior; all incurred expenses are due on the day of the event. The facility rental fee ranges $750–5,500 depending upon day and season. Catering is provided: Buffets, luncheons and dinners, including a custom-designed wedding cake, range $66–90/person. Tax, beverages, rentals and a 20% service charge are additional.

For business functions, social events and meetings, facility rental fees range $150–5,500 depending on the spaces rented. Food is provided; prices vary depending on menus and services selected. Call the sales department for specific rates.

AVAILABILITY: Year-round, daily, 7am–11pm, indoors. The Vineyard Lawn is available until 10pm.

SERVICES/AMENITIES:

Catering: in-house
Kitchen Facilities: n/a
Tables & Chairs: provided
Linens, Silver, etc.: provided
Restrooms: wheelchair accessible
Dance Floor: available
Bride's Dressing Area: yes, in Event Center only
AV/Meeting Equipment: full range, extra charge

Parking: large lot with parking attendants
Accommodations: no guest rooms
Outdoor Night Lighting: yes
Outdoor Cooking Facilities: no
Cleanup: provided
View: vineyards surrounded by rolling hills
Other: event coordination

RESTRICTIONS:

Alcohol: beer, champagne, spirits and Wente wine provided
Smoking: outside only
Music: amplified OK

Wheelchair Access: yes
Insurance: liability required
Other: no birdseed, rice or petals

The wedding vendors on our website are the best in the business. How do we know? Read page 553.

The Callippe Preserve Golf Course

Golf Course

8500 Clubhouse Drive, Pleasanton
925/426-6666 x4

www.playcallippe.com
events@playcallippe.com

● Rehearsal Dinners	● Corp. Events/Mtgs.
● Ceremonies	● Private Parties
● Wedding Receptions	Accommodations

You'll feel like you've stumbled upon an emerald tucked in between the tawny East Bay hills as you climb toward the lofty perch that is home to the Callippe Preserve Golf Course. A protected habitat for the beautiful California Callippe Silverspot Butterfly as well as the Tiger Salamander and the California Red-legged Frog, this graceful property carpeted in green and dotted with ancient live oaks and young sycamores has all the magic of Oz.

Nothing distracts from the beauty of the setting. The rambling, green and stone-colored California ranch-style clubhouse set on a promontory overlooking the entire Tri-Valley area is designed to enhance the natural ambiance. Most major celebrations take place on the airy Vista Patio, which presides over the spectacular golf course and valley panorama. This flexible space is enclosed on three sides, and the fourth can be draped to give the feel of a traditional indoor banquet room. On two sides, floor-to-ceiling windows slide open to allow balmy breezes to drift through. A broad, open-beam ceiling features lantern-style heat lamps that keep it cozy when those breezes cool. A delightful locale for cocktails, sit-down dinners, dancing or simply lounging with relaxed guests, it's bounded by the graceful curve of an adjoining two-tiered low deck. You'll want to linger out here as the well-trained staff serves up a California-style banquet as fresh and exhilarating as the surroundings.

Twinkling rope lights weave along the edge of the deck to illuminate its contours and the plantings of wild rose and fescue grasses that frame it. The perfect place for a band or quartet, the deck is also an excellent location for a small bar, welcome cocktails or additional seating. The wide lower deck a couple of steps below has a sweeping northern exposure and is ideal for stunning photos, romantic toasts, or late-night dancing under the stars.

After hours, the Vista Restaurant is also available for intimate private functions and offers club- and cabaret-style entertainment possibilities. It has a full granite bar, a princely two-sided stone fireplace, and a separate lounge area with wrought-iron chandeliers, redwood beam accents and saddle-brown leather couches. Your options are as limitless as the vistas. So, let your imagination soar here. The property's on-site coordinator and experienced banquet staff are adept at customization—and they're dedicated to making your dreams a reality. They'll help plan your event and allow you to sit back and enjoy the party at Callippe Preserve Golf Course. There's nothing like feeling on top of the world…

CEREMONY, EVENT/RECEPTION & MEETING CAPACITY: The site can accommodate 200 seated guests outdoors and on the mostly-enclosed Vista Patio. The Vista Restaurant can hold up to 70 seated or standing guests.

FEES & DEPOSITS: A deposit in the amount of the rental fee is required to reserve your date, and the balance is due 2 weeks prior to the event. The rental fee ranges $1,000–2,500 depending on the setup. Meals range $29–40/person. Tax, alcohol and a 20% service charge are additional.

AVAILABILITY: Year-round, weekends, anytime. Only one event per day.

SERVICES/AMENITIES:

Catering: in-house or BYO
Kitchen Facilities: none
Tables & Chairs: provided
Linens, Silver, etc.: provided or BYO
Restrooms: wheelchair accessible
Dance Floor: no
Bride's Dressing Area: no
AV/Meeting Equipment: CBA

Parking: large lot
Accommodations: no guest rooms
Outdoor Night Lighting: yes
Outdoor Cooking Facilities: BBQ CBA
Cleanup: caterer or renter
View: landscaped grounds, creek, canyon; panorama of fairways and hills
Other: event coordination

RESTRICTIONS:

Alcohol: in-house or BYO with corkage fee
Smoking: designated areas only
Music: amplified OK outdoors with restrictions

Wheelchair Access: yes
Insurance: not required

Casa Real at Ruby Hill Winery

Winery, Garden & Ballroom

410 Vineyard Avenue, Pleasanton
925/931-0200

www.casarealevents.com
info@casarealevents.com

●	Rehearsal Dinners	●	Corp. Events/Mtgs.
●	Ceremonies	●	Private Parties
●	Wedding Receptions		Accommodations

The name, Casa Real, means House of Royalty, and we have no doubt that you and your guests will feel to the manor born when you arrive at this dramatic property set in the heart of the Livermore Valley Wine Country.

Acres upon acres of vineyards frame the 20,000-square-foot villa. The beautiful Mediterranean-style fountain surrounded by roses is a paparazzi-pleasing backdrop for red carpet arrivals and departures. Enormous hand-carved mahogany doors with wrought-iron hinges open into the jaw-dropping Entrance Hall with its 32-foot ceiling, Italian tile floor and white limestone trim. Three huge chandeliers; artisan-crafted limestone niches, rosettes and medallions; and clerestory-style windows set high in the walls lend the space a classical, yet romantic, feel. It's a gallery fit for rows of marble statues or shining suits of antique armor, but you might be perfectly happy with a roomful of celebrants and a beautiful floral arrangement atop the mahogany table that sits at its center.

From this hall, five additional sets of massive mahogany doors lead in other directions. To the east, the similarly trimmed Amber Room with its honey and cocoa accents embraces you in an atmosphere of luxury and intimacy. Large enough for a sizeable indoor ceremony or sit-down gathering, its focal point is a 12-foot hand-carved limestone fireplace before which vows, performances and spirited toasts are surely in order. The Entrance Hall's north doors lead to the 9,000-square-foot Grand Salon, ideal for magnificent fêtes and feasts, with its soaring ceiling, mahogany bar and expansive windows. Twenty massive half-moon chandeliers, star-like pin lights, and sconces around the room's perimeter vary the mood; the champagne-colored Italian tile floor invites dancing; and handsome mahogany king's tables suggest banqueting in grand style.

No detail goes unattended in this regal oasis. In addition to the spacious, elegantly appointed restrooms, a posh chamber the size of a small condo (with couch, credenza, standing mirror, private bathroom and a granite-topped vanity that seats up to four) serves as a corporate closing room, a lounge for the bride and attendants or a peaceful semiprivate retreat.

For outdoor ceremonies, cocktails and other activities, the Sun Garden's terrace, walkways, limestone fountains and plants provide an idyllic setting. Views of the vineyards and the rolling East Bay hills abound, and a canopy of blue sky caps its protective walls. Within them Valencia orange trees, lavender, white tree roses and other beautiful blooms share space with lovely trees that border the garden's central lawn. And don't forget the historic Ruby Hill Winery right next door; it's a great spot for wine-tasting.

CEREMONY CAPACITY: The facility holds 320 seated guests indoors and 400 seated outdoors.

EVENT/RECEPTION CAPACITY: The site can accommodate 450 seated with a dance floor or 500 seated without.

MEETING CAPACITY: The site holds 600 seated guests.

FEES & DEPOSITS: A deposit equal to the rental fee or a minimum of $3,000, whichever is greater, is required to reserve your date. The rental fee ranges $1,000–5,000 depending on the day and time of the event. Meals with a full, 4½-hour bar start at $104/person. Tax and service charge are additional. A $750 ceremony setup fee is extra. Fees and policies are subject to change.

AVAILABILITY: Year-round. Sunday–Thursday, 8am–10pm; Friday and Saturday, 8am–11pm.

SERVICES/AMENITIES:

Catering: in-house

Kitchen Facilities: n/a

Tables & Chairs: provided

Linens, Silver, etc.: provided

Restrooms: wheelchair accessible

Dance Floor: yes

Bride's Dressing Area: yes

AV/Meeting Equipment: CBA, extra charge

Other: event coordination

Parking: large lot; directed or valet parking required for over 275 guests

Accommodations: no guest rooms

Outdoor Night Lighting: yes

Outdoor Cooking Facilities: n/a

Cleanup: provided

View: fountains, landscaped grounds, garden, courtyard, hills, valley and vineyards

RESTRICTIONS:

Alcohol: in-house

Smoking: outside only

Music: amplified OK with restrictions

Wheelchair Access: yes

Insurance: liability required

Castlewood Country Club

Golf Club

707 Country Club Circle, Pleasanton
925/485-2237

www.castlewoodcc.org
info@castlewoodcc.org

● Rehearsal Dinners	● Corp. Events/Mtgs.
● Ceremonies	● Private Parties
● Wedding Receptions	Accommodations

Once the site of the fabulous "La Hacienda Del Pozo de Verona" and the former estate of Phoebe Apperson Hearst, California's beloved hostess and first lady of philanthropy, the Castlewood Country Club still retains the aura of elegance and grace that were the hallmarks of its famous resident. The drive up Pleasanton Ridge, which overlooks the Amador Valley and is flanked by green fairways and gated estates, continues to generate a feeling of opulence and success. Giant palms line the Clubhouse approach, while the country club pool, built by Mrs. Hearst, sparkles like a huge aquamarine amid emerald lawns.

The princely porte-cochère that marks the entrance to the Clubhouse is reminiscent of the palatial 53-room California Mission-style mansion that once crowned the rise. This red carpet-style entrée through a beautiful colonnade is a fitting introduction to the spaces within.

Guests can gather in the handsomely furnished Grand Lobby with its soaring ceiling and majestic fireplace. Gleaming terracotta-colored floors reflect light in a way that adds warmth and splendor. The lobby leads to the Del Pozo Lounge, a 2,000-square-foot private prefunction space of castle-like splendor. A magnificent granite-and-marble bar in the back of the room draws guests in to relax with a cocktail in hand before stepping into the 6,000-square-foot Grand Ballroom. The room's 12-foot-high windows let in breathtaking valley and golf course views, and 10 massive Spanish-style chandeliers combine with other ambient lighting to halo festivities in just the right light. Event menus are customized by Castlewood's award-winning chef, and served up by a staff experienced in fine dining and topnotch service.

Let a waltz across the polished hardwood floors lead to the Del Pozo Terrace, where 1,600 additional square feet of function space and more stunning valley and woodland vistas expand the party possibilities. Perfect for pre-dinner or après-dinner drinks and tête-à-têtes, it's also an excellent ceremony space. For brides and grooms who wish to tie the knot on Castlewood's Oak Tree Lawn, the property's ancient oak tree, whose branches spread overhead like a lacy fan, is a spectacular natural backdrop for the wedding couple.

If the bride and her attendants need to freshen up, they can do so in quarters fit for a queen. Entrance is through the Ladies Lounge, where rich carpeting, card tables, wingback chairs and golf course views create an inviting vibe. The bathrooms feature vanities and wraparound counters with upholstered cream-and bronze-colored seating. The groom and his groomsmen also have their own space, but we're betting they'll spend little time there. After all, how often can you celebrate like a Spanish grandee in a 21st-century castle?

CEREMONY CAPACITY: The facility seats 200 guests indoors and 350 outdoors.

EVENT/RECEPTION CAPACITY: The site can accommodate 350 seated with a dance floor, 400 without, or 500 standing indoors.

MEETING CAPACITY: The site holds 450 seated guests.

FEES & DEPOSITS: A $5,000 deposit is required to secure your date. The rental fee ranges $1,000–5,000 depending on the day and time of the event and the space reserved. Meals start at $48/person. Tax, alcohol and a 20% service charge are additional.

AVAILABILITY: Year-round.

SERVICES/AMENITIES:

Catering: in-house or BYO
Kitchen Facilities: fully equipped
Tables & Chairs: provided
Linens, Silver, etc.: provided
Restrooms: wheelchair accessible
Dance Floor: provided
Bride's Dressing Area: yes
AV/Meeting Equipment: some provided, extra fee

Parking: large lot
Accommodations: no guest rooms
Outdoor Night Lighting: CBA
Outdoor Cooking Facilities: BBQ CBA
Cleanup: caterer or renter
View: fairways, landscaped grounds, pool area; panorama of hills and valley

RESTRICTIONS:

Alcohol: in-house, no BYO
Smoking: designated areas only
Music: amplified OK with restrictions

Wheelchair Access: limited
Insurance: liability required

The Club at Ruby Hill

Private Golf Club

3400 West Ruby Hill Drive, Pleasanton
925/461-3505
www.rubyhill.com
mjohnson@rubyhill.com

● Rehearsal Dinners	● Corp. Events/Mtgs.
● Ceremonies	● Private Parties
● Wedding Receptions	Accommodations

Judging by its beautiful entrance, with a Tuscan-style gatehouse, trellised driveway and meticulous landscaping, Ruby Hill is no ordinary golf club. In fact, what lies beyond the impressive gates is not just a golf course, but an exclusive private community surrounded by vineyards and spread over acres of open land. It's so exclusive that in order to take a peek at this lovely facility you have to make an appointment. However, no membership or sponsorship is required to host your event here.

The clubhouse and fairways are a short drive up the hill, and as you make your way to the top, you pass dozens of spectacular homes whose graceful architecture defines the development. Most of these houses are reminiscent of Italian villas, and when you finally reach the clubhouse, you're hardly surprised to find that it's the largest and most striking "villa" of them all.

Step through the arched front door into the Fireside Room and you're more than a little awestruck by the grand scale and inviting ambiance. The vast marble floor gleams softly, bathed in natural light from a stunning domed skylight overhead. Elegant conversational seating is arranged beneath the skylight and in front of a large stone fireplace. You can't help but notice rich details, like the crown molding, wall sconces and window trim, all seemingly fashioned from stone, and the eclectic antiques and art, which add a personal touch.

From the Fireside Room, walk down the regal staircase into the Main Ballroom, where indoor receptions and special events are held. The sheer grandeur of the space makes you want to sit down to fully appreciate the soaring 40-foot ceiling, custom chandelier and abundant light streaming in through a multitude of high windows and glass doors. Walls are painted a warm Tuscan wheat accented with creamy white trim, and the Florentine motif in the custom carpet swirls beneath your feet in muted earth tones.

Next to the Main Ballroom are a similarly appointed small private dining room for rehearsal dinners or meetings, and the Event Lounge, which is draped with chiffon and illuminated by twinkle lights and a chic chandelier. All three rooms open out onto an expansive arcaded patio that overlooks a formal garden and emerald lawn, as well as views of the golf course, the Livermore hills and Mt. Diablo.

The patio also overlooks a stunning oval terrace that's custom-made for al fresco ceremonies and receptions. Paved with smooth Napa Valley stone and enclosed by two wisteria-covered trellises, the terrace feels intimate despite the fact that it's completely open to the sky, the breeze and panoramic vistas.

Ruby Hill Golf Club is a glorious spot for any upscale affair or holiday party. And if you're interested in a corporate golf tournament, it has the first Jack Nicklaus-designed golf course in Northern California. The clubhouse was built to exacting standards so we're quite sure you'll feel right at home.

CEREMONY CAPACITY: The Fireside Room seats 200, the Ballroom 200, and the Terrace 300.

EVENT/RECEPTION CAPACITY: The Main Dining Room accommodates 200 seated or 300 standing. The Main Dining Room in conjunction with the adjoining outdoor patio can accommodate 350 seated. The Terrace holds 250 seated or 300 standing guests.

MEETING CAPACITY: Several spaces seat 8–45 guests.

FEES & DEPOSITS: A nonrefundable $3,000 deposit is required to reserve your date, and the estimated food & beverage total is due 1 month prior to the event. Meals range $40–50/person; tax, alcohol and a 20% service charge are additional. Customized menus are available.

AVAILABILITY: Year-round.

SERVICES/AMENITIES:

Catering: in-house, no BYO
Kitchen Facilities: n/a
Tables & Chairs: provided
Linens, Silver, etc.: provided
Restrooms: wheelchair accessible
Dance Floor: yes
Bride's Dressing Room: yes, 3-hours prior to the event
AV/Meeting Equipment: CBA, extra charge

Parking: large lot and valet
Accommodations: no guest rooms; nearby hotels with complimentary shuttle service
Outdoor Night Lighting: yes
Outdoor Cooking Facilities: yes
Cleanup: provided
View: vineyards, Jack Nicklaus Golf Course
Other: day-of event coordination available

RESTRICTIONS:

Alcohol: in-house; or BYO, corkage $18/bottle
Smoking: outside only
Music: amplified OK with restrictions

Wheelchair Access: yes
Insurance: not required
Other: no rice, birdseed or glitter

Want to find more venues and services? Check out our informative website, www.HereComesTheGuide.com.

293

Palm Event Center in the Vineyard

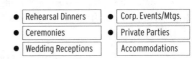

1184 Vineyard Avenue, Pleasanton
925/426-8666

www.palmeventcenter.com
info@palmeventcenter.com

- Rehearsal Dinners
- Ceremonies
- Wedding Receptions
- Corp. Events/Mtgs.
- Private Parties
- Accommodations

The ambiance here is purely palatial or maybe "palazzo," since the feeling you'll get is that you've stepped into the Italian countryside. Set on a 110-acre winery estate and fashioned in a size, scale and simplicity that emphasize the beauty and character of its vineyard setting, the Palm is certainly a magnificent place for a party.

The facilities are surrounded by vineyards and enjoy views of Mt. Hamilton and Ruby Hill. Guests arrive via a graceful palm-lined approach to find themselves in front of an imposing winery with its roots in the past. The atmosphere is one of privacy and refinement. Celebrations take place in the adjacent event venue, which has been built using antique brick recycled from an old historic winery. Carefully designed in a manner that blends wine country and Romanesque styles, it's a majestic edifice that bespeaks both taste and means.

The enchantment continues when you step into the Ballroom through the Palm's massive redwood doors. They're made from wine barrels that were aged over 50 years, and constructed by a master carpenter. Inside, a 24-foot-high ceiling and honey-colored Italian-tile floor define the grand scale of this spacious room. High Roman windows connect you with the outdoors: Look through them and you can see the tops of the palms. Weddings, fancy fundraisers, high-end dinner dances and corporate galas will all look impossibly posh in this sumptuous interior. Larger-than-life appointments include French oak barrels and four 800-pound mahogany king's tables ideal for presenting cakes, registration, buffets or banquets in royal style. Handsome portable screens can partition off any area, including the sleek tan-and-black granite bar. And the magnificent catering kitchen enables an all-star staff to turn out delicious contemporary cuisine, guaranteed to dazzle your palate. The sky's the limit on lighting, and this heaven of dual pin spots on adjustable dimmers is better than the stars! Even the seating is exquisite: ultra-comfy chairs are welcoming after a mad whirl (or two or three) around the ballroom.

On the eastern wall, huge floor-to-ceiling windows and glass doors open onto a sizeable, two-tiered patio, which can also be accessed from a trellis- and trumpet-vine-bordered walkway on the side of the building. Floored in tasteful gray stone and attractively lit, it's perfect for cocktails and hors d'oeuvres or for after-dinner drinks under the stars. The well-manicured lawn is another lovely gathering place, perhaps for a ceremony beneath a gorgeous redwood trellis, or for a convivial chat.

The cavernous Estate Room, lined with wine barrels and glittering tea lights, provides more space and is a beautiful setting for an indoor ceremony. This room can also host extra activities and sideshow attractions like a casino room, or double as a swanky lounge. Clean, crisp and cool, it's full of wine-cave romance and the fragrance of ripening vintages.

CEREMONY CAPACITY: The facility seats 300 guests indoors and 350 outdoors.

EVENT/RECEPTION CAPACITY: The Palm accommodates 350 seated with a dance floor, or 375 seated without.

MEETING CAPACITY: The site seats 375 guests.

FEES & DEPOSITS: A deposit equal to the rental fee or a minimum of $2,700, whichever is greater, is required to secure your date. The rental fee ranges $1,000–5,000 depending on day and time reserved. Meals with a full 4-hour bar package start at $98/person. Tax and service charge are additional. A $600 ceremony setup fee is extra. Fees and policies are subject to change.

AVAILABILITY: Year-round, daily, 8am–11pm.

SERVICES/AMENITIES:

Catering: in-house
Kitchen Facilities: n/a
Tables & Chairs: provided
Linens, Silver, etc.: provided
Restrooms: wheelchair accessible
Dance Floor: yes
Bride's Dressing Area: yes
AV/Meeting Equipment: CBA, extra charge

Parking: large lot; directed or valet parking required for over 275 guests
Accommodations: no guest rooms
Outdoor Night Lighting: yes
Outdoor Cooking Facilities: n/a
Cleanup: provided
View: vineyards, garden, hills, landscaped grounds, fountain
Other: event coordination

RESTRICTIONS:

Alcohol: in-house
Smoking: outside only
Music: amplified OK with restrictions

Wheelchair Access: yes
Insurance: liability required

Palm Pavilion

4501 Pleasanton Avenue, Pleasanton
925/426-7600
www.alamedacountyfair.com
fcater@alamedacountyfair.com

Event Center

● Rehearsal Dinners	● Corp. Events/Mtgs.
● Ceremonies	● Private Parties
● Wedding Receptions	Accommodations

Set on 267 beautifully landscaped acres in the heart of downtown Pleasanton, the Palm Pavilion is home to many events year-round, including weddings, private parties and corporate affairs.

Surrounded by its namesake trees, the versatile facility enables you to celebrate indoors and out. Inside, the golden oak bar, pale terracotta tiles and cream walls lend the space an inviting warmth, while a variety of lighting options make this large (5,000-square-foot) space feel surprisingly intimate. Generous windows on three sides showcase views of the golf course and main lawn area. Three adjoining patios—two open and one covered—let you and your guests revel in the balmy Pleasanton weather. In addition, the building is fully air-conditioned, and boasts up-to-date audiovisual technology.

Just a few steps away is the Wine Garden where ceremonies are held. Couples exchange vows on a raised platform near a burbling fountain, against a lush backdrop of flowers, ferns and other greenery. The stucco wall enclosing the garden ensures privacy.

If you're a bride on a budget, you won't find a better venue than the Palm Pavilion. The experienced staff will give you as much (or as little) assistance as you want, and they can handle everything from an upscale wedding to a quinceañera. Plus, they provide services and amenities you won't find at smaller facilities, such as acres of nearby parking, security, and plenty of privacy.

And because the Pavilion is part of the nonprofit Alameda County Fairgrounds, the revenue they generate goes back into maintaining and improving the property, ensuring that the grounds and buildings are always in tip-top shape.

With so much to offer, the Palm Pavilion could be the surprise perfect place for your special event!

CEREMONY CAPACITY: Various outdoor locations hold in excess of 2,000 guests; the Palm Pavilion seats up to 275.

EVENT/RECEPTION CAPACITY: Indoor spaces accommodate 225 seated or 275 standing guests. The Garden holds up to 200 seated or 250 standing.

MEETING CAPACITY: Various spaces hold up to 3,000 guests.

FEES & DEPOSITS: 50% of the estimated event total is required to reserve your date, and the balance is due 30 days prior to the event. The rental fee is $800 Sunday–Thursday and $1,400 Friday and Saturday. Meals start at $29/person. A 22% service charge and sales tax are additional.

AVAILABILITY: Year-round, daily, 8am–midnight.

SERVICES/AMENITIES:

Catering: in-house, no BYO
Kitchen Facilities: n/a
Tables & Chairs: provided
Linens, Silver, etc.: provided
Restrooms: wheelchair accessible
Dance Floor: yes, permanent
Bride's Dressing Area: CBA
AV/Meeting Equipment: some provided, more CBA

Parking: large lots
Accommodations: nearby partner hotels
Outdoor Night Lighting: yes
Outdoor Cooking Facilities: BBQ
Cleanup: provided
View: golf course, garden, park, grounds
Other: coordination available for fee; on-site florals, picnic area

RESTRICTIONS:

Alcohol: in-house
Smoking: outside only
Music: amplified OK with restrictions

Wheelchair Access: yes
Insurance: liability included

Elliston Vineyards

Winery

463 Kilkare Road, Sunol
925/862-2377
www.elliston.com
info@elliston.com

● Rehearsal Dinners	● Corp. Events/Mtgs.
● Ceremonies	● Private Parties
● Wedding Receptions	Accommodations

When gold rush pioneer Henry Ellis carved out an estate for himself in 1890, he picked a prime setting: a sheltered canyon tucked between two tree-covered ridges. Here he set up house in a three-story mansion constructed of thick sandstone from nearby Niles Canyon, and went about enjoying life in the country. Today his lovely homestead, now surrounded by vineyards, has become a prime setting for hosting weddings, receptions and private parties.

Garden-style ceremonies are held outdoors alongside the historic mansion, in a garden brimming with native flora and including an expansive lawn and gazebo. Stage your photos here, and you'll have some striking options for a backdrop—the century-old stone house, vibrant displays of azaleas and camellias and sprawling vineyards. But if you'd like to search for more photographic possibilities, go right ahead—there are plenty of photo opportunities at Elliston.

A short walkway takes you from the garden to the Terrace Room, a secluded 2,000-square-foot banquet room set into the hillside. Its vaulted ceiling and glass walls add to the feeling of spaciousness, while the surrounding deck gives guests a chance to dine al fresco at umbrella-shaded tables. A Victorian gazebo next to the deck is large enough for a bridal table or a quartet of musicians to serenade partygoers. The entire site is sheltered by oak, eucalyptus and olive trees, creating an ideal venue for you and your guests to celebrate.

Whether you're a bride planning your wedding or a wine aficionado, Elliston Vineyards is a destination worth seeking. Centrally located, with access from several East Bay freeways, you're close to civilization but you'd never know it—the quiet country atmosphere will give you the delicious feeling of being a million miles away.

CEREMONY CAPACITY: Outdoors, the South Lawn holds 225 seated; indoors the Terrace Room can accommodate 150 seated.

EVENT/RECEPTION CAPACITY: The Terrace Room and adjoining deck accommodate 225 guests, with 150 seated indoors and 75 seated outdoors.

MEETING CAPACITY: The facility holds up to 150 seated guests.

FEES & DEPOSITS: A nonrefundable $2,000 deposit is required when reservations are confirmed. 50% of the estimated event total is due 6 months prior to your function, with and additional 25% payment due 2 months prior. The remaining balance, with a confirmed guest count, is due on Friday 2 weeks prior. The food & beverage minimum, which applies to weekend evenings from April–October, is $9,500 on Saturday, and $7,500 on Friday or Sunday. The actual cost will depend on the menu and beverage package selected, and guest count. Luncheon and dinner menus, including hors d'oeuvres, start at $48/person for seated meals; buffets start at $46/person and require a 50-person minimum.

For meetings and conferences, a nonrefundable deposit is required when reservations are confirmed. Room fees range $500–750. Minimums may apply. Continental breakfast, full lunch and afternoon snack run $44/person.

AVAILABILITY: Year-round, daily.

SERVICES/AMENITIES:

Catering: in-house
Kitchen Facilities: n/a
Tables & Chairs: provided
Linens, Silver, etc.: provided
Restrooms: wheelchair accessible
Dance Floor: yes
Bride's Dressing Area: yes
AV/Meeting Equipment: projector screen, flip charts, DVD player and monitor

Parking: large lot, parking attendants
Accommodations: no guest rooms
Outdoor Night Lighting: yes
Outdoor Cooking Facilities: no
Cleanup: provided
View: vineyards and hills
Other: event planning and day-of coordination

RESTRICTIONS:

Alcohol: champagne, wine, beer and spirits packages provided, no BYO
Smoking: outside only
Music: amplified OK inside only

Wheelchair Access: yes
Insurance: not required
Other: no rice, birdseed or confetti

The Vineyards at Nella Terra Cellars

Winery

5005 Sheridan Road, Sunol
408/893-9463
www.nellaterra.com
info@nellaterra.com

- Rehearsal Dinners
- Ceremonies
- Wedding Receptions
- Corp. Events/Mtgs.
- Private Parties
- Accommodations

Take it from us: If you're planning a grand fête of any kind—wedding, fundraising gala, corporate celebration, holiday party, or glamorous social affair—you simply must check out this beautiful new venue tucked into the tawny Sunol Hills. It's only a few minutes from Highway 680 but seemingly worlds away...

You'll know you've arrived when you crest the gently rising terrain and spot the property's landmark 20-foot steel-rail barrel. From that vantage point you'll have an unimpeded and visually sumptuous view of Nella Terra Cellars' spectacular layout, which includes hillside vineyards, landscaped gardens, water features and walkways as well as stunning outdoor ceremony and reception sites and a dramatic peak-roofed white tent for entertaining indoors.

You can make your way down to the function areas in a number of ways, but our choice would be the property's regal 75-step staircase hewn from ancient vineyard stone. It descends in fairytale fashion past Viognier and Pinot Noir plantings. At its foot sits the elegant ceremony site with vine-draped arches at the entrance and a pergola backdropped by an idyllic creek-fed pond, trimmed in native grasses and flowers and stocked with hundreds of silvery fish. It's perfect for vows and romantic enough to inspire proposals, but dreamier still is an amble around the pond. The path leads across a bridge and past a small waterfall. Wood-hewn benches and catkins teased by dragonflies punctuate the walkway on the far shore where it meanders to end at the water's edge. There, a beautiful big bay tree offers shade and a lush spot for photos. It's a stunning place to pause, reflect or reconnect as you listen to the trill of waterfall, fountain and creek. And what a pleasure to breathe in the forest and floral scents while admiring the magnificent 360-degree vineyard surround!

But that's just a time-out. On the other side of the pond there's a party in progress. The sophisticated outdoor reception space is grand enough to support any gathering. Will it be cocktails, dinner, or other activities beneath the blue canopy of the sky or under the stars? Or do you want to move your guests inside? Use the vineyard's antique oak barrels and other props—highboy and farmhouse tables, lounge furniture, portable fire pits, Chiavari chairs, mirrors, lacy chandeliers and more—to transform the space to your specifications.

An enchanting Bride's changing room with hardwood floors, kitchenette, lounge area, bathroom, and private deck is another delightful bonus. Whatever your style, from rustic to royal, you'll find just what you need to realize your vision at this one-of-a-kind venue for your once-in-a-lifetime event.

CEREMONY CAPACITY: The site holds 300 seated guest outdoors.

EVENT/RECEPTION & MEETING CAPACITY: The site accommodates 300 seated or standing guests indoors and 300 standing outdoors.

FEES & DEPOSITS: 50% of the rental fee and 25% of the catering fees are required to secure your date, and the balance is due 10 days prior to the event. The rental fee starts at $7,500 and varies depending on the day and time reserved. Meals start at $46/person. Tax and a 20% service charge are additional.

AVAILABILITY: April–November (closed December–March).

SERVICES/AMENITIES:

Catering: in-house
Kitchen Facilities: n/a
Tables & Chairs: provided
Linens, Silver, etc.: provided
Restrooms: wheelchair accessible
Dance Floor: yes
Bride's & Groom's Dressing Area: yes
AV/Meeting Equipment: some provided
Other: WiFi access

Parking: large lot
Accommodations: no guest rooms
Outdoor Night Lighting: yes
Outdoor Cooking Facilities: BBQ CBA
Cleanup: provided
View: fountain, garden, landscaped grounds, fairways, lagoon, waterfall; panorama of fields, hills, mountains and vineyards

RESTRICTIONS:

Alcohol: in-house
Smoking: not allowed
Music: amplified OK

Wheelchair Access: yes
Insurance: liability required

This is important! Tell locations you're reading HERE COMES THE GUIDE and ask if our information is still current.

301

East Bay

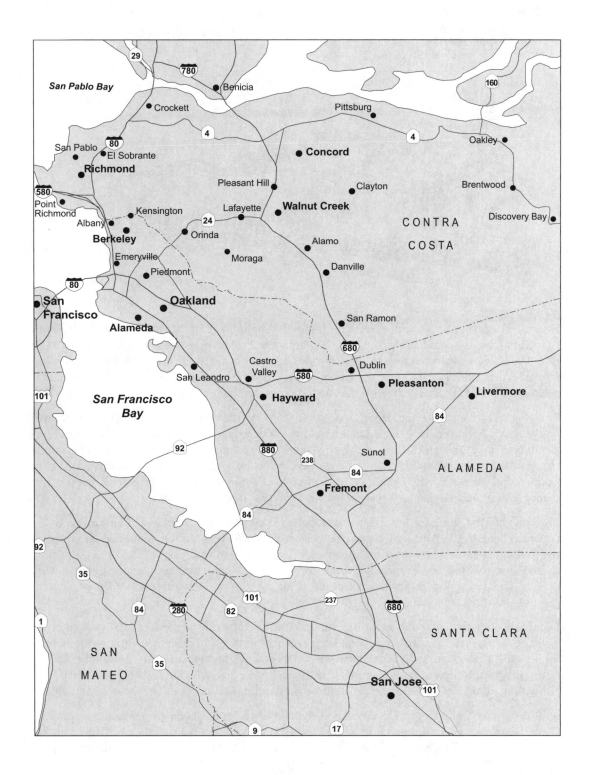

Grandview Pavilion

300 Island Drive, Alameda
510/865-5322

www.grandviewpavilion.com
info@grandviewpavilion.com

● Rehearsal Dinners	● Corp. Events/Mtgs.
● Ceremonies	● Private Parties
● Wedding Receptions	Accommodations

Fairy tales begin in places like this. Set in the tranquil community of Harbor Bay on historic Bay Farm Island in Alameda, the perfectly picturesque Grandview Pavilion does seem almost too good to be true. The lovely ivy-covered Mediterranean-style building sits just at the edge of the championship 36-hole Chuck Corica Golf Course, far enough away from the main complex to maintain an aura of seclusion without sacrificing the lush tree-dotted green and fairway views.

There's a soft sheen to the handsome Spanish-style doors that open onto the elegantly tiled foyer and spacious Ballroom. Full-size French windows cover the facing wall, bringing the Edenic surroundings inside. The backdrop of eucalyptus, pine trees and meticulously manicured lawns stands out against the neutral color scheme of cream-colored walls and white crown moldings and trim. Coppered chandeliers hang from the airy coffered ceilings, and the built-in granite, copper and mahogany bar and service area has back-to-back access from either room.

It's a magnificent stage for any high-end social or corporate event, but weddings are truly exceptional here. In the Ballroom, enormous mirrors overlook the polished, hand-laid cherrywood dance floor, amplifying the area and the energy. There's even a professional DJ booth seamlessly tucked away behind one retractable mirror for clutter-free entertaining. If dancing isn't on the agenda, the dance floor is an ideal place to set up a dramatic serpentine table showcasing an exquisite food presentation.

Did we mention that all the food for this venue is provided by one of the Bay Area's top caterers? *Grand Catering* has been wowing clients with excellent service and delectable dining experiences for decades. Their offerings look and taste like works of art. Whether your plans are simple (French bistro, BBQ, California cuisine) or extravagant (Asian fusion, luau with full roast pig, mashed potato bar with martini glass service), the eats will be outstanding—a true feast for the eyes and palate.

As if this weren't enough, the facility has recently added a spectacular tri-peaked tent pavilion. When the weather's warm, its clear "walls" are opened to let in balmy breezes. During cooler months or for evening events, the pavilion can be enclosed and heated for guests' comfort. But no matter what the season, this venue provides a garden experience with views of the surrounding flowers, plants and golf course. If you have your ceremony in the Garden Tent Pavilion, a white trellis at one end serves as an arch. Two indoor fountains create their own soothing music, while chandeliers and twinkle lights add an enchanting sparkle.

There's even a beautiful room for the bride and her attendants with pink champagne walls, soft moss-colored carpeting and private restrooms with peach marble accents, but our guess is the ladies will spend little time there.

CEREMONY CAPACITY: The Garden Tent Pavilion holds up to 200 seated guests.

EVENT/RECEPTION & MEETING CAPACITY: The Ballroom accommodates up to 288 seated guests with a dance floor or 450 standing. The total seated capacity for a reception is 420. The Garden Tent Pavilion can hold up to 120 seated guests.

FEES & DEPOSITS: For weddings, the rental fee is required to reserve your date; the estimated event total is due 30 days prior to the event. The rental fee ranges $1,600–3,800. The wedding reception food & beverage minimum is $50/person. Tax and a 20% service charge are additional.

For corporate meetings, the room rental fee starts at $500. Breakfast starts at $12/person, lunch at $18/person.

AVAILABILITY: Year-round, daily.

SERVICES/AMENITIES:

Catering: in-house, no BYO
Kitchen Facilities: n/a
Tables & Chairs: provided
Linens, Silver, etc.: provided
Restrooms: wheelchair accessible
Dance Floor: yes
Bride's Dressing Area: provided
AV/Meeting Equipment: full sound system, wireless mics, 2 LCD projectors, 2 built-in projection screens

Parking: large lot
Accommodations: no guest rooms
Outdoor Night Lighting: yes
Outdoor Cooking Facilities: CBA
Cleanup: provided
View: golf course
Other: event coordination

RESTRICTIONS:

Alcohol: in-house
Smoking: outdoors only
Music: amplified music indoors only, acoustic music OK outdoors

Wheelchair Access: yes
Insurance: not required

Bancroft Hotel

Boutique Hotel

2680 Bancroft Way, Berkeley
510/549-0113
www.bancrofthotel.com
kelly@bancrofthotel.com

● Rehearsal Dinners		● Corp. Events/Mtgs.	
● Ceremonies		● Private Parties	
● Wedding Receptions		● Accommodations	

Housed in a historic landmark building across the street from the University of California, the Bancroft Hotel has become one of the premier boutique hotels in the East Bay. Originally built in 1928 as the home of the College Women's Club, it was designed by Walter T. Steilberg, an associate of architect Julia Morgan (of Hearst Castle fame).

After a complete renovation of the property, the Bancroft Hotel had its much-acclaimed grand opening in 1994. Guests admired the handsome public spaces, graced with antiques, vintage-style furniture and period reproductions; furnishings in the Bancroft's 22 beautifully appointed guest rooms were reproduced from Walter Steilberg's original drawings, and many of the rooms are enhanced with balconies and views of the bay. There's an ambiance of timeless elegance, and whether you're dreaming of a celebration with an air of romantic nostalgia or quiet refinement, the Bancroft Hotel is an absolute must-see.

Most receptions unfold in the Great Hall, a glamorous event space inspired by the turn-of-the-century Arts and Crafts movement. This one-of-a-kind 4,000-square-foot room is lavished with floor-to-ceiling woodwork, period fixtures and stained-glass transoms. Gleaming hardwood floors and lofty ceilings add to the sense of tradition and grandeur, and two giant fireplaces provide warmth and atmosphere. The Hall actually has three distinct sections, which can be used for different aspects of your event. The raised hardwood stage at one end can hold musicians, a dance floor or the head table, while the recessed middle section can be transformed into an intimate dining space. Use the other end for additional reception seating, or for a buffet and bar setup. The Great Hall is not only spacious, but also extremely flexible—you could arrange your party in a variety of ways and still have it work fabulously.

The light and bright Steilberg Conference Room is distinguished by pale, gently curving walls and a magnificent fireplace trimmed in tile and rich mahogany. Windows at one end frame a pleasing view of the city and a slice of the San Francisco Bay in the distance. Another way to savor the vista is to sneak away to the Rooftop Terrace and share a champagne toast with your sweetie.

The Bancroft Hotel does have comfortable and attractive accommodations for your out-of-town relatives and friends—but why not reserve the entire boutique hotel exclusively for you and your guests for a destination weekend? A complete buyout gets you all the event spaces, guest rooms—even the parking lot! In fact, *Bancroft Catering* can customize all your meals to your liking throughout your stay, so you never really have to leave the hotel at all.

If you plan on "going green" for your wedding, then you'll appreciate the Bancroft's environmentally safe cleaning products, luxurious bamboo towels, organic linens and other "green" amenities.

Eco-weddings are a specialty, and the in-house culinary team offers earth-friendly tableware alternatives and organic menus. In 2011 all the guest rooms were renovated, and the lobby was redone, too. Check out its new look, featuring custom-designed, recycled tile and American clay walls.

Whether you're hosting a large bash or a cozy gathering, the Bancroft Hotel is a distinctive indoor wedding site with a conveniently located, yet very serene environment.

CEREMONY CAPACITY: Indoors, the hotel seats up to 250 guests. Three tiered sections in the Great Hall are available for smaller groups.

EVENT/RECEPTION CAPACITY: The facility holds 150–225 seated guests (depending on whether or not a dance floor is required), or 250 for a standing reception.

MEETING CAPACITY: The hotel accommodates 250 seated theater-style.

FEES & DEPOSITS: To secure your date, the entire rental fee is required as a deposit when you sign your contract. The rental fee runs $800–2,000 and varies depending on the season and day of the week. The entire hotel is available for a buyout. Luncheons start at $18/person, dinners at $40/person. Tax, alcohol and service charge are additional.

AVAILABILITY: Year-round, daily, anytime.

SERVICES/AMENITIES:

Catering: in-house
Kitchen Facilities: n/a
Tables & Chairs: provided
Linens, Silver, etc.: CBA, extra charge
Restrooms: wheelchair accessible
Dance Floor: provided
Bride's Dressing Area: CBA
AV/Meeting Equipment: banquet tables, flip charts; extra fee for TV and overhead projector

Parking: adjacent lot or valet CBA
Accommodations: 22 guest rooms
Outdoor Night Lighting: CBA
Outdoor Cooking Facilities: no
Cleanup: provided
View: SF Bay and Berkeley hills
Other: event coordination available

RESTRICTIONS:

Alcohol: in-house
Smoking: not allowed
Music: amplified OK until 10:30pm unless all guest rooms are booked by client

Wheelchair Access: event space only
Insurance: not required

Berkeley City Club

Historic Hotel and Social Club

2315 Durant Avenue, Berkeley
510/280-1532

berkeleycityclub.com
events@berkeleycityclub.com

- Rehearsal Dinners
- Ceremonies
- Wedding Receptions
- Corp. Events/Mtgs.
- Private Parties
- Accommodations

The Berkeley City Club, located just one block from the UC Berkeley campus, is a sensational landmark building and a proud member of Historic Hotels of America®. Although it's long been a private social club, the venue welcomes the public for a variety of social events as well as overnight stays in its 35 guest rooms.

Designed in 1929 by famed architect Julia Morgan, the popular club is like a miniature Hearst Castle. The Moorish Gothic-style building features landscaped inner courtyards and fountains, plus a wealth of graceful arches, domed ceilings, pillars, leaded-glass windows and doors, and art. Together they create a gorgeous backdrop for your wedding—and your photographs.

The detailing and craftsmanship are impressive throughout. The Drawing Room and Members' Lounge are large and gracious, with beamed ceilings, pianos, fireplaces, wall tapestries, tiled floors, Oriental carpets and sizable leaded-glass windows. The Ballroom, which has a stage, parquet floor, concert grand piano, and its own leaded-glass windows overlooking the courtyard, also has plenty of room for dancing along with your reception. For an outdoor affair, the sheltered Terrace is a wonderful spot on a warm day or evening. Many of these event spaces are connected to one another, and can be used individually or in combination.

The Camellia Courtyard is perfect for an intimate ceremony or cocktail reception. Filled with greenery and framed by the building's arches, it's evocative of a Mediterranean garden. A smaller, lushly planted fountain courtyard on the opposite side of the club lends itself to a cozy luncheon or rehearsal dinner. Even if you don't host an event in one of these courtyards, you'll definitely want to take advantage of their photogenic qualities for your wedding album.

Many couples like to host both their ceremony and reception here: The club's soaring architecture and private, contemplative areas provide a spiritual atmosphere for exchanging vows; at the same time, the versatile reception facilities and experienced staff ensure a flawless event.

Speaking of flawless, the club's hair salon and esthetician services make it easy for you and your bridesmaids to look and feel your best for the wedding. Whether you arrive the day before or the day of, you'll be able to relax while the on-site professionals take you from stressed to beautiful.

The Berkeley City Club is a tranquil oasis in this bustling college town. Family and friends who stay overnight will appreciate the newly renovated guest rooms, all of which offer outstanding views of the San Francisco Bay or Berkeley hills. Hotel guests also have special privileges: They can take a dip in the magnificent swimming pool, and enjoy the outstanding cuisine at Julia's, the club's modern American restaurant. From this conveniently located getaway, exploring Berkeley couldn't be easier: Famed Telegraph Avenue, museums, restaurants, the Theater District and public transit are all close by.

CEREMONY, EVENT/RECEPTION CAPACITY: Event spaces hold 14–200 seated guests. The Venetian Ballroom holds up to 350 standing guests.

MEETING CAPACITY: The Berkeley City Club has 5 meeting rooms that accommodate up to 250 seated theater-style or 125 seated classroom-style.

FEES & DEPOSITS: A nonrefundable deposit in the amount of the room rental is required when the reservation is confirmed; the balance and a final guest count are due prior to the function. The rental fee ranges $500–4,000 depending on the space and day selected. For a separate bar setup, a bartender fee will apply. Luncheons begin at $29/person and dinners at $36/person. Menus and event details can be arranged with the event coordinator. If your group would like to stay overnight, bed and breakfast rates will apply. Call for more information.

AVAILABILITY: Year-round, Tuesday–Friday, 8am–11pm and Saturday–Sunday, 9am–11pm. Closed Thanksgiving, Christmas and New Year's Day.

SERVICES/AMENITIES:

Catering: provided, no BYO
Kitchen Facilities: n/a
Tables & Chairs: provided
Linens, Silver, etc.: provided
Restrooms: wheelchair accessible
Dance Floor: yes
Bride's Dressing Area: no
AV/Meeting Equipment: full range CBA
Other: candelabras, fireplaces, pianos, event coordinator; complimentary amenities for overnight guests include a continental breakfast buffet

Parking: small lot, extra fee; valet or prepaid CBA
Accommodations: 35 guest rooms
Outdoor Night Lighting: yes
Outdoor Cooking Facilities: no
Cleanup: provided
View: indoor courtyards

RESTRICTIONS:

Alcohol: provided, no BYO
Smoking: not allowed
Music: amplified OK until 11pm, with restrictions

Wheelchair Access: yes
Insurance: liability required
Other: security sometimes required

Brazilian Room

Tilden Park, Berkeley (operated by East Bay Regional Parks)
510/544-3164
www.brazilianroom.org
brazil@ebparks.org

Historic Banquet Facility

Rehearsal Dinners	● Corp. Events/Mtgs.
● Ceremonies	● Private Parties
● Wedding Receptions	Accommodations

High in the hills of North Berkeley lies Tilden Park, popularly considered "the Jewel of the East Bay." Hiking trails with names like Seaview or Skyline wind past creeks, mineral springs, and sylvan meadows, up to the sweeping panorama offered at Inspiration Point. Just about every vista in Tilden Park is inspirational. Encompassing the Tilden Nature Area, most of the park's 2,077 acres serve as tranquil shelters for native plants and wildlife. Rangers here are serious about preserving this magnificent habitat—they even close one of their roads seasonally to protect migrating newts—and the result is a cornucopia of natural beauty. Visitors also enjoy the abundance of recreational activities, including steam trains, a golf course, and an antique merry-go-round. For generations of Bay Area residents, outings to Tilden Park have been part of a happy tradition, beginning with a youngster's first pony ride and perhaps culminating in a wedding ceremony at the historic Brazilian Room.

Once part of the 1939 Golden Gate Exposition on Treasure Island, the Brazilian Room was presented as a gift to the East Bay Regional Park District by the country of Brazil. The original interior hardwood paneling was kept intact, while a new exterior of local rock and timber was constructed by the Works Project Administration to permanently house the room.

To reach the Brazilian Room, follow Grizzly Peak Boulevard to Wildcat Canyon Road, and behold a cascading glen dotted with thick stands of fragrant pine, oak, and eucalyptus. Add to this scene a building of remarkable architectural achievement with its own beautiful garden, and you have a striking location for any celebration.

Wedding ceremonies are extremely popular on the flagstone patio, with its dramatic panorama of sloping lawn and tree-studded hillsides. After toasting the newlyweds, guests can sip their champagne among the colorful mix of lavender, foxglove, breath of heaven, and other flowers that make up the small garden adjoining the patio, or sample hors d'oeuvres under the cherry tree, abloom in April with perfumey-pink blossoms.

The setting at the Brazilian Room is just as lovely indoors as out. The building's Old English-style façade is defined by a trio of leaded-glass doors, each with dormer-style threshold. When guests move inside for the reception, they'll find that floor-to-ceiling leaded-glass windows that run along both sides of the hall. The rear windows offer a close-up look at the forest, evoking the romance of a light-filled mountain cabin. Dark wooden beams create a novel pattern on the ceiling, and polished wood flooring and a huge stone fireplace give the space additional rustic charm.

The serene pastoral surroundings at the Brazilian Room offer an environment free from noise and distraction, where nature's gifts are honored and preserved and the modern world is in harmony with the building's heritage. It's a place you'll want to make part of your own family tradition.

CEREMONY CAPACITY: The patio holds 180 seated; the main room up to 150 seated or 225 standing.

EVENT/RECEPTION CAPACITY: The main room accommodates 150 seated or 225 standing guests.

MEETING CAPACITY: The main room seats 150 conference-style or 225 theater-style.

FEES & DEPOSITS: A deposit is required to secure your date ($300 for a 7-hour block or $600 for a 12-hour block). A third of this deposit is refundable with more than 180 days' notice of cancellation. A signed contract is required within 7 days after the initial deposit, and the rental fee balance and cleaning & damage deposits are due 180 days prior to the event date. For events reserved fewer than 180 days in advance, the entire rental balance and all deposits are due when the contract is signed.

Weekend rates for Friday night, Saturday, Sunday and holidays (min. 7 hours) range $1,900–3,900 depending on the day and time frame reserved. Weekday rates range $375–900 depending on the day and length of time rented. The seasonal Sunday rate November through March is $1,900 for a 7-hour block between 9am and midnight; each additional hour is $250. For nonresidents of Alameda and Contra Costa counties, there is a surcharge that equals 20% of the room rental fee. Optional services are available at an extra charge.

AVAILABILITY: Saturday, Sunday and holidays 9am–4pm or 5pm–midnight; Friday evening 5pm–midnight; Friday day 8am–4pm; Monday, Wednesday, Thursday 8am–midnight; Sunday, November through March, 9am–midnight.

SERVICES/AMENITIES:

Catering: select from preferred list
Kitchen Facilities: ample
Tables & Chairs: provided
Linens, Silver, etc.: BYO
Restrooms: wheelchair accessible
Dance Floor: yes
Bride's Dressing Area: yes
AV/Meeting Equipment: PA, projector and screen, microphones, extra fee

Parking: complimentary lot
Accommodations: no guest rooms
Outdoor Night Lighting: yes
Outdoor Cooking Facilities: yes
Cleanup: caterer
View: great views of Tilden Park with lots of trees and relative privacy
Other: fireplace available, extra fee; wireless access available

RESTRICTIONS:

Alcohol: BYO; wine, beer or champagne only, kegs of beer restricted to patio and kitchen
Smoking: not allowed in the regional parks
Music: amplified OK indoors, outdoors with restrictions

Wheelchair Access: yes
Insurance: extra liability is required
Other: decorations restricted

Overwhelmed? Use the search criteria on www.HereComesTheGuide.com to narrow down your choices.

Claremont Club and Spa
A Fairmont Hotel

Landmark Hotel

41 Tunnel Road, Berkeley

510/549-8591

www.fairmont.com/claremont-berkeley
claremontcatering@fairmont.com

● Rehearsal Dinners	● Corp. Events/Mtgs.
● Ceremonies	● Private Parties
● Wedding Receptions	● Accommodations

The brilliant white, castle-like Claremont Club and Spa, A Fairmont Hotel has been a Bay Area landmark since 1915 when it debuted. Spread over 22 acres, the hotel is set high in the Berkeley Hills and commands one of the best views in the Bay Area. Along with its panoramic vista, the hotel's grand design, fragrant rose gardens and luxurious amenities have made it a perennial favorite for weddings.

Couples can host their entire event here, from a rehearsal dinner to a sublime honeymoon in a grand suite. The Lanai Room is a lovely indoor ceremony space and, when combined with the adjoining outdoor balcony, offers great photo opportunities. A variety of ballrooms—each with its own distinctive ambiance—accommodate groups of various sizes, so whether you're having an intimate gathering or a gala reception you'll find one that's ideal for your event.

The Claremont also boasts over 20,000 square feet of event space, plus three pools and 10 tennis courts. You'll definitely want to spend some time being pampered at the spa, where wedding packages include facials, hairstyling, manicures, pedicures and makeup application, ensuring that you'll be picture-perfect on your wedding day.

Planning your event here is stress-free, thanks to a team of wedding experts. And after the festivities wind down, you'll find an atmosphere of relaxation in the Claremont's guest rooms, which were renovated in 2015. All feature plush bathrobes, flat screen TVs, and WiFi. Many also provide exceptional views of San Francisco Bay.

Conceived as an English estate, this historic hotel and grounds have surrounded guests with elegance, sophistication and charm for nearly a century. So, whether you come here to get married in style or simply enjoy a delectable dinner for two, the Claremont is a peaceful and romantic retreat from the world.

CEREMONY CAPACITY: Indoor spaces hold 20–220 seated guests; outdoor spaces up to 180 seated.

EVENT/RECEPTION CAPACITY: The largest ballroom accommodates 300 seated with a dance floor, or 450 standing for a cocktail reception. Capacities for the 20 other rooms range 10–300 seated guests.

MEETING CAPACITY: There are 20 rooms that seat 20–400 theater-style, 30–275 classroom-style, or 8–60 conference-style.

FEES & DEPOSITS: For special events and weddings, a nonrefundable deposit in the amount of 25% of the estimated event total is required to hold your date.

The rental fee for an outdoor ceremony or one of the ballrooms starts at $2,500. Facilities are also available for a rehearsal dinner, day-after brunch or other wedding-related event. Food & beverage costs start at $110/person and vary based on the menu and bar arrangements. Tax and service charges are additional.

Fees for business functions and meetings vary depending on room(s) and services selected. Corporate day meeting packages are available; call for specific pricing.

AVAILABILITY: Year-round, daily, 6am–midnight.

SERVICES/AMENITIES:

Catering: in-house, no BYO
Kitchen Facilities: n/a
Tables & Chairs: provided
Linens, Silver, etc.: provided
Restrooms: wheelchair accessible
Dance Floor: provided
Bride's & Groom's Dressing Areas: CBA
AV/Meeting Equipment: full range AV

Parking: self-parking and valet
Accommodations: 276 guest rooms
Outdoor Night Lighting: CBA upon approval
Outdoor Cooking Facilities: BBQ
Cleanup: provided
View: entire East Bay and San Francisco Bay plus San Francisco skyline
Other: event coordination, spa, fitness center

RESTRICTIONS:

Alcohol: in-house
Smoking: outdoors only
Music: amplified OK indoors only

Wheelchair Access: yes
Insurance: required

The Faculty Club

Historic Campus Club

University of California at Berkeley
510/643-0834

www.berkeleyfacultyclub.com
events@berkeleyfacultyclub.com

● Rehearsal Dinners	● Corp. Events/Mtgs.
● Ceremonies	● Private Parties
● Wedding Receptions	● Accommodations

UC Berkeley has many picturesque settings, but the loveliest one may well be that of the Faculty Club. Located in the heart of campus, it's quietly ensconced in a grove of redwoods, oaks and maples next to meandering Strawberry Creek. Built in 1902 by the renowned architect Bernard Maybeck in traditional Arts and Crafts style, it's designed to create a cozy, intimate feeling.

The crowning glory of the club is the three-story Great Hall. With its vaulted ceiling, massive stone fireplace, and stained-glass windows featuring heraldic crests of the great universities of the world, it's reminiscent of many a European cathedral. Light from the floor-to-ceiling windows warms the redwood paneling and suffuses the Hall in a golden glow.

Two charming smaller spaces are also available for functions. The Heyns and Seaborg rooms (named respectively after a chancellor and a distinguished University Nobel Laureate) both have French doors leading to a private outdoor area with a garden view. The Seaborg Room is especially striking, with its open-beamed A-frame ceiling and wisteria-framed windows overlooking the peaceful Faculty Glade Lawn.

The Faculty Club has long been a favorite site for meetings, bar and bat mitzvahs, anniversary parties, class reunions, retreats and retirement dinners. But it really comes into its own during weddings. Many couples like to have the ceremony right outside on the Faculty Glade Lawn, then move into the Great Hall for the wedding feast. (The Heyns and Seaborg Rooms also have private terraces for al fresco ceremonies.) Aside from the building itself, the staff is the Faculty Club's greatest asset. They've been producing events since 1902, and they're experienced at accommodating a wide range of special requests. Do any of your guests have particular dietary needs? The Faculty Club can provide gluten-free, vegetarian or vegan dishes. For the ultimate in convenience, your family and friends are welcome to stay overnight in the club's hotel bedrooms (which are often reserved for visiting scholars). From these comfortable lodgings, it's just a quick walk down the stairs to the ceremony. Also, if the bride needs a room for changing, or for storing flowers or gifts, the club will provide one.

The Faculty Club's full catering service handles all the food & beverages—including the bar—and they offer menus for every type of event, from a brunch buffet to a formal sit-down dinner. Their catering staff hails from all over the world, and can create authentic cuisine from many countries including India, Mexico, Peru, Greece and Spain. The Faculty Club has been serving its members and guests for over 100 years, and will do everything possible to make your event successful and enjoyable.

CEREMONY CAPACITY: The Faculty Glade holds 250 seated guests; indoor spaces hold up to 200 seated.

EVENT/RECEPTION CAPACITY: The Great Hall accommodates 200 seated or 300 standing for a cocktail party.

MEETING CAPACITY: The club can seat 300 theater-style.

FEES & DEPOSITS: The room rental fee is required as a nonrefundable deposit to secure your date; the event balance is due 14 days prior to the event. The rental fee ranges $2,500–5,000 depending on the room selected. Catering is provided; meal prices range $50–95/person; beverages, alcohol, tax and a 20% service charge are additional.

AVAILABILITY: Year-round, daily, anytime (except days on which there is a Cal home football game).

SERVICES/AMENITIES:

Catering: in-house
Kitchen Facilities: n/a
Tables & Chairs: provided
Linens, Silver, etc.: provided
Restrooms: wheelchair accessible
Dance Floor: yes
Bride's & Groom's Dressing Areas: yes
AV/Meeting Equipment: BYO or CBA, extra charge

Parking: pay parking on campus evenings and weekends; reserved/hosted parking is available, restrictions may apply
Accommodations: 23 guest rooms
Outdoor Night Lighting: yes
Outdoor Cooking Facilities: no
Cleanup: provided
View: lawn, creek and garden
Other: event coordination, baby grand and upright pianos, wireless internet connection in hotel and banquet rooms

RESTRICTIONS:

Alcohol: in-house or BYO wine, corkage $18/ bottle
Smoking: not allowed
Music: amplified OK until 11pm

Wheelchair Access: except to Seaborg Room
Insurance: not required
Other: no rice or glitter; no nails, staples or tacks on walls

Hotel Shattuck Plaza

2086 Allston Way, Berkeley
510/845-7300

www.hotelshattuckplaza.com
sales@hotelshattuckplaza.com

Historic Boutique Hotel

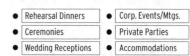

● Rehearsal Dinners		● Corp. Events/Mtgs.	
● Ceremonies		● Private Parties	
● Wedding Receptions		● Accommodations	

What's old and new and cool all over? It's the absolutely fabulous Hotel Shattuck Plaza, a venue that artfully blends its historic roots with a fresh, hip ambiance. Located in downtown Berkeley at the nexus of the city's cultural, gastronomic and academic centers, this recently renovated boutique hotel holds enormous appeal for those seeking a sophisticated, yet relaxed, place for their wedding or special event.

When you step into the lobby, you can't help but notice the high ceiling, sleek front desk, and pop of color from the bright red chandelier. It's a mix of elements that make the space feel open, airy, and even a bit playful, all at the same time. Throughout the hotel's interior, a bold, black-and-white motif perfectly plays off century-old architectural details like the original columns, cornices and decorative friezes. Look down at the checkerboard marble flooring and you'll see that they've even included a sly homage to the city's activist reputation with an inlaid peace sign.

To the right is a beautiful bar with sightlines to their much-lauded restaurant, FIVE. This stunning space can be completely cleared of furniture to create a breathtaking ceremony site. The soaring, coffered ceiling, dark wood floors, dazzling original 1900s glass-and-crystal chandelier, and floor-to-ceiling Palladium windows combine for sheer elegance. And talk about making an entrance—you'll walk down a long center aisle flanked by rows of towering classic columns!

Cocktails can be served outside on the brick-floored Courtyard, with a lower level for canapé displays and serving stations. If you prefer to raise a glass of bubbly indoors, there's the adjacent Historic Boiler Room, which has been transformed with a high tray ceiling, skylight, and double glass doors into an inviting spot for more intimate celebrations. Another option for smaller groups is the Whitecotton Room up on the sixth floor. Its graceful coved ceiling and a series of arched windows give this private hideaway a quiet charm—and downtown views.

But, for full-tilt glamour, you must see the Crystal Ballroom. Grand in scale, it features huge, fan-shaped, framed mirrors; a coffered ceiling; and lots of crystal chandeliers (of course). We especially love the chic, black-and-white striped wallpaper, which adds an inspired touch of haute design. The space comes with its own prefunction area, where you can serve cocktails and set up a photo booth or dessert bar.

After the party winds down, retreat to your complimentary honeymoon suite. Out-of-town guests will also enjoy staying overnight in their upscale rooms, savoring the hotel's innovative cuisine, and discovering everything Berkeley has to offer. The hotel is also a great home base for taking day trips to explore the Bay Area, like sightseeing in San Francisco or wine tasting in Napa and Sonoma.

CEREMONY CAPACITY: The hotel accommodates 200 seated guests indoors and 60 seated outdoors.

EVENT/RECEPTION CAPACITY: The hotel holds 200 seated or 250 standing indoors, and 60 seated or 100 standing outdoors.

MEETING CAPACITY: The hotel seats 300 theater-style.

FEES & DEPOSITS: 50% of the total event cost is required to reserve your date, and the balance is due 7 days prior to the event. The rental fee ranges $0–2,000 depending on the menu or package selected. Meals range $50–112/person. Tax, alcohol and a 22% service charge are additional.

AVAILABILITY: Year-round.

SERVICES/AMENITIES:

Catering: in-house
Kitchen Facilities: n/a
Tables & Chairs: provided
Linens, Silver, etc.: provided
Restrooms: wheelchair accessible
Dance Floor: portable provided
Bride's Dressing Area: yes
AV/Meeting Equipment: provided

Parking: garage or lot nearby
Accommodations: 199 guest rooms
Outdoor Night Lighting: yes
Outdoor Cooking Facilities: none
Cleanup: provided
View: cityscape, garden courtyard, bay
Other: event coordination

RESTRICTIONS:

Alcohol: in-house
Smoking: outdoors only
Music: amplified OK

Wheelchair Access: yes
Insurance: liability required

Lawrence Hall of Science

Public Science Museum

1 Centennial Drive, Berkeley
510/642-2275

www.lawrencehallofscience.org
hallrentals@berkeley.edu

●	Rehearsal Dinners	●	Corp. Events/Mtgs.
●	Ceremonies	●	Private Parties
●	Wedding Receptions		Accommodations

High in the Berkeley hills, the Lawrence Hall of Science boasts one of the best views in the Bay Area. The breathtaking panorama extends from the UC Berkeley campus to the ocean, Golden Gate and Bay Bridges, then stretches all the way to Sausalito and beyond. This coveted top-of-the-world setting, combined with dynamic event spaces, makes the museum an inspirational—and fun—wedding venue.

Several outdoor ceremony and reception sites take full advantage of the spectacular vista, beginning with the Plaza. Situated right beside the main entrance, this expansive stone patio is a favorite after-hours spot for exchanging vows against a glorious sunset. It's also the place to capture some unique photos, either in front of the huge Helix sculpture or atop Pheena, the iconic, life-sized whale, where there's enough room for the entire bridal party to get in on the shot!

If you prefer more seclusion—and the most jaw-dropping view—consider "The Forces That Shape The Bay" installation, a landscape of rock formations, native plantings, a waterfall and pond that surrounds a large grassy area and brings to life the story of nature. Say "I do" on a terrace perched at the edge of a bluff, which overlooks the stunning tableau spread out below. Afterwards, host cocktails on the sweeping lawn and mingle with your guests while strolling through the grounds. They even provide a telescope so that you can savor the amazing view up close. As for photo ops, the most popular backdrop may be the totem-like Sun Tower, a powerful sculpture that rises from the center of the lawn. (Worried about fog or rain? Don't, because there's an adjacent glass-walled Foyer for inclement weather.)

Once the museum closes, you'll have exclusive use of the facilities. Serve dinner in the high-ceilinged Lobby, and feel free to add your own decorative touches like dramatic uplighting, plasma balls, "geek chic" flower arrangements in lab beakers, or place cards written on periodic charts. Opt for a dance floor beside the tables or create a sultry nightclub with a "Cosmos" theme in the nearby "Science on a Sphere" exhibit. This area is highlighted by a six-foot orb on which you can project flashing animated images of earth, space, the oceans, or heavens.

A big perk of having any celebration here are the rotating exhibits featured throughout. So encourage your guests to wander and experiment—this is one museum where touching is definitely allowed. Go ahead and push your hand against the pin wall, make a paper airplane to see how far it flies under different conditions, or get a peek into life on the surface of Mars. No matter when you host your event, there's always something interesting to explore.

From start to finish, events coordinator Emma Duran-Forbes and her staff will make sure everything runs smoothly—as evidenced by the personal thank-you notes they consistently receive. When you add in reasonable rental fees, the freedom to bring your own caterer, and plentiful parking, it doesn't take a rocket scientist to discover why people love this place.

CEREMONY CAPACITY: The museum can accommodate 300 seated guests outdoors.

EVENT/RECEPTION CAPACITY: The museum holds 150 seated or 500 standing indoors and outdoors.

MEETING CAPACITY: The museum seats 275 theater-style.

FEES & DEPOSITS: 50% of the rental fee is required to secure your date and the balance is due 30 days prior to the event. The rental fee ranges $250–5,000, depending on the day of the event and the space reserved.

AVAILABILITY: Year-round, daily, after 5pm.

SERVICES/AMENITIES:

Catering: select from preferred list; or BYO with a $500 fee
Kitchen Facilities: none
Tables & Chairs: through caterer
Linens, Silver, etc.: through caterer
Restrooms: wheelchair accessible
Dance Floor: yes
Bride's & Groom's Dressing Areas: limited
AV/Meeting Equipment: available in specific meeting rooms

Parking: fee based
Accommodations: no guest rooms
Outdoor Night Lighting: limited
Outdoor Cooking Facilities: no
Cleanup: caterer or renter
View: San Francisco Bay, cityscape, Golden Gate Bridge

RESTRICTIONS:

Alcohol: BYO, permit required
Smoking: not allowed
Music: amplified OK with restrictions

Wheelchair Access: yes
Insurance: liability required
Other: no rice, glitter, or birdseed; decorations are restricted

---

Want to know WHAT TO ASK a potential location or vendor? Check out our Questions to Ask starting on page 21.

UC Botanical Garden

Botanical Garden

200 Centennial Drive, Berkeley
510/642-3352
botanicalgarden.berkeley.edu/rentals/
gardenrentals@berkeley.edu

- Rehearsal Dinners
- Ceremonies
- Wedding Receptions
- Corp. Events/Mtgs.
- Private Parties
- Accommodations

In the hills above UC Berkeley is a spectacular 34-acre garden of earthly delights, nestled in Strawberry Canyon and overlooking the San Francisco Bay. The Botanical Garden is home to over 12,000 different kinds of plants, including many rare and endangered species. A stroll through its varied environments takes you past a cloud forest, a Japanese pool with waterfalls, and even an orchid and carnivorous plant house! This place is more than just a collection of pretty flowers—it's a living museum.

Among all the natural splendor are several lovely sites for a celebration. Imagine saying "I do" in a grove of majestic redwood trees. Your guests are seated in a demi-amphitheater atop benches built into the earth itself. They anticipate your arrival, catching teasing glimpses of flowing white as you make your way up the forest path. Finally, you and your partner exchange vows, refreshed by air that's crisp and tinged with the scent of moist bark and leaves.

More intimate ceremonies are held in the Garden of Old Roses, a storybook bower with the visual allure of Monet's garden at Giverny. Rough-hewn steps climb down to a terraced knoll where your family and friends wait amidst a mix of lavender, blooming annuals, and antique roses. Opposite, masses of climbing roses cascade over the beams of a quaint wooden pergola. Completing the romantic vignette, a panorama of the bay unfolds beyond acres of sprawling foliage like a blue ribbon edging a flowery chintz gown.

The latest addition to the gardens is the historic Julia Morgan Hall, designed by the famous architect in 1911 and moved to its new home here in 2014. The building is perfect for small upscale receptions and rehearsal dinners, with an interior done entirely in warm, dark wood. The elegant main room features a fireplace and a floor-to-ceiling picture window that looks out to the attached deck and the California section of the garden beyond. It opens to both the deck and a charming sunroom, creating a wonderful indoor/outdoor flow between the spaces. Just steps from the Hall, the elevated Tour Deck provides an excellent spot for toasting the newlyweds while surveying the New World Desert garden below.

Another reception option is the Conference Center, set in the middle of the Palm and Cycad Garden above lush Strawberry Creek. Framed by luxuriant palms, rare cycads, and tree ferns, the center's broad tiled terrace makes a sunny place for pre-reception cocktails. Scenic backdrops for photos abound nearby—one that's particularly appealing is a footbridge spanning the green banks of the creek. Here, in the forest's dewy coolness, brightly colored dragonflies dart from delicate ferns to lily pads, and the silhouette of you and your partner is mirrored in the water below.

Inside the Conference Center are two adjoining rooms, each with greenhouse windows that let the sunshine in and showcase the surrounding greenery. You might have your banquet in one, do the cake cutting in the other, and then dance on the terrace. During cooler months, host everything indoors.

Whichever sites you choose in this horticultural wonderland, you can be sure of one thing: You're taking the concept of "a simple garden wedding" to a whole new level! And if you're planning a meeting, seminar, or private party, this unique venue works beautifully for those events, too.

CEREMONY CAPACITY: The Rose Garden seats up to 70, and the Redwood Grove up to 200.

EVENT/RECEPTION CAPACITY: The Conference Center (with the terrace) accommodates 100 seated or standing. Julia Morgan Hall holds 80 seated or standing (with deck), subject to seasonal and weather restrictions.

MEETING CAPACITY: Two spaces hold up to 80 seated theater-style.

FEES & DEPOSITS: A deposit based on the package selected is required to reserve your date, and the balance is due 1 month after the contract is signed. Wedding packages range $850–2,300 for a ceremony only, and $4,100–5,600 for a ceremony and reception. Pricing varies depending on the sites selected and day of the week. Hourly rental for non-wedding events is available during certain time blocks; contact the venue for more details.

AVAILABILITY: Various UC Botanical Garden sites are available year-round, 10am–midnight, subject to seasonal and weather restrictions.

SERVICES/AMENITIES:

Catering: select from list
Kitchen Facilities: kitchenette
Tables & Chairs: yes
Linens, Silver, etc.: BYO or through caterer
Restrooms: wheelchair accessible
Dance Floor: CBA, extra fee
Bride's Dressing Area: yes
AV/Meeting Equipment: WiFi and high-speed internet; additional equipment CBA

Parking: University lot, fees paid in advance
Accommodations: no guest rooms
Outdoor Night Lighting: yes
Outdoor Cooking Facilities: no
Cleanup: caterer or renter
View: botanical garden, creek, SF Bay, city, Golden Gate Bridge

RESTRICTIONS:

Alcohol: BYO, permit required
Smoking: not allowed
Music: amplified OK with restrictions

Wheelchair Access: limited
Insurance: liability required

Weddings and Special Events at UC Berkeley

Student Union

Bancroft & Telegraph, Berkeley
510/642-1141
eventservices.berkeley.edu
eventservices@berkeley.edu

● Rehearsal Dinners	● Corp. Events/Mtgs.
● Ceremonies	● Private Parties
● Wedding Receptions	Accommodations

Whether you're a Cal alum who wants to rekindle great college memories, or you're just looking for a unique wedding location in the East Bay, UC Berkeley offers some truly exceptional event spaces and services.

The iconic Campanile, the soaring clocktower that symbolizes this university, can turn your wedding ceremony into a one-of-a-kind experience. A long brick walkway, which runs down the center of the Campanile Esplanade, is lined with London Plane trees that form a lush canopy overhead during spring and summer. The bride makes her grand entrance down this natural aisle, joining her groom at the base of the Campanile where vows are exchanged as guests look on from their seats in the shade. Afterwards, cocktails are often served at a wide section of the walkway, and as night falls twinkle lights strung in the trees add sparkle to the entire Esplanade. If you want to give your guests a real thrill, rent the clock tower itself and invite everyone to ride the elevator to the top for a spectacular panorama of the East Bay as well as San Francisco, the bay and its bridges in the distance.

Another prime spot for al fresco ceremonies is Faculty Glade, an expansive lawn next to the historic Faculty Club. You can say "I do" under a spreading oak or in front of a stone bench, and then pose for photos among the redwoods at nearby Strawberry Creek. The setting is so lovely couples frequently host their reception here, too, at tables set up on the grass. Versatile and easily accessible, this area is equally popular for graduation parties, corporate bashes, outdoor banquets, and picnics.

For indoor celebrations, you have two completely different choices. The Anna Head Alumnae Hall, just off the main campus, will transport you back in time. Formerly a girls' school, this 1927 brown shingle gem comes with its own patio for mingling, and has an all-wood interior with a high, open-beamed trussed ceiling and a large stage. Although the building has been completely renovated to include plenty of audiovisual aids and adjustable lighting, period details like hand-painted stenciling and the original chandeliers have been retained.

In contrast, Pauley Ballroom is a modern space in the heart of Sproul Plaza. Paneled in oak, it boasts a 30-foot ceiling, hardwood dance floor, a view of the Campanile, and an extended patio that's perfect for a cocktail hour or barbecue. The star feature is a row of floor-to-ceiling windows that let guests peer over leafy treetops to far-reaching vistas of rolling hillsides and historic buildings. A divider wall allows you to split the room in two: Couples often have their ceremony in East

Pauley (one third), and use West Pauley (two thirds) for the reception. Brides can also reserve a changing room that's conveniently located on the conference level.

Planning an event at UCB is easy on you, thanks to UC's Event Services staff. With their "one-stop shopping" approach they'll handle all the details, from catering and table décor to extra AV equipment and rentals. Hosting your celebration here is easy on your guests too: This gorgeous campus is close to everything—hotels, public transportation, and lots of local attractions—so friends and family can spend more of their time celebrating with you.

CEREMONY CAPACITY: Indoors, Anna Head holds up to 275 seated guests. East Pauley Ballroom seats 250 and West Pauley Ballroom seats 450. Outdoors, the Campanile Esplanade accommodates 144 seated and Faculty Glade seats 200.

EVENT/RECEPTION CAPACITY: Anna Head holds up to 152 seated guests at round tables and 379 standing. Pauley Ballroom holds up to 550 seated when used in its entirety; East Pauley Ballroom holds 150 seated at rounds or 250 standing, and West Pauley holds 300 seated at rounds or 600 standing. Outdoors, the Campanile Esplanade accommodates 144 seated or 200 for a standing reception and Faculty Glade holds 200 seated or 600 standing.

MEETING CAPACITY: Anna Head seats up to 275 guests theater-style; East Pauley holds 250, West Pauley holds 450, and Pauley Ballroom in its entirety holds 900.

FEES & DEPOSITS: A deposit plus a signed contract and credit card on file are required to secure your date. The balance is due 30 days prior to the event. The rental fee starts at $500 and varies depending on the space(s) reserved. Meals range $15–60/person and up. Tax, alcohol and service charge are additional.

AVAILABILITY: Year-round, subject to University activities and availability.

SERVICES/AMENITIES:

Catering: provided by *ASUC SU Catering*
Kitchen Facilities: n/a
Tables & Chairs: provided indoors, CBA outdoors
Linens, Silver, etc.: provided, extra fee
Restrooms: wheelchair accessible
Dance Floor: yes
Bride's Dressing Area: yes
AV/Meeting Equipment: full-range indoors, CBA outdoors

Parking: on-street or on-site and nearby garages; guest passes available for purchase
Accommodations: nearby hotels
Outdoor Night Lighting: CBA
Outdoor Cooking Facilities: CBA
Cleanup: caterer or renter
View: cityscape and rolling hills

RESTRICTIONS:

Alcohol: CBA or BYO
Smoking: not allowed
Music: amplified OK indoors; OK outdoors with restrictions

Wheelchair Access: yes
Insurance: liability and proof of insurance required

Club Los Meganos - Trilogy at The Vineyards

Private Club

1700 Trilogy Parkway, Brentwood
925/809-7188

www.vineyardsweddings.com
vineyardsweddings@trilogyresort.com

● Rehearsal Dinners	● Corp. Events/Mtgs.
● Ceremonies	● Private Parties
● Wedding Receptions	Accommodations

Club Los Meganos at Trilogy at The Vineyards, which debuted in the summer of 2010, is, quite simply, spectacular. Even the drive up to the venue is a pleasure, as you pass olive groves, stately Italian cypress trees and a profusion of white roses and bright flowers. When you arrive at the club, situated just above a series of gentle hills neatly planted with grapevines, you sense that this place is something special.

The 34,000-square-foot club devotes an entire wing specifically to events: the Mount Diablo Events Center, named for the well-known peak visible from almost everywhere on the property. Interior spaces throughout are beautifully designed and incorporate rich woods, natural stone and sweeping expanses of glass in a way that's reminiscent of Frank Lloyd Wright. Outdoors, there's a nod to Mediterranean influences like the circular stone plaza, the tiered terracotta fountain and, of course, the surrounding landscape itself.

Ceremonies can be held on the Mt. Diablo Ceremony Lawn or at the Vineyards Reflection Pond. Both locations feature unobstructed views of the nearby hills in the foreground and Mount Diablo in the distance.

Serve cocktails and hors d'oeuvres on the Promenade, or indoors in the Reception Foyer. Here, as throughout the club, there's a masterful blend of contemporary design with an underlying homage to the Miwok tribe who once called this area home. Glass "NanoWalls," which reveal a spacious patio overlooking the gardens and water features, quickly fold away creating seamless access to the outdoors.

Dinner and dancing take place in the event center's versatile ballroom. Designed with a high, coffered ceiling and decorated in soothing shades of cocoa, cream and muted sky blue, the room has a sophisticated look. There's a view of Mount Diablo through more folding glass doors that open to the Promenade, creating a wonderful indoor-outdoor flow. A state-of-the-art AV system with drop-down screens and a gleaming wooden dance floor set the stage for a lively party.

For a unique rehearsal dinner or bridal shower, check out the Culinary Studio, a dream kitchen/ dining room where you have an opportunity to observe the chef in action, perhaps whipping up a special menu using ingredients from local orchards. Or, you can relax outside on the adjoining private patio with a glass of vino.

As if all this weren't enticing enough, both the bride and groom get to prepare for the day in the Hii/Komme Room.

CEREMONY CAPACITY: The Mt. Diablo Ceremony Lawn and Reflection Pond each accommodate up to 200 seated outdoors.

EVENT/RECEPTION CAPACITY: The facility seats 200 indoors and 200 outdoors.

MEETING CAPACITY: Meeting spaces hold 200 seated guests.

FEES & DEPOSITS: A $1,000 deposit is required to reserve your date, and the balance of the estimated event total is due 14 days prior to the event. The rental fee ranges $750–7,000 depending on the guest count, time of year and day of the week. Meals start at $39/person. Tax, alcohol and service charge are additional.

AVAILABILITY: Year-round, daily, afternoons and evenings. They host only one event per day.

SERVICES/AMENITIES:

Catering: in-house
Kitchen Facilities: n/a
Tables & Chairs: provided
Linens, Silver, etc.: provided
Restrooms: wheelchair accessible
Dance Floor: provided
Bride's Dressing Area: yes
AV/Meeting Equipment: provided

Parking: large lot
Accommodations: no guest rooms
Outdoor Night Lighting: yes
Outdoor Cooking Facilities: n/a
Cleanup: provided
View: garden, meadow, mountains, vineyards
Other: baby grand piano, spa services, event coordination

RESTRICTIONS:

Alcohol: in-house
Smoking: outdoors only
Music: amplified OK

Wheelchair Access: yes
Insurance: not required

Wedgewood Brentwood

Event Center at Golf Club

100 Summerset Drive, Brentwood
866/966-3009
www.wedgewoodbanquet.com
events@wedgewoodbanquet.com

Rehearsal Dinners	● Corp. Events/Mtgs.
● Ceremonies	● Private Parties
● Wedding Receptions	Accommodations

The lovely drive up to Wedgewood Brentwood is lined with stately royal palms, and really makes a grand first impression. Surrounded by acres of lushly landscaped grounds, the entire property has the look and feel of a relaxed, upscale country retreat.

High-end aesthetics greet you at every turn, beginning with the picturesque ceremony site: A classical Italian-style Pavilion, with six white columns topped with an ornate wrought-iron dome. Against a backdrop of graceful olive and Japanese maple trees and the scenic Brentwood Golf Course just beyond, this is quite an elegant stage for exchanging vows.

For the cocktail hour, guests stroll around the corner to the Terrace, a peaceful spot that enjoys views of the fairway, lakes and mountains. Meanwhile, the bridal party poses for pictures in the venue's numerous photogenic locales, such as a pond that overflows into a rushing waterfall and a nearby bridge spanning a profusion of pastel flowers. In settings like these, you're sure to capture plenty of suitable-for-framing images.

As the sun goes down, receptions gather in the high-ceilinged Ballroom, whose two walls of floor-to-ceiling windows frame the gorgeous vistas. Your own wedding colors will pop against the space's neutral hues of sandstone and adobe, and dimmable wrought-iron chandeliers help set the mood. The spacious Ballroom opens into a large bar area where four flat-screen TVs stand ready to host your digital displays—how about a real-time video of the wedding itself?

Given the caliber of this venue, you'll be surprised at Wedgewood's affordability. Their value-filled wedding packages can be customized to include your choice of wedding elements, from invitations to florals. What's more, you can count on the experienced staff's guidance, flexibility and attention to your specific needs. Your dedicated wedding planner will work with you throughout the entire process, from the first consultation until the last guest says goodbye. So all you have to do is relax and enjoy your own wedding.

CEREMONY CAPACITY: The site holds 300 seated guests indoors or outdoors.

EVENT/RECEPTION & MEETING CAPACITY: The facility can accommodate 300 seated or standing guests indoors, and 300 standing guests on the Terrace for a cocktail reception.

FEES & DEPOSITS: 25% of the estimated total event cost is required to reserve your date. An additional 25% is due 120 days prior to the event and the balance (based on your final guest count) is due 10 days prior. All payments are credited towards your final balance and are nonrefundable and nontransferable. All-inclusive, completely customizable wedding packages start at $46/person. Tax, alcohol and a 21–22% service charge are additional.

AVAILABILITY: Year-round, daily. Weddings generally take place in a 5-hour time block, but the event duration may vary depending on the day of the week. Event curfew is midnight, or 1am on New Year's Eve.

SERVICES/AMENITIES:

Catering: in-house
Kitchen Facilities: n/a
Tables & Chairs: provided
Linens, Silver, etc.: provided
Restrooms: wheelchair accessible
Dance Floor: provided
Bride's Dressing Area: yes
AV/Meeting Equipment: some provided

Parking: large lot
Accommodations: no guest rooms
Outdoor Night Lighting: yes
Outdoor Cooking Facilities: no
Cleanup: provided
View: fountain, fairways, landscaped grounds, mountains
Other: event coordination, in-house wedding cake and florals, clergy on staff

RESTRICTIONS:

Alcohol: in-house
Smoking: outdoors only
Music: amplified OK

Wheelchair Access: yes
Insurance: not required
Other: no rice, confetti or glitter; no open flames

The wedding vendors on our website are the best in the business. How do we know? Read page 553.

Oakhurst Country Club

Country Club

1001 Peacock Creek Drive, Clayton
888/626-8395

www.countryclubreceptions.com
eventdirector@oakhurstcc.com

- Rehearsal Dinners
- Ceremonies
- Wedding Receptions
- Corp. Events/Mtgs.
- Private Parties
- Accommodations

Located on a bench of land just above Ygnacio Valley and the growing city of Clayton, Oakhurst Country Club sits near the base of Mt. Diablo's steep and wild eastern rampart.

The vistas from its two event spaces, the west-facing Heritage and Diablo View rooms, are impressive. The larger Heritage Room takes in a sweeping panorama of the Diablo Valley, from Pleasant Hill to the Carquinez Strait. The smaller Diablo View Room scans the vividly chiseled profiles of Mt. Diablo's precipitous lesser-known side. A wide terrace that zigzags across the clubhouse's west side connects both rooms from the outside and is a highly popular feature with wedding parties. Besides its unfettered view of distant landscapes, the terrace provides a closer-in look at the club's azure-watered swimming pool, putting green and golf course.

Because it's surrounded by a visually arresting landscape, it's no surprise that Oakhurst hosts many outdoor wedding ceremonies. But exchanging vows outside also gets a boost from the club's attractive appearance. The clubhouse is fronted by a majestic porte-cochère, whose twin support pillars are clad in large flagstones and whose steeply angled roof rests atop big, bold wooden trusses. Couples often enjoy getting married next to this structure, which provides a dramatic architectural backdrop to the club's landscaped front.

When celebrants move indoors to the banquet rooms, they pass through an airy window-lined lobby that opens out to a 40-foot-high atrium. Those striking trusses you first see under the porte-cochère continue inside, adding yet another eye-catching element to the clubhouse's design.

Over the past decade Oakhurst has assembled an unflappable, well-organized, people-oriented staff, and developed a wide range of packages. Naturally, the many brides who've enjoyed worry-free weddings here have generated enthusiastic word of mouth about this site. To them, Oakhurst seems blessed with everything in just the right proportion: a savvy wedding team, plenty of options and flexibility, a memorable setting and fine architecture. That's a pretty nice combination to bring to your wedding day.

CEREMONY CAPACITY: The venue seats up to 250 guests indoors and 250 outdoors.

EVENT/RECEPTION & MEETING CAPACITY: Indoors, the Diablo View Room seats up to 70 guests with additional open terrace seating for 50. Heritage Room seats up to 170 with a covered terrace that seats up to an additional 72 guests.

FEES & DEPOSITS: A nonrefundable deposit, which is applied to your food & beverage total, is required to reserve your date. The amount of the deposit varies, depending on how far in advance you book. Payment terms for the balance also vary, and may be arranged on an individual basis. Wedding packages start at $44/person. Tax, alcohol and service charge are additional. Food & beverage minimums may apply. Menus and packages can be customized to fit your needs and budget. Call for details.

AVAILABILITY: Year-round, daily, 6am–2am.

SERVICES/AMENITIES:

Catering: in-house
Kitchen Facilities: n/a
Tables & Chairs: provided
Linens, Silver, etc.: provided
Restrooms: wheelchair accessible
Dance Floor: yes
Bride's Dressing Area: yes
AV/Meeting Equipment: provided, extra fee

Parking: large lot
Accommodations: no guest rooms
Outdoor Night Lighting: yes
Outdoor Cooking Facilities: yes
Cleanup: included
View: mountains, hills, fairways

RESTRICTIONS:

Alcohol: in-house
Smoking: outdoors only
Music: amplified OK

Wheelchair Access: yes
Insurance: not required
Other: no rice, birdseed or glitter

Crow Canyon Country Club

Country Club

711 Silver Lake Drive, Danville
925/735-5718
www.crow-canyon.com
kymberlie.avila@clubcorp.com

- Rehearsal Dinners
- Ceremonies
- Wedding Receptions
- Corp. Events/Mtgs.
- Private Parties
- Accommodations

Nestled against the foothills of Mt. Diablo and overlooking a championship 18-hole golf course, Crow Canyon Country Club offers a versatile combination of indoor and outdoor spaces for rehearsal dinners, wedding receptions, parties and business functions.

As you step into the club's impressive lobby, your eyes are drawn upward to the soaring ceiling with its glittering crystal chandelier. It's the ideal spot for mingling in conjunction with the adjacent lounge, which features a large granite bar, fireplace and big screen TV. Not surprisingly, the lounge is a popular hangout for grooms and their guys, who enjoy a little downtime relaxation here during the event.

Both the lobby and the lounge adjoin the Grand Ballroom, Crow Canyon's main reception area. Divisible into three sections, it can be configured to suit the size of your event. Natural light flows in through a wall of windows, and no matter where you're seated you have a fantastic view of the redwood-studded golf course and Mt. Diablo in the distance. Fifteen crystal-and-bronze chandeliers supply plenty of sparkle, and dimmers allow you to set the mood. The room's neutral palette is compatible with any color scheme, so by incorporating your choice of linens, flowers and other décor you can easily bring the look you envision to life. For added flexibility, a stage (great for the head table, a band or DJ) and hardwood dance floor are permanently set up in the center of the room.

The ballroom opens onto three patios, expanding your options even further. Use one or all of them for al fresco cocktails, additional seating, or simply as a place where guests can go for a little fresh air and a close-up view of the fairways and hills. The beauty of the club's layout is that all of these spaces are connected to each other, creating a wonderful indoor-outdoor flow.

In addition to the patios, Crow Canyon has several smaller rooms that lend themselves to intimate private parties, corporate luncheons or meetings, and indoor ceremonies. Speaking of ceremonies, couples often tie the knot on the golf course surrounded by mature redwoods and the wide blue sky.

Crow Canyon's Events Directors like to say "Yes!" to requests and are dedicated to making your wedding day the best one possible. They'll recommend preferred vendors or you can choose your own, and either way they'll work closely with them to ensure that your setup is perfect and everything runs smoothly. A variety of reception packages are available, and the club's catering team will customize your menu—including any dietary or cultural needs. You can even bring in an outside caterer with approval (and additional fees).

Among Danville's handful of special event venues, Crow Canyon Country Club stands out for its appealing spaces, wide range of services and attention to detail. Whether you have an informal affair or a sophisticated soirée in mind, this is one facility that can handle it from start to finish.

CEREMONY CAPACITY: The Club holds up to 300 guests outdoors and 400 indoors. Many options are available, including larger capacities. Call for details.

EVENT/RECEPTION & MEETING CAPACITY: The club can accommodate 10–330 seated or 15–500 standing guests indoors; outdoor patios adjoining almost every room provide additional event space.

FEES & DEPOSITS: The room rental fee ranges $300–1,800 and the food & beverage minimum ranges $350–15,000 depending on the day and time of the event and space rented. Food service is provided; catered events require 7 days advance confirmation of the guest count. Approximate per-person rates: breakfast $15–24, luncheon $16–30, dinner $28–60, with a variety of fun food reception stations. Customized menus are available. Alcohol, tax and a 20% service charge are additional.

AVAILABILITY: Year-round, daily, 6am–midnight. Extra hours may be added for an additional fee.

SERVICES/AMENITIES:

Catering: in-house or BYO, extra fee
Kitchen Facilities: fully equipped
Tables & Chairs: provided
Linens, Silver, etc.: provided
Restrooms: wheelchair accessible
Dance Floor: yes
Bride's Dressing Room: yes
AV/Meeting Equipment: overhead screen, LCD and slide projectors, monitor, phone lines, flip charts, wireless internet; all equipment extra charge

Parking: large lot, valet available
Accommodations: no guest rooms
Outdoor Night Lighting: yes
Outdoor Cooking Facilities: BBQ
Cleanup: provided
View: Mt. Diablo and golf course
Other: baby grand and upright pianos

RESTRICTIONS:

Alcohol: in-house or BYO wine, corkage $20/bottle
Smoking: outdoors only
Music: amplified OK indoors

Wheelchair Access: yes
Insurance: not required

Discovery Bay Golf and Country Club

Golf and Country Club

1475 Clubhouse Drive, Discovery Bay
925/634-0700
www.dbgcc.com
banquets@dbgcc.com

● Rehearsal Dinners	● Corp. Events/Mtgs.
● Ceremonies	● Private Parties
● Wedding Receptions	Accommodations

Down the long and winding road that leads through the tawny East Bay hills to where rivers gather to form the Sacramento Delta, you'll find a little Eden in the newly minted township of Discovery Bay. Set like an emerald at the heart of this gated community, the Discovery Bay Country Club offers a perfect slice of paradise at a highly affordable price.

Broad lawns, clouds of colorful flowers, and grand old pepper, willow, poplar, and ash trees greet guests as they approach the handsome clubhouse. Ceremonies and gatherings are often held on the exquisitely manicured front lawn, where a gentle slope provides a natural dais. Events held on the west patio enjoy a stunning view of Mt. Diablo. Serene and sophisticated, surrounded by shade trees and tickled by breezes and birdsong, the lawn, patio and clubhouse are brilliant environments for any affair.

Inside the bisque-colored Mediterranean-style building, sunlight waterfalls through the skylights and down the tall white columns of the property's atrium-style lobby. Just ahead, the spacious lounge with its broad bar, floor-to-ceiling windows and elegant baby grand Disklavier (it's like having a concert pianist on call!) offers gorgeous golf course views and comfortable seating. This is a spectacular place to greet guests or to entertain them with cocktails and hors d'oeuvres. The lounge also has its own stone patio screened by tall hedges and trees where partygoers can step into the sunshine. The facility's on-site coordinator and well-trained staff will ensure that everyone feels quite at home.

But the lawns, lobby and lounge are merely an introduction. The welcome extends to the property's beautiful dining room. You won't need to bring anything into this glamorous setting, with its softly colored carpets and walls, classic furnishings, and breathtaking views of the rolling fairways and lakes. Multiple levels of indoor lighting, including chandeliers, spots and recessed illumination in the handsomely coved ceiling will spotlight your event to perfection. Or you can shower your guests in sunlight on the outdoor veranda. Framed by the country club's verdant, meticulously groomed gardens and greens, this is a picturesque place for a wedding ceremony or *plein air* gathering or reception. The north- and west-facing panorama takes in Mt. Diablo and rarely fades to black without an extravagant sunset and its finale of twinkling stars.

Two smaller dining rooms make excellent choices for more intimate events—for showers and pre- or post-wedding celebrations—and there is a Bridal Suite Meeting Room that can be reserved for the bride and her entourage. Also available off the lobby, down a wide hall, are the club's carpeted, spa-quality locker rooms equipped with personal lockers, showers, hair dryers and toiletries, all of which allow the bridal party to relax and enjoy in the midst of the wedding day whirl.

CEREMONY & EVENT/RECEPTION CAPACITY: The site holds a maximum of 200 guests, seated or standing, indoors or outdoors.

MEETING CAPACITY: The conference room holds 20 seated guests.

FEES & DEPOSITS: A $1,000 deposit is required to reserve your date. The rental fee ranges $0–1,500 depending on the guest count. Rental fee is waived for events with 100 or more adult guests. Wedding meal prices range $55–75/person. Tax, alcohol and an 18% service charge are additional.

AVAILABILITY: Year-round. Weddings take place on Fridays, Saturdays and Sundays.

SERVICES/AMENITIES:
Catering: in-house
Kitchen Facilities: n/a
Tables & Chairs: provided
Linens, Silver, etc.: provided
Restrooms: wheelchair accessible
Dance Floor: provided
Bride's & Groom's Dressing Areas: yes
AV/Meeting Equipment: some provided

Parking: large lot, valet optional
Accommodations: no guest rooms
Outdoor Night Lighting: CBA
Outdoor Cooking Facilities: BBQ CBA
Cleanup: provided
View: golf course, mountains, lake, garden
Other: event coordination, bridal suite

RESTRICTIONS:
Alcohol: in-house or BYO wine with corkage fee
Smoking: outdoors only
Music: amplified OK indoors only

Wheelchair Access: yes
Insurance: not required

Hilton Garden Inn San Francisco/Oakland Bay Bridge

Hotel

1800 Powell Street, Emeryville
510/285-1712
www.sanfranciscooakland.stayhgi.com
kdesai@HGIEmeryville.com

- Rehearsal Dinners
- Corp. Events/Mtgs.
- Ceremonies
- Private Parties
- Wedding Receptions
- Accommodations

The Hilton Garden Inn SF/Oakland Bay Bridge is one of the East Bay's most appealing venues for special events. Conveniently located just minutes from the Bay Bridge, yet eons away from the urban hustle, it has easy access to every Bay Area attraction. Plus, the hotel presides over some of the region's most spectacular protected shoreline (think romantic walk along the water at sunset), and offers plenty of topnotch amenities and dining options.

Greet your guests in the hotel's attractive lobby. The sophisticated, residential-style environment is a great place for family, friends and colleagues to congregate and relax. The roomy, lobby-level lounge and the Great American Grill, with its airy indoor and outdoor seating, make for cheery meetings and reunions. A 3,200-square-foot, ballroom-capacity Conference Center on the ground floor can be divided into four separate sections, and is easily adapted to suit any number of social or corporate events. French doors off the lobby lead to an elegant cloistered space for more intimate private gatherings.

Want to set your sights higher? Let the elevators whisk you up 14 stories to the top floor of the hotel. Here you'll find the jewel in the crown of this handsome Hilton Garden Inn. Step into a spacious foyer carpeted in rich shades of rust and green. Registration can be set up here for events held in the Placer Room, with its wall of windows and view of the Berkeley hills. Or ascend the four granite-banistered steps at the end of the foyer to the 4,000-square-foot Top Of The Bay Ballroom. On the other side of the double doors you'll be welcomed with eye-popping, jaw-dropping, bridge-to-bridge views of the sparkling bay and the cities around it. Emeryville, Berkeley, Oakland, San Francisco, bridges, parklands, mountaintops, and marinas—you'll feel as if the entire Bay Area is within your grasp. This grand ballroom, which can be divided into two smaller salons, will turn any event into a gala.

Hilton Garden Inns get high ratings in customer satisfaction, and for good reason. They provide expert on-site wedding planning and catering staff, custom menu options and competitive pricing. They'll help you arrange an on-site ceremony, bridal shower or rehearsal dinner along with your reception, and take good care of all of your overnight guests. When the sun sets exquisitely upon your extravaganza, don't give up the glamour. Let the hotel staff shower you with that celebrated Hilton hospitality in the Premier Bridal Suite (with a parlor and two bedrooms!) or one of their other gorgeously appointed guest rooms.

CEREMONY, EVENT/RECEPTION & MEETING CAPACITY: The hotel accommodates 300 guests in the Top of the Bay Ballroom for a dinner reception with dance floor and can hold a total of 700 guests throughout the venue.

FEES & DEPOSITS: A 10% deposit is required to secure your date. 50% of the remaining event total is due 45 days prior to the event, and the balance is due 3 business days prior. The rental fee starts at $500; and pricing varies depending on the space reserved, the day and time of the event, and the guest count. Meals and packages start at $38/person; tax and service charge are additional.

AVAILABILITY: Year-round, daily, anytime.

SERVICES/AMENITIES:

Catering: in-house
Kitchen Facilities: n/a
Tables & Chairs: provided
Linens, Silver, etc.: provided
Restrooms: wheelchair accessible
Dance Floor: yes
Bride's Dressing Room: yes
AV/Meeting Equipment: on-site AV specialist

Parking: large lot
Accommodations: 278 guest rooms
Outdoor Night Lighting: CBA
Outdoor Cooking Facilities: no
Cleanup: provided
View: panorama of San Francisco skyline, Bay Bridge and Berkeley hills
Other: event coordination

RESTRICTIONS:

Alcohol: in-house
Smoking: outdoors only
Music: amplified OK indoors with restrictions

Wheelchair Access: yes
Insurance: required for outside vendors

Want to find more venues and services? Check out our informative website, www.HereComesTheGuide.com.

335

Lafayette Park Hotel & Spa

Boutique Hotel

3287 Mount Diablo Boulevard, Lafayette
925/299-4324
www.lafayetteparkhotel.com
weddings@lafayetteparkhotel.com

● Rehearsal Dinners	● Corp. Events/Mtgs.
● Ceremonies	● Private Parties
● Wedding Receptions	● Accommodations

Few hotels are given any kind of special recognition, so the fact that the Lafayette Park Hotel & Spa is one of the few in the East Bay to have received a Four Diamond Award should tell you something: namely, that they maintain an impeccable standard of comfort, ambiance and service. With its distinctive architecture—dormers, shuttered French windows, and peaked roofline—this local landmark looks like a French chateau. Behind its high walls, European charm abounds in lovely courtyards, a variety of event spaces, and a luxurious full-service health spa.

Just by walking around the hotel, you're struck by how its design and décor make you feel welcome. In the atrium-like lobby, sunlight streams in through windows 60 feet overhead, illuminating the sweeping oak staircase and white marble floor. On cool days, the couches in front of the oversize fireplace are the obvious place to relax. The warmth of wood is everywhere—even in the intricate inlaid floors in front of the elevators.

Step outside into the sunny Fountain Courtyard, and you quickly realize how idyllic this spot is for a ceremony or champagne reception. Enclosed by the golden walls of the hotel, the space becomes an Old World plaza with a trickling limestone fountain in its center, ringed by potted trees, clinging ivy and flowers.

From the Fountain Courtyard, it's a short walk inside to the Independence Ballroom where larger receptions and parties are held. The coffered ceiling is outfitted with handmade crystal chandeliers and spot lighting, which can be adjusted to create any mood.

Smaller ceremonies take place upstairs in the Wishing Well Courtyard. Named for the rose-entwined stone wishing well in its center, this petite patio is also embraced by the hotel's walls. As you gaze up at the shuttered windows, wrought-iron balconies and clinging ivy, you once again feel like you're in the middle of a French countryside inn. That European flavor carries over into the nearby George Washington Room, a more intimate reception space. Here, the Early American/ French décor features gilt-framed mirrors, marble-topped consoles and a deep green carpet set off by fleur de lis border designs.

The Diderot Library, with its packed bookshelves, 18th-century marble fireplace mantel and hardwood floor, is custom-made for rehearsal dinners, bridal showers, brunches and executive meetings.

A wonderful Lafayette Park amenity is their European Day Spa. In addition to providing an appealing selection of face and body treatments, the Spa features a fitness pavilion, a pool, a seasonal poolside café, an outdoor fireplace and a spa. The bride and her attendants will not be able to pass up an opportunity to indulge here before and even after (why not!) the Big Day. Everyone staying overnight will appreciate the nicely appointed rooms, many of which have their own wood-burning fireplaces. The hotel also offers a complimentary premium room for the honeymoon couple, and special rates for wedding guests.

Melding European elegance with California comfort, the Lafayette Park Hotel is indisputably one of the East Bay's favorite locations for weddings and special events.

CEREMONY CAPACITY: For seated groups, the Fountain Courtyard accommodates 160, the Wishing Well Courtyard 64, and the George Washington Room 130.

EVENT/RECEPTION CAPACITY: The hotel can accommodate 24–150 seated or 30–200 standing guests indoors, and 60–220 seated or 50–230 standing outdoors. The Independence Ballroom and Courtyard combined hold 300 seated or 350 standing guests.

MEETING CAPACITY: A variety of spaces seat 15–200 theater-style, or 8–45 conference-style.

FEES & DEPOSITS: 25% of the total wedding cost is due as a nonrefundable, nontransferable deposit to secure your date. The hotel's wedding packages include butler service hors d'oeuvres, beverages, linens, champagne toast, candle centerpieces and a premium guest room. The rental fee starts at $1,000 and varies depending on the spaces reserved. Wedding packages start at $115/person. Tax and service charges are additional. Fees for business functions vary depending on overnight rooms, services and menus selected.

AVAILABILITY: Year-round, daily. Weddings, 11am–4pm or 6pm–11pm; business functions, 8am–5pm or 6pm–11pm.

SERVICES/AMENITIES:
Catering: in-house
Kitchen Facilities: n/a
Tables & Chairs: provided
Linens, Silver, etc.: provided
Restrooms: wheelchair accessible
Dance Floor: yes
Bride's Dressing Area: CBA
AV/Meeting Equipment: full range

Parking: complimentary self-parking, valet available
Accommodations: 138 guest rooms
Outdoor Night Lighting: yes
Outdoor Cooking Facilities: no
Cleanup: provided
View: courtyard and pool
Other: event coordination

RESTRICTIONS:
Alcohol: in-house
Smoking: not allowed
Music: amplified within limits

Wheelchair Access: yes
Insurance: not required

Wildwood Acres

1055 Hunsaker Canyon Road, Lafayette
925/283-2600
www.wildwoodacres.com
events@wildwoodacres.com

- Rehearsal Dinners
- Ceremonies
- Wedding Receptions
- Corp. Events/Mtgs.
- Private Parties
- Accommodations

It's hard to believe, as you drive through the suburban sprawl that makes up most of Contra Costa County, that a rustic jewel like Wildwood Acres could exist here. Nestled in a wooded canyon only five miles from downtown Lafayette, it's suitable for a wide variety of events. Whether you're planning a country-style reception, family reunion, or frothy Victorian wedding with picture hats and parasols, Wildwood Acres can magically transform itself into the ideal venue.

The indoor facility is a 2,000-square-foot lodge with warm decorative flooring and a 60-foot garden mural. Open-beamed ceilings, Oriental rugs, and a stone fireplace with benches on either side make the room cozy. And, there's even a full-service bar. This would be an especially nice area for a Christmas party, an intimate wedding or other winter event.

The outdoor facilities, however, are what make Wildwood Acres so special. If you're getting married here, there's a lovely ceremony site up on a hill in a fern grotto, deep in a grove of towering bay trees and bigleaf maples. Exchange vows on a stone platform in one corner while your guests, seated in the adjacent open area, savor their surroundings. Afterwards, have your reception on two terraces, shaded by a natural canopy of alder and maple trees. A redwood gazebo houses the band, and there's plenty of room to kick up your heels on the sunken dance floor. All around, pottery urns overflowing with impatiens and ferns add spots of color, and winding paths lead to shady nooks containing wrought-iron or wooden benches.

CEREMONY, EVENT/RECEPTION & MEETING CAPACITY: The Lodge holds 165 seated or 250 standing guests; the Outdoor Area holds up to 400 guests seated or standing.

FEES & DEPOSITS: The facility rental fee ranges $80–600/hour depending on the day of the week and time of year. Complete catering packages, which include food, beer, wine, sparkling wine and setup, start at $99/person. Tax and an 18% service charge are additional.

Midweek business functions start at $36/person and include breakfast, lunch and nonalcoholic beverages. Tax and an 18% service charge are additional.

AVAILABILITY: Year-round. Sunday–Thursday, 7:30am–10pm; Friday–Saturday, 7:30am–2am.

SERVICES/AMENITIES:

Catering: in-house
Kitchen Facilities: n/a
Tables & Chairs: provided
Linens, Silver, etc.: provided
Restrooms: wheelchair accessible
Dance Floor: indoor and outdoor provided
Bride's & Groom's Dressing Areas: yes
AV/Meeting Equipment: full range

Parking: ample
Accommodations: no guest rooms
Outdoor Night Lighting: yes
Outdoor Cooking Facilities: n/a
Cleanup: provided
View: canyon, gardens
Other: event coordination

RESTRICTIONS:

Alcohol: in-house, no BYO
Smoking: designated areas only
Music: amplified OK

Wheelchair Access: yes
Insurance: not required

Hacienda de las Flores

Historic Home & Garden

2100 Donald Drive, Moraga
925/888-7045
www.moragahacienda.com
rents@moraga.ca.us

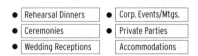

- Rehearsal Dinners
- Ceremonies
- Wedding Receptions
- Corp. Events/Mtgs.
- Private Parties
- Accommodations

An authentic Spanish-style mansion, the Hacienda de las Flores sits on land that was once the hunting ground for Miwok Indians. The historic town-owned structure is painted white with blue trim, and is surrounded by well-maintained park grounds. Inside the Hacienda, hardwood floors, beamed ceilings and a fireplace create a warm and inviting setting. Outdoors, a large lawn spreads out behind the building, enhanced by blue atlas cedar trees, pines, willows, palms and flowers. A circular flowerbed and fountain in the middle of the patio serve as the focal point for large parties or wedding receptions.

From the upper Hacienda lawn, flagstone stairs lead down to the Pavilion, a semicircular building with huge Corinthian columns overlooking a walled garden with lawn and patio. A set of large wrought-iron gates leads guests into the enclosure, where small seated functions or ceremonies can take place. Tranquil and secluded, the Hacienda offers one of the prettiest garden environments for special events in the East Bay.

CEREMONY CAPACITY: The Hacienda lawn holds 200 seated or standing guests, indoors the Hacienda holds 50 seated or 75 standing. The Pavilion accommodates 200 seated or standing outdoors and 50 seated or 60 standing indoors.

EVENT/RECEPTION CAPACITY: The Hacienda holds 200 guests outdoors, or 100 for a seated meal indoors throughout a few rooms. The Pavilion seats 50 inside and has an outdoor capacity of 150.

MEETING CAPACITY: There are 9 rooms that can accommodate 12–60 seated guests.

FEES & DEPOSITS: The event rental fee ranges $935–3,300 depending on the space selected, time of year and residency status. To reserve your date, half of the rental fee plus a refundable $750 security deposit and a nonrefundable $250 application fee are required. Remaining fees are due 6 months prior to the event. A deposit is required if you plan to use a non-preferred caterer or musicians. The damage deposit will be refunded within 60 days after the event provided all conditions have been met.

For weekday business meetings, fees vary depending on room(s) selected and include room setup. There is an additional fee for use of the Hacienda kitchen.

AVAILABILITY: For special events, Friday (2pm–11pm) and Saturday and Sunday (8 consecutive hours between 9am and 11pm); additional hours are available for the front end of events only. For weekday business meetings, the facility is available 8am–10pm.

SERVICES/AMENITIES:

Catering: select from preferred list

Kitchen Facilities: ample

Tables & Chairs: provided

Linens, Silver, etc.: through caterer

Restrooms: wheelchair accessible

Dance Floor: yes

Bride's Dressing Area: yes

AV/Meeting Equipment: no

Parking: lot and on-street

Accommodations: no guest rooms

Outdoor Night Lighting: access only

Outdoor Cooking Facilities: no

Cleanup: caterer, provided

View: fountain, lawns, flowerbeds and trees

RESTRICTIONS:

Alcohol: BYO wine, beer or champagne only

Smoking: outside only

Music: amplified OK with restrictions on speaker location

Wheelchair Access: yes

Insurance: included in fees

Other: decorations restricted; no birdseed, rice, confetti, flower petals, small feathers, loose glitter or mylar balloons

Camron-Stanford House

Lakeside Victorian Mansion

1418 Lakeside Drive, Oakland
510/874-7802
www.cshouse.org
aswift@cshouse.org

Rehearsal Dinners	●	Corp. Events/Mtgs.
● Ceremonies	●	Private Parties
● Wedding Receptions		Accommodations

Gracing the shore of Lake Merritt, the Camron-Stanford House is the last of the grand Victorian homes that once ringed the lake. Constructed in 1876, it derives its name from the Camrons, who were the first residents, and the Stanfords, who occupied it for the longest period. When the building was scheduled for demolition in the late 1960s, concerned citizens formed the Camron-Stanford House Preservation Association and spent the intervening years raising funds to return the home to its former splendor.

Elaborate molding and authentic wallpaper patterns and fabrics have all been used to match the originals as closely as possible. Rooms filled with period artifacts, antiques and photos take you back to the late 1800s. The only operational gas chandelier in Northern California is located here. Outside, a large rear veranda overlooks Lake Merritt. Receptions can take place in the house, on the veranda or on the expansive lawn that extends to the lake. An iron fence enclosing the site ensures privacy, while allowing guests to appreciate the colorful tapestry of boats, birds and joggers that surrounds them.

CEREMONY CAPACITY: The Veranda holds up to 90 seated guests; the veranda and lawn combined (facing the lake) hold 200 seated.

EVENT/RECEPTION & MEETING CAPACITY: The facility accommodates 50 guests inside or 200 outside.

FEES & DEPOSITS: A nonrefundable $200 deposit is required to book the facility. The rental fee, which ranges $1,000–4,000, varies depending on the space(s) selected and length of time rented. Additional hours are available at the rate of $250/hour.

AVAILABILITY: June 15–October 15, Saturdays (except by special arrangement).

SERVICES/AMENITIES:

Catering: BYO licensed
Kitchen Facilities: moderate
Tables & Chairs: seating for 100
Linens, Silver, etc.: BYO
Restroom: wheelchair accessible (ground level only)
Dance Floor: CBA
Bride's Dressing Area: CBA
AV/Meeting Equipment: available

Parking: on-street, lot
Accommodations: no guest rooms
Outdoor Night Lighting: provided
Outdoor Cooking Facilities: BYO
Cleanup: caterer
View: Lake Merritt and Oakland city skyline

RESTRICTIONS:

Alcohol: BYO
Smoking: not allowed
Music: amplified OK outside only

Wheelchair Access: limited
Insurance: proof required
Other: no tacks or tape; no candles, no flame-heated chafing dishes; no confetti or rice

This is important! Tell locations you're reading HERE COMES THE GUIDE and ask if our information is still current.

343

Chabot Space & Science Center

Space & Science Center

10000 Skyline Boulevard, Oakland
510/336-7421
www.chabotspace.org
rentals@chabotspace.org

- Rehearsal Dinners
- Ceremonies
- Wedding Receptions
- Corp. Events/Mtgs.
- Private Parties
- Accommodations

Looking for an out-of-this-world location to celebrate your wedding? Let the stars smile on you at Chabot Space & Science Center. In the evenings, this state-of-the-art science education center perched high in the Oakland hills makes a unique setting for private events.

The Center is surrounded by 13 wooded acres in Joaquin Miller Park, and its architecture takes full advantage of that fact: Numerous floor-to-ceiling windows, a glass skyway, and a catwalk-like loggia hugging the exterior, really make you feel like you're up in the trees. The two main buildings, the Spees and Dellums Buildings, are linked at the second floor by the skyway, and at ground level by an amphitheater and a courtyard with gardens. Exposed ceilings, black floors, and architectural details in green glass, aluminum and blond wood create a smart, polished look throughout the center.

Event spaces in the Spees Building include the MegaDome Theater, a café that provides a handy reception site, and a 242-seat planetarium featuring one of the world's most advanced immersive visualization systems. This allows them to take their audience on real-time jouneys to the edge of the known universe and back again. We were particularly taken with the idea of a celestial ceremony in the planetarium: Imagine getting married on a spot-lit stage beneath a 70-foot dome of gorgeous night sky thick with stars, while your guests sit spellbound in comfortable tiered seats. If you want to go all out, you can even make arrangements with the projectionist to create a sky that changes throughout the event.

Another appealing ceremony option—and one that will give every guest a great vantage point—is the semicircular amphitheater surrounded by trees. This is a particularly appropriate place to mark an important moment in time, as the amphitheater also functions as a nifty clock. At the top level of the amphitheater, the Pleiades Courtyard stretches back to the Spees Building café. Together, the two spaces make a convenient indoor/outdoor spot for serving post-ceremony refreshments. After dining, guests will enjoy strolling through the adjacent EnviroGarden, designed to showcase native plants.

You'll also want to consider serving cocktails in the sleek open spaces of the Spees Building. Although the Spees is a two-story structure, there are several areas where you can stand on the ground floor and gaze up unobstructedly to the top of the building. The most striking of these is the Rotunda, an atrium-like space capped by a huge octagonal skylight. During the day, light flowing in from the skylight illuminates a decorative green glass compass inlaid on the first floor.

If you set up musicians or a DJ on the Rotunda's circular "balcony," the music floats down to your guests mingling below.

Indoor receptions can take place in the exhibit spaces of the three-level Dellums Building, but the size and configuration of your event will depend on the current exhibits. The top floor of the Dellums opens to the outdoor plaza of the observatory complex. This is the highest point of the Center, and from here the sweeping bay views over the treetops are sure to wow your guests. The three domes house telescopes named "Leah," "Rachel" and "Nellie." You can arrange for access to the domes, and can actually hold a small sit-down dinner inside the larger of the two.

Chabot Space & Science Center is a stellar (sorry, we couldn't resist) location, not just for weddings, but for private and corporate events, too. And even if you aren't an astronomy buff, you'll delight in the sunset over the bay and the dazzling nighttime panorama of city lights twinkling below.

CEREMONY CAPACITY: The Obsevatory Complex and the Amphitheater each seat 150 guests, the planetarium seats up to 241, and the Dellums Building accommodates up to 300.

EVENT/RECEPTION CAPACITY: The facility can accommodate 150–500 seated or 200–1,000 standing guests indoors, and 100–150 seated outdoors.

MEETING CAPACITY: Galileo, Kepler and Copernicus can each seat up to 45 guests. The planetarium seats up to 241 theater-style, and the Tien MegaDome seats up to 205 theater-style.

FEES & DEPOSITS: 50% of the rental fee is required to secure your date. A refundable $1,000 cleaning deposit, along with the balance of the rental fee, is due 30 days prior to the event. The rental fee ranges $1,500–20,000 depending on the space(s) reserved. There is a discount for 501(c)(3) nonprofit groups.

AVAILABILITY: Year-round. Monday and Tuesday, 6am–midnight; Wednesday–Sunday, 5pm–midnight. Some seasonal restrictions apply; call for details.

SERVICES/AMENITIES:

Catering: select from preferred list
Kitchen Facilities: full kitchen
Tables & Chairs: BYO
Linens, Silver, etc.: BYO
Restrooms: wheelchair accessible
Dance Floor: built in or BYO
Bride's Dressing Area: yes
AV/Meeting Equipment: some provided

Parking: ample free parking on site
Accommodations: no guest rooms
Outdoor Night Lighting: limited
Outdoor Cooking Facilities: no
Cleanup: renter or caterer
View: panoramic and bay views
Other: use of exhibits; some event coordination provided

RESTRICTIONS:

Alcohol: licensed server required
Smoking: not allowed
Music: amplified OK

Wheelchair Access: yes
Insurance: extra liability required
Other: no balloons or confetti

Fairview Metropolitan

Golf Club

10051 Doolittle Drive, Oakland
510/944-0341
www.fairviewevents.com/metropolitan
metropolitan@fairviewevents.com

● Rehearsal Dinners	● Corp. Events/Mtgs.
● Ceremonies	● Private Parties
● Wedding Receptions	Accommodations

For red carpet treatment alongside the beautiful Metropolitan Golf Course, book your celebration at Fairview Metropolitan, a local favorite just minutes from downtown Oakland and the Oakland Airport.

Fairview Metropolitan has earned a reputation for its great value and scenic vistas. Plus, green weddings take note: the year-round Metropolitan Golf Course has been awarded sanctuary status by Audubon International. The entire property has a natural, spacious feel, and long views to the Oakland hills, the bay, downtown Oakland and the San Francisco skyline lend it an uplifting outlook and unhurried charm. Not only is Fairview Metropolitan a terrific venue for golf events, corporate functions and holiday parties, it's also become a popular choice for affordable East Bay weddings.

An expansive lawn, complete with a romantic gazebo and splashing fountain, is custom-made for wedding ceremonies next to the emerald-green fairways. While the wedding party poses for photos, guests follow a breezeway to the patio of the golf course's Sweet Spot Café where they mingle over cocktails. Bordered by attractive landscaping, the patio features uninterrupted views of the course and the bayside surroundings. Dinner and dancing take place nearby in two adjoining spaces: A sizable banquet room, with windows along two walls, that opens to a glamorous 3,000-square-foot tent. Outfitted with amenities such as a built-in bar, state-of-the-art sound system, dance floor, elegantly draped ceiling, carpeting, and cooling Casablanca fans, the tent is a fun and stylish "party central" that you can enjoy until midnight.

Of course, one of the most reassuring aspects of booking an event at this appealing East Bay location is the professionalism and service you'll receive in the hands of their expert staff. They provide a low-stress planning experience, with a choice of customizable wedding packages, some of which include invitations, flowers, wedding cake, and music, as well as the bar and a tempting menu. All their vendors have been carefully screened to ensure top quality, affordability and maximum satisfaction.

Will you choose the cream-white dendrobium orchids and bear grass in tall cylinder vases or the big bowls of floating roses, gerberas or gardenias? The stacked buttercream wedding cake with fresh flowers or the white-chocolate cake shaped like a gift box with a cascading ribbon? We can't list all of your options, but we can promise you this: You won't have to do any legwork, you'll know just what you're getting—and you won't lose track of the cost. The only thing you'll have to think about is where to go for your honeymoon!

CEREMONY CAPACITY: The center accommodates 350 indoors or outdoors.

EVENT/RECEPTION & MEETING CAPACITY: The center holds 350 seated or standing indoors.

FEES & DEPOSITS: 25% of the estimated total event cost is required to reserve your date. An additional 25% is due 120 days prior to the event and the balance (based on your final guest count) is due 10 days prior. All payments are credited towards your final balance and are nonrefundable and nontransferable. The ceremony fee is $750, and the venue rental for a reception starts at $1,500. Completely customizable wedding packages start at $39/person, and include invitations, DJ, dinner and more. For most packages, a champagne toast and wine with dinner are included and a hosted bar is extra. Tax is additional, but the service charge is included!

AVAILABILITY: Year-round, daily, 6am–midnight.

SERVICES/AMENITIES:

Catering: in-house
Kitchen Facilities: n/a
Tables & Chairs: provided
Linens, Silver, etc.: provided
Restrooms: wheelchair accessible
Dance Floor: provided
Bride's & Groom's Dressing Areas: CBA
AV/Meeting Equipment: some provided

Parking: large lot
Accommodations: no guest rooms
Outdoor Night Lighting: yes
Outdoor Cooking Facilities: no
Cleanup: provided
View: fairways, landscaped grounds, SF skyline
Other: event coordination, in-house wedding cake and florals, clergy on staff

RESTRICTIONS:

Alcohol: in-house
Smoking: outside only
Music: amplified OK

Wheelchair Access: yes
Insurance: not required
Other: no rice, confetti or glitter; no open flames

Highlands Country Club

Country Club

110 Hiller Drive, Oakland
510/849-0743
highlandscc@aol.com

● Rehearsal Dinners	● Corp. Events/Mtgs.	
● Ceremonies	● Private Parties	
● Wedding Receptions	Accommodations	

Suppose you wanted a place for your event that had a genuine "country club" ambiance, but you only had a limited budget. Where could you go? Well, you might want to take a little drive over to the Highlands Country Club.

Embraced by a sloping green sweep of lawn, and overlooking tennis courts and crystal-blue swimming pools, this architectural phoenix has literally risen from its ashes (the original club was destroyed in the 1991 Berkeley-Oakland Hills fire). The community surrounding the club has also been rebuilt, and few, if any, traces of the previous devastation are visible from the club itself.

What is visible from the club's Fireside Room is a panoramic view of the San Francisco Bay and adjacent communities that is so spectacular it almost makes additional decoration redundant. Hardwood floors, a neutral color scheme and large windows showcase the magnificent vista, while the soaring stone fireplace and antique brass chandeliers add a touch of friendly rusticity. There's even a small balcony that affords you the luxury of watching the sun set over the Golden Gate or the fog pour over the Berkeley hills as you sip champagne and enjoy the breeze. In front of the clubhouse, a sunny patio surrounded by verdant lawns and small trees is available for outdoor receptions. Although it's high up on a hill, this country club is fresh, unpretentious and quite down-to-earth.

CEREMONY CAPACITY: The Fireside Room, patio and gazebo each accommodate up to 100 guests, maximum.

EVENT/RECEPTION CAPACITY: The Fireside Room and patio combined hold up to 100 guests.

MEETING CAPACITY: The club accommodates 100 guests, maximum.

FEES & DEPOSITS: The rental fee is $1,200 and includes use of the Fireside Room, deck and patio areas for 4 hours; extra hours can be arranged. To secure your date, all of the nonrefundable rental fee plus a refundable $1,200 security deposit are required.

AVAILABILITY: Year-round, daily, 8am–11pm. Use of the deck and patio is seasonal. Only 1 event is booked per day.

SERVICES/AMENITIES:

Catering: BYO
Kitchen Facilities: moderately equipped
Tables & Chairs: provided
Linens, Silver, etc.: CBA or BYO
Restrooms: wheelchair accessible
Dance Floor: dining room or patio
Bride's Dressing Area: no
AV/Meeting Equipment: microphones, screen

Parking: on-street
Accommodations: no guest rooms
Outdoor Night Lighting: access only
Outdoor Cooking Facilities: BBQ
Cleanup: caterer or renter
View: East Bay hills and San Francisco Bay
Other: bar

RESTRICTIONS:

Alcohol: BYO
Smoking: outdoors only
Music: amplified OK indoors with volume limits

Wheelchair Access: yes
Insurance: certificate required
Other: no rice, birdseed, petals or glitter

Lake Chalet

1520 Lakeside Drive, Oakland
510/653-8282
www.thelakechalet.com
chaletevents@chaletmgmt.com

Waterfront Restaurant

- Rehearsal Dinners
- Ceremonies
- Wedding Receptions
- Corp. Events/Mtgs.
- Private Parties
- Accommodations

Ringed by a delicate necklace of lights and comprised of parkland, gardens, and historic civic structures, Lake Merritt and its environs is not only the vibrant heart of Oakland, it's a thriving urban wildlife sanctuary (the first official refuge in the U.S.). After a multiyear project to upgrade the lakeshore's landscaping and buildings, the city's "crown jewel" now has a waterfront restaurant worthy of its surroundings: the Lake Chalet.

Stepping down past colorful flowerbeds, you enter the handsomely restored edifice that was once the Lake Merritt Boathouse. It has never looked this grand. Charcoal-colored floors, blackened steel, lacquer-red metal and mahogany accents surround you in comfort and luster. The magnificent white marble bar that faces the water has become a hotspot for locals who gather here to enjoy an expansive view of the lake along with their cocktails.

The Chalet has also become a hotspot for special events. Larger parties reserve the Gondola Room, where three walls of windows frame panoramic views, and European-style balconies look out over the dock and lake. Private restrooms, kitchen, and bar; warm earth colors; hardwood floors and an atmosphere of ease and serenity make it an excellent setting for fabulous wedding receptions, as well as corporate events, fundraisers and cocktail parties. The bar here, like all the others indoors and out, offers the Chalet's exclusive handcrafted beers on tap.

Breezes blowing in through the windows draw you outside to the well-appointed patios, where a dock broad enough to accommodate a wedding ceremony, cocktail reception, or dinner reaches out into the placid lake waters. Outfitted with stylish furniture, palm trees, umbrellas and its own bar, this unique site has a resort-like feel. Wild ducks, snowy egrets, crested night herons and pelicans are among the protected birds that reside here, as do the gondolas that glide gracefully by. That's right—a taste of Venice has come to Lake Merritt! Gondola Servicio and its genial gondoliers are available for pickup and delivery during an event. Picture the bride's dramatic arrival or the newlyweds' departure in one of those slender black vessels. Better yet, capture the moment in photos!

For small mixers, meetings, rehearsal dinners or a hideaway for the bride, the Private Dining room is ideal. It features a fireplace, big-screen TV, and wine library, plus garden views and separate entrance for red carpet arrivals.

And yes, the food is also amazing. This place is, after all, run by the talented restaurateurs responsible for the Beach Chalet Brewery & Restaurant and the Park Chalet Coastal Beer Garden in San Francisco.

If your guests want to stay in town, there are lakeside, downtown and bayside hotels just a short ride away. Many of the city's most popular attractions—the Oakland Museum, Jack London Square, City Hall and the transbay ferries—are also nearby, but remember, Lake Merritt is home to some of the best of them: Children's Fairyland, the Rotary Nature Center, and of course, the marvelous Lake Chalet.

CEREMONY CAPACITY: The restaurant seats 120 guests.

EVENT/RECEPTION & MEETING CAPACITY: The facility can accommodate 120 seated or 150 standing for a reception, and up to 600 with a buyout.

FEES & DEPOSITS: 50% of the food & beverage minimum is required to reserve your date, and the balance is due in full on the day of the event. The rental fee ranges $150–5,000 depending on the space and services selected. Meals start at $39/person for lunch and $45/person for dinner. Tax, beverages and a 21% service charge are additional.

AVAILABILITY: Year-round, daily, 8am–midnight. After hours are optional, additional fee applies.

SERVICES/AMENITIES:

Catering: in-house
Kitchen Facilities: n/a
Tables & Chairs: provided
Linens, Silver, etc.: provided
Restrooms: wheelchair accessible
Dance Floor: provided
Bride's Dressing Area: no
AV/Meeting Equipment: some provided, CBA

Parking: large lot; valet available, extra fee.
Accommodations: no guest rooms
Outdoor Night Lighting: yes
Outdoor Cooking Facilities: none
Cleanup: provided
View: waterfront lake views, cityscape, landscaped grounds, garden

RESTRICTIONS:

Alcohol: in-house or BYO with corkage fee
Smoking: not allowed
Music: amplified OK

Wheelchair Access: yes
Insurance: not required

Overwhelmed? Use the search criteria on www.HereComesTheGuide.com to narrow down your choices.

Preservation Park

Victorian Homes

1233 Preservation Park Way, Oakland
510/874-7581
www.preservationpark.com
events@preservationpark.com

- Rehearsal Dinners
- Ceremonies
- Wedding Receptions
- Corp. Events/Mtgs.
- Private Parties
- Accommodations

Occupying two blocks just a heartbeat away from Oakland's City Center, Preservation Park is an eye-catching re-creation of a Victorian neighborhood. Sixteen Victorian homes have been beautifully restored and colorfully painted. The setting has been further enhanced with period park benches, ornate wrought-iron fences, old-fashioned street lamps and a bronze fountain from Paris.

The park's social center is the Pavilion, a graceful bandstand where ceremonies usually take place. While the bride and groom exchange vows on stage, their guests, seated on the lawn just below them, can appreciate the lovely landscaping and vintage architecture that surrounds them. Outdoor receptions are held in the adjacent Fountain Circle, a circular plaza with a large two-tiered fountain topped by the moon goddess Diana at its center. There's plenty of room for a band, or you could have an outdoor buffet on either side of the Pavilion.

If you're planning an indoor reception, two houses just off the Fountain Circle are available. The Ginn House, circa 1890, features two delightful light and airy parlors reminiscent of those in an English country home. Nile Hall, circa 1911, is a craftsman-style building with a sensational space for a grand and elegant party. It has a 30-foot-high ceiling, skylights, multiple windows, a stage and a theatrical lighting and sound system. This room is well designed, with soft colors, nice detailing and attractive appointments—and enough space to accommodate an extensive guest list. You can reserve one or both houses, as they're connected by a spacious interior hallway.

The park is not only popular for weddings, it's hosted a wide range of events. When you reserve the outdoor spaces, the entrance gates are closed to cars so you and your guests can savor the feeling of having this charming "town" all to yourselves. For a remarkable glimpse of old-time Oakland, pay a visit to Preservation Park—it's well worth the trip.

CEREMONY CAPACITY: Ginn House holds 80 seated, Nile Hall 200 seated, and the Pavilion Area 150–300 seated guests.

EVENT/RECEPTION & MEETING CAPACITY: Various rooms hold 10–150 seated guests indoors. The Pavilion Area accommodates up to 300 seated.

FEES & DEPOSITS: A $500 deposit is required to secure your date. The rental fee, which is payable 120 days prior to the event, is $1,325 for Nile Hall and $2,100 for Nile Hall plus the Ginn House. The rental fee for the outdoor Pavilion Area is $1,100–3,000 with setup.

AVAILABILITY: Year-round, daily, 8am–11pm. The outdoor Pavilion, May to mid-October.

SERVICES/AMENITIES:

Catering: select from preferred list or BYO licensed, extra charge

Kitchen Facilities: setup only

Tables & Chairs: provided, extra fee outdoors

Linens, Silver, etc.: provided by caterer

Restrooms: wheelchair accessible

Dance Floor: CBA

Bride's Dressing Area: CBA

AV/Meeting Equipment: sound equipment, WiFi, microphones, flip charts

Parking: on-street or city garage nearby

Accommodations: no guest rooms

Outdoor Night Lighting: yes

Outdoor Cooking Facilities: no

Cleanup: caterer

View: gardens and fountain

RESTRICTIONS:

Alcohol: in-house, no BYO

Smoking: outside only

Music: amplified OK

Wheelchair Access: yes

Insurance: may be required

Rotunda Building

Event Venue

300 Frank H. Ogawa Plaza, Oakland
510/410-6002

rotundabuildingoakland.com
mweventsinc@yahoo.com

- Rehearsal Dinners
- Ceremonies
- Wedding Receptions
- Corp. Events/Mtgs.
- Private Parties
- Accommodations

A shining example of how to renovate a cherished old building, The Rotunda in downtown Oakland is a jewel that's been polished to perfection. Built in 1912 as Kahn's, an elegant department store, it closed in 1984 but was placed on the National Register of Historic Places and later designated an Oakland Landmark. Meticulously restored in 2000, this Beaux Arts beauty now sparkles brightly as an upscale collection of office suites with a jaw-dropping event venue at its core.

Distinctive from the outside, it's positively fabulous inside. The palatial, circular Lobby boasts striking terrazzo flooring, tall plaster archways, and a ceiling that soars 120 feet overhead. Ringed by an ornate mezzanine and a series of upper tiers, the space draws your eye upward, first to the classic columns adorned with sculpted friezes and gilded embellishments and finally to the crowning glory—the stunning 5,000-square-foot elliptical dome of leaded glass. Illuminated by natural light flooding in during the day or awash in colorful lighting at night, it will take your breath away.

The main floor's majestic double-sided staircase, featuring original turn-of-the-century light fixtures, becomes the focal point for your dramatic entrance and ceremony. You can exchange vows at the base or up on the huge landing that also functions as a raised stage for toasts and entertainment.

After the "I do"s, everyone is invited to the mezzanine level for cocktails and hors d'oeuvres, before returning downstairs for dinner, dancing…and perhaps a show! With its grand proportions and general "wow" factor, The Rotunda is the perfect setting for something spectacular, like hosting a large ethnic wedding with all the accompanying pageantry, or a Cirque du Soleil-style aerial performance. Watching daring acrobats suspended from the dome execute gravity-defying feats will definitely give your friends and family something to remember.

And while we're talking about creating memorable moments here, you'll love being able to go up to the private rooftop for photos with City Hall and The Commons as your backdrop. You'll also love being treated like an A-lister from start to finish, thanks to the ace event management team. They can provide guidance and full-service planning for every aspect of your celebration, as well as recommendations on nearby hotels and sites to see in downtown Oakland and the Greater Bay Area.

CEREMONY CAPACITY: The facility accommodates 500+ seated guests indoors.

EVENT/RECEPTION CAPACITY: The facility holds 500 seated or 1,000 standing indoors

MEETING CAPACITY: The facility seats 350 for a meeting.

FEES & DEPOSITS: A $4,000 deposit is required to reserve your date and the balance is due 15 days prior to the event. The rental fee is $800/hour or $400/hour for nonprofit organizations.

AVAILABILITY: Year-round: weekdays, 4pm–10pm; Friday, Saturday and Sunday, 10am–midnight.

SERVICES/AMENITIES:

Catering: select from preferred list
Kitchen Facilities: fully equipped
Tables & Chairs: provided
Linens, Silver, etc.: provided
Restrooms: wheelchair accessible
Dance Floor: provided
Bride's Dressing Area: yes
AV/Meeting Equipment: CBA

Parking: garage or lot nearby
Accommodations: no guest rooms
Outdoor Night Lighting: access only
Outdoor Cooking Facilities: none
Cleanup: provided
View: cityscape, garden courtyard, bay
Other: event coordination

RESTRICTIONS:

Alcohol: in-house
Smoking: not allowed
Music: amplified OK indoors

Wheelchair Access: yes
Insurance: liability required

Sequoyah Country Club

Private Golf Club

4550 Heafey Road, Oakland
510/632-0243

www.sequoyahcc.com
catering@sequoyahcc.com

- Rehearsal Dinners
- Ceremonies
- Wedding Receptions
- Corp. Events/Mtgs.
- Private Parties
- Accommodations

It's easy to miss this very private venue, hidden high in the East Bay Hills amid rolling greens and gardens and the husky rustle of the giant sequoias—or *sequoyahs,* as the Native Americans called these massive redwoods.

Once the chic enclave of a privileged few, today this delightfully sequestered setting is open to anyone with the presence of mind to book it for a special celebration. Tuxedoes and evening gowns are no longer *de rigueur* here, but the style and panache that has distinguished the club since its inception remains. The graceful Spanish Colonial-style clubhouse, situated prominently above budding olive trees and bright beds of flowers, still plays host to spectacular parties.

At the top of the clubhouse steps, the front Patio seems the perfect place for guests to congregate. Its comfortable furnishings, several fire pits, and panoramic vista make it well suited for standing cocktails and passed hors d'oeuvres, but you may prefer to kick things off inside where other inspiring options await.

As you walk down the long Terrace Hallway, you can't help but appreciate the high, beamed ceiling; arches and columns; and lantern-style chandeliers—a combination of features that reflect the architectural charm of the building. The hallway opens onto the Terrace Room, a grand space that has clearly been designed with balls and extravaganzas in mind: Its vaulted, beamed ceiling, tremendous wrought-iron chandeliers, and wall of gleaming, wood-framed glass terrace doors convey an effortless elegance and refinement. The Terrace Room opens to a patio and pool, so guests can step outdoors on a moonlit evening and take in the cool night air.

The Terrace Room is bookended by the Terrace Bar and Boardroom (the groomsmen will love its woodsy feeling) and the fashionably bright and uplifting Sequoyah Room. These, like the larger Bay View Room across the hall, reflect the club's classy yet welcoming ambiance. There's even a cozy private chamber upstairs with a sitting area just outside. Here the country club's practiced and ultra-courteous staff can serve up a nerve-calming glass of champagne or quick bite for the bride and her entourage. This room can double as a pretty children's playroom, too.

For outdoor ceremonies or gatherings taking place on one of the East Bay's many sunny days, we suggest the picturesque Terrace Lawn. It's superlative spot for celebrants to bask in the property's stunning surroundings.

Indoors or out, Sequoyah Country Club provides an environment where you and your fortunate guests can flow smoothly from one event space to the next with ease, enjoying every moment to the fullest.

CEREMONY CAPACITY: The site holds 200 seated guests indoors and 250 seated outdoors.

EVENT/RECEPTION CAPACITY: The site can accommodate 360 seated or 450 standing indoors and 250 standing outdoors.

MEETING CAPACITY: Meeting spaces hold 100 seated guests.

FEES & DEPOSITS: A $2,000 deposit is required to secure your date, and the balance is due one week prior to the event. The rental fee ranges $300–2,000 depending on the space reserved and the day of the week. Meals range $30–52/person. Tax, alcohol and a 20% service charge are additional.

AVAILABILITY: Year-around, daily, 7am-midnight.

SERVICES/AMENITIES:

Catering: in-house
Kitchen Facilities: n/a
Tables & Chairs: provided
Linens, Silver, etc.: provided
Restrooms: wheelchair accessible
Dance Floor: portable provided
Bride's Dressing Area: yes
AV/Meeting Equipment: provided

Parking: large lot, valet available
Accommodations: no guest rooms
Outdoor Night Lighting: yes
Outdoor Cooking Facilities: BBQ CBA
Cleanup: caterer or renter
View: garden courtyard, fairways, pool area; panorama of Oakland and the peninsula
Other: grand piano, in-house wedding cake and florals

RESTRICTIONS:

Alcohol: in-house, or BYO with corkage fee
Smoking: designated areas only
Music: amplified OK indoors

Wheelchair Access: yes
Insurance: liability required

Skyline Community Church

Church

12540 Skyline Boulevard, Oakland
510/531-8212

www.skylineucc.org
office@skylineucc.org

●	Rehearsal Dinners	●	Corp. Events/Mtgs.
●	Ceremonies	●	Private Parties
●	Wedding Receptions		Accommodations

High in the Oakland hills, past handsome hillside residences, woodsy Joaquin Miller Park and the Chabot Space & Science Center, you'll find a pleasant surprise just off Skyline Boulevard. When you see the sign for Skyline Community Church, turn into the drive. Let it lead you up past the two lower parking lots on a sun-splashed, flower-flanked climb to the white wooden bell tower that signals your arrival at the church. Set on the crest of a hill that borders the East Bay Regional Park District, this quiet sanctuary sits under an expanse of blue sky and sunlight. Birds sing in the treetops. Gentle breezes stir the pines. Noise and commotion seem far, far away.

It's a charming venue for a wedding, retreat, or any other event where an open and affirming environment fits the bill. Couples of any faith or sexual orientation, are welcome, which makes it the perfect place for interfaith marriages and same-sex unions. You're also free to invite your own priest, rabbi, or other spiritual leader to officiate.

Receptions are generally held in the picturesque circular courtyard, outfitted with teak benches flanked by urns overflowing with succulents. The courtyard provides plenty of space for your DJ or band and dance floor, and can be set up with tenting, umbrella-shaded tables or whatever suits your celebration.

On one side of the courtyard, a little path that winds through the well-kept lawn ends in a heart-shaped pattern just in front of an old-fashioned gazebo with a peaked roof and weathervane that spins with the cooling winds. From here you can look down on a hillside lovingly planted and tended, like the other nicely landscaped parts of the property, by church members. The gazebo is an attractive spot to tie the knot, but you might want to save it for the cake cutting and photos and opt instead for a ceremony in the chapel on the opposite side of the courtyard.

Accessed by four large doors, the fan-shaped sanctuary has a beamed ceiling, parquet floor and a stunning wall of glass behind the altar that frames uninterrupted views of regional parkland and hills that roll toward Mt. Diablo. Acoustics in this hall are ethereal, making solo, a cappella, string or pipe organ (yes, this church has one!) performances sublime. Sea-blue carpeting leads down the stairs to the Meditation Room. It's a great spot for the groom and his guys to dress and meet with the pastor. The groom can then shake off any pre-wedding jitters in the serene labyrinth garden, which is also a beautiful site for photos. It even works perfectly for a tea ceremony prior to the wedding ceremony!

The bride and her attendants can get ready in the Friendship Room off the courtyard. Often used for fellowship and community gatherings, it features big windows, a compact adjacent kitchen, and double-mirrored cabinets with stage lighting that encourage plenty of primping.

Safe, private, relaxed and family-friendly, Skyline Community Church has much to offer children, too. Kids are encouraged to ring the church bell as the newlyweds leave the grounds. It's all so sweet and embracing…you and your guests will feel like you've found your own little piece of heaven.

CEREMONY CAPACITY: The Chapel holds a maximum of 240 seated guests; the Courtyard, 300 seated guests.

EVENT/RECEPTION & MEETING CAPACITY: The Courtyard holds up to 300 seated guests.

FEES & DEPOSITS: A $500 deposit is required to secure your date, and the balance is due 4 weeks prior to the event. The rental fee ranges $950–2,600 depending on the space reserved.

AVAILABILITY: Year-round. Monday through Saturday, 9am–11pm; Sunday, 1pm–11pm.

SERVICES/AMENITIES:

Catering: BYO
Kitchen Facilities: limited
Tables & Chairs: some provided
Linens, Silver, etc.: through caterer
Restrooms: wheelchair accessible CBA
Dance Floor: through caterer
Bride's & Groom's Dressing Areas: yes
AV/Meeting Equipment: digital projector and motorized screen with remote; WiFi

Parking: large lot, on-street
Accommodations: no guest rooms
Outdoor Night Lighting: yes
Outdoor Cooking Facilities: BBQ on site
Cleanup: caterer or renter
View: forest, mountains, valley, garden
Other: event coordination

RESTRICTIONS:

Alcohol: BYO wine, beer or champagne
Smoking: outside only at gazebo trellis
Music: amplified OK until 10pm

Wheelchair Access: limited
Insurance: liability required

Want to know WHAT TO ASK a potential location or vendor? Check out our Questions to Ask starting on page 21.

Snow Building at the Oakland Zoo

Event Venue

9777 Golf Links Road, Oakland
510/632-9525 x200
www.oaklandzoo.org
reservations@oaklandzoo.org

- Rehearsal Dinners
- Ceremonies
- Wedding Receptions
- Corp. Events/Mtgs.
- Private Parties
- Accommodations

The Oakland Zoo is unquestionably one of the Bay Area's most beloved attractions. It's a place where kids get to see wildlife up close for the first time, and grownups get to re-experience a little of that childhood magic. Couples looking for a unique location for their big day are also drawn here … and rewarded with more than warm memories: They discover that the zoo's light-filled Snow Building makes a really great—and very affordable—wedding venue.

Set off by itself on a hilltop perch, the modern, glass-walled building is surrounded by large swaths of grass, mature trees and best of all, sweeping views of the bay area and beyond. It's fronted by The Overlook, an expansive private terrace and lawn that's a favorite for ceremonies and cocktails thanks to mesmerizing panoramas from San Jose to the Bay Bridge and Golden Gate. Here, you can exchange vows beneath an arch with the city, water and mountains as your backdrop. Or, if you prefer more of a hushed, leafy setting, continue around to the Side Lawn and Terrace to say "I do" in front of a towering pine, then pose for portraits beneath a graceful magnolia. Follow with a reception al fresco, or opt to put up a tent aglow with chandeliers. (And you're welcome to mix and match with The Overlook area since you'll have exclusive use of the entire property).

The scenery is no less impressive inside, with great sightlines through windows that extend to the full height of the vaulted ceiling. Plenty of double glass doors allow for a true indoor/outdoor feel. The large space has a clean, neutral palette that works with virtually any style so you can add your own design flourishes. And the well-equipped kitchen gives you and your caterer-of-choice free rein to get creative. You'll also have sole use of the adjacent parking lot for your guests, and you can even arrange to hold your rehearsal up to two weeks in advance of the wedding.

Another special perk: The zoo's entrance is just a short stroll away, so it's easy to capture some one-of-a-kind photos.* How about a few fun shots as a new couple riding an ostrich or elephant (with all your attendants!) on the antique carousel? Or, gather the whole family in front of the bright pink flamingos. That way, when you reminisce, you'll feel even better knowing that events like yours helped raise revenue for animal care, conservation and education.

* Photo ops on the carousel or with live animals are subject to availability and there is an extra fee.

CEREMONY CAPACITY: The site accommodates 175 seated guests indoors or outdoors.

EVENT/RECEPTION CAPACITY: The venue holds 175 seated or 250 standing indoors or outdoors.

MEETING CAPACITY: The venue seats 175 theater-style.

FEES & DEPOSITS: A $325–350 deposit (Monday–Thursday) or a $525–600 deposit (Friday–Sunday) is required to reserve your date and the balance is due 2 months prior to the event. The rental fee starts at $660–700 (Monday–Thursday), $1,320–1,500 (Friday and Sunday), and $1,680–1,800 (Saturday). There is a $300 kitchen usage fee. Alcohol is allowed at non-youth events only. Prices are subject to change.

AVAILABILITY: Year-round.

SERVICES/AMENITIES:

Catering: BYO
Kitchen Facilities: fully equipped
Tables & Chairs: provided
Linens, Silver, etc.: BYO
Restrooms: wheelchair accessible
Dance Floor: provided
Bride's Dressing Area: yes
AV/Meeting Equipment: BYO

Parking: large lot
Accommodations: no guest rooms
Outdoor Night Lighting: limited
Outdoor Cooking Facilities: none
Cleanup: renter, some provided
View: panorama of the bay area, from San Jose to the Golden Gate Bridge
Other: fireplace available

RESTRICTIONS:

Alcohol: BYO
Smoking: outdoors only
Music: amplified OK indoors

Wheelchair Access: yes
Insurance: liability required
Other: birdseed OK outdoors only; no glitter, confetti, or balloon/bird releases

Temescal Beach House

Lakefront Event Facility

Temescal Regional Recreation Area, Oakland
510/544-3164
www.brazilianroom.org
brazil@ebparks.org

- Rehearsal Dinners
- Ceremonies
- Wedding Receptions
- Corp. Events/Mtgs.
- Private Parties
- Accommodations

A beach in the middle of Oakland? With water and sand and everything? Yes! And so much more, thanks to the East Bay Regional Park District, who developed this scenic gem as one of its first three parks back in 1938. Today, the 48-acre property is a neighborhood oasis where busy urbanites can experience nature's rejuvenating powers. Lake Temescal can even become your own private getaway when you rent the handsome Beach House for your wedding or special event.

It's a leisurely stroll from the parking area down to the Beach House, picnic lawns and lake, and your guests will find it a rewarding nature walk. The East Shore Trail gently curves through stands of oak and willow, revealing sensory surprises: A flicker of ginger turns out to be a red squirrel; native songbirds warble from the treetops; the air is scented with the spicy aroma of bay laurel. Water lilies grace the shoreline, while butterflies flit amongst the cattails.

As the path slopes downward, the trees part to reveal the Beach House set against a forested knoll, overlooking a sweep of sandy shore. The two-story building has a cut-stone foundation accented with a trio of arches on the lower floor. The upper story (which is the rental space) is all windows, promising a spectacular view. Constructed in 1940, the historic Beach House has the quality craftsmanship and relaxed, unpretentious style typical of the era. Two wide flights of stone steps lead you to the rear of the building, where a terraced garden provides a lush backdrop to a charming flagstone patio. Fragrant roses in creamy white, lipstick pink and deep scarlet bloom from spring to fall, a romantic addition to any wedding ceremony. The sound of rushing water beckons you to a nearby footbridge spanning a waterfall that cascades down to the lake. Boughs of oak, fern and colorful rhododendron encircle a small clearing just beyond the bridge. A stone bench invites you to survey the waterscape below, where snowy egrets and cormorants cavort in the lake, and majestic blue herons pose regally on the mossy bank.

As the evening grows cool, your guests can still enjoy the lakeside panorama as they retreat inside the Beach House, thanks to the long row of picture windows in the Lakeview Room and adjoining Fireside Room. Both spaces evoke an Americana theme, with gleaming hardwood floors, log cabin walls awash in an oh-so-pale mint green, and polished copper wall sconces. The Fireside Room also boasts a high ceiling with dark, rough-hewn open beams. A grand flagstone hearth at the far end crackles and glows with a gas-burning fire, keeping everyone toasty. Double French doors give a glimpse of the garden, and admit more natural light. Leave these doors open during your event, and you'll let in the soothing harmony of the waterfall and the songbirds.

The Beach House and its peaceful surroundings capture the gentle simplicity of the past, and when you come here for a visit you might find yourself daydreaming about the possibilities... *an intimate garden fête, complete with breezy broad-brimmed hats and elegant china... the nostalgic warmth of a holiday gathering around the fireplace... a picnic on the patio, while lake trout jump for dragonflies in the lazy summer twilight... or stealing a kiss from your sweetheart on the shore of the moonlit lake.* Be creative—whatever celebration you imagine, Temescal Beach House will make it wonderful.

CEREMONY CAPACITY: The Patio holds up to 130 seated guests.

EVENT/RECEPTION & MEETING CAPACITY: This location seats up to 80 guests.

FEES & DEPOSITS: A $100 deposit is required to secure your date. $50 of this deposit is refundable with more than 180 days' notice of cancellation. A signed contract is required within 7 days after the initial deposit.

The rental fee for Friday night, Saturday, Sunday, and holidays (min. 8 hours) ranges $900–1,500 depending on the day and time frame reserved. Each additional hour is $150. Weekday rates range $275–600 depending on the day and length of time rented. If you opt to bring your own food without a caterer, there is an additional fee. Evening non-catered events are prohibited. For nonresidents of Alameda and Contra Costa counties, there is a surcharge that equals 20% of the rental fee.

AVAILABILITY: Year-round, daily. Monday–Thursday, 8am–10pm; Friday, 8am–midnight; Saturday, 10am–midnight; Sunday, 10am–10pm.

SERVICES/AMENITIES:

Catering: select from preferred list
Kitchen Facilities: prep only
Tables & Chairs: provided
Linens, Silver, etc.: BYO
Restrooms: wheelchair accessible
Dance Floor: yes
Bride's Dressing Room: yes
AV/Meeting Equipment: projector, screen

Parking: large lot, fee charged April–Sept.
Accommodations: no guest rooms
Outdoor Night Lighting: patio only
Outdoor Cooking Facilities: no
Cleanup: through caterer
View: hills, lake, park
Other: fireplace available, extra fee; wireless access available

RESTRICTIONS:

Alcohol: BYO wine, beer or champagne
Smoking: not allowed in the regional parks
Music: amplified OK indoors, outdoors with restrictions

Wheelchair Access: yes
Insurance: extra liability is required

The Terrace Room
at the Lake Merritt Hotel

1800 Madison Street at Lakeside, Oakland
510/903-3580 Catering Department
www.theterraceroom.com
elizabeth@theterraceroom.com

Hotel and Conference Facility

● Rehearsal Dinners	● Corp. Events/Mtgs.
● Ceremonies	● Private Parties
● Wedding Receptions	Accommodations

Time has been good to the Lake Merritt Hotel. After three renovations in ten years, this classic 1927 Art Deco landmark is now filled with furnishings and accessories that enhance the building's striking architectural features.

The décor includes plush axminster carpeting, the design of which was inspired by a vintage fabric containing both a geometric pattern and exotic flowers in chestnut, gold, red and green; walls painted in a rich terracotta color; wrought-iron chandeliers; overstuffed Art Deco furniture covered in jewel-tone mohair fabric; and Lloyd Loom wicker chairs and cocktail tables.

The restoration extends to The Terrace Room, the hotel's restaurant and one of Oakland's premier entertainment sites. Twenty-foot, floor-to-ceiling windows along the entire front of this grand space offer an enchanting panorama of Lake Merritt, Lakeside Park and the Oakland hills. During the day the multilevel restaurant is bathed in light. At night, it has an intimate, almost cabaret feeling, and the view of the lake is spectacular: The dark surface of the water perfectly reflects the glittering Necklace of Lights gracing its perimeter.

The Terrace Room features a semicircular hardwood dance floor, and a sizable mural along one wall depicting Lake Merritt as it appeared over 40 years ago. A shiny black grand piano and Art Deco fixtures are nice finishing touches. In addition to its great location along Lake Merritt, the hotel provides a wide range of services, many of which can be specifically tailored to your special event.

CEREMONY CAPACITY: The Terrace Room holds 150 standing and/or seated guests.

EVENT/RECEPTION CAPACITY: The Terrace Room accommodates 220 seated without a dance floor, 190 seated with a dance floor, or 300 standing guests.

MEETING CAPACITY: The Terrace Room seats 220 without a dance floor, or 190 with a dance floor.

FEES & DEPOSITS: A nonrefundable $1,750 security deposit is required to reserve your date. An estimated 50% payment is required 2 months prior to your event and the balance is due 1 month prior. Full seated service, including food & beverage, starts at $35/person. Tax, administrative fee, and gratuity are additional.

AVAILABILITY: For special events, year-round, Saturdays 5pm–12am and Sundays 6pm–12am. The Terrace Room Restaurant and Lounge are also open to the public for dining: Monday–Friday, 11:30am–2pm for lunch; Monday–Wednesday, 5pm–8pm and Thursday & Friday, 5pm–9:30pm for dinner. Happy hour is Monday–Thursday, 5pm–10pm. Additionally, The Terrace Room serves brunch Saturday 10am–1:30pm and Sunday 10am–2:30pm.

SERVICES/AMENITIES:

Catering: in-house, no BYO

Kitchen Facilities: n/a

Tables & Chairs: provided

Linens, Silver, etc.: provided

Restrooms: wheelchair accessible

Dance Floor: yes

Bride's Dressing Area: no

AV/Meeting Equipment: podium

Parking: on-street

Accommodations: no guest rooms

Outdoor Night Lighting: access only

Outdoor Cooking Facilities: no

Cleanup: provided

View: Lake Merritt, Oakland hills, cityscape

Other: banquet captain on site

RESTRICTIONS:

Alcohol: in-house, or BYO wine and champagne only with corkage fee

Music: amplified OK with volume limits

Smoking: outdoors only

Wheelchair Access: yes

Insurance: required for vendors

Other: no food or beverages in lobby; no rice or confetti

Piedmont Community Church and Guild Hall

Community Hall

400 Highland Avenue, Piedmont
510/547-5700
www.piedmontchurch.org
jean@piedmontchurch.org

●	Rehearsal Dinners		Corp. Events/Mtgs.
●	Ceremonies	●	Private Parties
●	Wedding Receptions		Accommodations

You'll see the landmark bell tower of the beautiful Piedmont Community Church long before you arrive. Gleaming in the sunlight, the ivory-colored Mission-style building looks a bit like a wedding cake, set atop an ivy- and flower-covered rise overlooking the prosperous community that gives the venue its name.

An extensive renovation prior to the church's 100th-year anniversary added numerous features, making the facilities here even more guest-friendly. You can enter through a number of private and public stairways, ramps and drives, all of which lead to an expansive, landscaped inner courtyard that radiates around a colorful central fountain. This is, of course, the perfect place for an outdoor ceremony roofed in blue sky and skirted in blossoms. But you might want to use this area and the upper courtyard that surrounds it for music and cocktails, and instead get married in the church itself.

Nothing will prepare those attending for the regal ambiance within. Plush royal-blue carpet, dark pews cushioned in velvet, a lustrous, carved-beam ceiling, and two walls of stained-glass windows with floral motifs in brilliant, jewel colors evoke an Old World opulence. Couples tie the knot at an altar fit for a king and queen, beneath a rotunda brightened with lofty stained-glass windows. The church comes with a fabulous pipe organ hidden behind one altar wall, an organist, and acoustics that will naturally amplify even a whispered "I do." There are also separate spaces for the couple to get ready: the lounge-like Altar Guild Room for the groom; and a comfortable salon with mirrors, bathroom, vanity, private entrance and more for the bride and her retinue.

Across the courtyard, the welcoming Guild Hall provides a perfectly grand setting for a celebration of any kind. The beamed ceiling soars overhead, hardwood floors gleam golden, and pale sage-colored walls exude an embracing calm. Enormous windows can be left open on sunny days, and there's a generous stage for musicians. Another plus: a spacious commercial-quality kitchen that will surely please your caterer. Like the other structures on the property, Guild Hall has a private entrance, landscaped outdoor seating areas, and is flanked by graceful colonnades.

If your party is very large or very small, you may want to use the Clara Barton and Doris Murdock Rooms. Both open to the upper courtyard and provide parlor-like space for a guest lounge, additional buffet tables or a quieter, more intimate gathering. Panel doors separate the two rooms so that they can be used individually or together.

Sound heavenly? It is—especially when glasses are raised, toasts are made and the church bells chime for you.

CEREMONY CAPACITY: The sanctuary holds 300 seated guests, and the outdoor area seats 100.

EVENT/RECEPTION CAPACITY: Guild Hall can accommodate up to 200 seated guests.

MEETING CAPACITY: Meetings do not take place at this facility.

FEES & DEPOSITS: A deposit is required to secure your date, and the balance is due 30 days prior to the event. The rental fee ranges $1,750–3,975 depending on the space reserved, the length of your rental, and whether or not you are a Piedmont Community Church member. The fee includes clergy on staff, organist, complimentary event coordination for the rehearsal and ceremony, fireplace, grand piano, and a variety of tables and chairs.

AVAILABILITY: Year-round, daily; call for details.

SERVICES/AMENITIES:

Catering: BYO
Kitchen Facilities: fully equipped
Tables & Chairs: provided
Linens, Silver, etc.: CBA or through caterer
Restrooms: wheelchair accessible
Dance Floor: provided
Bride's Dressing Area: yes
AV/Meeting Equipment: n/a

Parking: on-street
Accommodations: no guest rooms
Outdoor Night Lighting: yes
Outdoor Cooking Facilities: none
Cleanup: provided
View: fountain, garden, landscaped grounds
Other: grand piano, clergy on staff, complimentary rehearsal and ceremony coordination

RESTRICTIONS:

Alcohol: BYO
Smoking: not allowed anywhere on the premises
Music: amplified OK indoors with restrictions

Wheelchair Access: yes
Insurance: liability required

The wedding vendors on our website are the best in the business. How do we know? Read page 553.

367

Piedmont Community Hall

711 Highland Avenue, Piedmont
510/420-3081
prdrentals@ci.piedmont.ca.us

Community Park Building

● Rehearsal Dinners	● Corp. Events/Mtgs.
● Ceremonies	● Private Parties
● Wedding Receptions	Accommodations

This facility is one of the most popular event venues in Northern California—and for good reason. The building is not only very attractive inside and out, but it has the added benefit of being situated in a lovely park setting.

Azaleas and camellias provide splashes of color near the circular landscaped plaza in front of the hall. Redwoods and flowering cherry trees shade portions of the plaza, and behind the building a stream and more trees complete the circle of greenery.

The garden is home to another structure, a Japanese Tea House that was relocated here after it was donated to the City of Piedmont. Couples can have a small ceremony in the Tea House, or brides can spend some quiet time here before the wedding or use it as a private place to dress and get ready for the big event. Two side walls of the Tea House are removable, so when the weather is mild, it's a terrific spot for an extra bar or hors d'oeuvres station.

Receptions take place in the Piedmont Community Hall, a splendid structure, Mediterranean in style with light taupe walls and terracotta tile roof. The hall's interior looks so sophisticated you'd never believe this is a city-owned facility. The main event space is a great party room, with a high, beamed ceiling, shining hardwood floors and chandeliers. Floor-to-ceiling windows allow lots of natural light and ensure that the "outdoor" feeling of the adjacent park carries over to your reception. This is a refined, nicely designed space, suitable for an elegant wedding, company party or corporate retreat. It's a popular spot, so remember to reserve early.

CEREMONY CAPACITY: The site holds up to 200 seated or standing guests indoors or outdoors.

EVENT/RECEPTION & MEETING CAPACITY: The site maximum is 200 guests. The hall accommodates 200 standing or 120 seated guests. The patio area holds 200 guests.

FEES & DEPOSITS: For events on Friday, Saturday, Sunday or holidays, a $1,000 security deposit is due 2 weeks after booking and is refundable 6 weeks after the event. Payment of the rental fee is due 90 days prior to the event. Weekend rental rates range $2,750–4,250 for an 8-hour block Friday–Sunday. Piedmont residents receive a discounted rate. Additional hours are available at $200/hour. For Monday–Thursday and off-season rates, please call for specifics.

Weekday rates for business functions vary depending on the event duration; call for more details.

AVAILABILITY: Year-round, daily, 8am–midnight (1 event per day). Call early—the summer months are booked quickly.

SERVICES/AMENITIES:

Catering: BYO
Kitchen Facilities: fully equipped
Tables & Chairs: provided
Linens, Silver, etc.: BYO
Restrooms: wheelchair accessible
Dance Floor: hardwood floor
Bride's and Groom's Dressing Area: restrooms
AV/Meeting Equipment: screen, microphones, PA system

Parking: on- and off-street
Accommodations: no guest rooms
Outdoor Night Lighting: yes
Outdoor Cooking Facilities: BYO
Cleanup: caterer or renter
View: park setting

RESTRICTIONS:

Alcohol: BYO beer, wine or champagne; must have controlled bar
Smoking: not allowed
Music: amplified OK

Wheelchair Access: yes
Insurance: liability required

Rockefeller Lodge

Historic Lodge

San Pablo, address withheld to ensure privacy.

510/235-7344 Deborah & Johnathan, Event Coordinators

www.rockefellerlodge.com
www.cateringwithpartytime.com
rocklodge1@gmail.com

● Rehearsal Dinners		● Corp. Events/Mtgs.
● Ceremonies		● Private Parties
● Wedding Receptions		Accommodations

Have you always wanted to do something a bit different? Maybe have a Victorian theme in one room and French lace and balloons in another? Or perhaps treat your guests to milk and cookies baked on the spot? Whatever your fantasy, the lodge's proprietors would love the challenge of making your special event a reality.

Tucked within a quiet, treelined San Pablo neighborhood, the historic, two-acre garden lodge is named for famed industrialist John D. Rockefeller who purchased the property around the turn of the century and turned it into his private hunting lodge. The brown-shingled building and its spacious interior retain a rustic dignity, thanks to hardwood floors, hand-hewn ceiling beams and a noteworthy fireplace: Rockefeller had it constructed of burnt bricks recovered from the 1906 earthquake. These days, receptions and company parties enjoy the rooms' cozy comfort all year round.

During its illustrious past, the property had once been a Japanese Buddhist temple and the current owners, the Marshall family, have retained the retreat's fragrant, woodsy serenity. Indeed, it's the lush grounds that attract most wedding couples. Winding brick paths and wisteria-covered arbors invite leisurely strolls, and splashing fountains lull guests into relaxed contentment. Wedding ceremonies are held on a red-bricked patio, with the couple saying their vows in a gazebo framed by redwoods. A patio area can host the reception, or during warmer months why not dine in the twinkle-lit gardens beneath a moonlit sky?

With its diverse past, versatile rooms and enchanting grounds, the lodge can accommodate a wide range of creativity. As it turns out, the Marshalls also run *Party Time Catering,* so they're just the folks to help you pull it all together, no matter what you envision.

CEREMONY & EVENT/RECEPTION CAPACITY: The lodge and grounds accommodate 410 seated guests; the lodge alone holds 140 seated. The entire site holds 350 for a reception.

MEETING CAPACITY: The lodge seats up to 140 guests.

FEES & DEPOSITS: A $600 security deposit is required to secure your date, and will be refunded after your event. The facility rental fee is complimentary for a 4-hour block Monday–Friday; it's $1,500 on Saturday, $600 on Sunday (day or evening), and complimentary for a Saturday morning event 11am–3pm. A 1-hour rehearsal can be arranged on Thursday evenings for $100. For events taking place November–March, except holidays, the base rental fee is reduced by 50%. Additional time is $200/hour. August–October: Variable rental rates apply.

Buffets for over 100 guests range $17–35/person. Catering for 50 people, minimum, starts at $22/person; tax and an 18% service charge are additional. Full payment is required 14 days prior to the event. There is a $5.50/person beverage service charge which includes labor, glasses and nonalcoholic beverages and a $1.50/person dessert service fee. Any menu can be customized. Additional pricing can be found at www.cateringwithpartytime.com.

AVAILABILITY: Year-round, daily, 10am–4pm or 5pm–11pm. Available for any 6-hour block of time on Sunday.

SERVICES/AMENITIES:

Catering: in-house, no BYO
Kitchen Facilities: n/a
Tables & Chairs: provided
Linens, Silver, etc.: provided
Restrooms: wheelchair accessible
Dance Floor: yes
Bride's Dressing Area: yes
AV/Meeting Equipment: BYO

Parking: 2 lots
Accommodations: no guest rooms
Outdoor Night Lighting: yes
Outdoor Cooking Facilities: no
Cleanup: provided
View: landscaped grounds and waterfalls
Other: full event planning

RESTRICTIONS:

Alcohol: BYO, service fee required
Smoking: outside only
Music: amplified OK inside only, 4-piece band limit

Wheelchair Access: yes
Insurance: certificate required when alcohol is served
Other: no rice or birdseed

The Bridges Golf Club

Golf Club

9000 South Gale Ridge Road, San Ramon
925/735-4253 x3 Special Events
www.thebridgesgolf.com
stijero@thebridgesgolf.com

- Rehearsal Dinners
- Ceremonies
- Wedding Receptions
- Corp. Events/Mtgs.
- Private Parties
- Accommodations

Perched on a gentle rise in the foothills of Mt. Diablo, the Bridges Golf Clubhouse looks every bit the Mediterranean villa, with its tiled roof, white walls and Moorish turrets. The interior has the feel of an exclusive country club, and from almost every window the view is a vision in green: acres of velvety fairways, rolling away into the distance. The setting is so lovely, you might easily forget that this place was built primarily for golf.

When you enter the clubhouse lobby, a pair of elaborate wrought-iron gates to your left opens into a swanky bar inside one of those exotic towers you noticed out front. The magnificent double-high coved ceiling boasts a massive chandelier that would seem at home in a Medici castle! The bar adjoins the Golfer's Patio, where guests can quaff cocktails under the shade of a sycamore while surveying the players on the links.

French doors and windows make up one wall of The Bridges' main dining area, appropriately christened the "View Room." Wall sconces and an antique-style chandelier produce a romantic candelabra effect, and together with the sunlight enhance the warm glow of the room's earth tones. A crosshatch of wooden ceiling beams harmonizes with the wood trim of the richly upholstered chairs and oak tables.

A veranda runs along the greens-side of the club, accessed by both the View Room and the adjacent Fireplace Room. Used separately, these two spaces are divided by a tasteful partition of wooden shutters topped with glass cutaways; to combine the rooms for a larger event, the partition is simply folded away. The ambiance of richness and comfort in the View Room also pervades the Fireside Room, a cozy space for a rehearsal dinner. Your focus here is drawn to a grand stone hearth with a novel design: The fireplace is actually double-sided, and doors lead to a curved patio that surrounds the hearth's outdoor face. They call this the "Back Fireplace," and if there's a chill in the evening air, simply snuggle up by the hearth and behold the picturesque panorama.

The club's most dramatic room is the Garden Pavilion, just a few steps from the clubhouse. It's a grand space, with a 25-foot ceiling, antique wrought-iron chandeliers and a wall of huge archways overlooking the fairways. Guests love to step through the center arch onto the "Looking Terrace," where they have a panoramic view of the greens, Mt. Diablo and the color-streaked sky as the sun sets behind the hills. The archways have tall French doors and windows, and the facility is climate controlled for year-round comfort. When the weather is perfect, however, you are still able to open the windows and let in the afternoon breeze. Set for an elegant reception, the Pavilion is breathtaking: Tables are covered with linens, flowers and votive candles; silver and crystal sparkle in the candlelight, and the whole room is filled with a warm glow. If you'd like a more informal ambiance, however, the Pavilion's flexibility can accommodate your creativity. Some couples have brought in lion or dragon dancers for entertainment, and one even hosted a luau with hula dancers. During the holiday season, Bridges transforms the Pavilion with festive decorations, but if you have a different look in mind the club's event coordinators will be happy to help you achieve it.

The Bridges Golf Club encourages "proper etiquette and the highest standards" on the golf course. This emphasis on quality and tradition is also reflected in the clubhouse and Pavilion, so whether you host a customized golf tournament, a conference or the most sophisticated wedding reception, your event will be first class all the way.

CEREMONY CAPACITY: The outdoor ceremony site on the First Fairway holds up to 300 seated guests. Indoors, the facility seats up to 200. Ceremonies only take place at The Bridges in conjunction with a reception.

EVENT/RECEPTION CAPACITY: The clubhouse accommodates 120 seated or 150 standing guests. The Garden Pavilion holds up to 300 seated or 400 standing, and the Cocktail Reception Patio holds 300 standing.

MEETING CAPACITY: The Fireside and View Rooms, combined, hold 80 guests seated theater-style. The Garden Pavilion seats 300 guests theater-style.

FEES & DEPOSITS: A nonrefundable $2,000 deposit is required to secure your date. 50% of the food & beverage minimum is due 9 months prior to the event, and the balance is due 2 weeks prior. The room rental fee ranges $300–3,000 depending on space reserved. Packages range $59–75/person; tax, alcohol and a 20% service charge are additional. Food & beverage minijmums apply and range $750–20,000 depending on space and time rented. Specials are available for Friday and Sunday bookings.

AVAILABILITY: Year-round, daily, 7am–2am.

SERVICES/AMENITIES:

Catering: in-house, or BYO
Kitchen Facilities: fully equipped
Tables & Chairs: provided up to 300 guests
Linens, Silver, etc.: provided
Restrooms: wheelchair accessible
Dance Floor: yes
Bride's Dressing Area: CBA
AV/Meeting Equipment: CBA, extra fee

Parking: large lot
Accommodations: no guest rooms
Outdoor Night Lighting: yes
Outdoor Cooking Facilities: CBA
Cleanup: provided
View: fairways, East Bay Hills, Mt. Diablo
Other: event coordination

RESTRICTIONS:

Alcohol: in-house or BYO, corkage $14/bottle
Smoking: outside only
Music: amplified OK

Wheelchair Access: yes
Insurance: not required

The Ranch at Little Hills

Ranch

18013 Bollinger Canyon Road, San Ramon
925/837-8158
www.littlehillsweddings.com
weddings@theranchatlittlehills.com

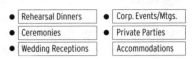

- Rehearsal Dinners
- Ceremonies
- Wedding Receptions
- Corp. Events/Mtgs.
- Private Parties
- Accommodations

Set on 25 gorgeous acres in the rolling hills of San Ramon next to the Las Trampas Regional Wilderness, The Ranch at Little Hills is a unique environment for weddings and events.

A path shaded by oaks leads to the lawn ceremony area, where you'll exchange vows on the beautiful Pergola Deck against a lush backdrop of trees. The nearby reception patio, encircled by enormous redwood and live oak trees, is especially romantic in the evening when twinkle lights add a festive glow and the stars glitter overhead.

If you prefer a more natural environment for your ceremony, you'll love the majestic oak tree site in Wildcat Canyon—it's truly tucked into the trees, which completely surround you. This spot will take your breath away, wow your guests, and make for extraordinary pictures. In fact, photo opportunities can be found at every turn throughout the grounds.

The Ranch at Little Hills provides a Bridal Suite that comes complete with a vanity and mirrors, as well as a comfy couch and chairs. There's also a Groom's Lounge with tables, a seating area, and an LED HD big screen TV (for guys who don't want to miss their favorite weekend sports event!)

All of the details of your special day will be attended to by your on-site wedding planner and coordinator, along with a courteous and professional staff. So whether you're planning a grand affair or an intimate celebration, The Ranch at Little Hills is the perfect place to start your happily ever after.

CEREMONY, EVENT/RECEPTION & MEETING CAPACITY: The facility holds 250 seated or standing guests outdoors.

FEES & DEPOSITS: The site rental fee, which starts at $3,995, is required to reserve your date, and the food & beverage balance is due 2 weeks prior to the event. Catering packages range $34–49/person and beverage packages range $15–20/person.

AVAILABILITY: April–November, flexible hours.

SERVICES/AMENITIES:

Catering: in-house
Kitchen Facilities: n/a
Tables & Chairs: provided
Linens, Silver, etc.: provided
Restrooms: wheelchair accessible
Dance Area: provided
Bride's Dressing Area: yes
AV/Meeting Equipment: CBA, extra fee may apply

Parking: large lot
Accommodations: no guest rooms
Outdoor Night Lighting: yes
Outdoor Cooking Facilities: BBQ on site
Cleanup: provided
View: canyon, hills, landscaped grounds
Other: picnic area, event coordination

RESTRICTIONS:

Alcohol: in-house
Smoking: designated areas only
Music: amplified OK outdoors with restrictions

Wheelchair Access: yes
Insurance: not required

Want to find more venues and services? Check out our informative website, www.HereComesTheGuide.com.

Wedgewood San Ramon

Event Center at Golf Club

9430 Fircrest Lane, San Ramon
866/966-3009
www.wedgewoodbanquet.com
events@wedgewoodbanquet.com

Rehearsal Dinners	● Corp. Events/Mtgs.
● Ceremonies	● Private Parties
● Wedding Receptions	Accommodations

At Wedgewood San Ramon, romantic settings are as much a part of the landscape as the surrounding foothills and pristine fairways of the adjacent golf course. An expansive lawn boasts a quaint white wedding gazebo, and a nearby lake with a rippling waterfall is graced by a 50-year-old weeping willow. On a sunny day, the majestic tree casts a cooling shadow across the guests as they await the bride's grand entrance. She and her attendants, meanwhile, have been preparing in front of floor-to-ceiling mirrors inside what the facility calls "the largest bridal dressing room in Contra Costa County." When the bride is ready, she waits in the banquet room for her cue and then steps through the French doors to follow the curving path down the aisle to her groom.

While the wedding party poses for photos against the venue's scenic backdrops, guests savor the picturesque outdoors on the patio during the cocktail hour. They can relax at umbrella-shaded tables or stroll along the lakeshore to watch the swans, herons, turtles and other wildlife. When it's time for the reception, everyone moves indoors to the Wedgewood Room, brightened by a bank of tinted windows that afford complete privacy while allowing everyone to enjoy the magnificent view out to the lake and golf greens. Recessed lighting, a gleaming dance floor, and a sunken bar create a sleek, contemporary vibe.

Wedgewood's helpful event planners have a reputation for delivering both value and personal service. Their all-inclusive wedding packages are fully customizable, and you can streamline your planning process by opting to include a DJ, cake, flowers, invitations and more. Wedgewood San Ramon also offers access to an 18-hole public golf course, plenty of parking, and an entire building reserved just for your event. Wedgewood has over 25 years of wedding-planning experience, and you can count on their expertise to make your celebration one you'll always remember.

CEREMONY CAPACITY: Outdoors, the lawn area holds 350 seated guests. Indoors, the Wedgewood Room seats 350.

EVENT/RECEPTION CAPACITY: The Wedgewood Room holds 350 guests for a seated or standing reception.

MEETING CAPACITY: Several spaces accommodate 50–350 seated guests.

FEES & DEPOSITS: 25% of the estimated total event cost is required to reserve your date. An additional 25% is due 120 days prior to the event and the balance (based on your final guest count) is due 10 days prior. All payments are credited towards your final balance and are nonrefundable and nontransferable. All-inclusive, completely customizable wedding packages start at $46/person. Tax, alcohol and a 21–22% service charge are additional.

AVAILABILITY: Year-round, daily, 6am–midnight.

SERVICES/AMENITIES:

Catering: in-house
Kitchen Facilities: n/a
Tables & Chairs: provided
Linens, Silver, etc.: provided
Restrooms: wheelchair accessible
Dance Floor: yes
Bride's Dressing Area: yes
AV/Meeting Equipment: some provided

Parking: ample lot
Accommodations: no guest rooms
Outdoor Night Lighting: yes
Outdoor Cooking Facilities: no
Cleanup: provided
View: lake, hills, fairways, waterfall, swans and ducks
Other: event coordination, in-house wedding cake and florals, clergy on staff

RESTRICTIONS:

Alcohol: in-house
Smoking: outside only
Music: amplified OK

Wheelchair Access: yes
Insurance: not required
Other: no rice, confetti or glitter; no open flames

Civic Park Community Center

1375 Civic Drive, Walnut Creek
925/256-3575
www.walnut-creek.org/rentals
rentals@walnut-creek.org

Community Center

● Rehearsal Dinners	● Corp. Events/Mtgs.	
● Ceremonies	● Private Parties	
● Wedding Receptions	Accommodations	

Romance is in the air at Civic Park Community Center. It blossoms in the rose gardens and flutters about the shade trees growing in this tranquil urban hideaway. It also resides in the Center's wedding gazebo, an inspiration not only for ceremonies, but for marriage proposals as well. Recently, a young man was so taken with the pretty structure he hung twinkle lights around it and hired a caterer to serve dinner for two beneath its canopy. Then, after he and his girlfriend toasted their love for each other with glasses of sparkling cider, he popped the question—and she accepted!

Located at the edge of Walnut Creek's busy downtown, the park and buildings that make up the community center feel surprisingly secluded. Mature sycamores and redwoods help screen out the sights and sounds of passing traffic. In many places the trees are so tall and thick you can barely see their tops. As you walk beneath their wide boughs or perhaps picnic on the lawn in their long, cool shadows, you have the pleasant impression you've stepped through the looking glass into the countryside.

Weddings have become so popular here they often have to be scheduled a year in advance. Along with the ceremony and reception sites, you can also reserve the center's Social Hall or Conference Room for a casual rehearsal dinner. These two small, unadorned rooms in the main building can be decorated in any style that suits you, and the Social Hall opens to a large commercial kitchen available for your use. On the day of the wedding, the carpeted lounge in the back of the building can be rented as a changing room for the bridal party. A big plus for many brides is the fact that all of the important wedding areas are just steps apart, making the transition from the changing room to the ceremony in the gazebo to the reception in the Assembly Hall easy and convenient.

Another plus is the simple architecture of the spacious Assembly Hall. The building's uncomplicated interior is a blank canvas awaiting your personal vision, and the neutral tones of the well-lit room blend easily with almost any décor. The six-foot banquet tables and metal-and-resin chairs provided by the center can be set up in any arrangement you choose. Many couples like to dress them up by renting special chair covers, tablecloths and table settings. A full Bose sound system, with speakers on all the overhead trestle beams, will have your guests swaying to the music wherever you place the dance floor.

With the exception of tacks, staples or nails in the wall, the transformation of the Assembly Hall is only limited by your imagination. One bride and groom expanded their reception outside the building by opening the room's 10-foot sliding glass door that leads to a small patio and the park beyond.

However you celebrate at the center, you'll love the flexibility of the spaces, and the park setting is sure to provide a beautiful backdrop.

CEREMONY, EVENT/RECEPTION & MEETING CAPACITY: Various indoor areas hold up to 250 seated banquet-style or 250 theater-style. Smaller events can also be accommodated. The gazebo and park area holds up to 300 guests seated or standing. (Chairs are not provided outdoors.)

FEES & DEPOSITS: A nonrefundable $500 deposit is required to reserve your date. The balance and security deposit are due in full 90 days prior to your event. The rental fee ranges $50–170/hour depending on the day and room rented. An additional $75 fee is charged if alcohol is served (indoors only).

AVAILABILITY: Year-round. Monday–Thursday, 8am–10pm; Friday and Saturday, 8am–1am; Sunday, 8am–midnight.

Weekend reservations may be made up to 1 year in advance. Weekday evenings may be scheduled on a limited basis depending on availability. Rental hours must include setup and cleanup time.

SERVICES/AMENITIES:
Catering: BYO
Kitchen Facilities: large commercial kitchen
Tables & Chairs: provided for indoor use
Linens, Silver, etc.: BYO or through caterer
Restrooms: wheelchair accessible
Dance Floor: yes
Bride's & Groom's Dressing Areas: may be available, extra fee
AV/Meeting Equipment: BYO

Parking: limited on site
Accommodations: no guest rooms
Outdoor Night Lighting: yes
Outdoor Cooking Facilities: BYO BBQ
Cleanup: caterer or renter
View: park, garden, landscaped grounds
Other: WiFi available (except Assembly Hall)

RESTRICTIONS:
Alcohol: BYO wine and beer only, permits required; not allowed at youth events
Smoking: outside parking areas only
Music: amplified OK indoors only

Wheelchair Access: yes
Insurance: may be required
Other: no birdseed, confetti, rice, rose petals, aerosol streamers, hay, sand or glitter; security required at all youth events

The Clubhouse at Boundary Oak

Banquet & Event Facility

3800 Valley Vista Road, Walnut Creek
925/934-3600 X21

www.playboundaryoak.com/weddings-events
kcolomb@playboundaryoak.com

- Rehearsal Dinners
- Ceremonies
- Wedding Receptions
- Corp. Events/Mtgs.
- Private Parties
- Accommodations

Nature abounds at this premier Walnut Creek venue, known for its wonderful views. Sitting on acres of manicured greens, it's bordered by open space and ringed by an extensive network of rustic, ridgeline trails.

The Clubhouse at Boundary Oak, named for a particularly majestic and artfully gnarled 350-year-old tree on the grounds, is just moments from town yet feels worlds away. From its hill-top perch it offers a front row seat to the location's expansive vistas.

Perhaps the best way to start off your momentous day in this city/country setting is to opt for an outdoor ceremony at one of two terrific sites. For peaceful panoramas that include the surrounding fairways, a towering stand of eucalyptus trees and a glimpse of Concord in the distance, exchange vows at the Lakeview Ceremony Site, set on a knoll beside the 9th-hole water feature and its impressive center fountain. If you prefer a more intimate alternative, get married on the Patio, which overlooks the putting green with the lake and fountain in the background.

You may be tempted to enjoy hors d'oeuvres and a glass of bubbly al fresco as well, but there are also several inviting spots inside the clubhouse. For example, the multilevel Mira Room adjoining the Patio has a long bar, wooden floors and great sunset views. Then, when you're ready for dinner, just step through the arched entryway into the Vista Room. This architecturally interesting space is cantilevered above the walkway below with three walls of windows that angle outwards, making the outdoors feel like part of the room. A pyramid-style ceiling completes the whole "mid-century modernist" feel.

If, however, your dream reception (or the size of your guest list) calls for something larger, take a short stroll through the Main Entrance Foyer—which doubles as a gallery displaying works by local artists—and start your festivities in the Atrium. In this bright space, anchored by a large permanent bar and rows of slanted skylights running the length of the ceiling, friends and family can mingle over cocktails. At dinnertime, three sets of double doors open to reveal the beautifully decorated Celebration Ballroom, which easily hosts 250 for dinner and dancing.

Before the day is over, the bride and groom may also want to have their photographer snap a picture of them standing beneath the spreading branches of the great oak. They'll have a classic photo that's not only representative of this lovely venue, but will provide a memorable addition to their wedding album.

CEREMONY CAPACITY: The venue accommodates 250 seated indoors or outdoors.

EVENT/RECEPTION CAPACITY: The clubhouse holds 250 seated or 400 standing.

MEETING CAPACITY: Meeting rooms seat 250 guests.

FEES & DEPOSITS: 25% of the estimated event total is required to confirm your date. The event balance and final guest count are due 14 days prior to the event. All events must meet a food & beverage minimum that varies depending on the date and time booked. Flexible wedding packages start at $48/person. Tax, alcohol and service charge are additional.

AVAILABILITY: Year-round, daily.

SERVICES/AMENITIES:

Catering: in-house
Kitchen Facilities: n/a
Tables & Chairs: provided
Linens, Silver, etc.: provided
Restrooms: wheelchair accessible
Dance Floor: yes
Bride's Dressing Area: yes
AV/Meeting Equipment: CBA

Parking: large lot
Accommodations: nearby partner hotels
Outdoor Night Lighting: access only
Outdoor Cooking Facilities: BBQ CBA
Cleanup: provided
View: garden, landscaped grounds, fountain, fairways, hills, lagoon, lake, mountains, valley

RESTRICTIONS:

Alcohol: in-house
Smoking: outdoors only
Music: amplified OK indoors with restrictions

Wheelchair Access: yes
Insurance: may be required

The Gardens at Heather Farm

1540 Marchbanks Drive, Walnut Creek
925/947-1678
www.gardenshf.org
rentals@gardenshf.org

Gardens and Education Center

●	Rehearsal Dinners	●	Corp. Events/Mtgs.
●	Ceremonies	●	Private Parties
●	Wedding Receptions		Accommodations

Natural. Beautiful. Versatile. The Gardens at Heather Farm spreads out over six landscaped acres full of colorful flowerbeds, herb and rock gardens and water features, and offers a variety of distinctive indoor and outdoor event spaces. Not surprisingly, it's one of the East Bay's most sought-after venues for weddings, parties, meetings, seminars, and other special occasions.

For a truly romantic ceremony, exchange vows at the Gazebo, designed with a unique, slate-tile roof and enhanced by climbing roses. The setting here is absolutely picture-perfect: The adjacent garden blooms continuously from spring through fall with thousands of vibrant roses that perfume the air, and the neighboring lake and fountains sparkle in the background.

Another option for saying "I do"—as well as hosting an al fresco reception, cocktail hour or luncheon—is the Meadow Lawn. This open, grass area is surrounded by Rugosa roses, pine trees and low shrubs and affords a lovely panoramic vista of the entire garden.

Cocktail hours and small receptions also take place at the Patio & Pavilion, a large terraced area bordered by a raised garden brimming with flowers and herbaceous plants. Custom-made for enjoying the outdoors, it comes with a caterer-friendly bar and granite-topped counter for serving appetizers and drinks, and a patio that accommodates table seating or dancing.

Indoor receptions are held in the bright and airy Camellia Room, featuring a beamed ceiling, hardwood floors (ideal for dancing) and large windows that bathe the room in natural light. You can personalize the space with decorative lights, draperies, lanterns or flowers ... or simply appreciate the gorgeous garden views. There's an adjacent bridal dressing room, plus a spacious wraparound deck that lets guests soak up the scenery and can also be used for food & beverage service.

These lush gardens will stimulate all your senses, and when you have your event here you get the added bonus of supporting a nonprofit public garden and nature education center.

CEREMONY CAPACITY: The site holds 150 seated guests indoors or outdoors.

EVENT/RECEPTION & MEETING CAPACITY: The facility accommodates 150 seated guests for dining. They offer customized floor plans that include dining, dancing and auditorium styles as well as standing formats for cocktail receptions, special events or company mixers. Some larger groups may be accommodated with custom floor plans utilizing their outdoor areas and wraparound deck.

FEES & DEPOSITS: A nonrefundable deposit of 50% of the rental fee is required to reserve your date; an $800 security deposit and the balance of the rental fee are due 6 months prior to the event. The weekday rental fee, Monday–Thursday, ranges $150–200/hour with a 4-hour minimum (off-peak season) or 6-hour minimum (peak season). The rental fee Friday–Sunday and holidays ranges $1,800–4,200 depending on the space rented and time of year. A garden ceremony setup on its own is $800. Extra hours are available for an additional fee, extra setup fees may apply.

AVAILABILITY: Year-round, daily. Sunday–Thursday, 9am–10pm; Friday–Saturday, 9am–midnight.

SERVICES/AMENITIES:

Catering: select from list

Kitchen Facilities: moderately equipped

Tables & Chairs: provided, including chairs for a ceremony

Linens, Silver, etc.: BYO

Restrooms: wheelchair accessible

Dance Floor: yes

Bride's Dressing Area: yes

AV/Meeting Equipment: podium, projection screen

Parking: complimentary lot and on-street

Accommodations: no guest rooms

Outdoor Night Lighting: yes, on deck and patio

Outdoor Cooking Facilities: BYO BBQ

Cleanup: caterer or renter

View: gardens, Mt. Diablo and pond

RESTRICTIONS:

Alcohol: BYO

Smoking: not allowed

Music: amplified OK indoors only

Wheelchair Access: yes

Insurance: proof of liability insurance required

Other: no confetti, rice, birdseed, flower petals, sparklers, or balloon releases

This is important! Tell locations you're reading HERE COMES THE GUIDE and ask if our information is still current.

383

Heather Farm Community Center

Community Center

301 North San Carlos Drive, Walnut Creek
925/256-3575
www.walnut-creek.org/rentals
rentals@walnut-creek.org

● Rehearsal Dinners ● Corp. Events/Mtgs.
● Ceremonies ● Private Parties
● Wedding Receptions ☐ Accommodations

Clark Gable was on the brink of becoming a major movie star when he came to Heather Farm in 1931 to make the motion picture *Sporting Blood*. Of course that was during the park's former life as a horse ranch and racetrack. The actor was so taken with the place he stabled his thoroughbreds there. Today Heather Farm shows little evidence of its equestrian past, but it retains a country-like atmosphere that draws visitors from all around the East Bay.

Tucked behind a hill on the outskirts of Walnut Creek, the 102-acre park is an oasis of shade trees, green grass and flower gardens. Meandering paths connect the picnic and nature areas with the swim center, tennis courts and athletic fields. With groves of trees and meadows separating the facilities from one another, it's almost as if each site is a park unto itself. And nestled in one of the most picturesque of these spots is Heather Farm Community Center.

Wedding receptions at the center are held in the Lakeside Room overlooking a large pond. One of our favorite features of this venue is its wraparound deck, which extends over the water. Guests who stroll out here are treated to an unobstructed view of ducks and geese swimming between the two large fountains that aerate the man-made lagoon. On the opposite shore, sycamores, oaks and pepper trees shade the extensive lawns and create a protective screen around the center. Some couples are so charmed by the scenery they hold their wedding ceremony on the deck followed by the reception inside.

The pond and fountains are also visible from the Lakeside Room through the wide windows along two walls. This spacious venue is enhanced by a coffered ceiling, and warmed by the fireplace nook, where friends and family can gather to toast the bride and groom. Pretty and unpretentious, the room requires very little decorating for those who want to keep their reception simple. Banquet and round tables, along with folding chairs, are provided with the reservation—the atmosphere, be it casual or elegant, is totally up to you.

And you won't have to worry about keeping your reception private in the middle of a park. Tall bushes and trees mask the entrance to the Lakeside Room from the rest of the park and the community center is closed to the public while you celebrate the day or night away.

CEREMONY CAPACITY: The Deck accommodates up to 100 guests; the Lakeside Room holds up to 200.

EVENT/RECEPTION & MEETING CAPACITY: The Lakeside Room accommodates 200 guests.

FEES & DEPOSITS: A nonrefundable $500 deposit is required to reserve your date. The balance and security deposit are due in full 90 days prior to your event. The rental fee ranges $50–170/hour depending on the room, day and time rented. An additional $75 fee is charged if alcohol is served.

AVAILABILITY: Year-round. Monday–Thursday, 8am–10pm; Friday and Saturday, 8am–1am; Sunday, 8am–midnight.

Weekend reservations may be made up to 1 year in advance. Weekday evenings may be scheduled on a limited basis depending on availability. Rental hours must include setup and cleanup time.

SERVICES/AMENITIES:

Catering: BYO

Kitchen Facilities: moderately equipped

Tables & Chairs: provided

Linens, Silver: BYO, or through caterer

Restrooms: wheelchair accessible

Dance Floor: yes

Bride's Dressing Area: may be available, extra fee

AV/Meeting Equipment: some provided, extra fee

Parking: ample on site

Accommodations: no guest rooms

Outdoor Night Lighting: yes

Outdoor Cooking Facilities: BYO BBQ

Cleanup: caterer or renter

View: pond, trees, garden, park, fountains

Other: WiFi available

RESTRICTIONS:

Alcohol: BYO wine and beer only, permits required; not allowed at youth events

Smoking: outside parking areas only

Music: amplified OK, indoors only

Wheelchair Access: yes

Insurance: may be required

Other: no confetti, rice, birdseed, rose petals, aerosol streamers, hay, sand or glitter; security required at all youth events; fountains cannot be guaranteed to function at all times

Shadelands Arts Center

Arts and Education Center

111 North Wiget Lane, Walnut Creek

925/256-3575

www.walnut-creek.org/rentals
rentals@walnut-creek.org

- Rehearsal Dinners
- Ceremonies
- Wedding Receptions
- Corp. Events/Mtgs.
- Private Parties
- Accommodations

There are quite a few reasons why Shadelands Arts Center has become a local favorite. Not only is it a great value for those looking for an affordable event venue, it's also one of the largest facilities in the East Bay (accommodating up to 300!) where you can bring the caterer of your choice.

Another plus is the building itself, which is easy to work with thanks to its neutral décor. The white interior is amenable to virtually any kind of decorating, and the high, open-beamed ceiling—often draped for weddings—gives the space a lofty feeling.

State-of-the-art sound and lighting systems (and an AV staff person on site during your event) enable you to create whatever ambiance you like. Whether you're having a live band or planning to listen to your own playlist through your iPod, the music will sound great because the room was designed for music or theater performances and the acoustics are excellent. You can also entertain your guests with a slideshow or video on the large projection screen. Use lighting in a variety of colors to create a particular mood or to highlight the ceiling or dance floor. Add to all these features a gleaming hardwood floor and a full catering kitchen and you have an event site that will satisfy all your needs.

Shadelands is perfectly suited for large weddings, because the entire event can be held in the main hall. If you require more space, the hall opens onto an enclosed patio that can be used for a ceremony, cocktail party or additional reception seating. It works well as a place for supervised activities for children, too.

For corporate functions, Shadelands supplies most of the equipment required for presentations: an LCD projector (extra fee), large projection screen, sound and lighting equipment—and complimentary WiFi.

The venue is also popular for fundraisers, as it provides different rooms for a silent auction and banking.

The center's staff are very accommodating, going out of their way to help you create the event you want while staying within your budget. And access to the fully equipped professional kitchen—with the option of bringing in your own caterer—are real benefits for couples planning a casual wedding or rehearsal dinner.

With its flexibility, ample parking and reasonable prices, Shadelands Arts Center is in demand. Its convenient location is also appreciated by guests coming from all over the Bay Area. If you want to host a wedding, private party or corporate event that's very much your own, this is definitely a location to consider.

CEREMONY CAPACITY: The Banquet Room holds 300 seated guests.

EVENT/RECEPTION CAPACITY: The Banquet Room can accommodate 300 seated at round tables.

MEETING CAPACITY: The Banquet Room seats 300 theater-style or 150 conference-style.

FEES & DEPOSITS: A nonrefundable $500 deposit is required to secure your date, and the balance and security deposit are due 90 days prior to the function. An additional $75 fee is charged if alcohol is served. The rental fee ranges $70–195/hour depending on the time frame of the event.

AVAILABILITY: Year-round: Monday–Thursday, 8am–10pm; Friday and Saturday, 8am–1am; Sunday, 8am–midnight. Rental hours must include setup and cleanup time. The venue may be booked up to 1 year in advance.

SERVICES/AMENITIES:

Catering: BYO
Kitchen Facilities: large, commercial
Tables & Chairs: provided
Linens, Silver, etc.: BYO or caterer
Restrooms: wheelchair accessible
Dance Floor: yes
Bride's & Groom's Dressing Areas: may be available, extra fee
AV/Meeting Equipment: full range, extra fee

Parking: ample on site
Accommodations: no guest rooms
Outdoor Night Lighting: yes
Outdoor Cooking Facilities: BYO BBQ
Cleanup: renter or caterer
View: landscaped grounds
Other: WiFi available

RESTRICTIONS:

Alcohol: BYO beer and wine only, permits required; not allowed at youth events
Smoking: outside parking areas only
Music: amplified OK, indoors only

Wheelchair Access: yes
Insurance: may be required
Other: security required at all youth events; no rice, birdseed, confetti, glitter, hay, sand, rose petals or aerosol streamers

Shadelands Ranch Museum

Museum

2660 Ygnacio Valley Road, Walnut Creek
925/935-7871
www.wchistory.com
wcshadelands@sbcglobal.net

Rehearsal Dinners	● Corp. Events/Mtgs.
● Ceremonies	● Private Parties
● Wedding Receptions	Accommodations

Stately shade trees tower above the lawn, gardens and terrace surrounding the former Penniman home at Shadelands Ranch Museum. From its curved glass bay windows to its classical white columns and wraparound veranda, the 1903 Colonial Revival house reflects the refinement and elegance of a bygone era when the handsome two-story home was the heart of a large fruit ranch in the Ygnacio Valley.

Today, Shadelands is lovingly maintained by the Walnut Creek Historical Society and the City of Walnut Creek. Citrus, pomegranate, walnut and quince still grow among the sycamores and redwoods shading the aptly named property. The fruit trees, along with the herb and vegetable gardens planted on the site, also serve as a reminder of Shadelands' rural past. While strolling the paths leading toward the patio and garden at the back of the house, it's easy to imagine the gracious hospitality that was once extended to guests of the ranch over 100 years ago. These days, events at Shadelands are held outdoors with the carefully restored house providing a charming backdrop.

On the expansive lawn at the back of the house, couples exchange vows in a gazebo encircled by roses. The garden setting is lovely on its own, or can be easily decorated to suit your taste. A spacious barked area along the side of the house is shaded by huge oak trees and outfitted with picnic tables, offering a venue with a more rustic feel. For an evening wedding, tiny lights can be woven through the trees, adding an enchanting ambiance to the occasion.

After the ceremony, the celebration continues on the adjoining patio. The terrace is large enough to accommodate tables for the reception and a DJ. Or, in keeping with the turn-of-the-(last)-century atmosphere, you might want to hire a band to play in the gazebo and have your guests dance on the patio.

Access to the inside of the house is limited to the kitchen, which is available as a bridal changing room or as a preparation site for the caterer. As committed as Shadelands is to keeping the ranch authentic to its early 20th-century style, the "old-fashioned" kitchen comes with a new gas range masquerading as a black wood-burning stove and a refrigerator camouflaged with wood paneling. Modern restrooms are adjacent to the new barn, just behind the circa 1902 water tank house and worker's cabin that border the garden.

Of the many reasons to hold your wedding and reception at the nonprofit Shadelands Ranch Museum, the most satisfying may be that the money you spend here goes toward preserving the history of Walnut Creek for future generations. Of course, at the same time, you and your betrothed will be making a little history of your own.

CEREMONY CAPACITY: The lawn area holds 250 seated guests.

EVENT/RECEPTION CAPACITY: The lawn area accommodates 250 seated or 400 standing guests.

MEETING CAPACITY: The location holds up to 250 seated guests for outdoor parties and meetings.

FEES & DEPOSITS: A $300 deposit and signed contract are required to secure your date, and the deposit is applied toward the rental fee. An additional refundable $500 damage deposit is also required. Payment in full of all fees is due 30 days before your event. The rental fee is $350/hour with a 3-hour minimum. There is a $200 setup/takedown and custodial fee, and a $100 fee for use of the kitchen (optional). 150 chairs and 30 tables are included with the rental fee; additional are available at $2 each.

AVAILABILITY: April–October.

SERVICES/AMENITIES:

Catering: BYO
Kitchen Facilities: fully equipped
Tables & Chairs: up to 150 chairs and 30 tables provided
Linens, Silver, etc.: BYO or caterer
Restrooms: wheelchair accessible
Dance Floor: patio available
Bride's Dressing Area: yes, in kitchen
AV/Meeting Equipment: tables and chairs

Parking: ample
Accommodations: no guest rooms
Outdoor Night Lighting: yes
Outdoor Cooking Facilities: BYO or caterer
Cleanup: renter or caterer, trash cans provided
View: landscaped grounds, garden, gazebo

RESTRICTIONS:

Alcohol: BYO, beer and wine only
Smoking: outside only
Music: amplified OK with volume limits, no amplifiers after 11pm

Wheelchair Access: yes
Insurance: proof of liability insurance required
Other: no rice, birdseed, confetti or nails

Solano County

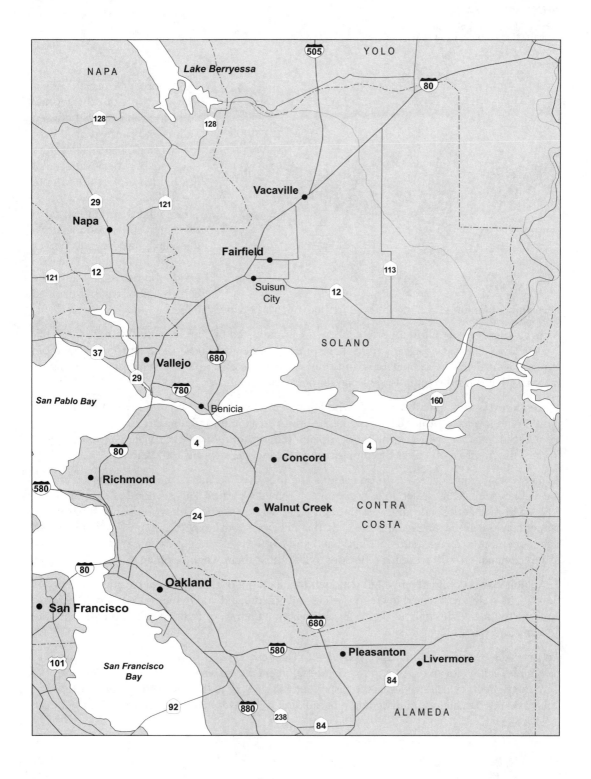

Hiddenbrooke Golf Club

Golf Club

1095 Hiddenbrooke Parkway, Solano County
707/558-0330 x206
www.hiddenbrookegolf.com
tsalvato@hiddenbrookegolf.com

- Rehearsal Dinners
- Ceremonies
- Wedding Receptions
- Corp. Events/Mtgs.
- Private Parties
- Accommodations

Most people who take the American Canyon exit off Interstate 80 in the rolling hills between Vallejo and Fairfield head west toward Napa. Few ever venture into the beautiful valley that lies hidden east of the turnoff, just half a mile over a ridge. Those who do find themselves on a graceful two-mile drive that dips, sweeps and curves through rolling hills down to Hiddenbrooke Golf Club, the centerpiece of a master-planned development minutes from the freeway in time, but a world away in feel.

Arriving guests are let off in a porte-cochère area dominated by four massive flagstone-faced pillars. A flower-lined arcade leads from there directly to the clubhouse banquet room. This room is posh, with high-quality materials and finishes that make it a perfect venue for weddings or meetings that run from semi- to pull-out-all-the-stops-formal.

The entrance is through tall twin dark wood doors, inset with top-to-bottom rows of square glass panels. The foyer's floor is a gleaming expanse of marble tiles, culminating in a floor-to-ceiling stone-faced fireplace, with a window occupying the top third of its back wall. Guests can sit in front of the fireplace and peer through the window at golfers on the 18th hole.

A glossy baby grand piano sits to one side of the fireplace and marks the entrance to an area of the clubhouse that can be set up to accommodate smaller parties. This section has several dining tables and looks out south and west through large windows. The dark-wood-paneled bar in the corner conveys an inviting feeling—exactly the ambiance you'd expect at a fine golf club. French doors open out to a large, sun-splashed patio and bar terrace. These areas are often available for use in conjunction with weddings. Be sure to ask about them when booking.

The clubhouse is dominated by high windows that look out over the golf course and to the ridges beyond. Its walls are finished in creamy white and accentuated with white wainscoting. There are large potted plants throughout the room, and warm paintings of farmlands and buildings evoke Tuscany and Napa.

An on-site wedding sales manager provides full, four-star service, from catering and menus to recommendations for transportation and entertainment. Ceremonies take place outdoors on the Ceremony Green, which overlooks the lush green hillsides, or in the enclosed Pavilion. A separate conference or banquet room in an adjacent building is ideal for business meetings and weddings.

Hiddenbrooke is an elegant refuge, the kind of place that inspires visitors to think they have stumbled onto some wonderful secret, and later to realize that for a few precious hours they were happily taken away from the cares and worries of the world.

CEREMONY CAPACITY: The Pavilion and recently renovated Ceremony Site each hold up to 250 guests.

EVENT/RECEPTION & MEETING CAPACITY: The Clubhouse seats 80 guests, the Brookside Room 50, and the Pavilion 250. For meetings, the Boardroom seats 16 guests conference-style.

FEES & DEPOSITS: A $1,000 deposit is required to reserve your date. Inclusive packages start at $50/person. Tax, alcohol and service charge are additional.

AVAILABILITY: Year-round, daily; 7am–10pm Sunday through Friday, til 11pm on Saturday.

SERVICES/AMENITIES:

Catering: in-house, no BYO
Kitchen Facilities: n/a
Tables & Chairs: provided
Linens, Silver, etc.: provided
Restrooms: wheelchair accessible
Dance Floor: no
Bride's Dressing Area: yes
AV/Meeting Equipment: CBA, extra charge

Parking: large lot
Accommodations: no guest rooms
Outdoor Night Lighting: CBA, extra charge
Outdoor Cooking Facilities: n/a
Cleanup: provided
View: 18-hole golf course
Other: event planning, baby grand player piano, golf tournaments

RESTRICTIONS:

Alcohol: in-house, or BYO wine with corkage fee
Smoking: outside only
Music: call for details

Wheelchair Access: yes
Insurance: not required
Other: no rice, confetti or birdseed

Overwhelmed? Use the search criteria on www.HereComesTheGuide.com to narrow down your choices.

Sacramento, Central Valley and Chico

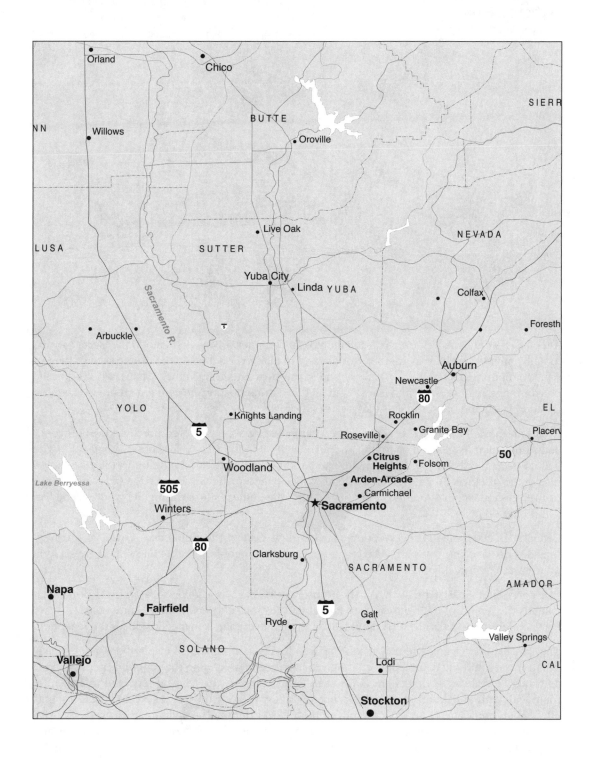

Granite Bay Golf Club

Golf Club

9600 Golf Club Drive, Granite Bay
916/791-7578 x110

www.granitebayclub.com
kelle.collier@clubcorp.com

- Rehearsal Dinners
- Ceremonies
- Wedding Receptions
- Corp. Events/Mtgs.
- Private Parties
- Accommodations

Although it's only a half hour from Sacramento, this premier private golf club in the Sierra Nevada foothills might as well be in another world—and in many ways it is. As the centerpiece of the up-scale community of Granite Bay, it's a serene haven surrounded by luxury estates, woods, granite outcroppings, mature oaks, and lakes. With all this natural beauty, the club is a fabulous venue for a wedding, but the big surprise is that it's also affordable.

Events are hosted in the classically designed clubhouse, where a covered porch and white wood-and-stone columns give it a charming, old-fashioned feel. The view from here is spectacular: The golf course spreads out below, encircling a sparkling lake and continuing on to the tree-dotted hills in the distance. To the right, a cart path winds over a rustic wooden bridge (a favorite photo op) and disappears into the trees. And then there's the endless sky, covering the whole scene like a vast blue dome.

Ceremonies take place in the Wedding Garden right next to the clubhouse. A wall of greenery provides privacy, and vows are exchanged beneath a wrought-iron arch while seated guests look on from the impeccably manicured lawn.

The party starts just steps away on the Conservatory Patio, the expansive covered porch that extends the length of the Conservatory and is the best place to enjoy the picture-postcard view. Post-ceremony cocktails are served out here, and then everyone is invited inside for the reception.

The Conservatory is an extremely flexible space, thanks to a number of inspired design elements. White trusses and ductwork support a high, peaked ceiling, lending the room an industrial-chic ambiance. Overhead skylights are covered by shade screens that can be retracted to flood the room with natural light during the day, while bistro lights along the trusses create a "starry night" effect after sundown. Dimmers control the mood, and draping or uplighting can be added for a more dramatic atmosphere. Want to show a photomontage or video? A built-in projector and dropdown screen are at your fingertips.

Three smaller rooms are used in a variety of ways. The wood-lined Library, highlighted by a floor-to-ceiling stone fireplace and a baby grand piano that plays itself, is perfect for a cozy ceremony or rehearsal dinner. The two Colt Rooms (and patio) can be combined for an indoor ceremony, and Colt Room I frequently serves as a lovely bridal changing room, complete with fireplace, wood paneling, and bookshelves. Each of these spaces takes on a romantic glow when lit by dozens of candles.

Making it all come together is the club's exceptional Private Event Director, Kelle Collier. She oversees everything from your first meeting to the end of your celebration, and will do whatever she can to bring your vision to life. She'll even personally accompany you and your photographer on a golf cart ride around the property to show you the most photogenic spots to pose for pix!

As ecstatic couples have raved, "If you want to impress your guests, then this is the place for you!" ... "The beauty and the staff are incredible and the food here is TOPNOTCH" ... "Our experience was amazing!"

CEREMONY CAPACITY: The facility seats 100 indoors and 240 outdoors, theater-style.

EVENT/RECEPTION CAPACITY: The club accommodates 240 guests seated banquet-style or 300 standing indoors, and 70 seated banquet-style or 240 standing outdoors.

MEETING CAPACITY: Meeting spaces hold up to 240 seated banquet-style.

FEES & DEPOSITS: A deposit is required to reserve your date. The rental fee ranges $150–1,500 depending on the day of the week and room selected. Buffets start at $26/person for lunch or $30/person for dinner, and plated meals start at $24/person for lunch or $30/person for dinner. Tax, alcohol, and a service charge are additional. Hosted bar packages and no-host bars are available.

AVAILABILITY: Year-around, Tuesday–Sunday. Closed Mondays.

SERVICES/AMENITIES:
Catering: in-house
Kitchen Facilities: n/a
Tables & Chairs: provided
Linens, Silver, etc.: provided
Restrooms: wheelchair accessible
Dance Floor: provided
Bride's Dressing Area: yes
AV/Meeting Equipment: provided

Parking: large lot
Accommodations: no guest rooms
Outdoor Night Lighting: yes
Outdoor Cooking Facilities: no
Cleanup: provided
View: fountain, garden, hills, landscaped grounds, meadow; panorama of fairways and lake
Other: event coordination

RESTRICTIONS:
Alcohol: in-house
Smoking: outdoors only
Music: amplified OK

Wheelchair Access: yes
Insurance: not required

DoubleTree By Hilton Sacramento

Hotel

2001 Point West Way, Sacramento
916/924-4900

www.doubletreesacramento.com
rlsa_ds@hilton.com

● Rehearsal Dinners	● Corp. Events/Mtgs.
● Ceremonies	● Private Parties
● Wedding Receptions	● Accommodations

Fresh-baked chocolate chip cookies offer a warm welcome when you check in at the DoubleTree by Hilton Sacramento, but it's the friendly staff and newly renovated ballrooms that truly make this venue an excellent choice for a destination wedding or special event.

The hotel can accommodate almost any size group or function: Each of its three ballrooms has a unique style, as well as its own entrance, foyer and convenient parking for easy access.

If you're planning an outdoor wedding ceremony, the Capital Patio is an ideal spot. Adjoining the Capital Ballroom, it's bordered by a gentle creek and overlooks a lush garden and rolling lawn. The bride makes her grand entrance through the garden and across a quaint footbridge that spans the creek. A petal-strewn aisle leads to the patio, and a wooden arbor where vows are exchanged in the shade of sheltering trees. Both the bridge and arbor can be decorated with flowers, fabric or garlands coordinated with your color scheme to give it a personal touch. In the evening, twinkle lights add a magical quality to the setting.

A favorite option for intimate receptions or rehearsal dinners is the tented Event Pavilion and patio. In spring and summer the pavilion is normally left open-sided, but even during cooler weather when its "walls" are drawn down, you still feel warm, comfortable and connected to the surrounding greenery through clear acrylic windows. Couples hosting their reception in the pavilion can tie the knot just a few steps away beneath a delicate wrought-iron gazebo.

Seasoned event professionals will help orchestrate your celebration, from offering vendor recommendations to day-of coordination. Several wedding packages as well as customized menus are available. Certain ethnic cuisines, including Indian and Middle Eastern, may be prepared and brought in by a licensed caterer.

The hotel has 448 oversized guest rooms with balconies, which means all your friends and family can stay in one place. And whether they're lounging by the hotel pool, shopping in the nearby mall or taking in the historic attractions of Old Sacramento, your guests will enjoy their free time almost as much as attending your wedding.

CEREMONY CAPACITY: The site seats 1,300 guests indoors and 350 outdoors.

EVENT/RECEPTION CAPACITY: The facility can accommodate 830 seated or 1,500 standing indoors and 200 seated or 250 standing outdoors.

MEETING CAPACITY: Meeting spaces hold 1,300 seated guests.

FEES & DEPOSITS: 25% of the estimated total event cost is required to secure your date, with the balance due 10 days prior to the event. The rental fee ranges $500–5,000 depending on the space(s) reserved. Meals range $30–68/person. Tax, alcohol and a 22% service charge are additional.

AVAILABILITY: Year-round, daily.

SERVICES/AMENITIES:

Catering: in-house, or BYO (ethnic cuisine only)
Kitchen Facilities: limited
Tables & Chairs: provided
Linens, Silver, etc.: provided
Restrooms: wheelchair accessible
Dance Floor: provided, portable CBA
Bride's Dressing Area: CBA
AV/Meeting Equipment: CBA

Parking: large lot, valet/self-parking
Accommodations: 448 guest rooms
Outdoor Night Lighting: yes
Outdoor Cooking Facilities: BBQ CBA
Cleanup: provided
View: fountain, garden, landscaped grounds, pool area, waterfall
Other: grand piano, event coordination

RESTRICTIONS:

Alcohol: in-house, or BYO with corkage fee
Smoking: outside only
Music: amplified OK with restrictions

Wheelchair Access: yes
Insurance: liability required

Wedgewood Sterling Hotel

Banquet Center

1300 H Street, Sacramento
866/966-3009

www.wedgewoodbanquet.com
events@wedgewoodbanquet.com

Rehearsal Dinners	●	Corp. Events/Mtgs.	
● Ceremonies	●	Private Parties	
● Wedding Receptions	●	Accommodations	

Gracing the corner of a pretty treelined street in Downtown Sacramento, just blocks away from the Governor's Mansion and State Capitol, the historic Sterling Hotel instantly grabs your attention with its authentic Victorian charm. Built in 1894 as a luxury residence, it was transformed into a boutique hotel in 1988. Today its nostalgic glamour and prime location make it an in-demand venue for landmark celebrations.

Intimate weddings begin on the second floor with a ceremony in the Chandelier Room, named for the four glittering crystal chandeliers suspended from the high ceiling. Tall windows softly draped in creamy gauze fabric filter in natural light, and the lovely space needs little decoration, save for flowers at the altar. If your party is larger, exchange vows in the sumptuous Sterling Ballroom on the ground floor, or outdoors on the cozy brick patio. Wedgewood can also arrange a romantic ceremony nearby in the Capitol Rose Garden, where fragrant blooms, a rose petal aisle, and a three-tiered fountain create an enchanting setting. For something really impressive, say "I do" on the majestic Capitol steps, with a grand façade of Romanesque arches and pillars as a stately backdrop.

Wherever you wed, the favorite spot for the cocktail hour is the hotel's Cellar Lounge. Guests soak up a distinctive "wine cellar" ambiance along with their hors d'oeuvres, surrounded by faux terracotta walls, wine casks, and a rustic concrete bar.

The elegance quotient goes up a few notches in the adjoining Sterling Ballroom, a stunning reception space with an inspired mix of period details and modern flair. A series of beautiful floor-to-ceiling arches inset with beveled-glass panels run along two walls and evoke the building's turn-of-the-century heritage. They also reflect light from alabaster chandeliers overhead, giving the room extra sparkle. Perhaps the ballroom's most striking element is a gorgeous backlit, stained-glass rotunda. Couples often pose below it while their photographer snaps some colorful—and unique—shots for their album.

Two more perks you'll appreciate: on-site accommodations and a sophisticated bridal changing room with an abundance of marble and mirrors.

Weddings here are overseen by Wedgewood Wedding & Banquet Centers, who boast a 30-year reputation for delivering both value and personal service. These experts offer all-inclusive wedding packages that are fully customizable, so you can mix and match items that best suit your vision and budget. Their helpful staff will oversee everything from start to finish, which means you get to relax and spend your time enjoying the festivities.

CEREMONY CAPACITY: The site can seat 200 guests indoors and outdoors.

EVENT/RECEPTION CAPACITY: The site holds 200 seated or standing indoors and 125 seated or standing outdoors.

MEETING CAPACITY: Meeting spaces seat 200 guests.

FEES & DEPOSITS: 25% of the estimated total event cost is required to reserve your date. An additional 25% is due 120 days prior to the event and the balance (based on your final guest count) is due 10 days prior. All payments are credited towards your final balance and are nonrefundable and nontransferable. All-inclusive, completely customizable wedding packages start at $46/person. Tax, alcohol and a 21–22% service charge are additional.

AVAILABILITY: Year-round, daily, until 11pm.

SERVICES/AMENITIES:

Catering: in-house
Kitchen Facilities: n/a
Tables & Chairs: provided
Linens, Silver, etc.: provided
Restrooms: wheelchair accessible
Dance Floor: provided
Bride's Dressing Area: yes
AV/Meeting Equipment: provided

Parking: large lot
Accommodations: 16 guest rooms
Outdoor Night Lighting: access only
Outdoor Cooking Facilities: no
Cleanup: provided
View: cityscape, fountain, garden patio, landscaped grounds, old-growth trees
Other: event coordination, on-site wedding cake and florals

RESTRICTIONS:

Alcohol: in-house
Smoking: designated areas only
Music: amplified OK indoors

Wheelchair Access: yes
Insurance: not required

Wine Country

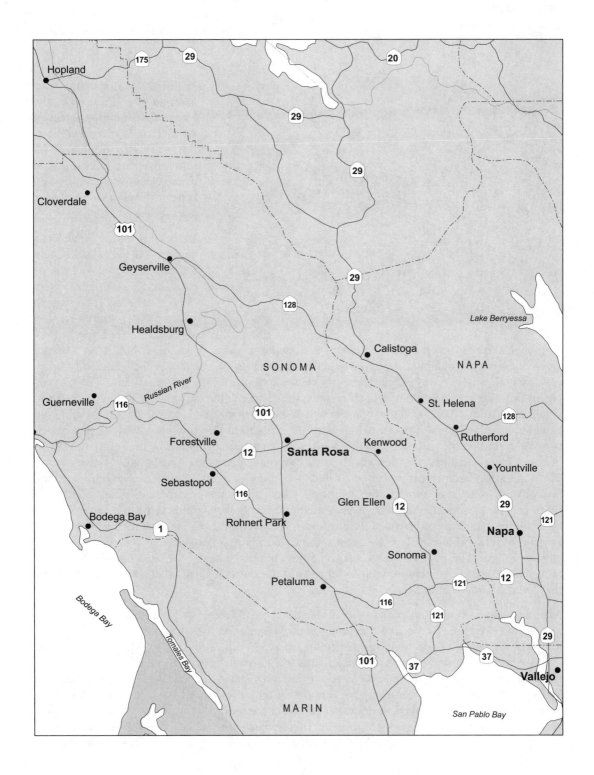

Hans Fahden Vineyards

Winery

4855 Petrified Forest Road, Calistoga
707/942-6760

www.hansfahden.com
mary@hansfahden.com

● Rehearsal Dinners	● Corp. Events/Mtgs.
● Ceremonies	● Private Parties
● Wedding Receptions	○ Accommodations

High in the mountains between Santa Rosa and Calistoga, the Hans Fahden family has created an incredible place with outdoor sites elegant enough for satin gowns and tuxedos, and a marvelous indoor facility with some of the most extraordinary features we've ever seen.

Even at first glance, the winery's gardens and event facilities are quite lovely, but like a Fabergé egg, their outward beauty is only a prelude to a wealth of creativity, craftsmanship and aesthetic richness within.

Your special event may start in the Teahouse, a quaint wooden structure covered with wisteria, grapevines and red climbing roses. Small gatherings can use the Teahouse for ceremonies or receptions, but larger groups mingle there before descending into the gardens below. The gardens are an exquisite combination of French country style and wildlife habitat, and if they remind you of an Impressionist painting, it's no coincidence. Winery owners and landscapers Antone and Lyall Fahden relied heavily on Monet's paintings of the gardens at Giverny when they designed their own. As you travel the path down to the pond, your senses are tantalized by the sights and smells of roses, irises, petunias, pansies, cornflowers, poppies, ornamental grasses and native shrubs. The garden has been cleverly planted so that something different blooms each month, creating one wave of color after another. In late spring, roses take center stage; other floral "coming attractions" include matilija poppies, oleander, zinnias, sunflowers and blue pitcher sage. Midway between the Teahouse and pond, a terraced lawn bordered by a volcanic-ash rock wall and beds of pink evening primroses, lavender, roses and California poppies serves as a ceremony site for large weddings. The covered bridge spanning the lily pond can also be used for weddings, and brings you close to a variety of wildlife—thanks to the ducks, egrets, quail and mourning doves that call the gardens home.

After exchanging vows, join your guests in the winery building, a long graceful structure whose mellow wood exterior and peaked, sage-green roof blend with the rugged mountainside behind it. Inside, a gray slate floor, high beamed ceiling of grooved pine and redwood, and cream walls give the room a simple beauty that complements the glory of the gardens viewed through French doors. In one corner, a grand piano provides background music as your guests nibble appetizers and sip champagne. Just when everyone thinks that their eyes simply couldn't take in any more beauty, the 400-pound Douglas fir doors at one end of the room are thrown open to reveal a wine cave containing candlelit tables set for dinner. This amazing cave is like the jewel within a Fabergé egg: gorgeous, surprising and utterly unique. Formed of volcanic ash rock, the T-shaped cave's walls are lined with wine barrels; metal fixtures with grape-leaf cutouts and twinkle-light-wrapped poles provide subtle lighting. At the T's apex, two wine barrels support a massive arrangement of fresh flowers; above, gold candle sconces in floral designs await lighting. When these sconces are lit, along with the candelabras on the tables and the twinkle lights, Ali Baba's cave itself could not be more enchanting. Magical doesn't even begin to describe an event here—as you sit down to dinner, surrounded by flowers, flickering shadows and the piquant smell of aging wine, you'll feel as if you're part of a breathtaking fairy tale. And, unlike limestone caves, this cave's volcanic-ash rock adjusts to body temperature when occupied, so you can wear the most daring *décolleté* gown and never have to throw a jacket over your shoulders.

If you're thinking that Hans Fahden sounds like a wonderful place, but you're not planning to get married anytime soon, keep in mind that the winery can accommodate all types of events, from a gala celebration to a business seminar. But we can't help feeling that the site's stunning visual appeal may be most appreciated at a wedding. So, brides, if your fantasy includes a vision of you in a magnificent Vera Wang gown against a backdrop of pristine natural beauty, you owe yourself a visit to Hans Fahden Winery. They can make your dream wedding a beautiful reality!

CEREMONY CAPACITY: The Monet garden seats 120; the Teahouse seats 50; multiple garden settings for Enchating Elopements are available during the week.

EVENT/RECEPTION CAPACITY: The Grand Room and outdoor patio combined accommodate 120 guests; the Wine Cave seats 120. During winter months, December–March, the facility accommodates up to 85 guests.

MEETING CAPACITY: The Grand Room seats 100 guests, the Wine Cave seats 120.

FEES & DEPOSITS: For an À la Carte wedding, a $2,500 deposit is required to reserve your date; the balance is due 10 days prior to the event. The rental fee is $7,500 on weekdays including Friday, $7,000 on Sunday, and $8,500 on Saturday. All-inclusive wedding package rates for 100 guests are $27,500 for weekdays including Friday, $27,000 for Sunday, and $28,600 for Saturday. A $3,000 deposit is required to reserve your date, and the balance is due 10 days prior to the event.

AVAILABILITY: Year-round, daily, 10am–10pm.

SERVICES/AMENITIES:

Catering: select from preferred list
Kitchen Facilities: prep only
Tables & Chairs: round tables, 120 Chiavari chairs, 120 white padded ceremony chairs
Linens, Silver, etc.: BYO
Restrooms: wheelchair accessible
Dance Floor: textured cement floor
Bride's & Groom's Dressing Areas: yes
AV/Meeting Equipment: BYO

Parking: on-site lot
Accommodations: private honeymoon cottage sleeps 4, lodging in Calistoga is 5 minutes away
Outdoor Night Lighting: market lighting and Japanese lanterns
Outdoor Cooking Facilities: BBQ
Cleanup: caterer
View: vineyards, Mayacamas mountains
Other: day-of coordinator, piano, rentals valued at $7,350+ included w/rental fee

RESTRICTIONS:

Alcohol: full bar available, wine provided or BYO, no corkage fee with 1 case minimum purchase
Smoking: outdoors only
Music: DJs only, no bands allowed

Wheelchair Access: limited
Insurance: certificate required
Other: no rice, birdseed, confetti, sparklers or butterfly releases

Solage
Auberge Resorts Collection

Resort and Spa

755 Silverado Trail, Calistoga
707/226-0813

www.solagecalistoga.com
sol.weddings@aubergeresorts.com

●	Rehearsal Dinners	●	Corp. Events/Mtgs.
●	Ceremonies	●	Private Parties
●	Wedding Receptions	●	Accommodations

As you approach Napa Valley's northern limit the terrain becomes bolder, with lush, densely wooded hills. At the heart of this striking landscape you'll find Solage, a very green, very stylish, very accommodating resort & spa. Created with an exquisite sense of space and flow, Solage provides all the comforts you expect of a posh resort in an atmosphere of relaxed luxury.

Best of all, Solage is a place where you can orchestrate as elaborate a wedding as you like—without all the stress that can come with it. That's because the powers that be here are masters at banishing pre-wedding jitters: They can arrange to have your party arrive a day or two early and unwind in accommodations that cluster around what is essentially a private courtyard. They'll also give you an opportunity to walk through the wedding and reception site two hours before your ceremony to make sure that everything is just the way you want it.

The prime wedding venue is Solage's main pavilion, Solstice, an expertly designed space that lends itself to any kind of decorative theme you can imagine. Huge floor-to-ceiling glass doors open to a terrace and lawn that face the soaring Palisades Mountains and a glimpse of Mt. St. Helena, the Bay Area's tallest peak. Brides often make a dramatic entrance onto the lawn from Solstice to begin their ceremony. Solage sets up a bar and post-ceremony cocktail hour in the adjoining courtyard, then invites guests back into Solstice for dinner and dancing.

Speaking of dinner, Solage's Michelin Star-rated restaurant, Solbar, will be catering your reception. Executive Chef Brandon Sharp and his team are happy to customize your menu, incorporating farm-fresh, seasonal ingredients into unique, flavorful dishes. Even their dessert choices are unexpected, from the Brown Butter Financier Cake with warm fruit compote to the Butterscotch Pudding with amaretti-pine nut cookies and crème fraîche.

The resort's standout architecture has been coined "Napa barn meets San Francisco loft." Solage's sleek barn-like buildings, with their steep roofs, clapboard siding and artful use of metal and glass, all overlook courtyards or lawns. Oaks, olive trees, Canary Island date palms, lavender and herbs grow profusely. Everything—furniture, fountains and art—is attractively simple and made from the very best products. Another bonus is that Solage is a thoroughly green-oriented resort, employing sustainable building materials and state-of-the-art power generation and conservation.

The spa, encompassing 20,000 square feet and 14 private treatment rooms, is downright sensational, offering an array of facials, body treatments and massages in tranquil surroundings, including geothermal pools and their signature mud bar (fresh mud—nothing recycled!). Many brides relax here pre- and post-celebration. Some even arrange for private yoga classes the morning of their wedding.

In addition to on-site spa indulgences, bocce ball, fitness facilities and swimming, Calistoga's restaurants and shops are a five-minute bike ride away (two complimentary cruiser bikes come with each overnight accommodation). There's also easy highway access—and close proximity—to Napa's finest wineries, as well as neighboring Alexander and Dry Creek Valleys.

This is a chic, sophisticated retreat with an astounding variety of services, all delivered with a true "yes" mentality. Solage's greatest attribute, however, is making you feel more content in body and mind than you ever dreamed possible.

CEREMONY, EVENT/RECEPTION & MEETING CAPACITY: The resort holds 200 seated or 230 standing guests indoors and 250 seated or 500 standing outdoors.

FEES & DEPOSITS: An $8,000 deposit is required to reserve your date. A portion is due 90 days prior to the event and the balance is due 14 days prior. The rental fee ranges $3,000–8,000 depending on the dates and space selected. Food & beverage pricing ranges $200–285/person. Tax, alcohol and a 22% service charge are additional.

AVAILABILITY: Year-round, daily, 6am–midnight.

SERVICES/AMENITIES:

Catering: provided
Kitchen Facilities: n/a
Tables & Chairs: provided
Linens, Silver, etc.: provided
Restrooms: wheelchair accessible
Dance Floor: no
Bride's Dressing Area: CBA
AV/Meeting Equipment: provided
Other: spa services, complimentary bikes, event coordination

Parking: large lot, complimentary valet
Accommodations: 89 guest rooms
Outdoor Night Lighting: yes
Outdoor Cooking Facilities: BBQ CBA
Cleanup: provided
View: garden courtyard, mountains, landscaped grounds

RESTRICTIONS:

Alcohol: provided
Smoking: designated areas only
Music: amplified OK

Wheelchair Access: yes
Insurance: liability required

Want to know WHAT TO ASK a potential location or vendor? Check out our Questions to Ask starting on page 21.

The Highlands Estate

Bed & Breakfast

33430 Highway 128, Cloverdale
707/894-9500

www.thehighlandsestate.com
weddings@thehighlandsestate.com

● Rehearsal Dinners	● Corp. Events/Mtgs.
● Ceremonies	● Private Parties
● Wedding Receptions	● Accommodations

The view from The Highlands Estate's hilltop perch stretches out for miles across the Anderson and Alexander Valleys, with rolling hills, vineyards, and farms creating a pastoral scene that seems lifted out of an Impressionist painting. Deer, wild turkeys, and a variety of birds are frequent visitors to the property, and lucky guests may also receive an enthusiastic welcome from the Estate's resident pups, Daisy and Henry.

A full-service bed and breakfast is housed in the gracious, Victorian-inspired home at the Estate's center. Off the soaring foyer is a cheerful dining room where guests gather for daily breakfasts, and coffee is offered throughout the day. A cozy living area with a fireplace beckons you to settle in with a glass of wine and a board game, while downstairs, you'll find a billiard room, cinema with plush stadium seating, and a gym. Four finely appointed guest rooms boast en suite bathrooms, whimsical décor, and views of the grounds and distant hills.

As your guests begin to arrive for your wedding, they're directed to an ample parking area near the base of the Estate's 21 green acres. From there, they take a short, pretty stroll up a gently sloped path past Syrah vines, olive and fruit trees, toward a grassy ceremony site facing the valleys and mountains. (A courtesy shuttle is available for those who don't wish to walk.) The area is comfortably shaded in the afternoon, and a four-posted wooden arbor on a small platform functions as your altar or chuppah. Rock speakers placed around the lawn's perimeter provide music and sound amplification, ensuring an unobstructed view.

Once you've exchanged vows, The Four Seasons Barn stands ready to host a memorable reception. This spacious structure has a corrugated metal roof and siding, a high ceiling with exposed ductwork and wagon wheel chandeliers, and gorgeous farm tables, handmade by the owner. For an open-air cocktail hour or dinner, there's a large patio strung with market lights just outside. The barn blends the best of rustic charm and modern conveniences—it's insulated and climate-controlled, with indoor restrooms, two catering areas (one inside, one outside), handicapped parking, and a sweetly decorated bonus room that may be used as a dressing suite, ketubah signing area, or babysitting space.

Intimate ceremonies can be also held beneath the branches of the Estate's remarkable centuries-old oak tree, set on a majestic spot that allows you to take in the entire valley. Late afternoon weddings here are especially lovely, when the sun setting beyond the eastern mountains creates a truly magical picture. Parties with fewer than 40 guests can then move to a reception on the B&B's deck, overlooking the pool and pond.

All of the lighting at The Highlands Estate is dark-sky compliant, so before retiring to your honeymoon suite be sure to sit out on the deck to gaze as long as you like at the canopy of stars.

CEREMONY, EVENT/RECEPTION & MEETING CAPACITY: The estate can accommodate up to 200 guests.

FEES & DEPOSITS: 50% of the venue rental fee is required to secure your date, and the balance is due 60 days prior to the event. The rental fee for weddings starts at $4,750 and varies depending on the day, time, space reserved, and guest count.

Rates for business functions, meetings or other types of events vary. Please contact the venue for more details.

AVAILABILITY: Year-round, daily.

SERVICES/AMENITIES:

Catering: BYO
Kitchen Facilities: prep only
Tables & Chairs: CBA
Linens, Silver, etc.: BYO
Restrooms: wheelchair accessible
Dance Floor: provided
Bride's Dressing Area: yes
AV/Meeting Equipment: BYO

Parking: large lot, up to 75 cars; shuttle service required December–March
Accommodations: 4 guest rooms
Outdoor Night Lighting: yes
Outdoor Cooking Facilities: none
Cleanup: caterer or renter
View: forest, garden courtyard, pond, landscaped grounds, meadow, pool area; panorama of rolling hills and vineyards
Other: 12 wine barrels

RESTRICTIONS:

Alcohol: BYO, licensed server required
Smoking: not allowed
Music: amplified OK indoors with restrictions

Wheelchair Access: yes
Insurance: liability required

deLorimier Winery

Boutique Winery

2001 Highway 128, Geyserville
707/433-3303 x103
www.delorimierwinery.com
isabelle@wilsonartisanwines.com

- Rehearsal Dinners
- Ceremonies
- Wedding Receptions
- Corp. Events/Mtgs.
- Private Parties
- Accommodations

A shining example of a boutique winery, deLorimier is also a wonderfully bucolic venue for a romantic wedding. Located in the Alexander Valley along the renowned "wine trail," it's surrounded by gentle rolling hills planted with Bordeaux varietals—the occasional horse in a field makes it all even more picture-perfect.

Neat rows of Cabernet grapevines line the gravel road that leads up to their expansive courtyard where couples often exchange vows. This peaceful locale, enhanced by a sculptural boulder fountain, is nestled between the weathered-wood Barrel Room and the craftsman-style Tasting Room. Seasonal blooms and a graceful red maple add a burst of color to the perimeter. And running the length of the far side, an elaborate arbor covered with lush greenery stands in front of acres of well-tended vines. In short, it's a sublime stage for a quintessential Wine Country ceremony.

You may want to linger here with cocktails around the fountain, but most brides invite their guests into the modern Tasting Room. Its polished stone floor, high pitched ceiling and walls of windows provide an open, airy feel. The large center bar acts like a magnet for mingling, while a floor-to-ceiling fireplace and paintings by local artists draw your eye around the entire space. If you'd like to delight the oenophiles in your group, arrange to serve flights of deLorimier's award-winning Cabs and Meritage.

Your main reception takes place on the back lawn, a wide swath of soft grass that's bordered by more vineyards and looks out over countryside panoramas. Strings of twinkle lights add sparkle to the festivities, and there's an ample patio for dancing under the stars. The all-important cake-cutting ceremony becomes even more memorable when presented in the private, glass-enclosed Club Room, which is especially cozy with the fireplace lit on a cool evening.

As the hour gets late and you don't want the mood to end just yet, you'll be very happy that you've decided to stay for the weekend. (In fact, many couples even stay the night before so they can be relaxed for the big event). deLorimier has two beautifully furnished king suites with pastoral vistas, as well as a three-bedroom farmhouse so you can have out-of-town guests join you … or put them up at nearby inns operated by the winery's owners. And if you really want to immerse yourselves in the Sonoma Valley vibe, take advantage of the option to host a rehearsal dinner or post-wedding brunch at any one of their sister wineries.

CEREMONY, EVENT/RECEPTION & MEETING CAPACITY: The site holds up to 24 seated or 50 standing guests indoors and 150 seated or standing outdoors.

FEES & DEPOSITS: 50% of the total event cost is required to reserve your date, and the balance is due 4 months prior to the event. The rental fee ranges $3,000–8,000 depending on the type of event, timeline and guest count. An additional Wine Cellar purchase is based on 1/2 a bottle/person; Wine Club discount applies.

AVAILABILITY: Year-round, daily, 5pm–10pm. Additional hours prior to 5pm are available for $1,000 each.

SERVICES/AMENITIES:

Catering: select from preferred list
Kitchen Facilities: fully equipped
Tables & Chairs: provided
Linens, Silver, etc.: through caterer
Restrooms: wheelchair accessible
Dance Floor: yes
Bride's & Groom's Dressing Areas: no
AV/Meeting Equipment: BYO

Parking: large lot
Accommodations: 5 guest rooms
Outdoor Night Lighting: yes
Outdoor Cooking Facilities: no
Cleanup: caterer
View: fountain, garden patio, hills; panorama of Alexander Valley Vineyards and mountains

RESTRICTIONS:

Alcohol: in-house
Smoking: designated areas only
Music: amplified OK

Wheelchair Access: yes
Insurance: liability required

Beltane Ranch

11775 Sonoma Highway, Glen Ellen
707/833-4233

www.beltaneranch.com
anne@beltaneranch.com

Private Estate and Ranch

● Rehearsal Dinners	● Corp. Events/Mtgs.
● Ceremonies	● Private Parties
● Wedding Receptions	○ Accommodations

The story behind Beltane Ranch is an interesting one: Its origins date back to 1892, when a black woman from New Orleans named Mary Ellen Pleasant came to Sonoma's fabled Valley of the Moon and built the existing house as a way to escape—and celebrate—the great business success she had enjoyed in San Francisco.

It's easy to see what drew her to erect her home on this spot. A narrow drive flanked by old trees, vineyards, grassy fields and beautiful hand-built stone walls leads up to Beltane, which nestles beneath venerable oaks atop a gentle slope. The house Mary Ellen created is a two-story, five-room, wooden confection, graced with delicate lathed railings and Victorian-style wood trim as well as grand verandas outfitted with wicker furnishings. The front of the residence is bordered by a flower garden enclosed by a classic white picket fence.

Next to the house are two lawns used for ceremonies. The larger one, which has views of the vineyard, is edged with flowerbeds, low stone walls and towering oaks. A stage for the DJ in one corner is festooned with strings of lights that create a festive glow at night. The smaller lawn right behind the house is a bit more intimate. It's especially appealing when a musician, positioned in one corner of the adjacent upstairs veranda, provides soft music during the ceremony. A garden area near the trellised entrance to the main house often hosts small receptions. There's also a rustic horse barn that makes a charming setting for rehearsal dinners and other small gatherings of up to 60.

When brides who've wed here talk about what they liked, the first thing they cite is Beltane's authenticity. A still-working ranch that raises cattle, grows olives and grapes, and produces its own wine, Beltane evokes Old Sonoma from the days before the county became an upscale destination. The lovingly maintained old house has nothing slick about it. Its vibrant gardens have evolved over the years and seem part of the landscape. Bridal party members often enjoy breakfast fruit harvested from raspberry bushes planted decades ago by the owner's grand aunt. Another attractive feature is the stand-alone cottage, a Berber-carpeted hideaway that has a firebox, sitting area, private bath, and a small garden and deck overlooking the main lawn.

Brides also appreciate Beltane's seasoned staff, many of whom have been at the property for at least 15 years. One dividend of the ranch's reputation for great service is that quite a few newlyweds return for their anniversaries. (The ranch has even welcomed the children of couples who've been married here.)

Beltane's newest service is its in-house catering. Their chef will custom-design and prepare a menu for up to 50 guests that showcases their sustainable estate-grown organic produce, olive oil and wine pairings. Now you can have a very special meal not just for an intimate wedding, but for a rehearsal dinner and brunch, too!

Beltane remains one of the loveliest old ranch houses in California. Owned by the same family since the 1930s and surrounded by 1,000 acres of open-space preserve, the ranch's 100 acres are the ideal place to hold a true Sonoma County country wedding. Everything here—the venue and its surroundings—blends seamlessly to create a perfect pastoral stage.

CEREMONY, EVENT/RECEPTION & MEETING CAPACITY: Beltane Ranch can accommodate up to 150 seated or standing guests outdoors, up to 60 seated or standing in the rustic barn, and 14 seated or standing indoors.

FEES & DEPOSITS: One third of the rental fee is required to reserve your date. The next third is due 3 months prior to the event, and the final third is due 2 weeks prior. Event packages include exclusive use of the bed & breakfast, lawns and surrounding garden areas; Garden Cottage accommodations for the bride & groom during their stay; and a full breakfast for all B&B guests (the 5 B&B rooms must be booked and paid for during the wedding). The rental fee for a summer wedding is $12,500 for up to 75 guests, $15,000 for 76–125, or $17,500 for 126–150. The midweek and off-season fee ranges $4,200–7,400. One- or two-night packages for intimate weddings and special events of up to 50 people are available starting at $2,500. Purchase of 1 case of Beltane Ranch wine per 20 guests is required; non-Beltane Ranch wines, beer and other alcohol may also be brought in. In-house catering is available for up to 50 guests, and meals start at $105/person. Tax, alcohol and service charge are additional. Catering for events of 51–150 guests is provided by outside caterers (choose from list). Beltane Ranch Vineyards & Winery is certified 100% sustainable by the California Sustainable Winegrowing Alliance.

AVAILABILITY: Outdoor events are held from May through October. Intimate weddings and barn events available year-round. Events may be held from 4pm–10pm.

SERVICES/AMENITIES:

Catering: in-house or select from list
Kitchen Facilities: prep only
Tables & Chairs: provided
Linens, Silver, etc.: through caterer
Restrooms: not wheelchair accessible
Dance Floor: provided
Bride's Dressing Area: yes
AV/Meeting Equipment: CBA

Parking: large lot
Accommodations: 6 guest rooms
Outdoor Night Lighting: garden arbors, lawn and trees
Outdoor Cooking Facilities: caterers only
Cleanup: provided
View: mountains, vineyards, forest, garden

RESTRICTIONS:

Alcohol: Beltane Ranch wine purchase required; OK to BYO other beverages and alcohol
Smoking: outdoors only
Music: amplified OK outdoors with restrictions

Wheelchair Access: limited
Insurance: extra liability required

The wedding vendors on our website are the best in the business. How do we know? Read page 553.

B.R. Cohn Winery

Winery

15000 Highway 12, Glen Ellen
707/302-3574
www.brcohn.com/weddings
brcohn@paulaleduc.com

● Rehearsal Dinners	● Corp. Events/Mtgs.
● Ceremonies	● Private Parties
● Wedding Receptions	○ Accommodations

Just 45 minutes north of the Golden Gate Bridge in the heart of Sonoma Valley, B.R. Cohn Winery offers a multitude of possibilities in a romantic Wine Country atmosphere. Olive trees, whose graceful branches shade the road leading up to the winery, are a fitting introduction to this pastoral location.

From the top of the hill, it's a short walk down to the outdoor Amphitheater, a spectacular ceremony site with a large stage and terraced lawn. Couples exchange vows on the stage beneath an enormous oak tree. Behind them is a stunning natural backdrop: acres of lush Cabernet vineyards and a full view of the Sonoma Mountains. Guests seated on the stage or lawn have the perfect vantage from which to enjoy the lovely panorama.

Nearby is another gorgeous venue to tie the knot: Oak Hill. Set in the middle of a vineyard, this rustic spot is shaded by 300-year-old oaks and manzanita trees and so private that all you hear is the occasional chirping of birds. Guests have a 360-degree view of the surrounding grapevines, and on hot days a soft breeze keeps them comfortable. Nature provides ample "decoration" so you don't need to add anything—except perhaps some rose petals for the aisle.

A third choice is the Poolside Arbor. Ideal for smaller ceremonies and cocktail receptions, it features landscaped gardens and fruit trees and has a view of the olive grove, vineyards and mountains in the distance.

When it's time to dine, most couples invite their guests to the Olive Grove for an al fresco celebration. This expansive lawn is shaded by more than a dozen 140-year-old French Picholine olive trees. Flowers make a colorful border, while tiny lights woven throughout every other tree create nighttime sparkle. Although this grove is usually used for receptions, it's equally beautiful for ceremonies.

In addition to its numerous event spaces, B.R. Cohn provides a charming cottage for the bride, her entourage and her family. Outfitted with an antique vanity, full-length mirror and couches, it's a cozy place to primp and relax.

Nestled between the Mayacamas and Sonoma Mountains, B.R. Cohn Winery's 90 acres possess a wealth of beauty, tranquility and options. Add to that fine wines and the expertise of *Paula LeDuc Fine Catering* and you have everything you need for an outstanding event.

CEREMONY & EVENT/RECEPTION CAPACITY: The winery holds up to 250 seated or standing guests outdoors. Indoor capacity is a tented terrace area that holds up to 50 seated or 75 standing.

MEETING CAPACITY: Meeting spaces accommodate 50 seated guests.

FEES & DEPOSITS: The rental fee and 50% of the catering total is required to secure your date. The rental fee ranges $2,500–10,000 depending on the day of the week. Catering is provided exclusively by *Paula LeDuc Fine Catering* and pricing starts at $340/person. Event services, such as lighting, flooring, portable restrooms and guest shuttles are additional.

AVAILABILITY: Year-round, daily, flexible hours. Outdoor spaces are available April–November, weather permitting.

SERVICES/AMENITIES:

Catering: provided by *Paula LeDuc Fine Catering*

Kitchen Facilities: prep area only

Tables & Chairs: through caterer

Linens, Silver, etc.: through caterer

Restrooms: wheelchair accessible

Dance Floor: CBA

Bride's Dressing Area: yes

AV/Meeting Equipment: through caterer

Parking: ample, complimentary; shuttles or valet required for 150 or more guests

Accommodations: no guest rooms

Outdoor Night Lighting: yes

Outdoor Cooking Facilities: no

Cleanup: caterer

View: vineyards, olive trees, Sonoma Mountains, landscaped grounds

RESTRICTIONS:

Alcohol: in-house wine, beer by *Paula LeDuc Fine Catering*

Smoking: not allowed

Music: amplified OK outdoors until 10pm

Wheelchair Access: yes

Insurance: certificate of liability required

Dawn Ranch Lodge

Ranch & Lodge

16467 Highway 116 , Guerneville
707/869-0656

www.dawnranch.com
weddings@dawnranch.com

- Rehearsal Dinners
- Ceremonies
- Wedding Receptions
- Corp. Events/Mtgs.
- Private Parties
- Accommodations

Dawn Ranch Lodge has been a favorite of vacationers since the early 1900s, when The San Francisco and North Pacific Railroad delivered guests right to the new resort's doorstep. The train station's long since gone, but people are still falling in love with this enchanting Guerneville getaway.

Tucked against the Russian River, the Lodge features clusters of sweet white cabins and cottages dotted throughout the towering redwoods, and the original buildings have been artfully updated with a thoughtful eye toward retaining their nostalgic charm.

Couples often kick off their wedding weekend with a meet-and-greet at The Boathouse. This historic, late 1800s building, with its inviting, rustic interior and adjacent lawn, is a popular spot for both welcome and after-parties. The area has been used for a variety of activities—games, shrimp broils, barbecues, and s'mores by the campfire following a float on the river. You might also gather guests for drinks and mingling around the pool; it's beautifully lit in the evening, and a band shell with an elevated deck can serve as a stage and dance floor, or be set with lounge furniture.

Rehearsal dinners are held in the original Lodge, whose warm wood dining room and bar are now home to the venue's restaurant, Agriculture Public House. Their innovative, comforting fare focuses on ingredients that are sustainable and locally sourced … in many cases, *very* locally, from the proprietor's ranch in Napa as well as right outside in Dawn Ranch's own kitchen garden. For an especially memorable treat, host your rehearsal dinner inside the gates of the garden, accompanied by the thriving plants that contributed to your meal.

You can exchange vows in The Meadow, with giant redwoods creating a breathtaking natural backdrop, or in The Orchard, where fruit and walnut trees provide seclusion and shade. Both areas will also accommodate either an open-air or tented reception, with a cocktail hour and lawn games on the nearby River Lawns. In the spring and summer, these spaces are alive with flowers and blooming trees, while autumn and winter bring striking color changes to the surrounding foliage.

Wedding packages are designed to give you privacy, flexibility, and plenty of time to enjoy the place. The "Ultimate Wedding Weekend" grants couples exclusive use of the grounds from Friday through Sunday, while the "Orchard Package", available May through October, offers a choice of a Friday, Saturday, or Sunday event. Both options guarantee enough cabins to house a large group, so you're able to make the most of your days at this timeless vintage treasure.

CEREMONY CAPACITY: The site holds 120 seated indoors and up to 400 seated outdoors.

EVENT/RECEPTION CAPACITY: The site accommodates 65 seated or 120 standing guests indoors and 400 seated or standing outoors.

MEETING CAPACITY: Meeting spaces seat up to 65 guests.

FEES & DEPOSITS: The site fee, which ranges $7,500–15,000, depending on the time of year, day of the week and spaces rented, is required to reserve your date. Menus start at $85/person. Buffet-style, plated, or family-style menus are available. Alcohol and cabin rental are additional.

Note: Bar services and catering are provided exclusively by Dawn Ranch Lodge, and all catering is done on site. Please call for details.

AVAILABILITY: Year-round, daily. Tours by appointment.

SERVICES/AMENITIES:

Catering: in-house
Kitchen Facilities: n/a
Tables & Chairs: included in some packages
Linens, Silver, etc.: included in some packages
Restrooms: wheelchair accessible
Dance Floor: included in some packages
Bride's Dressing Area: yes
AV/Meeting Equipment: BYO
Other: 15 acres, river access, full-service resort, event coordination included in some packages

Parking: large lot, on street
Accommodations: 53 guest rooms
Outdoor Night Lighting: included in some packages
Outdoor Cooking Facilities: none
Cleanup: provided
View: river, garden, landscaped grounds, meadow, pool area; panorama of hills and redwood trees

RESTRICTIONS:

Alcohol: in-house
Smoking: designated areas only
Music: amplified OK with restrictions

Wheelchair Access: limited
Insurance: not required

Madrona Manor

Historic Inn

1001 Westside Road, Healdsburg
707/433-1542 X111

www.madronamanor.com
arielle@madronamanor.com

- Rehearsal Dinners
- Ceremonies
- Wedding Receptions
- Corp. Events/Mtgs.
- Private Parties
- Accommodations

"Madrona Manor"...the very name sounds like something out of a romantic novel, and if romance is what you're looking for, you've come to the right place. Built in 1881 by Sonoma County businessman John Paxton as a family residence, it became an inn during the 1980s and earned a spot in the National Register of Historic Places. Current owners Bill and Trudi Konrad worked diligently to restore this landmark to its former splendor, and they've succeeded admirably.

This elegant boutique hotel is a classic example of Victorian architecture with period scrollwork, a mansard roof, dormer windows and columned verandas. The property occupies eight acres of prime Sonoma County real estate, whose tangled woodlands have been lovingly coaxed into a garden showplace with fountains, rolling lawns, herb gardens, a citrus grove and a rainbow of seasonal flowers.

The manor's interior shows the same attention to detail and eye for authenticity as the grounds. The first-floor rooms all have fireplaces, crystal chandeliers, carved sideboards and turn-of-the-century art. The Palm Terrace is a large covered veranda, whose wicker furniture, potted palms and cheerful upholstery make it reminiscent of a Victorian conservatory.

Madrona Manor offers three types of wedding packages, and each one makes ample use of the manor's felicitous environs. The favored ceremony site is the capacious Wedding Lawn, bordered by masses of flowers and towering sycamores.

The Victorians were known for their elaborate multicourse repasts, and Madrona Manor is as authentic in this as it is in everything else. Thanks to Chef Jesse Mallgren, the venue has a prestigious one-star Michelin rating. Chef Mallgren's considerable talents and renowned seasonal menus are at your disposal. Another talented staff member is Arielle Larson, the Director of Special Events, who is adept at creating breathtakingly romantic destination weddings.

Madrona Manor is also available during the week and in the off-season. Of course, nonwedding events such as celebratory dinners or corporate functions are also welcome. If your love life could use a jump-start, you don't have to wait for Valentine's Day—just take a trip to Madrona Manor, where romance is in the air all year round.

CEREMONY & EVENT/RECEPTION CAPACITY: The facility can accommodate 200 guests.

MEETING CAPACITY: The manor has various rooms that can hold 15–28 seated conference-style or theater-style.

FEES & DEPOSITS: For weddings, 50% of the facility fee, which ranges $1,500–15,000, is required to book your date. Meals range $75–105/person. Tax, alcohol and a 20% service charge are additional.

AVAILABILITY: February–December.

SERVICES/AMENITIES:

Catering: in-house, no BYO
Kitchen Facilities: n/a
Tables & Chairs: provided
Linens, Silver, etc.: provided
Restrooms: wheelchair accessible
Dance Floor: yes
Bride's Dressing Area: yes, during the day
AV/Meeting Equipment: projector, screen, conference phone and broadband

Parking: complimentary
Accommodations: 22 guest rooms
Outdoor Night Lighting: yes
Outdoor Cooking Facilities: no
Cleanup: provided
View: estate gardens, Dry Creek Valley
Other: personal coordinator provided

RESTRICTIONS:

Alcohol: in-house
Smoking: designated areas outside
Music: amplified OK indoors only

Wheelchair Access: yes
Insurance: not required
Other: no rice, birdseed, confetti or sparklers

Soda Rock Winery

Historic Old West Town

8015 Highway 128, Healdsburg
707/433-3303 x103

www.sodarockwinery.com
isabelle@wilsonartisanwines.com

- Rehearsal Dinners
- Ceremonies
- Wedding Receptions
- Corp. Events/Mtgs.
- Private Parties
- Accommodations

Even though we're accustomed to seeing an exuberant array of Wine Country event sites in a wide range of architectural styles, Soda Rock Winery is showstoppingly different. It looks like the Hollywood set of a Wild West town…except that this is the real deal. Or at least it was in the 1860s when these fabulous old buildings housed the general store, post office and pretty much all of downtown Soda Rock. But leave it to the Wilson family, owners of 9 distinctive wineries, to lend a hip, modern sensibility to their faithful restoration of this standout venue.

The centerpiece is the two-story winery building, which resembles the exterior of the Alamo and is fronted by a large Courtyard Plaza with a fountain. Surrounded by seasonal gardens and a view to hills and vineyards, this is an excellent spot for an outdoor ceremony or reception. If you'd like something more rustic, a bride favorite is walking down the aisle beside the 100-year-old barn with more vineyards behind it. Even if you don't exchange vows here, you simply must pose for photos inside the barn: The weathered wood with all its knotholes lets streams of light filter in, creating a dreamy, ethereal effect. Your photographer will be in heaven and your wedding album will be even more memorable!

While Soda Rock's exterior is all original stone, once you enter the main winery building you're in for a surprise and a treat. The interior has been gutted and turned into a setting that's the ultimate in industrial chic. Cool and spacious, the Tasting Room and Lounge feature some things old…and some things new: The exposed beam ceiling, vintage carved wooden bar, and viticulture artifacts (like antique barrels and an early bottling machine), mix beautifully with marble accents, sleek leather chairs and contemporary art.

After cocktails (and their artisan wine, of course), you can move to the dual-level Ballroom. Its soaring, wood trestle ceiling, polished cement floor and enormous century-old ageing barrels make this quite unlike your standard ballroom. It's a most wonderful blank canvas, ready for your personal stamp. Whether you prefer it airy and open or wish to add lanterns, drapery and dramatic lighting, this space (and the adjacent Vineyard Room) can be transformed to suit virtually any vision.

Soda Rock also has four private rooms—including the Water Tower Suite with 360-degree vineyard views—that can be used as bridal changing suites. And if you're just not ready to say goodbye to friends and family yet, there's always the option to host a post-wedding brunch (think rehearsal dinner, too) at any of the Wilson family's other award-winning locations.

CEREMONY & EVENT/RECEPTION CAPACITY: The facility can accommodate 250 guests.

MEETING CAPACITY: Meeting spaces hold 200 seated guests.

FEES & DEPOSITS: 50% of the total event cost is required to reserve your date and the balance is due 4 months prior to the event. The rental fee ranges $3,000–10,000 depending on the activity, timeline and guest count. An additional wine cellar purchase is based on 1/2 bottle per person; Wine Club discount applies.

AVAILABILITY: Year-round, daily, 5pm to 10pm. Additional hours prior to 5pm are available for $1,500 each.

SERVICES/AMENITIES:

Catering: select from preferred list
Kitchen Facilities: prep only
Tables & Chairs: provided
Linens, Silver, etc.: through caterer
Restrooms: wheelchair accessible
Dance Floor: yes
Bride's Dressing Area: no
AV/Meeting Equipment: BYO

Parking: large lot
Accommodations: no guest rooms
Outdoor Night Lighting: yes
Outdoor Cooking Facilities: no
Cleanup: caterer
View: fountain, garden patio, hills, landscaped grounds; panorama of Alexander Valley Vineyards and mountains

RESTRICTIONS:

Alcohol: in-house
Smoking: designated areas only
Music: amplified OK with restrictions

Wheelchair Access: yes
Insurance: liability required

Want to find more venues and services? Check out our informative website, www.HereComesTheGuide.com.

421

Villa Chanticleer

Historic Venue

900 Chanticleer Way, Healdsburg
707/318-9925
www.villachanticleer.com
bhughes@villachanticleer.com

- Rehearsal Dinners
- Ceremonies
- Wedding Receptions
- Corp. Events/Mtgs.
- Private Parties
- Accommodations

Among the trees and manicured lawns of this 17-acre park you'll find Villa Chanticleer, a charming venue that will put you in mind of a gentler, more graceful time.

Built in 1910 as a country resort, the Villa has a rich history of hosting weddings, receptions, parties and community events. Guests appreciate not only the peace and beauty of the lovely surroundings, but the facility's thoughtful amenities as well—both the Villa and Annex have been outfitted with a state-of-of-the-art audiovisual system to enhance your event.

When you arrive on the Villa grounds, take a moment to enjoy the large trees, mature landscape, fresh air and birdsong. As you cross the stone steps to enter the Villa, notice the wide veranda shaded by a handsome, wisteria-draped arbor. Inside, you're welcomed by an open, gracious foyer. The bar area directly ahead is conveniently U-shaped and surrounded by eight large booths, perfect for a cocktail hour or small family affair.

The doors to your right lead to the Dining Room; those on your left open to the Ballroom. Each 3,000-square-foot room features redwood paneling, light-toned hardwood floors and bucolic views. In the Dining Room, generous picture windows frame panoramic vistas of the Alexander Valley below and Geyser Peak in the distance. From the Ballroom, you can see the veranda, lawn, and hillside covered in oaks, maples and bay laurel trees. A centrally located, modern commercial kitchen is easily accessible from both spaces, adding to their versatility.

A short walk from the Villa is the elegant Wedding Garden. Wrought-iron gates invite you into the two-level secluded lawn bordered by terraced flowerbeds and redwood trees. A quaint gazebo may serve as either a backdrop or the focal point for your ceremony.

The Annex and the Picnic/Barbecue area are excellent for casual events such as family reunions, baby showers, company picnics and rehearsal dinners.

This multifaceted facility provides a memorable setting for large or intimate gatherings, and the price is quite attractive. No wonder Villa Chanticleer has been a favorite of wedding couples and their guests for generations.

CEREMONY CAPACITY: The Ballroom and Dining Room each accommodate 250 seated guests; the Wedding Garden holds up to 250 guests; and the Annex holds 120 seated guests.

EVENT/RECEPTION CAPACITY: The Dining Room and Ballroom each hold 250 seated banquet-style, or 200 seated at 60-inch round tables. The Annex (which is a smaller building located next to the Main Villa) accommodates 120 seated or 150 for a standing reception. Outdoor picnic facilities accommodate 200 people and the bar area up to 150 guests.

MEETING CAPACITY: For corporate functions, the entire building holds up to 600 seated guests.

FEES & DEPOSITS: The Villa's 12-hour rental fee ranges $1,675–6,000 depending on day of the event. Fees for the Wedding Garden (available Friday–Sunday) range $850–1,500 depending on the day. The rental fee for the Villa Annex is approximately half that of the Villa. An hourly rate is also available for both buildings; call for details. Rental fees are due when reservations are confirmed. A security/damage deposit is required: $1,000 for the Wedding Garden or the Villa, and $600 for the Annex. This fee is due 60 days prior to your event and will be refunded 6–8 weeks after the event. There is a rental fee for use of the picnic area along with a $200 security/damage deposit.

AVAILABILITY: Year-round, daily, including some holidays. The Wedding Garden is available Friday–Sunday only.

SERVICES/AMENITIES:
Catering: BYO licensed caterer
Kitchen Facilities: commercial
Tables & Chairs: provided
Linens, Silver, etc.: china and silver available, extra fee; BYO linens
Restrooms: wheelchair accessible
Dance Floor: yes
Bride's Dressing Area: yes
AV/Meeting Equipment: PA, easels, screen, podium, stage, LCD projectors

Parking: large lot, 130 spaces
Accommodations: no guest rooms
Outdoor Night Lighting: no
Outdoor Cooking Facilities: BBQ
Cleanup: caterer responsible for kitchen; other cleaning handled by venue, extra fee
View: nearby mountain range

RESTRICTIONS:
Alcohol: in-house or BYO beer and wine
Smoking: outdoors only
Music: amplified OK indoors only

Wheelchair Access: yes
Insurance: liability provided, extra fee
Other: no rice, birdseed, metallic balloons, streamers or confetti

Red Barn Ranch

Ranch

16181 Mountain House Road, Hopland
707/272-0611
www.redbarnranchevents.com
redbarnranchevents@gmail.com

● Rehearsal Dinners
● Ceremonies
● Wedding Receptions
● Corp. Events/Mtgs.
□ Private Parties
□ Accommodations

This charming, family-run venue is nestled in the foothills south of Hopland, just a few miles from Highway 101. It sits on 100 acres of rolling hills dotted with centuries-old oak trees, and features a babbling creek, turtle pond, gardens, a small vineyard, and its postcard-perfect namesake red barn. The ranch's owners, the third generation of the Rorabaugh Family to live here, have spent the past 20 years transforming this former sheep and dairy farm into a wonderfully flexible, rustic event location.

The Barn itself is over 100 years old, and throughout its restoration the owners were careful to preserve and repurpose many original farm elements. Wagon wheel fans are hung from the rafters, and an elevated platform once used for sheep now holds a sound system connected to speakers positioned throughout the ranch. There's a sheltered, open-air catering area just off the barn, along with a large Santa Maria-style barbecue wagon—your hosts will even provide the wood!

Across from the Barn, a small red shed has been given new life as the adorable Southern Belle Saloon. It's become a favorite place for a bar, and is equipped with a commercial-grade ice maker, climate controls, and a large window fitted with an exterior shelf for serving. Next to the Saloon, there's an oversized fire pit, big enough for a crowd to gather around and roast s'mores.

Options for use of the outdoor areas are virtually unlimited. Three spacious lawns, as well as a patio adjoining the Barn, can host your ceremony, reception, and cocktail hour in any configuration you choose. With so much land, there's ample room for lawn games, a photo booth, and an al fresco lounge area—the hosts love to see couples express their creativity when deciding how to make the ranch their own.

The property is almost entirely solar powered, and a gravity-flow system uses rainwater collected in the ponds to keep the grounds and gardens green year-round. Red Barn Ranch also provides couples with a list of trusted local vendors in an effort to support Hopland's economy.

The Rorabaugh Family suggests making the most of your weekend by organizing a creekside campout for your family and friends. Alternatively, they offer trailer parking for those who might not want to "rough it". Your rental package gives you access to the grounds from Friday through Sunday—just the right amount of time to relax and make memories in this special place.

CEREMONY, EVENT/RECEPTION & MEETING CAPACITY: The site accommodates 500 seated or standing guests outoors.

FEES & DEPOSITS: A $2,000 deposit is required to reserve your date and the balance is due 30 days prior to the event. The rental fee is $7,000. No hard alcohol is allowed on the premises.

AVAILABILITY: Year-round, daily, noon–midnight.

SERVICES/AMENITIES:

Catering: BYO
Kitchen Facilities: prep only
Tables & Chairs: some provided
Linens, Silver, etc.: BYO
Restrooms: wheelchair accessible
Dance Floor: provided
Bride's Dressing Area: yes
AV/Meeting Equipment: provided

Parking: large lot
Accommodations: 3 guest rooms
Outdoor Night Lighting: yes
Outdoor Cooking Facilities: BBQ on site
Cleanup: caterer or renter
View: panorama of rolling hills, oak trees, vineyard, pond, creek, fields, cows, lawns, and railroad
Other: tent and trailer camping, fire pit, horse-shoes, mister systems, wine barrels, stage

RESTRICTIONS:

Alcohol: BYO
Smoking: designated areas only
Music: OK outdoors

Wheelchair Access: no
Insurance: liability required

Carneros Resort and Spa

Resort and Spa

4048 Sonoma Highway, Napa
707/299-4967 Wedding Specialist
www.carnerosresort.com
eharris@carnerosresort.com

- Rehearsal Dinners
- Ceremonies
- Wedding Receptions
- Corp. Events/Mtgs.
- Private Parties
- Accommodations

Nestled among 28 acres of rolling hills, grapevines, and unspoiled farmland, the Carneros Resort and Spa is a one-of-a-kind setting. The venue's architectural style is based on cues from the local countryside—barns, silos and ranchers' cottages—but rendered with a shot of industrial soul. The result is a clean, modernist aesthetic—and the perfect balance of rustic charm and unpretentious luxury.

Beautifully landscaped walking paths meander through flowering gardens with fountains to all the facilities on the property. At The Arbor, their premier ceremony location, you can exchange vows against a backdrop of Napa Valley vineyards and distant mountains. This site also boasts a number of enhancements, including a lovely trellis, water feature, lush plantings—even drought-tolerant, heel-friendly turf!

A wide range of inspiring event locations can accommodate the size and style of almost any celebration. The Napa and Sonoma Ballrooms showcase the resort's unique design with their soaring peaked roofs, handcrafted barn-board walls, and state-of-the-art lighting and sound. Both ballrooms, which can be divided into smaller sections for more intimate events, are filled with natural light and open onto the Carneros Courtyard through multiple sets of French doors.

The Carneros Courtyard is custom-made for outdoor gatherings. Along with its spacious lawn and stone fireplace, it's wired for sound and has festival lighting. It's a dream spot for an open-air cocktail reception or post-dinner cigars and cognac by a roaring fire.

For rehearsal dinners or smaller weddings and private events, reserve the Hilltop Restaurant. Its patios flank the signature infinity-edged pool, and whether you're entertaining inside the restaurant or out, you'll enjoy a breathtaking view of the hills and surrounding vineyards.

Wine tasting is a favorite pastime in the valley, but the resort offers a long list of other tempting activities. Let's start with eating: In addition to the Hilltop Dining Room, the FARM and The Boon Fly Café round out a trio of great on-site restaurants. Get the blood moving with a yoga class, a round of bocce ball, or a swim in the lap pool (where you can recover from your exertions by lounging on the elevated deck beneath a cooling shade trellis). The Fitness Barn, overlooking the pool, provides plenty of equipment and features retractable walls to take advantage of the Napa weather. For a more relaxing approach to improving your well being, head to the Spa at the Resort. Here, you'll find an extensive menu of massages, body treatments, facials, products, and much more—all in a tranquil, healing environment.

At the end of a thoroughly satisfying day, your own little hideaway awaits. Indulge in an outdoor shower for two on your private patio with a view of bucolic vineyards and rolling hills. Then luxuriate in the heated slate floors, 800-thread-count sheets, and a match-ready fireplace. Although The Carneros Resort and Spa is only an hour from San Francisco, you'll feel like you've traveled to another world, a place where beauty and serenity reign and every one of your sophisticated desires is catered to.

CEREMONY, EVENT/RECEPTION & MEETING CAPACITY: The Resort holds up to 175 guests indoors or outdoors, seated or standing.

FEES & DEPOSITS: 50% of the estimated event total is required to secure your date. An additional 25% is due both 9 and 6 months prior to the event, and the balance is due 14 days prior. The rental fee ranges $8,000–12,000 depending on the space reserved. The food & beverage minimum starts at $200/person. Tax and a 20% service charge are additional.

AVAILABILITY: Year-round, daily, anytime.

SERVICES/AMENITIES:

Catering: in-house
Kitchen Facilities: n/a
Tables & Chairs: provided
Linens, Silver, etc.: provided
Restrooms: wheelchair accessible
Dance Floor: provided
Bride's Dressing Area: CBA
AV/Meeting Equipment: CBA
Other: spa services

Parking: large lot
Accommodations: 86 cottages and private homes
Outdoor Night Lighting: yes
Outdoor Cooking Facilities: BBQ CBA
Cleanup: provided
View: garden, meadow, mountains, vineyards, hills, pool

RESTRICTIONS:

Alcohol: in-house
Smoking: outdoors only
Music: amplified OK indoors; outdoors, acoustic only with volume restrictions

Wheelchair Access: yes
Insurance: not required

Fairview Napa

Event Center at Golf Club

2295 Streblow Drive, Napa
707/255-4333
www.fairviewevents.com/napa
napa@fairviewevents.com

- Rehearsal Dinners
- Ceremonies
- Wedding Receptions
- Corp. Events/Mtgs.
- Private Parties
- Accommodations

In one of the most popular (and pricey) destination wedding regions in the country, it's rare to find a venue of such exquisite beauty and affordability as Fairview Napa. Fairview Events provides couples with exceptional value and personalized service, and their Napa site, set amidst 350 scenic acres of Kennedy Park Golf Course, really exceeds expectations.

It all starts with the verdant Ceremony Lawn. Scented by white and pink roses, it features a soothing water wall and a low stone fence along one side for privacy. An old-fashioned lamppost and a pair of oak barrels adds Wine Country flavor to the wedding aisle. Exchange vows beneath a redwood arbor against a lush background of evergreens and feathery maples that rustle in the afternoon breeze. If you time it right, you can say "I do" as the sunset paints the sky beyond the trees.

Afterwards, invite everyone to savor the idyllic scenery with cocktails and appetizers on the lawn or on the nearby view-filled patio. Meanwhile, you and your spouse can hop into a golf cart with your photographer to explore the emerald fairways, artfully landscaped with bridges, ponds and even a romantic iron bench for two, shaded by a spreading Monterey Pine. Several neighboring locales also contribute to a creative "best of" Napa photo album: a vineyard, a formal garden complete with antique sundial, and an abandoned railroad track marked by a vintage crossing signal.

Then it's time to make your entrance into the spacious and private Pavilion. This 3,000-square-foot, climate-controlled reception area has a high, peaked ceiling draped in white and lit by chandeliers. The corner bar is built on a base of wine casks, and walls of picture windows frame a lovely vista of rolling greens, old-growth oak trees and the surrounding hills. Modern AV equipment is neatly tucked away, leaving lots of room for the large built-in dance floor. And since you're tucked away in the forested parkland with only the local wildlife for neighbors, you can keep the music (and the party!) going until midnight.

As always with Fairview, you'll have a wide range of menu options and can customize everything to fit your taste and budget. Choose one of their all-inclusive packages that cover all the details, from invitations to cake, or mix and match the elements to create the package that's right for you.

The helpful staff will oversee your celebration from start to finish, so you can relax and enjoy your own vision of the perfect Wine Country wedding.

CEREMONY, EVENT/RECEPTION & MEETING CAPACITY: The facility accommodates up to 220 guests, indoors or outdoors.

FEES & DEPOSITS: 25% of the estimated total event cost is required to reserve your date. An additional 25% is due 120 days prior to the event and the balance (based on your final guest count) is due 10 days prior. All payments are credited towards your final balance and are nonrefundable and nontransferable. The ceremony fee is $1,000, and completely customizable wedding packages start at $49/person. These include invitations, DJ, dinner, and more. For most packages, a champagne toast and wine with dinner are included and a hosted bar is extra. Tax and a 22% service charge are additional.

AVAILABILITY: Year-round, daily, event hours 6am–12am.

SERVICES/AMENITIES:

Catering: in-house
Kitchen Facilities: n/a
Tables & Chairs: provided
Linens, Silver, etc.: provided
Restrooms: wheelchair accessible
Dance Floor: provided
Bride's Dressing Area: yes
AV/Meeting Equipment: some provided

Parking: large lot
Accommodations: no guest rooms
Outdoor Night Lighting: yes
Outdoor Cooking Facilities: no
Cleanup: provided
View: garden, landscaped grounds; panorama of fairways, hills, lakes and old-growth oak trees
Other: event coordination, in-house wedding cake and florals, clergy on staff

RESTRICTIONS:

Alcohol: in-house
Smoking: outdoors only
Music: amplified OK with restrictions

Wheelchair Access: yes
Insurance: not required
Other: no rice, confetti or glitter; no open flames

This is important! Tell locations you're reading HERE COMES THE GUIDE and ask if our information is still current.

429

Silverado Resort and Spa

Resort & Spa

1600 Atlas Peak Road, Napa
707/257-5469
silveradoresort.com/weddings
sales@silveradoresort.com

- Rehearsal Dinners
- Ceremonies
- Wedding Receptions
- Corp. Events/Mtgs.
- Private Parties
- Accommodations

The gracious plantation-style mansion at the heart of Silverado Resort and Spa has been welcoming guests to this picturesque corner of the Napa Valley since the 1870s. As you drive down the long, private entrance road lined with magnolia and palm trees, it's easy to feel transported to another time and place—one with a seamless blend of Southern hospitality and casual California charm.

The resort's most popular spot for weddings, especially during warmer months, is The Grove, an outdoor venue at the center of the South Golf Course that's surrounded by majestic, ancient oaks. A grassy aisle leads to a soaring natural arch formed by tree branches, and during quiet moments of your ceremony guests may even be able to hear the gentle babbling of Milliken Creek. After exchanging vows, you'll dine and dance under the stars in a romantic brick courtyard strung with market lights.

The Arbor offers another al fresco ceremony location, with an elevated path curving down to a secluded sunken courtyard encircled by rose bushes and trailing vines. From here, invite your guests to a reception in your choice of three indoor spaces. Or, consider hosting your entire wedding in The Mansion Gardens, a 30,000-square-foot indoor/outdoor event center adjacent to the stately mansion. As of Fall 2016, it will feature an enormous permanent open-sided pavilion, a stage, and a small vineyard (this *is* Wine Country, after all, so taking photos among the vines is a must!)

Those with a traditional indoor affair in mind can opt for the Grand Ballroom, a classically lovely space with a 15-foot ceiling, crystal chandeliers and plush carpeting, as well as a large dance floor. A row of French doors opens to the Fairway Deck, a hardwood terrace shaded by a sweeping fabric awning. It's an enchanting spot for your cocktail hour, with a view of the golf course and the sunset over the Vaca Mountain Range.

More intimate weddings can be hosted in the stylish Royal Oak and Vintners' Court rooms. They have floor-to-ceiling windows overlooking the grounds; artful, modern Wine Country-inspired décor; and access to the airy Terrace. A recently remodeled annex provides a selection of conference-style rooms that can be used as day-of prep areas for the bride and groom, or rented for a luncheon or day-after brunch.

There are over 370 guest accommodations at Silverado, ranging from basic hotel-style rooms to "homestyle" cottages large enough for families. The on-site Silverado Market & Bakery lets guests stock up on wine and snacks from beloved local artisans, while The Grill serves breakfast, lunch, and dinner focusing on sustainable, farm-to-fork fare. And with two PGA golf courses, an incredible world-class spa with full salon services, hiking and biking trails nearby, ten swimming pools, ten tennis courts, bocce ball, and countless wineries to tour, you and your guests will have no trouble finding activities to create the perfect Napa Valley weekend.

CEREMONY CAPACITY: The site can seat 350 indoors or 250 outdoors.

EVENT/RECEPTION CAPACITY: The facility holds 350 seated or 400 standing indoors, and 250 seated or 300 standing outdoors.

MEETING CAPACITY: The facility can accommodate 400 seated guests.

FEES & DEPOSITS: 25% of the anticipated food & beverage total is required to reserve your date and the balance is due with the signed contract. Rental fees range $1,500–10,000 depending on the day and time of the event and the space rented. Meals range $129–235/person. Tax, alcohol and a 22% service charge are additional.

AVAILABILITY: Year-round, daily, 6am–1am.

SERVICES/AMENITIES:

Catering: in-house
Kitchen Facilities: n/a
Tables & Chairs: provided
Linens, Silver, etc.: provided
Restrooms: wheelchair accessible
Dance Floor: portable provided
Bride's Dressing Area: yes
AV/Meeting Equipment: CBA

Parking: large lot
Accommodations: 370 guest rooms
Outdoor Night Lighting: yes
Outdoor Cooking Facilities: none
Cleanup: provided
View: garden, hills, landscaped grounds, valley, vineyards; panorama of mountains and fairways
Other: event coordination

RESTRICTIONS:

Alcohol: in-house
Smoking: not allowed
Music: amplified OK with restrictions

Wheelchair Access: yes
Insurance: not required

SpringHill Suites by Marriott-Napa Valley

Hotel

101 Gateway Road East, Napa
707/251-4060

www.springhillsuitesnapavalley.com
tayanique.harding@marriott.com

- Rehearsal Dinners
- Ceremonies
- Wedding Receptions
- Corp. Events/Mtgs.
- Private Parties
- Accommodations

Located a mere ten minutes from downtown Napa, this custom-built hotel from Marriott is the ideal spot to host your dream Napa wedding without the big Napa cost. Romantic gardens, a private vineyard, gracious reception areas, and a relaxed atmosphere create a setting where you'll want to gather friends and family to celebrate … then linger to explore the best of the Wine Country, just a picturesque drive away.

The hotel's inviting lobby instantly draws you in with its warm Tuscan hues, soft leather chairs, exposed-beam ceiling and modern stone fireplace. French doors and a wall of windows overlook a covered patio and the venue's beautifully landscaped grounds. This series of lush gardens, bordered with lavender, white roses and colorful seasonal blooms, are connected by meandering walkways and dotted with trees.

Springhill's lovely ceremony site features large, twin lawns separated by a wide center aisle so that everyone seated on them has a clear view of your entrance. You'll exchange vows beneath a lattice arch set in front of a charming fountain wall, reminiscent of something you'd see in an Italian piazza. In the background, tall trees frame the rolling Napa Hills.

This spacious outdoor plaza allows ample room for serving cocktails and hors d'oeuvres on the grass or patio areas. Dinner and dancing follow in the Tented Pavilion, which has a large dance floor and a draped, high-peaked ceiling. You can remove the walls for an open-air effect, affording glorious views of the gardens as well as glowing pink sunsets fanning over the hotel's Mediterranean roofline. A fire pit on the other side of the lawn makes a nice place for a nightcap or quiet conversation.

If you prefer an indoor reception, start with a red carpet entry into the Chardonnay Foyer and Ballroom, both designed with high ceilings and impressive glass chandeliers. The smaller, more intimate Bordeaux or Merlot Rooms might be perfect for your rehearsal or welcome dinner, or can serve as your bridal room.

Since only one wedding takes place at a time, you have your choice of several event locales. The certified wedding coordinator on site can help you with everything from choreographing the flow and choosing the décor to planning your menu and selecting preferred vendors. (There's a full catering kitchen at the hotel so you also have the option of bringing in your own caterer).

Some packages include a complimentary suite for the newlyweds, along with discounts for out-of-town guests who will appreciate the roomy accommodations with separate sitting areas, flat screen TVs, i-docks, wet bars and free WiFi. There's also a wine bar in the lobby and a free breakfast buffet to fortify you before a day of sightseeing … or just lounging by the pool beneath swaying palm trees.

CEREMONY CAPACITY: The site accommodates 120 seated guests indoors, and 230 seated outdoors.

EVENT/RECEPTION & MEETING CAPACITY: The facility holds 120 seated or 150 standing indoors, and 225 seated or 250 standing outdoors.

FEES & DEPOSITS: A $1,000 deposit is required to secure your date and the remaining balance is due 7 days prior to the event. Event space rental fees range $750–3,500 depending on the day and time reserved, and event room selected. Meals range $25–120/person. Tax, alcohol and a 20% service charge are additional.

AVAILABILITY: Indoors, year-round daily, 6am–midnight; outdoors, May–October, 9am–11pm.

SERVICES/AMENITIES:
Catering: in-house, BYO, or choose from list
Kitchen Facilities: fully equipped
Tables & Chairs: provided
Linens, Silver, etc.: provided
Restrooms: wheelchair accessible
Dance Floor: portable provided
Bride's Dressing Area: yes
AV/Meeting Equipment: provided or CBA
Other: event coordination

Parking: large complimentary lot
Accommodations: 100 guest rooms
Outdoor Night Lighting: yes
Outdoor Cooking Facilities: BBQ on site
Cleanup: caterer or renter
View: canyon, fountain, garden, courtyard, landscaped grounds, pool area; panorama of green rolling hills

RESTRICTIONS:
Alcohol: in-house, or BYO with corkage fee
Smoking: outdoors only
Music: amplified OK

Wheelchair Access: yes
Insurance: not required

The Westin Verasa Napa

Resort Hotel

1314 McKinstry Street, Napa

707/257-5153

www.westinnapa.com/weddings
jperkins@westinnapa.com

● Rehearsal Dinners	● Corp. Events/Mtgs.
● Ceremonies	● Private Parties
● Wedding Receptions	● Accommodations

Located at the nexus of foodie heaven, premium vineyards and small-town charm, The Westin Verasa Napa is the epitome of relaxed luxury, offering beautiful surroundings and exceptional service. Add in crème de la crème dining created by one of the country's most prominent—and Michelin-starred—chefs and you'll elevate your wedding celebration to a sublime experience.

Designed like a rambling, Craftsman-style lodge, the hotel makes generous use of natural rock, pale woods and lots of glass. Its open, airy lobby keeps things low-key and sophisticated with an emphasis on quality materials like slate floors, thick rugs and soft leather sofas arranged near a polished stone fireplace. A four-sided bar in front of a wall of windows is a magnet for mingling, while the outdoor Fireside Plaza and its fountain topped with flames makes a fun setting for an inspired wine & tapas reception.

Each of The Westin's two ceremony areas has a distinctive flavor. Garden lovers will gravitate to the Oval Lawn, a grassy expanse hugged on three sides by the hotel. You'll exchange vows beneath a billowing canopy framed by towering palms, while overlooking the lush banks of the Napa River with the Mayacama Mountains in the distance. Enjoy cocktails on the adjacent bocce ball courts before taking a short country stroll along the river to your reception site.

For larger groups, there's the Solera Courtyard, a spacious plaza next to the Amphora Ballroom. It's a captivating locale with stone flooring, rock-and-wood pillars, flower-filled ceramic urns and border landscaping that mixes bamboo, red maple and a host of native plants to great effect. This is especially true at the semicircular end of the courtyard, where a curved wall set off by abundant greenery make an ideal backdrop for tying the knot. Savor some chilled bubbly and mouth-watering appetizers under strands of starry twinkle lights before moving inside to one of the reception rooms, each with a wine-related name like Barrique, Cepage, Domaine and Amphora. Muted, neutral tones will appeal to the most discerning brides, as will the coffered ceilings and shirred fabric light fixtures.

But no description of this destination resort would be complete without emphasizing the glorious food that is a highlight of any event here. Under the guidance of Chef Ken Frank, all ingredients are locally sourced and combined to perfection. The presentation is spectacular, but awakening your taste buds is the raison d'être of the menu (which can be completely customized). For the ultimate gourmet affair, book the La Toque Terrace, an intimate private dining room adjoining Frank's much-lauded restaurant.

In one of literature's most famous lines of poetry, Omar Khayyam suggested that "A jug of wine, a loaf of bread and thou" is all you need to be happy. But if he were alive today—and planning a wedding—he'd probably add The Westin Verasa Napa to the list. Their gorgeous rooms, friendly staff, gustatory delights and proximity to all the region's attractions will make you very, very happy indeed.

CEREMONY CAPACITY: The hotel seats 180 indoors and 250 outdoors.

EVENT/RECEPTION CAPACITY: The resort accommodates up to 180 seated or 230 standing guests indoors, and up to 250 seated or 350 standing outdoors.

MEETING CAPACITY: Meeting spaces hold up to 200 seated guests.

FEES & DEPOSITS: 50% of the food, beverage and setup costs are required to secure your date, and the balance is due 30 days prior to the event. The rental fee ranges $500–5,000 depending on the space, day and time reserved. Morning meals range $28–52/person, noon meals range $45–86/person, and evening meals range $89–122/person. Tax, alcohol and a 23% service charge are additional.

AVAILABILITY: Year-round, daily.

SERVICES/AMENITIES:

Catering: Michelin Star-awarded, in-house and off-site
Kitchen Facilities: n/a
Tables & Chairs: provided
Linens, Silver, etc.: provided
Restrooms: wheelchair accessible
Dance Floor: custom provided
Bride's Dressing Area: yes
AV/Meeting Equipment: provided, business center

Parking: valet required
Accommodations: 180 guest rooms
Outdoor Night Lighting: yes
Outdoor Cooking Facilities: no
Cleanup: provided
View: mountains, river, garden courtyard, landscaped grounds, pool area
Other: event coordination, in-house wedding cake, in-house florals, in-house DJ, in-room spa services, Jacuzzi, workout room

RESTRICTIONS:

Alcohol: in-house
Smoking: not allowed
Music: amplified OK with restrictions

Wheelchair Access: yes
Insurance: liability required
Other: no confetti, rice or birdseed; wedding coordinator required for ceremonies and receptions

Fairview Sonoma County

100 Golf Course Drive, Rohnert Park

707/591-5313

www.fairviewevents.com/sonoma-county
sonomacounty@fairviewevents.com

- Rehearsal Dinners
- Ceremonies
- Wedding Receptions
- Corp. Events/Mtgs.
- Private Parties
- Accommodations

Situated in the middle of Rohnert Park, a friendly community just south of Santa Rosa and an hour north of San Francisco, Fairview Sonoma County offers both class and outstanding value. The Club overlooks the 36-hole Foxtail Golf Course dotted with leafy trees, and all you see from the banquet center's 125 feet of floor-to-ceiling windows are velvety greens, the occasional golfer, and a duck or two heading for the pond just off the 9th hole.

Yes, only a short stroll from the banquet hall lies a calm green pond looking newly transplanted from the English countryside. Complete with weeping willows, waterfowl and a lacy white gazebo bordered by roses, it's an idyllic setting for exchanging vows. In addition to being very pretty, this waterside spot accommodates 300 seated guests, all comfortably facing away from the sun.

Weddings are held year-round, and are equally lovely during the afternoon, when the garden scenery is on full display, or as the sun sets in the evening. (In winter, couples wed inside before an arch and floral displays the facility sets up.) The bride makes her grand entrance from the banquet room's double-doors and all eyes are upon her as she proceeds along a curving walkway to the gazebo. While the couple poses for pictures afterwards, guests walk up a red carpet into the banquet center, a 3,300-square-foot, airy white hall filled with natural light from the expanse of windows. Everyone enjoys appetizers and drinks in the bar area until the newlyweds are announced and take their place at the head table. Catering options run the gamut from a casual buffet to formal sit-down dinner with gourmet fare. You can even add extras like a cappuccino bar or chocolate-covered strawberries. And rare among venues: There are no noise restrictions, so you can party until midnight!

To save you both money and stress, Fairview Sonoma County offers all-inclusive packages that can include a DJ and MC, invitations, wedding cake, florals, hosted bar and more. But if you want to design your own package, the helpful wedding pros are happy to customize to suit your particular needs. For example, a Russian couple enjoyed borscht at their reception, and a Vietnamese pair held a tea ceremony. Some couples have released butterflies during the ceremony, while one even rolled their Harley out to the gazebo for photos.

Although Fairview Sonoma County is popular for weddings, it also hosts rehearsal dinners, golf tournaments, fundraisers, retirement parties and civic luncheons. Charming and unpretentious, Fairview combines affordability with an ease of execution that makes it quite a desirable spot for Wine Country celebrations.

CEREMONY CAPACITY: The venue accommodates up to 300 seated guests both indoors and in the outdoor ceremony area.

EVENT/RECEPTION CAPACITY: The center holds up to 300 seated or standing indoors.

MEETING CAPACITY: The center accommodates up to 300 seated theater-style.

FEES & DEPOSITS: 25% of the estimated total event cost is required to reserve your date. An additional 25% is due 120 days prior to the event, and the balance (based on the final guest count) is due 10 days prior. All payments are credited towards the final balance and are nonrefundable and nontransferable. The ceremony fee is $599, and completely customizable wedding packages start at $36/person. For most packages, a champagne toast and wine with dinner are included and a hosted bar is extra. Tax and a 22% service charge are additional.

AVAILABILITY: Year-round, daily until midnight.

SERVICES/AMENITIES:

Catering: in-house
Kitchen Facilities: n/a
Tables & Chairs: provided
Linens, Silver, etc.: provided
Restrooms: wheelchair accessible
Dance Floor: yes
Bride's Dressing Area: yes
AV/Meeting Equipment: some provided

Parking: ample on site
Accommodations: no guest rooms
Outdoor Night Lighting: yes
Outdoor Cooking Facilities: no
Cleanup: provided
View: fairways, pond, mountains
Other: event coordination, in-house wedding cake and florals, clergy on staff

RESTRICTIONS:

Alcohol: in-house
Smoking: outdoors only
Music: amplified OK

Wheelchair Access: yes
Insurance: not required
Other: no rice, confetti or glitter; no open flames

Overwhelmed? Use the search criteria on www.HereComesTheGuide.com to narrow down your choices.

437

Auberge du Soleil

Luxury Inn & Restaurant

180 Rutherford Hill Road, Rutherford

707/967-3141

www.aubergedusoleil.com
emily.coyne@aubergeresorts.com

- Rehearsal Dinners
- Ceremonies
- Wedding Receptions
- Corp. Events/Mtgs.
- Private Parties
- Accommodations

Nestled in a 33-acre sunlit olive grove on the slopes of Rutherford Hill, Auberge du Soleil is not only one of wine country's most iconic venues, it's also one of its most romantic. In addition to breathtaking views, its five-star accommodations, service, and Michelin Star-rated culinary program have made it a magical destination for weddings.

No matter where you celebrate here, you're surrounded by beauty. The Terrace is an idyllic spot for exchanging vows and mingling over cocktails. From its airy hillside perch, this spacious deck overlooks a spectacular view of tree-covered hills and the Napa Valley stretching all the way to the horizon. The adjoining Vista Rooms, which open to the Terrace through multiple French doors, share the same view and provide a warm, casually elegant space for a reception.

Smaller ceremonies are held in La Pagode, an open-air, Asian-inspired pavilion tucked away among centuries-old olive trees, vineyards, and a sculpture garden. An exquisite dinner follows in the Maison d'Arbre, otherwise known as "The Treehouse". Located above the main level of the hotel, it's a unique private dining room with large windows and French doors that open to its own deck and a Napa Valley panorama.

At Auberge du Soleil, your experience will be as rewarding as the venue itself. Their team of professionals makes planning your wedding stress-free by providing plenty of personal attention along with their expertise. Exceptional cuisine is a priority at the inn, which specializes in Mediterranean-inspired food that showcases the freshest, seasonal ingredients from local and regional vendors. Renowned Executive Chef Robert Curry will customize a menu especially for you, and oversee its preparation by his talented culinary staff. To complement your meal, Wine Director Kris Margerum is happy to create the perfect pairing using selections from the hotel's award-winning wine cellar.

With a setting as picturesque as this one, you and your guests will want to savor it as long as possible. So why not stay an extra night or two? The accommodations at Auberge du Soleil are a delight: Terraced down the hillside, a series of earth-toned maisons house 50 guest rooms and suites, each with its own fireplace, private outdoor terrace, and views of the Napa Valley. You'll be treated to a spacious bathroom with a separate shower and soaking tub, custom-crafted bath products, sumptuous Italian linens, down bedding and duvets…and complimentary guest amenities including wine, fruit, snacks, espresso and more.

Luxurious, yet in harmony with nature…chic, yet cozy…tranquil, healing, and oh-so-lovely. Auberge du Soleil indulges and satisfies all the senses, which is why it has captivated guests for over three decades and will continue to do so for years to come.

CEREMONY CAPACITY: The Terrace holds 120 guests, and La Pagode accommodates up to 30.

EVENT/RECEPTION CAPACITY: Vista Rooms I and II, combined, hold 120 guests. Maison d'Arbre seats 30 guests.

MEETING CAPACITY: Please contact the venue for info on hosting corporate meetings.

FEES & DEPOSITS: 25% of the estimated event total is required to confirm your date. An additional 50% of the estimated total is due 60 days prior to the event and the estimated balance is due 7 days prior, with any remaining balance payable upon departure. The facility fee ranges $1,500–8,000 based on the date, time, and event spaces reserved. It includes: exclusive use of your selected private dining space, tables, Italian linens, Chiavari chairs, Riedel crystal stemware, silver, dance floor, staffing, complimentary valet parking (for parties up to 30), a dedicated private dining manager to assist with day-of event coordination, and more. Meals start at $80/person for brunch and $110/person for dinner. Beverages, tax and a 20% service charge are additional.

AVAILABILITY: Year-round, daily, 6am–midnight. Weddings take place 10am–3pm or 5pm–11pm.

SERVICES/AMENITIES:

Catering: in-house, no BYO

Kitchen Facilities: n/a

Tables & Chairs: provided

Linens, Silver, etc.: provided

Restrooms: wheelchair accessible

Dance Floor: yes

Bride's & Groom's Dressing Areas: CBA

AV/Meeting Equipment: CBA

Parking: valet

Accommodations: 50 guest rooms and suites

Outdoor Night Lighting: yes

Outdoor Cooking Facilities: no

Cleanup: provided

View: panorama of Napa Valley and vineyards

RESTRICTIONS:

Alcohol: in-house, no BYO

Smoking: area CBA

Music: amplified OK with approval

Wheelchair Access: elevator

Insurance: not required

Farmstead at Long Meadow Ranch

Restaurant & Farm

738 Main Street, St. Helena
707/963-4555
www.longmeadowranch.com/events
events@longmeadowranch.com

- Rehearsal Dinners
- Ceremonies
- Wedding Receptions
- Corp. Events/Mtgs.
- Private Parties
- Accommodations

Consistently ranked one of the top restaurants in Napa Valley, this nirvana for foodies is also an exceptional wedding locale. Their beautifully planted edible gardens and intriguing mix of indoor and outdoor venues make this downtown St. Helena hotspot the ultimate farm-to-table experience.

The verdant property juxtaposes the old with the new: The original Gothic farmhouse is now a general store and tasting bar for their award-winning wines and olive oils, and the restaurant—once a nursery barn—boasts architectural chandeliers made from repurposed antique tractor parts. Copious trees and vegetation offer shade as well as bursts of color, but, with Long Meadow Ranch's commitment to responsible farming, nearly everything that grows here makes its way onto the menu.

Nature is the backdrop for ceremonies at this charming retreat. One romantic site features a vine-covered Pergola, but for something a bit more rustic exchange vows in the Apple Meadow, a swath of tall grass bordered by sweet apple trees. If you've got a small party, say "I do" in front of Farmstead's graceful walnut tree.

The expansive Lawn, adorned with white roses, rosemary, and espalier apple trees and surrounded by vineyards, is a wonderful spot for a large sit-down dinner or an intimate gathering of friends and family under strands of festive twinkle lights. It also has a canopy-covered stage at one end (another ceremony option!) and is outfitted with a private covered patio that's ideal for a cocktail reception.

One of the highlights of an al fresco reception can be a Live Fire experience, where the chefs spring into action to cook right in front of the guests. Carnivores in your crowd will be impressed at how they can roast an entire pig or lamb to perfection, but vegans take heart—they also grill the salad. Homemade marshmallows and Scharffen Berger chocolate are provided so your friends and family can make their own s'mores as they sit around a bonfire.

If you'd prefer to move indoors, the Barn is sleek and chic with a minimalist aesthetic that includes a polished concrete floor (excellent for music and dancing till 12:30am!), high ceiling and exposed overhead grid with mini spotlights. An entire wall of multi-paned glass overlooks the vineyards, plus access to the covered patio creates a nice indoor/outdoor flow. The smaller Potting Shed can serve as your Bridal Suite or a cozy scene for a rehearsal dinner.

Whichever setting you choose, your dining experience is sure to please. Executive Chef Stephen Barber's extensive background in Southern cooking forms the basis for Farmstead's innovative menu that elevates comfort food to the sublime. Fresh, seasonal, Long Meadow Ranch ingredients combined with a team of culinary experts—including a charcuterie specialist—means that long after the bouquet has been tossed you'll still be reminiscing about that great meal.

CEREMONY & EVENT/RECEPTION CAPACITY: The Barn holds 75 for a seated reception, 120 theater-style, or 175 standing guests indoors and 300 seated or 500 standing outdoors.

MEETING CAPACITY: Meeting spaces seat 75 guests.

FEES & DEPOSITS: 50% of the food & beverage minimum is required to reserve your date and the balance is due 15 days prior to the event. The facility fee varies based on your guest count and the day and time rented. Family-style meals range $30–85/person. Tax, alcohol and a 20% service charge are additional.

AVAILABILITY: Year-round, daily.

SERVICES/AMENITIES:

Catering: in-house
Kitchen Facilities: n/a
Tables & Chairs: provided
Linens, Silver, etc.: provided
Restrooms: wheelchair accessible
Dance Floor: yes
Bride's Dressing Area: yes
AV/Meeting Equipment: CBA

Parking: shuttle service required for parties of 30 or more
Accommodations: no guest rooms
Outdoor Night Lighting: yes
Outdoor Cooking Facilities: BBQ on site
Cleanup: provided
View: fountain, grounds, mountains, valley; panorama of vineyards and gardens
Other: wireless internet

RESTRICTIONS:

Alcohol: in-house
Smoking: not allowed
Music: amplified OK with restrictions

Wheelchair Access: yes
Insurance: liability required

Meadowood Napa Valley

Resort

900 Meadowood Lane, St. Helena
707/967-1223
www.meadowood.com
weddings@meadowood.com

- Rehearsal Dinners
- Ceremonies
- Wedding Receptions
- Corp. Events/Mtgs.
- Private Parties
- Accommodations

Driving to the exclusive Meadowood Napa Valley property is indeed a pleasure. A narrow tree-shaded lane flanked by forested hillsides leads you into the sophisticated estate, which offers wine experiences, cooking classes, sporting venues, an all-suite spa, a health and fitness center, swimming pools and beautifully appointed guest rooms.

The superbly designed buildings are reminiscent of New England during the early 1900s, with white balconies, gabled roofs and gray clapboard siding. All is secluded on 250 acres in the heart of Napa Valley.

The sprawling, multi-tiered clubhouse accommodates small private parties and large celebrations with equal ease. It's set high on a slope, overlooking lush green fairways and manicured lawns. The spacious Vintners and Woodside Rooms are available for receptions, luncheons or dinners with dancing. The Vintners Room is particularly fabulous, with a high ceiling, stone fireplace and outstanding views. On request, the adjacent lawn can be set up with tables and tents for an outdoor affair.

This estate provides everything you need for a stellar event—award-winning cuisine, impeccable service, deluxe accommodations and an environment to match.

CEREMONY CAPACITY: The resort can accommodate 6–1,000 guests seated outdoors or 6–100 seated indoors.

EVENT/RECEPTION CAPACITY: The Golf Course accommodates 1,000 seated guests. The Vintners Room seats 120 indoors, and the lawn area accommodates up to 250 seated. The Woodside Room seats 45 with a dance floor and 60 guests without. The Woodside Lawn accommodates 75 seated guests.

MEETING CAPACITY: Please inquire for further information about corporate events.

FEES & DEPOSITS: For weddings, the facility fee is $2,000–12,000 depending on the day and time of year, and includes ceremony coordination, rehearsal and setup, china, glassware and floor-length white or ivory table linens with overlays and napkins. Votive candles and bistro lights are provided for evening events. Catering services are provided. Lunch buffets and barbecues start at $78/person, 3-course luncheons start at $76/person, and 4-course dinners start at $148/person. Tax and a 20% service charge are applied to the final total.

For business functions or other events, fees vary depending on room(s) selected and services required; call for more specific information.

AVAILABILITY: Year-round, daily, anytime. Call for details.

SERVICES/AMENITIES:

Catering: in-house, no BYO

Kitchen Facilities: n/a

Tables & Chairs: provided

Linens, Silver, etc.: provided

Restrooms: wheelchair accessible

Dance Floor: CBA in Vintners & Woodside rooms

Bride's Dressing Area: CBA

AV/Meeting Equipment: CBA

Parking: multiple lots, valet CBA

Accommodations: 99 guest rooms and suites

Outdoor Night Lighting: yes

Outdoor Cooking Facilities: provided

Cleanup: provided

View: rolling green hills overlooking old-growth forest

Other: spa and fitness facilities, golf, croquet, tennis, wine experiences, cooking classes

RESTRICTIONS:

Alcohol: in-house, or BYO wine with $40 corkage fee

Smoking: outside only

Music: amplified OK indoors, outdoors with restrictions

Wheelchair Access: yes

Insurance: required for hired vendors

Hilton Sonoma Wine Country

Hotel

3555 Round Barn Boulevard, Santa Rosa

707/569-5529

www.hiltonsonomahotel.com
stssc-salesadm@hilton.com

- Rehearsal Dinners
- Ceremonies
- Wedding Receptions
- Corp. Events/Mtgs.
- Private Parties
- Accommodations

Set on 13 acres of beautifully landscaped grounds dotted with eucalyptus and redwood trees, Hilton Sonoma Wine Country is known for its rustic charm and resort-style atmosphere. The property overlooks the city of Santa Rosa and the rolling hills of Sonoma County, a wine region that's not only famous for its viticulture, but has also hosted generations of family celebrations, weddings and getaways.

The hotel offers a variety of spaces for your event. Say your vows on the picturesque Nectar Lawn with the historic Red Barn as your backdrop, or, if your group is large, reserve the grassy, hedge-lined Harvest Meadow. There are three ballrooms to choose from for your reception, with the Sonoma being the most popular. It opens to a lovely terrace that's available year-round thanks to outdoor heaters.

Hilton Sonoma Wine Country's cuisine incorporates fresh, local, and seasonal ingredients, and their menus can be customized to fit your vision. Your personal Wedding Specialist will also work closely with you, making planning a breeze. And whatever wedding package you select, you'll receive a complimentary guest room for the wedding couple for two nights.

Your guests will appreciate that they can stay and play on the hotel's private grounds before and after the wedding day. Spacious accommodations, which are spread out over the property, feature many upgraded room types and amenities. Several rooms come with a deck and make fantastic gathering areas for families and friends to relax and enjoy each other's company. In addition, this full-service hotel provides a kid-friendly junior Olympic pool, elegant dining in Nectar Restaurant, and close proximity to wineries, breweries, shopping and entertainment.

With its prime location, flexible event spaces, topnotch service, and wealth of things to do, it's no surprise that this Hilton is a favorite for both special events and weekend retreats.

CEREMONY & EVENT/RECEPTION CAPACITY: Both indoor and outdoor spaces hold up to 250 seated or 350 standing guests in one area.

MEETING CAPACITY: Several spaces accommodate 20–250 seated guests.

FEES & DEPOSITS: 20% of the estimated total is required to reserve your date, and the balance is due 10 working days prior to the event. The rental fee, which starts at $700 for an indoor wedding and $1,200 for an outdoor wedding, varies depending on the day, time and season. Meals start at $53/person for lunch and $67/person for dinner. Tax, alcohol and a 21% service charge are additional.

Rates for business functions, meetings or other types of events vary. Please contact the venue for more details..

AVAILABILITY: Year-round, daily, anytime.

SERVICES/AMENITIES:

Catering: in-house
Kitchen Facilities: n/a
Tables & Chairs: provided
Linens, Silver, etc.: provided
Restrooms: wheelchair accessible
Dance Floor: yes
Bride's Dressing Area: no
AV/Meeting Equipment: provided, extra fee

Parking: large lot, complimentary self-parking
Accommodations: 250 guest rooms
Outdoor Night Lighting: CBA, extra fee
Outdoor Cooking Facilities: no
Cleanup: provided
View: hills, cityscape, grounds
Other: event coordination, assistance with rentals

RESTRICTIONS:

Alcohol: in-house
Smoking: outdoors only
Music: amplified OK

Wheelchair Access: yes
Insurance: required

Want to know WHAT TO ASK a potential location or vendor? Check out our Questions to Ask starting on page 21.

Hyatt Vineyard Creek Hotel

Hotel

170 Railroad Street, Santa Rosa
707/636-7200
www.vineyardcreek.hyatt.com
sonom-rfp@hyatt.com

- Rehearsal Dinners
- Ceremonies
- Wedding Receptions
- Corp. Events/Mtgs.
- Private Parties
- Accommodations

Located in the heart of Wine Country, just blocks from Santa Rosa's Historic Railroad Square and a short drive from over 200 nearby wineries, the Hyatt Vineyard Creek Hotel is a venue you and your guests will love. You can host your entire celebration here, and whether you're planning a local or destination wedding the hotel is the perfect home base for exploring the region. It offers a wide variety of event sites along with an attentive staff that can help you design an intimate dinner, a gala reception, or a spectacular al fresco affair in their divine gardens.

Nestled behind the hotel, the dual gardens are true treasures. The verdant Knights Valley Garden includes an expansive lawn and is highlighted by an impressive 80-foot water wall that borders one side. There's a curved trellis at the far end, which many brides use as an altar, and a wisteria-covered arbor that's ideal for a shaded rehearsal dinner or cocktail hour, followed by a reception on the grass. Another flower-covered arbor separates this locale from the even larger Sonoma Valley Garden. Planted with fragrant roses and lavender, it's framed by an array of lush trees and punctuated with dramatic sculptures. You can pose for photos amongst the rows of vines in a small vineyard, or in front of the wonderfully photogenic "Bridge". This striking wood-and-iron trestle, part of the Prince Memorial Greenway running behind the property, is worth exploring with your photographer (check out the stone steps and creek, too!).

Where the gardens meet the hotel, you'll find the Dry Creek Patio, a romantic spot for dancing or a cool-weather ceremony in front of the flickering fireplace. French doors open to the light and airy Dry Creek Valley Ballroom, with delicate sconces and soft pastel tones. Both this space and the Russian River Valley Ballroom, with its adjoining courtyard, enjoy lovely views and are just right for mid-sized celebrations. But if you decide to go big, then the Alexander Valley Ballroom and its large prefunction foyer are for you. Modern chandeliers, state-of-the art audiovisual equipment and room for 500 of your nearest and dearest give you the grand setting you desire.

Whatever your needs, their experienced Wedding Specialist—who also serves as your "day of" coordinator—can guide you every step of the way, from choosing décor and lighting packages to customizing your menu. She can also assist with other activities or services, like booking a welcome dinner for your bridal party at their casual-chic Brasserie Restaurant and Lounge. She's happy to reserve accommodations for out-of-town guests, too.

And don't forget—in addition to your complimentary wedding-night suite, you're earning bonus points that you can redeem for a honeymoon at any Hyatt Hotel and Resort worldwide. Now that's a nice way to start your marriage!

CEREMONY CAPACITY: The hotel can accommodate 500 seated guests indoors or outdoors.

EVENT/RECEPTION CAPACITY: The site holds 450 seated or 600 standing guests indoors and outdoors.

MEETING CAPACITY: Meeting spaces accommodate 500 seated guests.

FEES & DEPOSITS: 25% of the total event cost is required to secure your date and the balance is due 10 business days prior to the event. The rental fee ranges $500–2,000 depending on the guest count and the space reserved. Meals range $60–100/person. Tax, alcohol and service charge are additional.

AVAILABILITY: Year-round, daily, 6am–midnight.

SERVICES/AMENITIES:

Catering: in-house
Kitchen Facilities: n/a
Tables & Chairs: provided
Linens, Silver, etc.: provided
Restrooms: wheelchair accessible
Dance Floor: portable provided
Bride's Dressing Area: yes
AV/Meeting Equipment: some provided, more CBA

Parking: large lot, on-street, valet available
Accommodations: 155 guest rooms
Outdoor Night Lighting: yes
Outdoor Cooking Facilities: no
Cleanup: provided
View: gardens, wisteria trellis, 80-foot water wall, small vineyard, sculpture garden
Other: event coordination

RESTRICTIONS:

Alcohol: in-house
Smoking: designated areas only
Music: amplified OK with restrictions

Wheelchair Access: yes
Insurance: not required

Mayacama

Private Golf Club

1240 Mayacama Club Drive, Santa Rosa
707/569-2921

www.mayacama.com
rreynoso@mayacama.com

● Rehearsal Dinners	● Corp. Events/Mtgs.
● Ceremonies	● Private Parties
● Wedding Receptions	☐ Accommodations

Your Mayacama experience begins the moment you pass through the gated entry to the exclusive private residence resort where the golf club resides. From here it's a leisurely two-mile drive to your destination—just enough time to leave the rest of the world behind, soak up the serenity of a native landscape dotted with discreet luxury villas, and prepare to be wowed when you arrive at the clubhouse.

The sprawling Mediterranean-style compound at the top of the hill is truly special. Fronted by a circular drive, it boasts a dramatic domed entryway with arched iron gates that open into the sublime Courtyard Terrace. Shady, colonnaded walkways hug the perimeter and a soaring Mission-style tower rises like a citadel against the back wall. This bold, al fresco locale offers an inviting welcome for your guests and will later serve as the setting for your dinner reception.

But first, there's the all-important wedding ceremony and Mayacama has a wonderful spot for it: a sunkissed patio extending out from the hillside just below the clubhouse. While the couple says "I do," guests enjoy an added pleasure—a sweeping view of the rolling fairways, forested hills, and deep blue lake of the Jack Nicklaus-designed golf course spread out before them. After vows are exchanged, everyone walks to the back of the patio and steps through a pair of ivy-framed wooden doors that mark the entrance to "The Cave." Built into the hill, this elegant underground wine cellar is a cool, stone-floored space that's perfect for champagne toasts. A staircase inside the cellar leads back up to the clubhouse where the festivities continue.

Guests gather at the rear of the clubhouse for a cocktail reception on the multi-tiered Back Terrace. Breathtaking, 270-degree panoramic views include manicured fairways in front, the Mayacama foothills to the left and the occasional hawk circling above. It would be tempting to spend your entire celebration right here, but then you'd miss dining in that romantic Courtyard Terrace you saw upon arrival.

And romantic it is: Candlelit tables are arranged amidst ancient olive trees beneath the night sky, and more candles flicker along the edge of the central fountain. While your family and friends are reveling in this heavenly place, they'll feast on inspired California cuisine and local wines. Mayacama's seasonal and customizable menus center on fresh organic fruits and vegetables, locally raised meats and poultry, and fresh herbs from their own gardens. Sonoma's bounty of artisan cheeses and olive oils are key ingredients, too.

When dessert is finished, dancing commences in the adjoining Living Room, where a high, crossbeam ceiling, lots of glass and comfy sofas near a fireplace make this space both open and intimate. And since it also flanks the Back Terrace, guests can easily step outside, get cozy next to the blazing fire pit, and savor a cognac under the stars.

Tally up the commanding vistas, striking architecture, impeccable décor—and some pre-wedding pampering at their top-of-the-line spa—and it's obvious to anyone why Mayacama is a winning choice for a memorable event.

CEREMONY CAPACITY: The site accommodates 300 seated guests outdoors.

EVENT/RECEPTION CAPACITY: The facility holds 85 seated or 150 standing indoors and 300 seated or 450 standing outdoors.

MEETING CAPACITY: Meeting spaces seat up to 40 guests.

FEES & DEPOSITS: 25% of the total event cost is the nonrefundable deposit required to reserve your date, and the balance is due 10 days prior to the event. The site fee starts at $8,000 and varies depending on the day and time of the event, the guest count, and the spaces rented. Meals start at $100/person. Tax, alcohol and a 20% service charge are additional. A day-of coordinator is required.

AVAILABILITY: Year-round, daily.

SERVICES/AMENITIES:
Catering: in-house
Kitchen Facilities: n/a
Tables & Chairs: some provided, more CBA
Linens, Silver, etc.: some provided, more CBA
Restrooms: wheelchair accessible
Dance Floor: provided
Bride's Dressing Area: yes
AV/Meeting Equipment: some provided, more CBA

Parking: valet required
Accommodations: no guest rooms
Outdoor Night Lighting: CBA
Outdoor Cooking Facilities: BBQ on site
Cleanup: provided
View: forest, pond, garden, fountain, lake; panorama of mountains, fairways and valley
Other: in-house wedding cake, spa services

RESTRICTIONS:
Alcohol: in-house
Smoking: designated areas only
Music: amplified OK

Wheelchair Access: yes
Insurance: liability required

Oakmont Golf Club

Golf Course and Clubhouse

7035 Oakmont Drive, Santa Rosa
707/537-3671
www.weddingsinsonoma.com
heather@oakmontgc.com

● Rehearsal Dinners	● Corp. Events/Mtgs.
● Ceremonies	● Private Parties
● Wedding Receptions	Accommodations

Located in the heart of the Wine Country, the Oakmont Golf Club is just one hour north of San Francisco and 10 minutes from downtown Santa Rosa. Nestled under weeping willows and majestic oaks, it affords panoramic views of the Mayacama Mountains and the entire Sonoma Valley. Host your wedding here, and you'll appreciate not just the lovely setting but the event spaces and affordable cuisine as well.

The outdoor ceremony site takes advantage of the beautiful scenery—you exchange vows next to a tree-and-grass-fringed pond about 250 yards from the clubhouse. Guests are seated under shade trees facing the pond and waterfall, which serve as a marvelous backdrop during the ceremony. A storybook bridge beneath a canopy of tall willows spans the pond and makes a charming photo op.

Then it's just a short walk back to the clubhouse for the rest of the celebration. Cocktails are served on the expansive terrace overlooking the 18th green. While guests are toasting the newlyweds, they also get to enjoy the gorgeous landscape: the golf course's groves of mature firs, sycamores, maples and redwoods, with Hood Mountain and the Mayacamas in the distance. In the evening, family and friends can gather around wine-barrel fire pits beneath strings of festive bistro lights.

When it's time for the reception, three sets of double doors open into the spacious ballroom, which can be divided into smaller sections if desired. During the day, natural light flows in thanks to floor-to-ceiling windows that frame vistas of Oakmont's award-winning golf course and the surrounding mountains. The club's impressive bar, which is right down the hallway from the ballroom, also rewards with huge picture windows that look out onto the fairways and peaks.

Their all-inclusive wedding packages offer a wide range of options that cover all the essentials—plus a menu tasting, complimentary round of golf for two, and a day-of coordinator to ensure that everything runs smoothly.

Oakmont is easy to get to, easy on the eyes, and easy on the budget. All these assets have made it a local favorite, and it's certain to be a favorite with you, too.

CEREMONY CAPACITY: The 18th-hole site accommodates 300 guests.

EVENT/RECEPTION & MEETING CAPACITY: The ballroom holds up to 250 seated (300 with use of the terrace).

FEES & DEPOSITS: A $1,500 deposit is required to reserve your date. The rental fee starts at $2,000, and varies depending on the day and time of year. Meals start at $46/person. Tax and a 20% service charge are additional.

AVAILABILITY: Year-round, daily, 6am–11pm.

SERVICES/AMENITIES:

Catering: in-house

Kitchen Facilities: n/a

Tables & Chairs: provided

Linens, Silver, etc.: provided

Restrooms: wheelchair accessible

Dance Floor: yes

Bride's Dressing Area: yes

AV/Meeting Equipment: some provided, more CBA

Parking: ample on site

Accommodations: no guest rooms

Outdoor Night Lighting: yes

Outdoor Cooking Facilities: BBQ on site

Cleanup: provided

View: mountains, fairways, hills, fountain, lake

Other: wedding coordination for rehearsal and day of event

RESTRICTIONS:

Alcohol: in-house or BYO wine with corkage fee

Smoking: outdoors only

Music: amplified OK with volume restrictions

Wheelchair Access: yes

Insurance: not required

Paradise Ridge Winery

Winery

4545 Thomas Lake Harris Drive, Santa Rosa
707/528-9463
www.prwinery.com
events@prwinery.com

● Rehearsal Dinners	● Corp. Events/Mtgs.
● Ceremonies	● Private Parties
● Wedding Receptions	○ Accommodations

So sweeping is the view from the western veranda at the Paradise Ridge Winery that a bride can get an inkling of what it's like to be an eagle, suspended above hillside vineyards and oak groves, gazing for miles over the Russian River Valley. Yet the winery is just minutes from downtown Santa Rosa in the heart of Sonoma County wine country. Its proximity to the city, as well as its spectacular scenery, draws locals who flock here for sunset wine tasting on the veranda. Wedding parties come to the 156-acre family-run estate, too, and not just for the view. Owners Walter Byck and the late Marijke Byck-Hoenselaars combined the European traditions of Marijke's Dutch homeland with their own artistic tastes to create a unique setting for celebrations.

The centerpiece of the winery is a spacious, two-story building whose stucco walls, loggia, and mahogany veranda echo early California architecture. Built for special events, it houses the Vineroom (the estate's tasting room), the Nagasawa Cellar, and a professional catering kitchen. Guests drive up to the winery through pastures, vineyards, and the unique four-acre "Marijke's Grove" of artwork set among the oaks. The highlight of the Grove is a two-story-high sculpture of the word LOVE that can be seen from the Winery's covered veranda, where family and friends get together before being seated for the ceremony on the Poetry Terrace, a terracotta patio with two bridal stages—and a spectacular wine country vista.

A separate deluxe changing room is reserved for the bride and her entourage, so they can relax and sip champagne before the big moment. The bride makes her grand entry through the Vineroom's double doors onto the veranda, and then descends eight steps to the Poetry Terrace, which is shaded by colorful crepe myrtle trees. The groom makes his own entrance from the loggia, because the owners feel it's his special day, too.

After the ceremony, guests mingle on the Poetry Terrace and enjoy estate-bottled wines, champagne and hors d'oeuvres. As dusk descends, twinkle lights provide a romantic touch. When it's time for the reception, the doors to the Vineroom are thrown open. An oversized gas fireplace and dramatic Italian chandeliers add charm, and floor-to-ceiling windows capture magnificent sunsets over a vineyard panorama. At night, ambient lighting casts a honeyed glow over the room. If you're hosting a large gala, additional tables can be placed on the wraparound veranda, which shares an indoor/outdoor bar with the Vineroom. Wedding parties usually dance on the Vineroom's oak floor, but you can also set up a band on the Poetry Terrace. With the city lights winking in the distance and the moon cresting over the hillside, it's absolutely glorious.

While most couples prefer a sunset wedding during the warmer months, winter weddings here are also lovely. The Nagasawa Cellar is a novel option for an intimate ceremony in front of the grand, wood-burning fireplace. Your caterer, selected from the winery's preferred list, will help you create delicious pairings from the estate's vintages.

At the close of the festivities, friends and family gather in the winery's European-style courtyard for a traditional send-off of the newlyweds, whose marriage has been magnificently launched at this sophisticated venue.

CEREMONY CAPACITY: The Poetry Terrace holds 250 seated; the Nagasawa Cellar, 150.

EVENT/RECEPTION CAPACITY: The winery holds 250 seated or 250 standing indoors, and 110–250 seated or 250 standing outdoors.

MEETING CAPACITY: Several spaces accommodate 40–250 seated guests.

FEES & DEPOSITS: Half of the rental fee is required to confirm your date. The rental balance is due 4 months prior to the event; a beverage deposit and a refundable $1,000 security deposit are due 30 days prior. The rental fee ranges $5,500–9,500 depending on the guest count, day of the week and time of year. Wine, champagne and beer are charged on consumption, with the estimated total payable 30 days in advance. In January, February and March, the winery offers 50% off the facility fee. For business meetings or seminars on other days, the rental fee varies depending on the guest count, day of week and time of day. Weekday minimums start at $1,500; call for details.

AVAILABILITY: Year-round, daily. Special events and business functions, 8am–1am.

SERVICES/AMENITIES:
Catering: select from list
Kitchen Facilities: fully equipped
Tables & Chairs: provided
Linens, Silver, etc.: through caterer and winery
Restrooms: wheelchair accessible
Dance Floor: wood floor/terrace
Bride's Dressing Area: yes
AV/Meeting Equipment: podium, microphone, audio system, screen

Parking: ample on site, complimentary
Accommodations: no guest rooms
Outdoor Night Lighting: yes
Outdoor Cooking Facilities: pizza oven
Cleanup: caterer and facility
View: vineyards and Russian River Valley; panoramic west-facing sunset views

RESTRICTIONS:
Alcohol: wine, beer and champagne provided
Smoking: designated area outdoors
Music: amplified OK with volume limits, outside until 10:30pm

Wheelchair Access: yes
Insurance: additional liability required
Other: no confetti, glitter, rice, birdseed, bubbles; children must be supervised

---

The wedding vendors on our website are the best in the business. How do we know? Read page 553.

Vintners Inn

4350 Barnes Road, Santa Rosa
707/566-2607

www.vintnersinn.com
weddings@vintnersinn.com

Restaurant and Hotel

- Rehearsal Dinners
- Ceremonies
- Wedding Receptions
- Corp. Events/Mtgs.
- Private Parties
- Accommodations

Stepping onto the grounds of this 92-acre estate is a little like going through the proverbial looking glass—you're just a few minutes north of bustling Santa Rosa, but you appear to have entered a small village in Tuscany. Suddenly you're enveloped by vineyards, flowerbeds, courtyards, and fountains in a tranquil setting artfully designed to enhance peace of mind.

A grand bell tower and French fountain mark the entrance to Vintners Inn Event Center, created especially with weddings in mind. The interior features a beautifully detailed ceiling, an abundance of windows, wood and stone surfaces, vibrant wall coverings and rich fabric furnishings. Outdoor terraces are surrounded by rows of grapevines, gardens, orchards and a multitude of flowers. An expansive prefunction area doubles as a wedding chapel for indoor ceremonies. Mirrored stone alcoves on either side of the room are filled with candles and flowers, adding warmth and beauty to the space. When the weather is balmy, however, most couples prefer to tie the knot under the Wedding Pavilion, a gorgeous ceremony spot at the edge of a vineyard. A simple structure of four tall white columns topped by a wooden trellis frames the leafy vineyard backdrop and provides shade as you say your vows. Guests enjoy this quintessential Wine Country tableau from their seats on the adjacent lawn.

The *pièce de résistance* of the center is the Rose Ballroom, a 3,200-square-foot space with walls of windows overlooking the gardens. The richly decorated room features a 15-foot ceiling, impressive iron chandeliers and plush Axminster carpeting throughout. It's also equipped with state-of-the-art audiovisual systems, including theater-sized screens that automatically drop down for a DVD or video presentation. The Ballroom opens onto a trellised veranda and stone fireplace, flanked by gardens and lawn.

The estate is also home to the nationally renowned restaurant, John Ash & Co., and the deluxe, Four-Diamond Vintners Inn, a 44-room boutique hotel housed in three separate villas. A short stroll across manicured lawns and tile pathways takes you from restaurant to hotel, and gives you a sense of just how close you are to some of the most important things in life: good food and wine, a soft (and elegant) place to lay your head at night, and a tangible connection to nature. Walk out of your guest room and in one minute you can be standing in the vineyards or sitting on the restaurant's wisteria-draped rear terrace, touching the tendrils of grapevines just inches away.

The restaurant, which receives the *Wine Spectator's* Best of Award of Excellence year after year, showcases California cuisine. Its menu changes seasonally to take advantage of fresh, locally grown foods, and dishes are paired with an award-winning wine list featuring some 500 wines. Because the cuisine is such an integral part of this venue's appeal, bridal couples work with the chef to select a multicourse menu and design their own wedding cake. Hors d'oeuvre choices might include Ahi Tuna Sashimi on Wonton Chips with Avocado Tartar or Lamb and Rosemary Meatballs, while entrées range from Pan Seared Salmon with White Bean Purée to Grilled Pork Chops with Cheddar Cheese Grits, Braised Cabbage and Madeira Sauce.

Many guests want to fully experience the Wine Country, and plan an overnight stay at the inn. Nearby attractions include more than 200 Sonoma County wineries, hot-air balloon tours, golf, tennis, fishing, and even whale-watching and kayaking on the coast.

CEREMONY & EVENT/RECEPTION CAPACITY: The Event Center holds up to 250 seated or 500 standing guests, indoors or outdoors.

MEETING CAPACITY: The Event Center seats up to 240 conference-style.

FEES & DEPOSITS: 50% of the estimated event total is required to secure your date, and the balance is due 120 days prior to the event. Any remaining balance is due at the conclusion of the event. The rental fee ranges $3,500–10,000 depending on the space reserved and guest count. Multi-course meals start at $65/person. Wedding cake, tax, alcohol and a 20% service charge are additional.

AVAILABILITY: Year-round, daily, 9am–midnight.

SERVICES/AMENITIES:

Catering: in-house
Kitchen Facilities: full kitchen
Tables & Chairs: provided
Linens, Silver, etc.: provided
Restrooms: wheelchair accessible
Dance Floor: CBA
Bride's Dressing Area: yes
AV/Meeting Equipment: full range CBA

Parking: large lot, valet available
Accommodations: 44 guest rooms
Outdoor Night Lighting: yes
Outdoor Cooking Facilities: BBQ CBA
Cleanup: provided
View: vineyards, gardens, landscaped grounds
Other: bocce ball court, jogging trail through the vineyards, working vegetable gardens, dining terraces

RESTRICTIONS:

Alcohol: in-house, or BYO wine with corkage fee
Smoking: outdoors only (restricted by county ordinance)
Music: amplified OK with restrictions

Wheelchair Access: yes
Insurance: not required

Sova Gardens

Garden and Event Facility

5186 South Gravenstein Highway, Sebastopol
707/795-4747 Denise Looney
www.sovagardens.com
information@sovagardens.com

- Rehearsal Dinners
- Ceremonies
- Wedding Receptions
- Corp. Events/Mtgs.
- Private Parties
- Accommodations

It would take a pleasurable lifetime to discover all of the treasures hidden alongside Sonoma County's country lanes—the tucked away redwood groves, the small farms growing heirloom vegetables, the quiet studios of hardworking artists. One of those gems is Sova Gardens, a wedding venue that combines the best of indoor and outdoor amenities. Although it's located just yards off the highway to Sebastopol, you'd be hard pressed to spot it along the road. When you do find it, you'll be pleased you did.

Sova's wide lawns and rustic-style structures create a relaxed country feel. The first buildings that catch your eye are the water tower and the yellow-shingled, two-story 1906 farmhouse beside it. Faithfully and beautifully restored, the four-bedroom house—right next to the ceremony site—is a lovely backdrop for photos. The farmhouse is also available for weekend rentals.

Sova's long main facility and the place where most people enter the venue is called the Tavern Building. Converted from an early 20th-century chicken coop, it's a combination banquet and reception hall, club, lounge and bar (featuring an early 1900s bar from the old Santa Rosa Hotel). With its many windows, hardwood floors, red curtains, goldenrod walls and dark furniture, the Tavern is both an excellent stand-alone indoor space for winter ceremonies, and a welcoming retreat where guests can mingle and rest on warm days. (The commercial kitchen here is like catnip to local caterers—all they have to bring is the food!)

An arbor festooned with small lights extends from one end of the Tavern Building and looks out over the smaller of the site's two lawns as well as a grove of fragrant redwoods. Beyond, Sova's 10,000-square-foot lawn seems to extend forever, sloping gently from the Tavern Building toward a line of ornamental trees and rose-garlanded wooden fences. The lawn is intensely green—almost emerald—and its spaciousness makes it easy for guests to circulate and socialize. A three-tiered fountain splashes at its exact center, and potted flowers and ornamental palms flank it almost everywhere. The view extends to distant pastures, farm buildings and houses, adding to the very bucolic ambiance.

Photographers love Sova. One great photo op is the waterwheel at the base of the tower. With its lush pond, filled with reeds and blooming plants, the site is like a grand wishing well. Other choice spots for photos are under the redwoods, next to a rose garden, by the centerpiece fountain, in a rustic barn or at the edge of the smaller lawn overlooking a dance pavilion. The pavilion, easily accessed by a ramp or stairway, is outfitted with custom lighting and chandeliers. It's also bordered by ornamental trees, dazzling sunflowers and colorful vines.

Sova Gardens has an easygoing rural vibe, with all of the openness, informality and charm a bride might want as she imagines her perfect country wedding day.

CEREMONY & EVENT/RECEPTION CAPACITY: The site accommodates 200 seated or 300 standing guests outdoors.

MEETING CAPACITY: Meeting spaces hold 250 seated guests.

FEES & DEPOSITS: A nonrefundable deposit of 50% of the venue rental fee is required to reserve your date, and the balance is due 90 days prior to the event. The rental fee ranges $2,500–6,500 depending on the space selected and time and date of the event.

AVAILABILITY: Year-round, daily. Outdoor events must conclude by 10pm.

SERVICES/AMENITIES:

Catering: select from preferred list
Kitchen Facilities: fully equipped
Tables & Chairs: provided
Linens, Silver, etc.: through caterer
Restrooms: not wheelchair accessible
Dance Floor: provided
Bride's Dressing Area: yes
AV/Meeting Equipment: CBA

Parking: large lot
Accommodations: can rent Farmhouse
Outdoor Night Lighting: yes
Outdoor Cooking Facilities: BBQ on site
Cleanup: provided
View: gardens, landscaped grounds, pond, fountain, meadow

RESTRICTIONS:

Alcohol: BYO, no corkage fee
Smoking: allowed outdoors only
Music: amplified OK

Wheelchair Access: yes
Insurance: liability required

Vine Hill House
at O'Connell Vineyards

3601 Vine Hill Road. Sebastopol
707/823-8590

www.vinehillhouse.com
info@vinehillhouse.com

Private Guest House and Gardens

- Rehearsal Dinners
- Ceremonies
- Wedding Receptions
- Corp. Events/Mtgs.
- Private Parties
- Accommodations

It takes practically no time at all for Vine Hill House to rejuvenate the flagging spirit and lower the blood pressure of anyone beleaguered by city stresses. As you head through the Russian River Valley on a picturesque two-lane, country highway, and up the hill through apple orchards and vineyards, you can't help but wonder what awaits you. By the time you've reached the guest house and gardens, the fragrant air and country quiet have already begun to smooth your rough edges.

Enter through a small gate to the left of the guest house and into the garden, and any remaining tenseness melts away. What you see before you is a landscape of uncommon beauty. Set on a slight rise, the garden has an almost 360-degree view of the surrounding hills, covered with apple orchards and row upon perfect row of premium-quality grapevines. You can see distant Mount St. Helena to the north and the coastal mountain range stretching south.

Fortunately for you, this breathtaking setting can be the backdrop for your celebration. You won't need much in the way of decoration, since nature's already done such a great job. And what nature hasn't done, owners Dan and Jan O'Connell have. The handsomely landscaped grounds are tidy and well-groomed: One part of the garden is covered with plush lawns bordered by flowerbeds, densely planted with brightly-hued blooms; another section is planted with a small grove of firs, redwoods, oaks and madrones.

Weddings in this little bit of heaven are particularly sweet. The bride makes her entrance either from the guest house or through the entry gate, and walks along the garden path to a peaceful ceremonial lawn. Seated guests have the dual pleasure of watching the ceremony and taking in the spectacular view. For receptions, the manicured lawn is turned into an al fresco dining room, filled with linen-clad tables shaded by market umbrellas. No matter where you sit, you're treated to an eyeful of rolling hills, vineyards and endless sky. Later on, dance under stars and stately oak and redwood trees. And if the weather becomes uncooperative, tents or canopies can be arranged so that you don't have to worry about the elements.

Vine Hill House sits in the center of the gardens, and is a real charmer. Built in the late 1800s, the house was originally a two-story stagecoach stop, located further down the hill. Restored as a classic single-story, 1920s-style cottage around 90 years ago, it was relocated up the hill in 1957 to its present-day setting. The updated, fully furnished house has a large sunny kitchen, living room, and two bedrooms with private bathrooms. Each sunlit room has windows overlooking gardens, vineyards or orchards. During events the bridal party has exclusive use of the guest house to get ready, or to just relax. The house and gardens are also great for corporate meetings, picnics, nonprofit events, company seminars or retreats.

This is a place where you and your guests can slow down, relax and take in the changing landscape: blossoming apple trees and fields of mustard flowers in the spring; warm breezes and the sounds of frogs and crickets in summer; a blaze of color and the excitement of the annual harvest and crush in the fall.

CEREMONY, EVENT/RECEPTION & MEETING CAPACITY: Outdoors, the site accommodates up to 225 guests; indoors, 20 guests.

FEES & DEPOSITS: A nonrefundable payment of $2,800 and a signed contract are required to reserve your date. The balance is payable in 2 installments due 8 months and 3 months prior to the event. For a 6-hour wedding (April–November), the site fee ranges $5,895–8,295 for up to 150 guests. Overtime runs $800/hour. In addition, a portion of the wine served at the event must be purchased from O'Connell Vineyards. Please call for more detailed information.

For meetings and nonprofit events, call for more details.

AVAILABILITY: Outdoor events, April 1–November 30, 10am–10pm.

SERVICES/AMENITIES:

Catering: select from list
Kitchen Facilities: fully equipped
Tables & Chairs: provided, plus market umbrellas
Linens, Silver, etc.: CBA, extra charge
Restrooms: wheelchair accessible
Dance Floor: yes
Bride's Dressing Area: yes
AV/Meeting Equipment: BYO

Parking: ample on site
Accommodations: no guest rooms
Outdoor Night Lighting: yes
Outdoor Cooking Facilities: caterer's kitchen facility
Cleanup: caterer
View: vineyards, apple orchards, Sonoma hills
Other: tents/canopies can be arranged; heaters provided

RESTRICTIONS:

Alcohol: BYO, no corkage fees
Smoking: outdoors, designated areas only
Music: amplified OK with volume restrictions

Wheelchair Access: yes
Insurance: certificate required

Fairmont Sonoma Mission Inn and Spa

Resort & Spa

100 Boyes Boulevard, Sonoma
707/938-9000
www.fairmont.com
smi.weddings@fairmont.com

● Rehearsal Dinners	● Corp. Events/Mtgs.
● Ceremonies	● Private Parties
● Wedding Receptions	● Accommodations

As you turn off Sonoma's main street and into Fairmont Sonoma Mission Inn and Spa's ten acres of trees, manicured lawns and colorful gardens, the abrupt transition from bustling city to quiet retreat takes you by surprise. And once you begin to stroll around the grounds, your surprise turns into delight.

The Inn occupies a site once considered a sacred healing ground by Native Americans, who discovered the natural underground hot mineral waters here. Today, it continues to be not just a mecca for those seeking an antidote to stress, but a premier location for all types of special events.

An abundance of lawns are available for ceremonies, cocktail receptions and seated dinners. Among them are the Creekside Lawn, bordered by a creek and encircled by trees; the vast Breezeway Lawn, set off by flowerbeds; and the South Lawn, shaded by beautiful trees. Some of the lawns can be tented for more intimate outdoor parties.

Indoor spaces are often used in conjunction with the lawns. For example, you might exchange vows on the Creekside Lawn, then host cocktails on the private fountain patio adjoining the Sonoma Valley Room, before stepping into the ballroom for your reception. When you open the French doors to this dramatic setting, it makes a fantastic first impression: elegantly set tables glow with candles, creating an enchanting ambiance. The room also boasts golden walls, a high open-beamed ceiling with chandelier, and a wood-burning fireplace.

Perhaps the most popular venue is Vintage Hall. Located at the resort's Sonoma Golf Club, it provides the exclusivity of a private club and plenty of room for a larger wedding. Couples exchange vows on the Oak Tree Lawn beneath a spreading oak, or on the adjacent Courtyard steps. After post-ceremony toasts in the Courtyard, everyone moves into the Hall for a reception with a view: floor-to-ceiling windows overlook the spectacular 177-acre, 18-hole championship golf course. As night falls, guests often walk outside to mingle on the expansive veranda—it's the perfect spot to savor an after-dinner drink by the fire pit, while watching the sun set over the fairways. Plus, the party can continue even out here until midnight!

Food at the Inn is given as much attention as your event and your comfort. Fresh regional produce, cheeses, and meats are the main ingredients that go into everything, from simple hors d'oeuvres to sumptuous seated dinners. Exquisite wedding cakes are also made in-house. Your Wedding Specialist will oversee every aspect of your celebration, from assisting with planning to arranging overnight accommodations. And on top of everything else, guests have access to the Spa's full range of therapeutic and pampering services (their salon does makeup, hair, mani/pedis, and facials!) to help them look and feel their best. Many brides book the Spa Loggia, a private balcony, for a bridal party spa day.

When the festivities have concluded, the newlyweds can retire to their complimentary honeymoon suite, complete with romantic turndown service. And if they've opted for the "Wedding Weekend", they'll wake up the next morning with a couple of equally enticing choices: spend the day relaxing with friends and family and indulging at the inn … or go and explore all that Sonoma has to offer.

CEREMONY CAPACITY: Outdoors, the Creekside Lawn seats 200; the Oak Tree Lawn at the Sonoma Golf Club seats 200. Indoors, the Sonoma Valley Room seats 150 and Vintage Hall accommodates 200 seated.

EVENT/RECEPTION CAPACITY: The Sonoma Valley Room accommodates 140 seated, Vintage Hall holds 180 seated, and the Pavilion holds 250 seated. Outdoors, the Oak Tree Lawn seats 180.

MEETING CAPACITY: Multiple venues hold 10–200 seated guests.

FEES & DEPOSITS: The site fee ranges $4,000–9,000 and includes: on-site ceremony location with white folding chairs; cocktail hour site; reception site with tables, Chiavari chairs, white linens, china, silverware, printed menus, dance floor; formal menu tasting; and complimentary honeymoon suite for the wedding night.

AVAILABILITY: Year-round, daily, anytime.

SERVICES/AMENITIES:
Catering: in-house
Kitchen Facilities: n/a
Tables & Chairs: provided
Linens, Silver, etc.: provided
Restrooms: wheelchair accessible
Dance Floor: provided
Bride's Dressing Area: multiple options
AV/Meeting Equipment: full range AV

Parking: valet or self-parking
Accommodations: 226 guest rooms
Outdoor Night Lighting: yes
Outdoor Cooking Facilities: yes
Cleanup: provided
View: grounds, gardens, golf fairways and mountains
Other: coordination, wedding cakes, honeymoon planning assistance

RESTRICTIONS:
Alcohol: in-house
Smoking: outdoors only
Music: amplified OK indoors until 11pm, acoustic OK outdoors until 10pm, (both OK until midnight at Sonoma Golf Club)

Wheelchair Access: yes
Insurance: not required

Want to find more venues and services? Check out our informative website, www.HereComesTheGuide.com.

461

Viansa Sonoma

Winery

25200 Arnold Drive, Sonoma
707/341-7002
www.viansa.com
events@viansa.com

●	Rehearsal Dinners	●	Corp. Events/Mtgs.
●	Ceremonies	●	Private Parties
●	Wedding Receptions		Accommodations

If you've ever gone wine tasting in Sonoma, you probably noticed Viansa as you drove into the county, or maybe you caught a glimpse of it on your way back home. If, however, you actually stopped to visit the winery, chances are you didn't get much further. This place is so wonderful, it's easy to spend hours here—sampling the wines, having lunch, shopping in the Italian Marketplace and just strolling the grounds. Set atop a hill overlooking the Valley of the Moon and resembling a Tuscan Villa, Viansa embraces you with Italian hospitality and satisfies all your senses.

The Villa (aka the winery building), with its tiled roof, terracotta walls and shuttered windows is your first taste of Tuscany. A series of French doors along the left wing open onto a circular courtyard, flanked by olive trees and grapevines; colorful flowerpots encircle the fountain in the center and mark the perimeter.

To the right of the Villa a stone-walled staircase takes you past the thriving grapevines on either side up to a huge bronze door at the top. As you pass through the doorway, you enter a thoroughly enchanting hilltop "village." To one side is an intimate fountain courtyard, enclosed by ivy-clad walls and shaded by silvery olive trees. A few steps further are the expansive Main Lawn, a picnic area beneath a trellis laced with grapevines, and the Italian Marketplace. Everywhere you look you'll see bright red geraniums spilling out of planters, wrought-iron benches and, of course, the delicate presence of olive trees shimmering in the sun.

Once the winery closes to the public, Viansa is yours to enjoy. Get married in the circular courtyard or candlelit wine cellar. If you like the festive ambiance of the Marketplace, serve sparkling wine here while your guests mingle amongst vibrant displays of wines, mustards, olive oils, pestos and other gourmet delicacies. The venue's newest reception space is the versatile Pavilion. Available year-round, it provides breathtaking panoramic views of the Sonoma Valley, the estate vineyards, and coastal wetlands.

Before the sun sets completely, take a walk up to Upper Lawn, the highest point of the property. From the edge of the plateau you have a fantastic vista of Viansa's 91 acres of restored wetlands far below. This seasonal home to one million ducks, shorebirds and golden eagles also attracts avid bird watchers during peak migrations every spring.

The people at Viansa have long felt that Americans should be able to enjoy wine and food together, just as Italians have done for centuries. Guests who dine here appreciate the extraordinary amount of care that goes into the cuisine and service, and they have responded with their patronage: 80% of the winery's event business is word of mouth. At Viansa, they've not only created an exquisite environment for celebrating, they've made it possible for each guest to have an unforgettably delicious Italian experience.

CEREMONY CAPACITY: The Courtyard and the Lawn each accommodate up to 220 seated guests.

EVENT/RECEPTION & MEETING CAPACITY: Indoors, the facility holds 220 guests.

FEES & DEPOSITS: The rental fee and 50% of the catering total are required upon booking the estate. The rental fee ranges $2,500–12,000 depending on the day of the week reserved. Catering is provided exclusively by *Paula LeDuc Fine Catering* and pricing starts at $350/person. Event services, such as lighting, flooring and guest shuttles, are additional.

AVAILABILITY: The winery is open year-round. Weddings take place in the evenings only; call for details.

SERVICES/AMENITIES:

Catering: provided by *Paula LeDuc Fine Catering*
Kitchen Facilities: n/a
Tables & Chairs: provided
Linens, Silver, etc.: provided
Restrooms: wheelchair accessible
Dance Floor: area provided
Bride's Dressing Area: yes
AV/Meeting Equipment: CBA, extra fee

Parking: large lot
Accommodations: no guest rooms
Outdoor Night Lighting: yes
Outdoor Cooking Facilities: no
Cleanup: provided
View: Sonoma Valley, mountains, vineyards, wetlands preserve
Other: event coordination

RESTRICTIONS:

Alcohol: wine and beer only provided, no BYO
Smoking: outside only
Music: amplified OK

Wheelchair Access: yes
Insurance: certificate required
Other: no rice or birdseed

Brix

Restaurant

7377 St. Helena Highway, Yountville
707/944-2547
www.brix.com
matt@brix.com

- Rehearsal Dinners
- Ceremonies
- Wedding Receptions
- Corp. Events/Mtgs.
- Private Parties
- Accommodations

Brix may sit right on Napa Valley's main highway, but once you're inside you're in some sort of Wine Country Dreamtime where nothing matters except good food, good wine and the sharing of both with family and friends. (By the way, "Brix" is a term used by wine growers that refers to the percentage of sugar in ripening grapes.)

Brix is surrounded by vineyards, but behind the restaurant is a huge kitchen garden, formally laid out in the European style. Many of the fruits, vegetables and herbs used in Brix's cuisine are grown here—you frequently see a white-garbed sous-chef gathering ingredients for an order. Here, too, you can hold a ceremony amid the flowers and fruit, with a vista of the vineyards stretching out across the valley to the foot of the western mountains.

Intimate receptions often take place in the Oakville Room, a deliciously inviting space with an abundance of wood details that succeeds in being both elegant and informal. At the far end, a _trompe l'oeil_ mural makes you think you're looking through a large picture window at an authentic Wine Country landscape. Along one side of the room, a grand mirror reflects the lovely scene on the opposite side: tall windows framing a serene view of the adjacent tree-filled patio.

The restaurant's largest event area is the Vineyard Reception Site. This al fresco space, which was literally carved out of the Kelleher Family Vineyards, enjoys sweeping views of nearby grapevines and the Mayacamas Mountains beyond—the quintessential Wine Country setting. Here, you're seated on Chiavari chairs at tables regally set with Riedel stemware, St. Andrea silverware and Villeroy & Boch bone china. The food, the service and the ambiance will make you feel totally pampered.

The secluded Cottage is perfect for a small reception or rehearsal dinner. In this cozy nest, guests dine at a long table where conversation is fueled by the delectable fare. French doors on the western wall open to a private patio, an ideal place to start your celebration off with cocktails and appetizers. It's also a heavenly spot for a little after-dinner unwinding—simply step outside to watch the sun set, smoke a cigar or savor the gorgeous scenery.

In addition to growing a significant percentage of the produce used in the restaurant, Brix bakes their own bread and smokes their own salmon. Other ingredients are procured in season, and as fresh as possible. The wine list is graced by some of Napa's most prestigious vintages—it annually wins the Wine Spectator Best of Award of Excellence and the International Restaurant & Hospitality Diamond Award.

Warm, relaxed and intimate: if these words describe the wedding your heart desires, Brix awaits you…

CEREMONY CAPACITY: 240 outdoors at the vineyard site.

EVENT/RECEPTION CAPACITY: The Vineyard Dining Area holds up to 240 guests. Indoors, the Oakville Room holds up to 60, the Cottage up to 30, and the Reserve Cellar up to 12 guests.

MEETING CAPACITY: The Oakville Room seats up to 80 guests conference-style.

FEES & DEPOSITS: A deposit is required to reserve your date. Meals range $38–68/person. Tax, alcohol and a 20% service charge are additional.

AVAILABILITY: Year-round, for lunch and dinner Monday–Saturday and brunch and dinner on Sunday.

SERVICES/AMENITIES:

Catering: in-house
Kitchen Facilities: n/a
Tables & Chairs: provided
Linens, Silver, etc.: provided
Restrooms: wheelchair accessible
Dance Floor: patio or CBA
Bride's Dressing Area: yes
AV/Meeting Equipment: BYO

Parking: shuttle required for groups over 40
Accommodations: no guest rooms
Outdoor Night Lighting: terrace
Outdoor Cooking Facilities: yes
Cleanup: provided
View: vineyards, garden, mountains

RESTRICTIONS:

Alcohol: in-house
Smoking: outside only
Music: amplified OK

Wheelchair Access: yes
Insurance: not required

Santa Cruz Area

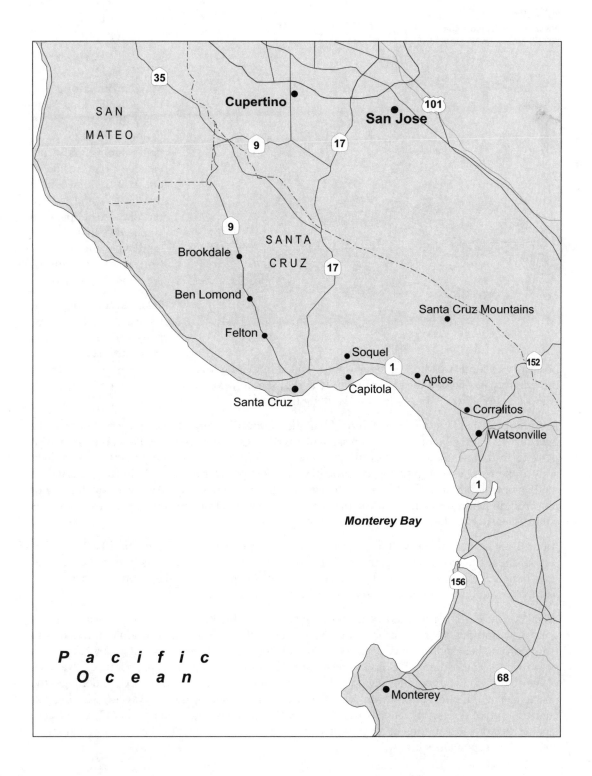

Seascape Beach Resort

Oceanfront Resort

1 Seascape Resort Drive, Aptos
831/662-7140

www.seascaperesort.com
weddings@seascaperesort.com

- Rehearsal Dinners
- Ceremonies
- Wedding Receptions
- Corp. Events/Mtgs.
- Private Parties
- Accommodations

Spread out along the bluffs overlooking Monterey Bay, this resort definitely lives up to its name. From almost any vantage point, inside or out, you have sweeping ocean vistas, and if you're one of those people who comes alive in the sea air (and who isn't?), you'll find the surroundings here quite rejuvenating.

Take the ceremony spot, for example: It's an expanse of lawn on top of a bluff, set against a postcard-beautiful backdrop of cypress trees and shimmering sea. The miniforest at the edge of the property is a favorite place for the bride and groom to have their pictures taken, and a short path leads down to the beach for a walk along the sand.

Receptions are held indoors in a variety of banquet rooms. The largest, the Seascape Room, has a light, airy feel and fabulous ocean views. Smaller weddings take place in the Riviera Room, which has one wall of windows that face the bay and another that overlooks the treetops. A skylight adds to the natural light in the space. Probably the most popular room for intimate gatherings is the Bayview Room. It not only faces the ocean, but has its own terrace. For a very small party or rehearsal dinner, reserve the Peninsula Room. It, too, benefits from an abundance of windows as well as views of the bay and tree-studded bluff.

All of these spaces, along with additional rooms, are also available for meetings. Each one has state-of-the-art audio, video, computer, high-speed internet and modem connections. Another huge benefit are the in-house professional meeting, wedding and special event planners who will assist you with the planning and execution of your event.

Whether you're getting married or hosting a meeting, conference or retreat here, Seascape is a great place to bring your guests for an extended stay. All of the accommodations (from suites to two-bedroom beach villas) have decks or patios, kitchenettes and fireplaces, and many have direct ocean views. You can go for a dip in one of three heated pools and hot spas, or take advantage of the tennis courts, gym and Olympic-size pool at the Seascape Sports Club. Sanderlings, the on-site restaurant, offers dining with sweeping ocean vistas. Nearby there are award-winning golf courses, and, of course, the Santa Cruz/Monterey/Carmel coastline is one of the most spectacular stretches of coast in the country. So, if you're tempted to turn your event into a vacation, go ahead—Seascape makes it easy.

CEREMONY CAPACITY: The Wedding Bluff accommodates 250 seated guests.

EVENT/RECEPTION CAPACITY: The resort holds 50–250 seated indoors.

MEETING CAPACITY: 8 rooms accommodate 35–400 guests.

FEES & DEPOSITS: For weddings or special events, a nonrefundable $2,000 deposit is required to reserve your date. Ceremony site fees start at $1,250. Wedding packages start at $105/person including catering and room rental. Seated meals for non-wedding special events or business functions start at $35/person; alcohol, tax and a 23% service charge are additional.

For weekday special events or meetings, the banquet room rental fee ranges $600–1,200/day, with catering à la carte. Meeting packages are available that include meals, refreshment breaks, banquet/meeting room rentals and basic audiovisual.

AVAILABILITY: Year-round, daily, 7am–11pm. Wedding receptions are held on Saturdays and Sundays in the Seascape Room, 4pm–9:30pm; or in the Riviera or Bayview Rooms, 1pm–6:30pm. For meetings or conferences, please call the sales department.

SERVICES/AMENITIES:

Catering: in-house, no BYO

Kitchen Facilities: n/a

Tables & Chairs: provided

Linens, Silver, etc.: provided

Restrooms: wheelchair accessible

Dance Floor: provided

Bride's & Groom's Dressing Areas: rentable suites

AV/Meeting Equipment: fully equipped

Parking: on-site for 500 guests

Accommodations: 285 suites and villas

Outdoor Night Lighting: yes

Outdoor Cooking Facilities: no

Cleanup: provided

View: Pacific Ocean panorama

Other: coordination, theme and beach events, complimentary night stay for bride & groom

RESTRICTIONS:

Alcohol: in-house, no BYO

Smoking: outdoors only

Music: amplified OK with limits

Wheelchair Access: yes

Insurance: not required

Other: no rice, confetti, birdseed or uncontained candles

Seascape Golf Club

Golf Club

610 Clubhouse Drive, Aptos
888/998-6276

www.countryclubreceptions.com
www.seascapegc.com
privateeventdirector@seascapegc.com

● Rehearsal Dinners		● Corp. Events/Mtgs.
● Ceremonies		● Private Parties
● Wedding Receptions		Accommodations

Santa Cruz and its environs have long been renowned for spectacular scenery. Clusters of forested hillsides hug a shoreline that teems with marine life and rainbow-hued flora, and the favorite pastime of locals seems to be watching for that twilight moment when the setting sun kisses the blue surf. Santa Cruz's quaint suburbs boast small-town charm aplenty, attracting artisans, tourists and nature-seekers by the thousands. Yet, like the monarch butterflies that flutter among the region's many eucalyptus groves, Santa Cruz has undergone a transformation during the last decade or so, shedding its Bohemian persona in favor of a laid-back sophistication. You'll want to take advantage of the area's attributes for your special celebration, and one of the nicest spots to do this lies in the beachside village of Aptos.

From Highway 1, head shoreward into a quiet residential neighborhood tucked away in the coastal highlands. Here you'll find the appropriately named Seascape Golf Club, perched on a bluff facing the Pacific. The cream-colored building has an arched colonnade running along the front, accented with flowering herbs and shrubs; a towering pine stands at one end, while a willow spills its languid boughs over the other, contributing to Seascape's lush allure.

Seascape is known for its "Weddings on the Green," ceremonies on the manicured grass of the 10th tee. To reach this magic spot from the parking lot, follow a flight of mariner-style stairs with ropes for banisters down to a delightful garden hollow. Landscaped slopes dotted with cheery surprises of color cradle a swath of lawn, ample enough for an enchanting ceremony for 240 guests. Set an archway, gazebo or columns just so, and your friends and family will enjoy a sweeping vista of the redwood-studded fairways. Then, while you newlyweds pose for scenic wedding photos, guests enjoy an open-air cocktail hour on an adjacent lawn, set up with umbrella-shaded tables.

For the dinner and dancing phase of your event, Seascape brings the party inside to the Monarch Room. This breezy, sun-washed space comes with a high ceiling and clerestory windows; ornate bronze chandeliers lend a dash of formality. The airy mood is enhanced by a neutral palette and a ribbon of windows that wraps around the room's outer edge, embracing a view that extends over swaying treetops and gently rolling fairways. Those reluctant to forsake the outdoors simply walk out to the terrace where garden benches invite a quiet respite, the better to watch the stars illuminate the sky.

A short walkway connects the Monarch Room to the Clubhouse, another attractive space for smaller events (or as a foul-weather backup for the ceremony and cocktail hour). The Clubhouse's natural wood ceiling conveys a relaxed-yet-refined quality. Windows frame the pretty golf course panorama, with the blue expanse of the Pacific just beyond. Set café tables and chairs on the Clubhouse's adjoining terrace, and guests can delight in the salty tang of the sea air.

Also delightful are Seascape's "package deals," which let you mix and match your event options. Seascape even offers "A Little Tyke's Reception," which provides a party room, buffet and entertainment for the kids—all you bring is the babysitter.

CEREMONY, EVENT/RECEPTION & MEETING CAPACITY: The club holds up to 240 seated or 300 standing guests.

FEES & DEPOSITS: A nonrefundable deposit, which is applied to your food & beverage total, is required to reserve your date. The amount of the deposit varies depending on how far in advance you book. Payment terms for the balance also vary, and may be arranged on an individual basis. Packages start at $22/person. Tax, alcohol and service charge are additional. Food & beverage minimums may apply. Menus and packages can be customized to fit your needs and budget. Call for details.

AVAILABILITY: Year-round, daily, 7am–11pm.

SERVICES/AMENITIES:

Catering: in-house
Kitchen Facilities: n/a
Tables & Chairs: provided
Linens, Silver, etc.: provided
Restrooms: wheelchair accessible
Dance Floor: yes
Bride's & Groom's Dressing Areas: yes
AV/Meeting Equipment: CBA

Parking: large lot
Accommodations: no guest rooms
Outdoor Night Lighting: yes
Outdoor Cooking Facilities: no
Cleanup: provided
View: Pacific Ocean, fairways
Other: event coordination

RESTRICTIONS:

Alcohol: in-house
Smoking: outdoors only
Music: amplified OK

Wheelchair Access: yes
Insurance: not required

This is important! Tell locations you're reading HERE COMES THE GUIDE and ask if our information is still current.

Monarch Cove Inn

Inn

620 El Salto Drive, Capitola
831/464-1295
www.monarchcoveinn.com
monarchcoveinn1@gmail.com

- Rehearsal Dinners
- Ceremonies
- Wedding Receptions
- Corp. Events/Mtgs.
- Private Parties
- Accommodations

We're going to ask you to participate in a guided meditation: Relax, breathe deep, and envision your private sanctuary … a place of perfect beauty, peace, and contentment…. Did you conjure up an image of the seashore? Then slow your breathing to the rhythm of the waves…. Or perhaps you see yourself in a pretty garden, filled with butterflies, songbirds and delicate blossoms? Then let the sweetly fragrant air fill your senses…. Now, imagine combining these two idyllic havens into one spectacular seaside garden venue…. Can you picture a romantic wedding at such a divine spot? Wake up! Your dream has come true—at the Monarch Cove Inn.

Poised on an ocean bluff, the Monarch Cove Inn looks out onto a breathtaking curve of forested shoreline, home to flocks of pelicans and the bright butterflies that inspired the inn's name. Yet the enviable location of this dove-colored Victorian is only part of its allure. The delightfully understated architecture has just enough period features—gabled roof, angled bay windows—to evoke the grace of the past, yet is not so ornate as to make modernists uncomfortable. Originally built in 1895 as a private retreat for two wealthy British families, in the '20s the property passed to an oil magnate who added quaint cottages for his celebrity visitors, like silent film star Mary Pickford (it is even rumored that Al Capone once spent the night!). Today, the Monarch Cove Inn offers a variety of genial accommodations—as well as an enchanting site for an oceanview wedding.

The inn's vintage façade is framed against a backdrop of swaying treetops and flowering greenery. Listen closely and you can hear the rush of the tide just beyond. Off to one side, a serpentine path meanders through an informal English garden, where a parade of fluffy hydrangeas, wild lavender and California poppies charms the eye. Here, a winsome statue peeks out from behind a hedge; there, a canopy of climbing heirloom roses makes an inviting hideaway. Finally, the path comes to a large clearing, and you find yourself face to face with the sea; when the sun dispels the morning mist, the breathtaking azure panorama stretches all the way to Monterey.

The clearing comprises a carpet of green lawn that sweeps along the cliffs, and an expansive wooden deck that takes center stage. Couples say their vows on the deck or the lawn, with the splashing surf just below. A hidden path leads down to an area called The Terrace (really a swath of grass perched below the gardens) where guests sip cocktails and savor the refreshing sea breeze.

Next, everyone moves to the deck for the reception. Whether styled elegant, casual or somewhere in between, the picture-postcard setting will have everyone wearing an "I'm-in-Heaven" smile.

The wedding party usually takes over the inn for the weekend, and though continental breakfast is brought to each room, you can arrange for an al fresco brunch the next morning out on the deck. To experience the inn's nighttime ambiance, host a rehearsal dinner beginning with a blazing sunset, followed by a candlelight soirée. Recently renovated lodging includes spacious suites and private cottages, some with Jacuzzi and fireplace, all with dynamic views. One thing is certain: Whatever room is yours for the night, the Inn will make you feel at home.

CEREMONY, EVENT/RECEPTION CAPACITY: The inn accommodates up to 125 guests outdoors, 50 of whom must be lodged at the venue. Lodging requirements vary depending on the number of guests and the day of the week that the event is held. Please call for more details.

MEETING CAPACITY: The inn seats up to 25 guests indoors.

FEES & DEPOSITS: A $2,500 deposit is required to reserve your date, and the balance is due 90 days prior to the event. The venue rental fee ranges $3,995–4,500 depending on the day of the week. Saturday weddings require the rental of all 11 rooms for 2 nights, plus an additional room deposit. Catering packages start at $75/person for 75-99 guests, $65/person for 100 or more guests and include equipment rentals. The service charge is included! Tax is extra. Smaller events may use outside caterers upon approval. Alcohol is BYO with no corkage fee.

AVAILABILITY: Year-round, daily, noon–6pm.

SERVICES/AMENITIES:

Catering: in-house for large parties.
Kitchen Facilities: prep only
Tables & Chairs: provided
Linens, Silver, etc.: provided with in-house caterer
Restrooms: wheelchair accessible
Dance Floor: on deck
Bride's Dressing Area: CBA
AV/Meeting Equipment: BYO

Parking: limited on site; off-site lot provided, shuttle recommended
Accommodations: 11 guest rooms
Outdoor Night Lighting: limited, BYO
Outdoor Cooking Facilities: BYO
Cleanup: caterer or renter
View: ocean panorama, garden, hills
Other: wedding planner/coordinator available

RESTRICTIONS:

Alcohol: BYO, no corkage fees
Smoking: outside only
Music: acoustic music OK, or use of preferred vendor with volume restrictions

Wheelchair Access: limited
Insurance: not required

Shadowbrook

Restaurant & Gardens

1750 Wharf Road, Capitola
831/475-1222

www.shadowbrook-capitola.com
weddings@shadowbrook-capitola.com
banquets@shadowbrook-capitola.com

- Rehearsal Dinners
- Ceremonies
- Wedding Receptions
- Corp. Events/Mtgs.
- Private Parties
- Accommodations

Shadowbrook is unlike any place we've ever seen and, truth be told, you can't really see it until you're actually in it. Almost completely hidden at the base of a steep, beautifully land-scaped hillside, the site has a tantalizing aura of mystery and romance. We were intrigued. Instead of descending via the unique cable car, we walked down one of the winding garden paths through a riot of palms, ferns, colorful flowers, waterfalls and koi-filled ponds.

Originally built in the 1920s as a log cabin summer house, the restaurant now consists of seven distinctly different rooms and three patios spread out in tiers above Soquel Creek. The garden theme, so meticulously executed outside, is carried throughout the interior. Greenery is visible everywhere, from vines clinging to the ceilings in the Main Dining Room to the almost-100-year-old cypress growing through the ceiling of the Garden Room. And then there's your choice of views: gardens, woods, the quietly flowing creek or all of the above. It's no surprise that Shadowbrook continues to be voted "One of the Top 100 Romantic Restaurants" in the country by various publications year after year.

Shadowbrook has hosted weddings since the early 1950s, and the recently remodeled Rock Room Bar and Lounge is a sublime spot for exchanging vows. While its massive wooden beams, impressive stone fireplace and stone walls convey a comforting sense of history, it's the partially glass ceiling and wall that make ceremonies here truly magical. Through the glass everyone can watch the bride's entrance as she walks down a garden path, framed by the gorgeous landscape. Outdoor ceremonies on the private Creekside Patio are also blessed by nature: Held at the water's edge, they're enveloped in a lush mix of ferns, flowers and coastal redwoods. At dusk, the surrounding treescape comes alive with twinkle lights.

Every room at Shadowbrook has its own individual charms, and many can be used for rehearsal dinners or other private events. The Fireside Room dates back to 1947, and the original stone fireplace, redwood walls, and Craftsman-style lighting fixtures preserve its rustic feel. A lovely choice for an intimate event is the Redwood Room, featuring redwood beams and wainscoting, and a sun-drenched private brick patio next to the chef's herb garden. The Owner's Private Reserve Room will make you feel like you have the restaurant all to yourself, as a fire blazes in the river rock fireplace. Larger groups who still want a sense of privacy will appreciate the Wine Cellar

Room, boasting a brick fireplace and a collection of fine wines on display. Last, but certainly not least, is the Greenhouse Room, which delights the senses with an abundance of plants and light. Windows along its entire length afford a view of the creek and open to let in fresh coastal breezes.

People are drawn to world-famous Shadowbrook by its incomparable ambiance, but they also come for the food. Chef de Cuisine Roger Gowen utilizes regional products, organic ingredients, and hormone-free meats to provide diners with consistently high-quality cuisine. Each menu is tailored to your tastes, and thanks to the very talented on-site pastry chef, Robyn Wood, you can even order custom wedding and celebration cakes.

Shadowbrook is popular for many reasons, one of them being its strong emphasis on customer service. As the Banquet and Events Manager says, "We're far more interested in having you tell us what you want, rather than us telling you what you can have."

CEREMONY CAPACITY: The Redwood Room patio accommodates up to 26 guests. The Creekside Patio and the Rock Room each hold up to 100 guests.

EVENT/RECEPTION & MEETING CAPACITY: For large events, wedding receptions or personal preference, you may reserve the entire restaurant (which accommodates up to 220 seated guests) when it is not open to the public. For rehearsal dinners and smaller social or business functions, you may reserve private areas or rooms within the restaurant. The Greenhouse Room holds 60 guests, the Wine Cellar Room 46, the Redwood Room 26, and the Owner's Private Reserve Room 18.

FEES & DEPOSITS: For weddings and larger events, there is a facility fee of $2,500 for exclusive use and $500–2,000 for semi-private use. For smaller social or business events during regular operating hours, private room rental fees range $100–500 depending upon the size of the room. The deposit required to book most events is equal to the food & beverage minimum or the facility fee/room rental fee, whichever is higher. Three-course meals start at $50/person. Alcohol, tax and service charges are additional.

AVAILABILITY: Daily, 9am–10pm. Earlier hours for business meetings can be arranged.

SERVICES/AMENITIES:

Catering: in-house
Kitchen Facilities: n/a
Tables & Chairs: provided
Linens, Silver, etc.: provided
Restrooms: wheelchair accessible
Dance Floor: in lounge area
Bride's & Groom's Dressing Areas: yes
AV/Meeting Equipment: PA, microphones, projection screen; other CBA for a fee

Parking: ample, complimentary
Accommodations: no guest rooms
Outdoor Night Lighting: on patio and paths
Outdoor Cooking Facilities: no
Cleanup: provided
View: Soquel Creek and gardens

RESTRICTIONS:

Alcohol: in-house, or BYO with corkage fee
Smoking: patio only
Music: amplified OK indoors with volume limits; outdoors, acoustic only

Wheelchair Access: yes
Insurance: not required
Other: no rice or birdseed

Chaminade Resort & Spa

Resort & Spa

One Chaminade Lane, Santa Cruz
831/465-3452 or 831/465-3409
www.chaminade.com/santacruz_wedding
weddings@chaminaderesortspa.com

- Rehearsal Dinners
- Ceremonies
- Wedding Receptions
- Corp. Events/Mtgs.
- Private Parties
- Accommodations

Set high on a mountain bluff overlooking forested hills, Chaminade Resort & Spa is a sublime Mediterranean-style retreat blessed with a stunning view of Monterey Bay and the Santa Cruz Mountains. The historic estate has a refreshing, contemporary flair, mingling the best of Old World elegance and modern luxury. The original Mission-style buildings, constructed in the 1930s, have been expanded into a gracious resort set in the midst of meticulously tended gardens and embraced by 300 acres of native oak, redwood and eucalyptus.

Naturally, such romantic surroundings make Chaminade a prime spot for weddings. Have your ceremony on the Courtyard Terrace, an intimate setting reminiscent of a Spanish plaza, complete with a tranquil tiered fountain. Couples recite their vows atop a slightly elevated stage, canopied by an arbor laced with climbing roses and seasonal wisteria. In the background, a sweeping vista of native woodland and the brilliant blue bay accents the photo-worthy moment. Another pretty possibility is the Sunset Patio, which guests enter through an archway of bougainvillea. As the bride and groom recite their vows, they're framed by a dramatic panorama of rolling hills and the Pacific on the horizon.

Large receptions are held in the Santa Cruz Ballroom. A high, soffited ceiling arches overhead, while windows on three sides overlook the wooded valley and the sea in the distance. The ballroom has a generous dance floor and access to its own balcony. Smaller celebrations gather in the Sunset Room, with arched floor-to-ceiling windows that bring the outside in; another choice is the Seascape Room, which adjoins the Fireside Patio and shares the same spectacular views of the forest and ocean.

Lavish and varied wedding packages offer a number of bride-pleasing amenities, such as complimentary valet parking for all your guests and custom wedding cakes.

After the festivities wind down, you and your guests will discover that the accommodations here are as enticing as the scenery. Newly renovated guest rooms have been updated in the eclectic, bohemian style of the artisan community of Santa Cruz. Newlyweds will also appreciate the lush views from their patio, where they can savor a little late-morning lingering.

Another feel-good feature: Chaminade Resort is a certified "Green Business." This commitment extends to their spa, which has a holistic approach to relaxation and rejuvenation, and only uses natural products. Throw a private spa party for your bachelorette gathering, or choose the couples massage and indulge in some pampering for you and your groom; the spa also has special bridal options, including makeup consultation and application.

With an on-site pool, hot tub, tennis courts and miles of beautiful hiking trails, there's plenty to keep everyone entertained. Off property, you can stroll on a beach, go wine tasting, rock climb or board a yacht for a sunset cruise.

You'll be able to relax and truly enjoy yourself, knowing you've entrusted your celebration to experienced professionals, dedicated to providing world-class hospitality down to the tiniest detail. Along with the outstanding facilities and gorgeous location, a "dream come true" wedding at Chaminade Resort & Spa is virtually a sure thing.

CEREMONY CAPACITY: The Courtyard Terrace holds 230 seated and the Sunset Patio up to 180 seated.

EVENT/RECEPTION & MEETING CAPACITY: The facility seats 230 guests indoors or outdoors.

FEES & DEPOSITS: For weddings, a nonrefundable $3,500 deposit is required; the estimated balance is due 14 days prior to the event. Additional deposits may be required based on the guest count. Please inquire for details regarding guest minimums.

All-inclusive wedding packages include site rental fees, setup, cleanup, all furniture and linens, professional event coordination, generous hors d'oeuvres, entrées (buffet or sit-down), deluxe wedding cake, and complimentary valet parking. Packages range $114–154/person; beverages, tax and service charges are additional. Special rates are available for overnight accommodations for the wedding couple and guests.

For other types of events, please call for details.

AVAILABILITY: Year-round, weekends. An indoor location is available in the event of rain.

SERVICES/AMENITIES:
Catering: in-house, no BYO
Kitchen Facilities: n/a
Tables & Chairs: provided
Linens, Silver, etc.: provided
Restrooms: wheelchair accessible
Dance Floor: included in package
Bride's Dressing Area: yes
AV/Meeting Equipment: provided
Other: on-site wedding cake, spa services, tennis courts, hiking trails, event coordination

Parking: complimentary valet, on-site lot
Accommodations: 156 guest rooms
Outdoor Night Lighting: yes
Outdoor Cooking Facilities: BBQ CBA
Cleanup: provided
View: garden patio, pool area, fountain, landscaped grounds; panorama of forest, valley, Pacific Ocean and rolling hills

RESTRICTIONS:
Alcohol: in-house, no BYO
Smoking: outdoors only
Music: amplified OK indoors, acoustic only outdoors

Wheelchair Access: yes
Insurance: not required
Other: no rice or birdseed

Hollins House at Pasatiempo

20 Clubhouse Road, Santa Cruz

831/459-9182

www.pasatiempo.com/weddings
mseifert@pasatiempo.com

Banquet Facility

● Rehearsal Dinners	● Corp. Events/Mtgs.
● Ceremonies	● Private Parties
● Wedding Receptions	Accommodations

The Hollins House, built in 1929 by championship golfer Marion Hollins, is located above the Pasatiempo Golf Club in the Santa Cruz Mountains, not far from Highway 17. Approached through acres of green fairways, the house is situated atop a knoll and offers panoramic views of Monterey Bay. You can reserve either the entire facility or just the Hollins Room and Patio.

The Main Dining Room is very long, with high ceilings, big mirrors and picture windows with views of the garden and ocean beyond. There's also a fireplace and hardwood parquet dance floor. The Tap Room is a more informal space, a cocktail lounge with a long brass bar, fireplace and windows overlooking garden and ocean. The adjacent garden is narrow, with a lawn bordered by profusely blooming impatiens. A medium-sized patio, surrounded by wisteria and situated next to the Hollins Room, is a picturesque place for an outdoor reception. The Hollins Room is an intimate private dining room with a big mirror, fireplace, chandelier, rounded bay windows with bench seat and a vista of the Pacific Ocean framed by nearby oak trees. The banquet coordinator will assist you with all of your event arrangements, from flowers to specialized menus.

CEREMONY CAPACITY: The Garden with gazebo holds 225 seated guests.

EVENT/RECEPTION CAPACITY: The entire facility accommodates 80–250 seated or standing guests in the summer and fall and 175 during cooler months. The Hollins Room and Patio, combined, hold 30 seated guests.

MEETING CAPACITY: The Hollins Room accommodates 10–30 seated conference-style; the Main Dining Room seats 50 conference- or theater-style.

FEES & DEPOSITS: A nonrefundable $3,000 deposit for the entire Hollins House or $500 deposit for the Hollins Room is required to secure your date. The total balance is due 14 days prior to the event, along with the final guest count. The facility fee for the entire Hollins House ranges $3,500–5,500, depending on the season. For the Hollins Room and Patio, it's $500. The ceremony setup fee is $900.

Hors d'oeuvres/buffets run approximately $62/person and seated meals for up to 100 guests run $45–65/person. You may customize your menu with help from the chef and in-house event coordinator. For parties of 50 or more, a $300 security guard is required. Alcohol, tax and a 22% service charge are additional. There's also a $2/person outside dessert charge.

For meetings, Hollins House offers customized packages that may include continental breakfast, full lunch and dinner, plus tee times when available.

AVAILABILITY: For weddings, the entire Hollins House is available Friday and Saturday 4pm–11pm or Sunday 2pm–9pm. Earlier time frames can be accommodated. Meeting availability is 8am–4pm Monday–Friday, and Tuesday–Saturday evenings 6pm–11pm.

SERVICES/AMENITIES:

Catering: in-house, no BYO

Kitchen Facilities: n/a

Tables & Chairs: provided

Linens, Silver, etc.: provided

Restrooms: wheelchair accessible

Dance Floor: yes, large

Bride's Dressing Area: yes

AV/Meeting Equipment: AV, extra charge

Parking: large lots

Accommodations: no guest rooms

Outdoor Night Lighting: yes

Outdoor Cooking Facilities: BBQ CBA

Cleanup: provided

View: Monterey Bay and Pasatiempo Golf Course

Other: meetings with golf

RESTRICTIONS:

Alcohol: in-house

Smoking: outside only

Music: amplified OK

Wheelchair Access: yes, ramp

Insurance: not required

Overwhelmed? Use the search criteria on www.HereComesTheGuide.com to narrow down your choices.

479

Amphitheatre of the Redwoods
at Pema Osel Ling

2013 Eureka Canyon Road, Corralitos
831/761-6270
www.polmountainretreat.com
info@polmountainretreat.com

Retreat & Conference Center

- Rehearsal Dinners
- Ceremonies
- Wedding Receptions
- Corp. Events/Mtgs.
- Private Parties
- Accommodations

The Amphitheatre of the Redwoods is part of the Pema Osel Ling Retreat Center, a name that means "Lotus Land of Clear Light." The phrase conjures up images of a mystical mountain paradise, and it's an apt vision: Sequestered on over 102 acres of redwood forests, open meadows and gardens, this natural haven provides a sense of tranquility that's often missing from the frenzy surrounding a wedding. That peaceful easy feeling begins as you start the drive up Eureka Canyon into the wilds of the Santa Cruz Mountains. Dense woods with mist-shrouded treetops, fern grottoes and an occasional deer prepare you for the center's rustic yet welcoming ambiance.

With a variety of on-site accommodations ranging from large family homes to cozy cabins and campsites, you will want to take over the entire center for your own destination wedding weekend. Guests often meet up first at the Orchard House, a two-story lodge with a fireplace and a towering redwood growing right up through the front deck. Greet everyone with the center's signature mint iced tea, hand out maps and itineraries, and let the fun begin.

The retreat center has two extraordinary locations for ceremonies. The Amphitheatre of the Redwoods is a real-life "fairy ring"—a circle of redwoods born from one "grandmother" tree that survived a storm. Underground, all the trees' roots intertwine for added strength—just as you and your groom will support each other during your marriage. As you exchange vows, the wind whistles through the branches and the cry of blue jays and chattering squirrels makes you feel like you're in the middle of nowhere. A soaring canopy of magnificent redwoods stretches heavenward, the boughs weaving patterns against the blue sky. What an inspired place to say "I do"! For a more spacious ceremony site, get married at the Bay View Meadow and Terrace. With guests seated on the treelined meadow, bride and groom wed on a redwood deck at the edge of a hillside. Behind them, green thickets soften the view, while the distant blue waters of Monterey Bay wink in the sunlight.

Receptions are celebrated in the Gallery Meadow. Choose the configuration of canopies and extras you want, and the center's event pros will make it happen. The Celebration Hall, a ranch-style A-frame that opens to a lawn and plaza, offers an indoor/outdoor option. Several more benefits are worth noting. One is the knowledgeable staff, who'll assist you in structuring your agenda to include yoga, massage, hikes, bonfires, pool parties or whatever you can dream up. Then there's the award-winning gourmet catering. From vegan to prime rib, the on-site culinary team will not only whip up a delicious wedding feast, but also offers brunch, picnic lunch, rehearsal dinner, late night snack, and s'more packages.

Their late curfew lets you party until 2am indoors, and there's no corkage fee so you can bring your own libations. What there is at this retreat is beautiful scenery, friendly banquet staff and a refuge of freedom and renewal to call your own.

The Pema Ling Osel Retreat Center is a nonprofit run by the Vajrayana Foundation that preserves the spiritual, cultural and artistic traditions of Tibetan Buddhism. Couples who choose Amphitheatre of the Redwoods or any other of the retreat center's event venues have the added pleasure of supporting the foundation's mission to cultivate the Buddhist ideals of peace and compassion in the world.

CEREMONY CAPACITY: Outdoors, the Amphitheatre holds 150–160 seated, and the Bay View Meadow holds 300 seated. Indoors the site can accommodate 100–150 depending upon the setup.

EVENT/RECEPTION CAPACITY: The center accommodates 80 for receptions and 100 for all other dining events seated indoors and 300 or more seated or standing outdoors.

MEETING CAPACITY: Meeting spaces hold 100 seated guests, and 150 seated theater-style.

FEES & DEPOSITS: A $1,000 deposit is required to reserve your date. 40% of the estimated event total is due within 3 weeks of the initial deposit, and the balance is due 90 days before the event date. The rental fee ranges $2,950–6,950 depending on the day and duration of the event, and the time of year. Wedding meals start at $75/person and include tables, chairs, linens, napkins, china, flatwear, water glasses, full buffet, lemonade or iced tea, appetizers, coffee & tea, setup, cleanup, trash removal and servers. Other meals range $18–51/person. Tax and a 20% service charge are additional.

AVAILABILITY: Year-round, daily, anytime.

SERVICES/AMENITIES:

Catering: in-house
Kitchen Facilities: available for light cooking & snacks only
Tables & Chairs: provided
Linens, Silver, etc.: provided
Restrooms: wheelchair accessible
Dance Floor: portable available
Bride's Dressing Area: yes
AV/Meeting Equipment: CBA
Other: event coordination, pool, fire pit

Parking: large lot
Accommodations: 52 beds in various cabins and houses; camping space for 25 tents
Outdoor Night Lighting: yes
Outdoor Cooking Facilities: n/a
Cleanup: provided
View: courtyard, landscaped grounds, fountain, garden, pond, forest, valley, canyon; panorama of hills, coastline and ocean

RESTRICTIONS:

Alcohol: BYO, no corkage fee
Smoking: in designated areas only
Music: amplified OK outdoors until 10pm and indoors until 2am

Wheelchair Access: yes
Insurance: liability required

Kennolyn's
Hilltop Hacienda & Stone Creek Village

Address withheld to ensure privacy. Soquel

831/479-6700

www.kennolyn.com
weddings@kennolyn.com

Special Event & Retreat Center

- Rehearsal Dinners
- Ceremonies
- Wedding Receptions
- Corp. Events/Mtgs.
- Private Parties
- Accommodations

From an enviable vantage atop the scenic Santa Cruz Mountains, Kennolyn offers a can't-miss choice of two unique venues, each with its own personality and considerable charm. The first is the Hilltop Hacienda Estate, which overlooks lush redwood forests and the crystal blue Monterey Bay. This handsome property not only has a fabulous view, but it's so quiet and tranquil up here that you feel like you've really gotten away from it all, even though it's just a short drive from town.

The Hacienda not only includes a main event space, but also a private home that sleeps up to 10. You enter this Spanish-style building through a sun-drenched courtyard, with a four-tiered fountain bubbling in its center and pots of vibrant flowers all around. Ceremonies are magnificent out on the Hacienda Lawn, a grand sweep of green that faces a spacious terracotta-tiled terrace, accented with Mediterranean-style landscaping. Receptions inside the banquet room are equally welcoming. Spacious and unpretentious in design, it has a wood-beamed ceiling with wrought-iron chandeliers that convey elegant simplicity. At one end of the room, a lofty fireplace mantel of rich chocolate brown provides a striking contrast to the light tan walls. Sets of white French doors along two sides open onto either the courtyard or a heavenly patio that faces the bay. When the sun goes down, you can extend the day's warmth by lighting a fire in the hearth. As you might imagine, weddings here are delightful, and for corporate seminars or retreats you'd be hard pressed to find a more restful spot.

Located in another part of this 300-acre redwood paradise is Stone Creek Village, a miniature "town" reminiscent of a bygone era when logging and mining were going concerns. The Village is the perfect destination for a family reunion or a casual, weekend-long wedding for up to 100 guests. For a ceremony in the forest, the rustic redwood amphitheater includes log seating built right into the hillside, and "I do's" are exchanged in front of a mystical backdrop of towering trees. Stone Creek Village's main gathering space is the old-fashioned Lodge, with its great river rock fireplace. Indoor and outdoor dining areas include a Town Square and fire pit, ripe with event possibilities.

Your guests can experience a nostalgic stay in the Village's cabin cottages, appointed with antiques, down comforters and vintage stoves. Before and after the wedding, friends and family have plenty of activities to enjoy: lounge by the Village's swimming pool; organize team challenges on the tennis, basketball and volleyball courts; or simply follow the lilting invitation of resident songbirds to explore the hiking trails that lead into the surrounding forest.

From welcome refreshments to day-after brunch, Kennolyn's hospitality and gorgeous setting will bring beauty and serenity to any event.

CEREMONY & EVENT/RECEPTION CAPACITY: Hilltop Hacienda Estate seats up to 300 and Stone Creek Village seats up to 120 guests.

MEETING CAPACITY: Meeting spaces hold up to 100 seated guests.

FEES & DEPOSITS: To reserve your date, 25% of the anticipated event total is required as a nonrefundable deposit. Another 25% payment is due 90 days prior to the event date. The balance plus a refundable damage deposit are payable 10 days prior. Wedding packages start at $67/person and include a private consultation with Kennolyn's professional wedding coordinator, event coordination on the wedding day, hors d'oeuvres, buffet or plated meal, setup and cleanup, tables, chairs and linens, plus an invitation to Kennolyn's Wedding Day Overview. Beverages, facility fee, tax and a 20% service charge are additional.

AVAILABILITY: Year-round.

SERVICES/AMENITIES:

Catering: in-house, no BYO

Kitchen Facilities: n/a

Tables & Chairs: provided

Linens, Silver, etc.: provided

Restrooms: wheelchair accessible

Dance Floor: courtyard

Bride's & Groom's Dressing Areas: yes

AV/Meeting Equipment: CBA

Parking: ample, several lots

Accommodations: 30 cabin cottages and suites

Outdoor Night Lighting: yes

Outdoor Cooking Facilities: BBQ

Cleanup: provided, renter cleans decorations

View: vistas of Monterey Bay and Santa Cruz, redwood forest

Other: event coordination, carriage rides, full range of sports activities

RESTRICTIONS:

Alcohol: in-house, no BYO

Smoking: designated areas only

Music: amplified OK until 10:00pm

Wheelchair Access: most areas, not all

Insurance: not required

Other: no pets, glitter, rice or birdseed; decorations OK with approval

Monterey and Carmel

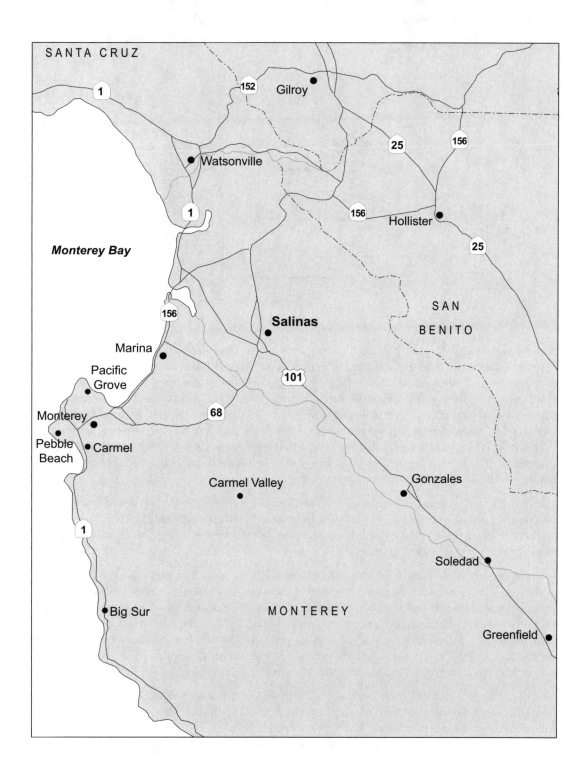

Carmel Valley Ranch

One Old Ranch Road, Carmel
831/620-6408 or 855/687-7262

www.carmelvalleyranch.com
weddings@carmelvalleyranch.com

Resort

- Rehearsal Dinners
- Ceremonies
- Wedding Receptions
- Corp. Events/Mtgs.
- Private Parties
- Accommodations

As we drive through the gate of Carmel Valley Ranch, a large black-tailed deer nonchalantly saunters in front of our car. It's a perfect welcome to this exclusive country hideaway, whose nearly 500 acres of rolling foothills are a breathtaking embodiment of the valley's timeless allure. Fragrant lavender wildflowers pop from green meadows, rare California condors glide overhead, and countless oak trees play host to warbling sparrows and Steller's jays. Just beyond, the tawny Santa Lucia Mountains take on a rosy-mauve glow as the sun dips below the horizon. So careful were the designers to maintain ecological harmony that the resort buildings seem almost sculpted into the pastoral surroundings by Mother Nature herself. The golf course is accredited by the Audubon Society, and native wildlife wanders undisturbed throughout the grounds.

The Ranch's fresh design puts a playful spin on Carmel's signature style: The décor is a warm expression of natural textures and earth tones, punctuated by the occasional rich, fruit-inspired hue or contemporary pattern. An extra layer of luxe has been added, making this already impressive venue keenly desirable for any celebration.

In the Ranch's hub, the Lodge, an open lobby and reception areas flow into the view-filled lounge and restaurant. Here, walls of picture windows look out to a turquoise pool and deck, framed by landscaped hillsides and a stand of oaks dripping with Spanish moss. Two sophisticated ballrooms, which adjoin a partially covered wraparound terrace, face the oak canopy. A tall stacked-stone fountain splashes water into a rectangular pool, turning the terrace into a refreshing place for cocktail mixers. Social hours can also convene beneath an adjacent pavilion. For an exciting rehearsal dinner, invite your guests into the Adventure Kitchen for a live cooking demo.

One of the resort's multiple ceremony sites is the River Lawn, a sweep of grass crowned by a froth of seashell-pink climbing roses and flanked by 100-year-old sycamore trees. A backdrop of forested hills completes the pretty tableau. And since we're in the heart of Carmel Valley Wine Country, why not wed on the resort's signature Vineyard Lawn—it's bordered by acres of grapevines and enjoys views of the Santa Lucia Mountains and a lovely water feature.

For a reception with an indoor-outdoor flow, reserve the Golf Clubhouse. It boasts its own terrace next to the Valley Lawn (another ceremony site with lush mountain and canyon views). A charming spot for an intimate al fresco dinner is the Organic Garden. Fragrant year-round with the scent of herbs, it's surrounded by lavender fields and overlooks the Santa Lucia Mountains. Wherever you celebrate on the property, you'll appreciate the staff's personalized, unobtrusive service and expertise in organizing your destination event weekend.

After the festivities, savor some alone time in your spacious luxury suite; actually, ALL the accommodations are suites with cathedral ceilings, cozy fireplaces and balconies for soaking up the valley vista. Though the rooms convey a soothing understated elegance, they include up-to-the-minute amenities embodying the latest technological advances.

If this isn't enough pampering, the resort's Spa Aiyana, a 10,000-square-foot facility, offers an exhilarating menu of services and includes a salon, fireplace suites and treetop fitness center. Ahhh, what a sublime way to round out your extraordinary Carmel Valley Ranch experience!

CEREMONY CAPACITY: The resort accommodates up to 250 seated indoors and 400 outdoors.

EVENT/RECEPTION CAPACITY: The resort holds 220 seated indoors and 300 outdoors; 300 standing indoors and 400 outdoors.

MEETING CAPACITY: The resort accommodates 250 seated guests.

FEES & DEPOSITS: A deposit equal to the site fee plus 10% of the estimated food & beverage cost is required to reserve your date. The balance is due according to the customized deposit schedule agreed upon in your contract. The site fee starts at $2,500 and varies depending on the venue selection. Dinners start at $90/person. Tax, alcohol and a 21% service charge are additional.

AVAILABILITY: Year-round, daily, 6am-11pm.

SERVICES/AMENITIES:

Catering: in-house
Kitchen Facilities: n/a
Tables & Chairs: provided
Linens, Silver, etc.: provided
Restrooms: wheelchair accessible
Dance Floor: provided, portable CBA
Bride's & Groom's Dressing Areas: CBA
AV/Meeting Equipment: provided

Parking: large lot, self-parking, valet parking
Accommodations: 181 guest suites
Outdoor Night Lighting: CBA
Outdoor Cooking Facilities: BBQ CBA, pizza oven
Cleanup: provided
View: landscaped grounds, garden, forest, mountains, golf course, vineyards
Other: spa services

RESTRICTIONS:

Alcohol: in-house
Smoking: outside only
Music: amplified OK with restrictions

Wheelchair Access: yes
Insurance: not required

Hyatt Carmel Highlands

Oceanside Inn

120 Highlands Drive, Carmel
831/620-6234
www.highlandsinn.hyatt.com
hyatthighlandscatering@hyatt.com

- Rehearsal Dinners
- Ceremonies
- Wedding Receptions
- Corp. Events/Mtgs.
- Private Parties
- Accommodations

Built in 1916 in the Carmel Highlands just south of Carmel, this particular Hyatt Hotel is one of the most sought-after event locations in California. Noted for its panoramic views and extraordinary cliffside setting, the hotel provides an idyllic environment for a special celebration.

After its multi-million-dollar renovation, this venue is more stunning than ever. Commanding one of the world's most spectacular vistas, with exploding waves crashing 200 feet below, the hotel offers a variety of first-class facilities for either business functions or weddings. For outdoor ceremonies, a redwood deck complete with contemporary gazebo is perched just above the rocky cliffs overlooking the Pacific.

After the ceremony guests are escorted into a variety of reception areas—each is elegant, with comfortable furnishings and outstanding views. The hotel's chefs are renowned for culinary excellence, and the extensive wine and champagne list frequently garners the Grand Award from *Wine Spectator*. The staff can organize a traditional party or a more creative event for the adventuresome. If you're looking for a very special place for one of life's great moments, the incomparable Hyatt Carmel Highlands should be high on your list.

CEREMONY CAPACITY: The outdoor gazebo accommodates 120 seated guests. In case of inclement weather, your wedding coordinator can offer options.

EVENT/RECEPTION & MEETING CAPACITY: The property can accommodate 12–175 seated guests indoors. The gazebo and deck hold up to 120 seated outdoors.

FEES & DEPOSITS: A deposit equal to the amount of the site fee, which ranges $3,000–10,000, is due upon signing of the event contract. Luncheons start at $95/person, dinners at $115/person; alcohol, tax and a 21% service charge are additional. A final confirmed guest count and entrée choices is due 2 weeks before the event, with adjustments accepted along with the final payment 3 working days before the event.

AVAILABILITY: Year-round, daily, anytime.

SERVICES/AMENITIES:

Catering: in-house, no BYO
Kitchen Facilities: n/a
Tables & Chairs: provided
Linens, Silver, etc.: provided
Restrooms: wheelchair accessible
Dance Floor: CBA, extra charge
Bride's Dressing Area: CBA
AV/Meeting Equipment: full range CBA, extra fee

Parking: complimentary valet
Accommodations: 48 guest rooms
Outdoor Night Lighting: limited
Outdoor Cooking Facilities: n/a
Cleanup: provided
View: coastline panorama at the gateway to Big Sur

RESTRICTIONS:

Alcohol: in-house
Smoking: outdoors only
Music: amplified restricted

Wheelchair Access: limited
Insurance: may be required

Want to know WHAT TO ASK a potential location or vendor? Check out our Questions to Ask starting on page 21.

Wedgewood Carmel

4860 Carmel Valley Road, Carmel
866/966-3009
www.wedgewoodbanquet.com
events@wedgewoodbanquet.com

Event Center at Golf Club

Rehearsal Dinners	●	Corp. Events/Mtgs.
● Ceremonies	●	Private Parties
● Wedding Receptions		Accommodations

The Spanish Colonial buildings of Wedgewood Carmel are spread out on a spacious plateau over-looking the lovely green fairways of Rancho Cañada Golf Course. At this serene country club in sun-splashed Carmel Valley, you won't find any pretensions—just friendly professional service and appealing event spaces. The nicely landscaped grounds are dotted with tall oaks and fragrant pine trees. A small pond fringed with bamboo and golden poppies is silhouetted against forested hillsides, a picturesque backdrop for wedding ceremonies. But if you prefer, Wedgewood can also arrange a beach wedding just a short drive away on Carmel's Monastery Beach. Here the staff sets up chairs and an archway right on the sand. Afterward, the celebration continues back at the club.

Social hours are usually held in the Fountain Courtyard, accented by garden beds brimming with cheerful blooms. A splashing fountain in the center of the plaza provides hacienda flair. Guests mingle in the shade beneath a covered patio with a stone wood-burning fireplace, or in the tastefully appointed foyer just inside, before retiring to one of the adjacent banquet rooms for the reception.

The commodious Fiesta Ballroom hosts receptions beneath a high wood-beam ceiling inset with skylights. Elaborate Mission-style chandeliers convey Old World elegance, and expansive picture windows make it seem as if your celebration is set among oak groves and camellia bushes. Smaller gatherings enjoy the Merienda Room, with similar décor and windows framing the cascading fair-ways, adorned with clusters of trees and flowers and surrounded by the majestic hills. You can admire the view up close on the Merienda's outdoor patio, which is also a great spot for cocktails or even a wedding ceremony.

Despite its first-class scenic setting, Wedgewood Carmel is surprisingly affordable. The Wedge-wood Wedding and Banquet Centers are known for offering a range of customizable, inclusive event packages that take you from champagne toast to after-dinner coffee--a budget-pleaser and a time-saver. If you want to make golf part of your weekend, you'll get discounted rates for that as well. And with its prestigious Carmel Valley location, Wedgewood Carmel will make your guests feel even more privileged to attend your special event.

CEREMONY CAPACITY: The site seats up to 400 indoors or on the Clubhouse Lawn.

EVENT/RECEPTION & MEETING CAPACITY: The Fiesta Ballroom accommodates up to 400 seated or 550 standing guests, and the Merienda Ballroom up to 175 seated or standing. These spaces can be divided into smaller sections for meetings or intimate events.

FEES & DEPOSITS: 25% of the estimated total event cost is required to reserve your date. An additional 25% is due 120 days prior to the event, and the balance (based on your final guest count) is due 10 days prior. All payments are credited towards your final balance and are nonrefundable and nontransferable. All-inclusive, completely customizable wedding packages start at $49/person. Tax, alcohol and a 21–22% service charge are additional.

AVAILABILITY: Year-round, daily, 7am–midnight.

SERVICES/AMENITIES:

Catering: in-house
Kitchen Facilities: n/a
Tables & Chairs: provided
Linens, Silver, etc.: provided
Restrooms: wheelchair accessible
Dance Floor: yes
Bride's Dressing Area: yes
AV/Meeting Equipment: some provided

Parking: large lot
Accommodations: no guest rooms
Outdoor Night Lighting: yes
Outdoor Cooking Facilities: CBA
Cleanup: provided
View: golf fairways, valley, mountains; ceremony site has ocean view
Other: event coordination, in-house wedding cake and florals, clergy on staff

RESTRICTIONS:

Alcohol: in-house
Smoking: outside only
Music: amplified OK

Wheelchair Access: yes
Insurance: not required
Other: no rice, confetti or glitter; no open flames

Gardener Ranch

Ranch

114 West Carmel Valley Road, Carmel Valley
831/298-7360
www.gardenerranch.com
admin@gardenerranch.com

- Rehearsal Dinners
- Ceremonies
- Wedding Receptions
- Corp. Events/Mtgs.
- Private Parties
- Accommodations

Tucked in the sunny hills of Carmel Valley, Gardener Ranch's 24 tranquil acres flourish alongside the banks of the Carmel River. With a rich history of hosting presidents and celebrities, the picturesque property has recently been renovated and reimagined as a welcoming retreat for family reunions, company getaways and—of course!—destination weddings. Reserve for a weekend or longer, and the ranch becomes your own private paradise where you can wed, dine, and stay amid laid-back refinement.

One of the ranch's most clever innovations is Bridal Camp, a spacious bungalow where bridal parties can prep in style. Feminine, functional and fun, Bridal Camp has thought of everything: director chairs facing a wall of mirrors and makeup counters; comfy slipcovered sofas for lounging and girl-talk; a salon with hairstylist and manicure stations; a gym and massage room; and a swanky Groom's Room, too.

Ceremonies unfold with rustic beauty out on Woodlands Lawn, a blanket of soft grass surrounded by towering oaks and sycamores. At one end, graceful willow branches form a natural arch, a lovely spot to say "I do." You can add your own signature touches—whimsical signage, crystals dangling from tree limbs, a flower-decked chuppah—but the site is equally captivating left au naturel.

After the first kiss, the bridal party explores the venue's photogenic grounds, while guests amble over to the nearby Clubhouse Patio for cocktails. Cushioned lounge furniture, market umbrellas and a fire pit are clustered around a sparkling swimming pool, a scene made even more glamorous with the addition of market lights or Chinese lanterns. As dusk turns to evening, everyone adjourns to the Dining Room, a flexible L-shaped space that's at once homey and elegant: A vaulted light-wood ceiling sports a dazzling crystal chandelier, and a fire ablaze in a cozy brick hearth is reflected in gilded mirrors and multipaned windows. There's even a grand piano on hand for dinner serenades.

When it's time to kick things up a notch, move the reception into the skylit Breakfast Room, where black-and-white tiles beneath your feet become a retro-chic dance floor. Inevitably, guests drift back to the pool deck to take in a resplendent country sky.

Five unique lodges spread out among the meadows make overnight stays a genuine treat. Newlyweds usually opt for the secluded River Cottage: Its quaint stylings and private waterfront deck inspire romance. By contrast, the luxurious Main House—a 3-bedroom residence with its own pool and three fireplaces—makes a lively gathering place. Enjoy the ranch's on-site activities, including croquet or bocce ball; or venture forth to tour local wineries, take a horseback ride or hike scenic mountain trails.

For all that there is to do, you're likely to find the Ranch's simple pleasures to be the most endearing…treelined paths that reveal an old-fashioned tree swing…colorful birds on the wing or splashing in a fountain…a serene mountain silhouette that hugs the property like an earthy embrace. This kind of ineffable charm needs to be experienced to be fully appreciated, and your landmark occasion offers the perfect opportunity to do just that.

CEREMONY, EVENT/RECEPTION & MEETING CAPACITY: The facility can accommodate 150 seated or 200 standing guests indoors, and 200 seated or standing outdoors.

FEES & DEPOSITS: 50% of the total event cost is required to reserve your date. 25% is due 6 months prior to the event and the remaining 25% is due 45 days prior. The rental fee ranges $1,000–49,500 depending on the season, the number of guests and the length of your stay. Weekend wedding packages start at $25,000 and include overnight accommodations for up to 50 guests. Tax applies to overnight accommodations only. There is no other tax or service charge.

AVAILABILITY: Year-round.

SERVICES/AMENITIES:

Catering: BYO
Kitchen Facilities: n/a
Tables & Chairs: some provided
Linens, Silver, etc.: BYO
Restrooms: wheelchair accessible
Dance Floor: yes
Bride's Dressing Area: yes
AV/Meeting Equipment: BYO
Other: grand piano, picnic area, propane heaters, fire pit, hammocks, swing

Parking: large lot, shuttle CBA for groups with over 106 vehicles
Accommodations: 5 houses hold up to 50 guests
Outdoor Night Lighting: access and clubhouse patio string lights
Outdoor Cooking Facilities: no
Cleanup: caterer
View: fountain, garden patio, landscaped grounds, meadow, pool area; panorama of hills, oak trees, river and willows

RESTRICTIONS:

Alcohol: BYO
Smoking: outdoors only
Music: amplified OK with restrictions

Wheelchair Access: limited
Insurance: liability required

Holman Ranch, Vineyard & Winery

Historic Private Estate

Address withheld to ensure privacy. Carmel Valley
831/659-2640
www.holmanranch.com
info@holmanranch.com

- Rehearsal Dinners
- Ceremonies
- Wedding Receptions
- Corp. Events/Mtgs.
- Private Parties
- Accommodations

High atop the sunny hills of Carmel Valley rests Holman Ranch and Vineyard, a historic private estate blessed with a treasure chest of scenic jewels and a rich legacy of hosting society's elite that dates back to the 1920s. In 2006, the 400-acre spread was adopted by the Lowder family, who completed a loving restoration that retains the ranch's Old World character while adding up-to-the-minute luxuries, cool winery caves, and vineyards along with enhanced interiors and lavish outdoor spaces that make the most of the spectacular view-filled grounds.

An oak-lined road climbs to the ranch's pond and stables, where guests park and are shuttled to the hilltop entrance. Arriving at the Main Plaza, visitors get a captivating first impression: a mélange of red-tile roofs, landscaped walkways, shade trees and glimpses of grapevines against a mountain panorama. Finally, eyes rest on the Hacienda itself, an architectural gem crafted of Carmel stone and oak, with tile and metal details. This easy blend of grand Spanish style and relaxed California attitude conveys a rustic elegance.

Both varied and flexible, Holman Ranch holds a myriad of possibilities … so why not stage each phase of your event in a different spot? While the bride and her attendants primp and prep in one of the suites, the groom and his pals gather in the handsome Game Room—complete with an antique bar and jukebox—to calm pre-wedding nerves over a game of pool or darts. Ceremonies are gorgeous on the Hacienda Lawn, which sweeps to the edge of a hillside studded with Pinot Noir grapevines. Wedding guests have an endless view of the Carmel Valley, alive with chaparral, oak trees and hawks soaring overhead. As the sunset burnishes the Santa Lucia Mountains, the couple says their vows atop the Ceremony Veranda, a stone platform that seems suspended above the valley floor.

Afterwards, the social hour commences on the nearby Stone Terrace, which is ringed with olive trees. Many couples opt to serve appetizers along with a special tasting of Holman Ranch's unique estate-produced olive oils and wines—oenophiles will especially appreciate that the vintages maintain the grape's integrity from vine to bottle. Everyone is free to relax in the adjoining Great Room, whose vaulted ceiling, fireplace and player piano contribute to a comfortable, homey ambiance.

Receptions bask in the warm valley twilight out on the Rose Patio, dressed with rose bushes and potted citrus trees. Family-style rehearsal dinners might prefer the Arbor, a magnificent wooden promenade lined by olive trees and young grapevines that lend it a Mediterranean flair. Then, move the party to the barn-style Carriage House, where an explosion of twinkle lights along whitewashed rafters creates the illusion of dancing beneath a star-filled sky. When it's time to cut the cake, many couples prefer to stage this time-honored ritual back outside beneath the charming arbor, which also adds a lush frame for photos.

And let yourself think beyond the wedding: Host a casual welcome dinner down the hill at Holman's acclaimed restaurant and bar, Will's Fargo. Or have a barbecue at the ranch that includes bocce ball or horseshoes so the families can get acquainted before the main event. You can even throw a pool party, complete with umbrella drinks and beach balls. Weekend event packages include use of 10 recently restored guest rooms, including a 2-bedroom/2-bath private house with its own cozy kitchen. Altogether, the ranch can accommodate up to 38 overnight guests. The inviting home-away-from-home experience comes with a deluxe Continental-plus breakfast and the ranch's recreation facilities.

From a refined, one-of-a-kind event to laid-back fun, Holman Ranch Vineyard & Winery can arrange it all, and oh so well.

Holman Ranch is shown by appointment only. Please call to schedule a visit.

CEREMONY CAPACITY: The site can accommodate 400 seated guests.

EVENT/RECEPTION CAPACITY: Outdoors, the Rose Patio holds 150 seated and the Main Plaza seats 400. Indoors, the Carriage House holds 150 seated guests.

MEETING CAPACITY: The Conference Room holds 10 seated around a boardroom table with executive chairs; the Carriage House seats 200.

FEES & DEPOSITS: A nonrefundable deposit of one third of the site and room rental fees is required to reserve your date. A second nonrefundable deposit totaling 50% of the balance is due 6 months before the event. The remaining balance is due 1 month prior. The site rental fee ranges $500–20,000 depending on the time of year, day of the week, number of guests, type of package or event, and hours of rental. Rental of the 10 guest rooms, which is required for weekend events during high season (May–October), starts at $8,000 plus tax for a 3-day/2-night package and includes access to the pool, game room and fitness center.

AVAILABILITY: Year-round, anytime. Off-season rates apply November–April.

SERVICES/AMENITIES:

Catering: select from preferred list
Kitchen Facilities: prep only for caterer use, full kitchen for overnight guests
Tables & Chairs: provided for up to 150 guests
Linens, Silver, etc.: through caterer
Restrooms: 5 are wheelchair accessible, 6 total
Dance Floor: provided
Dressing Area: yes
AV/Meeting Equipment: some provided

Parking: large lot, limited to 100 cars
Accommodations: 10 guest rooms
Outdoor Night Lighting: yes
Outdoor Cooking Facilities: caterer or rental
Cleanup: caterer and renter
View: vineyards, panoramic views of Carmel Valley and the Santa Lucia Mountains
Other: player piano, pool, game room, vineyard tours, heaters and market umbrellas; estate-grown wine and olive oil available

RESTRICTIONS:

Alcohol: BYO, served through licensed caterer or bartending service with minimum estate wine purchase
Smoking: designated areas only
Music: amplified OK with restrictions

Wheelchair Access: yes
Insurance: required

Quail Lodge and Golf Club

Golf Club

8000 Valley Greens Drive, Carmel Valley
831/620-8833

www.quaillodge.com
weddings@quaillodge.com

- Rehearsal Dinners
- Ceremonies
- Wedding Receptions
- Corp. Events/Mtgs.
- Private Parties
- Accommodations

With 850 acres of lush gardens, tree-shaded lakes, rolling meadows, and a beautifully designed golf course, Quail Lodge has been a favorite Carmel Valley venue for over 50 years and a premier destination for weddings and other special events.

Located on the sunny side of the Monterey Peninsula in the scenic Carmel Valley, Quail Lodge offers a wonderful selection of indoor and outdoor settings, including Quail Meadows, a popular and picturesque ceremony site that takes advantage of the glorious weather. A peaceful lake plays host to the occasional blue heron or covey of resident quail, and tree-covered hillsides form a gentle wave along the horizon. Whether you add a flower-laden bridal arch or let the scenery form the backdrop, this splendid spot will take your breath away.

Quail's other scenic venues feature naturally inspired settings that are perfect for receptions, parties, and rehearsal dinners. From their intimate private rooms and outdoor terrace, you and your guests can enjoy tranquil garden and poolside views. Receptions for larger groups are held in the elegant Peninsula Ballroom, which boasts a cathedral ceiling and three walls of windows that showcase the spectacular surroundings. Wherever you gather, friends and family will be treated to exemplary service and the finest-quality fare. The chefs at Quail Lodge specialize in delicious local, organic California cuisine, and they lavish the same care on their event meals as they do at Edgar's, their popular on-site restaurant.

Not only will your loved ones leave your celebration feeling happy and satisfied, they'll also appreciate getting to extend their visit by staying in one of the Lodge's newly renovated California Ranch-style rooms or suites. Resort activities abound, from tennis to swimming to a genuine Land Rover Driving School. And if your guests would like to unwind with a round of golf the day before or after your festivities, Quail's recently refined 18-hole championship golf course is one of the most walkable and player-friendly courses on the Monterey Peninsula.

Quail possesses all the elements for a stellar destination event, but it's their professional planners who weave these elements together in a way that matches your vision. Combining attention to detail with creative sparkle, they'll transform your special occasion into something truly memorable.

CEREMONY CAPACITY: Outdoors, the Quail Meadows area seats up to 600. Indoors, the Peninsula Ballroom holds 300 seated theater-style, and more intimate rooms can accommodate 30–100 seated guests.

EVENT/RECEPTION CAPACITY: Indoors, the Peninsula Ballroom holds 200 seated or 300 standing; the Oak Room 30 seated or 50 standing; the Garden Room 50 seated or 70 standing; The Covey 80 seated.

MEETING CAPACITY: There are 3 rooms that can seat 30–300 theater-style, 26–60 boardroom-style or 24–200 classroom-style.

FEES & DEPOSITS: For special events, a nonrefundable $2,500 deposit is required to reserve your space. A customized payment schedule is developed with final payment due 30 days prior to the event. The rental fee ranges $500–$6,000. Catering packages start at $85/person; tax, alcohol and a 20% service charge are additional.

AVAILABILITY: Year-round, daily, including holidays.

SERVICES/AMENITIES:

Catering: in-house, no BYO
Kitchen Facilities: n/a
Tables & Chairs: provided
Linens, Silver, etc.: provided
Restrooms: wheelchair accessible
Dance Floor: provided
Bride's & Groom's Dressing Area: Yes
AV/Meeting Equipment: full range, extra fee

Parking: large lots
Accommodations: 93 guest rooms
Outdoor Night Lighting: CBA
Outdoor Cooking Facilities: no
Cleanup: provided
View: fairways, lakes, ponds, valley, hills

RESTRICTIONS:

Alcohol: in-house, or corkage $25/bottle
Smoking: designated areas
Music: amplified OK indoors only

Wheelchair Access: yes
Insurance: not required

The wedding vendors on our website are the best in the business. How do we know? Read page 553.

Club Del Monte
at Monterey's Naval Postgraduate School

1 University Circle, Monterey

831/656-1049

navylifesw.com/monterey/dining/catering
mwrcatering@nps.edu

Historic Landmark

- Rehearsal Dinners
- Ceremonies
- Wedding Receptions
- Corp. Events/Mtgs.
- Private Parties
- Accommodations

Club Del Monte is an Art Deco jewel set amongst 25 acres of sprawling lawns dotted with oak, cypress, and pine. Constructed in 1926 as an elegant hotel, the building resembles a Spanish-Moorish citadel and has a gently commanding air. Frequented for decades by celebrities and socialites, the hotel was finally acquired in 1951 by the Navy for its Postgraduate School. Today, this illustrious landmark is once again making an impression, this time as a standout special occasion venue.

Your guests will feel like royalty when welcomed with cocktails in the Quarterdeck Lounge. This majestic lobby was built on a palatial scale, with soaring 30-foot ceilings, crosshatched with hand-painted wooden beams. Two rows of stone columns grace both sides of the room, framing a towering floor-to-ceiling window that overlooks the estate-like grounds.

Proceed to the glittering Barbara McNitt Ballroom for a formal dinner-dance, and be transported back to the era when movie stars like Jean Harlow and Clark Gable danced the night away inside these very walls. Then as now, the room's main attraction was an ornately tiled wall fountain with cascading water, quite the glamorous statement piece—especially when backlit with colorful lighting. Elaborate tilework bordering floor-to-ceiling arched windows at either end of the room brings the Moorish influence inside, and gives the Ballroom a spicy, exotic ambiance. Other Art Deco details include the lacy plasterwork ceiling, huge wrought-iron chandeliers and matching wall sconces.

The Ballroom opens onto a Veranda that overlooks European-inspired rose gardens and the Peacock Lawn, a favorite site for wedding ceremonies. Stretches of grass offer spacious seating, while manicured hedges, an occasional peacock and the stately building form a handsome backdrop for exchanging vows.

Smaller gatherings might celebrate on La Novia Terrace, a sun-splashed venue that's wonderful for an open-air ceremony or cocktail hour. This terrace adjoins La Novia Room, similar in elegance to the Ballroom but on a more intimate scale. Its rich wood trim and hand-painted wooden ceiling beams are distinctively vintage touches. Finally, the mid-sized El Prado Banquet Room has a grand, historic feel, enhanced by the cherrywood dance floor, dark wood beams and arches that surround your event in high style. Beautiful chandeliers and coordinating sconces bathe the space in a soft, warm luster.

Club Del Monte holds a treasure trove of site options, along with noteworthy catering; and as you'd expect from a naval facility, everything here is top rank.

Note: Since this is a military facility, private events require prior approval. Please contact the Catering Department for more information.

CEREMONY CAPACITY: The facility accommodates up to 400 seated or standing guests on the lawn.

EVENT/RECEPTION CAPACITY: Indoors, several rooms hold 25–600 seated or 25–1,000 standing.

MEETING CAPACITY: The Ballroom holds 600 seated at rounds of 10 or 500 seated theater-style; the La Novia Room holds 80 at rounds of 10, 75 theater-style. The El Prado seats 140.

FEES & DEPOSITS: For weddings and receptions, a nonrefundable deposit of $550–1,600 (depending on the room reserved), is required to book the facility. 75% of the estimated event total is payable 4 weeks prior to the function, and the balance is due 1 week prior.

Catering starts at $45/person, with a $3/person cake-cutting fee. Wine, champagne and a 19% service charge are additional.

Weekday meeting fees vary depending on the catering services required.

AVAILABILITY: Year-round, daily. Weddings can be booked 11am–4pm or 6pm–11pm; conferences or other special events, 7am–4pm or 6pm–11pm. Extra hours are available for an additional charge.

SERVICES/AMENITIES:

Catering: in-house, no BYO
Kitchen Facilities: n/a
Tables & Chairs: provided
Linens, Silver, etc.: provided
Restrooms: wheelchair accessible
Dance Floor: yes
Bride's Dressing Area: yes, additional fee
AV/Meeting Equipment: CBA

Parking: on-base lot; weekday carpooling recommended for large events
Accommodations: military or Department of Defense cardholders only
Outdoor Night Lighting: no
Outdoor Cooking Facilities: no
Cleanup: provided
View: of lawns and gardens

RESTRICTIONS:

Alcohol: in-house, no BYO
Smoking: outside only, 20 feet away from building
Music: amplified OK

Wheelchair Access: yes
Insurance: not required
Other: no rice, birdseed, glitter, confetti, bubbles or wall decorations

Hyatt Regency Monterey Hotel & Spa

Hotel

1 Old Golf Course Road, Monterey
831/657-6540
www.monterey.hyatt.com
hyattmontereycatering@hyatt.com

- Rehearsal Dinners
- Ceremonies
- Wedding Receptions
- Corp. Events/Mtgs.
- Private Parties
- Accommodations

Walking past the fountain entryway into the Hyatt Regency Monterey's Fireplace Lounge, you instantly feel yourself relaxing amid the resort's sophisticated comforts, natural materials and soothing earth tones. Take it from us, the sky-lit Lounge is an inviting spot to while away a pleasant hour, quaffing a local vintage from their wine cellar along with tasty appetizers by their acclaimed farm-to-table bistro, TusCA Ristorante.

While the innovative food and drink are delicious, the resort boasts a bounty of recreational activities, like their full-service Racquet Club, 2000-square-foot Fitness Center and neighboring Del Monte Golf Course. Two sparkling pools surrounded by gardens beckon swimmers and sunbathers alike. Rent a bicycle to tour the scenic grounds, or take the trails that skirt the nearby bay up to historic Cannery Row. (The hotel's Les Clefs d'Or Concierge can arrange everything from Aquarium tickets to wine tasting.)

With so much to entice and entertain, you don't need an excuse to visit this resort. But if you've come to celebrate a special occasion, then you'll be delighted by the expert service and range of venue options.

The Regency Grand Ballroom, the largest in the county, can host a gala dinner for 600 and still have plenty of room for dancing. Soft teal blue-and-beige décor reflect Monterey's serene coastal palette; high ceilings with inset lighting bays and a bank of windows provide gentle illumination. The adjoining foyer opens to a terrace with a retractable awning, perfect for an indoor/outdoor social hour. Though not quite as large, the Monterey Grand Ballroom still holds up to 400 guests. While the Regency takes its inspiration from the sea and sky, the Monterey recalls the region's mountains and meadows: Rustic hues are enlivened with a sunny yellow reminiscent of springtime daffodils. An adjacent patio increases your staging possibilities.

Open-air receptions are sometimes celebrated on the Garden Terrace, which can also be tented. The bridal party and guests reserve the rooms overlooking this courtyard, and this clear-sided pavilion becomes your own party central.

Your nearest and dearest will thank you for their mini-vacation, which includes plush, contemporary accommodations. Newlyweds receive a complimentary suite for their wedding night, but for the ultimate indulgence splurge on a Villa, a four-bedroom oasis with its own private lanai and swimming pool! This secluded hideaway can host your rehearsal dinner or cocktail party in high style.

One more awesome amenity: While at some hotels the spa seems like an afterthought, this Hyatt's new Marilyn Monroe Spa knows just what women want. In addition to relaxing massages, brides and their entourages receive movie-star treatment in the "Glamour Room," which offers Marilyn-inspired makeup and hair styling. Meanwhile the groom and his pals unwind at the award-winning Knuckles Sports Bar, where brews, billiards and bro-time can be enjoyed until the wee hours.

From arrival straight on through to Farewell Brunch, your destination wedding weekend at this luxurious resort is an inspired way to savor a memorable Monterey experience.

CEREMONY CAPACITY: The facility seats up to 1,000 guests indoors and 500 outdoors.

EVENT/RECEPTION CAPACITY: The facility holds 800 seated or 1,200 standing guests indoors and 300 seated or 450 standing outdoors.

MEETING CAPACITY: Meeting spaces can accommodate up to 1,200 seated guests.

FEES & DEPOSITS: 20% of the total event cost is required to reserve your date and the balance is due 10 days prior to the event. The rental fee ranges $500–2,000 depending on the ceremony space reserved. Meals range $80–125/person. Tax, alcohol and a 23% service charge are additional.

AVAILABILITY: Year-round.

SERVICES/AMENITIES:

Catering: in-house
Kitchen Facilities: n/a
Tables & Chairs: provided
Linens, Silver, etc.: provided
Restrooms: wheelchair accessible
Dance Floor: portable provided
Bride's Dressing Area: CBA
AV/Meeting Equipment: provided

Parking: large lot
Accommodations: 550 guest rooms
Outdoor Night Lighting: CBA
Outdoor Cooking Facilities: BBQ CBA
Cleanup: provided
View: forest, garden, fairways, landscaped grounds
Other: event coordination

RESTRICTIONS:

Alcohol: in-house
Smoking: designated areas only
Music: amplified OK with restrictions

Wheelchair Access: yes
Insurance: liability required

InterContinental The Clement Monterey

Waterfront Hotel

750 Cannery Row, Monterey
831/642-2009
www.ictheclementmonterey.com
icreservation@pahotel.com

- Rehearsal Dinners
- Ceremonies
- Wedding Receptions
- Corp. Events/Mtgs.
- Private Parties
- Accommodations

Throughout the years, Monterey's timeless natural beauty has been the inspiration for artists, poets and novelists alike. Recently, a downtown renaissance has put a glamorous polish on historic districts like Cannery Row, and author John Steinbeck would be amazed to see these formerly rough-and-tumble dockside streets dramatically transformed into a thoroughly modern boulevard. Today's Cannery Row is alive with fashionable boutiques, delectable eateries, upscale galleries and a vibrant street scene that attracts visitors from all over the world. And right next door, at the heart of the action, sits the celebrated Monterey Bay Aquarium.

Can this quaint yet oh-so-now slice of paradise get any better? Yes, it can. InterContinental The Clement Monterey was designed as a serene coastal retreat for personal rejuvenation and spectacular private celebrations.

Wedding ceremonies are staged on an expansive courtyard facing the sapphire-blue waters of the bay. Two fire pits provide an ambient glow, particularly romantic at sunset. Couples say their vows with the bay in the background, while seabirds trace graceful curves on the horizon, and otters and sea lions frolic in the waves.

With such a picturesque setting, have your social hour out in the fresh ocean air as well. While the bridal party poses for pictures, guests enjoy the hotel's boardwalk and pier, which extends out over the bay. Cut-outs along the wooden pier reveal tantalizing peeks directly down at the teeming underwater world of the Monterey Bay Sanctuary.

As twilight descends, retire indoors to admire the vista from another perspective. The Pacific Ballroom is a refined setting for a bayside gala, replete with picture windows that capture a panorama of the moonlit ocean. Bring the sparkle indoors by decorating with lights—the banquet staff can customize your event according to your wishes. The view will be even more impressive from the Ocean Terrace Ballroom, located upstairs. It's an intimate space that boasts a bayview terrace.

The resort's equally impressive public spaces are tranquil and welcoming, thanks to the stylish use of wood and other natural materials, along with décor in soothing shades of green and blue, evocative of the sea and sky. One of the most notable spaces is the Reading Room, warmed by a contemporary stone-faced fireplace. Adjacent to the Reading Room, the Library serves as a private dining salon that's perfect for formal rehearsal dinners.

One of the benefits of a destination event at InterContinental The Clement Monterey is that friends and family can have a minivacation, because there's simply no end to the area's fun-filled activities. Hotel accommodations feature up-to-the-minute amenities, and many have fireplaces, ocean views and balconies. Their on-site spa pampers with the latest in beautification and wellness treatments. VIP Babysitting is also available for children, enabling parents to enjoy the wedding celebration.

This magnificent hotel, which opened in May 2008, has become extremely popular for special events. Reserve your space now to take advantage of Monterey's legendary allure.

CEREMONY CAPACITY: The resort holds 240 seated indoors or outdoors.

EVENT/RECEPTION & MEETING CAPACITY: The facility accommodates 240 seated indoors or outdoors.

FEES & DEPOSITS: A nonrefundable deposit of 25% of the estimated food & beverage total plus 100% of the facility fee is required to confirm your event, and is due within 14 days of contract signing. 50% of the estimated remaining balance is due 120 days prior to the event, and the balance is due 14 days prior. The facility fee ranges $1,000–5,000 depending on the space(s) rented. Wedding packages range $87–107/person. Tax and a 21% service charge are additional and subject to change.

AVAILABILITY: Year-round, daily, 10am–11pm.

SERVICES/AMENITIES:

Catering: in-house
Kitchen Facilities: n/a
Tables & Chairs: provided
Linens, Silver, etc.: provided
Restrooms: wheelchair accessible
Dance Floor: provided
Bride's Dressing Area: yes, extra charge
AV/Meeting Equipment: available

Parking: valet and self-parking
Accommodations: 208 guest rooms
Outdoor Night Lighting: available
Outdoor Cooking Facilities: no
Cleanup: provided
View: ocean
Other: spa, 24-hour fitness center, pool, Jacuzzi, babysitting

RESTRICTIONS:

Alcohol: in-house
Smoking: not allowed
Music: amplified OK with restrictions

Wheelchair Access: yes
Insurance: required for vendors

Memory Garden

Garden

20 Custom House Plaza, Monterey
831/649-3445, Grapes of Wrath Events
www.grapesofwrath.com
grapes@grapesofwrath.com

● Rehearsal Dinners	● Corp. Events/Mtgs.
● Ceremonies	● Private Parties
● Wedding Receptions	Accommodations

Stroll through Monterey's downtown historic district, and you'll find it studded with secret gardens. Each of them is private and within walking distance of hotels ranging from bed & breakfast to 4-star. Memory Garden, in the Monterey State Historic Park is perhaps the most intriguing of them all.

Framed on three sides by tall adobe walls with graceful arched cutouts and on the fourth by the Pacific House, an elegant 1847 Spanish-Colonial style building, it's a grand plaza suitable for all kinds of events. Four 75-year-old magnolias shade the plaza, their branches casting an intricate web of shadows on the ground. In spring and summer the trees also provide a gorgeous floral display, along with the other flowers planted along the perimeter. A fountain burbling in the courtyard's center soothes the ear, while sea breezes supply natural air-conditioning.

Corporate picnics, luncheons and dinners are popular here, but the Garden is especially lovely for weddings. The site can accommodate a formal dinner for 300 guests, yet it's warm and intimate enough for a casual gathering of 50.

If you're getting married in the Garden, you may choose as your backdrop the massive arched wooden gate at the entrance, the wisteria-covered pergola along the southwest wall or the towering cedar opposite the pergola.

Afterwards, the open configuration of the Garden lends itself to lively hors d'oeuvre stations followed by either a seated dinner or a buffet beneath the trees. And you don't need a lot of decorations—a simple thread of color can pull together the surrounding foliage and architecture, creating a beautiful setting with little effort. Floral arrangements on the tables can be as elaborate as exotic blooms in a wrought-iron centerpiece or as understated as a terracotta pot with greenery. For evening events, permanent subtle lighting in the trees makes it easy to create a fairy-tale or Old California atmosphere.

To get just the right food for your celebration, turn to *Grapes of Wrath Events*. They have lots of experience orchestrating events in the Garden, and will cook up a California Cuisine-style feast to satisfy your taste (and that of all your guests!). You might want to start off with an hors d'oeuvre griddle, featuring crab cakes, towers of layered polenta, and pesto risotto cakes, or indulge in the ultimate California treat—a sushi boat filled with assorted maki! Bright, fresh flavors are the hallmark of their main dishes, too. Choices from Monterey Bay include grilled salmon with a Mediterranean tapenade, fresh albacore with a mango salsa or maybe braised halibut in ginger and orange. These are often paired with a medium rare sirloin with rich Cabernet mushrooms, or perhaps Castroville chicken, perfectly seasoned with artichokes, wine and herbs.

After checking out the local seasonal produce, *Grapes of Wrath* might serve up grilled vegetables, a crunchy sugar snap pea salad, or heirloom tomatoes with fresh mozzarella and basil…all colorful reminders that Monterey is in California's premium growing region.

Two more elements for a successful event are great music and good wine, and *Grapes of Wrath* staff can help you with both. As full-service caterers, they'll match you up with musicians and other vendors that best fit your vision, provide excellent (and affordable) wines, and coordinate the day of your event.

We don't know how this garden got its name, but it was an inspired choice—when your party is over, you'll walk away with a wedding's worth of wonderful memories.

CEREMONY, EVENT/RECEPTION & MEETING CAPACITY: The garden holds 275 seated or 400 standing guests for a cocktail reception.

FEES & DEPOSITS: A nonrefundable $150 processing fee and a refundable $500 damage deposit are required to obtain your permit. Rental fees range from $1,150 for a ceremony to $3,150 for a weekend ceremony and reception that includes 7 hours of event time and 3 hours of setup and breakdown.

Grapes of Wrath Events has been hosting events at the Memory Garden for years, however, you may bring in the caterer of your choice. All menus created by *Grapes of Wrath Events* are custom-designed; for menus and pricing go to www.grapesofwrath.com. There is no cake-cutting fee and beverages are provided at retail cost.

AVAILABILITY: Year-round, daily, 9am–10pm, weather permitting. Setup must be done within the time stated on your permit.

SERVICES/AMENITIES:
Catering: Grapes of Wrath or BYO
Kitchen Facilities: no
Tables & Chairs: through caterer
Linens, Silver, etc.: through caterer
Restrooms: wheelchair accessible
Dance Floor: through caterer
Bride's Dressing Area: nearby hotels, none on site
AV/Meeting Equipment: through caterer

Parking: covered garage within 2 blocks
Accommodations: nearby hotels
Outdoor Night Lighting: yes
Outdoor Cooking Facilities: yes
Cleanup: caterer
View: garden
Other: walking distance to Wharf, downtown and hotels; event coordination available through caterer

RESTRICTIONS:
Alcohol: provided, or BYO
Smoking: designated areas only
Music: amplified OK with limits

Wheelchair Access: yes
Insurance: required, CBA through caterer or arrange your own
Other: no rice, picking flowers, etc.

Want to find more venues and services? Check out our informative website, www.HereComesTheGuide.com.

505

Monterey Beach House

285 Figueroa Street, Monterey
831/648-7240
www.centralcoastevents.com
info@centralcoastevents.com

Historic Beach House

● Rehearsal Dinners	● Corp. Events/Mtgs.
● Ceremonies	● Private Parties
● Wedding Receptions	Accommodations

If you love the sea, you've probably fantasized about spending time at a private beach house with the sand right outside your door and seals and pelicans as your only neighbors. You've pictured yourself admiring ocean views and spectacular sunsets from your front porch, and gathering friends and family around an evening bonfire, with the sublime setting putting everyone in a summertime state of mind no matter what the season.

Well, the event professionals at Central Coast Events (CCE) can make your fantasy a reality—at least for your wedding day. They've been arranging festivities-to-remember for years, and many of the most memorable have happened at the historic Monterey Beach House.

Located next to a waterfront park and wharf, and within walking distance to Monterey hotels and activities, the beach house is a simple cloud-colored building trimmed in sailor blue. The steps of its broad front deck descend onto the sand, and since CCE lays claim to its own stretch of this pristine shoreline, they'll set up your event right at the water's edge.

Ceremonies are accompanied by a palm treelined wedding aisle, white chairs, a wooden wedding arch and the blue Pacific. Drinks and appetizers are served on the deck, and while the bridal party poses for scenic photos the staff sets up the outdoor reception. The usual motif includes tiki torches, a bonfire and colorful beach chairs, and the beach site can accommodate up to 1,000 guests. Want fire and hula dancers? Ask, and Central Coast Events will make it happen. This is also one of the only local beaches that allow cocktails—so bring on the paper umbrellas!

Inside the beach house, social hours and receptions are anything but dull thanks to a myriad of novelty attractions, like ping pong, pool, and an optional "surf's up" photo backdrop—all sure-fire icebreakers. If you opt for an elegant ambiance, the staff can remove the games and have everything looking fancy as you please. The newly renovated interior features light, faux-finished floors and draped ceilings with twinkle lights. The neutral palette allows you to dress up the beach house for a sophisticated soirée, but some couples embrace the beach theme by choosing from a wide array of tropical-colored linens and other vibrant décor. Just ask the staff for help and ideas!

A stage at one end of the room is outfitted with a rear projection screen and a state-of-the-art lighting and sound system. Amp up the entertainment by booking the house DJ or band, who will "wow" your guests with cool tunes and a light show.

CCE's menus offer a fine selection of California coastal-cuisine dishes that are both hearty and delicious. Entrées are prepared fresh during your event on a large outdoor grill; favorites include oak-grilled tri-tip, and guava-glazed salmon with grilled pineapple salsa. Whatever you choose, your guests are sure to be satisfied.

And here's a thought: If you're planning a formal affair at another Monterey venue, why not change things up by reserving the Monterey Beach House for your rehearsal dinner? Their event packages and high-caliber service add up to convenience, value, and guaranteed good times. Lots of venues can host a wedding…but if you want a party, then this is the place.

CEREMONY & MEETING CAPACITY: The site seats 200 guests indoors and 300 outdoors.

EVENT/RECEPTION CAPACITY: The facility can accommodate 200 seated or 500 standing indoors and 400 seated or 600 standing outdoors.

FEES & DEPOSITS: A nonrefundable $2,000 deposit is due at the time of booking. 100% of the estimated total is due 30 days prior to the event, and any remaining balance is due on the business day following the event.

Their wedding package is $100/person and includes the site fee, beach ceremony, beach party reception, choice of 4 menu options, cake-cutting, assorted beverages and bar setup, and more. Alcohol is additional.

AVAILABILITY: Year-round, daily, 11am–4pm or 6pm–11pm.

SERVICES/AMENITIES:

Catering: in-house
Kitchen Facilities: on site
Tables & Chairs: provided
Linens, Silver, etc.: provided or CBA
Restrooms: wheelchair accessible
Dance Floor: provided
Bride's Dressing Area: CBA
AV/Meeting Equipment: some provided

Parking: city lot ($1.50/hour fee)
Accommodations: no guest rooms
Outdoor Night Lighting: CBA, extra fee
Outdoor Cooking Facilities: BBQ on site
Cleanup: provided
View: ocean/bay
Other: clergy on staff, event coordination

RESTRICTIONS:

Alcohol: in-house, or BYO wine with corkage fee
Smoking: outdoors only
Music: amplified OK with restrictions

Wheelchair Access: yes
Insurance: not required
Other: no rice, birdseed or fake petals on beach

Monterey Plaza Hotel & Spa

Oceanfront Resort

400 Cannery Row, Monterey
831/646-1700

www.montereyplazahotel.com
weddings@montereyplazahotel.com

- Rehearsal Dinners
- Ceremonies
- Wedding Receptions
- Corp. Events/Mtgs.
- Private Parties
- Accommodations

There's something about being next to the ocean that most of us find irresistible. Maybe it's the bracing aroma of sea air, or the way the light glints off the waves. Whatever it is, you experience that special "something" here at the Monterey Plaza Hotel & Spa. Built right at the water's edge, the Plaza takes advantage of a spectacular bayside setting that's just a heartbeat away from the world-renowned Monterey Bay Aquarium and Cannery Row.

The plaza's 17,000 square feet of event space encompasses an array of sophisticated banquet rooms enhanced by Mediterranean-inspired furnishings. A recent $3 million renovation has brought fresh polish to the décor, and ensured that all the amenities are state-of-the-art—including advanced audiovisual and wireless capabilities. Aesthetic upgrades, like decorative crown moldings and Villeroy & Boch plateware and silver, add extra elegance to your affair.

Ceremonies at the resort are held on either of two sun-splashed terraces, both embracing panoramic vistas of the Pacific. On the Lower Terrace, the bride captures every eye as she descends the main staircase to a broad, tiled deck; on the sprawling Upper Plaza, the wedding processional walks beneath a white trellis, set off by terracotta planters brimming with flowers. Then vows are exchanged under a simple arch with the ocean and sky as a blue-on-blue backdrop.

Afterwards, most receptions take place in the Monterey Bay Room or the Dolphins Room. The latter is so close to the water you can see otters floating by and hear the gentle lapping of the waves. Both rooms mirror the earthy palette of the coastal milieu—deep marine blues and greens, terracotta reds, and warm, sun-kissed golds. Scenic artwork adorns the walls, complementing the gorgeous floor-to-ceiling bay view. For a more formal gala, the Cypress Ballroom has teakwood paneling, new custom chandeliers and its own terrace overlooking the seascape.

Rich with history and diverse activities, Monterey is a sightseer's paradise; and with the plaza's exceptional hospitality, your guests will appreciate the fact that you've chosen it as their home base—especially when they experience the hotel's rooftop spa! This is the place to relax before the big celebration (or unwind after), by indulging in a massage, facial, or one of the spa's signature treatments. The spa even boasts an outdoor sundeck complete with fireplace and whirlpool tubs, where you can enjoy a light lunch along with the invigorating salt-laced breezes.

Newlyweds often opt to stay in a spacious luxury suite, featuring a fireplace and oceanview deck. The accommodating staff can even transform your suite into a celebratory setting for a cocktail party or a post-wedding brunch. However, we highly recommend a romantic candlelight dinner for two on your private deck, where you can raise your glasses to the glorious sunset coloring the horizon, the boundless sea, and each other.

CEREMONY CAPACITY: The Lower Terrace accommodates 120 guests seated in rows and a few more standing guests; the Upper Plaza holds 300 guests seated in rows.

EVENT/RECEPTION CAPACITY: Various rooms seat 30–300 with dancing.

MEETING CAPACITY: There are 11 conference rooms (17,000 square feet of meeting space), which accommodate up to 250 guests.

FEES & DEPOSITS: The rental fee for a 5-hour event ranges $850–2,500, depending on the banquet room reserved. It is payable, along with the $2,000–2,500 ceremony site fee, when reservations are confirmed. The event balance (based on the estimated food & beverage total) is due 10 working days prior to the function. Meals start at $75/person. Additional evening hours may be purchased at $500/hour. Alcohol, tax and a 21% service charge are additional. Note that overnight accommodations for the bride and groom can be arranged at a special rate for up to two nights.

AVAILABILITY: Year-round, daily, until 10pm.

SERVICES/AMENITIES:

Catering: in-house, no BYO

Kitchen Facilities: n/a

Tables & Chairs: provided

Linens, Silver, etc.: provided

Restrooms: wheelchair accessible

Dance Floor: provided

Bride's & Groom's Dressing Areas: CBA

AV/Meeting Equipment: some provided, other CBA extra fee

Parking: valet, extra fee

Accommodations: 290 guest rooms

Outdoor Night Lighting: additional CBA

Outdoor Cooking Facilities: CBA

Cleanup: provided

View: Monterey Bay and Pacific Ocean

RESTRICTIONS:

Alcohol: in-house, no BYO

Smoking: outside only

Music: amplified OK with volume restrictions

Wheelchair Access: yes

Insurance: required for outside vendors only

Other: no glitter, birdseed or rice

The Perry House

201 Van Buren Street, Monterey
831/647-0114
www.perryhousemonterey.com
info@eventsbyclassic.com

Bayview Event Facility

- Rehearsal Dinners
- Ceremonies
- Wedding Receptions
- Corp. Events/Mtgs.
- Private Parties
- Accommodations

Overlooking the Monterey Bay, the historic Perry House—an eye-catching Queen Anne-style Victorian—is just right for an elegant yet homey celebration.

Originally built in 1860 by ship captain Manuel Perry, this popular landmark has served as an art gallery, tearoom, flower shop and even a costume museum. Embracing a fresh vision of the site's potential, *The Events by Classic Group* purchased the Perry House in 2010, and their stunning renovation has re-imagined the vintage home as a premier wedding venue.

Ceremonies are held in the garden, a manicured lawn bordered by the Main House and the Carriage House. A stately white pergola anchors the seaward side, framing the wedding couple as they say "I do" amidst flowery landscaping and a filtered backdrop of sea and sky.

After the vows, the cocktail hour kicks off in the Carriage House, a convivial spot complete with cocktail seating, a fireplace and a state-of-the-art audiovisual system. One wall of windows gazes into a quiet, shade-dappled corner of the garden; another wall displays sepia-toned photos of Monterey's bygone days. The highlight of the space, however, is a breathtaking dome ceiling of amber-and-pistachio-hued stained glass evoking the room's Art Deco heritage as well as a sense of occasion.

Just outside, a rustic stone and brick oven produces delicious wood-fired pizzas. In fact, all event cuisine is grilled or cooked to order, creating a savory aroma that melds with the salty tang of the ocean air. Equally inviting are dreamy panoramas of sailboat-filled harbors and wooded heights, which are best viewed from the cascade of balconied stairways of the Main House. As twilight descends, a sigh-inducing sunset gives way to a glittering skyscape of stars and city lights.

The Perry House becomes even more enchanting at night, when a profusion of fairy lights sparks across porch railings, tree trunks and rooflines. This is when the action usually shifts to the Captain's Room on the lower floor of the Main House, where receptions flow freely from bay windowed nooks out onto the terrace.

Yet another intriguing gathering place is the second-story Harbor View Lounge, a virtual sanctuary of 18th-century opulence that's also used for the bridal party's pre-wedding prep. This spacious suite has a luxurious sitting area and an adjoining boudoir with a sumptuous bed worthy of royalty. Newlyweds often retreat to the Lounge to survey the revels unfolding below, or to share some private time.

Like its sister property, Gatherings, the Perry House is an all-inclusive venue. The experts at *The Events by Classic Group* are known for going out of their way to produce personalized events with five-star catering and superb service. Their specialty is innovative roaming receptions, where food stations are strategically placed throughout the property to encourage a lively atmosphere and maximum mingling.

Blessed with enduring charm, the Perry House overflows with character, warmth and thoughtful touches, and is well on its way to creating a romantic, new legacy.

CEREMONY CAPACITY: The garden seats 130 guests outdoors.

EVENT/RECEPTION CAPACITY: The facility holds 80 seated indoors and 130 seated or standing outdoors.

MEETING CAPACITY: Meeting spaces hold 60 seated guests.

FEES & DEPOSITS: A $2,500 deposit is required to reserve your date. 50% of the estimated event total is due 120 days prior to the event and the balance is due 10 days prior. The rental fee ranges $1,690–6,320 depending on various factors such as season, day of week, time of day, and whether you book a ceremony with your reception. Meals range $84–99/person. Tax, alcohol and a 20% service charge are additional.

AVAILABILITY: Year-round, daily; Friday & Saturday until 10pm; Sunday–Thursday until 9pm.

SERVICES/AMENITIES:

Catering: in-house
Kitchen Facilities: n/a
Tables & Chairs: provided
Linens, Silver, etc.: provided
Restrooms: some wheelchair accessible
Dance Floor: provided
Bride's Dressing Area: yes
AV/Meeting Equipment: some provided
Other: fire pit, speakers throughout the property, complimentary event coordination

Parking: garage across street
Accommodations: no guest rooms
Outdoor Night Lighting: yes
Outdoor Cooking Facilities: grill and outdoor pizza oven
Cleanup: provided
View: fountain, garden, landscaped grounds; panorama of cityscape, bay and harbor

RESTRICTIONS:

Alcohol: in-house, or BYO with corkage fee
Smoking: designated areas only
Music: amplified OK indoors

Wheelchair Access: yes
Insurance: liability required

Tarpy's Roadhouse

Restaurant

2999 Monterey-Salinas Highway, Monterey

831/655-2999

www.tarpys.com
banquet@tarpys.com

- Rehearsal Dinners
- Ceremonies
- Wedding Receptions
- Corp. Events/Mtgs.
- Private Parties
- Accommodations

We know what you're thinking: How appealing can a place be with the word "roadhouse" in its name? Well, in this case, very appealing indeed. Though this historic stone building and its five beautifully landscaped acres boast a colorful Old West past, it's now known for delicious food, an eclectic atmosphere, and an enchanting array of event spaces.

Guests enter the property beneath a large cut-stone archway, and stroll to Tarpy's truly original ceremony site: the Courtyard, an open-air plaza sheltered by high weathered stone walls laced with ferns, trees and climbing vines. Many a bride has peeked out the upstairs window that overlooks the Courtyard and experienced butterflies of excitement as she watched friends and family take their seats. Finally, she makes her grand entrance down an ivy-lined stone staircase brimming with vibrant geraniums, and across a petal-strewn aisle to meet her groom. Against this natural, rustic backdrop, the newlyweds share their first wedded kiss.

The cocktail hour (or indeed any sunset gathering) is nothing short of magical on the Library Patio, a terracotta-paved terrace where guests savor refreshments amidst a captivating mélange of textures, colors and scents. One of the patio's walls is ingeniously built into the hillside, with nooks abloom with flowers and aromatic herbs. Meanwhile, the bridal party explores the grounds' photogenic settings—and there are plenty to choose from. A velvety carpet of grass surrounded by redwoods, pines and blossoming greenery is a picturesque backdrop for group portraits, and couples can't resist the old-fashioned white gazebo and quaint wishing well. On another lawn, there's a scenic pond with a spraying fountain.

The restaurant itself boasts a variety of pleasing spaces for receptions and rehearsal dinners, and some can be used in combination. Two of the cozy indoor rooms adjoin the charming Front Porch, where wooden tables and metal chairs cluster beneath a stone-and-wood arbor laced with passionflower vines. In the Shell Room, soft cream walls and crisp white linens impart a relaxed elegance, while a fireplace constructed entirely of seashells provides a whimsical counterpoint. The Vintner's Room displays award-winning local wines, contemporary art and views of the lush gardens. Upstairs, the Library is a spacious, private room with an open-beam ceiling, country-style chandeliers and a welcoming hearth. Inevitably, as the night unfolds, the party spills back out onto the Library Patio for dancing.

Your celebration is overseen by Tarpy's own Certified Wedding Venue Planner, who'll gladly assist with menu planning and vendor recommendations, as well as keep things running smoothly.

Whatever your special occasion, Tarpy's is sure to fill the bill. And don't worry, you won't find any shady characters drinking bathtub gin at this roadhouse—just delighted diners enjoying the congenial vibe.

Tarpy's also does off-site catering, and is a Certified By The Guide *vendor (which means they've passed our very tough reference check with flying colors.) You can read more about their catering services on HereComesTheGuide.com.*

CEREMONY CAPACITY: The site seats 50 indoors and 70 outdoors.

EVENT/RECEPTION CAPACITY: Tarpy's accommodates 80 seated and 110 standing indoors; 110 seated or standing outdoors.

MEETING CAPACITY: The facility seats 80 guests.

FEES & DEPOSITS: 50% of the estimated event total is required to reserve your date. The balance is due on the day of the event. Rental fees may apply depending on event specifications. Meals range $36–92/person. Tax, alcohol and a 21% service charge are additional.

AVAILABILITY: Year-round, daily, 8:30am–midnight.

SERVICES/AMENITIES:

Catering: in-house, no BYO
Kitchen Facilities: n/a
Tables & Chairs: provided
Linens, Silver, etc.: provided
Restrooms: wheelchair accessible
Dance Floor: CBA
Bride's & Groom's Dressing Areas: CBA
AV/Meeting Equipment: some provided

Parking: large lot
Accommodations: no guest rooms
Outdoor Night Lighting: yes
Outdoor Cooking Facilities: no
Cleanup: provided
View: forest, garden, pond
Other: clergy on staff

RESTRICTIONS:

Alcohol: in-house, or BYO wine with corkage fee
Smoking: outside in parking lot only
Music: amplified OK with volume restrictions

Wheelchair Access: yes
Insurance: not required
Other: no glitter, birdseed or rice

This is important! Tell locations you're reading HERE COMES THE GUIDE and ask if our information is still current.

513

Gold Country and Yosemite

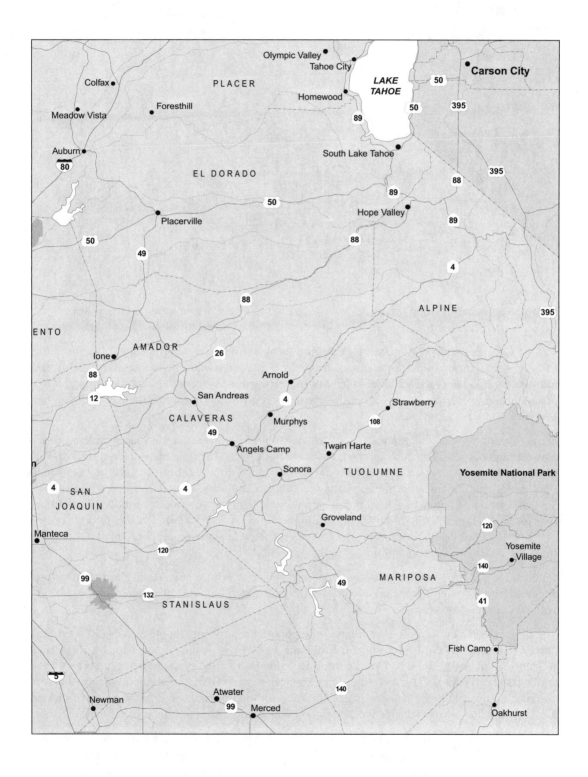

Tenaya Lodge at Yosemite

Mountain Resort

1122 Highway 41, Fish Camp
877/247-9249
www.tenayalodge.com
tenayaweddings@delawarenorth.com

- Rehearsal Dinners
- Ceremonies
- Wedding Receptions
- Corp. Events/Mtgs.
- Private Parties
- Accommodations

With its magnificent soaring peaks, backwoods trails and legendary panoramas, Yosemite National Park is a cherished natural treasure. It's also a destination wedding locale like no other.

One of the most congenial places at Yosemite to tie the knot is Tenaya Lodge, the first hotel to bring the luxuries of a classic resort to this awe-inspiring wilderness. The newly refreshed, four-diamond lodge is a resplendent blend of the earthy and the contemporary, featuring natural materials like wood, stone and leather that create a rich, warm ambiance. The overall impression is one of refined comfort.

Tenaya's event spaces also embody rustic elegance, and put Yosemite's scenic wonders on display during your fête. The Terrace, a second-story deck fringed with feathery pine trees, makes a lovely outdoor ceremony site. After the vows, guests descend a flight of stairs to the open-sided Pavilion for another angle on the gorgeous scenery. Cocktails and dinner are served beneath the Pavilion's wood ceiling, which is trimmed with twinkle lights. If you prefer an indoor celebration, then reserve the 10,000-square-foot Grand Ballroom. Tasteful and modern, it boasts floor-to-ceiling windows that look out to the stunning mountains carpeted in sugar pines. For a smaller reception, book the Forest View Room, affording equally beautiful vistas.

Intimate ceremonies are magical in the Wedding Garden, a private lawn nestled among trees and enclosed by a wooden fence and a stone archway. The staff can also arrange an off-the-beaten-path ceremony—just ask.

The lodge is a haven for green weddings—the banquet rooms are Double Silver LEED-certified, and the cuisine is local and sustainable. Tenaya has five seasonal dining choices: the casual Jackalope's Bar and Grill for fun after-parties; Parkside Deli for delicious grab-and-go options; the family-friendly Timberloft Pizzeria; the Sierra Restaurant, which includes an outdoor patio with fire pit; and the upscale Embers for romantic fireside dining and exquisite organic seasonal menus. Each of these has its own distinctive atmosphere and can be reserved for your rehearsal dinner.

Yosemite's rugged grandeur, made famous by photographer Ansel Adams' indelible images, will enhance your own wedding photos, too. Tenaya's knowledgeable event planning professionals are happy to point out the best backdrops, as well as arrange activities for your guests. Nature lovers can ride horses, hike to a waterfall, or simply take in the spectacular sunsets and dazzling starscapes. Sports enthusiasts might want to golf, bike, or ice skate. Meanwhile, the bride will probably opt to unwind at Ascent Spa. Bridal spa packages, along with 12 treatment rooms, steam rooms and a sauna, offer a wealth of pampering.

Guests will appreciate the updated accommodations in the Main Lodge: All 240 rooms and suites now have a rustic contemporary design, luxury bedding, plush carpet and many more amenities. For the newlyweds, we recommend one of the secluded cottage-style rooms with fireplaces for quality alone time. Think of Tenaya Lodge at Yosemite as "Happiness in the High Sierras!"

CEREMONY CAPACITY: The site seats 400 guests indoors and 350 outdoors.

EVENT/RECEPTION CAPACITY: The facility can accommodate 400 seated or 900 standing indoors and 200 seated or 350 standing outdoors.

MEETING CAPACITY: Meeting spaces hold up to 1,200 seated guests.

FEES & DEPOSITS: A maximum $2,500 deposit is required to reserve your date and the balance is due 30 days prior to the event. The rental fee ranges $700–2,700 depending on the day and time of the event and the space rented. Wedding packages range $145–180/person. Tax, alcohol and a 20% service charge are additional.

AVAILABILITY: Year-round, daily, 10am–midnight.

SERVICES/AMENITIES:
Catering: in-house
Kitchen Facilities: n/a
Tables & Chairs: provided
Linens, Silver, etc.: provided
Restrooms: wheelchair accessible
Dance Floor: portable provided
Bride's Dressing Area: yes, guest room/suite
AV/Meeting Equipment: some provided
Other: grand piano, spa services, event coordination

Parking: large lot, complimentary valet
Accommodations: 302 guest rooms, suites and cottages
Outdoor Night Lighting: yes
Outdoor Cooking Facilities: none
Cleanup: provided
View: garden, landscaped grounds; panorama of forest and mountains

RESTRICTIONS:
Alcohol: in-house or BYO wine or champagne with corkage fee
Smoking: designated areas only
Music: amplified OK with restrictions

Wheelchair Access: yes
Insurance: not required

Monte Verde Inn

18841 Foresthill Road, Foresthill
530/888-8123

www.monteverdeinn.net
monteverde@foothill.net

Inn & Garden

- Rehearsal Dinners
- Ceremonies
- Wedding Receptions
- Corp. Events/Mtgs.
- Private Parties
- Accommodations

If you're looking for a very special place, it's in Foresthill, a small hamlet about 40 minutes northeast of Sacramento. Here you'll find the historic Monte Verde Inn, which is, in a word, wonderful.

The property was originally a gathering spot for Native Americans, and after gold was discovered in 1849, it became a toll station and respite for travelers. A private residence was built on the site in 1936, and today this stately Georgian-style manor is a gracious reminder of the past. A glassed-in sun porch covers the front of the manor house, and makes a sparkling backdrop for photos of the bridal party.

The landscaped grounds have the feel of an English country estate: A long entry drive, lined with flowering plum trees, draws you back in time. Manicured lawns, 100-year-old quince trees and a veritable tapestry of flowers (changed seasonally according to the whim of the owners) invite you to celebrate amid a garden of earthly delights. For ceremonies try the patios—they're surrounded by tall cedars that form an informal outdoor cathedral. At night, "fairy lights" and turn-of-the-century streetlights create a glittering halo around dancing couples.

Guests can also enjoy the inn's inviting interior, whose large open rooms feature an array of architectural embellishments and antiques. Spacious, newly refurbished guest rooms occupy the second floor. They're prettily decorated and have high ceilings, hardwood floors and Oriental carpets. The inn offers a wedding package that accommodates up to 16 overnight guests, and includes champagne and snacks, plus a full breakfast. For a nominal charge, you can invite other friends or family staying nearby to join you for this "morning after" get-together.

Food is a top priority here, and the inn's professional chef prepares all meals using only the freshest, highest-quality ingredients.

All these elements combined—the enchanting grounds, delicious cuisine, quaint accommodations, and enthusiastic service—create the Monte Verde Inn's successful mix of country charm and elegance.

NOTE: Monte Verde Inn is an LGBT-friendly venue.

CEREMONY CAPACITY: The patio accommodates 225 seated or standing guests; indoors, the inn holds 100.

EVENT/RECEPTION CAPACITY: 100 guests maximum indoors; up to 225 seated outdoors.

MEETING CAPACITY: The inn holds up to 100 seated guests.

FEES & DEPOSITS: 25% of the estimated event total is required to secure your date. Rates start at $84/person and include rental of the inn for 5 hours; rehearsal; all setup for ceremony and reception; color-coordinated, fresh floral centerpieces for all tables; wedding cake; hors d'oeuvres; full buffet and nonalcoholic beverages. Note that all food is prepared from fresh ingredients on the premises. Alcoholic beverages, tax and a 21% service charge are additional.

AVAILABILITY: Year-round, daily.

SERVICES/AMENITIES:

Catering: in-house, no BYO

Kitchen Facilities: n/a

Tables & Chairs: provided

Linens, Silver, etc.: provided

Restrooms: wheelchair accessible

Dance Floor: patio

Bride's Dressing Area: yes; also CBA for bridal party

AV/Meeting Equipment: BYO

Parking: 2 large lots

Accommodations: 6 guest rooms

Outdoor Night Lighting: yes

Outdoor Cooking Facilities: no

Cleanup: provided

View: garden and forests

Other: event coordination included

RESTRICTIONS:

Alcohol: in-house; wine, beer and champagne only

Smoking: outside only

Music: amplified OK

Wheelchair Access: outdoor access only, limited indoor access

Insurance: not required

Wedgewood Sequoia Mansion

Historic Mansion

643 Bee Street, Placerville
866/966-3009

www.wedgewoodbanquet.com
events@wedgewoodbanquet.com

Rehearsal Dinners	● Corp. Events/Mtgs.
● Ceremonies	● Private Parties
● Wedding Receptions	Accommodations

From its perch atop a wooded knoll, this historic Victorian mansion immediately commands attention with its multi-gabled roof, wraparound porch, and beautiful period details. Originally built as a residence in 1853, today this outstanding example of Gold Rush-era elegance continues to glitter as an utterly charming special event venue managed by Wedgewood Wedding & Banquet Centers.

Getting married at the mansion is like being the heroine of a historic novel. The upstairs Bridal Room, decorated with gilded mirrors and rich red velvet, affords a peek out the window to watch as guests arrive. A graceful dual staircase descends to the main floor, where the bride proceeds to her choice of three ceremony sites. The first is a glass-enclosed, light-filled stone Veranda, a cozy space that recalls a bygone era and overlooks a charming garden lawn. Next is the sprawling lawn itself, which enjoys a backdrop of the mansion's quaint façade and the snow-dusted mountains in the distance. Lastly, there's a lush forest retreat around the corner, where towering sequoias, pines, and a lily pond seem right out of a fairy tale.

Each of these picturesque locales, as well as the mansion's lovely interior, can also be used for taking romantic photos while guests mingle in the Dining Room and adjoining bar. With dark wood accents, comfortable couches, and magnificent hand-carved 19th-century fireplaces, these handsome spaces are ideal for serving cocktails or a selection of wines from the nearby Nello Olivo Vineyards. The Nello Olivo Wine Cellar and Tasting Room is actually housed in the mansion's basement, and makes a novel social hour option.

For a regal reception, the magnificent Empire Room sets the perfect tone of nostalgic glamour. Eight glass-and-brass Victorian-style chandeliers drop from the soaring, open-beamed cathedral ceiling, casting a warm glow over elegantly decked tables and the hardwood dance floor. Off to one side, there's a draped stage for entertainment or a sweetheart table, and the adjoining Veranda can house the buffet or wedding cake.

Wedgewood Sequoia Mansion offers all-inclusive wedding packages that are both customizable and affordable, ensuring that you'll enjoy both great service and exceptional value along with a truly unique setting. Whether it's adding your personal touches to the décor or creating your menu, the Wedgewood event pros will do their best to help you realize your dream wedding.

CEREMONY CAPACITY: The venue holds 250 seated guests indoors or outdoors.

EVENT/RECEPTION CAPACITY: The Sequoia Mansion accommodates 250 seated or standing guests indoors.

MEETING CAPACITY: The mansion seats up to 250.

FEES & DEPOSITS: 25% of the estimated event total is required to reserve your date. The next 25% is due 120 days prior to the event and the balance is due 10 days prior. All payments are credited towards your final balance and are nonrefundable and nontransferable. All-inclusive, completely customizable wedding packages start at $46/person. Tax, alcohol and a 21–22% service charge are additional.

AVAILABILITY: Year-round, daily, 7am–midnight.

SERVICES/AMENITIES:
Catering: in-house
Kitchen Facilities: n/a
Tables & Chairs: provided
Linens, Silver, etc.: provided
Restrooms: wheelchair accessible
Dance Floor: yes
Bride's & Groom's Dressing Areas: yes
AV/Meeting Equipment: some provided

Parking: large lot, limited
Accommodations: no guest rooms
Outdoor Night Lighting: yes
Outdoor Cooking Facilities: no
Cleanup: provided
View: forest
Other: event coordination, in-house wedding cake and florals, clergy on staff

RESTRICTIONS:
Alcohol: in-house
Smoking: outdoors only
Music: amplified OK

Wheelchair Access: yes
Insurance: not required
Other: no rice, confetti or glitter; no open flames

Wedgewood at David Girard Vineyards

Garden Winery

741 Cold Springs Road, Placerville
866/966-3009

www.wedgewoodbanquet.com
events@wedgewoodbanquet.com

Rehearsal Dinners	●	Corp. Events/Mtgs.
● Ceremonies	●	Private Parties
● Wedding Receptions		Accommodations

California's gold rush ended more than a century and a half ago, but these days there's something just as seductive luring people to El Dorado County. Acres and acres of countryside planted with grapevines have created a "new" wine country with lots of buzz. And since nothing says romance quite like a vineyard wedding, it's pretty exciting that the event wizards at Wedgewood have teamed up with one of the area's best-reviewed and most beautiful wineries.

Situated in the foothills of the Sierra Nevada Mountains, David Girard Vineyards' hilltop perch offers an idyllic retreat with Tuscan-style architecture and inspiring views in every direction. The rolling contours of this 85-acre property are reminiscent of France's Rhone Valley, where warm days and cool nights produce memorable vintages. In this case, the setting produces memorable celebrations as well.

An impressive, gated entrance sets the tone as you wind your way up to a Shangri-La site for your ceremony: the lush, leafy, and very private Hilltop Amphitheater. An expansive emerald lawn spreads out in front of a forest of mature oaks, and a long center aisle leads to the curved colonnade altar with its raised stage. Surrounded by greenery and picture-postcard panoramas, it's a magical spot for sharing your vows.

Afterwards, guests are welcomed to the Viticulture Galleria, a spacious reception hall with a clean, modern aesthetic and touches of Mediterranean chic. A 30-foot ceiling, exposed crossbeams, polished concrete floor, and artistic barrel chandeliers blend as seamlessly as one of David Girard's highly rated wines. An adjacent terrace and retractable glass doors provide an indoor/outdoor flow for your cocktail hour, as well as lovely vistas of the colorful garden and vineyards. Plus, the building's iconic bell tower, with its tall arched cut-outs, gives your photographer lots of options for framing incredible shots, as do the property's scenic lakes, fountains and waterfall.

And for those wanting to turn their wedding into a getaway, a selection of nearby hotels and B&Bs will serve as a home base for exploring gold rush ghost towns, historic Victorian landmarks, and the great outdoors.

But David Girard Vineyard is much more than a stunning location at the gateway to the Sierras and Lake Tahoe. When you host your event here, you'll also receive Wedgewood's top-rated service, exemplified by their attention to detail, convenient one-stop shopping, and delicious menus expertly paired with DGV's exceptional wines. Their affordable all-inclusive packages mean that you can enjoy the style and exclusivity of a vineyard wedding at a fraction of what you'd expect to pay!

CEREMONY CAPACITY: The winery holds 300 seated guests outdoors.

EVENT/RECEPTION CAPACITY: The winery accommodates 300 seated or standing guests indoors and 300 standing outdoors.

MEETING CAPACITY: Meetings do not take place at this facility.

FEES & DEPOSITS: 25% of the estimated event total is required to reserve your date. The next 25% is due 120 days prior to the event, and the balance is due 10 days prior. All payments are credited towards your final balance and are nonrefundable and nontransferable. All-inclusive, completely customizable wedding packages start at $10,500 for up to 100 guests, and include facility rental, appetizers and meal, hosted beer and wine, specialty reception lighting, invitations and accessories bundle, DJ, and more. Tax and a 22% service charge are additional. Certain revenue minimums will apply depending upon the event date and time.

AVAILABILITY: Year-round, daily. Event curfew is 10pm.

SERVICES/AMENITIES:

Catering: in-house
Kitchen Facilities: n/a
Tables & Chairs: provided
Linens, Silver, etc.: provided
Restrooms: wheelchair accessible
Dance Floor: provided
Bride's Dressing Area: yes
AV/Meeting Equipment: some provided, more CBA

Parking: large lot
Accommodations: no guest rooms
Outdoor Night Lighting: access only
Outdoor Cooking Facilities: no
Cleanup: provided
View: panorama of vineyards and surrounding countryside
Other: on-site wedding cake and florals

RESTRICTIONS:

Alcohol: in-house
Smoking: designated areas only
Music: amplified OK

Wheelchair Access: yes
Insurance: not required

Overwhelmed? Use the search criteria on www.HereComesTheGuide.com to narrow down your choices.

Tahoe Area

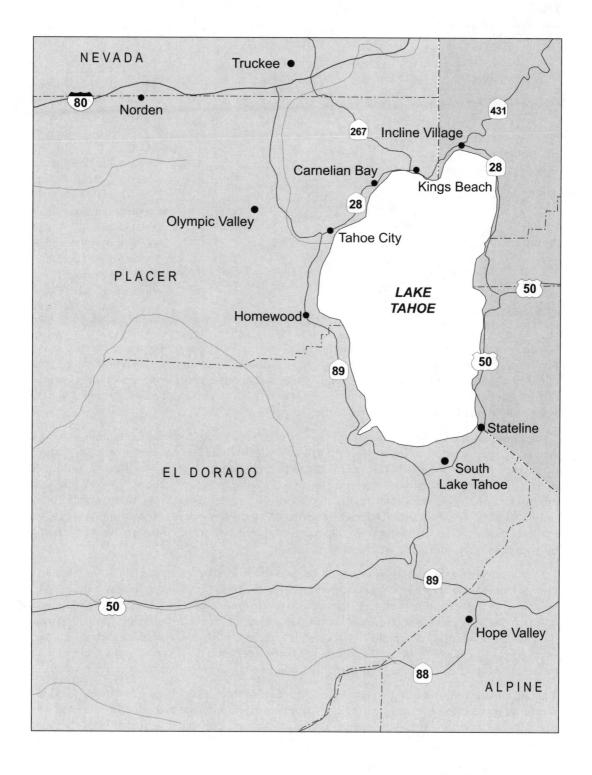

Big Water Grille

Lakeview Restaurant

341 Ski Way, Incline Village
775/833-0606

www.bigwatergrille.com
john@bigwatergrille.com

- ● Rehearsal Dinners
- ● Ceremonies
- ● Wedding Receptions
- ● Corp. Events/Mtgs.
- ● Private Parties
- □ Accommodations

Catching just a glimpse of Lake Tahoe, with its brilliant color and amazing clarity, can take your breath away. But big views of Big Blue, as the country's only alpine lake is affectionately known, can sometimes be hard to find for your wedding day festivities. That is, until you get to Big Water Grille, a North Shore mecca where your nearest and dearest can revel for hours in what are arguably the area's most spectacular and unobstructed vistas.

Located just a quarter mile from Diamond Peak in Incline Village and two miles from the Hyatt, Big Water Grille masterfully balances being a special destination with being a favorite dining spot of the locals. Clad in river rock, the residential building is perched on a slope above the shoreline. A clean, modern interior with high ceilings flows into three levels, and from every angle, soaring glass walls showcase irresistible views of the lake.

There's enormous flexibility in planning how to use the restaurant for your celebration, but most wedding parties are drawn first to the inviting outside deck. Here, you can exchange vows, framed by majestic pines as the sparkling water is tinted by the sunset. Then pop the bubbly, and invite friends and family to toast your union while also drinking in nature's beauty. Afterwards, your guests can easily move inside to the bar and lounge for butler-passed hors d'oeuvres (ahi tuna poke a favorite!) and customized specialty cocktails. The centerpiece of this welcoming space is a massive stone fireplace that's not only warm and cozy, but also makes a perfect photo backdrop for your ceremony during the winter months.

Dinner is served in the Dining Room, built on two levels to take advantage of that ever-present view, which now faces some strong competition from the highly acclaimed, mouth-watering presentations from their culinary staff. Dishes emphasize fresh seasonal produce, and are extremely flavorful and light. The restaurant also offers signature Santa Maria-style barbecue, brought in from their sister-restaurant, Gus' Open Pit Barbecue. It features tri-tip, ribs, chicken and more, cooked over red oak and served with all the trimmings. (Gus' caters, too, so if you're hosting an event on the lakefront or elsewhere, they can cook their fabulous comfort food to order at your location.)

To complement your meal, Big Water Grille's wine list includes a variety of vintages from around the world in a range of prices. In fact, if you're planning an intimate reception or rehearsal dinner, consider reserving the Wine Cellar, a sophisticated private setting separate from the Main Dining Room.

After dinner, guests usually move the party back up to the lounge. With its polished wood floor and comfy sofas, this area provides a great clubby atmosphere for dancing, as well as cake-cutting in front of the striking hearth. Another option: romantic stargazing out on the deck in the crisp mountain air.

And since this is Nevada, where there are no restrictions on when to end your music or have last call, you can start your celebration later in summer to catch the sunset and then party the night away.

CEREMONY CAPACITY: The restaurant holds 100 standing guests indoors in front of the fireplace and 30 seated or 100 standing outdoors.

EVENT/RECEPTION CAPACITY: The restaurant accommodates 120 seated or 135 standing indoors and 30 seated or standing outdoors on the deck.

MEETING CAPACITY: Meeting spaces hold 100 seated guests.

FEES & DEPOSITS: 50% of the food & beverage minimum is required to reserve your date, and the balance is due at the end of the event. The rental fee ranges $0–750 depending on your event needs. Meals range $48–100/person. Tax, alcohol and a 20% service charge are additional.

AVAILABILITY: Year-round, daily, until 1am. Please call for details.

SERVICES/AMENITIES:

Catering: in-house
Kitchen Facilities: n/a
Tables & Chairs: provided
Linens, Silver, etc.: provided
Restrooms: wheelchair accessible
Dance Floor: provided
Bride's Dressing Rooms: CBA
AV/Meeting Equipment: some provided

Parking: large lot
Accommodations: no guest rooms
Outdoor Night Lighting: yes
Outdoor Cooking Facilities: no
Cleanup: provided
View: panorama of Lake Tahoe and mountains
Other: event coordination

RESTRICTIONS:

Alcohol: in-house
Smoking: not allowed
Music: amplified OK

Wheelchair Access: yes
Insurance: not required

North Tahoe Event Center

8318 North Lake Boulevard, Kings Beach

530/546-7249

www.northtahoeevents.com
sales@northtahoeevents.com

Lakeside Event Center

● Rehearsal Dinners ● Corp. Events/Mtgs.
● Ceremonies ● Private Parties
● Wedding Receptions Accommodations

The North Tahoe Event Center, set in a desirable spot on Lake Tahoe's less crowded North Shore, is a unique venue with nothing between it and the deep blue waters of the lake except a wide stretch of pristine beach. This versatile facility offers a variety of appealing spaces, and can accommodate both large and small events with ease.

The Lakeview Suite, with its wall of floor-to-ceiling windows, affords a stunning backdrop for your wedding: the serene, azure lake and surrounding peaks dusted with snow. And because the room opens onto the expansive Lakeview Terrace, during those glorious months from late spring to early fall you can host your ceremony or cocktail hour outside and then move back inside for the reception, creating a wonderful indoor/outdoor flow. As evening falls, the terrace is also a premium spot to savor a romantic sunset or watch the moon rise over the eastern Sierras, casting a golden shimmer upon the lake.

Larger private events and corporate functions are held in the 4,800-square-foot Timberline Room. Although it's perfect for an elaborate gala of up to 300 guests, it can be sectioned for more intimate gatherings. There are several additional spaces that work well for childcare, a buffet setup or a staging area. Some of the Event Center's other features include a large mirrored bridal dressing room, professional in-house catering, and a spacious commercial kitchen if you bring in your own caterer.

Both you and your guests will love the chance to experience Tahoe's year-round recreation—skiing, mountain biking, golf, kayaking, paddle boarding and hiking. There are also less strenuous but equally satisfying activities like fine dining, shopping, and visiting art galleries—especially along the newly renovated and pedestrian-friendly beachfront commercial center in Kings Beach.

With its prime location, flexibility, affordability and glorious view, the North Tahoe Event Center has developed quite a following among those who wish to celebrate in one of the country's most popular destinations.

CEREMONY CAPACITY: Several rooms accommodate up to 350 seated or standing guests indoors. The Lakefront Terrace holds 350 seated or standing outdoors.

EVENT/RECEPTION & MEETING CAPACITY: Various rooms hold up to 350 seated or 500 standing guests indoors. The Lakefront Terrace can accommodate 250 seated and 350 standing outdoors.

FEES & DEPOSITS: A deposit of 50% of the estimated total is required to confirm your date. The balance is due 2 weeks prior to the event. The rental fee ranges $1,100–9,000 depending on the guest count and space reserved. If you bring your own caterer, there is an extra fee. Use of the in-house caterer requires a deposit (applied to the final catering invoice) to retain those services. In-house catering starts at $32/person. Tax, alcohol and service charges are additional.

AVAILABILITY: Year-round, daily, 9am–midnight.

SERVICES/AMENITIES:

Catering: in-house or BYO
Kitchen Facilities: commercial
Tables & Chairs: provided
Linens, Silver, etc.: place settings and glassware provided with in-house caterer
Restrooms: wheelchair accessible
Dance Floor: available upon request, extra fee
Bride's Dressing Area: yes (large or small available)
AV/Meeting Equipment: large screens, easels, AV, LCD projectors, WiFi, conference calls, high-speed internet available

Parking: large lot, extra fee
Accommodations: available nearby
Outdoor Night Lighting: yes
Outdoor Cooking Facilities: BBQ grill
Cleanup: provided
View: Lake Tahoe and Sierras
Other: vendor referral list available

RESTRICTIONS:

Alcohol: in-house or BYO
Smoking: designated areas
Music: amplified OK indoors

Wheelchair Access: yes
Insurance: required
Other: no rice, confetti or artificial flower petals

Resort at Squaw Creek

Luxury Resort

400 Squaw Creek Road, Olympic Valley

530/584-4097

www.squawcreek.com
info@squawcreek.com

- Rehearsal Dinners
- Ceremonies
- Wedding Receptions
- Corp. Events/Mtgs.
- Private Parties
- Accommodations

Spectacular Resort at Squaw Creek encompasses 195 hillside acres of relaxation, indulgence and breathtaking beauty at the base of Squaw Valley. Just minutes from Lake Tahoe, this all-season resort makes the most of its magnificent surroundings: towering granite peaks and ponderosa pines dusted with snow in the winter, and sunlit meadows and starlit skies during the milder months.

Such a magical setting is perfect for special celebrations, and this award-winning AAA Four Diamond resort, decked out in glass, wood and granite, boasts over 47,000 square feet of distinctive indoor and outdoor event space.

Both ceremonies and receptions are held outside on the resort's multilevel terraces. One is a vast lawn, where you can exchange vows in front of a stunning 250-foot waterfall that cascades into a stream that ripples down to the pool. Another choice spot is the spacious spa deck, which has its own stone fireplace and also overlooks the verdant valley below and forested mountains on the horizon. Or tie the knot right on the golf greens, surrounded by a grove of pine trees and serene alpine panoramas.

After the ceremony, couples can move the party into one of the restaurants or chic ballrooms, each with its own unique character. The Six Peaks Grille, for example, boasts soaring floor-to-ceiling windows that frame the glorious scenery. The expansive Grand Sierra Ballroom hosts up to 500 guests, and comes with a prefunction space that's great for serving champagne and appetizers.

And speaking of food: Dining at the resort is an elegant and varied affair. From rehearsal dinners to bridal party luncheons, the special events manager and executive chef can help you create a menu that delights your guests, while keeping your budget in mind. Resort at Squaw Creek sources food from local farms and artisan purveyors, as well as its own vegetable garden. The executive chef and mixologist infuse food and cocktails with authentic Tahoe flavors and herbs right from their garden. Thanks to their on-site pastry chef, you can customize your choice of dessert, whether it's a gorgeous wedding cake or a gourmet dessert bar with all of the fixings.

Your friends and family will also appreciate the resort's 405 well-appointed accommodations, which feature suites with kitchenettes and fireplaces. And there are plenty more attractions: For starters, how about a world-class spa and fitness center, boutique promenade, and swimming pools with spas that are heated year-round! Other fun on-site activities include a championship golf course, tennis, biking, hiking, snowboarding, and cross-country skiing—plus you have ski-in/ski-out access to the adjacent ski area!

However you envision your destination wedding, you and your guests can bask in the resort's warm hospitality from welcome refreshments all the way through your post-wedding brunch. And you might even be tempted to stay on for a High Sierra honeymoon!

CEREMONY CAPACITY: The Spa Deck seats 200 theater-style; the Pavilion seats up to 300 theater-style; and the Golf Course accommodates up to 150 guests subject to the time of day and season.

EVENT/RECEPTION CAPACITY: The Ballrooms accommodate 200–500 seated or 700 standing guests; Montagnas holds up to 80 seated, Six Peaks Grille up to 100 seated, and Cascades Restaurant up to 200 seated.

MEETING CAPACITY: Event spaces seat 20–500 guests.

FEES & DEPOSITS: 25% of the estimated food & beverage total plus the rental fee is required to secure your date. A deposit schedule will be determined for your remaining balance. The rental fee starts at $2,000, and varies depending on the day of the week, time of day and space reserved. Wedding packages start at $111/person and can be customized. Wedding services include a ceremony arbor arch, professional AV services, and a complimentary fireplace suite for the couple on their wedding night. A 23% service charge and tax are additional.

AVAILABILITY: Year-round, daily, flexible hours between 6am and 2am.

SERVICES/AMENITIES:
Catering: in-house
Kitchen Facilities: n/a
Tables & Chairs: provided
Linens, Silver, etc.: provided
Restrooms: wheelchair accessible
Dance Floor: provided
Bride's & Groom's Dressing Areas: CBA
AV/Meeting Equipment: provided, extra fee may be required

Parking: large lots; valet available, extra fee
Accommodations: 405 guest rooms & suites
Outdoor Night Lighting: yes
Outdoor Cooking Facilities: BBQ CBA
Cleanup: provided
View: mountains, forest, fairways, meadow
Other: children's program, spa services, heated swimming pool, Jacuzzis, bike rentals, golf, tennis courts, guided hiking

RESTRICTIONS:
Alcohol: in-house, or BYO with corkage fee
Smoking: outside only
Music: amplified OK with restrictions

Wheelchair Access: yes
Insurance: recommended

MontBleu Resort Casino and Spa

Resort & Casino

55 Highway 50, Stateline
775/586-2074
www.montbleuresort.com
avopalensky@montbleuresort.com

- Rehearsal Dinners
- Ceremonies
- Wedding Receptions
- Corp. Events/Mtgs.
- Private Parties
- Accommodations

Some couples are looking for a wedding venue that focuses on fun and excitement. Others crave beautiful scenery so that they can enjoy the great outdoors. For those who want it all—and in one place—there's MontBleu Resort.

This lively hotel is located just a short stroll from Lake Tahoe's stunningly picturesque southern shore. Fresh from a $25 million renovation, it offers everything you and your guests could possibly need, from the bridal shower and rehearsal dinner to the reception and post-wedding entertainment.

Ceremonies take place in their twelfth-floor Wedding Chapel, which is truly a room with a view: huge windows overlook the crystalline waters of the glacier lake. For your reception, you can choose from an array of options thanks to over 16,000 square feet of flexible event space. For example, the Evergreen and Aspen Ballrooms can be combined for a large group, or divided for a more intimate celebration. They feature 14-foot ceilings and state-of-the-art sound and tech, and you're welcome to customize the décor—add draping, dramatic lighting, and other personal touches to create your own ambiance. If you're looking to emphasize the "party" in wedding party, check out Opal, their vibrant casino lounge where you can stop in for cocktails, rent it out for a VIP-style reception, or join the night owls for dancing until dawn.

There's so much to do here that it's easy to turn your wedding into an extended getaway. On-site activities start with getting pampered at the Spa, swimming in their fabulous lagoon-style indoor pool, and checking out the action in the casino. At the adjacent theater, you can attend a concert (country, reggae, and rock are often booked) or perhaps catch the act of a stand-up comedian. Looking for something a bit more athletic or even Zen? Try a round of golf at the course next door, mountain bike around the lake, kayak on water so clear it will actually take your breath away, or simply take a peaceful hike among the tall trees.

The event and catering teams will help make your wedding as stress-free as possible. Packages include great menu options, as well as assistance with booking photographers, flowers, music, and even an officiant for your ceremony. They can also arrange discounted room blocks and transportation both locally and to the nearby airport, so that all you have to do is relax and enjoy.

CEREMONY CAPACITY: The Wedding Chapel holds 110 seated guests indoors.

EVENT/RECEPTION CAPACITY: The site accommodates 500 seated or 1,200 standing guests indoors.

MEETING CAPACITY: Meeting spaces can seat 20–1,500 guests.

FEES & DEPOSITS: A $250 deposit is required to reserve your date and the balance is due 30 days prior to the event. Venue rental fees for a 5-hour event start at $85 for the Chapel and $250 for the Reception Room, and vary depending on the day of the event and the guest count. Luncheons range $19–28/person, dinners range $28–46/person depending on the menu selected. Tax, alcohol and an 18% service charge are additional.

AVAILABILITY: Year-round, daily, 10am–6pm for the Chapel, 6am–3am for the Reception Room.

SERVICES/AMENITIES:

Catering: in-house
Kitchen Facilities: n/a
Tables & Chairs: provided
Linens, Silver, etc.: provided
Restrooms: wheelchair accessible
Dance Floor: portable provided
Bride's Dressing Area: yes
AV/Meeting Equipment: provided

Parking: large lot, valet available
Accommodations: 438 guest rooms
Outdoor Night Lighting: CBA
Outdoor Cooking Facilities: none
Cleanup: provided
View: forest, fountain, fairways; panorama of lake and mountains from the 9th floor and above
Other: clergy on staff

RESTRICTIONS:

Alcohol: in-house
Smoking: designated areas only
Music: amplified OK indoors

Wheelchair Access: yes
Insurance: not required

Want to know WHAT TO ASK a potential location or vendor? Check out our Questions to Ask starting on page 21.

The Tahoe Wedding Collection

Northstar, Heavenly and Kirkwood, Lake Tahoe

530/562-3830

www.tahoeweddingcollection.com
blfox@vailresorts.com

Mountain Resorts

● Rehearsal Dinners	● Corp. Events/Mtgs.
● Ceremonies	● Private Parties
● Wedding Receptions	● Accommodations

Lake Tahoe, where Mark Twain once said the air is so pure it's what angels breathe, consistently makes every "must-see" list. So how fabulous is it that The Tahoe Wedding Collection offers three distinct, premier mountain resorts here—each with its own unique style, charm and price point to suit any destination wedding!

The aptly named Heavenly juxtaposes awe-inspiring panoramas of Tahoe's sapphire waters with the excitement of nearby casinos and nightlife. Let your spirit soar as you ride the gondola up to the three-tiered Blue Sky Terrace to exchange vows against a backdrop of the dazzling lake. Then linger over cocktails before continuing up the mountain for a reception at Tamarack Lodge. The angled roofline and floor-to-ceiling windows give you unobstructed views of the mountains from its open, airy interior, where tables are made from local pines and soft light glows from forged iron chandeliers. If you're planning summer nuptials and crave lots of privacy, board the aerial tram for a mile-long, scenic ascent to Lakeview Lodge. Here, your outdoor ceremony boasts a top-of-the-world tableau of shimmering water and a spectacular sunset, followed by dinner and dancing indoors or under the stars.

Those who revel in the great outdoors will love Kirkwood. Off the beaten path, this rustic retreat lets you unplug, relax, and share the full "beauty of nature" experience with friends and family. Say "I do" in a meadow blooming with wildflowers and surrounded by the rugged peaks of the Sierras. Meander down wooded pathways for photos amid towering trees or nearby crystalline lakes, then convene at the Off The Wall Bar and Grill for a spirited celebration. Centrally located in the village, this quintessential lodge features a large bar, fireplace, antler chandeliers and a wall of windows that frame truly awesome sunsets. An adjacent patio provides a nice indoor/outdoor flow for dinner and dancing. Your event coordinator can also arrange a BBQ, cocktails and taco bar, and picnics and games on the plaza or around the fire pit during subsequent days.

But for high-end luxury with a laid-back ambiance, nothing beats Northstar! This elegant yet relaxed resort is actually a full-scale village perched on Tahoe's north shore. An amazing array of stunning event spaces, an award-winning executive chef, upscale shops, hip restaurants, a theater, skating/roller rink—even a 5-star Ritz-Carlton complete with indulgent spa—offer everything you could want for the wedding of your dreams. And best of all, there are over 3,000 acres of gorgeous ski and alpine terrain. At the heart of the village is the Overlook Pavilion, an ideal spot with romantic tenting for an outdoor wedding that blends convenience with privacy and mountain views. For something a bit loftier, take the gondolas 8,000 feet up to the glass-walled Zephyr Lodge and savor those sweeping vistas of the Pacific Crest and dramatic sunsets over Castle Peak. Need something more intimate? Check out TC's Pub or Tavern 6330.

Whichever resort you choose, the team at The Tahoe Wedding Collection can help you choose the right package and guide you every step of the way from menu planning and décor to arranging accommodations and fun activities for your guests. With so many options, they've got you covered.

CEREMONY & MEETING CAPACITY: Each venue can seat up to 125 guests indoors and 250 outdoors.

EVENT/RECEPTION CAPACITY: The venues each hold up to 250 seated or 500 standing, indoors or outdoors.

FEES & DEPOSITS: A deposit is required to secure your date, and the balance is due 30 days prior to the event. The venue rental fee starts at $1,000 and varies depending on the day, time, space reserved, and guest count. Meals range $25–69/person. Tax, alcohol and a 20% service charge are additional.

Rates for business functions, meetings or other types of events vary. Please contact the venue for more details.

AVAILABILITY: Year-round, daily.

SERVICES/AMENITIES:

Catering: in-house
Kitchen Facilities: fully equipped
Tables & Chairs: provided
Linens, Silver, etc.: provided
Restrooms: wheelchair accessible
Dance Floor: portable provided
Bride's Dressing Area: yes
AV/Meeting Equipment: provided

Parking: large lot
Accommodations: 500 guest rooms
Outdoor Night Lighting: yes
Outdoor Cooking Facilities: BBQ on site
Cleanup: provided
View: forest, fairways, landscaped grounds; panorama of mountain ranges and Lake Tahoe
Other: picnic area, event coordination

RESTRICTIONS:

Alcohol: in-house, or BYO with corkage fee
Smoking: designated areas only
Music: amplified OK

Wheelchair Access: yes
Insurance: not required

Granlibakken Tahoe

Resort & Conference Center

725 Granlibakken Road, Tahoe City
530/581-7312

www.granlibakken.com
annieevans@granlibakken.com

- Rehearsal Dinners
- Ceremonies
- Wedding Receptions
- Corp. Events/Mtgs.
- Private Parties
- Accommodations

The pursuit of love and the thrill of adventure have drawn folks to Granlibakken Valley for more than 75 years. In the 1920s, tourists tobogganed down its slopes. In the '30s and '40s, Olympic hopefuls soared off Tahoe's first ski jump, which was built here. Then in 1947, Norwegian Ski Jumper Kjell "Rusty" Rustad arrived on the scene. Smitten with the place, he built a log cabin ski hut near the base of the alpine canyon. In the decades since, Granlibakken has grown into a modern, all-season resort and conference center. Today Rustad's hut has become a favorite spot for bonfires, barbecues and casual rehearsal dinners. And though the jump site is no longer in use, couples still come to this 74-acre mountain getaway to take their own jump into matrimony.

Tie the knot just outside the Main Conference Center and Lodge, where a stand of pine and fir trees lends privacy to a landscaped patio with an elevated stage. If you want to have your reception on the same patio, the staff will set it up with umbrella-shaded tables.

You can also eat, drink, and be married in any of the Center's three main rooms. Guests celebrating in the spacious Granhall enjoy the view of trees through the room's wide windows or from the adjoining patio. Within the sedate Mountain Ballroom, neutral tones blend easily with traditional wedding décor and heavy sliding panels can be opened or closed to accommodate the size of your group. For a warm ceremony on a snowy day, the massive fireplace in Cedar House provides a cozy backdrop. The nearby cedar deck makes a casual setting for a post-ceremony cocktail hour, while the newlyweds take the short drive to the lake for photographs.

The Big Pine Lodge, just a bouquet toss further up the hill, is a mini mountain retreat by itself. A vaulted open-beam ceiling and stone fireplace add old-lodge ambiance, and with a living room, bridal changing room, kitchen, and seven guest rooms, it's an ideal hideaway for close family and friends. You can have an intimate rehearsal dinner in the main room, and later host your entire wedding outdoors on the expansive lush lawn. Surrounded by flowers and tall pines, it features a stunning two-tiered stone ceremony stage with rock stairs flowing down both sides. There's also enough space to dine al fresco at tables shaded by umbrellas.

Granlibakken's staff will make sure your celebration unfolds just as you imagine it. A wedding reception requires a minimum two-night stay; barbecues and banquets are typically prearranged with the resort's event coordinator; and a hot breakfast buffet is included for all overnight guests. The facility's lodges and townhouses offer comfortable rooms and suites decorated to complement the resort's natural setting, and there's plenty to do: Play on one of the five tennis courts, or relax in the heated swimming pool and hot tub; hike the well-traveled footpaths up to the Tahoe Rim Trail or down into Tahoe City; or, in the tradition of those who've come to the valley for both love and a winter adventure, ski with your new spouse down Granlibakken's fir-sheltered slopes.

Note that wedding ceremonies held at Granlibakken must be followed by a reception on site. However, you can get married elsewhere, and still host your reception here.

CEREMONY CAPACITY: Indoors or out, Granlibakken holds up to 350 seated guests.

EVENT/RECEPTION CAPACITY: Several spaces hold up to 350 seated or 400 standing guests.

MEETING CAPACITY: Groups of up to 350 seated guests can be accommodated.

FEES & DEPOSITS: The room rental fee and/or the wedding package cost is required to secure your date. Rental fees range $500–7,000 depending on the spaces reserved and season. Meals range $30–65/person. Tax, alcohol, and an 18% service charge are additional. Wedding packages are available that include 2 nights' lodging and breakfast for up to 14 guests. Inquire for details!

AVAILABILITY: Year-round, daily, 6am–10pm.

SERVICES/AMENITIES:

Catering: in-house, no BYO
Kitchen Facilities: n/a
Tables & Chairs: provided
Linens, Silver, etc.: provided
Restrooms: wheelchair accessible
Dance Floor: CBA, extra charge
Bride's Dressing Area: included in wedding package
AV/Meeting Equipment: yes

Parking: ample on-site
Accommodations: 180 guest rooms
Outdoor Night Lighting: yes, extra charge
Outdoor Cooking Facilities: BBQs, extra charge in some areas
Cleanup: provided
View: forest, hills, mountains
Other: event coordination

RESTRICTIONS:

Alcohol: in-house or BYO with corkage fee
Smoking: designated areas only
Music: amplified OK

Wheelchair Access: limited
Insurance: not required
Other: no rice, birdseed or confetti

The Lodge Restaurant & Pub
at Tahoe Donner

12850 Northwoods Boulevard, Truckee

530/582-9643

www.tahoedonner.com/weddings
groupsales@tahoedonner.com

Restaurant & Banquet Facility

- Rehearsal Dinners
- Ceremonies
- Wedding Receptions
- Corp. Events/Mtgs.
- Private Parties
- Accommodations

Set in the Sierra Nevada Mountain Range near Donner Lake, The Lodge Restaurant & Pub is a wonderful place to celebrate your destination special event amid breathtaking pastoral beauty. This popular restaurant and banquet center is the cornerstone of Tahoe Donner, an exclusive planned community with its own golf course and access to a wealth of outdoor recreational opportunities. Many of these activities, such as the equestrian center, biking, skiing, camping, golf and more, are also open to the public.

The Lodge, designed with floor-to-ceiling windows overlooking towering pines and the rugged mountain golf course, highlights the glories of the natural world in a classic Tahoe-style ambiance.

Spring through fall, wedding ceremonies can be held at one of The Lodge Restaurant & Pub's picturesque sites. The Pavilion Area, just outside the restaurant, offers a beautiful arbor overlooking the wooded mountains. Say "I do" right on the grass, then enjoy cocktails and appetizers al fresco followed by your reception in the adjacent tiled Pavilion. This spacious peaked tent, luxuriously draped in pleated white fabric, is compatible with any style of décor and the clear sides all around let the outside in.

For a more intimate ceremony, cocktail party or dinner, host it in the landscaped Grotto, which features a waterfall and also provides some lovely photo opportunities.

In the winter months, all of The Lodge Restaurant & Pub's interior spaces are warm and inviting, with alderwood trim and high, open-beamed ceilings. Huge picture windows capture the dynamic view, which is especially compelling in winter when the trees and mountains wear a dusting of snow, creating a magnificent panoramic landscape.

The Sage and Aspen Rooms on the second story are cozy settings for rehearsal dinners, family reunions, or birthday parties. Both overlook the 18th green and the Aspen Room has a fireplace. The attractive downstairs banquet room is a private reception option in any season. And last but not least, The Lodge's pub is available, too, as a fun spot for the after-party.

With the rustic splendor of its environs, pleasing architecture and gracious hospitality, The Lodge Restaurant & Pub at Tahoe Donner is a standout venue for any event.

CEREMONY CAPACITY: The Lodge accommodates 60 seated indoors and 200 seated outdoors.

EVENT/RECEPTION & MEETING CAPACITY: The facility holds 150 seated and 200 standing indoors; 200 seated and 350 standing outdoors.

FEES & DEPOSITS: $1,000 and a signed contract are required to secure your date. 20% of the estimated event total is due 6 months prior to your date, and the balance is due 1 month prior. The venue rental fee ranges $500–4,300 depending on the space reserved. Meals start at $50/person. Fees do not include tax, alcohol and gratuity, which are additional.

AVAILABILITY: May–October, outdoors/tent, 8am–10pm. Indoor spaces are available year-round, 6am–10pm.

SERVICES/AMENITIES:

Catering: in-house
Kitchen Facilities: n/a
Tables & Chairs: provided
Linens, Silver, etc.: provided
Restrooms: wheelchair accessible
Dance Floor: CBA
Bride's & Groom's Dressing Areas: CBA
AV/Meeting Equipment: some provided

Parking: free, provided
Accommodations: hotels, motels, rental homes and camping nearby
Outdoor Night Lighting: yes
Outdoor Cooking Facilities: BBQ CBA
Cleanup: provided
View: river, forest, mountains, fairways

RESTRICTIONS:

Alcohol: in-house
Smoking: not allowed
Music: amplified OK indoors or outdoors with restrictions

Wheelchair Access: yes
Insurance: not required

Index

Event Venues

---

a

b

c

d

e

f

g

h

i

j

k

l

m

n

o

p

q

r

W

All of the Event Services profiled on HereComesTheGuide.com have been

1. We only represent the best professionals in the biz.

The professionals featured on our website aren't plucked from a random Google search. They're a carefully selected group of vendors who we'd recommend to our friends and business associates without hesitation.

2. Because we're picky, you don't have to worry about who to hire for your event.

We've thoroughly checked the professional track record of our event pros so you can be as confident about their abilities as we are. The companies we highlight have passed our reference check with flying colors, and we're honored to represent each of them. They've all been *Certified By The Guide.* To see all of our prescreened vendors, go to HereComesTheGuide.com.

3. Getting into Here Comes The Guide is tough.

The service providers we represent are topnotch. We put each one through a rigorous reference check, which involves interviewing up to 30 other event professionals and couples. We contact every single reference and ask about the professionalism, technical competency and service orientation of the advertiser in question.

When you invest 7–10 hours talking to that many brides and professionals, you get a crystal clear picture of who's doing a superb job and who isn't. Those candidates who received consistent, rave reviews made it into HereComesTheGuide.com's VENDOR section. Those who didn't were (nicely) turned down.

About the Authors

Jan Brenner has co-authored and edited all of Hopscotch Press' books. Although she received a BA in English from UC Berkeley, she backed into writing only after spending ten years in social work and four in publishing. Along the way she got a couple of other degrees that have never been put to official use. A lifelong dilettante, she's quasi-conversant in 3.1 languages, dabbles in domestic pursuits, and spends an inordinate amount of time hanging out with her dog Luigi.

Jolene Rae Harrington has been with Hopscotch Press since she first fell in love with their groundbreaking publications while planning her own beach wedding in 1995. In addition to co-authoring and editing the *Here Comes The Guide* books, she serves as Director of Creative Content for HereComesTheGuide.com and is a frequently quoted expert on the bridal industry. Beyond her work at Here Comes The Guide, Jolene's writing credits range from an award-winning television script to a best-selling children's computer game. She lives in her native Southern California with her husband and various animal children.

Virtual tours let you visit event sites without leaving home!

Use your computer to visit hundreds of venues without ever leaving home. Each tour gives you a 360-degree view of a location's event spaces—it's like standing in the middle of the room and turning in a complete circle so you can see everything. By taking a "tour" online, you can quickly decide if the location you're viewing is a good fit for you.

See a variety of spaces

360-degree moving images

Virtual tours at HereComesTheGuide.com

Dresses by Designer Loft, New York; Photo by Judy Pak

HereComesTheGuide.com also lists Designer Wedding Dress Trunk Shows and Sample Sales!

Trunk Shows offer you a chance to shop a designer's entire collection during a personal consultation with style experts—it's free, and frankly, it feels fabulous to be the center of attention. Many of these events also offer sales incentives.

Sample Sales feature deep discounts on in-stock bridal gowns. Though sizes and styles are more limited, it's a fantastic way to get a dreamy designer look for less.

And don't forget: There are also Trunk Shows and Sample Sales for fashion accessories, bridesmaid dresses, cocktail dresses and formalwear for Moms, too!

Notes

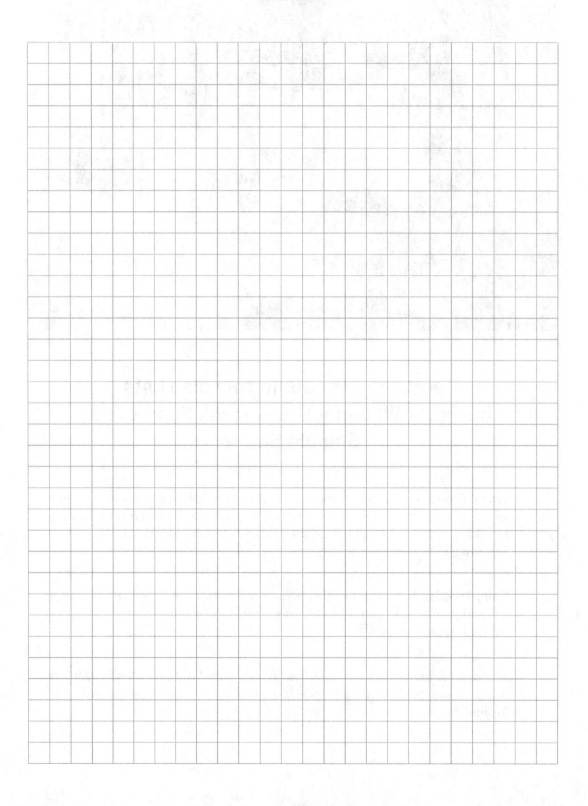

Notes

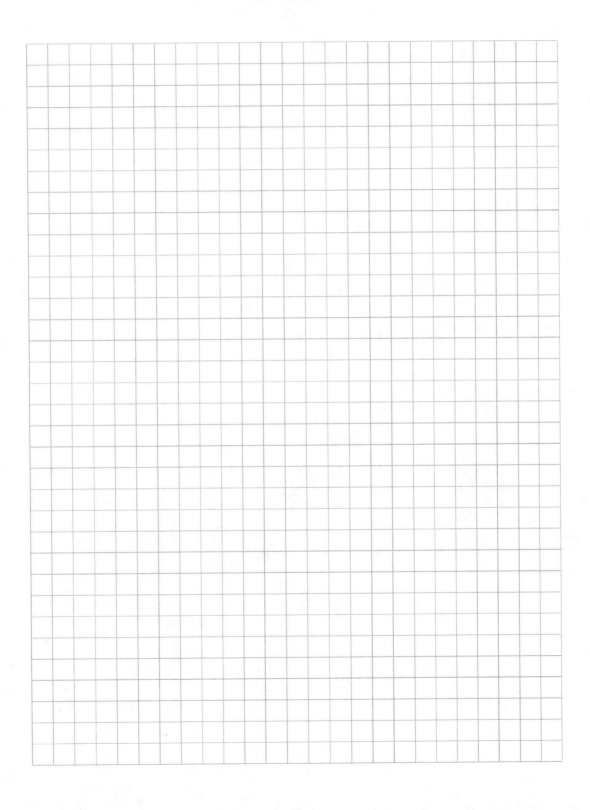

Notes

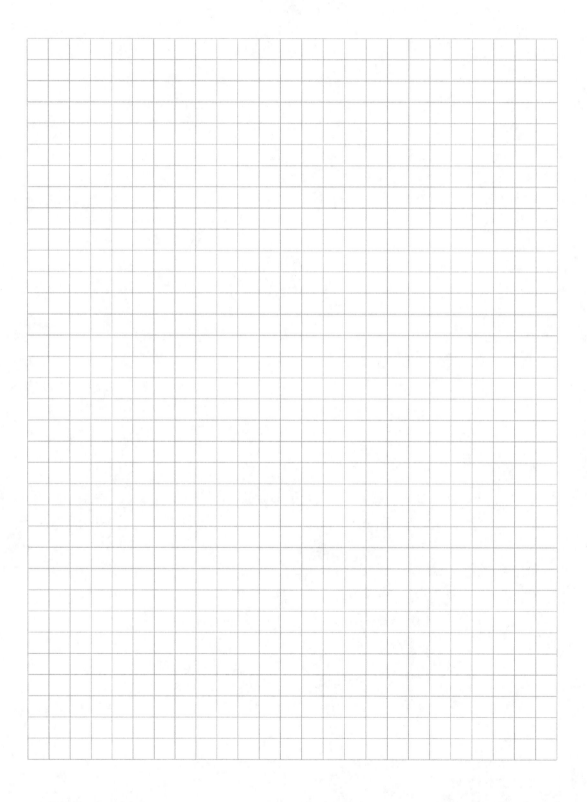

Notes